William Nealy

MENASHA RIDGE PRESS
Your Guide to the Outdoors Since 1982
an imprint of AdventureKEEN

The Nealy Way of Knowledge: Twenty Years of Extreme Cartoons

Printed in the United States of America

Published by
MENASHA RIDGE PRESS
Your Guide to the Outdoors Since 1982
an imprint of AdventureKEEN

2204 First Ave. S., Ste. 102
Birmingham, Alabama 35233
800-678-7006, FAX 877-374-9016
adventurewithkeen.com

ISBN 978-1-63404-374-8 (pbk); ISBN 978-1-63404-375-5 (ebook)

PUBLISHER'S NOTE

What you hold in your hands is a book of William Nealy's art, pulled from the gnarliest Class VI rapids of time . . . almost lost forever.

But now Nealy's zany illustrations have been bound and bandaged together in a new monumental collection, including books and cartoons long out of print. Nealy's full-speed downhill no-holds-barred art has been reset and brought back to life like never before.

This is the craziest collection of cartoons since Nealy first put paddle to water and pen to paper. The result is a hilarious slice of the outdoor community as extreme and cutting as Nealy was himself.

Many of the illustrations have not been seen since they were first published. Now they're back and will certainly delight old and new Nealy fans alike.

We are proud at Menasha Ridge Press and AdventureKEEN to help return Nealy's art and irreverent illustrations to the bookshelf. Nealy had a gift for teaching, storytelling, and capturing the beauty of the rivers he sketched and the people he loved. His humorous approach to telling the twisted tales of paddlers, mountain bikers, hikers, campers, inline skaters, and skiers everywhere is a gift to all participating in the weird, wonderful world of outdoor sports.

You can learn more about William, his art, and his many books at thewilliamnealy.com.

SINCERELY,
THE MENASHA RIDGE
PRESS TEAM

To Holly,
The love of my life

Huge thanks to some of the people who've helped me over the years: John Barbour, Bob Sehlinger, James Jackson, Dave Van Kleek, Bob Gernandt, John Lane, Tom Schlinkert, Cliff Earle, Bunny Johns, James & Katie Torrence, Jimm East, Howard DuBose, Henry Unger, Bruce Tiller, Tom Stout, Diff Ritchie, Frank Fleming, J. T. Lemmons, Daniel Wallace, Herb Kincey, Bud Zehmer, Joan Wallace, Brian & Coleman, Tammy Knight, Slim Ray, Charlie Walbridge, Gary Winterhalter, Ernie Aziz, David Bilstrom, Basie Settle, Magpie, and especially my **Mom**!

Table of Contents

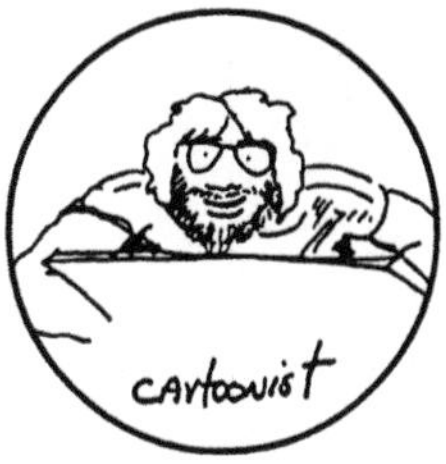
cartoonist

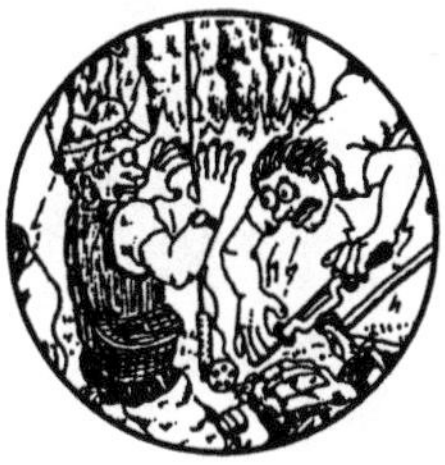

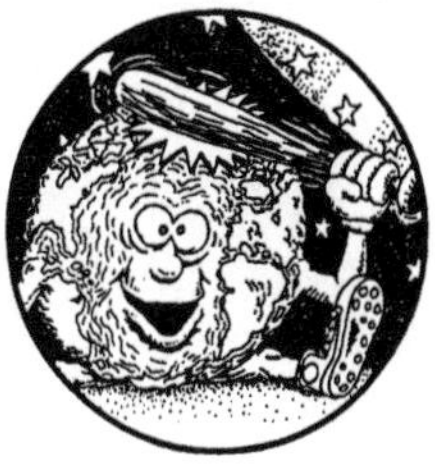

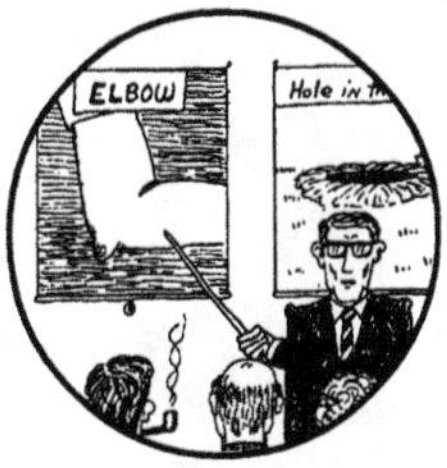
ELBOW
Hole in th

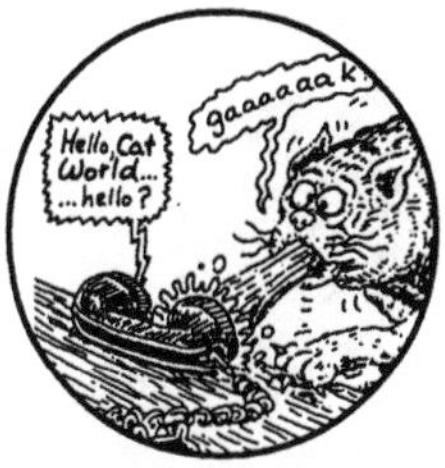
Hello, Cat World... ...hello?
gaaaaaak

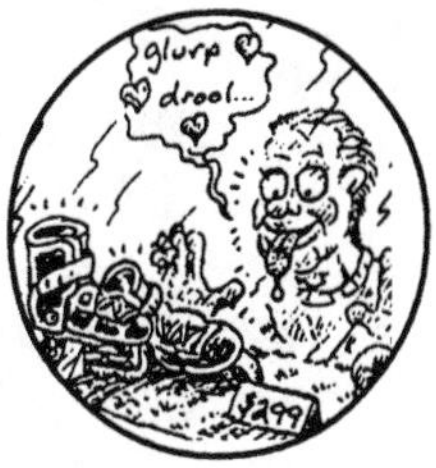
glurp drool...
$299

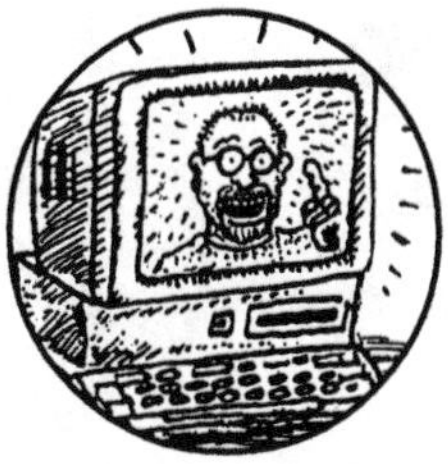

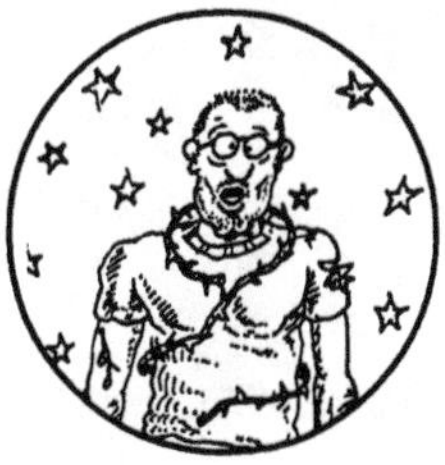

Introduction

Whenever I meet people who want to talk about my work, they usually start by asking me how in the world I come up with all my **zany ideas**. "What an imagination!" they exclaim. Sadly, I must confess that most of my material is autobiography. I swam a lot of rapids, wrecked a lot of bikes, and busted my head with astonishing frequency. Then I wrote it all down, usually in step-by-step diagram form. I document most of my life this way. For instance, last year I was standing on a rickety barstool trying to silence a beeping smoke alarm. Suddenly the seat broke and I dropped into the stool frame and toppled onto the floor. I was trapped like a rat but able to destroy the !6?★:@! smoke alarm in situ.

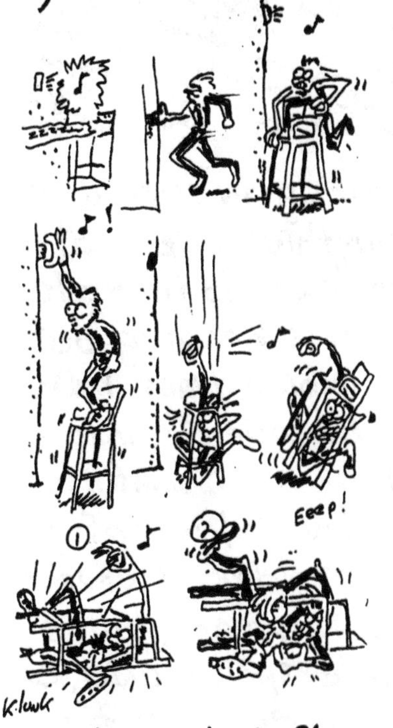
Eeep!
Klunk

I try to use every aspect of my life, past and present, in my drawings. Like everyone, the experiences of my childhood continue to influence my adult life. The art I do today is inextricably linked to where I grew up and what was happening when I was a kid. It was a riot, literally.

I was born in North Carolina but we moved to Birmingham, Alabama when I was a year old. Thanks to the steel mills, Birmingham was one of the smoggiest and most polluted places on the planet. The high particulent count, combined with severe childhood asthma, led me to spend a lot of time confined indoors, drawing and playing with my three-legged dog, Prince. I "raised" an assortment of animals in my suburban bedroom. My mom said that I could have anything as a pet except a **rhinoceros** or a **cat** and I took her up on it. We had chameleons crawling on the living room drapery, snakes dozing in the bathtub of our only bathroom, and all sorts of rodents reproducing at phenomenal rates. The importance of animals in my life has always been reflected in my cartoons. These days our country home continues to be a regular animal embassy, guarded by pigs.

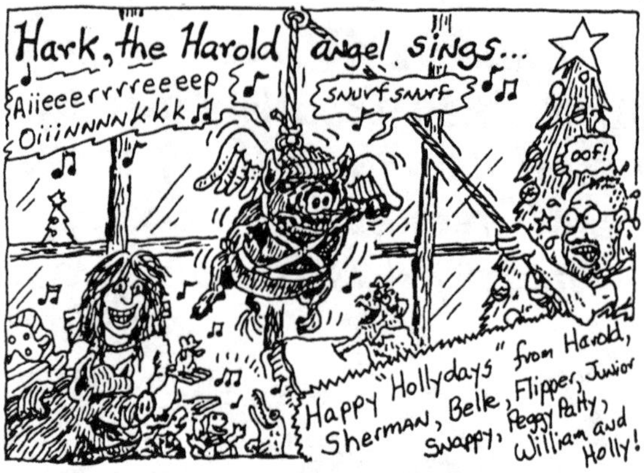
Hark, the Harold angel sings...
Aiieeerrrreeeep
Oiiinnnnkkk
SNUFFSNUFF
OOF!
Happy "Hollydays" from Harold, Sherman, Belle, Flipper, Junior Snappy, Peggy Patty, William and Holly!

My asthma kept me from participating in "normal" kid activities like football, baseball, and anything else that involved a lot of full-tilt running. I had to learn to recreate at my own speed so I spent a lot of time hanging out in the woods, hunting, fishing, and climbing trees. I was a boy scout, excelling in what used to be called "Woodcraft." My scouting experiences made me feel most comfortable in the woods and so I became an outdoor kind of guy. Although my asthma improved as I got older, I never developed a fondness for team sports. Instead, I was drawn to individualistic pursuits like spelunking, canoeing, climbing, and skiing. As it turned out, these activites became the focus of my adult cartoon career.

Like most boys, I was packed with aggression. Since I couldn't discharge these impulses with "the guys" who got to attack one another under the guise of P.E., I did it with **art**. Drawing was something I could do under any circumstances and it allowed me to express myself and my frustrations. The most despised elementary school teachers and coaches were the subjects of my earliest, sickest caricatures. They became reptiles, blood-oozing fiends, or evil despots. Later, they became the casualties strewn about on bloody battlefields.

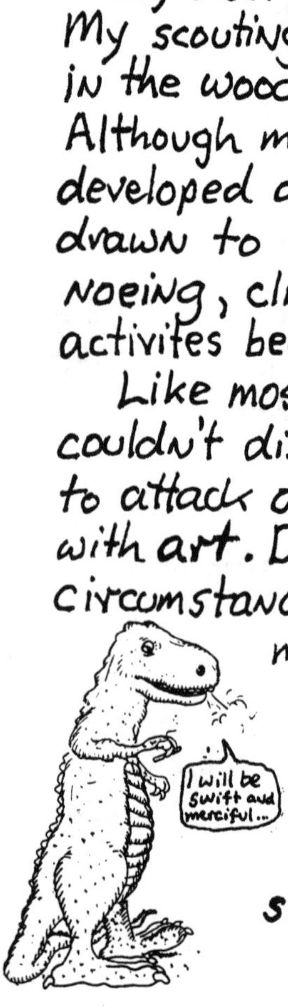
I will be swift and merciful...

Growing up in Birmingham in the sixties

was like getting a **kid doctorate** in race, violence, politics and the environment. George Wallace was the governor and "Bull" Connor was our Chief of Police. Nightly on the TV news we watched as our police force attacked peaceful civil rights demonstrators, including hundreds of little black kids our age. Firemen used firehoses to blow people down the street. Cops sicced their attack dogs on kids who didn't move quite fast enough. At church twice a week we listened to white preachers explain how segregation was god's own plan. When I asked if I could invite a black friend to church I was told "No, they have their own churches." This social madness was not lost on me and became fodder for political & religious satire.

Before
After

Why Klansmen Wear Hoods...

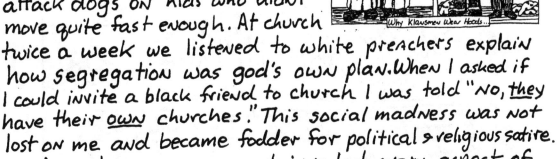

As a teenager my art invaded every aspect of my life. I was drawing all the time and cartoons became my second language, sometimes my first. In junior high I used cartoons to express the **zeitgeist** of typical pubescent males... **Killer Urinals!**

THE STRANGE CASE OF THE MEN'S ROOM OF DEATH
Help me
MEN
AAIEEE
SUDDENLY..
Wha... A Clamp?
FLUSH
-Clunk-
It's got me?
Twist Crunch
FROOSH

Oh God... It's pulling Me IN... Help... AIEEEE!
Gurk Crunch
my wife... my kids... my Job... Help Help... EAARG!
Glug Glug Glug

Helicopters were popular too!

we're off!
YAAAA
?

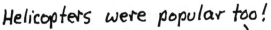

In high school I used my cartoons to explain to myself the weird world around me. By this time I'd fallen in love with Holly, my editor, muse and lifelong girlfriend. At 16, however, rather than actually speak the **icky love words**, I sent her cartoons of my affection...

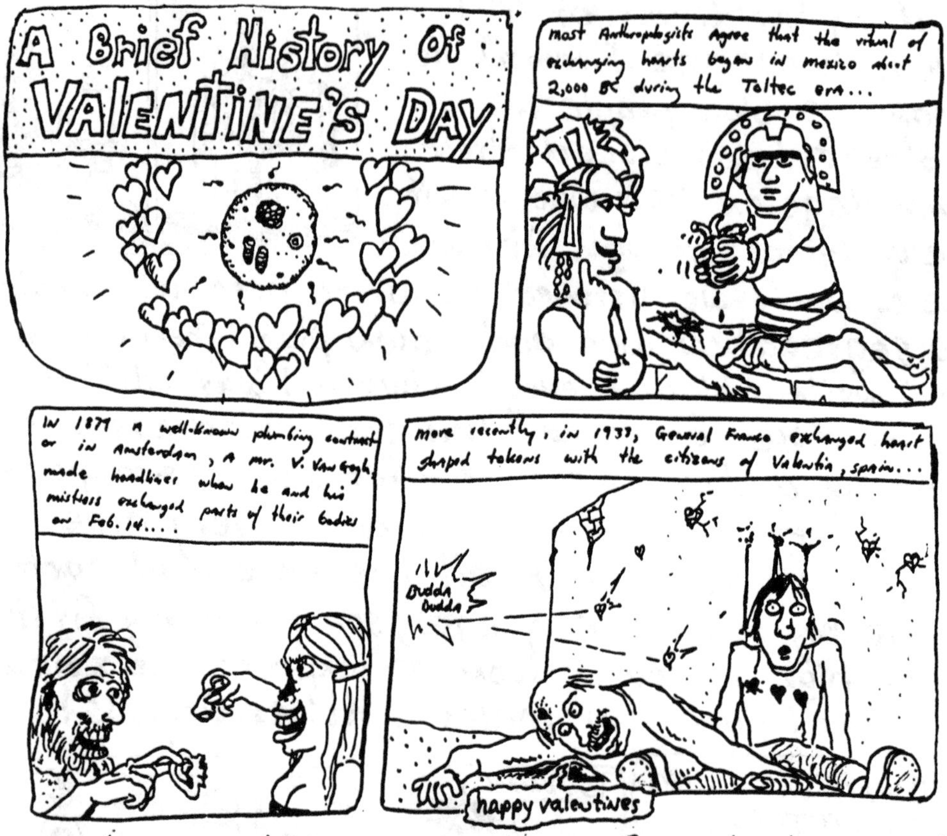

A Brief History Of
VALENTINE'S DAY
most Anthropologists agree that the ritual of exchanging hearts began in mexico about 2,000 BC during the Toltec era...
In 1877 a well-known plumbing contractor in Amsterdam, a mr. V. Van Gogh, made headlines when he and his mistress exchanged parts of their bodies on Feb. 14....
more recently, in 1937, General Franco exchanged heart shaped tokens with the citizens of Valentia, spain...
Budda Budda
happy valentines

This cartoon contains many of my favorite teenage themes blood and guts, bullets and their sound effects, politics, and a little anatomy. My token reference to "love" is shown by the traditional attack of the sperm on an egg surrounded by a picket of hearts... how romantic!

In the late 60's and early 70's, Holly and I comprised about 1/10 of Birmingham's tiny peacenik hippie population. We went to great lengths to look bizzare, which isn't that far in Alabama. We were way far out and like generations of teens before us, secretly enjoyed the uproar we caused, though we feigned selfrighteous indignation at the negative attention. Occasionally things got a little out of control and we would become the intended objects of threats, projectile spitting and worst of all, gun waving. In a unilateral effort to encourage a thoughtful pause in hostilities, I made a very limited edition (2) of **Charlie Manson Fan Club** t-shirts, Holly & I being the sole members. Then (or now for that matter) there was nothing more certain to set you apart from the flower people than the appearance of a friendly affiliation with Mr. Manson. Nobody messed with us anymore. Art 1, rednecks 0.

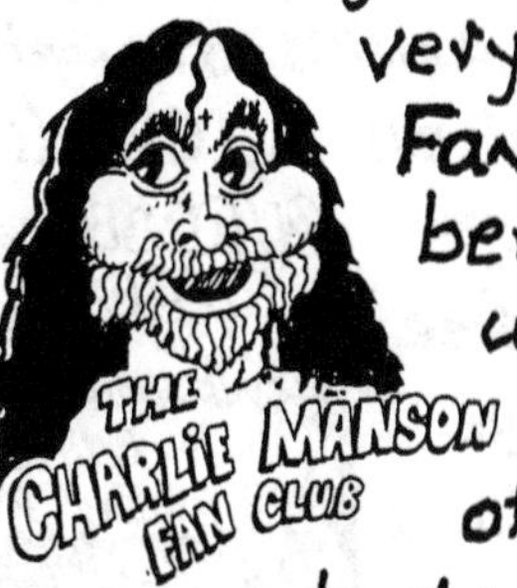
THE
CHARLIE MANSON
FAN CLUB

We were teenage political activists, as much for the scene as for the cause. I frequently did cartoons for underground newspapers. Holly's presence in my life happened to coincide with a series of adventures & misadventures in "higher" education. First, I dropped out of high school in the 11th grade. It wasn't Holly's fault that high school **sucked**. For me, every day was a battle. My teachers and classmates didn't find my shoulder-length hair and provocative t-shirts at all endearing. All my class notes became boredom-induced cartoon extravaganzas like this. (left- an actual page from my "civics" notebook.)

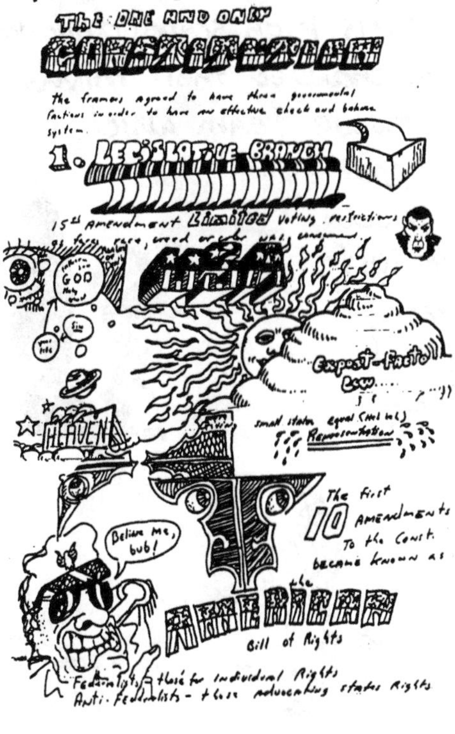
The one and only
The framers agreed to have three governmental factions in order to have an effective check and balance system.
1. Legislative Branch
15th Amendment Limited voting restrictions
GOD
Expost-facto law
Heaven
Small states equal (not b.) Representation
The first 10 amendments to the Const. became known as the
Bill of Rights
Believe me, bub!
Federalists - those for individual Rights
Anti-Federalists - those advocating states Rights

My high school experience was especially frustrating for me; until then learning had always been something I loved and did well. In 1971, despite my disillusionment with the educational system, (and a crappy dropout **job**), I decided to get out of Alabama and somehow go to college. I wrote

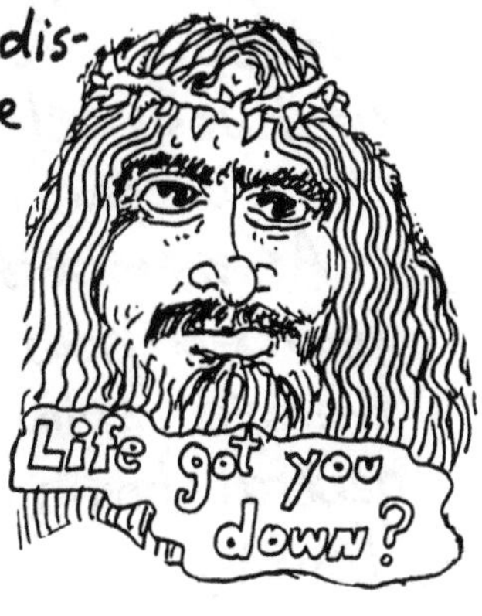
Life got you down?

lots of letters to colleges and to my surprise, I actually got permission to go to England and audit undergraduate classes at Oxford. I was going to be a "roads scholar"! The first cartoon I ever sold was to Oxtale, one of Oxford's alternative newsmagazines. Strangely enough, they wanted all my Charlie Manson material. Oxtale paid me 6 tax-free pounds ($12.00) a page for cartoons, in cold, hard cash!

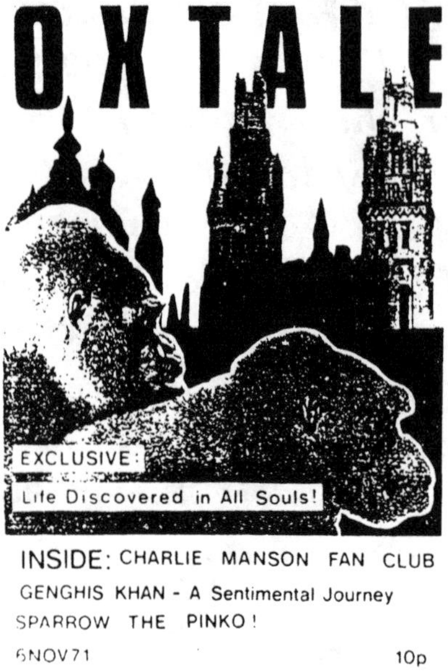
OXTALE
EXCLUSIVE:
Life Discovered in All Souls!
INSIDE: CHARLIE MANSON FAN CLUB
GENGHIS KHAN - A Sentimental Journey
SPARROW THE PINKO!
6NOV71
10p

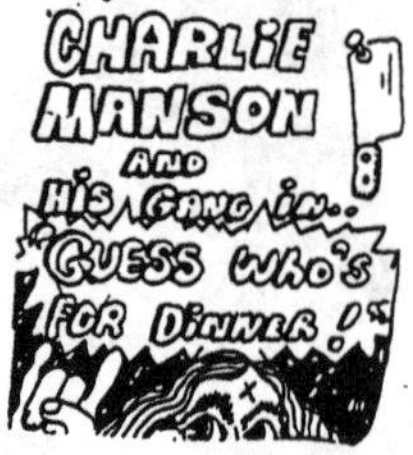
CHARLIE MANSON
AND
HIS GANG IN..
GUESS WHO'S FOR DINNER!

Even though things were going well, after one term I decided to return home. I missed Holly desperately and besides, I was running out of money. Thrilled as I was that Oxtale was publishing me regularly, it was impossible to live on $24 a month. Being a genuine starving artist was nowhere near as cool as I had anticipated. Most importantly, I had been accepted at St. Johns College as a real college student, sans high school diploma. I needed to get out there before they changed their minds!

St. Johns had a great search and rescue team which I immediately joined. It was my first opportunity to do some real climbing and mountaineering. Ironically, I had just successfully dodged the Draft and suddenly I found myself jumping out of Huey helicopters onto mountaintops on paramilitary-style "missions"!

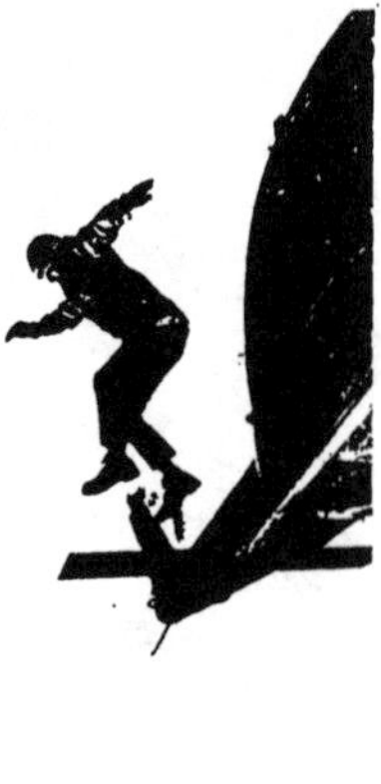

As members of the S&R team, we learned how to rappel, treat hypothermia, splint broken bones, and, in general, how to deal with wilderness trauma (usually our own!). My experiences in New

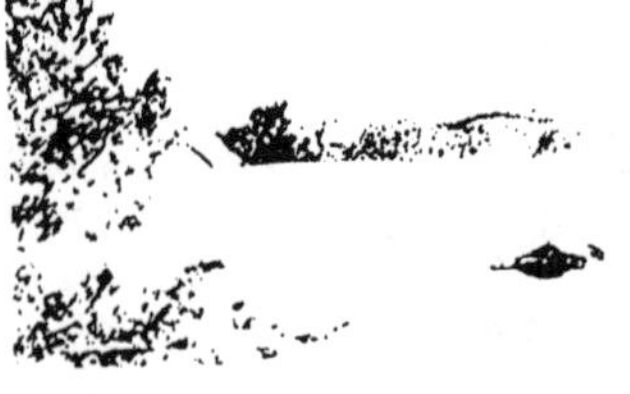

Mexico were the beginning of what has become a lifelong interest in anatomy, kinetics, and emergency medicine. Paramedic training has made it easier for me to visualize the physiology and body mechanics required to learn and to illustrate the complex physical moves involved in adventure sports. I can also envision the first aid procedures I will need to repair my buddies and myself while learning.

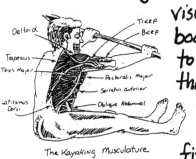

Ticep
Bicep
Deltoid
Trapezius
Teres Major
Pectoralis Major
Serratus anterior
Latissimus Dorsi
Oblique Abdominal
The Kayaking Musculature

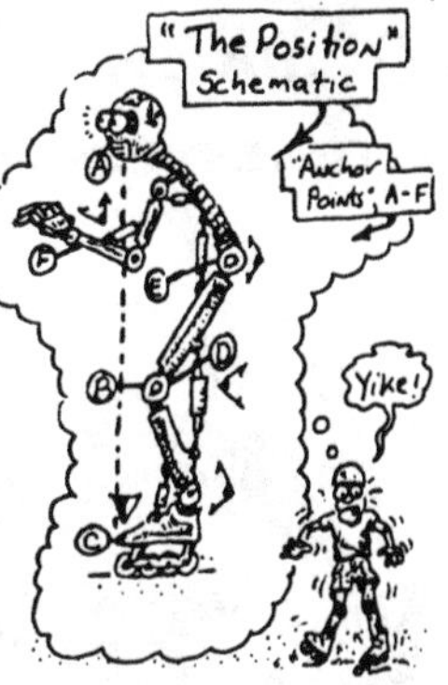

"The Position" Schematic
"Anchor Points", A-F
Yike!

My father died after my freshman year at St. Johns and I decided to return to Alabama to help out my mom. Holly hated Emory U. so we both transferred to a small liberal arts college in Birmingham to be together again. Being over-familiar with Birmingham, we spent all our spare time out of town hiking, camping, climbing, and boating.

We bought an ABS canoe from some good friends who had just opened the Liquid Adventure Canoe Shop in town. We didn't know exactly what we were doing on the maiden voyage when we wrapped our new canoe around a tree on a floodstage river, nearly drowning in the process. This was extremely exciting... we were hooked!

In the spring of 1976, Liquid Adventure opened a small outpost on the Locust Fork River in North Alabama. We spent all our spare time up there building the shop, guiding canoe trips and paddling a lot. I did whitewater cartoon t-shirts for the shop. Unfortunately the locals were unfamiliar with the beneficial economic effects of adventure tourism and didn't like river hippies at all! They vandalized cars, dropped trees and strung barbed wire across the rapids. Not <u>too</u> surprising given the culture clash. It was a **big surprise** when the shop "mysteriously" burned to the ground and KKK posters were nailed to the ruins.

The Liquid Adventure Canoe Shop.

Before
After

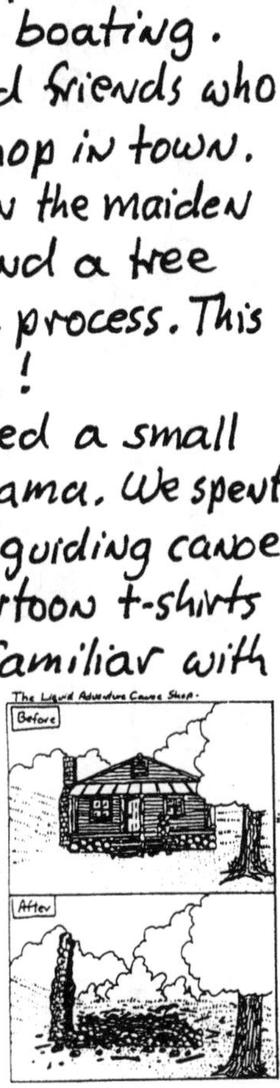

We got the message. Deciding to become refugees from war-torn Alabama, we moved to Chapel Hill, NC, which is to the South as Berkeley is to the West. We deserved a break. After we got settled, I added fly fishing and mountain biking to my outdoor repertoire. Way back then in mountain bike prehistory you couldn't just go out and buy a "mountain bike". You had to construct your own, part by part, on an old Schwinn cruiser frame.

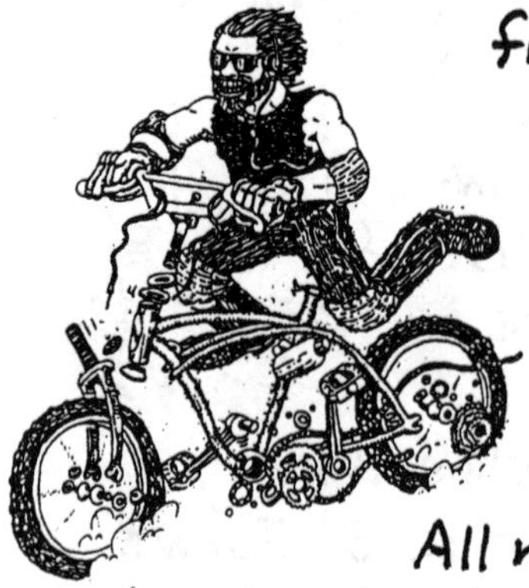

All my new interests and equipment needs cost a lot more money than we had. Holly was in graduate school and teaching at U.N.C. As generous as her stipend was (ha!), it wasn't enough to keep me in up-to-date equipment for even one of my chosen sports.

As with most people who live outside the mainstream culture (where all the money seems to be), I had to start thinking about how to make a living. By now I was 25 and the grown-ups were acting like I was supposed to be one of them. Naturally, I did this cartoon to give some order to my alternative career choices. ⤺

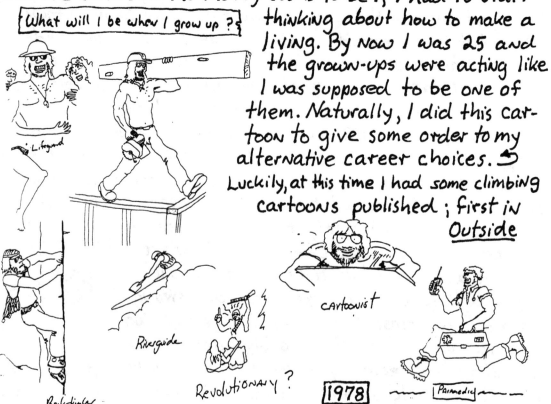

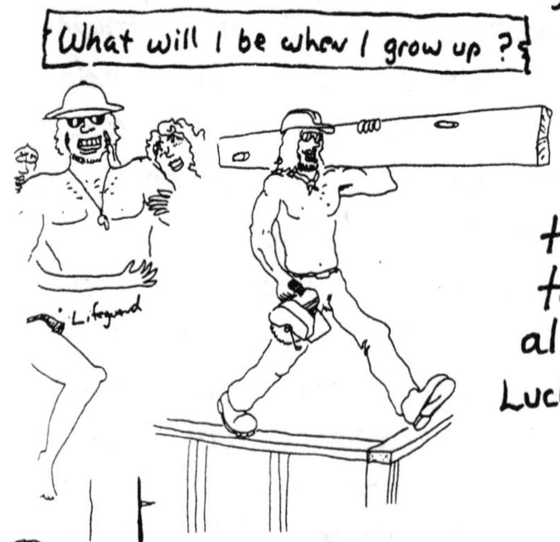
What will I be when I grow up?
Lifeguard

Luckily, at this time I had some climbing cartoons published; first in <u>Outside</u>

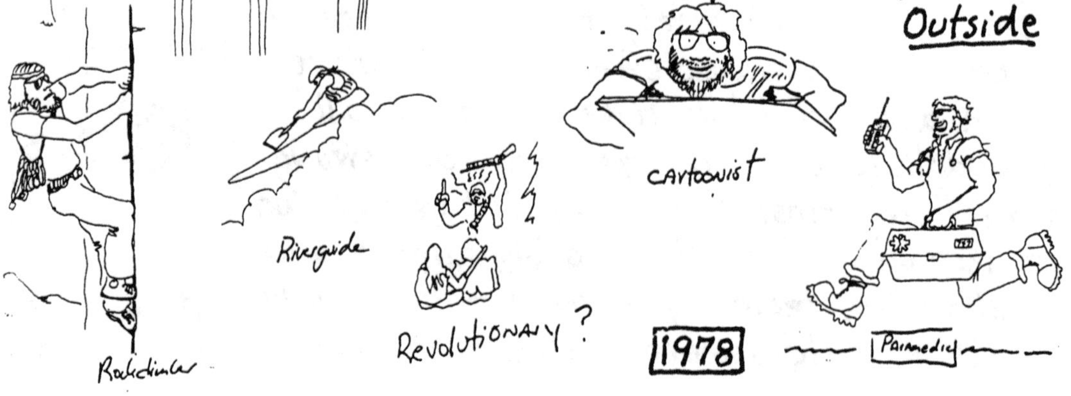
Rockclimber
Riverguide
Revolutionary?
Cartoonist
1978
Paramedic

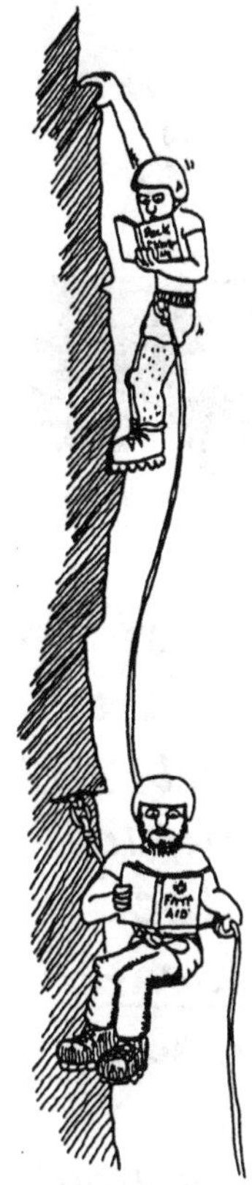

magazine by winning a contest for "the most outrageous climbing device or product". They published my "suck-em-ups" drawing and paid me $6.00! Off Belay, the now defunct but righteous climbing journal, published a few drawings and 'toons. After these minor but tantalizing successes I was beginning to wonder if I could actually make it as a professional climbing/kayaking illustrator/cartoonist. A "Real Job" loomed on the horizon...

Stalling, I got a job in a tiny paddle shop (7'x 30'), renting canoes to students so they could drink beer and get trashed on the nearby Haw River. I spent so much time giving directions to the put-in and drawing diagrams of rapids on scraps of paper that I finally just drew a big poster of the river. It was a river caricature with detailed rapid diagrams and prototypical boater wipe-out cartoons. By the end of that paddling season I realized I'd sold over a hundred maps of a river nobody had ever heard of. Now I began to consider whether I could sell enough maps to make a living at it. If so I would have to map rivers with more commercial viability than the Haw. Figuring I had nothing to lose I drew a map of the closest commercially rafted river, the Nantahala River. I'd swum it numerous times and knew every rock and riffle. We stopped at Nantahala Outdoor Center on our way to Birmingham for Christmas with the drawing. I had no appointment but hoped somebody would take a look at it and, ideally, order a few dozen maps on consignment.

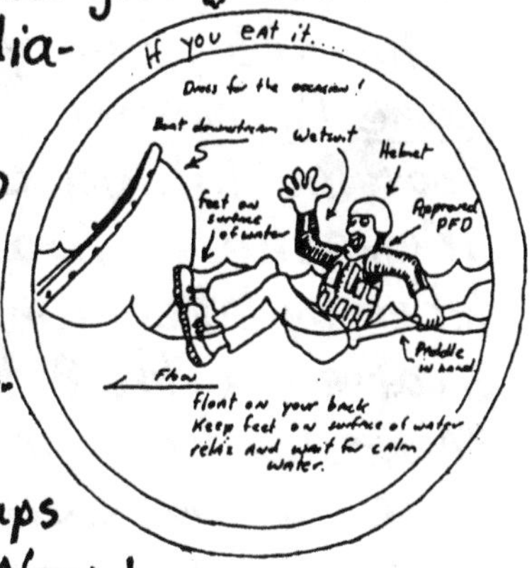

If you eat it...
Wetsuit
Helmet
Feet on surface of water
Approved PFD
Paddle in hand
Flow
Float on your back
Keep feet on surface of water
relax and wait for calm water.

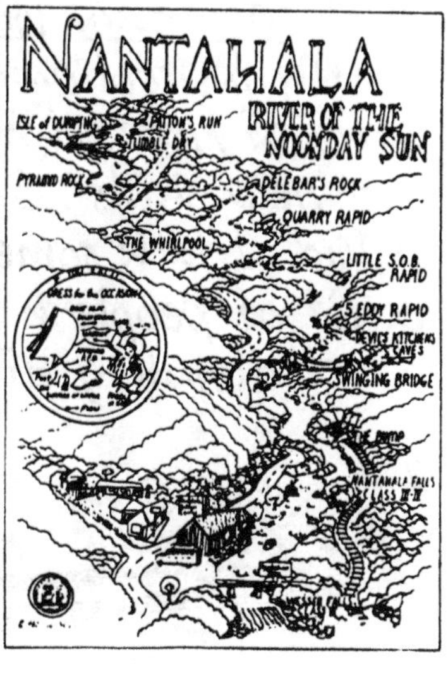

NANTAHALA
RIVER OF THE NOONDAY SUN
PATTON'S RUN
TUMBLE DRY
DELEBAR'S ROCK
QUARRY RAPID
THE WHIRLPOOL
LITTLE S.O.B. RAPID
SWINGING BRIDGE

John Barbour, the store manager, looked at the map and ordered **1,000!** Leaving the store I finally knew what I would do when I grew up.

I named my company **Class VII** which was Euro-boater lingo for a rapid that's a suicide run. By 1981 I'd mapped 10 classic southeastern rivers. At a raft show in February

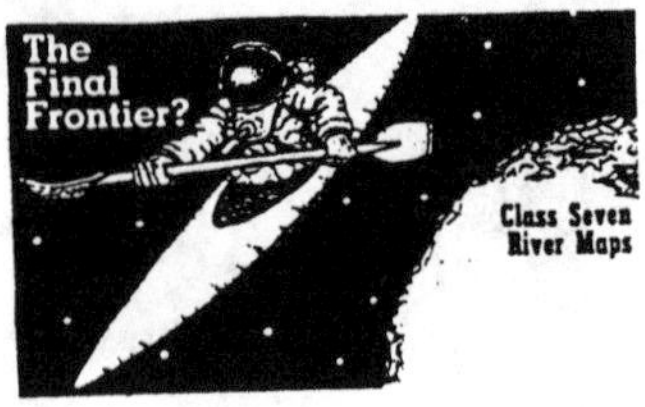
The Final Frontier?
Class Seven River Maps

I was approached by Bob Sehlinger, who had just started his own publishing company. He asked if I was interested in doing a book of my maps for him to publish. I literally slid down the wall onto the floor, knocking over a paddle display. I nodded: **yes, I was interested!**

In 1983, two years after publishing my Whitewater Home Companion, Bob, Holly, and I started a new outdoor publishing company, Menasha Ridge Press. "Menasha" is Iroquois for "...word that must be spelled-out-letter-by-letter-whenever spoken on the telephone". We started with 8 titles including my map book. Today Menasha has over 100 titles in print, 10 of which were written and illustrated by me. After doing two volumes of river maps I wrote 4 outdoor humor books on whitewater, skiing, and mountain biking, as well as three instructional books (Kayak, Inline, and Mountain Bike).

My instructional books are basically spruced-up versions of notes I make to myself in the process of learning new skills. Since I didn't participate in athletics as a kid, I lack some skills and body memories a lot of people have. This results in a vast quantity of crash and burn experiences (i.e.- "material") for me to draw upon for my diagrams & cartoons. The basic goal of my instructional

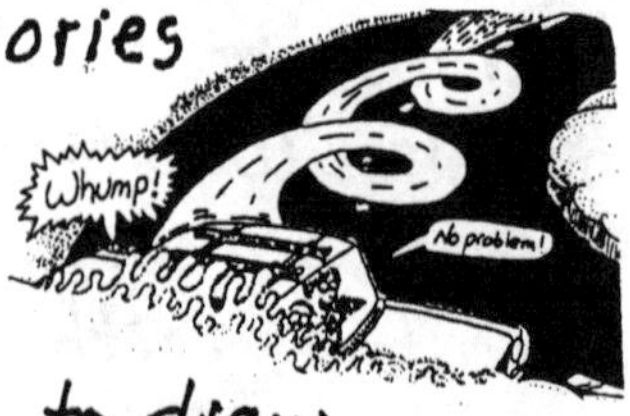
Whump!
No problem!

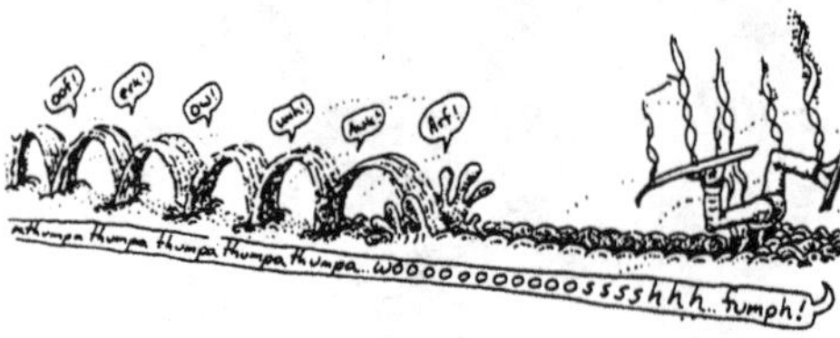

books is to teach you how NOT to get trashed as much as I did learning each skill level. As my skills improve in the course of the book, I also experience **NOT** getting trashed so I can illustrate learning success. "Learning successes" are rarely as funny and entertaining as colorful beginner crash and burns.

Sometimes I get blocked and can't for the life of me remember if anyone likes my work or thinks it's even remotely funny. Holly reminds me in no uncertain terms that yes, I am funny and lots of people do appreciate my cartoons & illustrations. Holly is my muse, when she's not being anal compulsive and reorganizing my life. She even comes up with some of the cartoons that I do, especially really bad puns. (above)

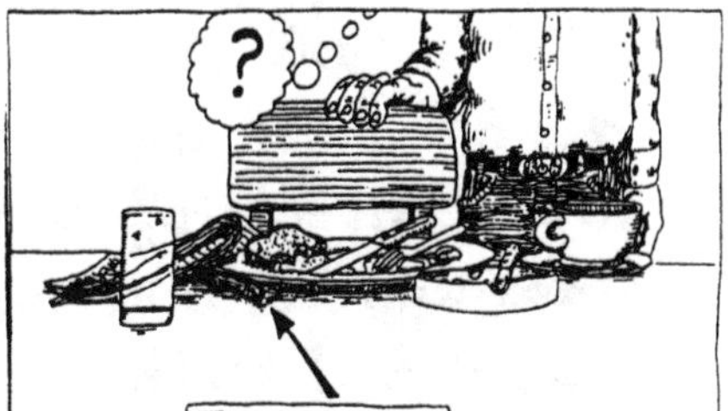
?
The Missing Link

She also edits everything I write and even though it really pisses me off when she deletes my **favorite paragraph** (including the story I wanted to tell here about Lazlo, the mad gypsy I roomed with in the Rome youth hostel in 1971 who smashed Michelangelo's "Pieta" a week after I left Italy and was a really interesting character (I thought!). I eventually agree that her suggestions are right, usually...

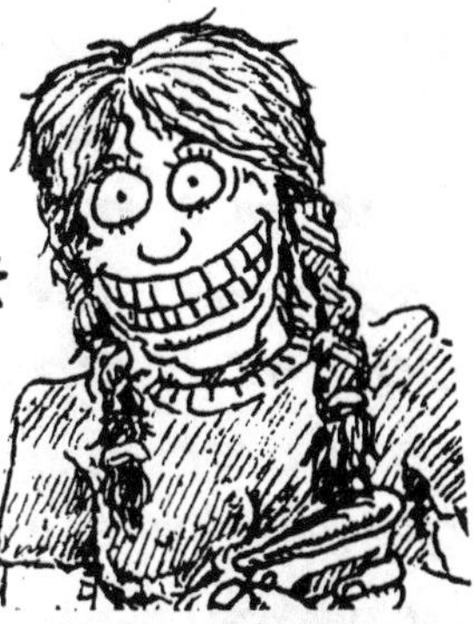

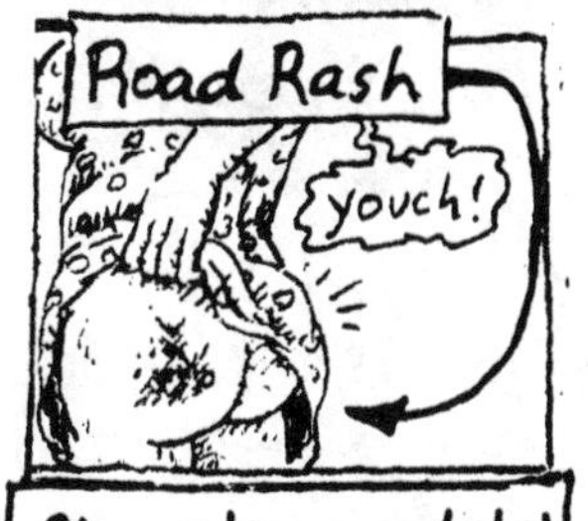
Road Rash
youch!
She also models!

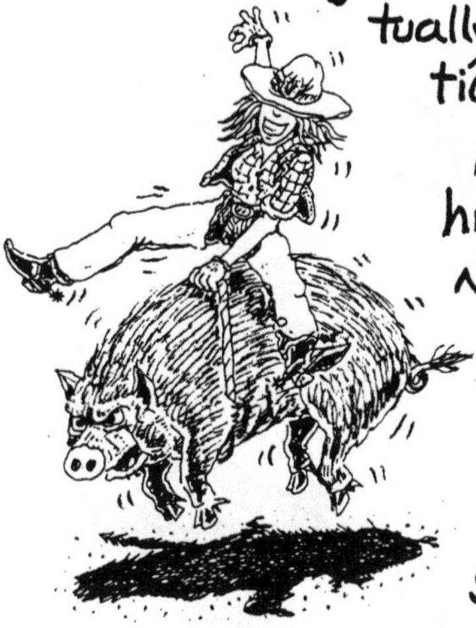

Holly was my climbing, hiking, and paddling partner until 1977, two years after she was diagnosed with Rheumatoid Arthritis (1975). During her final year of paddling she resorted to duct-taping her ruined hands to her paddle because she couldn't grip. This gave me and our paddling buddies conniption fits because of the danger she was putting herself in. It was a forced retirement, by me. She still accompanys me on paddling trips when she's able. She's remained incredibly conversant on all aspects of the sports we used to do. She can hold her own in any campfire debate. After editing my skating book, <u>Inline</u>, she swears that if she only had a body-splint and a pair of orthopedic street skates she'd kick my ass on any ramp or halfpipe. I have no doubt that she would.

We've lived together since 1974, "in sin" until just $1\frac{1}{2}$ years ago. Nowdays we live in the woods outside of Chapel Hill with our dog, two potbellied pigs, a passel of turtles, lizards, snakes, and the occasional marsupial. I still regularly get crunched on my mountain bike or inline skates. I still paddle whitewater and ski, albeit in an ultra-conservative manner these days. I even map the occasional river, bike trail, or ski resort. I'm teaching my nine year-old nephew, Basie, to climb and boat. He's already showing signs of Vulgarianism (!). So, these days when I mess up and find myself flying head-over-heels through the air, in those precious seconds before the inevitable crash-landing, I comfort myself with this thought...

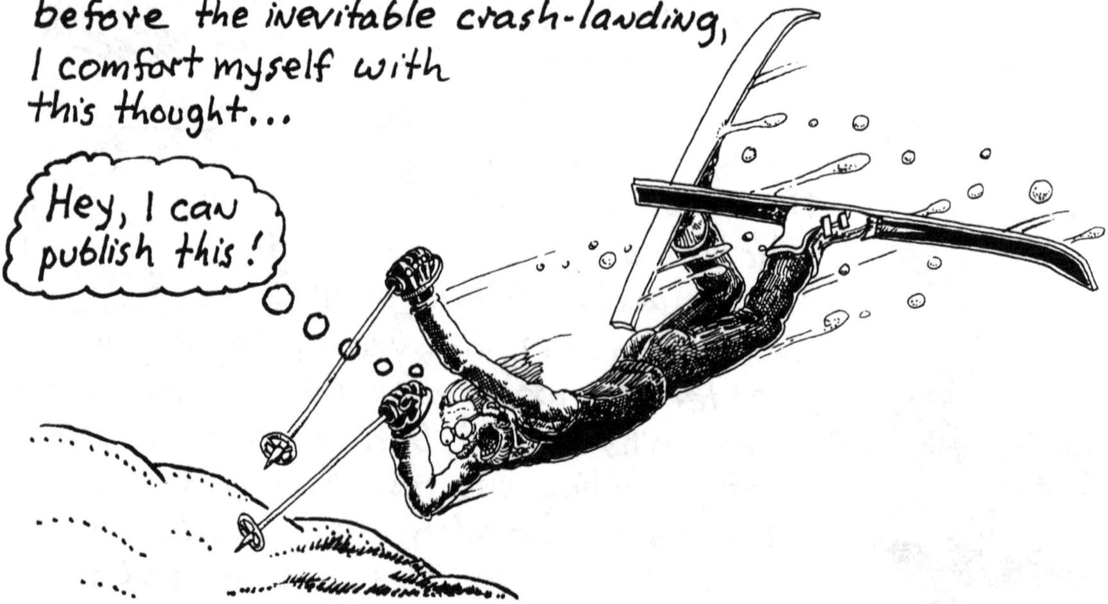
Hey, I can publish this!

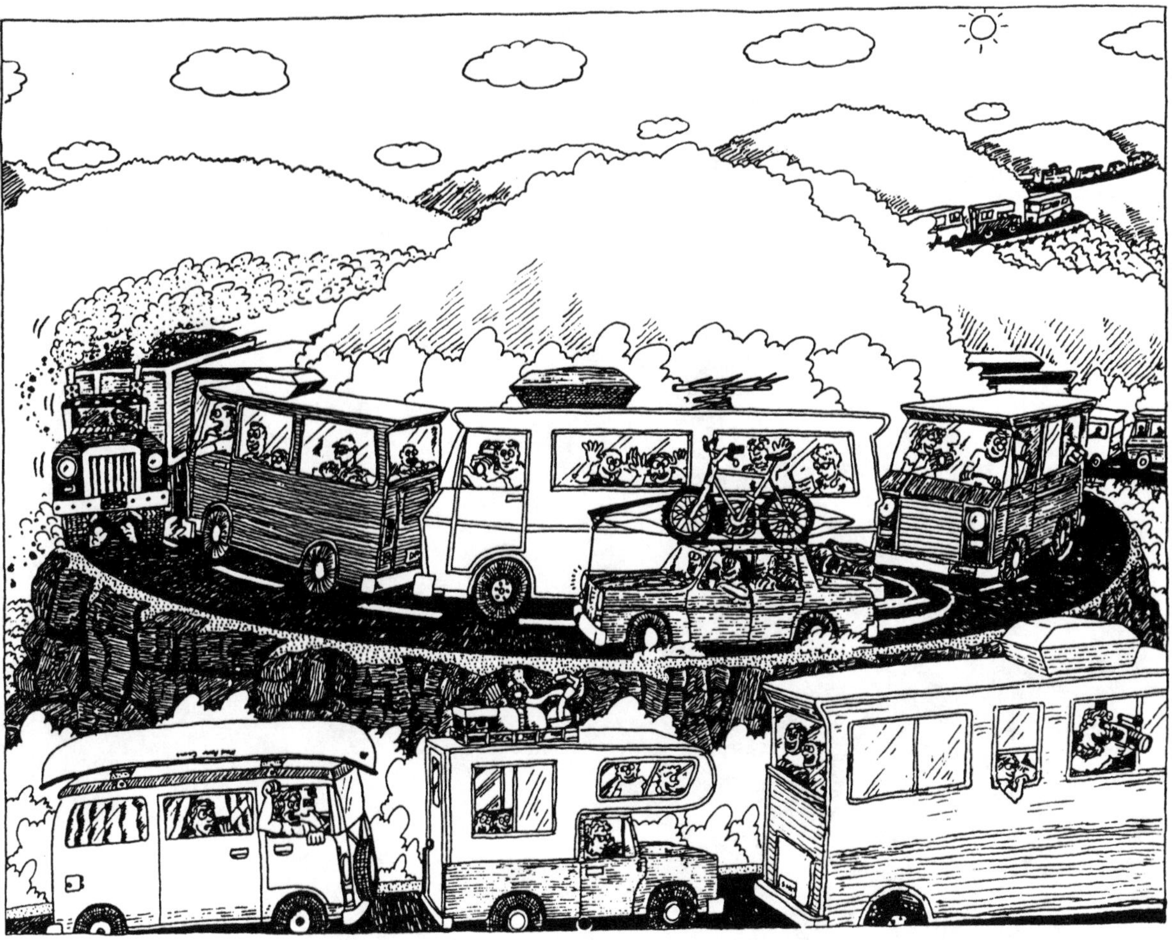

Blue Ridge Parkway, 1980. Holly is still a helluva mountain driver...

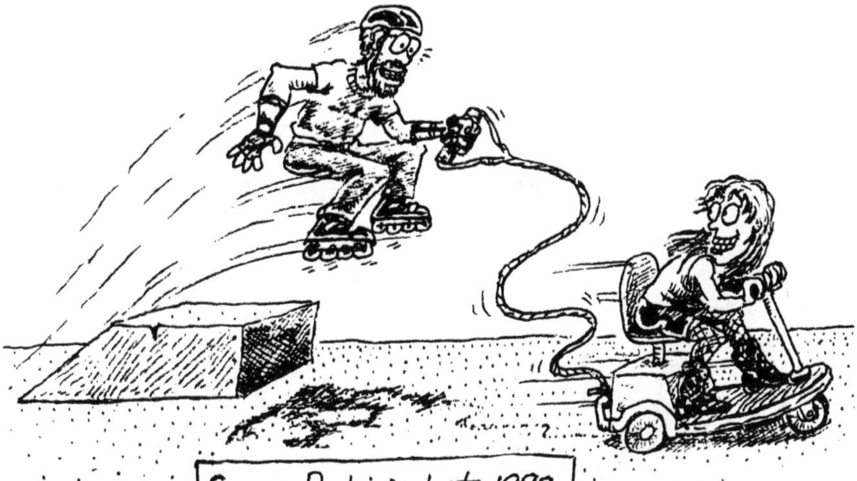

Some Parking Lot, 1999

Ah, Wilderness...

Extreme Cartoons By The Master Of Disaster

Running Rivers

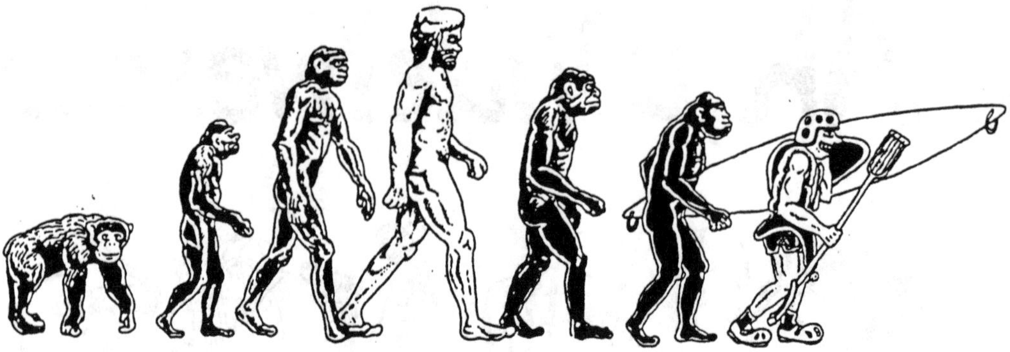

Does Kayaking have a hidden metaphysical agenda? You Decide...

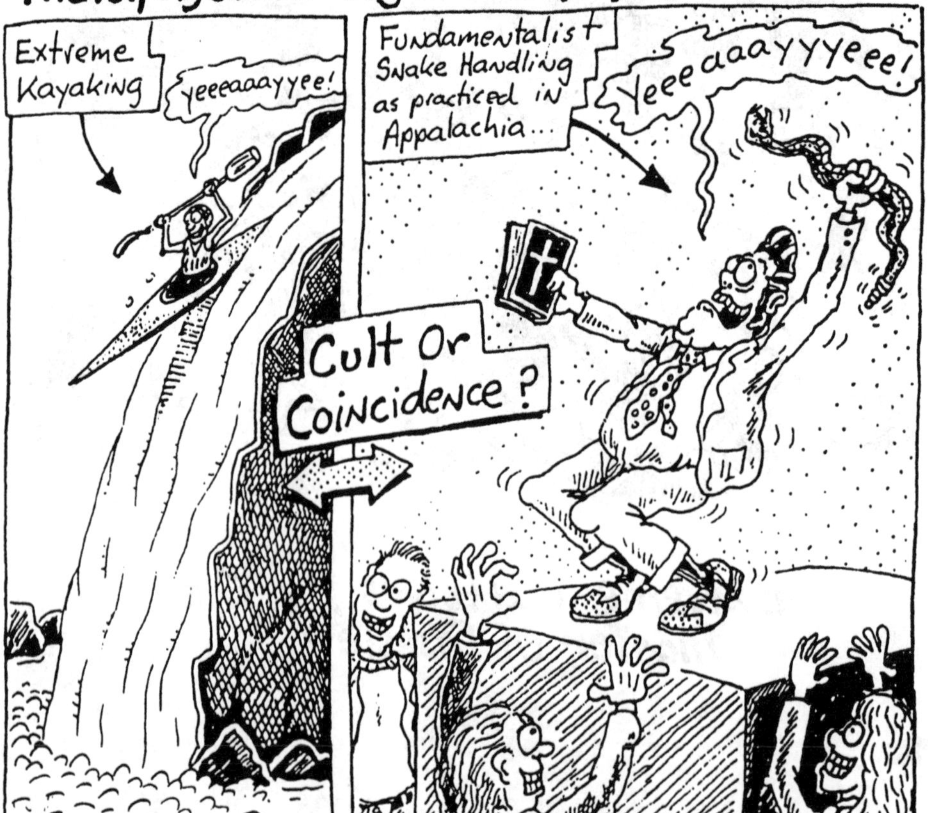
Extreme Kayaking
yeeeaaayyee!
Fundamentalist Snake Handling as practiced in Appalachia...
Yeeeaaayyyeee!
Cult Or Coincidence?

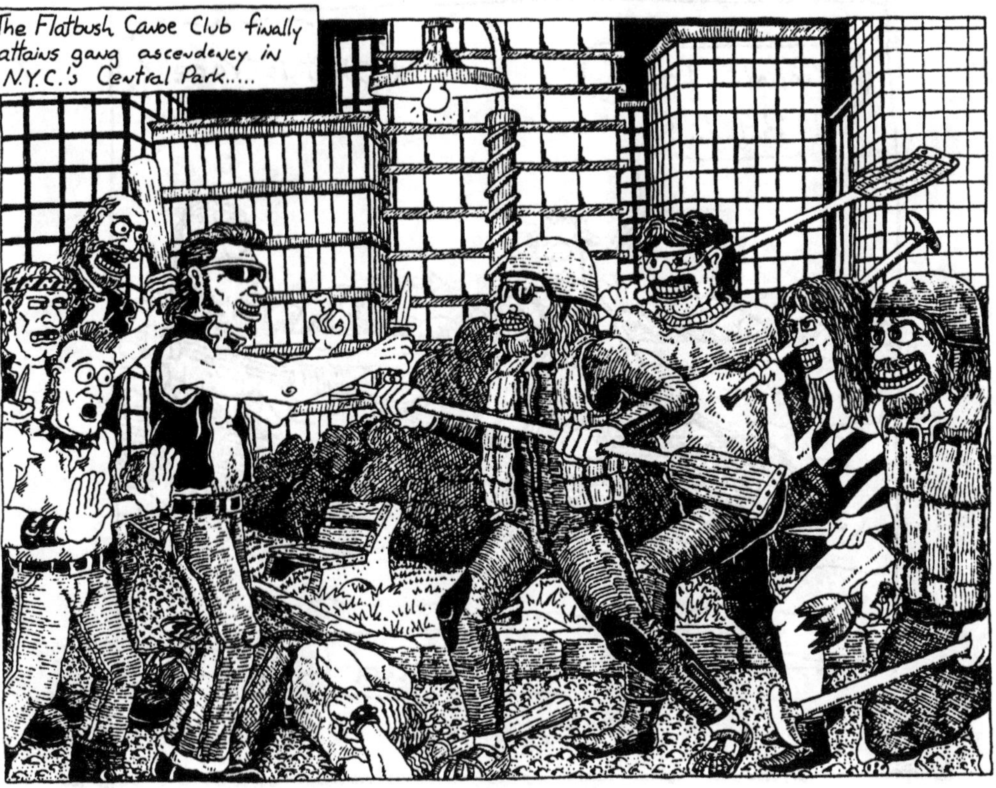
The Flatbush Canoe Club finally attains gang ascendency in N.Y.C.'s Central Park.....

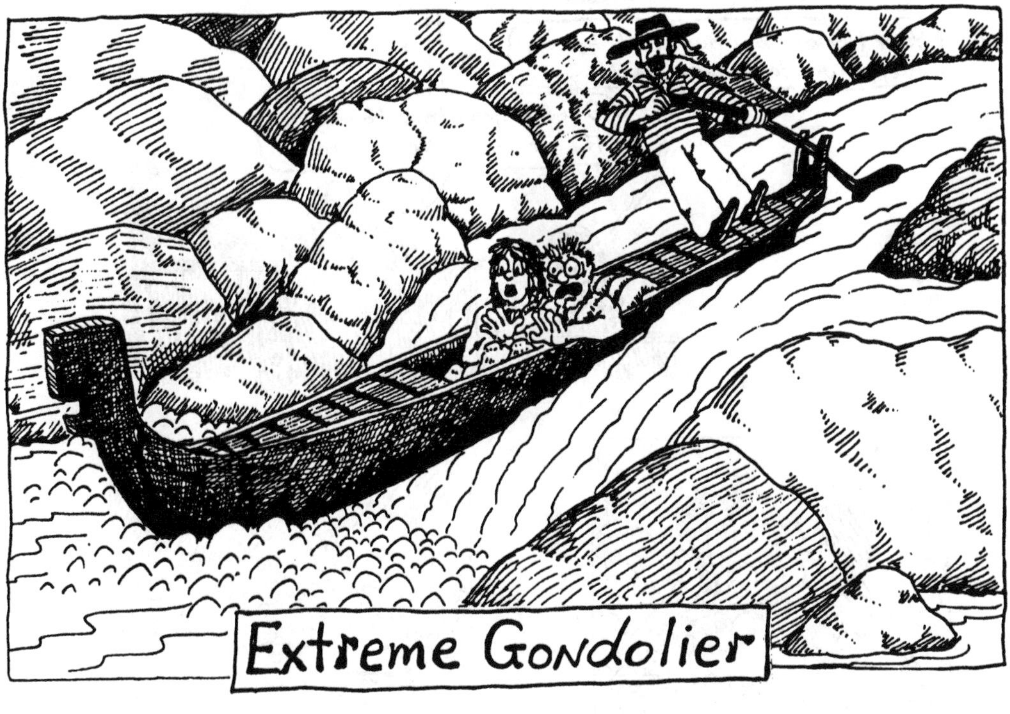
Extreme Gondolier

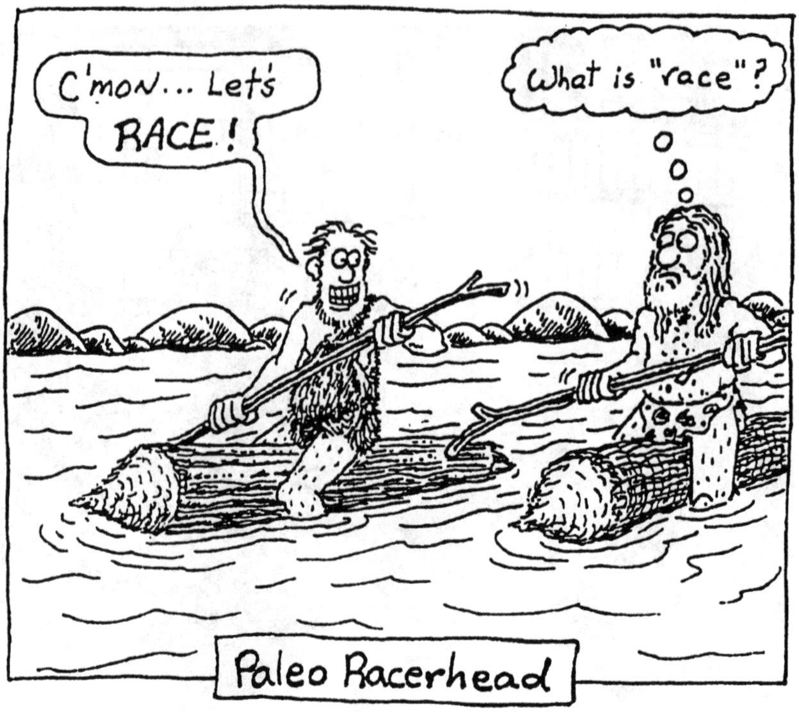
C'mon... Let's RACE!
What is "race"?

Paleo Racerhead

Whitewater divorce - What happens when one member of a couple gets fed up with tandem open boating and buys a kayak, C-1 or solo canoe.

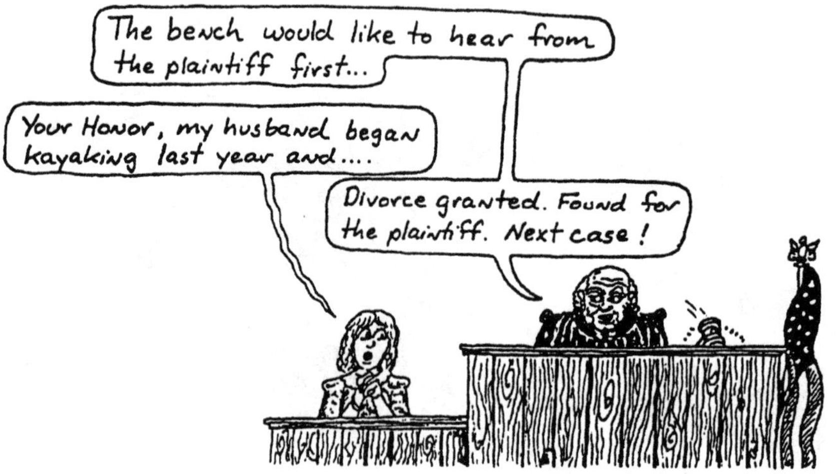
The bench would like to hear from the plaintiff first...
Your Honor, my husband began kayaking last year and....
Divorce granted. Found for the plaintiff. Next case!

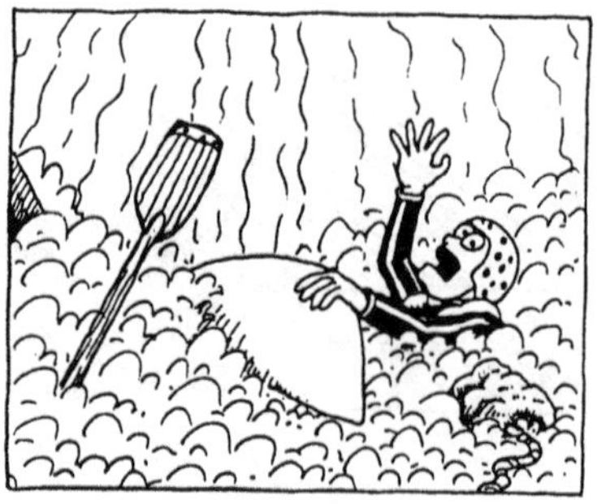

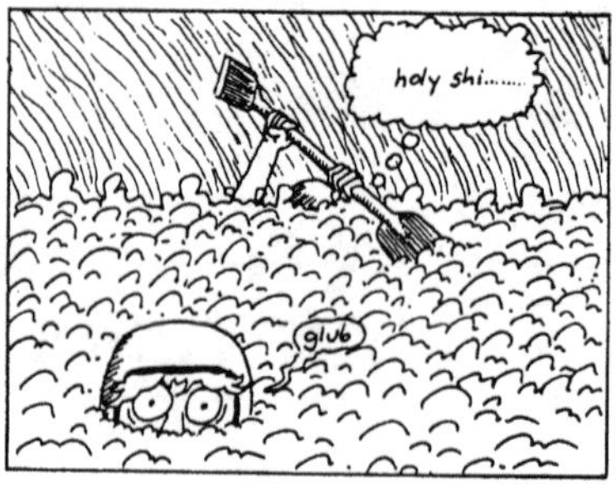
holy shi......
glub

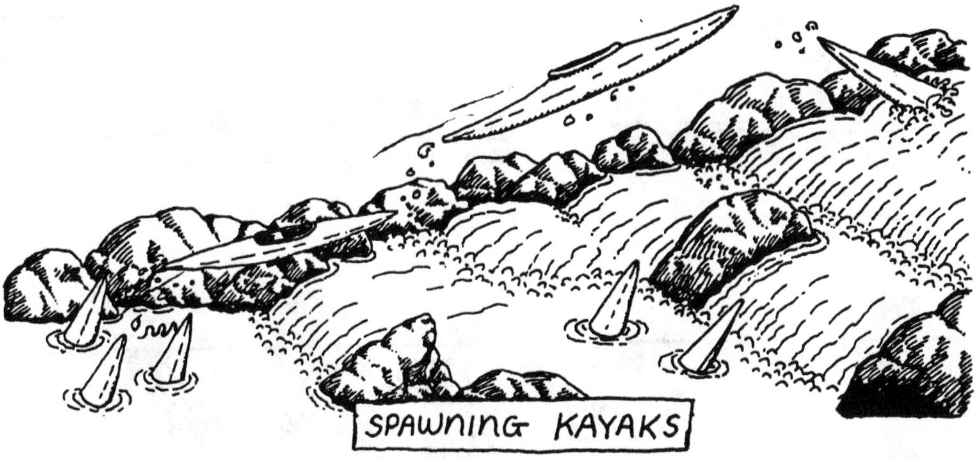
SPAWNING KAYAKS

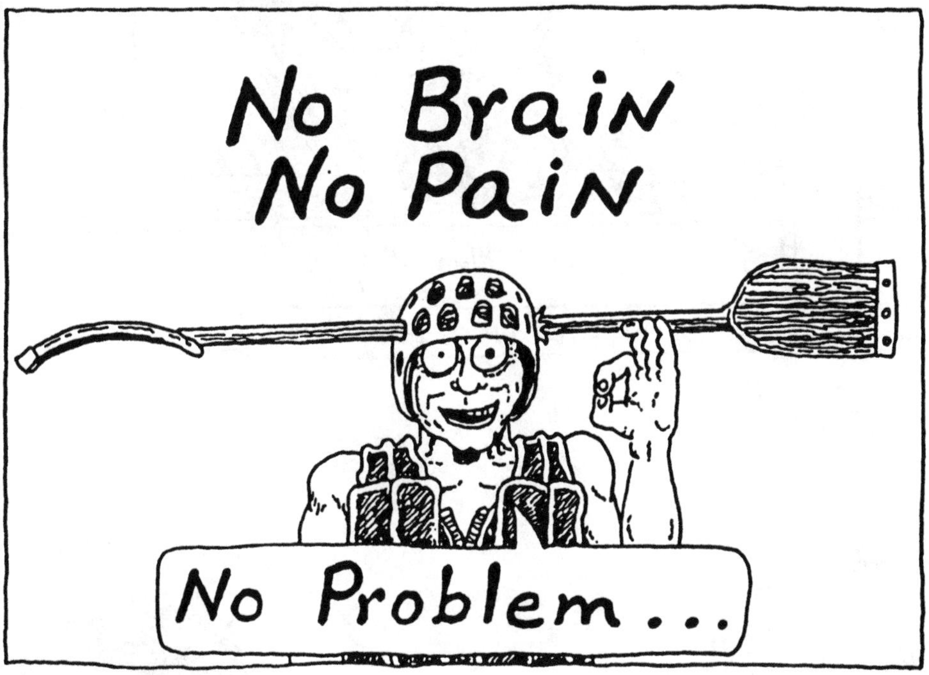
No Brain
No Pain
No Problem...

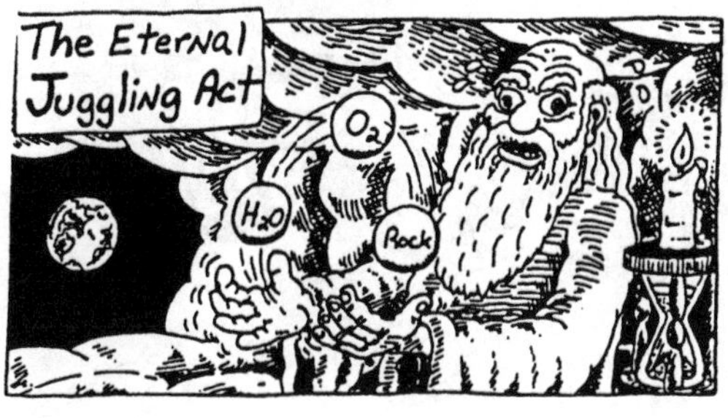
The Eternal Juggling Act
O_2
H_2O
Rock

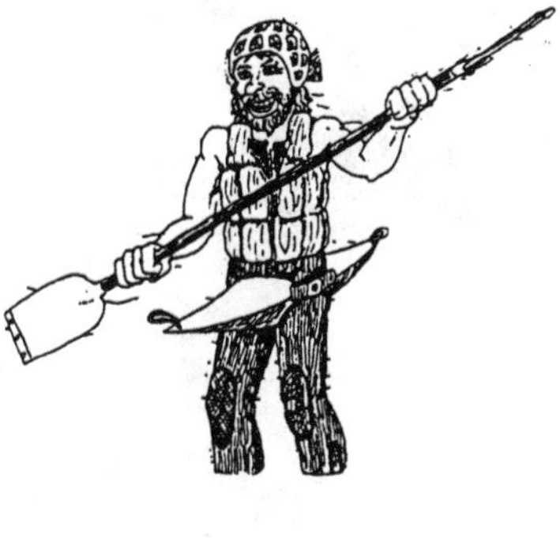

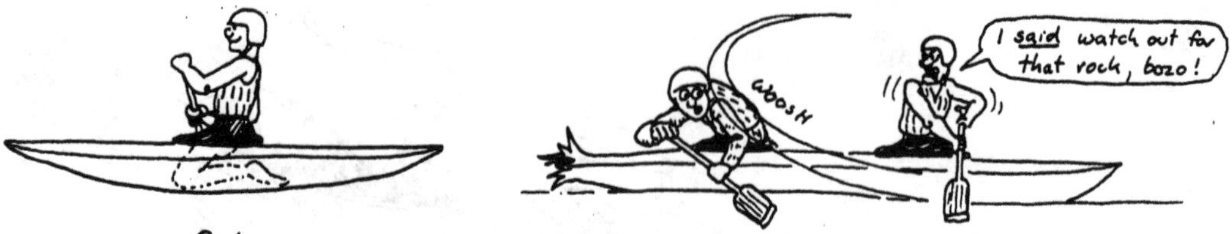
WOOSH
I said watch out for that rock, bozo!

C-1

C-2

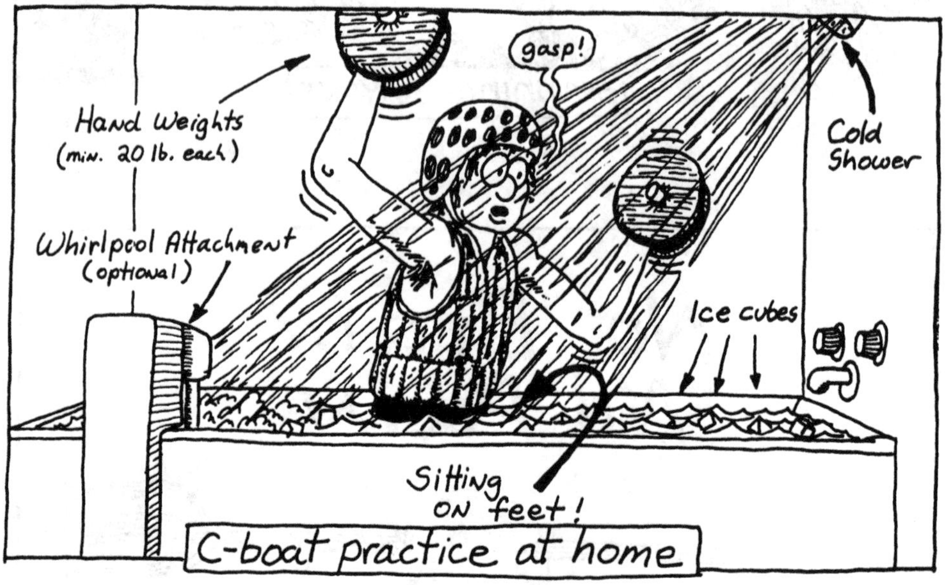
gasp!
Hand Weights
(min. 20 lb. each)
Cold Shower
Whirlpool Attachment
(optional)
Ice cubes
Sitting on feet!
C-boat practice at home

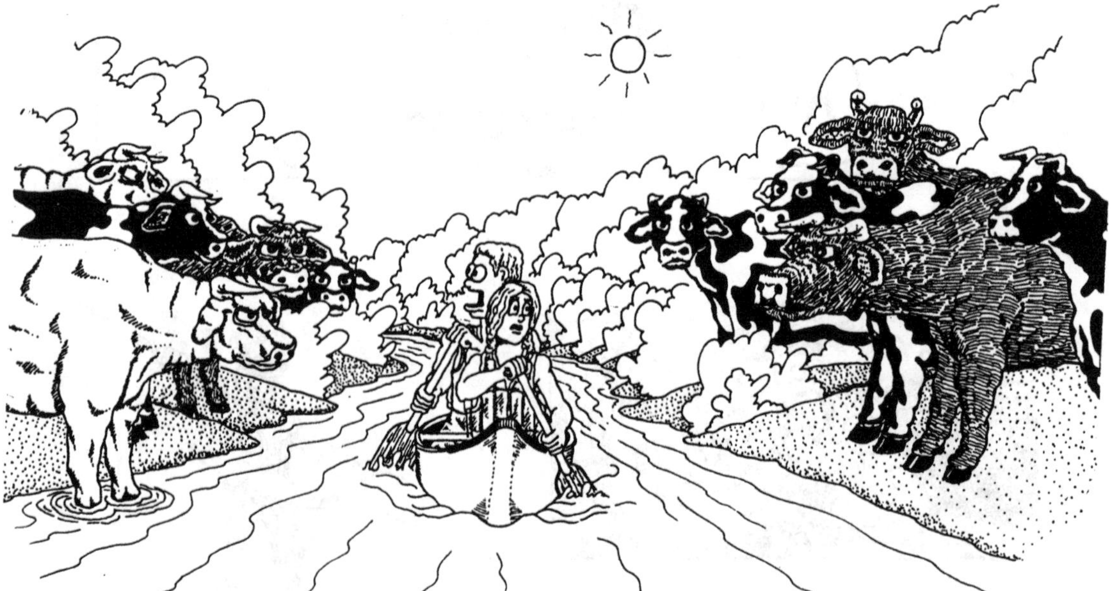

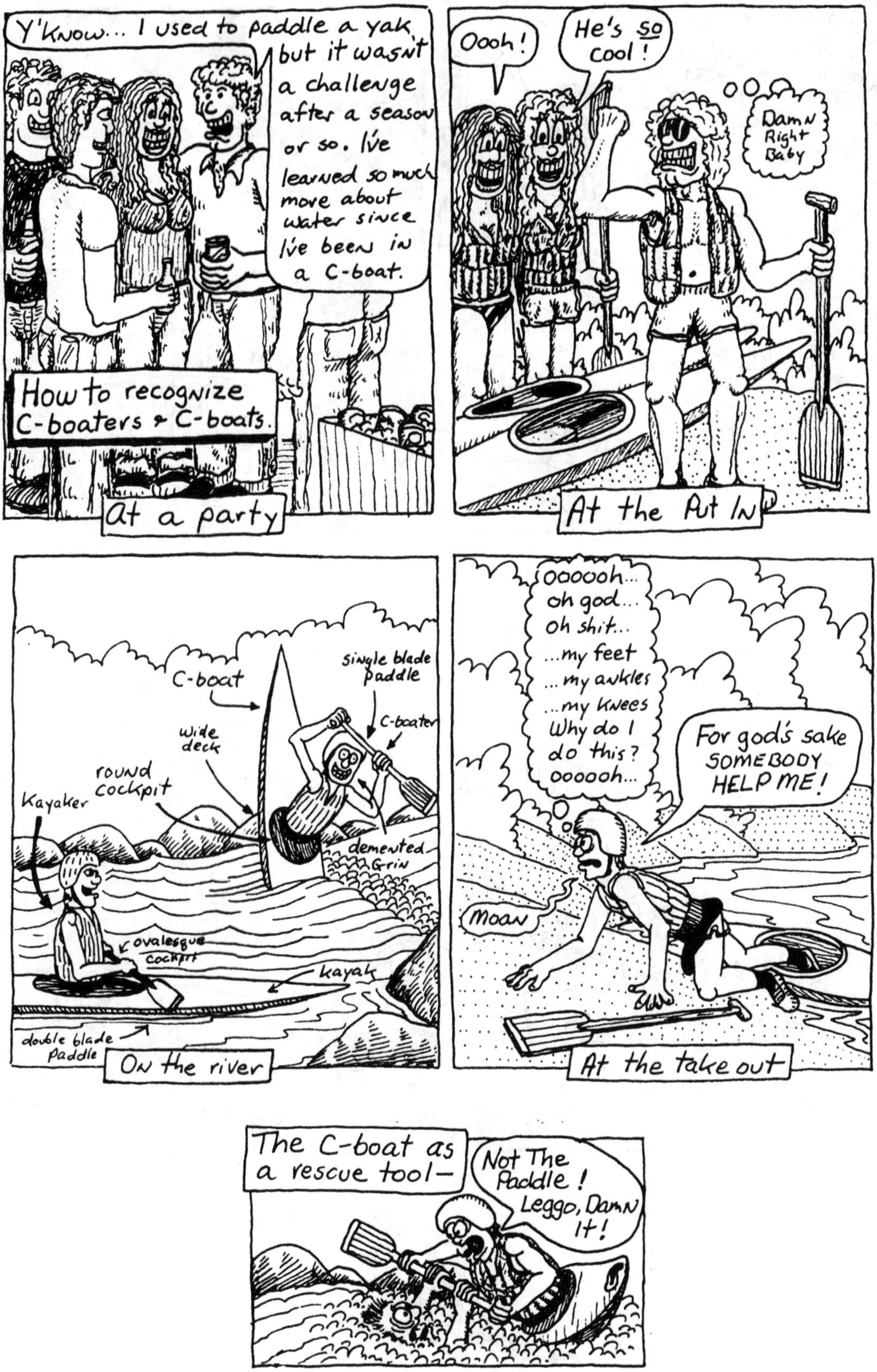
Y'Know... I used to paddle a yak, but it wasn't a challenge after a season or so. I've learned so much more about water since I've been in a C-boat.
How to recognize C-boaters & C-boats.
At a party
Oooh!
He's so cool!
Damn Right Baby
At the Put In
C-boat
single blade paddle
C-boater
wide deck
round cockpit
Kayaker
demented Grin
ovalesque cockpit
kayak
double blade Paddle
On the river
oooooh... oh god... oh shit... ...my feet ...my ankles ...my knees Why do I do this? oooooh...
For god's sake SOMEBODY HELP ME!
Moan
At the take out
The C-boat as a rescue tool—
Not The Paddle! Leggo, Damn it!

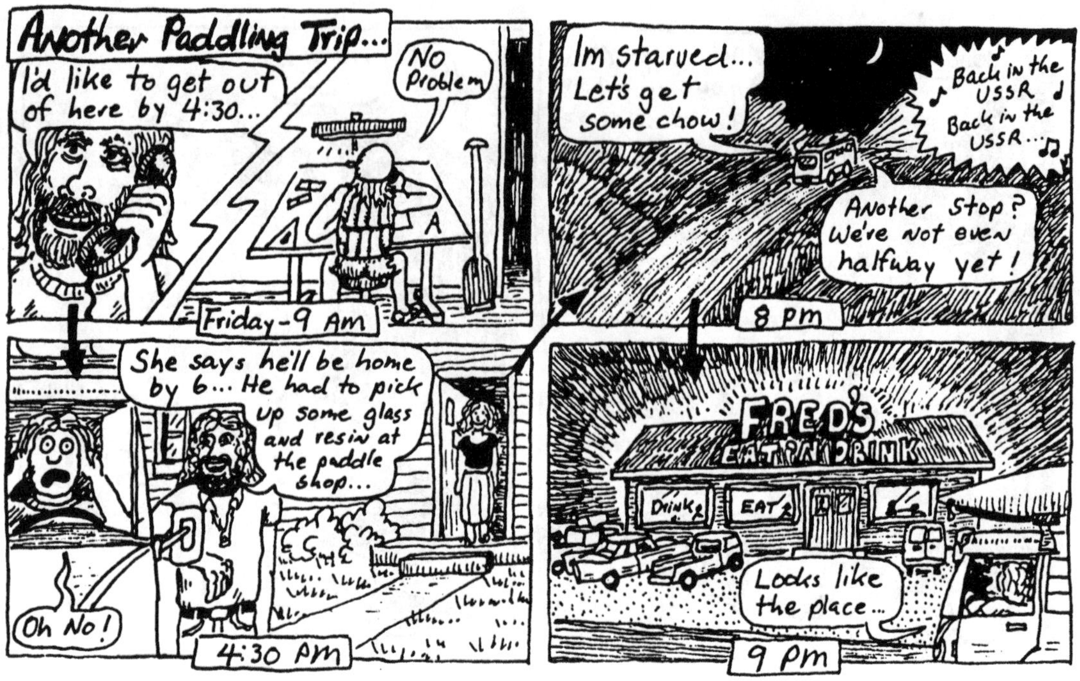
Another Paddling Trip...
I'd like to get out of here by 4:30...
No Problem
Friday-9 AM
Im starved... Let's get some chow!
Back in the USSR Back in the USSR...
Another Stop? We're not even halfway yet!
8 pm
She says he'll be home by 6... He had to pick up some glass and resin at the paddle shop...
Oh No!
4:30 PM
FRED'S
DRINK
EAT
Looks like the place...
9 pm

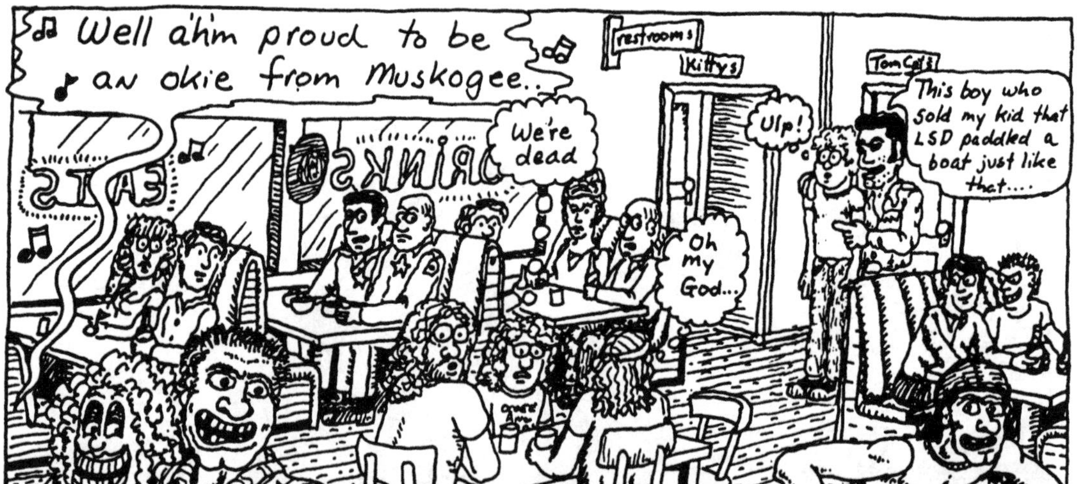
Well a'him proud to be an okie from Muskogee..
restrooms
Kittys
TomCats
We're dead
Ulp!
This boy who sold my kid that LSD paddled a boat just like that...
Oh my God...
Tee hee
You betcha Jim-Bob!
Hey Ed... Play that'un about th' Faggot Trucker! Har Har Har

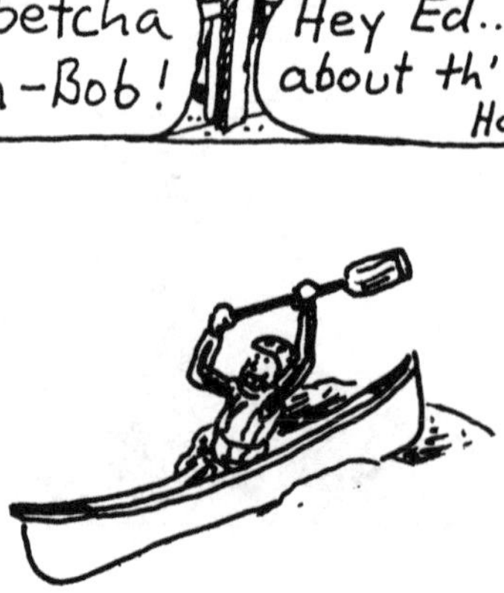

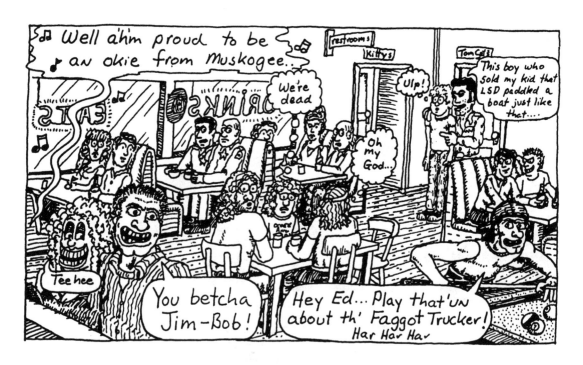

Moments Later..
Come back here, you Hippies!
Har Har
How far now?
A "mere" 200 miles...
11 pm
Sardines & Beer would suit me just fine..
U-TOTE EM
You fellers goin' fishin'?
Yeah!
You bet!
really..
ICEE
ICE
10 pm
When are we going to get to the camping area?
Soon... real soon
I think he's lost.
ZZZ
I've only camped here 25 times... shut up!
12 pm
We're here!
Zzzz!
Zzzz..
Zzzz
Wake up, guys - It's time to go to sleep!
1 Am
Where ARE we?
Well.. it's not West Hell, so it must be East Hell.
Kilgore National Forest, Bozo.
Anybody seen my tent pegs?
1:30 Am

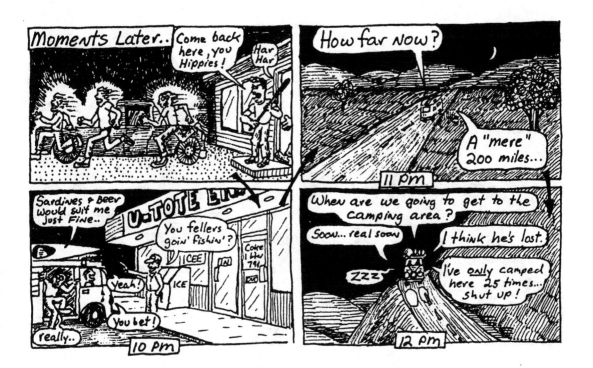

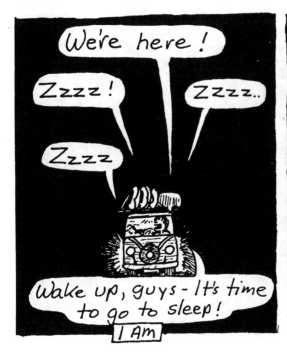

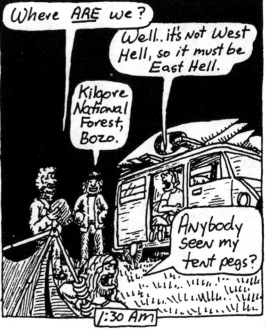

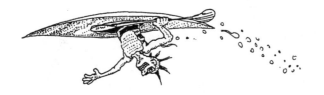

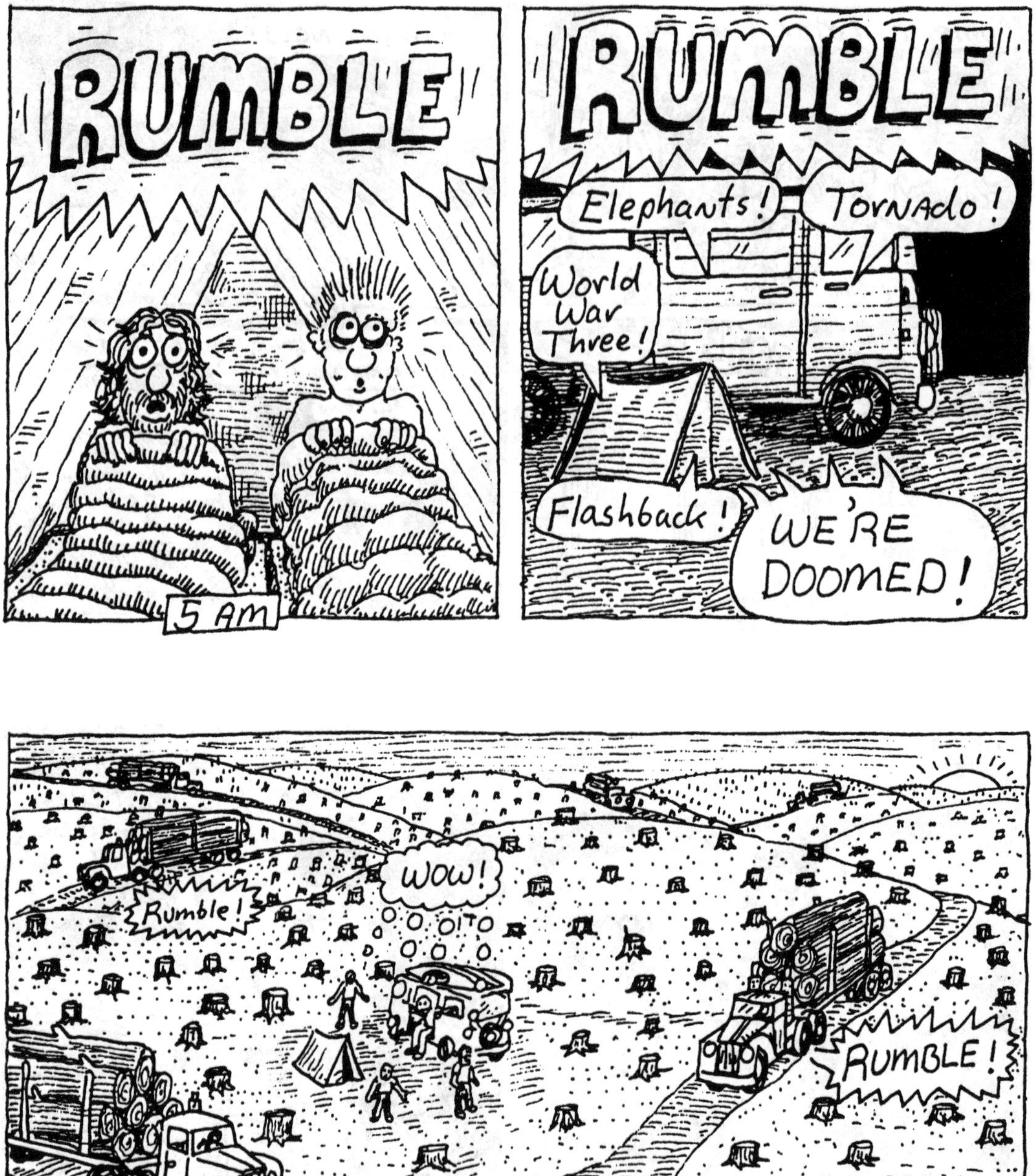
RUMBLE
5 AM
RUMBLE
Elephants!
Tornado!
World War Three!
Flashback!
WE'RE DOOMED!
WOW!
Rumble!
RUMBLE!
RUMBLE
Author's Note: This is a True story!

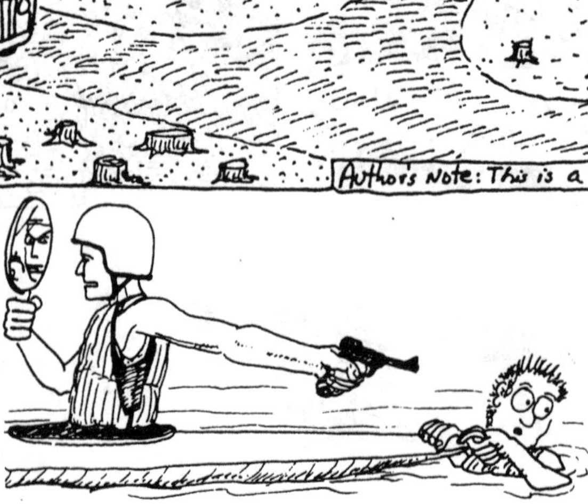

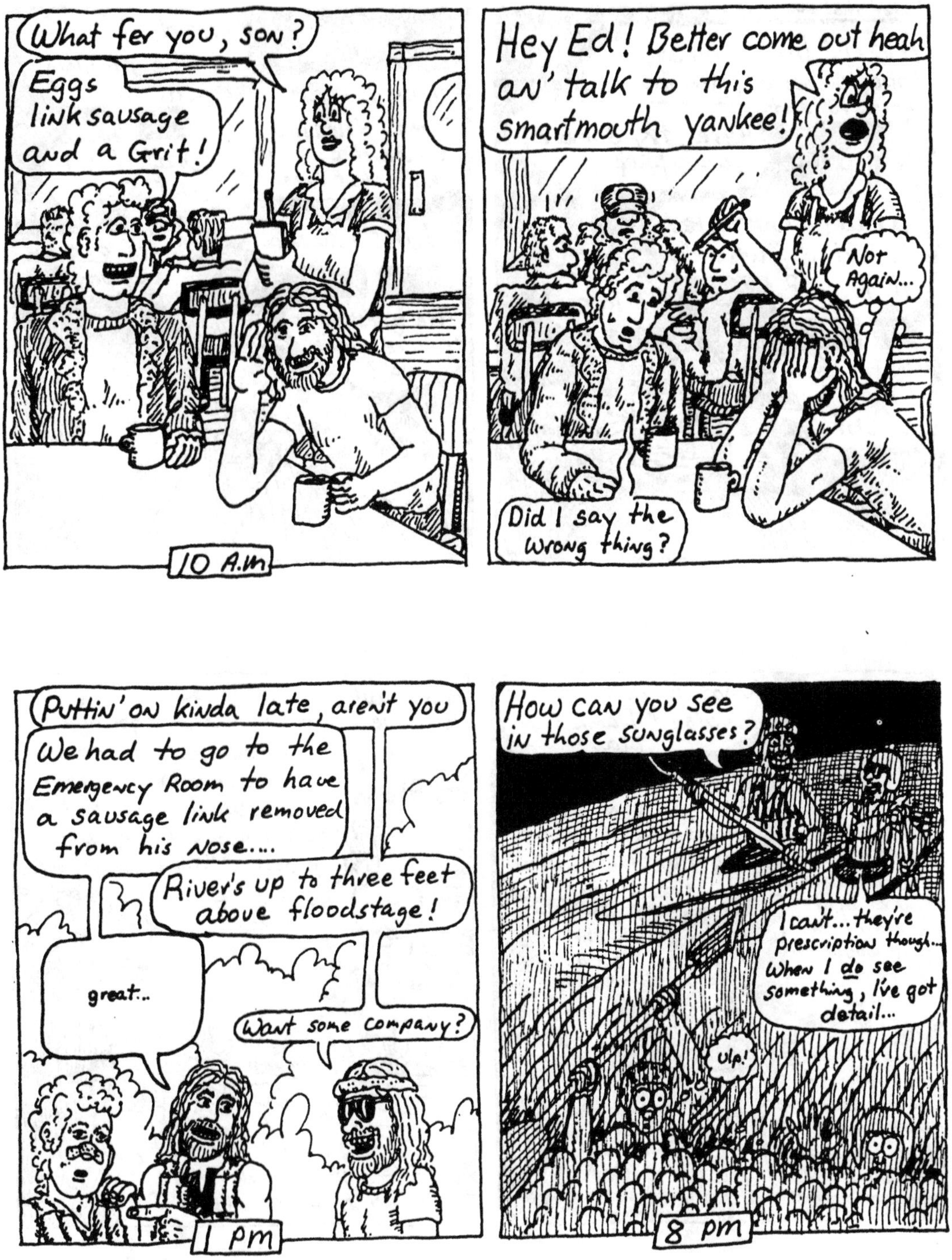
What fer you, son?
Eggs link sausage and a Grit!
10 A.M
Hey Ed! Better come out heah an' talk to this smartmouth yankee!
Not Again...
Did I say the wrong thing?
Puttin' on kinda late, aren't you
We had to go to the Emergency Room to have a sausage link removed from his Nose....
River's up to three feet above floodstage!
great..
Want some company?
1 pm
How can you see in those sunglasses?
I can't... they're prescription though... When I do see something, I've got detail...
Ulp!
8 pm

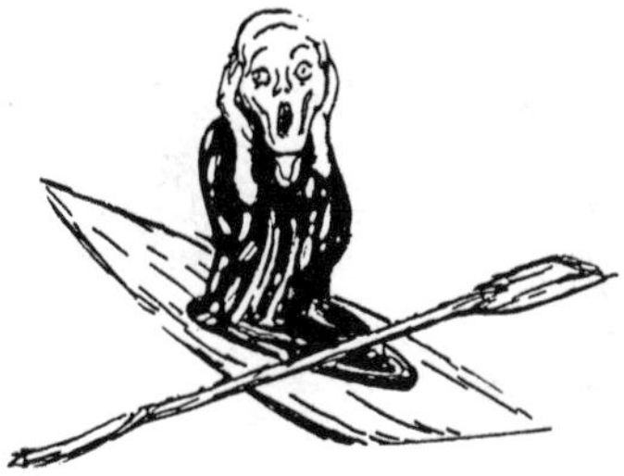

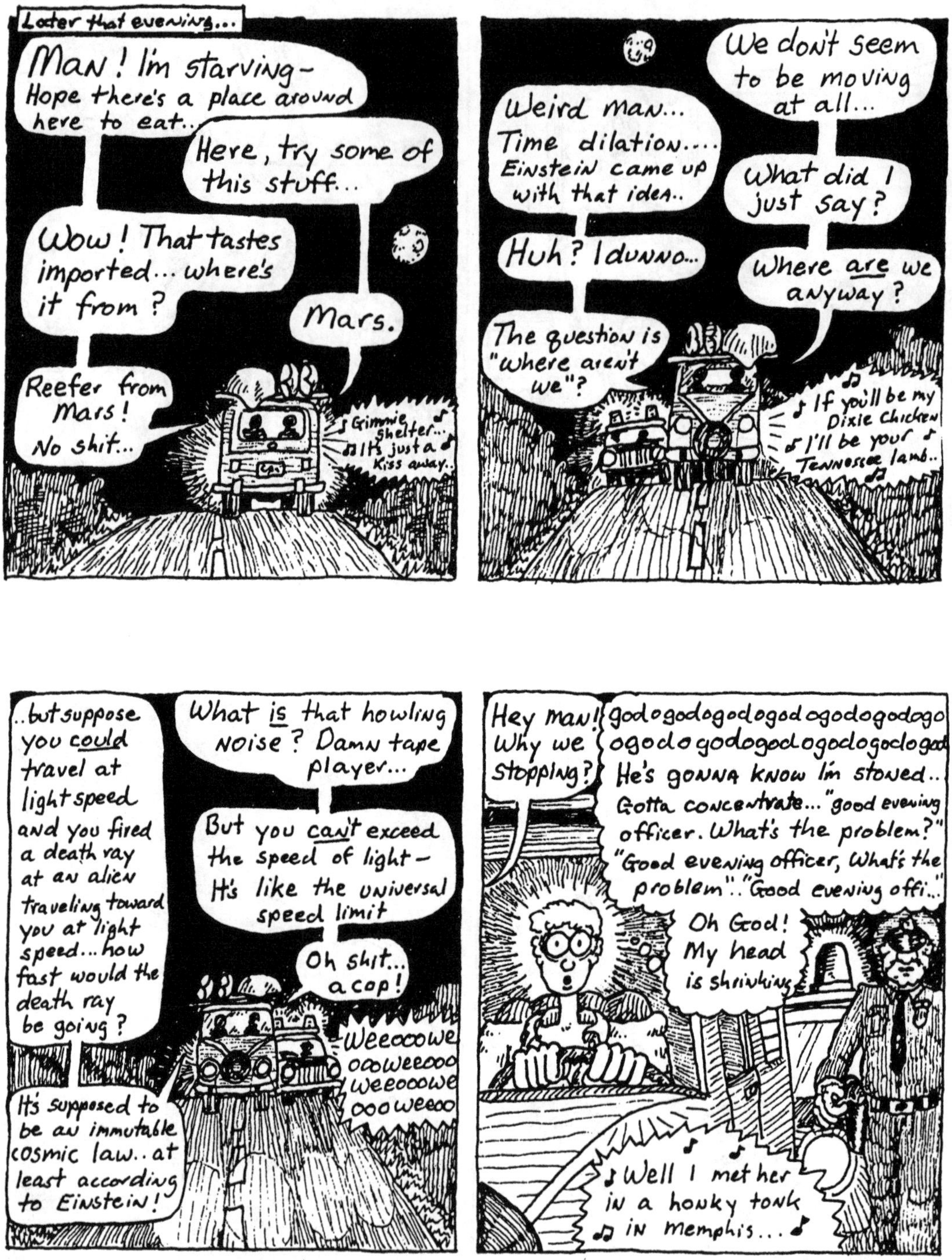
Later that evening...
Man! I'm starving- Hope there's a place around here to eat..
Here, try some of this stuff...
Wow! That tastes imported... where's it from?
Mars.
Reefer from Mars! No shit...
Gimmie Shelter... It's just a Kiss away..
Weird man... Time dilation.... Einstein came up with that idea..
Huh? Idunno...
The question is "where aren't we"?
We don't seem to be moving at all...
What did I just say?
Where are we anyway?
If you'll be my Dixie Chicken I'll be your Tennessee lamb..
..but suppose you could travel at light speed and you fired a death ray at an alien traveling toward you at light speed... how fast would the death ray be going?
What is that howling noise? Damn tape player...
But you can't exceed the speed of light- It's like the universal speed limit
Oh shit... a cop!
Weeooowe ooweeooo weeooowe ooweeoo
It's supposed to be an immutable cosmic law.. at least according to Einstein!
Hey man! Why we stopping?
godogodogodogod ogodogodogo ogodogodogodogodogodogod
He's gonna know I'm stoned.. Gotta concentrate..."good evening officer. What's the problem?" "Good evening officer, What's the problem". "Good evening offi..
Oh God! My head is shrinking
Well I met her in a honky tonk in memphis...

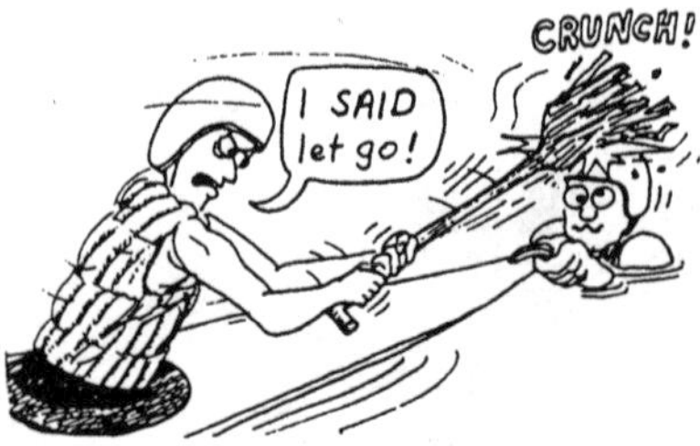
CRUNCH!
I SAID let go!

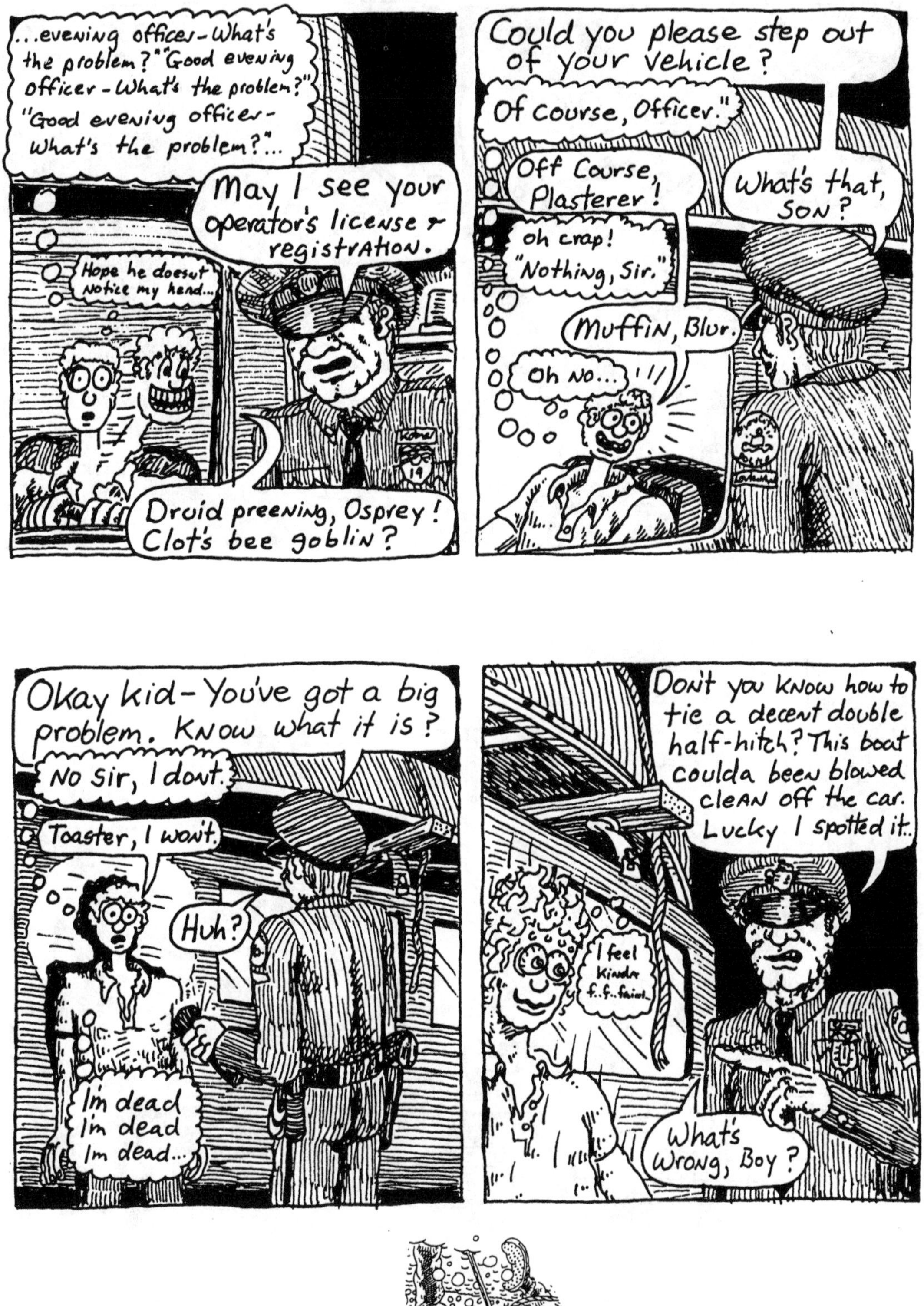
...evening officer-What's the problem?" "Good evening officer-What's the problem?" "Good evening officer-What's the problem?"...
May I see your operator's license & registration.
Hope he doesnt Notice my head...
Druid preening, Osprey! Clot's bee goblin?
Could you please step out of your vehicle?
Of course, Officer."
Off Course, Plasterer!
What's that, SON?
oh crap! "Nothing, Sir."
Muffin, Blur.
Oh no...
Okay kid- You've got a big problem. Know what it is?
No sir, I dont.
Toaster, I wont.
Huh?
Im dead Im dead Im dead...
Dont you know how to tie a decent double half-hitch? This boat coulda been blowed clean off the car. Lucky I spotted it..
I feel kinda f..f..faint..
What's Wrong, Boy?

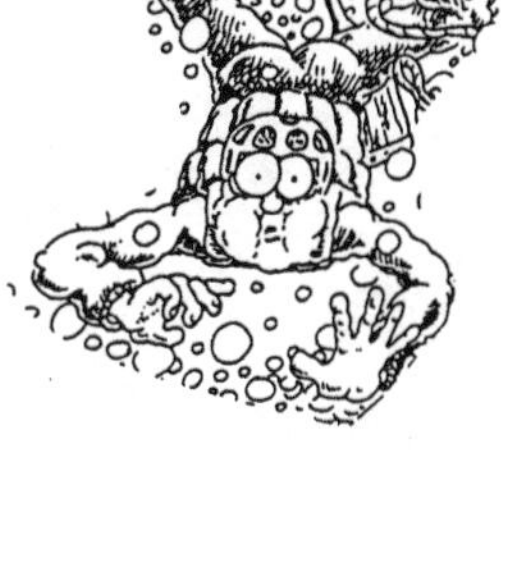

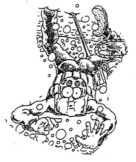

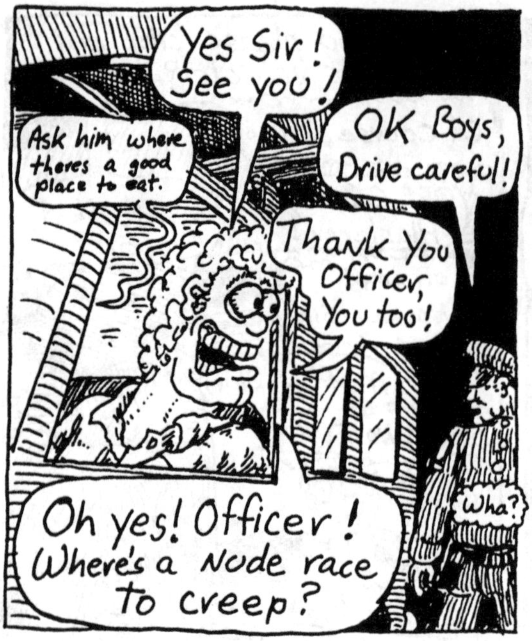
Yes Sir! See you!
Ask him where theres a good place to eat.
OK Boys, Drive careful!
Thank You Officer, You too!
Oh yes! Officer! Where's a Node race to creep?
Wha?

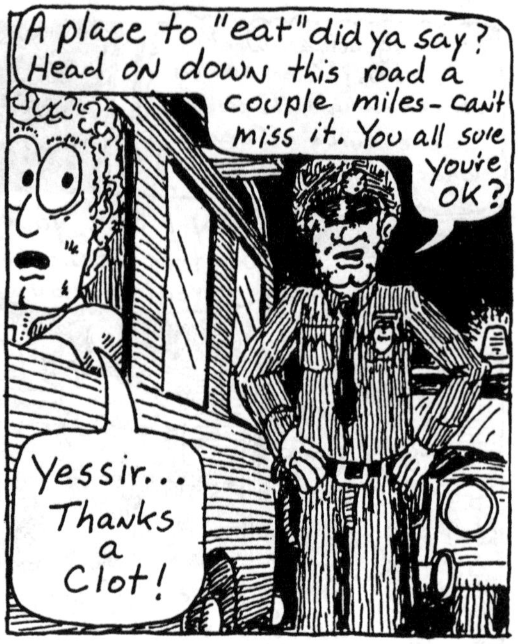
A place to "eat" did ya say? Head on down this road a couple miles - can't miss it. You all sure you're OK?
Yessir... Thanks a Clot!

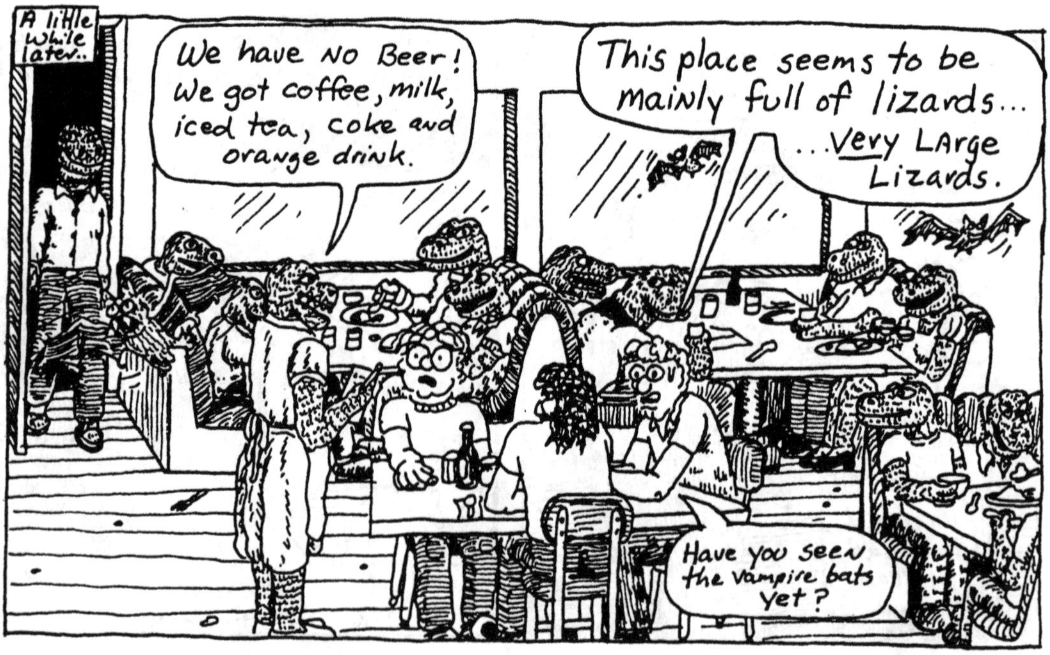
A little while later..
We have No Beer! We got coffee, milk, iced tea, coke and orange drink.
This place seems to be mainly full of lizards... ...Very Large Lizards.
Have you seen the vampire bats yet?

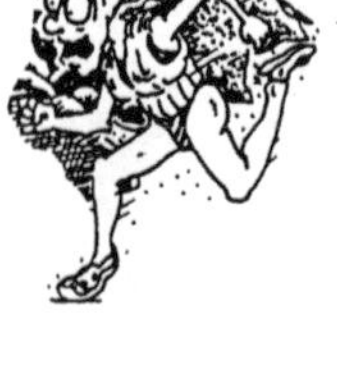

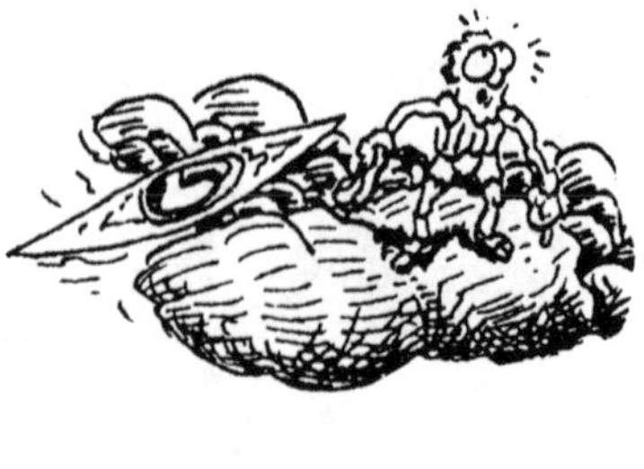

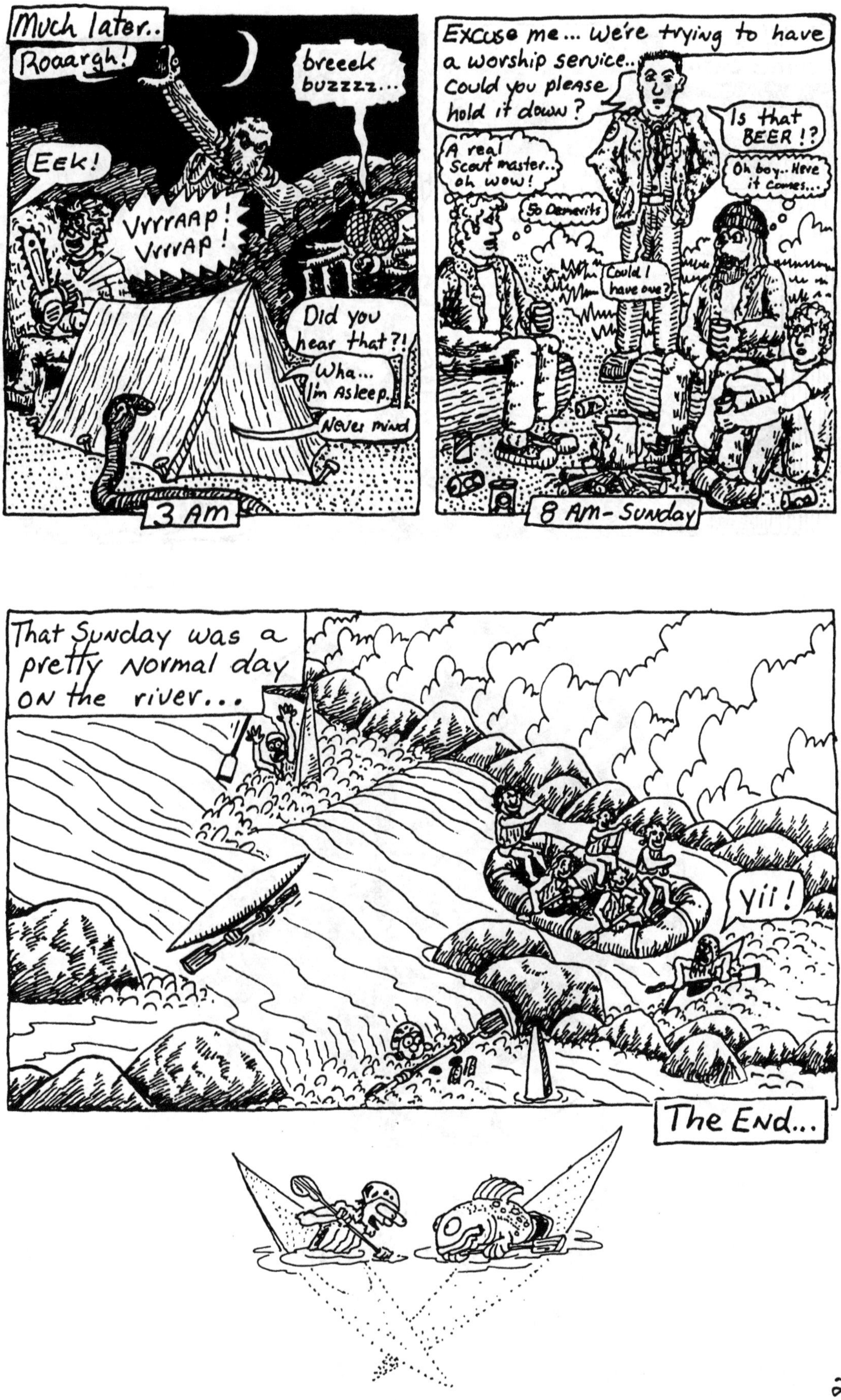

Much later..
Roaargh!
breeeek buzzzz...
Eek!
Vvvraap! Vvvrap!
Did you hear that?!
Wha... I'm Asleep..
Never mind
3 AM
Excuse me... we're trying to have a worship service.. could you please hold it down?
A real Scout master.. oh wow!
Is that BEER!?
Oh boy.. Here it comes...
50 Demerits
Could I have one?
8 AM - Sunday
That Sunday was a pretty Normal day on the river...
yii!
The End...

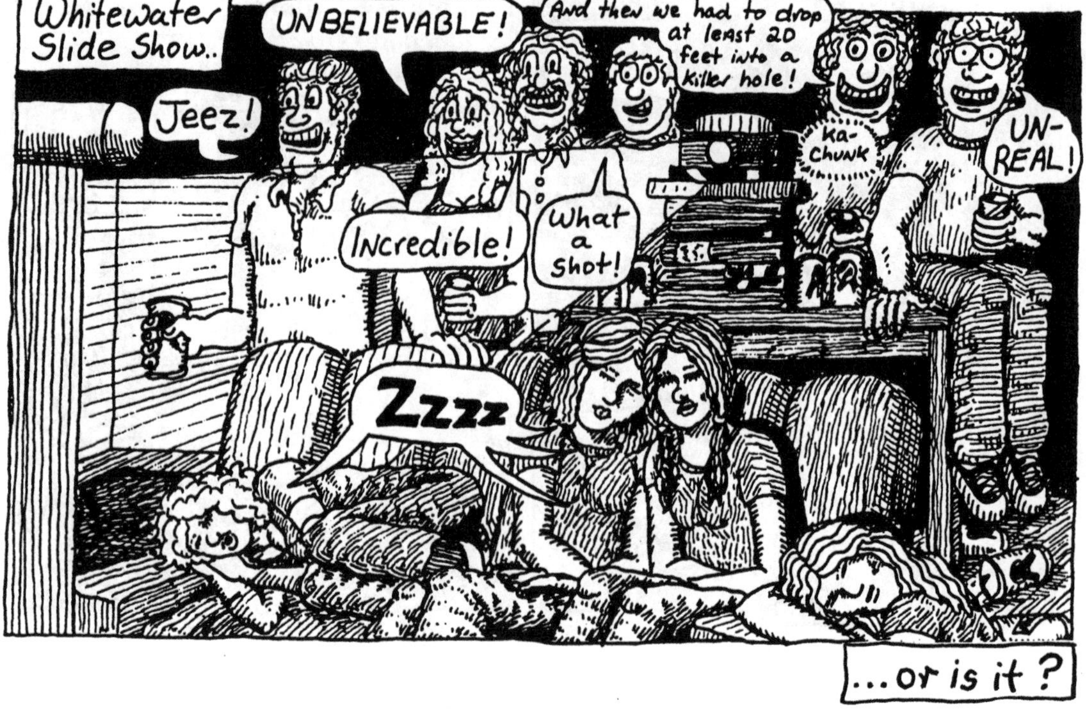
Whitewater Slide Show..
UNBELIEVABLE!
And then we had to drop at least 20 feet into a killer hole!
Jeez!
KA-CHUNK
UN-REAL!
Incredible!
What a shot!
Zzzz
...or is it?

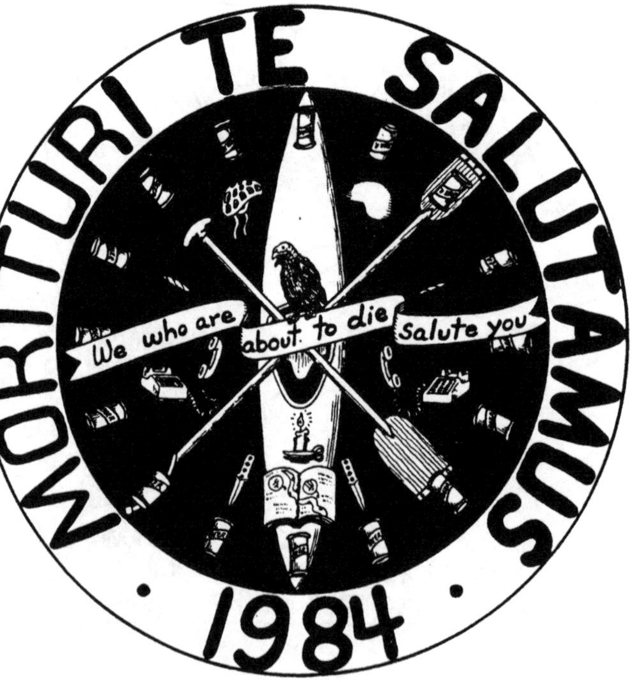
MORITURI TE SALUTAMUS
We who are about to die salute you
· 1984 ·

S & M University of
Whitewater Sciences

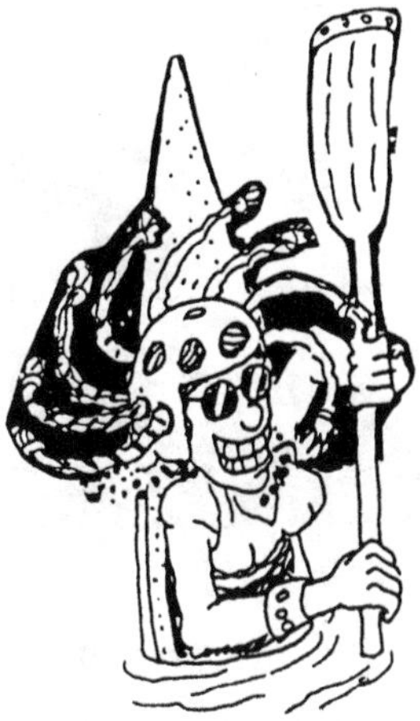

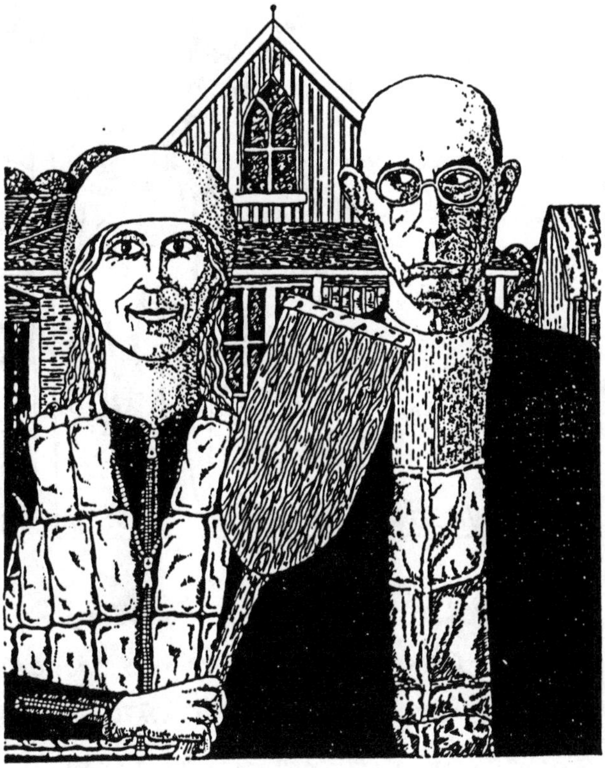

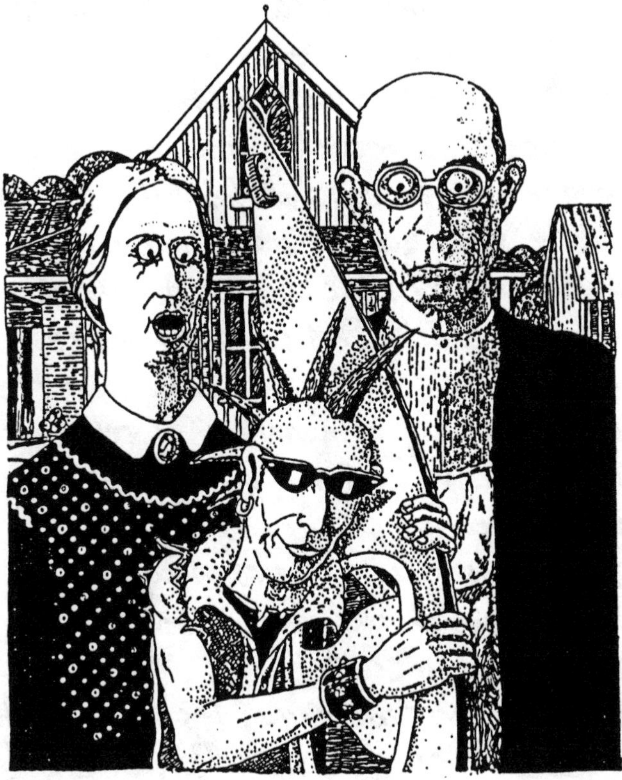

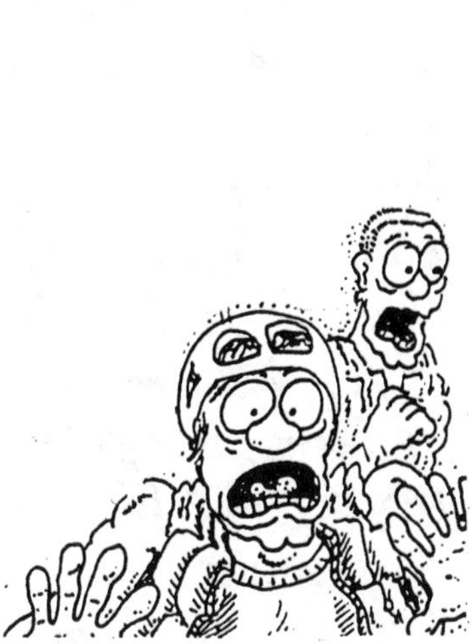

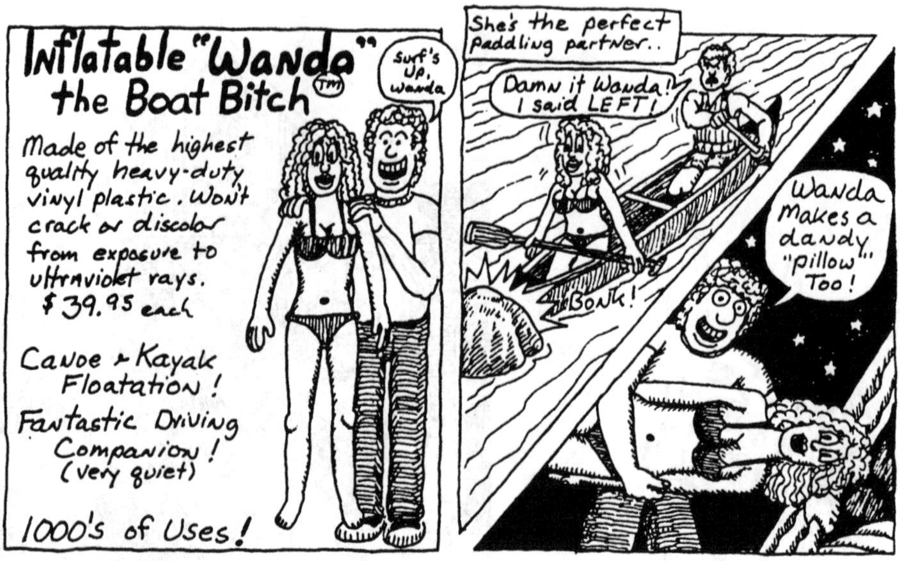
Inflatable "Wanda" the Boat Bitch™
Made of the highest quality heavy-duty vinyl plastic. Won't crack or discolor from exposure to ultraviolet rays. $39.95 each
Canoe & Kayak Floatation!
Fantastic Driving Companion! (very quiet)
1000's of Uses!
Surf's up, Wanda
She's the perfect paddling partner..
Damn it Wanda! I said LEFT!
BONK!
Wanda makes a dandy "pillow" too!

"Wanda" has turned out to be my most controversial whitewater cartoon gag. It has angered many women boaters. Yes, it's **sexist**, but it's making fun of **men**, not women! Let me expound: when I go on river trips, at night I usually end up sitting around some campfire drinking, swapping lies, and meeting lots of new boaters. It's definitely the **best** part the whitewater day and a great **ritual**. Occasionally, however, I witness a display that makes me grind my teeth in **anger**. Some **stud** (he thinks) has brought a "**babe**" along on the trip as a convienience so he'll have a **cook**, a **maid**, and somebody to **shag** (preferably within evergone elses' earshot). She'll also run shuttle and buy groceries while the **real men** run the river & have fun. She may be allowed to sit in the bow of a canoe while being verbally abused by **Mr. Stud**. This cartoon makes fun of **guys** who think a woman is a thing, not a person; the type of guy who might actually enjoy a meaningful relationship with an **inflatable love-doll** ("...if she only could drive, she'd be perfect"). How **pathetic** could a guy **be !?**

Yes, I do make fun of women & men, rafters & kayakers, rednecks & hipsters, whales & woodchucks and, above all, **myself!** I'm an **equal opportunity cartoonist**. This cartoon makes fun of **male jerks**, not **women!** It's like shooting fish in a barrel, but it's <u>fun</u>! Can you spell "I.R.O.N.Y."?

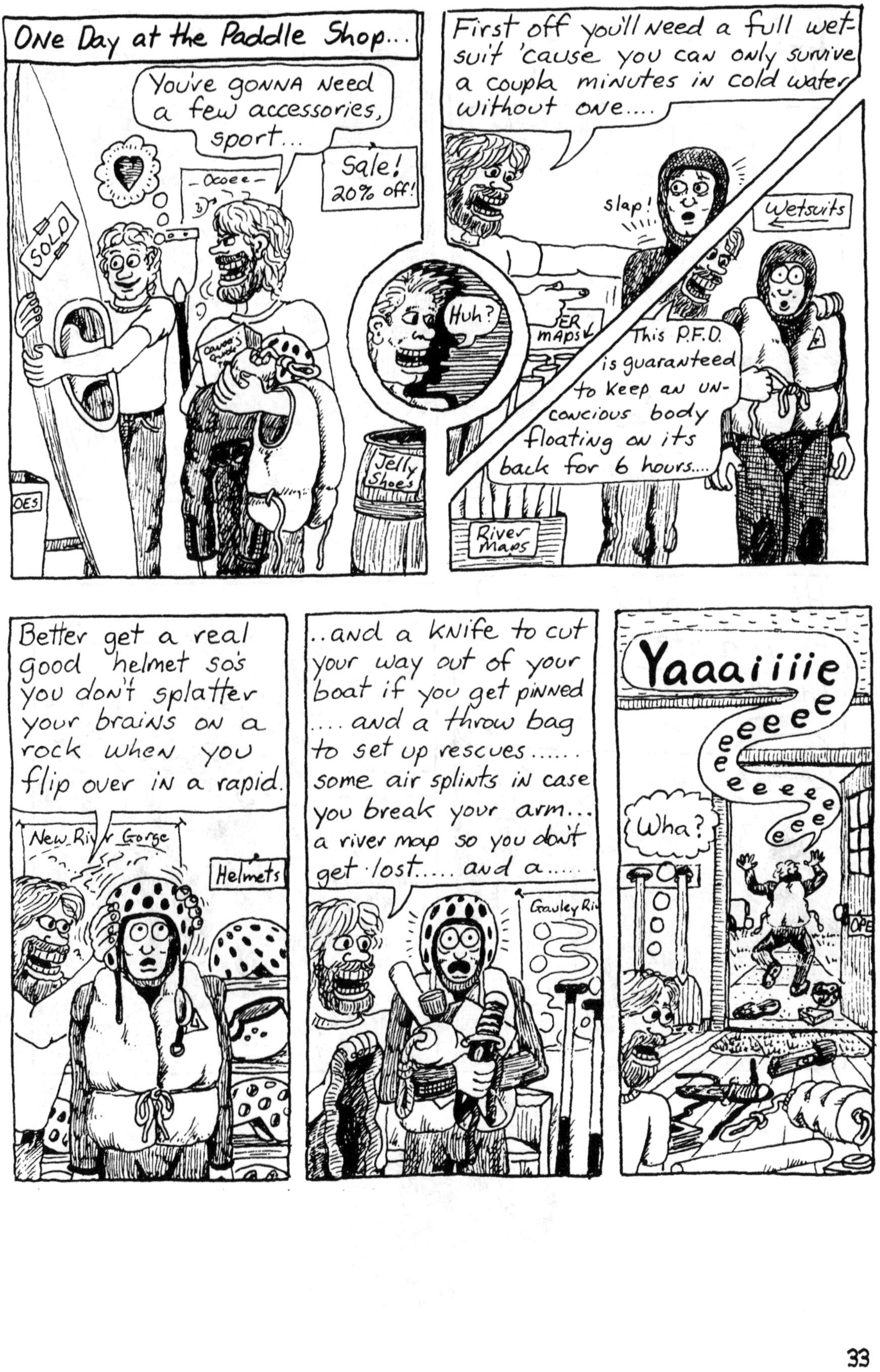

One Day at the Paddle Shop...
You've gonna need a few accessories, sport...
SOLD
Sale! 20% off!
Huh?
Jelly Shoes
First off you'll need a full wet-suit 'cause you can only survive a coupla minutes in cold water without one....
slap!
Wetsuits
maps
This P.F.D. is guaranteed to keep an unconcious body floating on its back for 6 hours....
River Maps
Better get a real good helmet so's you don't splatter your brains on a rock when you flip over in a rapid.
New River Gorge
Helmets
..and a knife to cut your way out of your boat if you get pinned ....and a throw bag to set up rescues...... some air splints in case you break your arm... a river map so you don't get lost..... and a.....
Yaaaiiiie eeeeeeeeeeeeee
Wha?

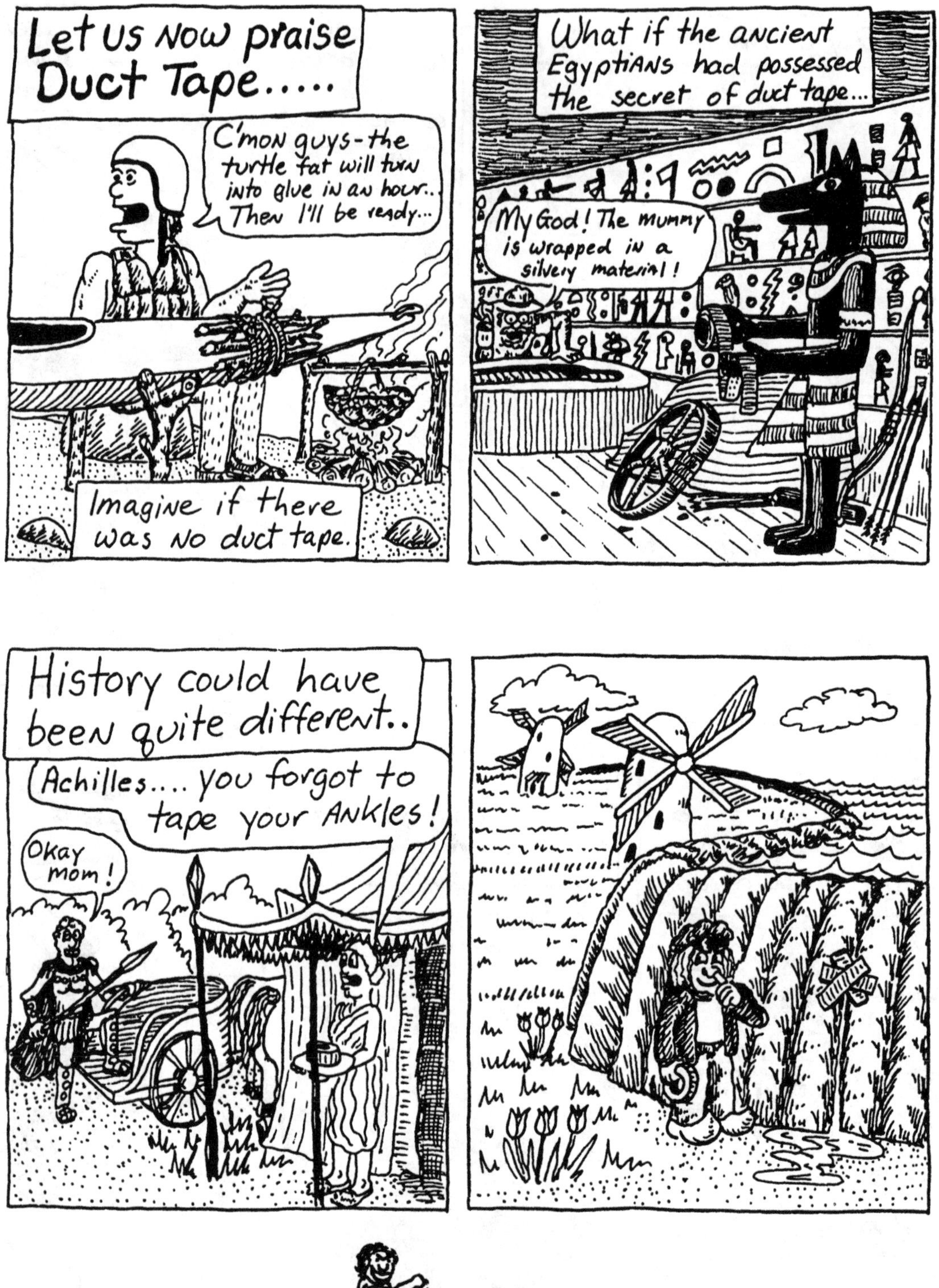
Let us now praise Duct Tape.....
C'mon guys-the turtle fat will turn into glue in an hour.. Then I'll be ready...
Imagine if there was no duct tape.
What if the ancient Egyptians had possessed the secret of duct tape...
My God! The mummy is wrapped in a silvery material!
History could have been quite different..
Achilles.... you forgot to tape your Ankles!
Okay mom!

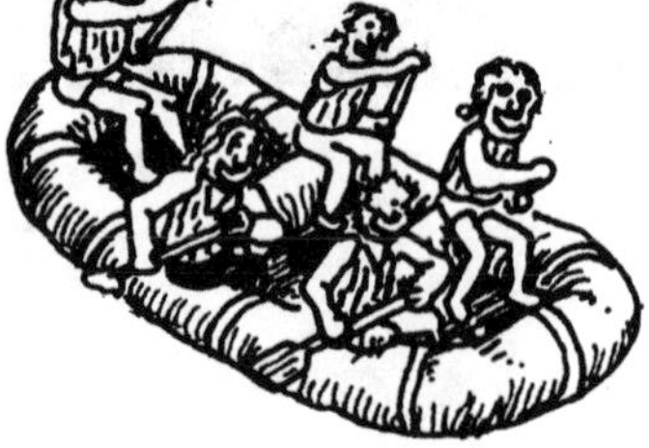

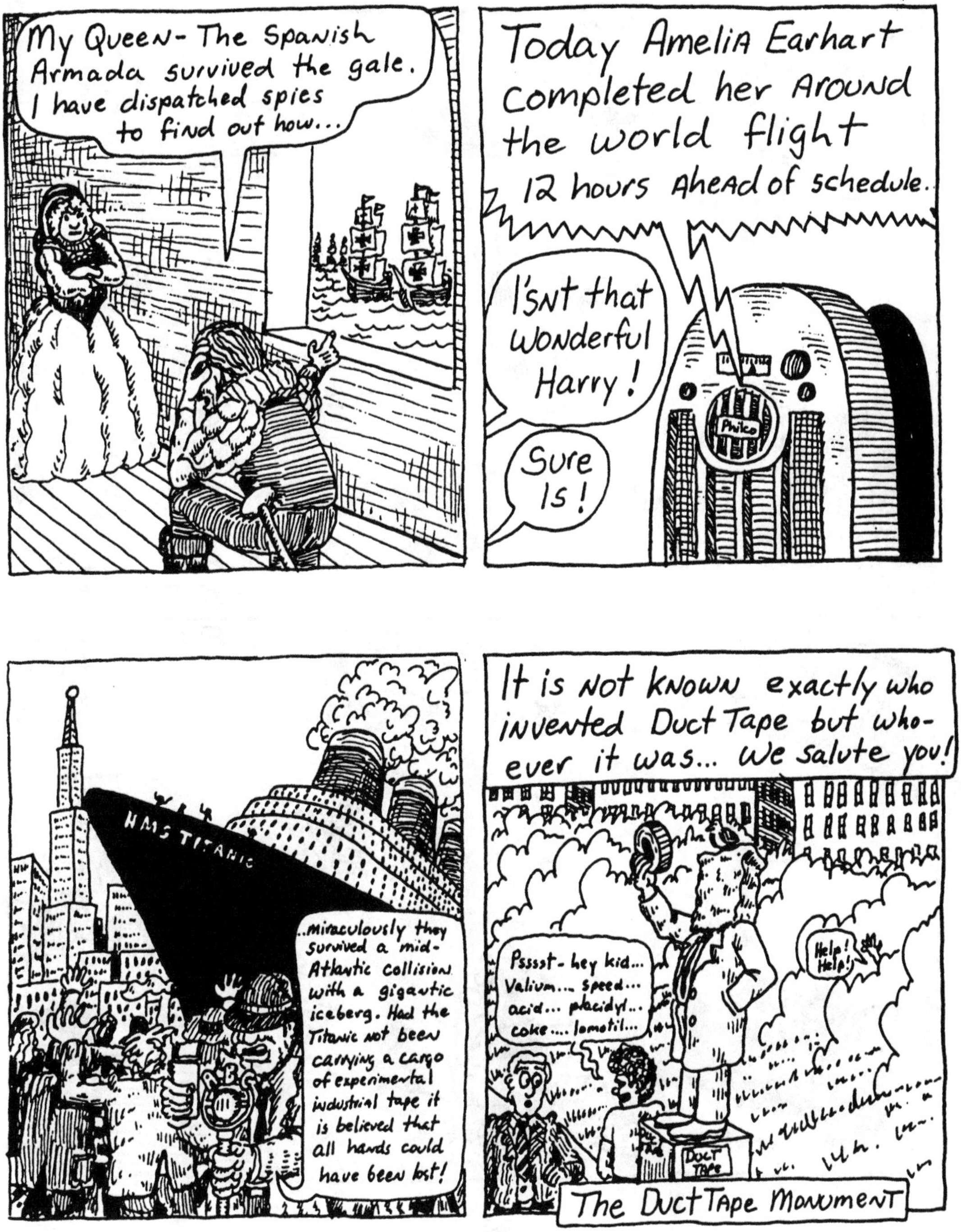
My Queen- The Spanish Armada survived the gale. I have dispatched spies to find out how...
Today Amelia Earhart completed her Around the world flight 12 hours Ahead of schedule.
I'snt that Wonderful Harry!
Sure Is!
Philco
HMS TITANIC
...miraculously they survived a mid-Atlantic collision with a gigantic iceberg. Had the Titanic not been carrying a cargo of experimental industrial tape it is believed that all hands could have been lost!
It is Not known exactly who invented Duct Tape but who-ever it was... We salute you!
Psssst- hey kid... Valium... speed... acid... placidyl... coke.... lomotil...
Help! Help!
DUCT TAPE
The Duct Tape Monument

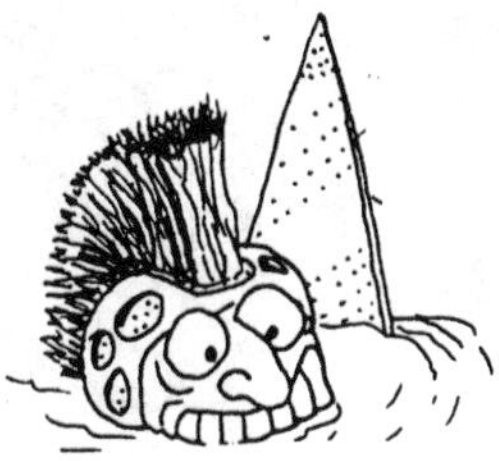

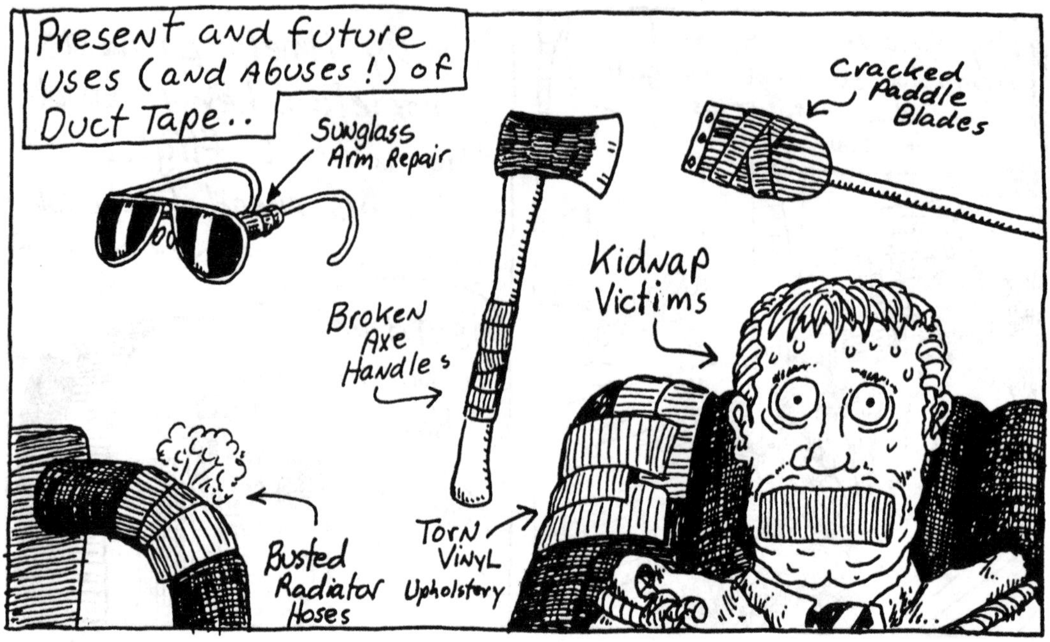
Present and future uses (and Abuses!) of Duct Tape..
Sunglass Arm Repair
Cracked Paddle Blades
Kidnap Victims
Broken Axe Handles
Busted Radiator Hoses
Torn Vinyl Upholstery

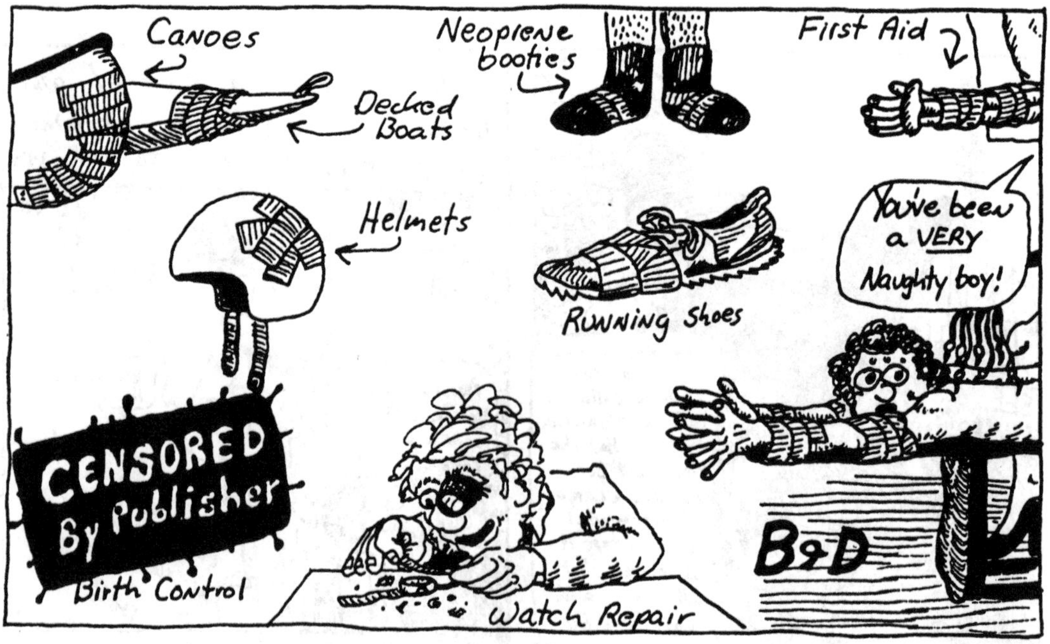
Canoes
Neoprene booties
First Aid
Decked Boats
Helmets
You've been a VERY Naughty boy!
Running Shoes
CENSORED By Publisher
Birth Control
Watch Repair
B&D

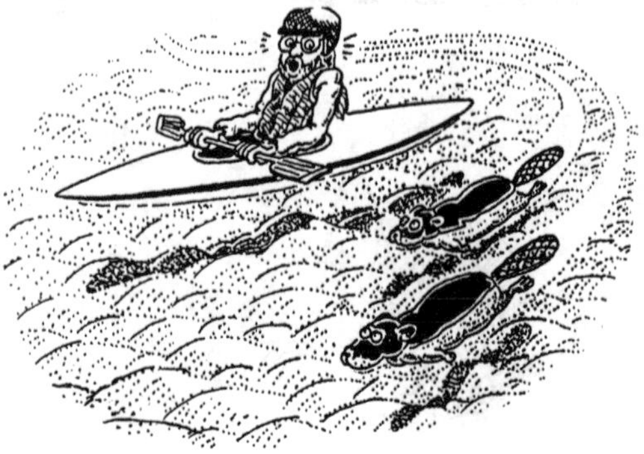

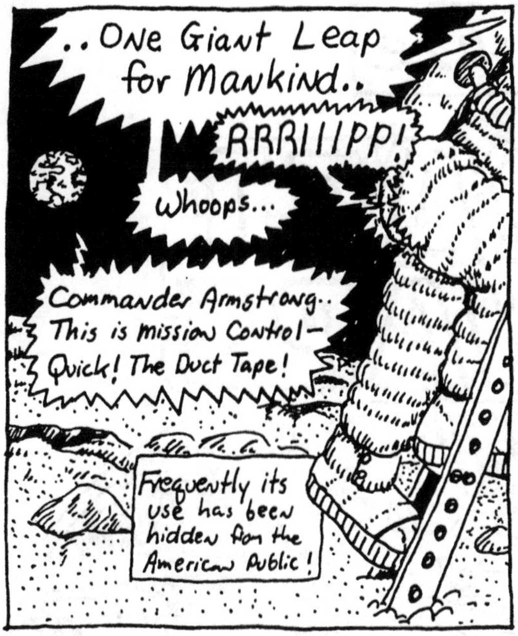

..One Giant Leap for Mankind..
RRRIIIPP!
Whoops...
Commander Armstrong.. This is mission Control- Quick! The Duct Tape!
Frequently its use has been hidden from the American Public!

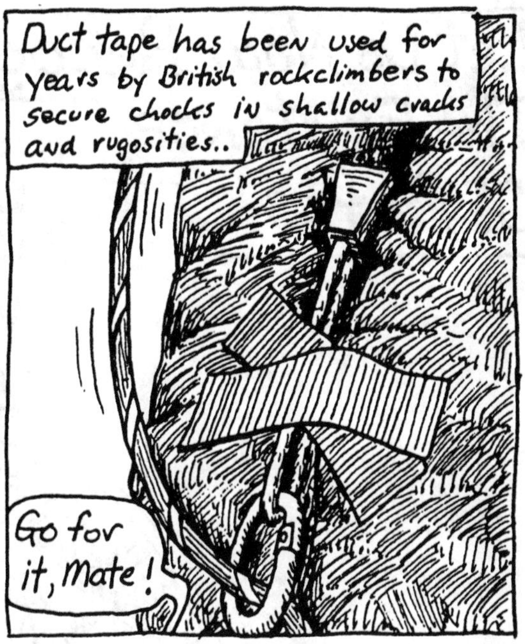

Duct tape has been used for years by British rockclimbers to secure chocks in shallow cracks and rugosities..
Go for it, Mate!

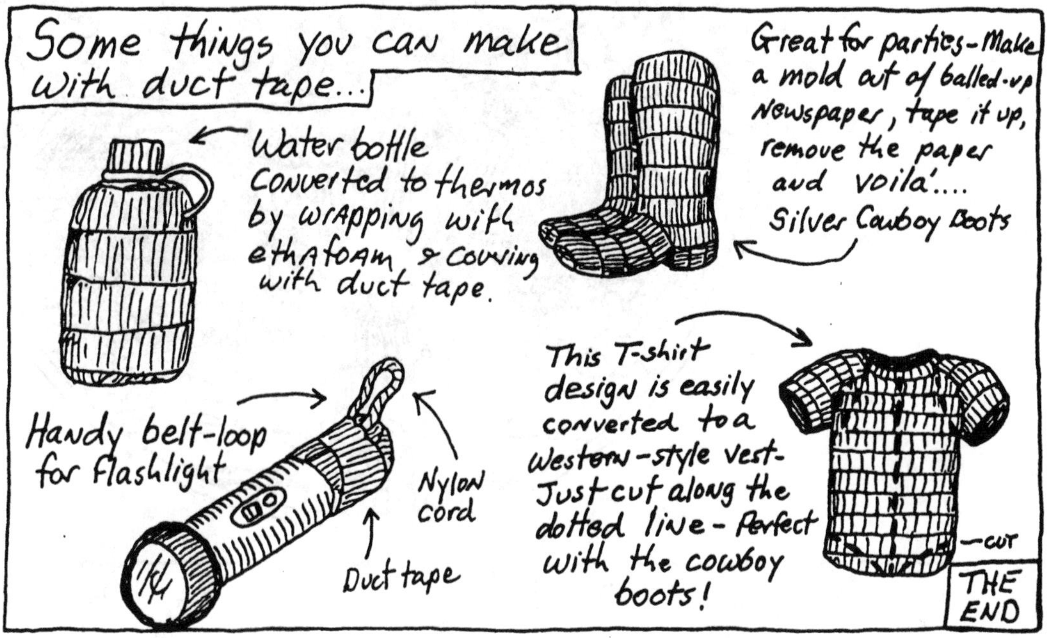

Some things you can make with duct tape..
Great for parties - Make a mold out of balled-up Newspaper, tape it up, remove the paper and voila'.... Silver Cowboy Boots
Water bottle converted to thermos by wrapping with ethafoam & covering with duct tape.
This T-shirt design is easily converted to a Western-style vest- Just cut along the dotted line - Perfect with the cowboy boots!
CUT
Handy belt-loop for flashlight
Nylon cord
Duct tape
THE END

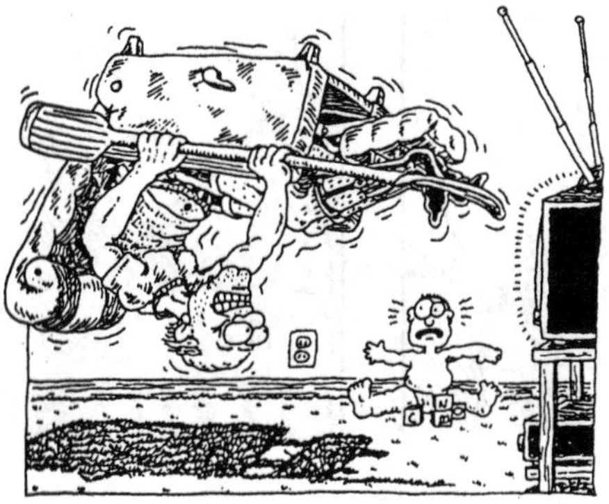

Let Us Now Recognize The Existence Of Rafts...

RAFT WARS

Budda Budda
AWK!
OOF

The next raft that runs over me...
.. Gets this!
SPROING
click!

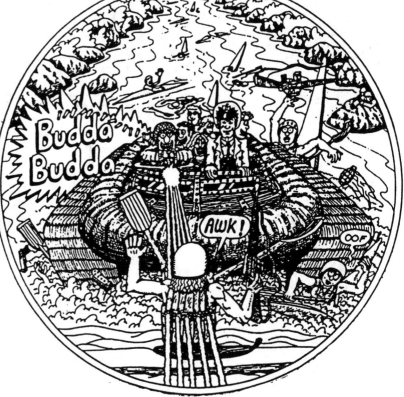

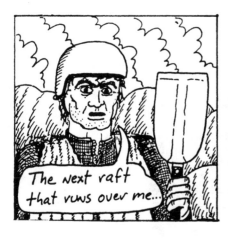

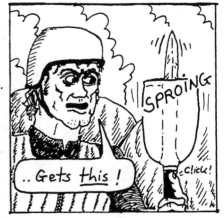

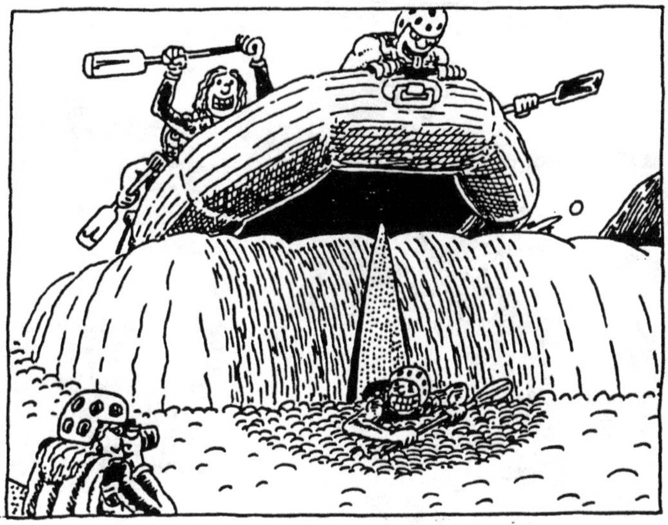

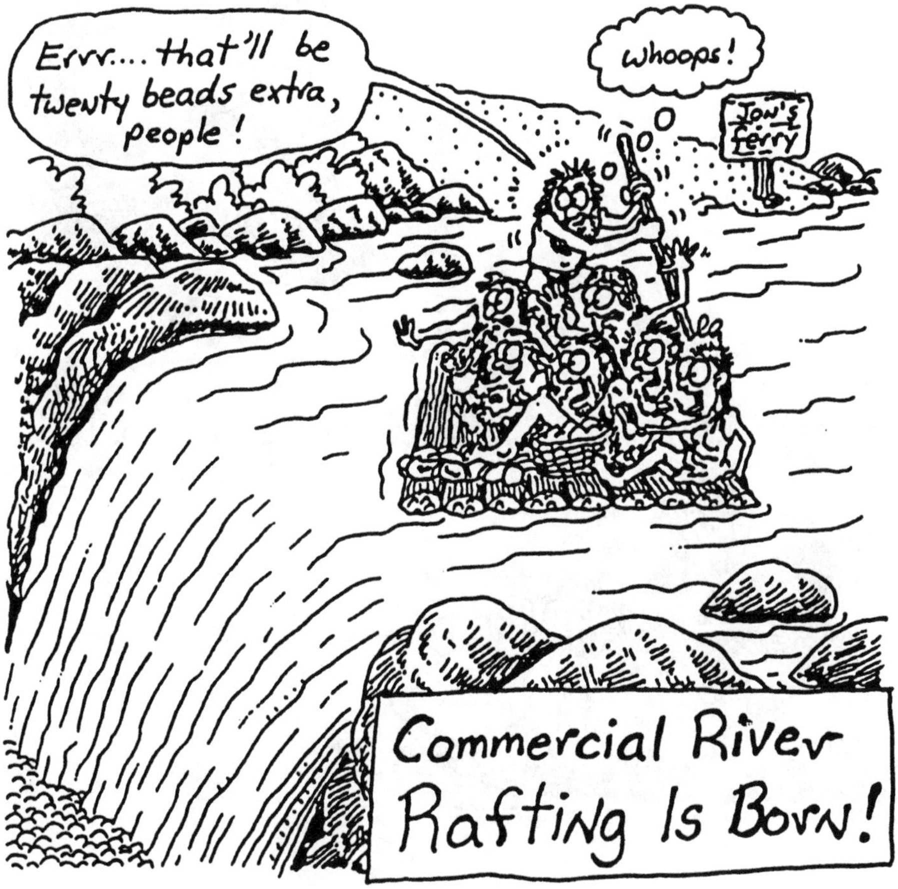
Errr.... that'll be twenty beads extra, people!
whoops!
Jon's Ferry
Commercial River Rafting Is Born!

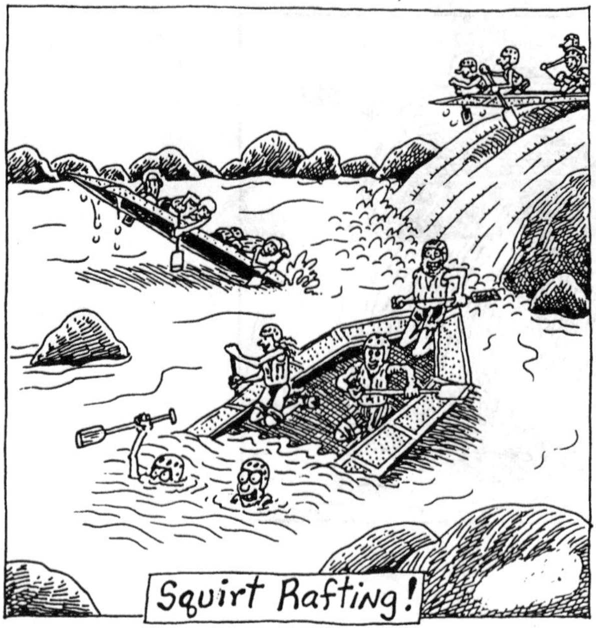
Squirt Rafting!

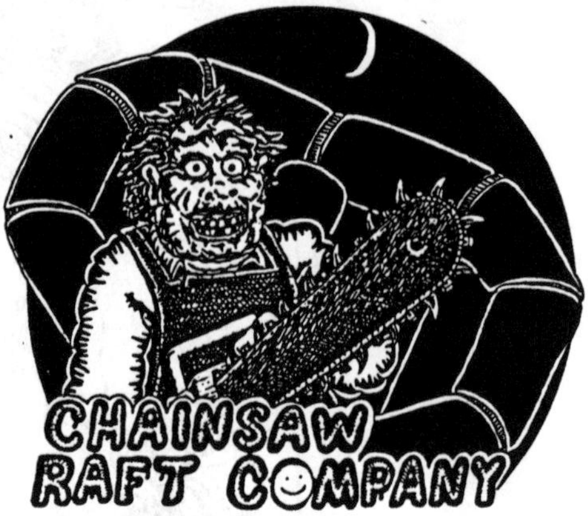
CHAINSAW
RAFT COMPANY

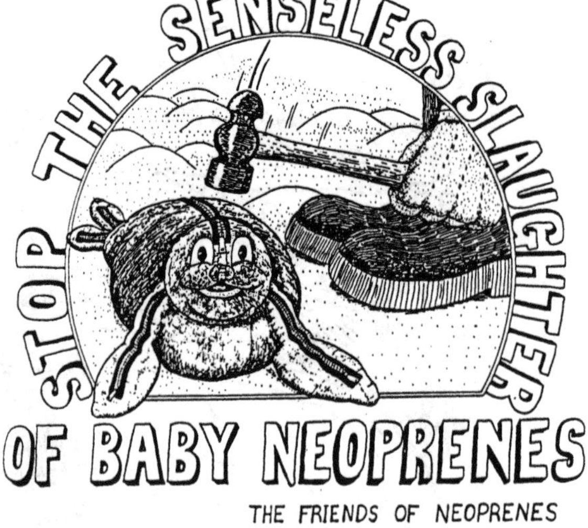
STOP THE SENSELESS SLAUGHTER
OF BABY NEOPRENES
THE FRIENDS OF NEOPRENES

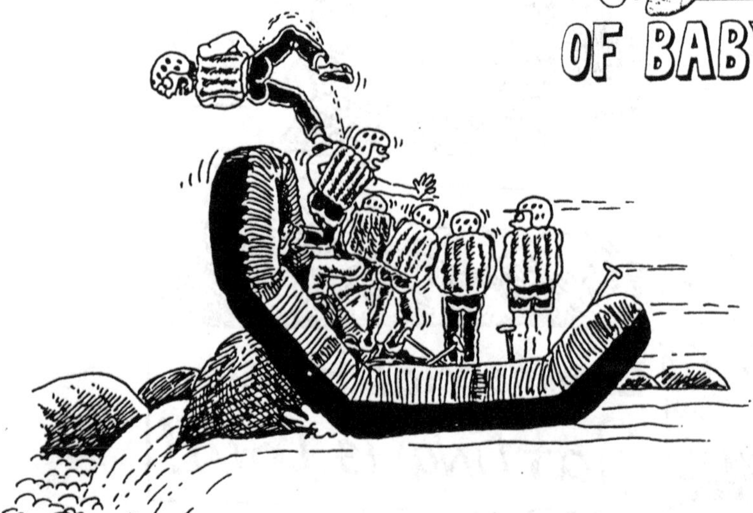

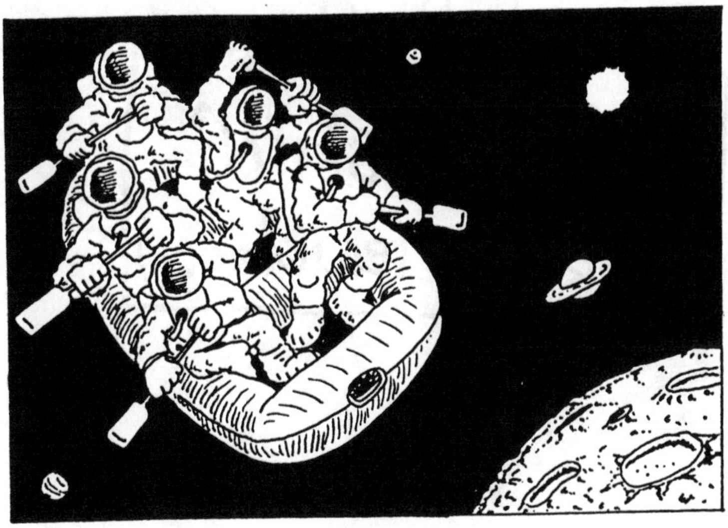

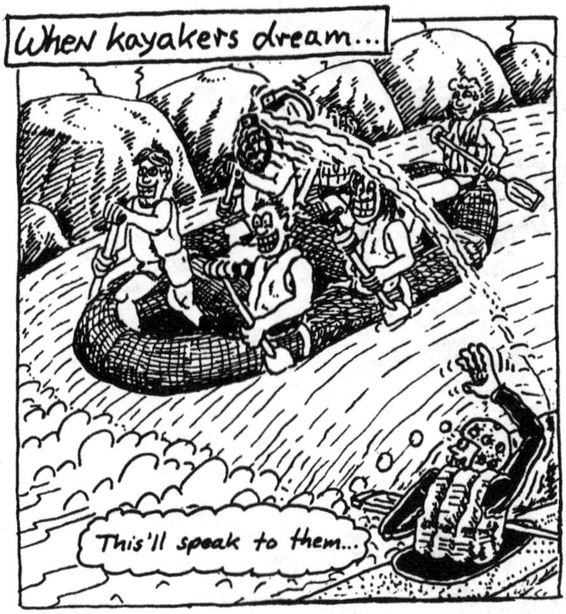
When kayakers dream...
This'll speak to them...

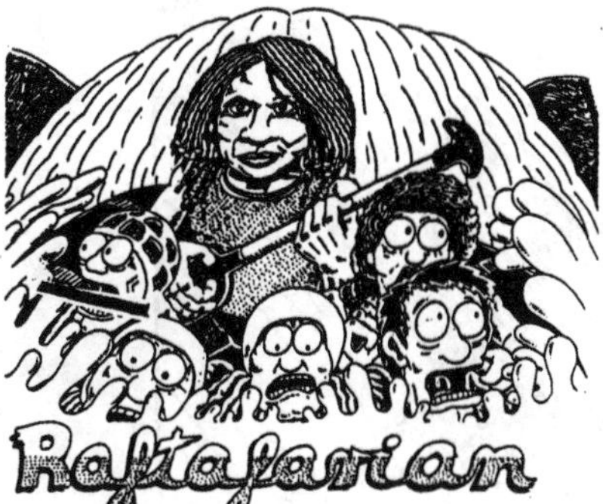
Raftafarian

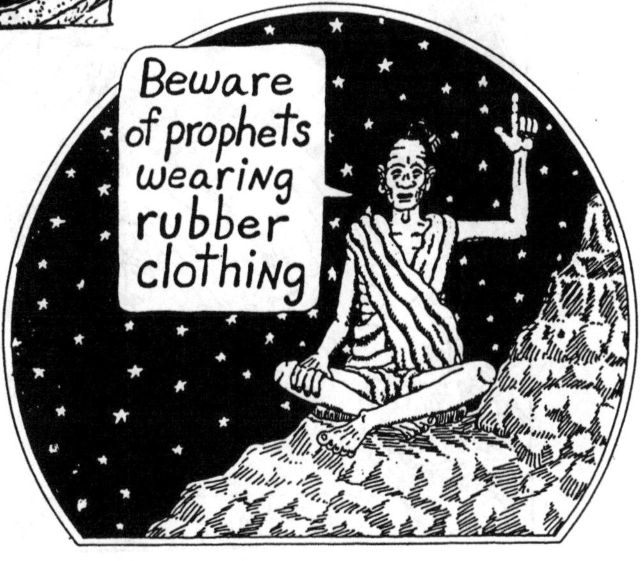
Beware of prophets wearing rubber clothing

Gone Fishin'
(back in a few daze)

Extreme Fly Fishing

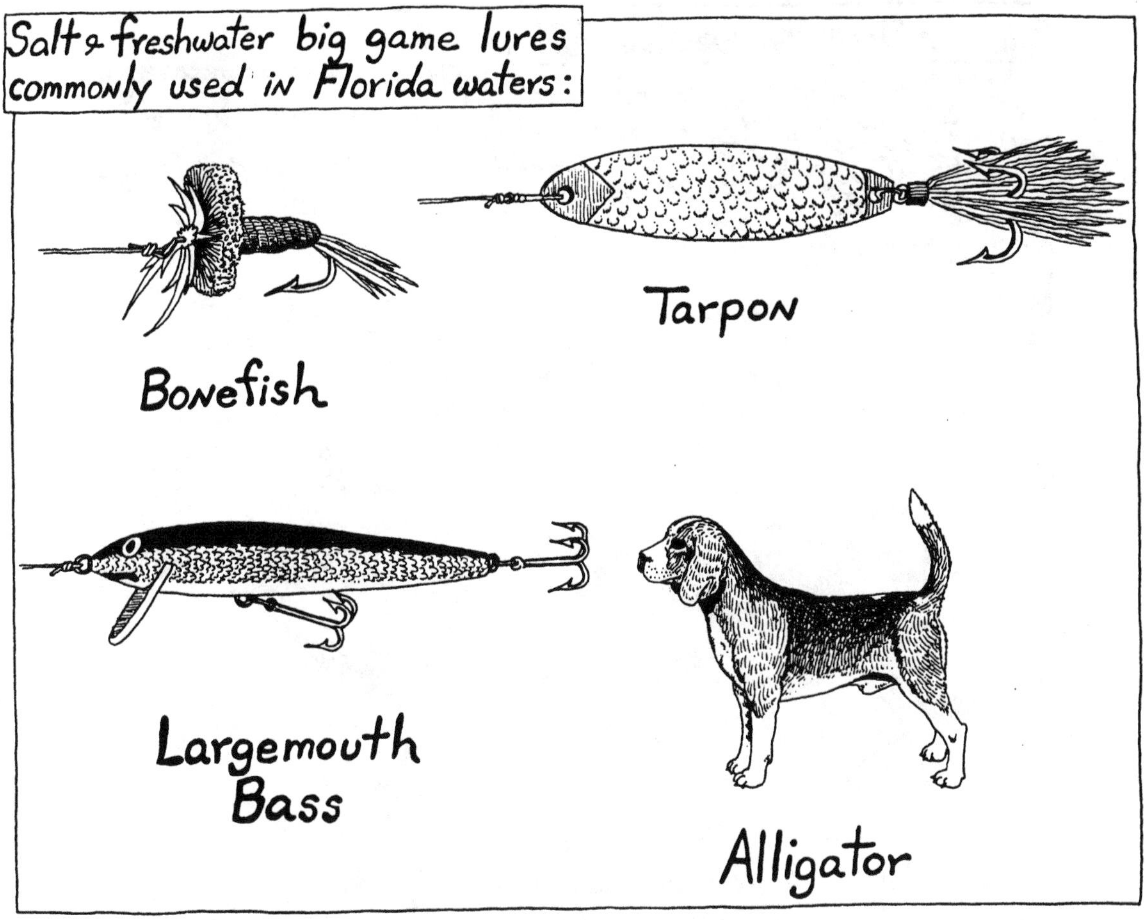
Salt & freshwater big game lures commonly used in Florida waters:
Bonefish
Tarpon
Largemouth Bass
Alligator

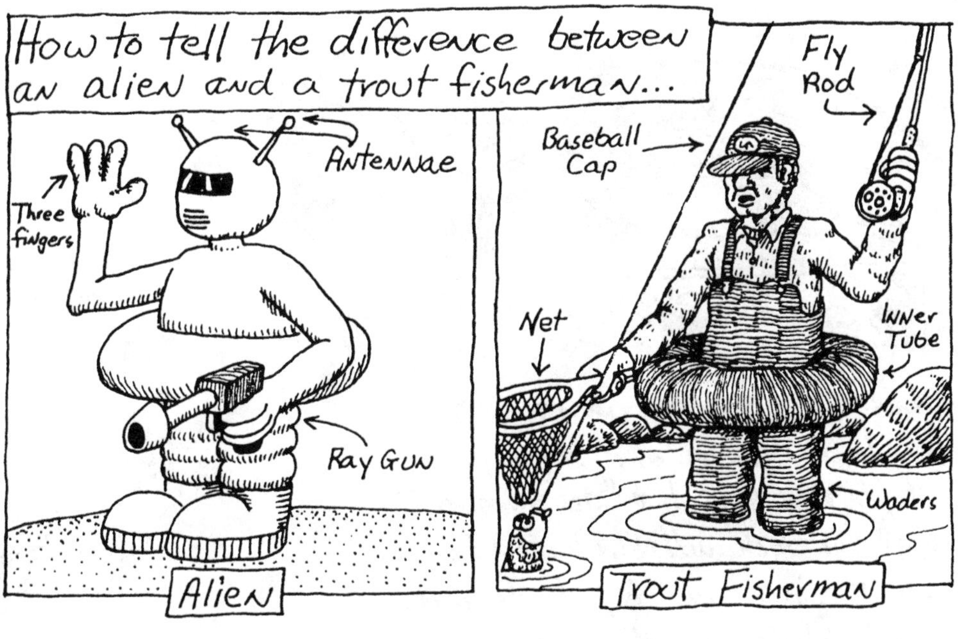
How to tell the difference between an alien and a trout fisherman...
Three fingers
Antennae
Ray Gun
Alien
Fly Rod
Baseball Cap
Net
Inner Tube
Waders
Trout Fisherman

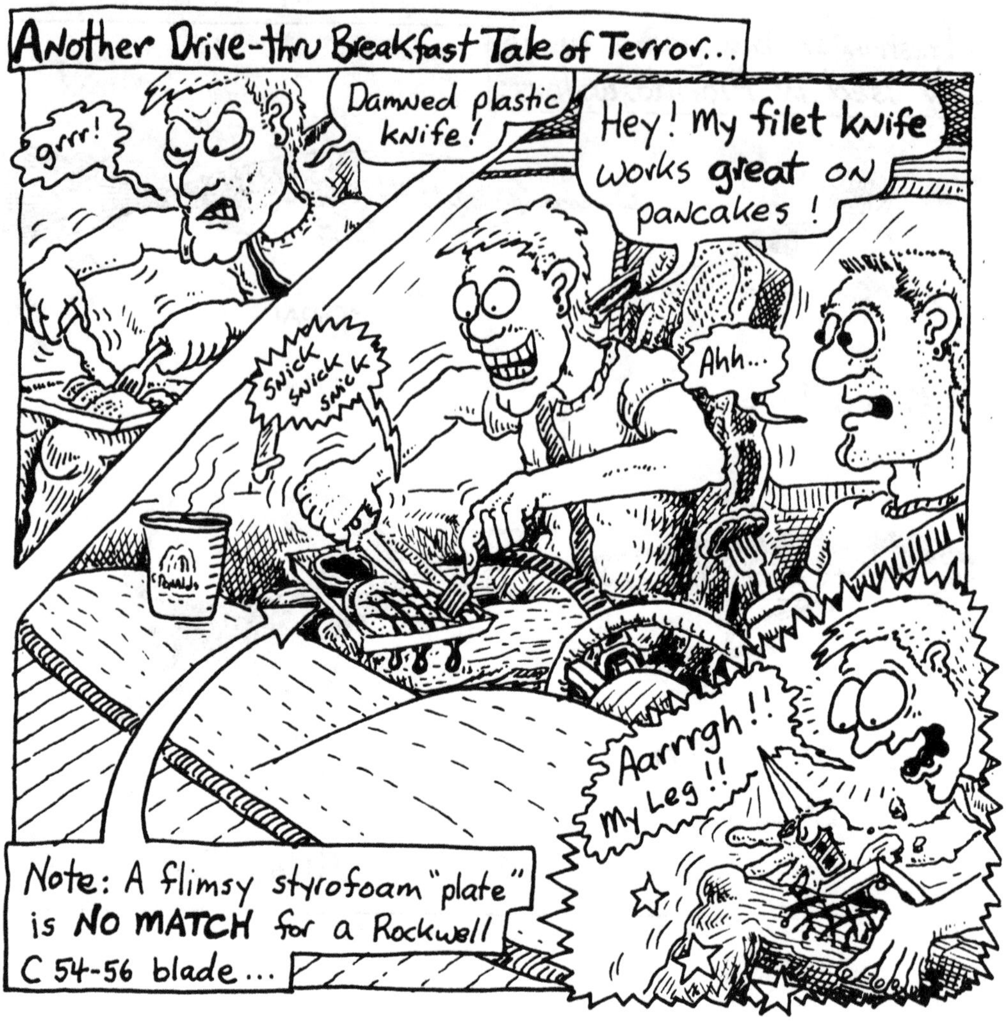
Another Drive-thru Breakfast Tale of Terror...
grrr!
Damned plastic knife!
Hey! My filet knife works great on pancakes!
SNICK SNICK SNICK
Ahh...
Note: A flimsy styrofoam "plate" is NO MATCH for a Rockwell C 54-56 blade...
Aarrrgh!! My Leg!!

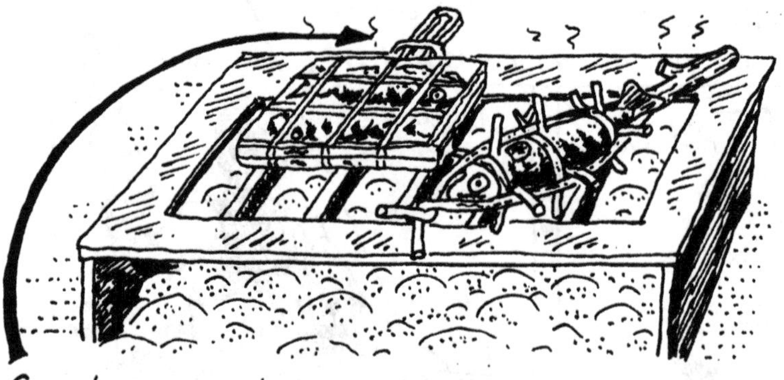

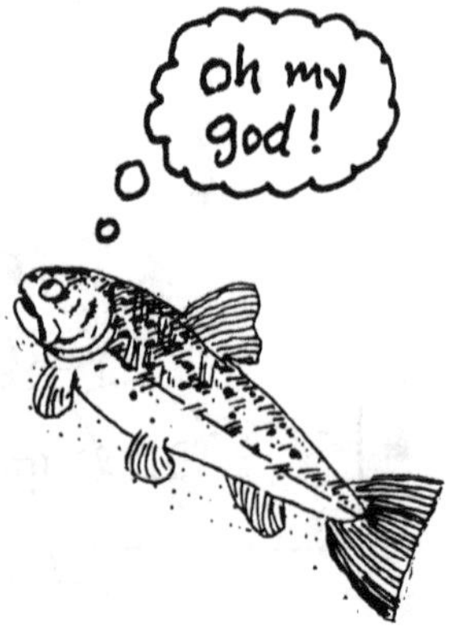
Oh my god!

Grill over coals and baste with butter, lemon juice and lemon pepper. Do not place fish on hot "government" grills, as the fish will stick and fall apart when you try to turn it. Cook till flaky and golden brown.

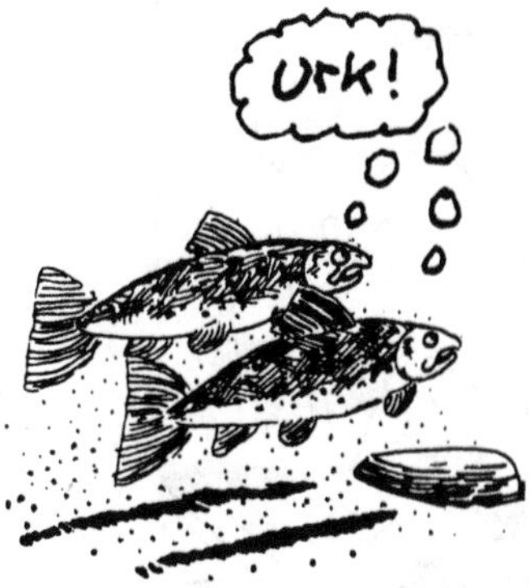
Urk!

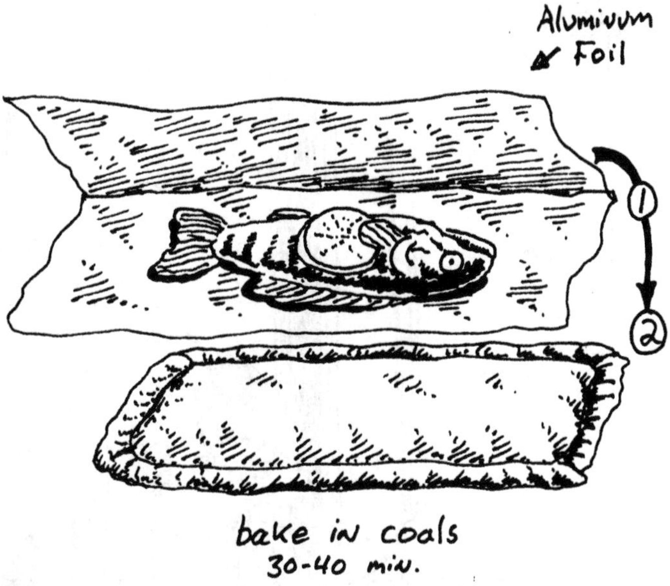
Aluminum Foil
1
2
bake in coals
30-40 min.

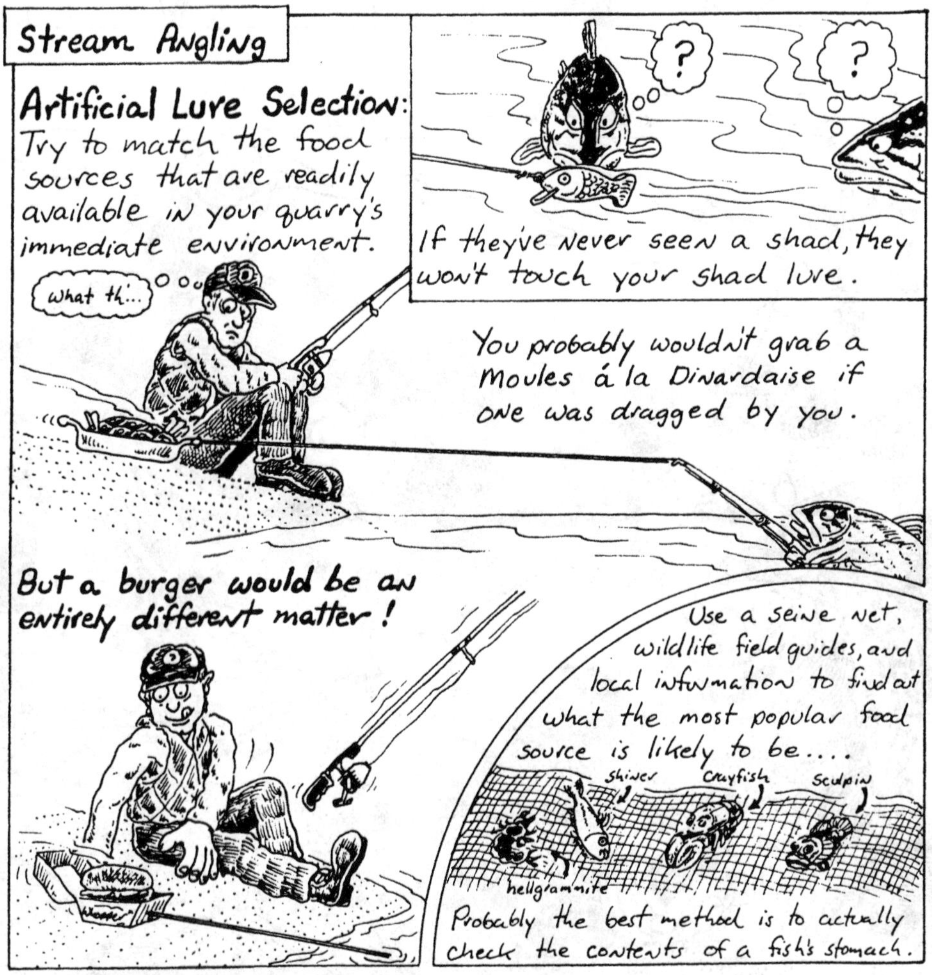
Stream Angling
Artificial Lure Selection:
Try to match the food sources that are readily available in your quarry's immediate environment.
?
?
If they've never seen a shad, they won't touch your shad lure.
what th...
You probably wouldn't grab a Moules á la Dinardaise if one was dragged by you.
But a burger would be an entirely different matter!
Use a seine net, wildlife field guides, and local information to find out what the most popular food source is likely to be....
shiner
crayfish
sculpin
hellgrammite
Probably the best method is to actually check the contents of a fish's stomach.

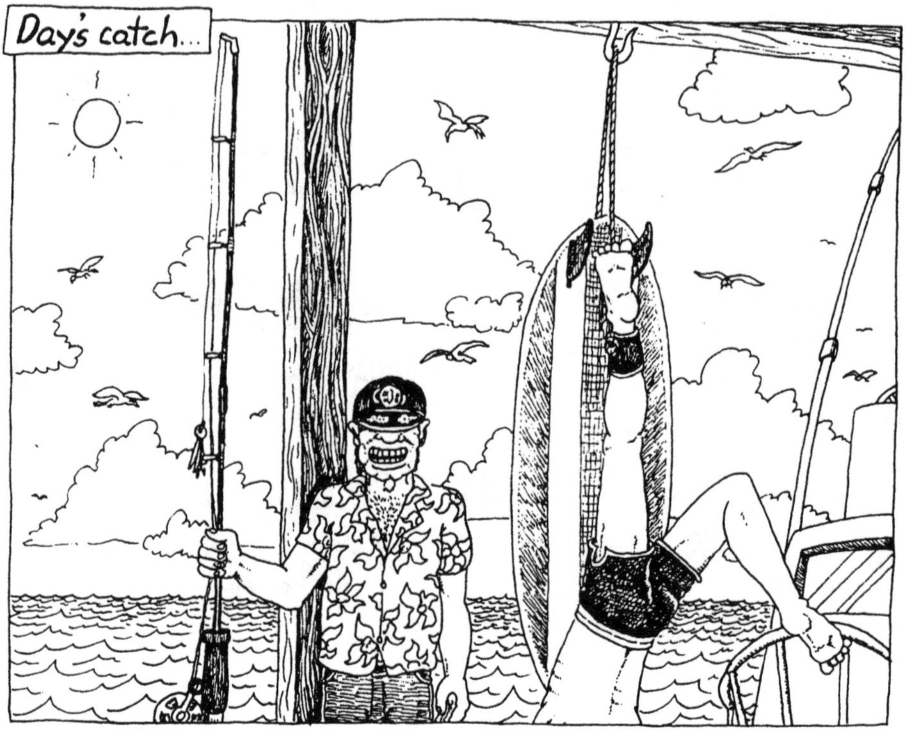
Day's catch...

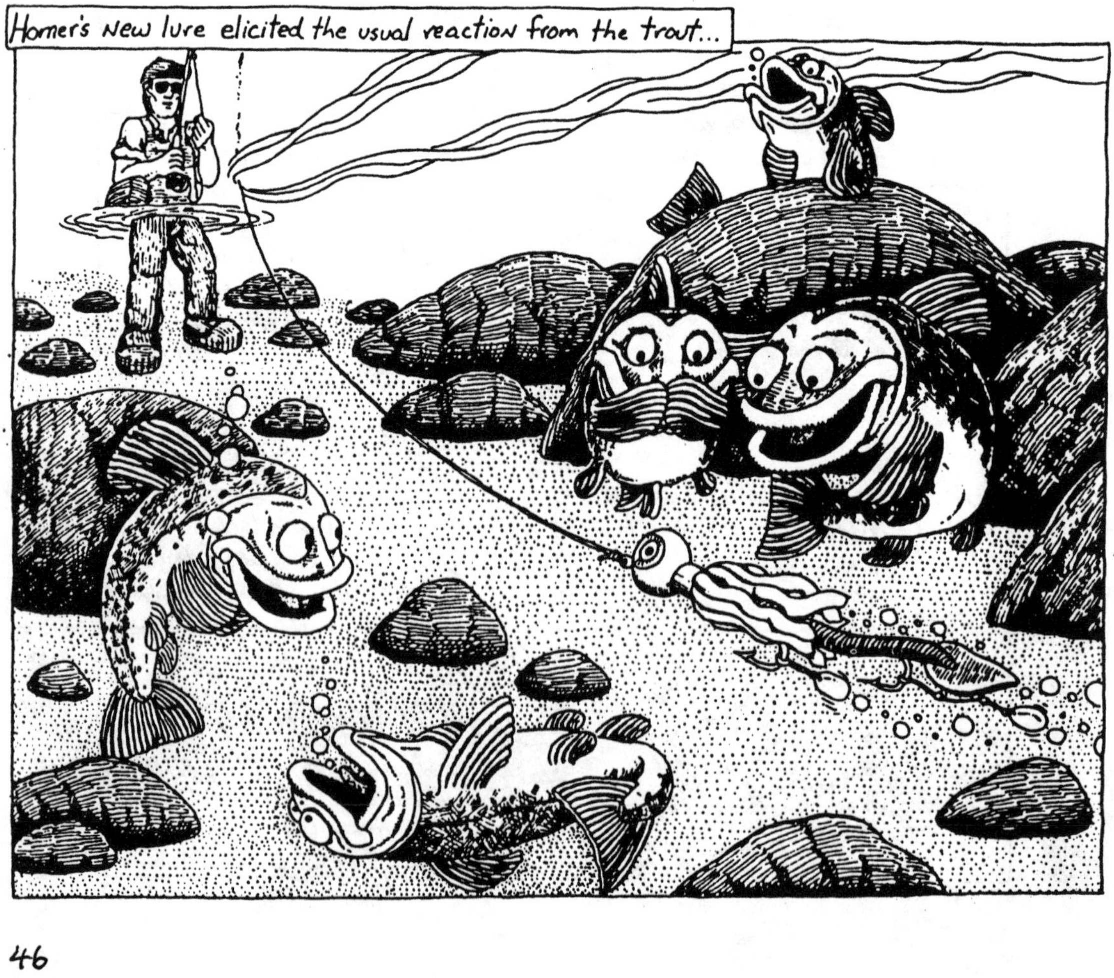
Homer's new lure elicited the usual reaction from the trout...

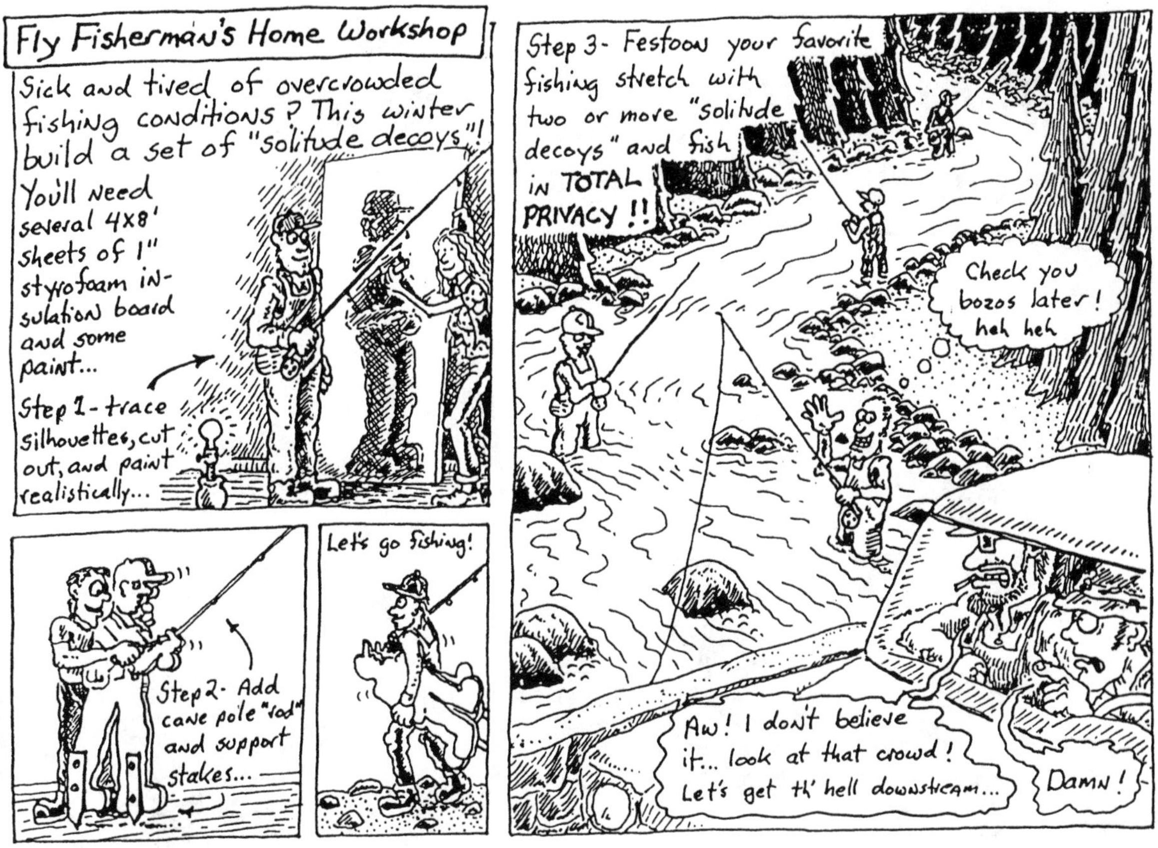
Fly Fisherman's Home Workshop
Sick and tired of overcrowded fishing conditions? This winter build a set of "solitude decoys"!
You'll need several 4x8' sheets of 1" styrofoam insulation board and some paint...
Step 1 - trace silhouettes, cut out, and paint realistically...
Step 2 - Add cane pole "rod" and support stakes...
Let's go fishing!
Step 3 - Festoon your favorite fishing stretch with two or more "solitude decoys" and fish in TOTAL PRIVACY!!
Check you bozos later! heh heh
Aw! I don't believe it... look at that crowd! Let's get th' hell downstream...
Damn!

Give a man a fish
and he will eat today...
Teach a man to fish
and he'll sit in a boat
and drink beer all day. ANON.

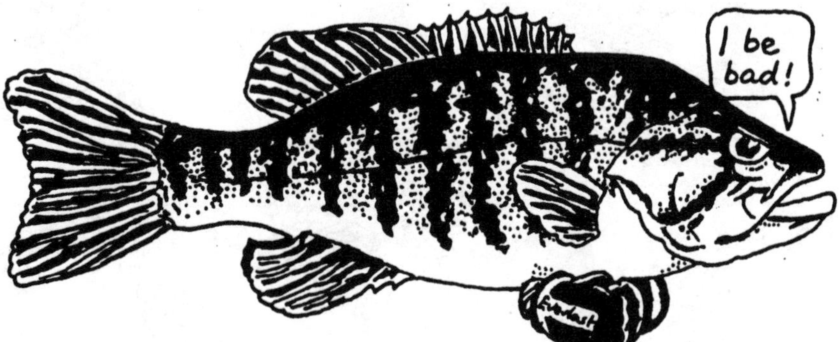
I be bad!

Typical Smallmouth Bass

Kill Kill Kill! (gone huntin')

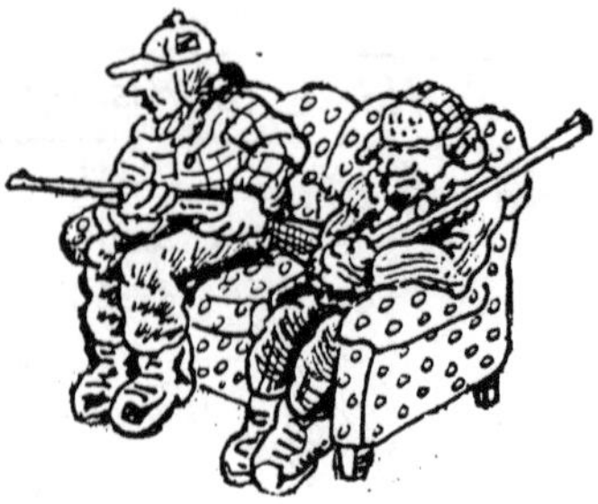

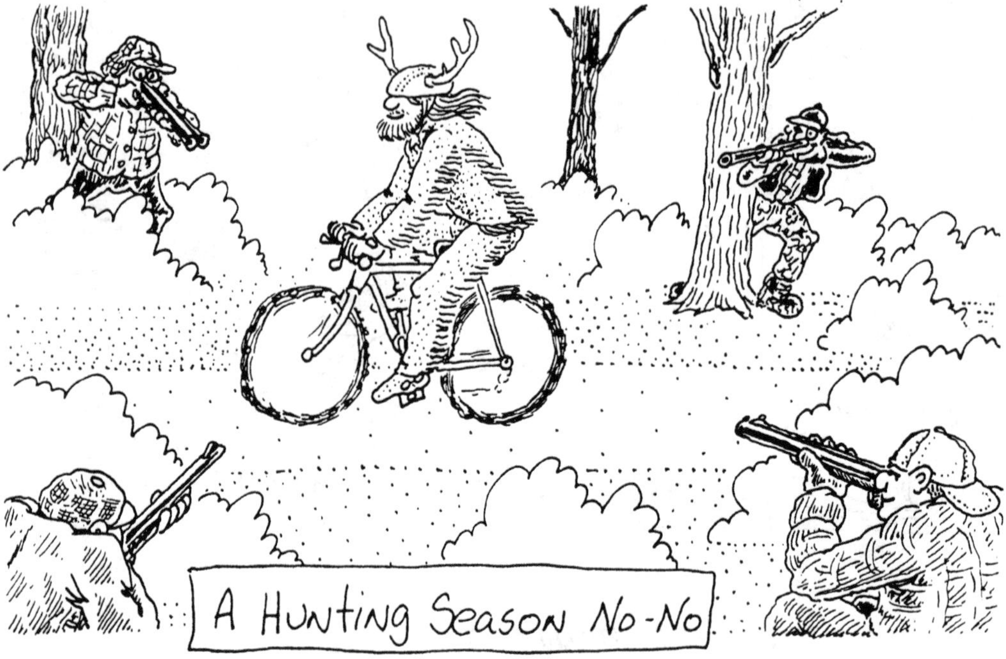

A Hunting Season No-No

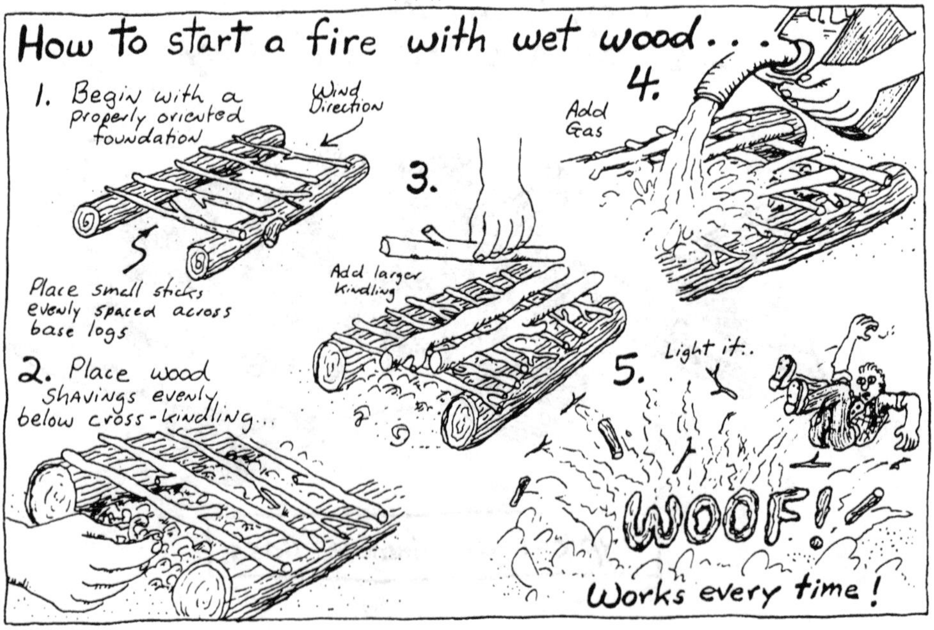
How to start a fire with wet wood . . .
1. Begin with a properly oriented foundation
Wind Direction
Place small sticks evenly spaced across base logs
2. Place wood shavings evenly below cross-kindling . . .
3.
Add larger kindling
4.
Add Gas
5.
Light it.
WOOF!
Works every time!

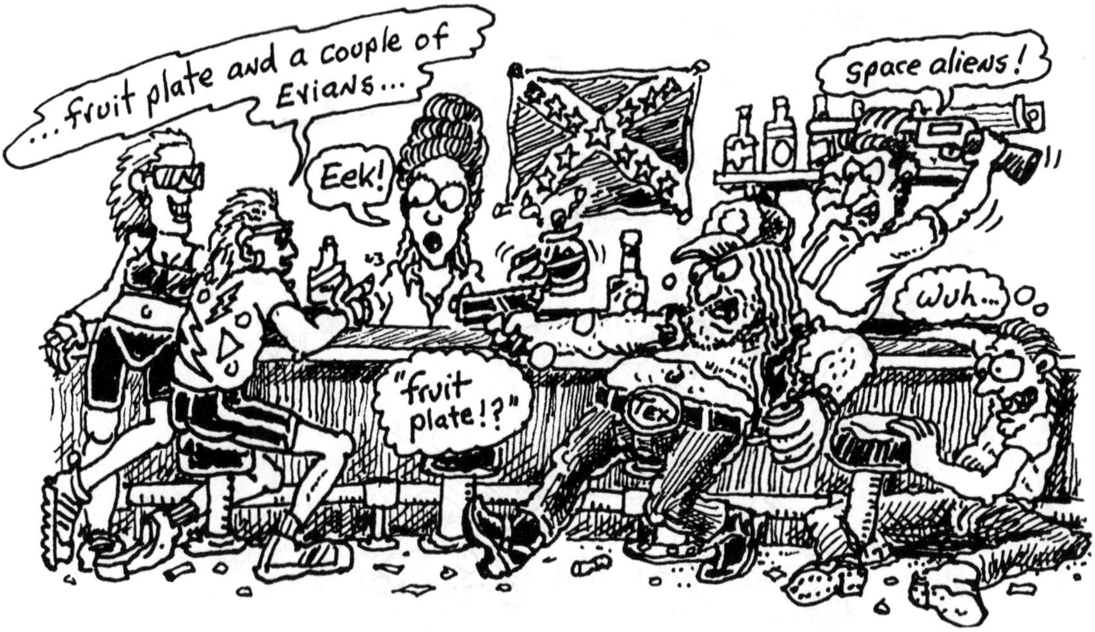
...fruit plate and a couple of Evians...
Eek!
Space aliens!
Wuh...
"fruit plate!?"
Tex

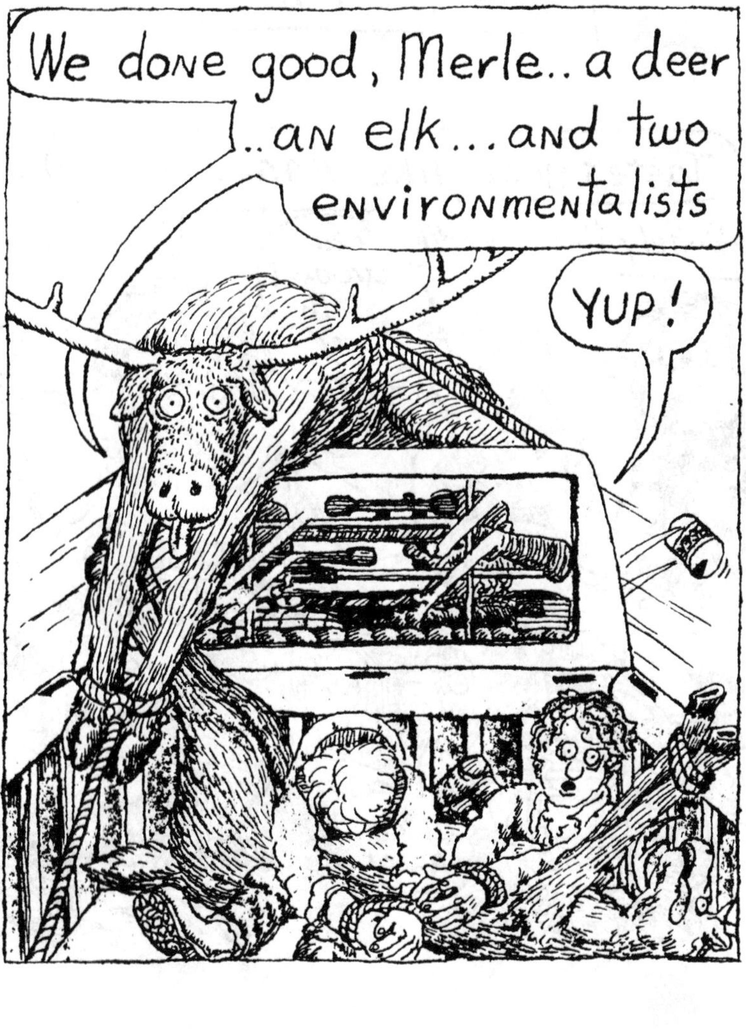
We done good, Merle.. a deer ..an elk...and two environmentalists
YUP!

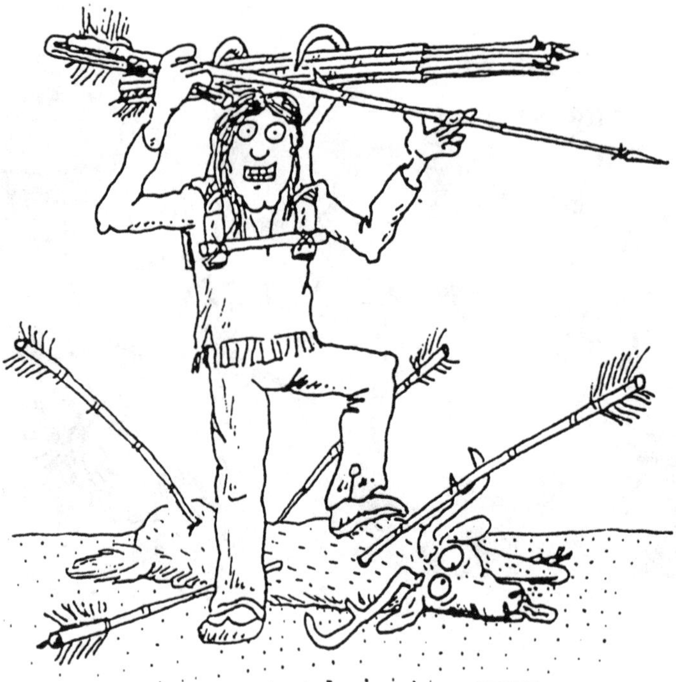

Semi-Auto AtlAtl

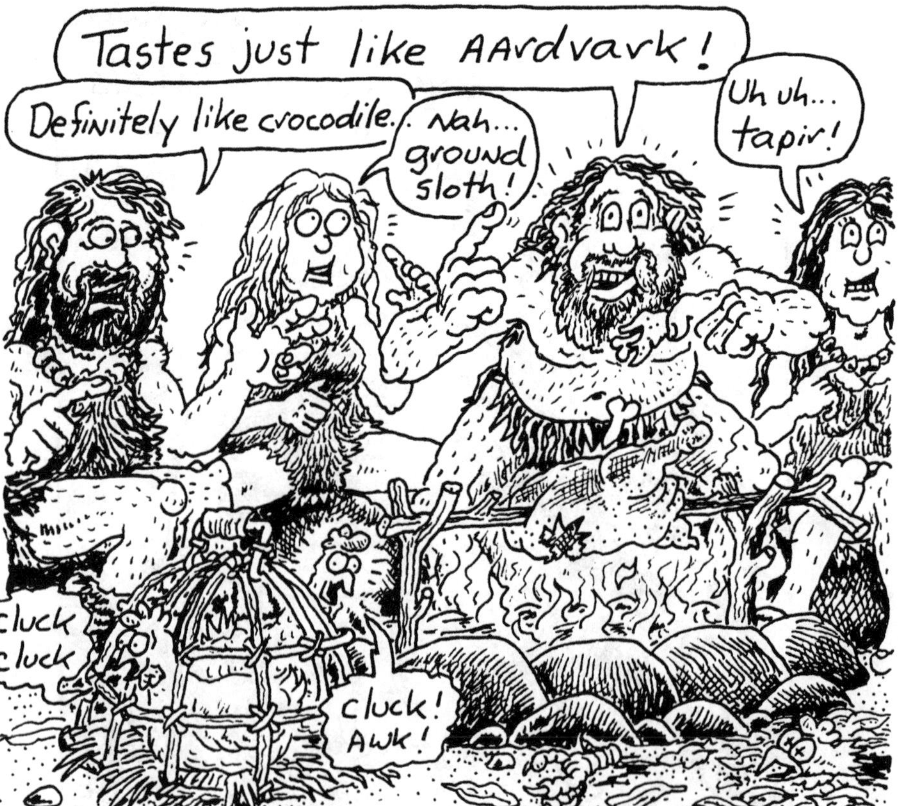
Tastes just like AArdvark!
Definitely like crocodile.
Nah... ground sloth!
Uh uh... tapir!
cluck cluck
cluck! Awk!

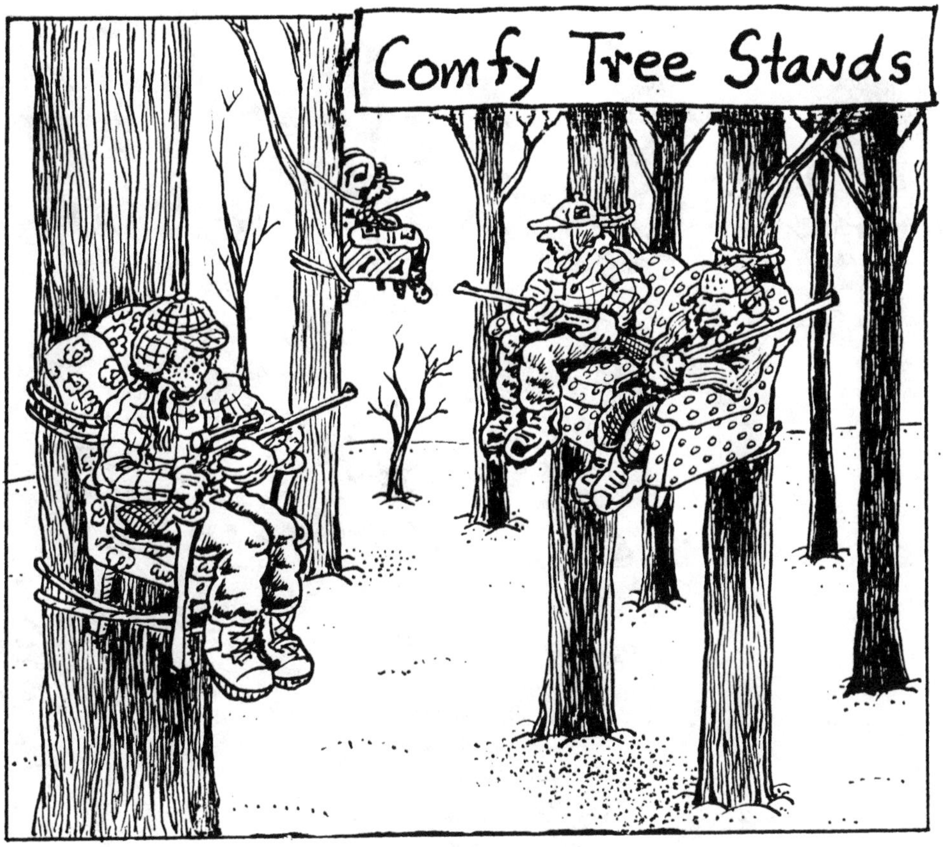
Comfy Tree Stands

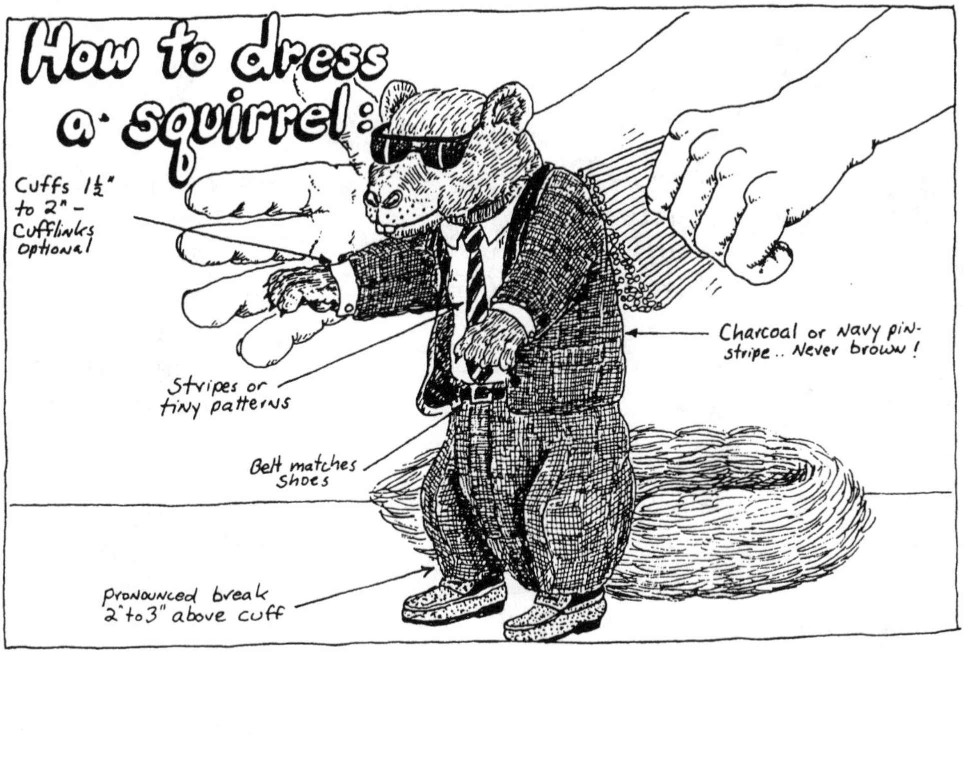
How to dress a squirrel:
Cuffs 1½" to 2" – Cufflinks optional
Charcoal or Navy pin-stripe.. Never brown!
Stripes or tiny patterns
Belt matches shoes
pronounced break 2" to 3" above cuff

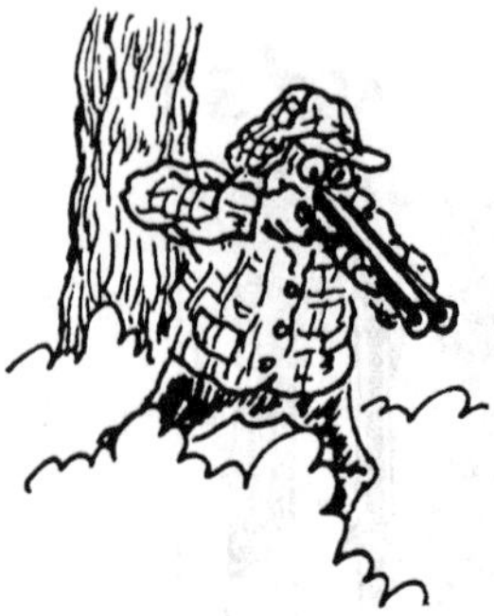

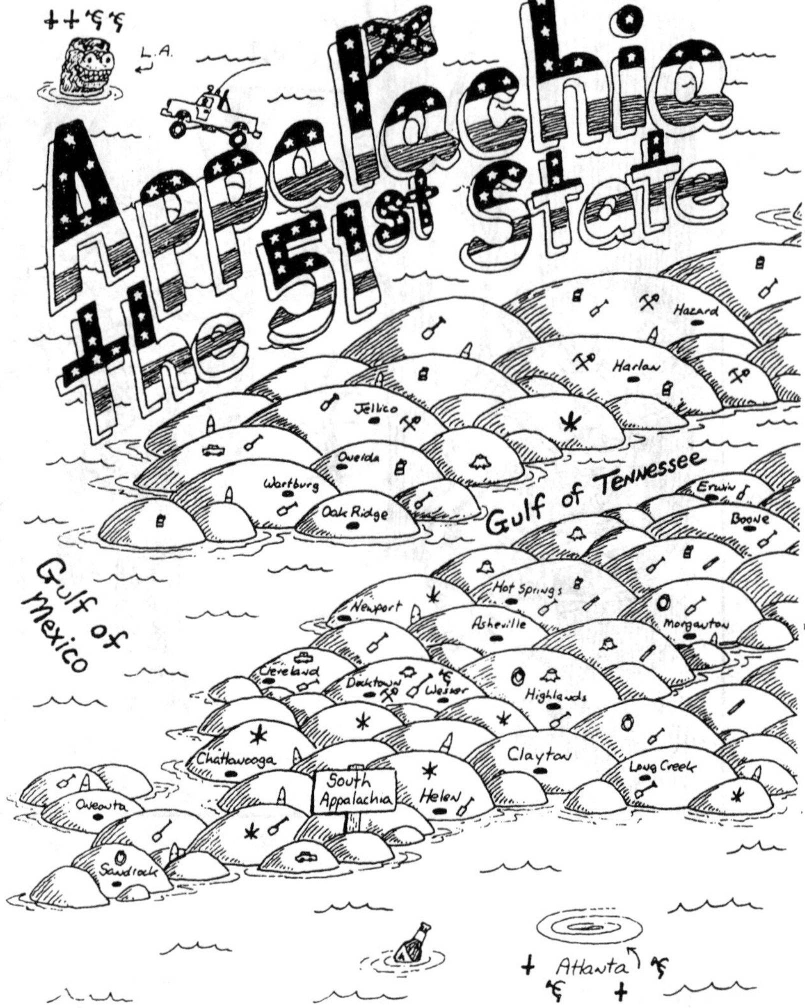

Appalachia
The 51st State
L.A.
Hazard
Harlan
Jellico
Oneida
Wartburg
Oak Ridge
Gulf of Tennessee
Erwin
Boone
Gulf of Mexico
Hot Springs
Newport
Asheville
Morganton
Cleveland
Ducktown
Webster
Highlands
Chattanooga
Clayton
Long Creek
South Appalachia
Helen
Oneonta
Sandrock
Atlanta

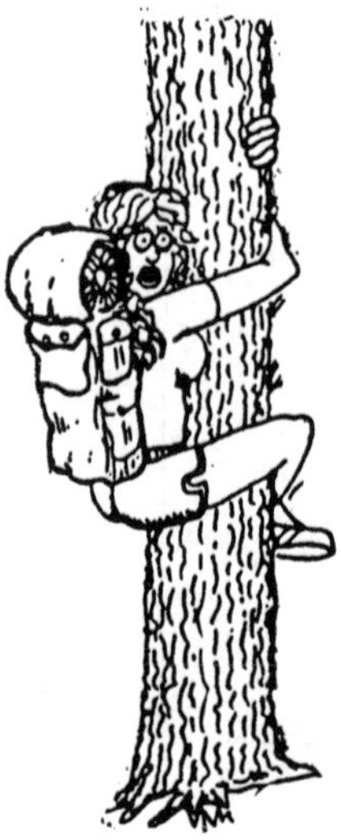

Urban Dislikes:

handguns
southern cooking
Merle Haggard

harsh drug laws
clearcuts
rednecks
bass fishing
professional wrestling
Smith & Wesson
Walmart
jacked-up 4x4 pickup trucks

Appalachian Dislikes:

gun control
granola
...that feller you can't call "Prince" no more
speed limits
wilderness areas
pencil-necked city boys
trout fishing
Ally McBeal
The Clintons
L.L. Bean
BMW

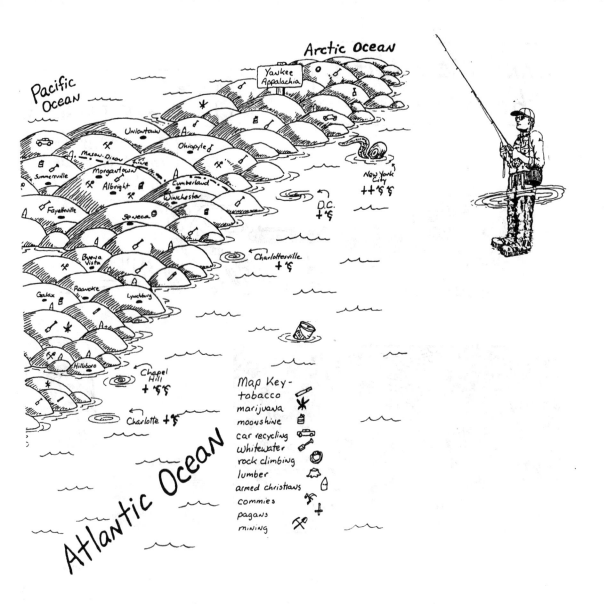

Arctic Ocean

Yankee Appalachia

Pacific Ocean

Uniontown
Ohiopyle
Mason-Dixon Line
Morgantown
Summerville
Albright
Cumberland
Winchester
Fayetteville
Seneca
Buena Vista
Roanoke
Galax
Lynchburg
Hillsboro
Chapel Hill
Charlotte

New York City

D.C.

Charlottesville

Atlantic Ocean

Map Key -
tobacco
marijuana
moonshine
car recycling
whitewater
rock climbing
lumber
armed christians
commies
pagans
mining

Urban Likes:
New York City
Antiques Roadshow
laptop computer
sushi
perrier
aerobics
Annie Hall
kayaks
Wall Street Journal
Sierra Club
wild rivers
ecstasy
wok

Appalachian Likes:
McDonalds
NFL Football
weedeater
quarterpounder @ cheese
Bud
shootin' the assault rifle
Smokey & the Bandit VI
bass boats
Guns And Ammo
NRA
recreational lakes
Skoal
chainsaw

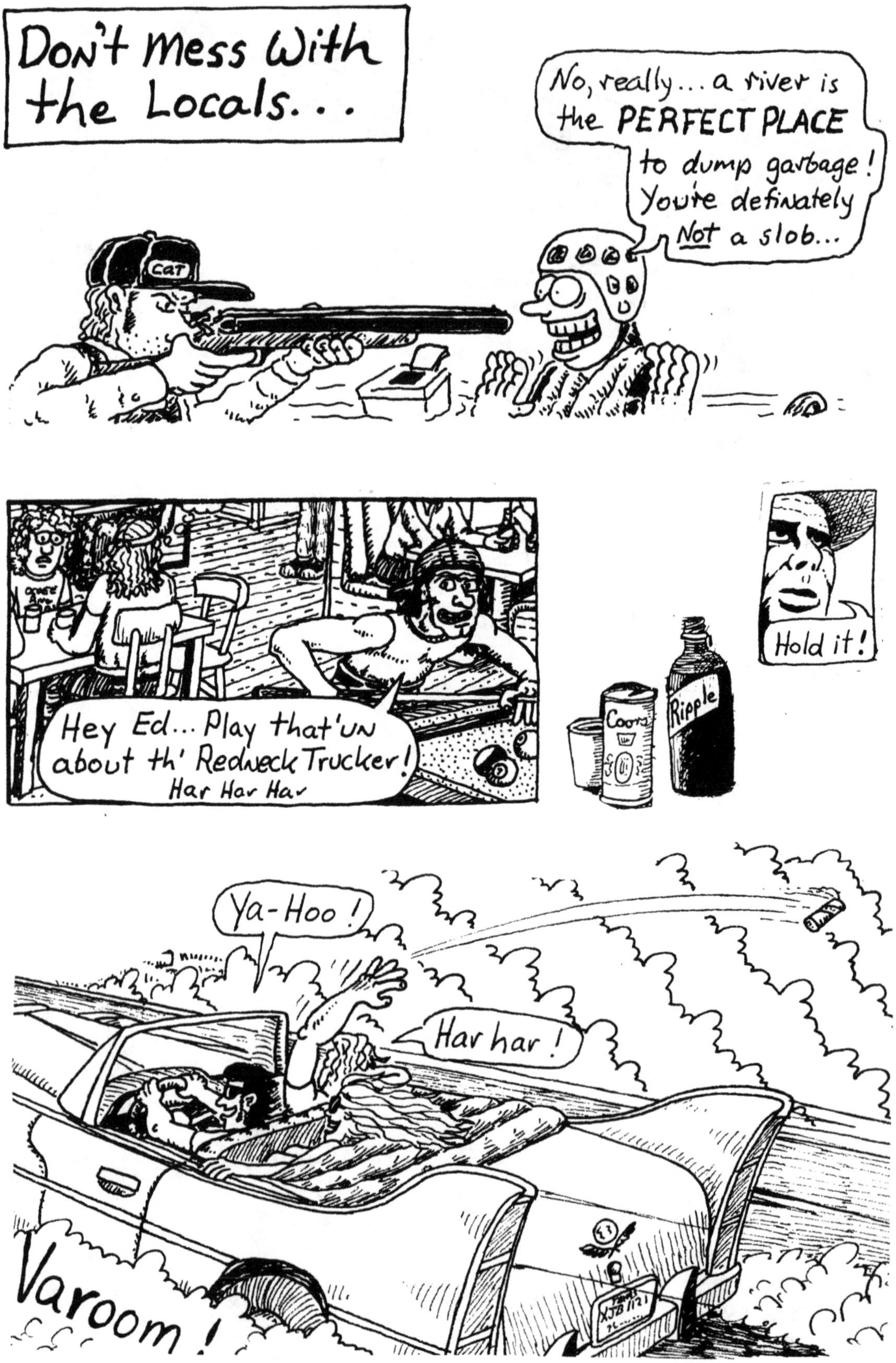
Don't Mess With the Locals...
No, really... a river is the PERFECT PLACE to dump garbage! You're definately Not a slob...
CAT
Hey Ed... Play that'UN about th' Redneck Trucker! Har Har Har
Coors
Ripple
Hold it!
Ya-Hoo!
Har har!
Varoom!

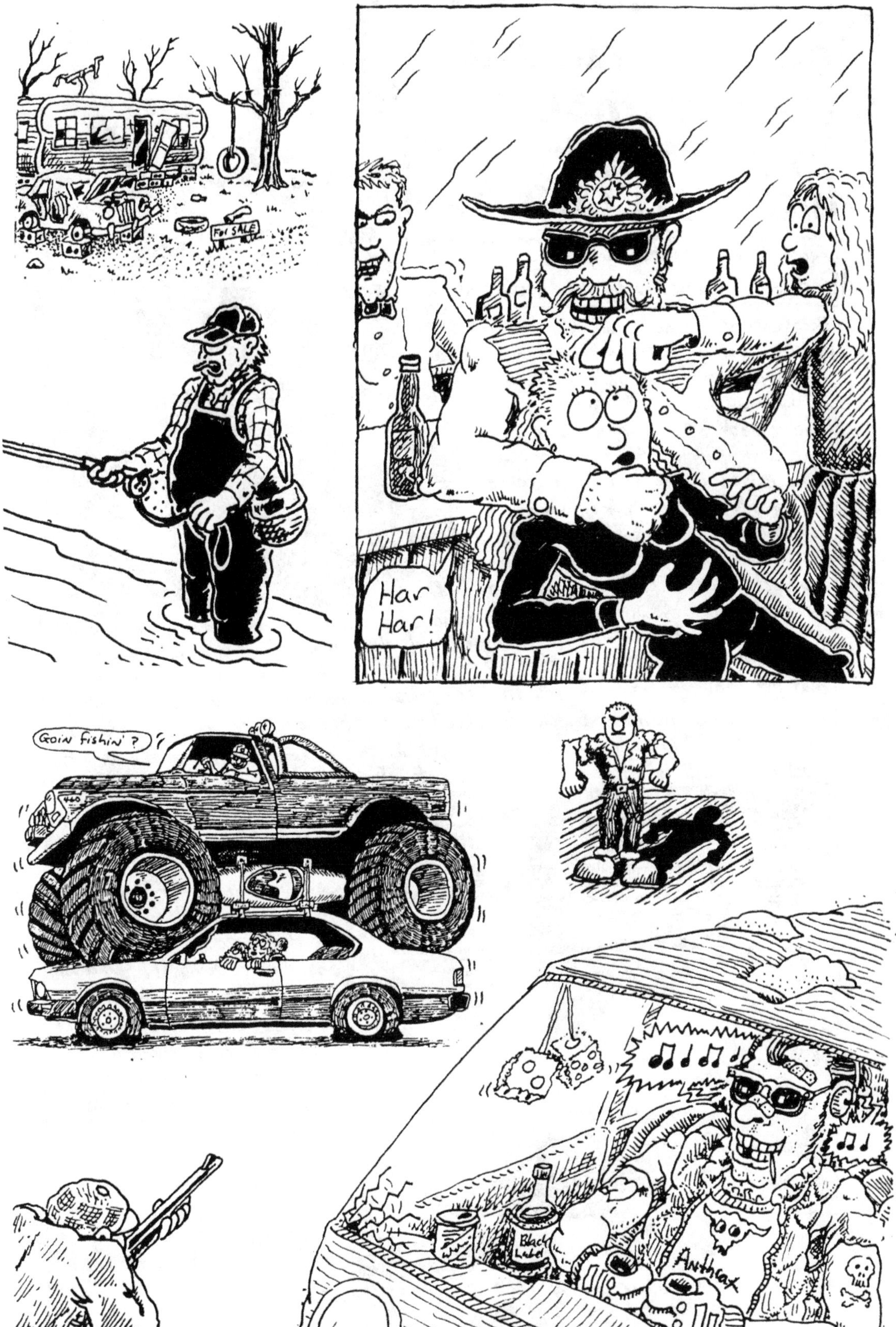
For SALE
Har Har!
Goin fishin'?
Black Label
Anthrax

You shor do have a purty mouth...

Hiking & Camping...

Funhog Paranoia Serie's, Part I

Roadside Camping In The Mountains

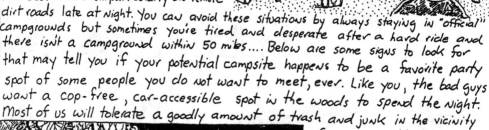

If'n it weren't fer that beard you'd look jes like mah wife...

ulp!

Good shootin', Joe Bob!

Pow!

sh-t!

Occasionally, fun hogs will find themselves seeking "non-designated" roadside campsites while recreating in the mountains. Unfortunately, poor site selection can get you in deep shit with people who could have been extras in the movie "Deliverance"! [See opposite] While 99% of indigenous mountain folks are wonderful people, encounters with the 1% criminal types are best avoided... particularly on remote dirt roads late at night. You can avoid these situations by always staying in "official" campgrounds but sometimes you're tired and desperate after a hard ride and there isn't a campground within 50 miles.... Below are some signs to look for that may tell you if your potential campsite happens to be a favorite party spot of some people you do not want to meet, ever. Like you, the bad guys want a cop-free, car-accessible spot in the woods to spend the night. Most of us will tolerate a goodly amount of trash and junk in the vicinity of a one-night camp site (we're tired & desperate, remember?) but too much of certain types of trash can tell us to get the hell out of the area, if we are observant. Obviously you don't want to camp in or next to a site thats ankle-deep in beer cans and AK-47 brass. If this site is on a dead-end road or loop even if you camp 2 miles back up the road the mutants will be cruising by all night on their way to their party spot. Thus, it's always worth checking out not only the campsite but the general vicinity as well.

What do you think?

I think if we don't stop drivin' around I'm gonna die!

Numerous shell casings and shot-up cans & appliances... very bad sign!

Ancestral matting ground.. bad sign!

Jo & Tom '89

Tina + Bob 91

Stolen wire burned to recover copper... <u>very</u> bad sign!

To be continued....

56

Funhog Paranoia Series, Part II

Roadside Camping In The Mountains

So, you found a roadside campsite, built a fire & kicked back to enjoy a cold brew before bed... a jacked-up pick-up truck full of feral locals drinking whiskey pulls up. What do you do?! Unless you're the Tactical Mtn. Bike Team from Ft. Bragg, N.C. (with an M-16 or two stashed in your duffle bags) you may want to consider splitting, A.S.A.P.! At best they will drink all your beer, piss on your tent and fall into your campfire, generally keeping you up all night. At worst.... well, use your imagination. Be friendly (but not too friendly, especially if there's women with you), make up a good excuse to go and **SPLIT**! Good Excuses To Split: ① My girlfriend just got bit by a funny-looking spider... where's the nearest hospital? ② The game warden just came by and told us to get moving... ③ Watch out... SNAKES! We musta stirred up a nest of copperheads settin' up camp... we're gettin' the hell outa here! Etc., etc...

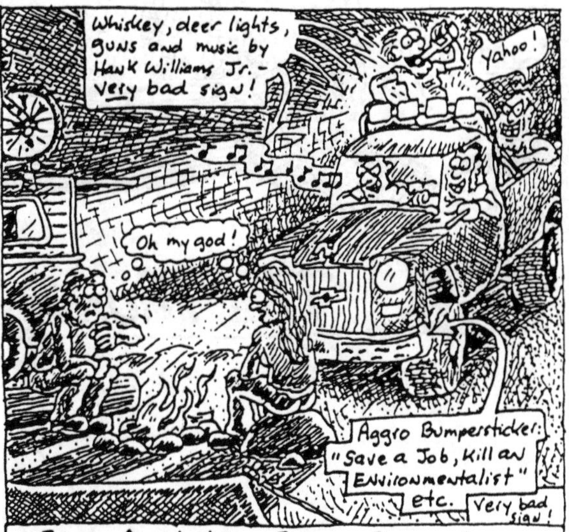

Whiskey, deer lights, guns and music by Hank Williams Jr. - very bad sign!
Yahoo!
Oh my god!
Aggro Bumpersticker: "Save a Job, Kill an Environmentalist" etc.
Very bad sign!

Basic Appalachian Danger Recognition

Actually there are worse things than drunk rednecks with guns to encounter late at night in the boonies... ① MetaGeeks!! Almost always from Ohio, Florida or New Jersey*, these guys will **DRIVE YOU NUTS!**

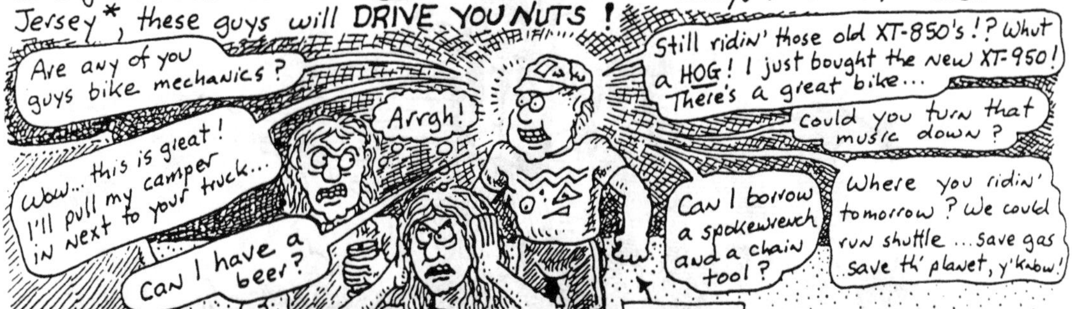

Are any of you guys bike mechanics?
Arrgh!
Still ridin' those old XT-850's!? Whut a HOG! I just bought the new XT-950! There's a great bike...
Could you turn that music down?
Wow... this is great! I'll pull my camper in next to your truck...
Can I have a beer?
Can I borrow a spokewrench and a chain tool?
Where you ridin' tomorrow? We could run shuttle... save gas save th' planet, y'know!

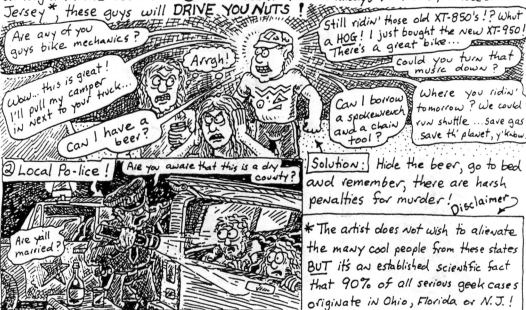

Solution: Hide the beer, go to bed and remember, there are harsh penalties for murder!

② Local Po-lice!

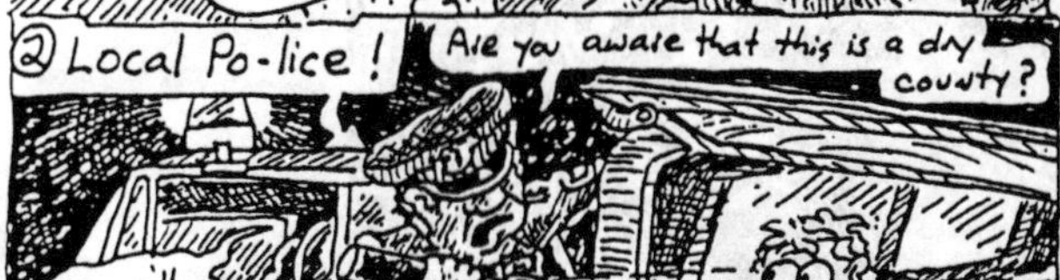

Are you aware that this is a dry county?
Are y'all married?

Disclaimer

* The artist does not wish to alienate the many cool people from these states BUT it's an established scientific fact that 90% of all serious geek cases originate in Ohio, Florida or N.J.!

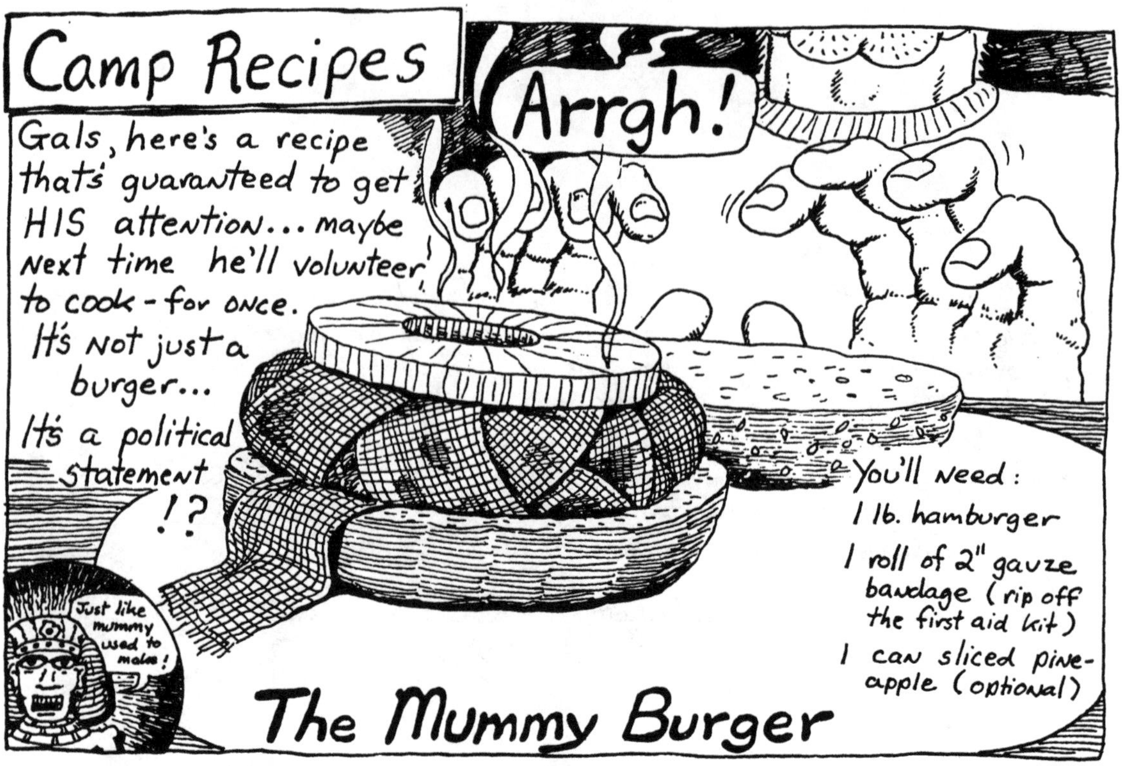
Camp Recipes
Gals, here's a recipe that's guaranteed to get HIS attention... maybe next time he'll volunteer to cook - for once.
It's not just a burger...
It's a political statement !?
Arrgh!
Just like mummy used to make!
You'll need:
1 lb. hamburger
1 roll of 2" gauze bandage (rip off the first aid kit)
1 can sliced pineapple (optional)
The Mummy Burger

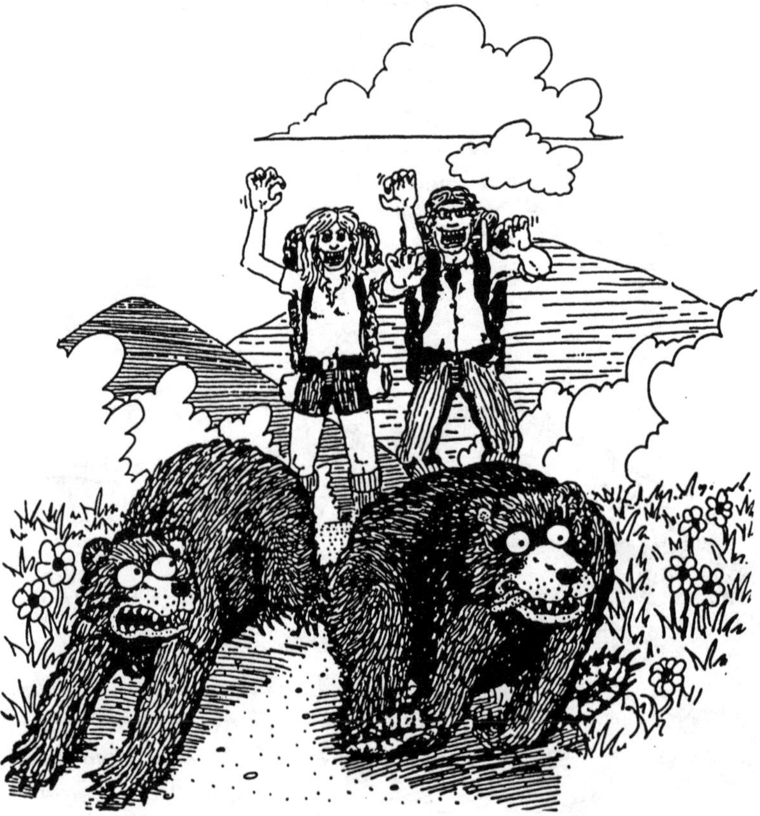

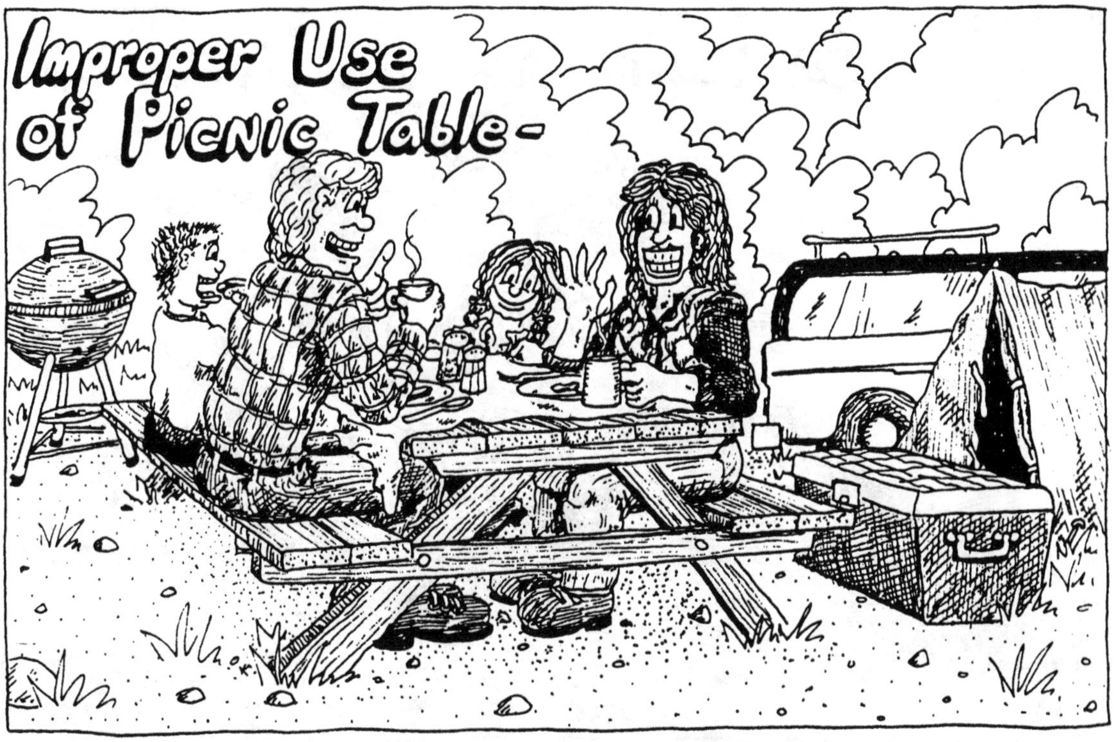
Improper Use of Picnic Table-

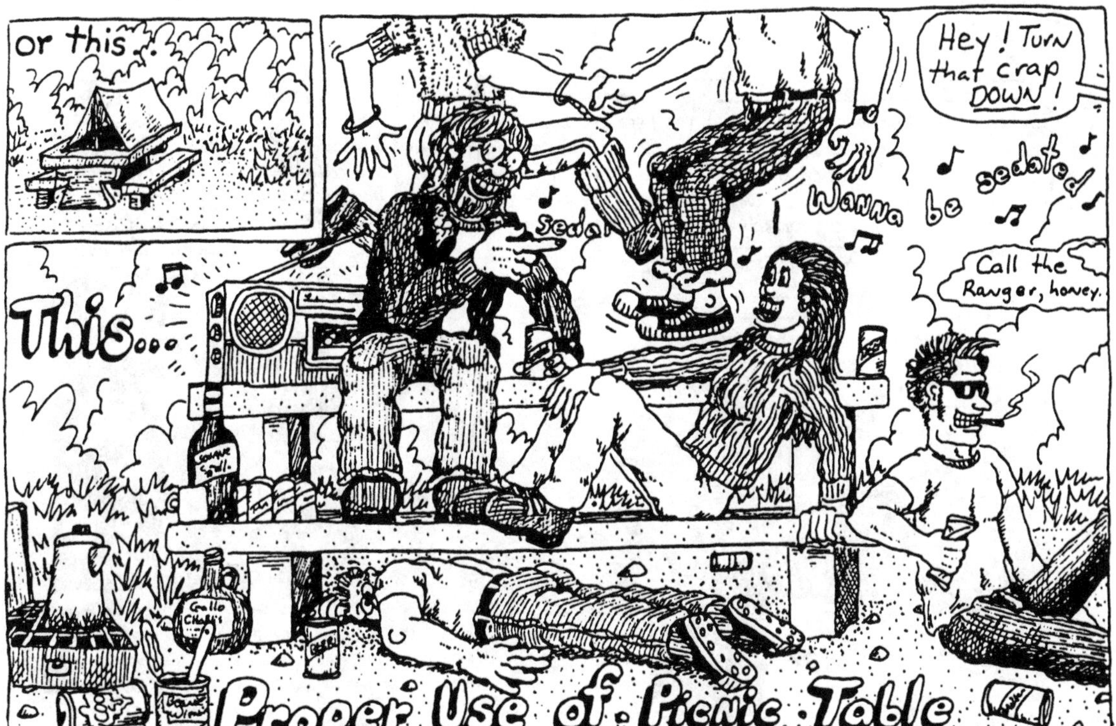
or this..
This...
Hey! Turn that crap DOWN!
sedat
Wanna be sedated
Call the Ranger, honey.
Proper Use of Picnic Table

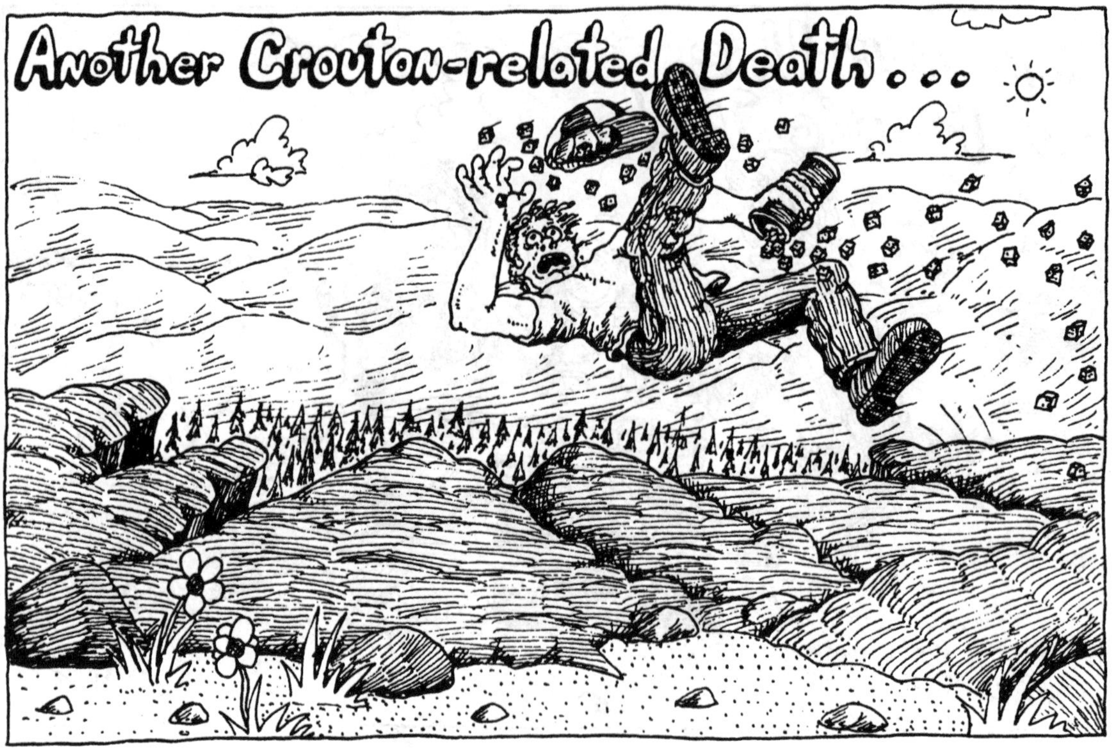
Another Crouton-related Death...

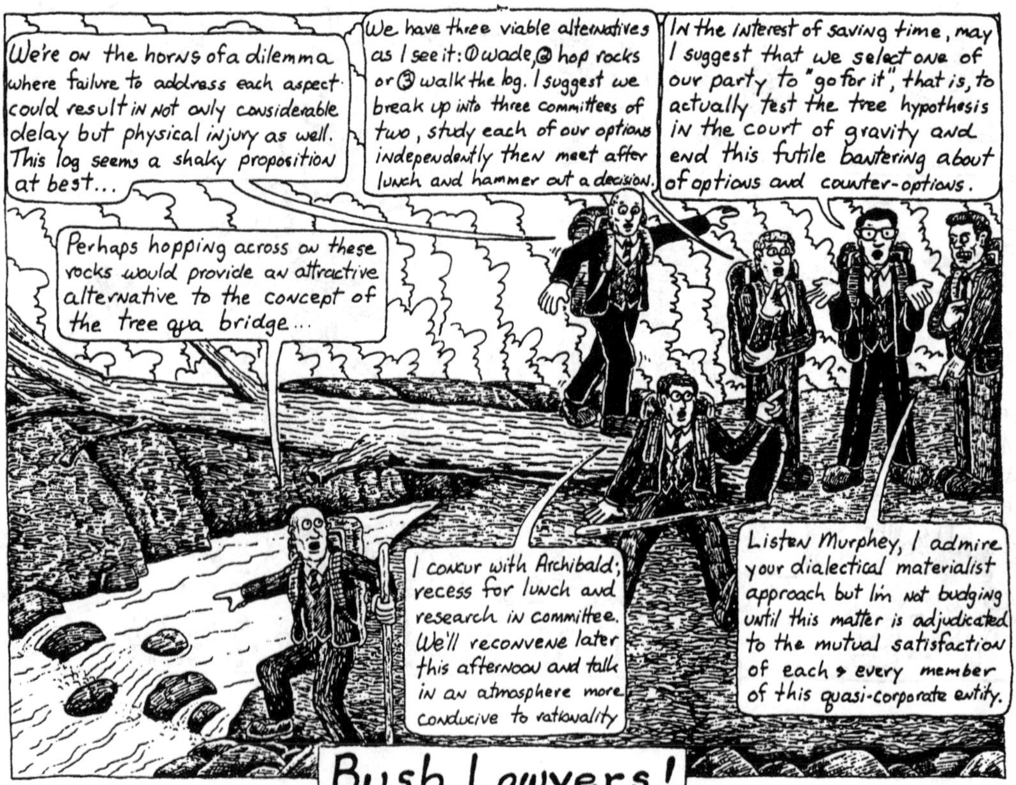
We're on the horns of a dilemma where failure to address each aspect could result in not only considerable delay but physical injury as well. This log seems a shaky proposition at best...
We have three viable alternatives as I see it: ① wade, ② hop rocks or ③ walk the log. I suggest we break up into three committees of two, study each of our options independently then meet after lunch and hammer out a decision.
In the interest of saving time, may I suggest that we select one of our party to "go for it", that is, to actually test the tree hypothesis in the court of gravity and end this futile bantering about of options and counter-options.
Perhaps hopping across on these rocks would provide an attractive alternative to the concept of the tree qua bridge...
I concur with Archibald; recess for lunch and research in committee. We'll reconvene later this afternoon and talk in an atmosphere more conducive to rationality
Listen Murphey, I admire your dialectical materialist approach but I'm not budging until this matter is adjudicated to the mutual satisfaction of each & every member of this quasi-corporate entity.
Bush Lawyers!

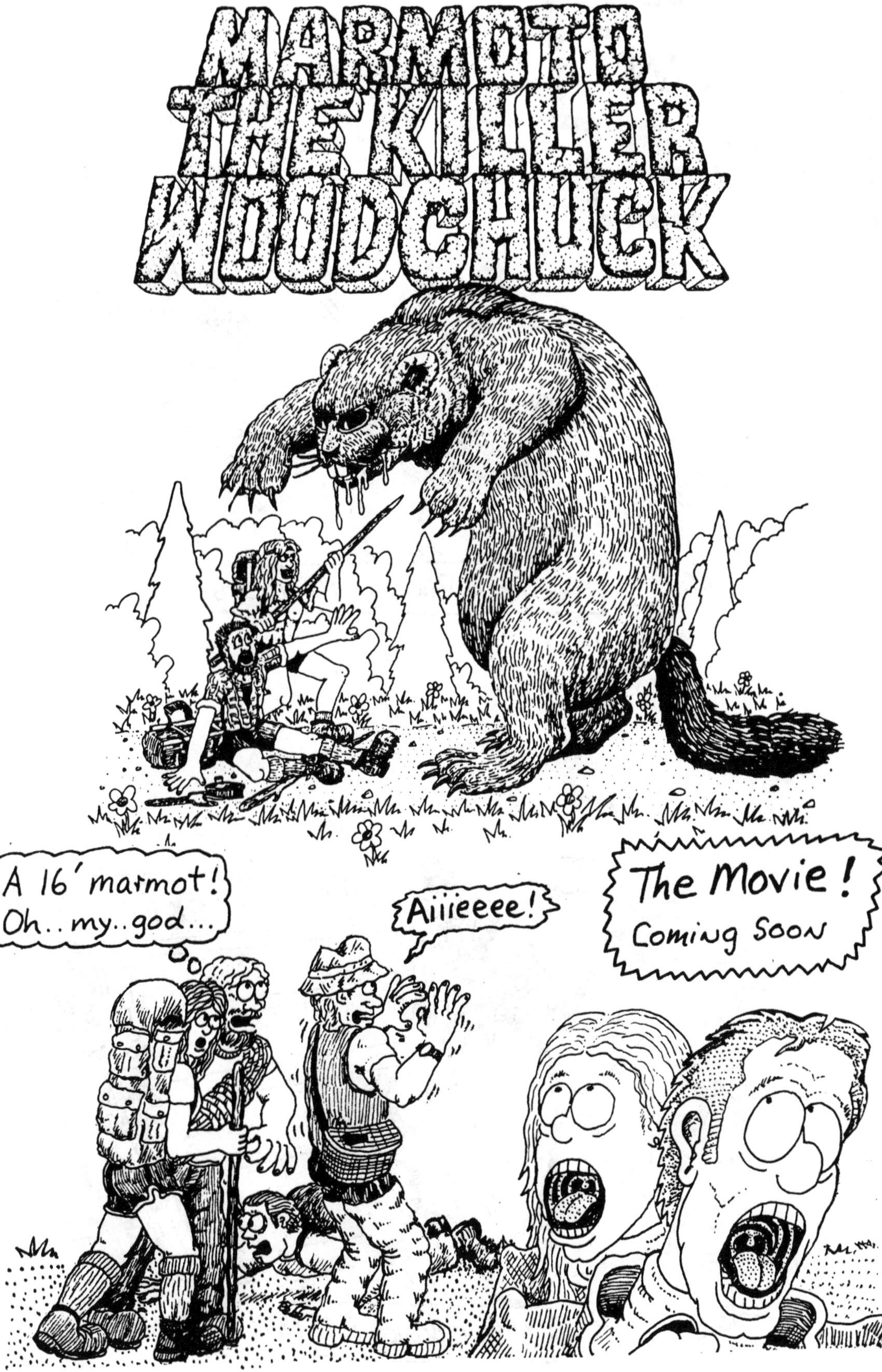
MARMOTO THE KILLER WOODCHUCK
A 16' marmot! Oh..my..god...
Aiiieeee!
The Movie! Coming Soon

Surfin' Turf...

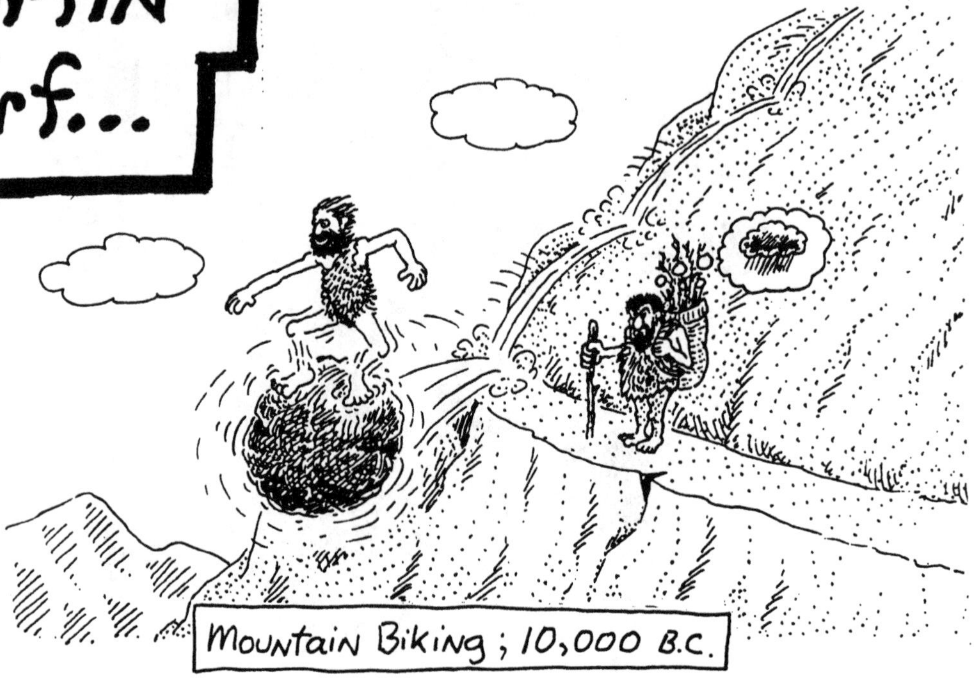
Mountain Biking; 10,000 B.C.

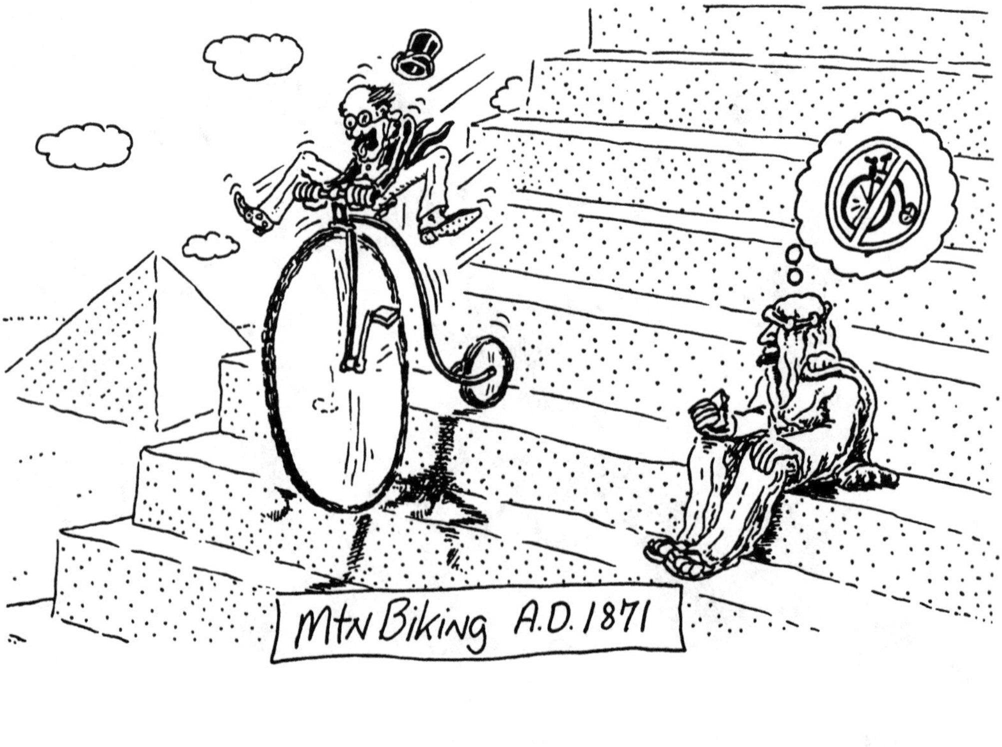
Mtn Biking A.D. 1871

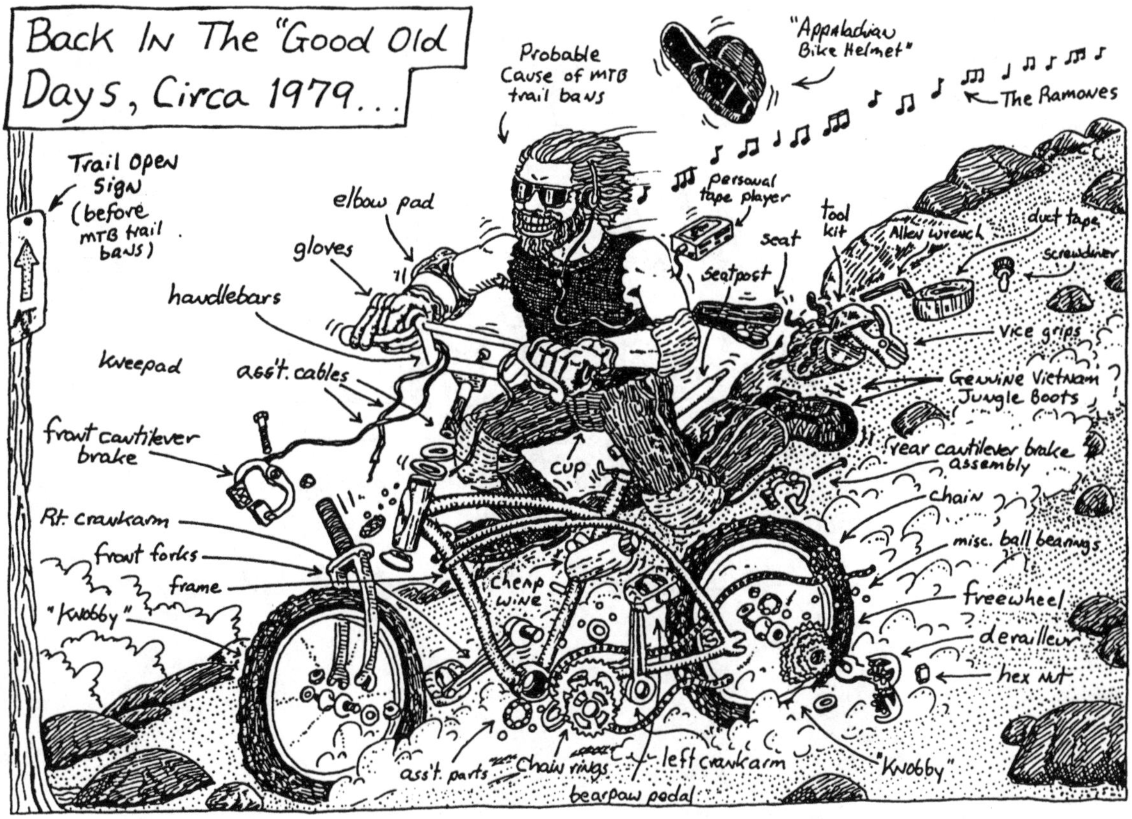
Back In The "Good Old Days, Circa 1979...
Probable Cause of MTB trail bans
"Appalachian Bike Helmet"
The Ramones
Trail open sign (before MTB trail bans)
A.T.
elbow pad
personal tape player
tool kit
Allen wrench
duct tape
screwdriver
gloves
seat
seatpost
handlebars
vice grips
kneepad
ass't. cables
Genuine Vietnam Jungle Boots
front cantilever brake
cup
rear cantilever brake assembly
Rt. crankarm
chain
front forks
Cheap wine
misc. ball bearings
frame
freewheel
"Knobby"
derailleur
hex nut
ass't. parts
chain rings
left crankarm
"Knobby"
bearpaw pedal

1983

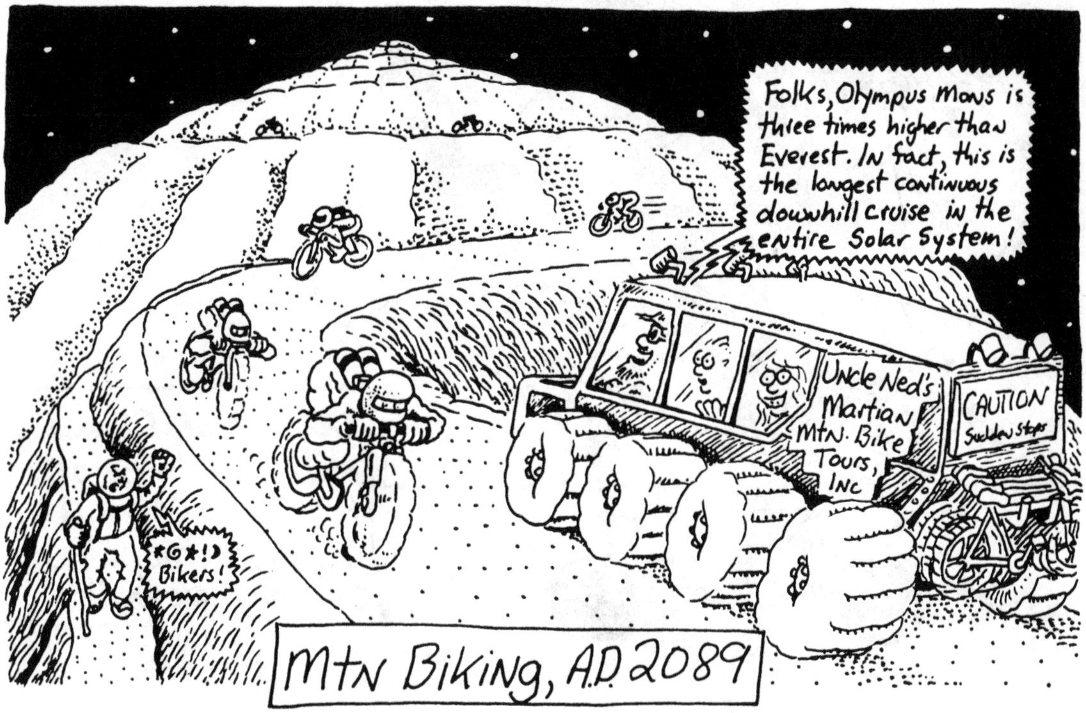
Folks, Olympus Mons is three times higher than Everest. In fact, this is the longest continuous downhill cruise in the entire Solar System!
Uncle Ned's Martian Mtn. Bike Tours, Inc
CAUTION Sudden Stops
G!! Bikers!
Mtn Biking, A.D. 2089

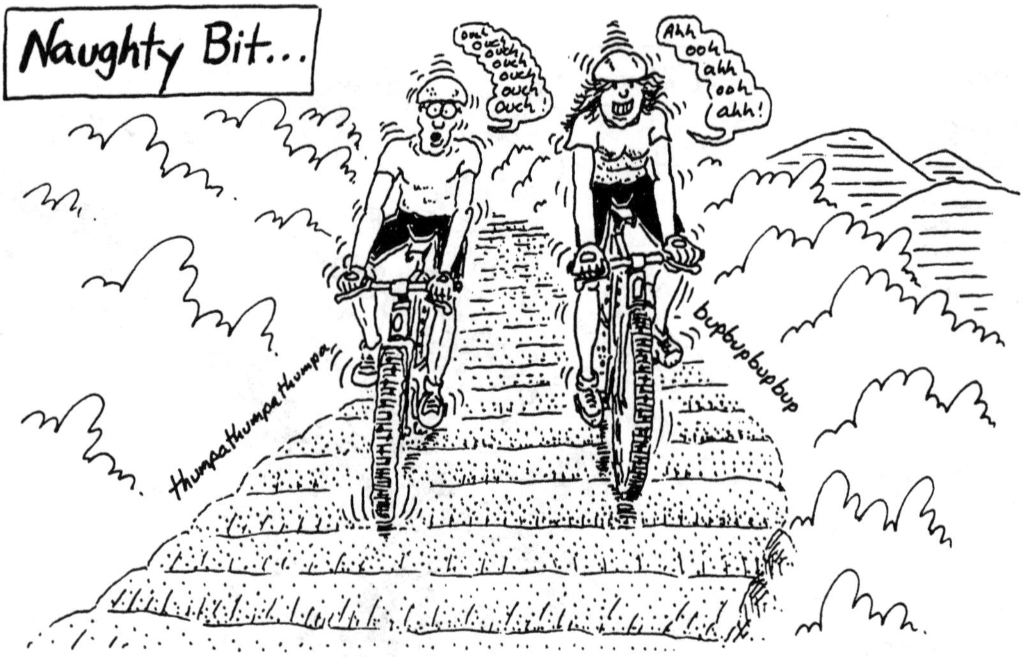
Naughty Bit...
ouch ouch ouch ouch ouch ouch ouch!
Ahh ooh ahh ooh ahh!
thumpathumpathumpa
bupbupbupbup

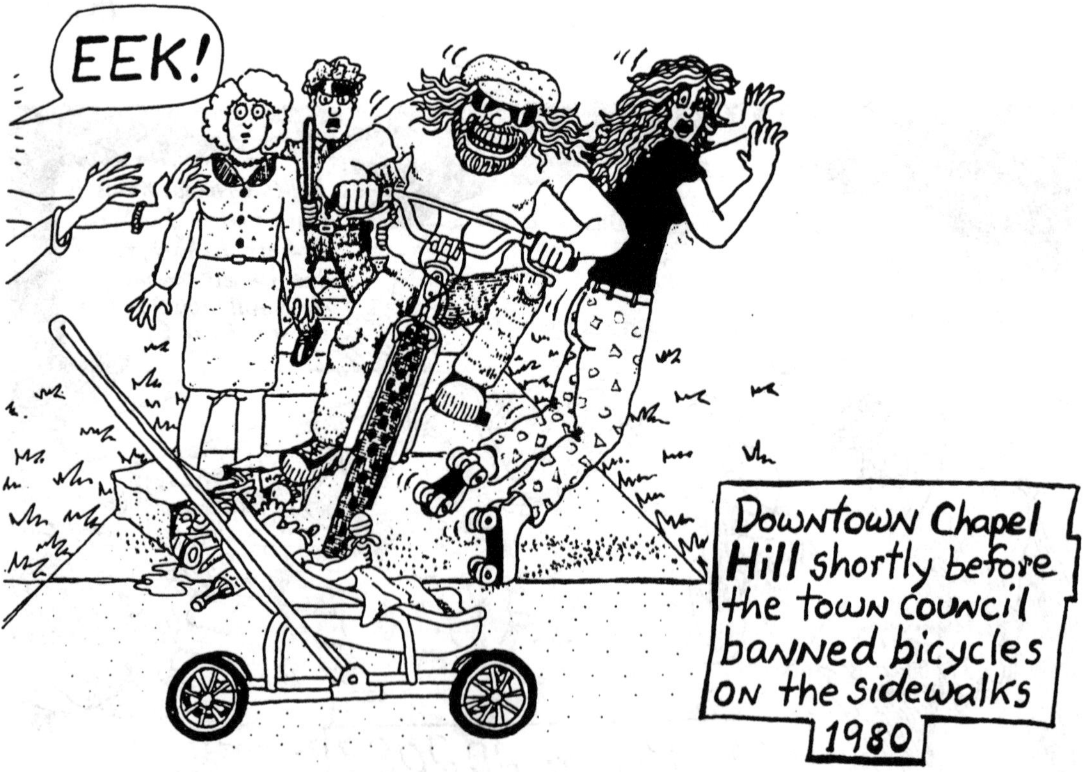
EEK!
Downtown Chapel Hill shortly before the town council banned bicycles on the sidewalks
1980

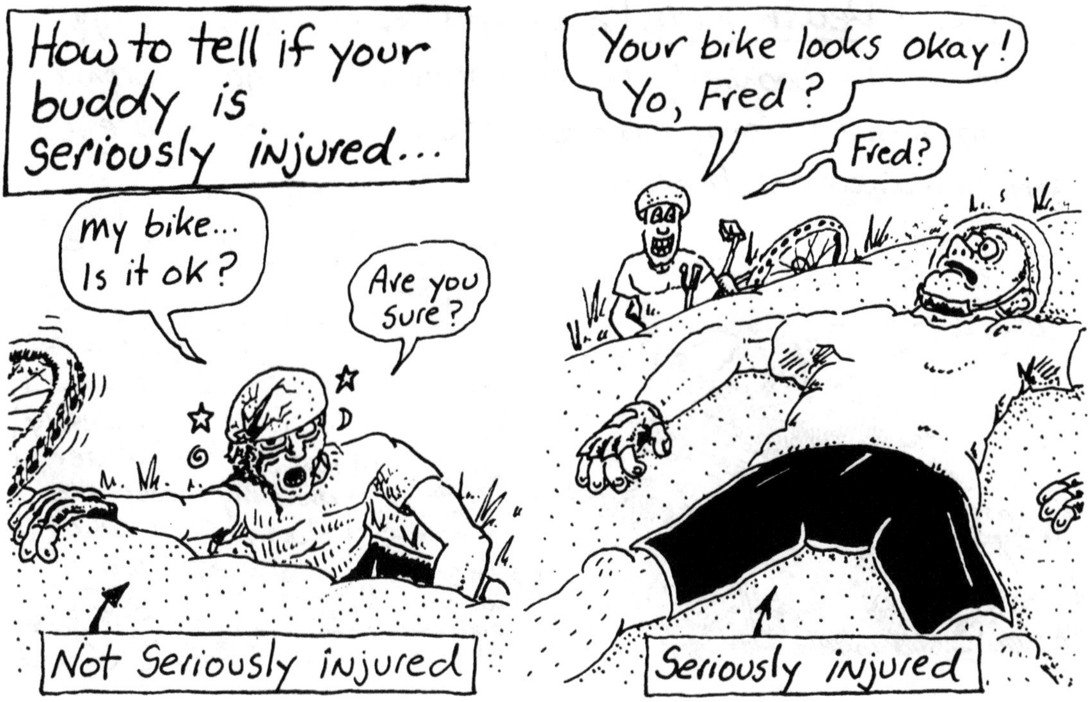
How to tell if your buddy is seriously injured...
my bike... Is it ok?
Are you sure?
Not Seriously injured
Your bike looks okay! Yo, Fred?
Fred?
Seriously injured

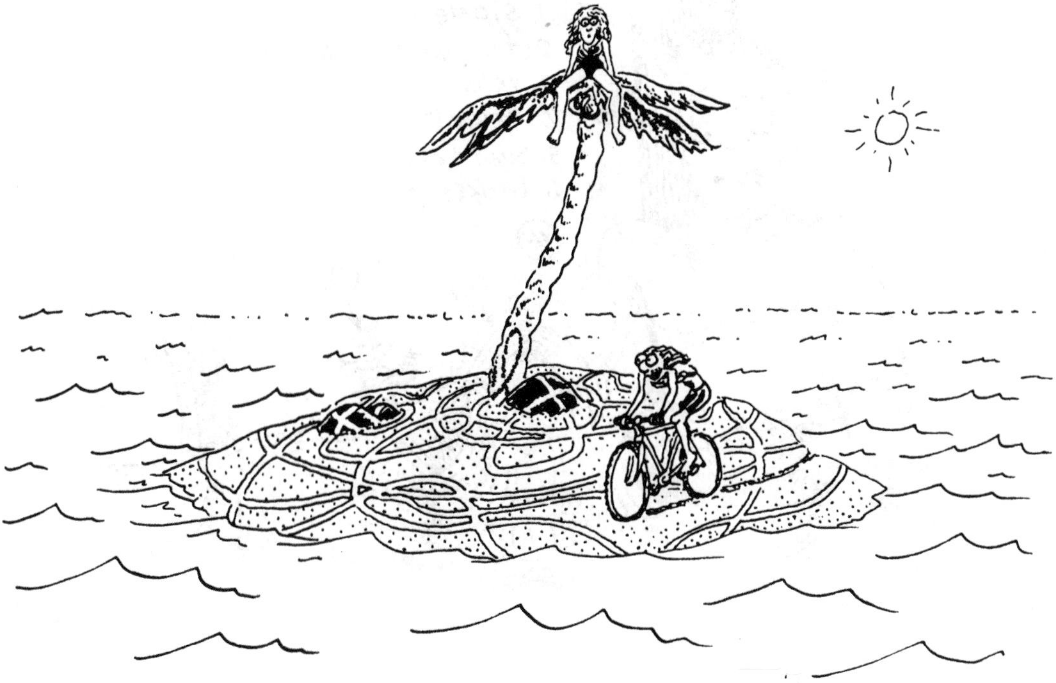

Bataan Death Ride

a.k.a. "Hell Cruise", "Exploratory", "Humping the Boonies", etc. A pleasure cruise gone wrong due to misdirection, misinformation, or misadventure. Or any combination thereof.

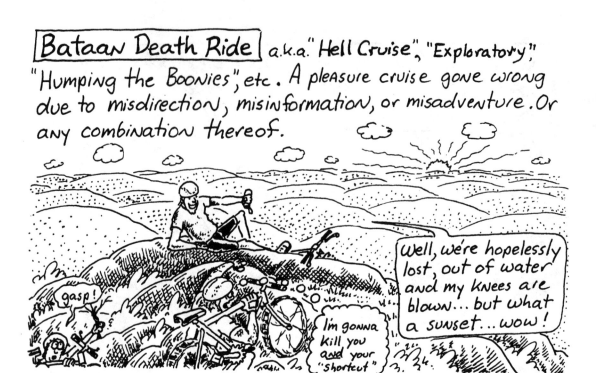

Well, we're hopelessly lost, out of water and my knees are blown... but what a sunset... wow!

gasp!

I'm gonna kill you and your "shortcut"

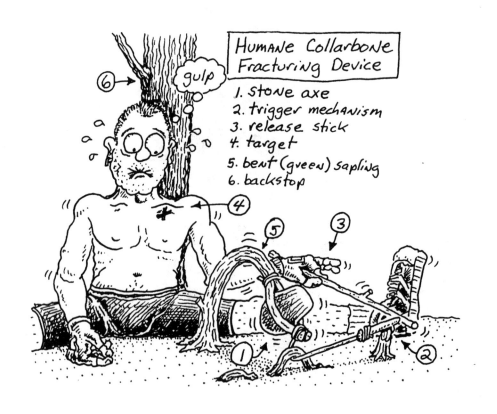

Humane Collarbone Fracturing Device

1. stone axe
2. trigger mechanism
3. release stick
4. target
5. bent (green) sapling
6. backstop

gulp

All about Seat Height

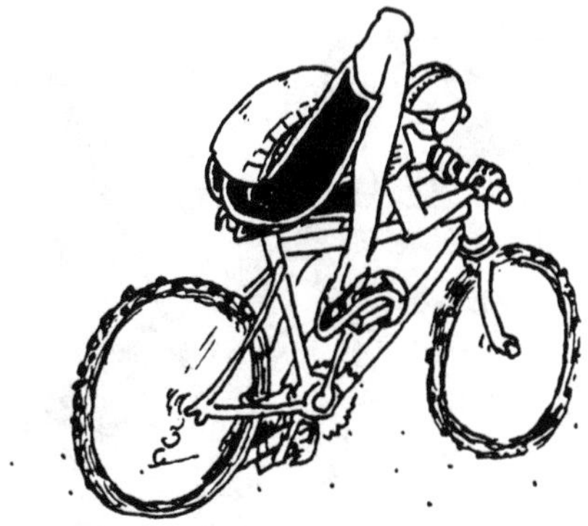

Seat too low

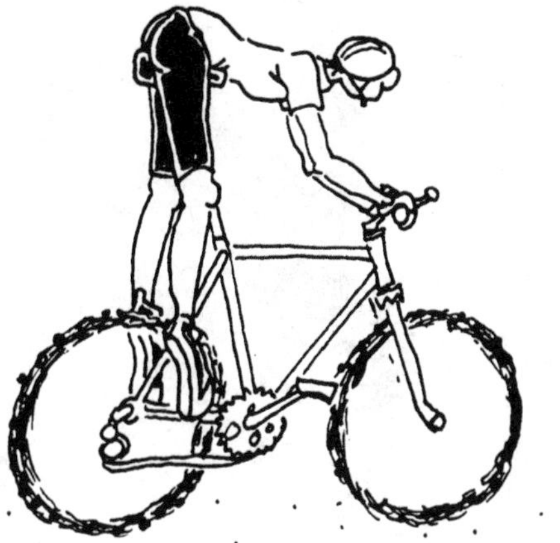

Seat too high

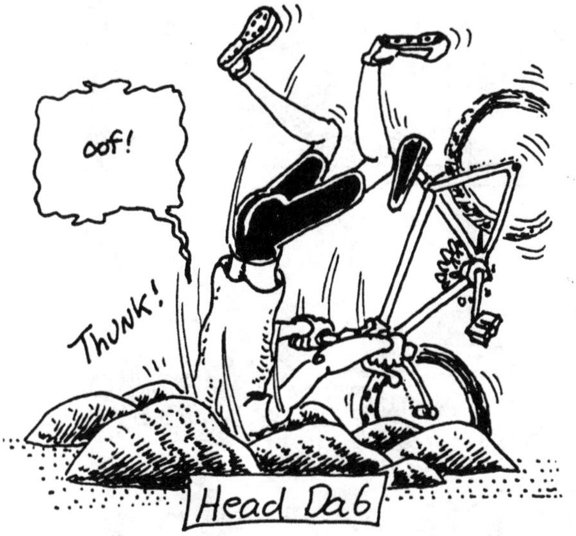
oof!
THUNK!
Head Dab

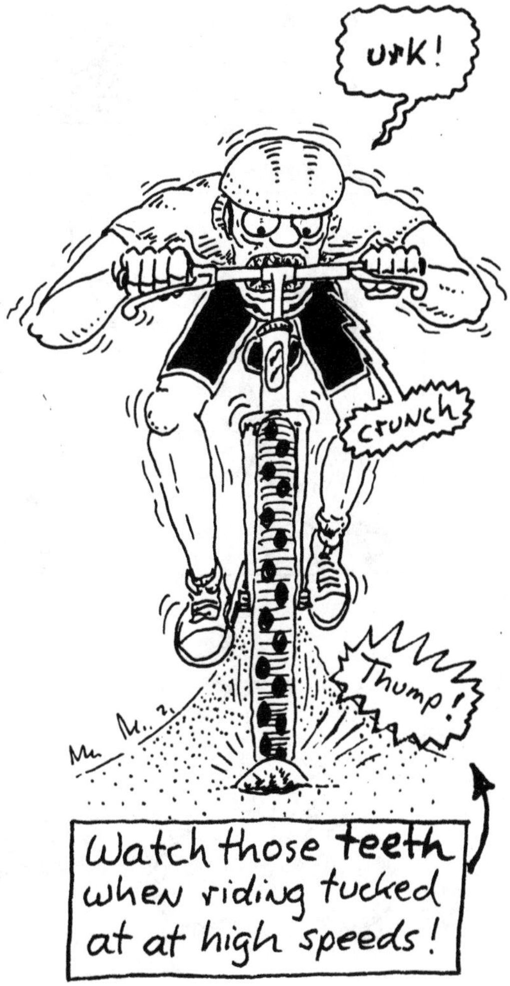
URK!
CRUNCH
Thump!

Watch those teeth when riding tucked at at high speeds!

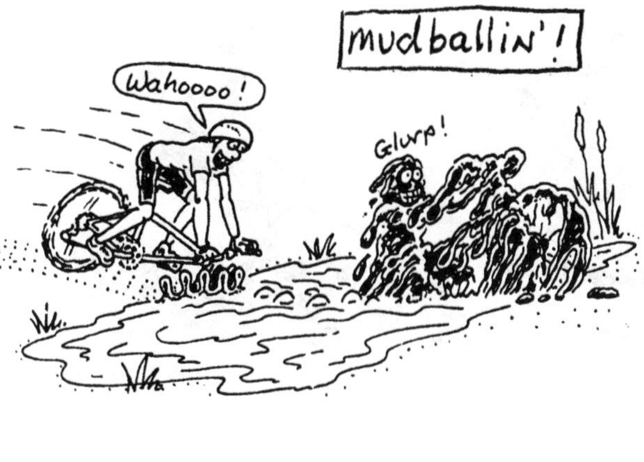
mudballin'!
Wahoooo!
Glurp!

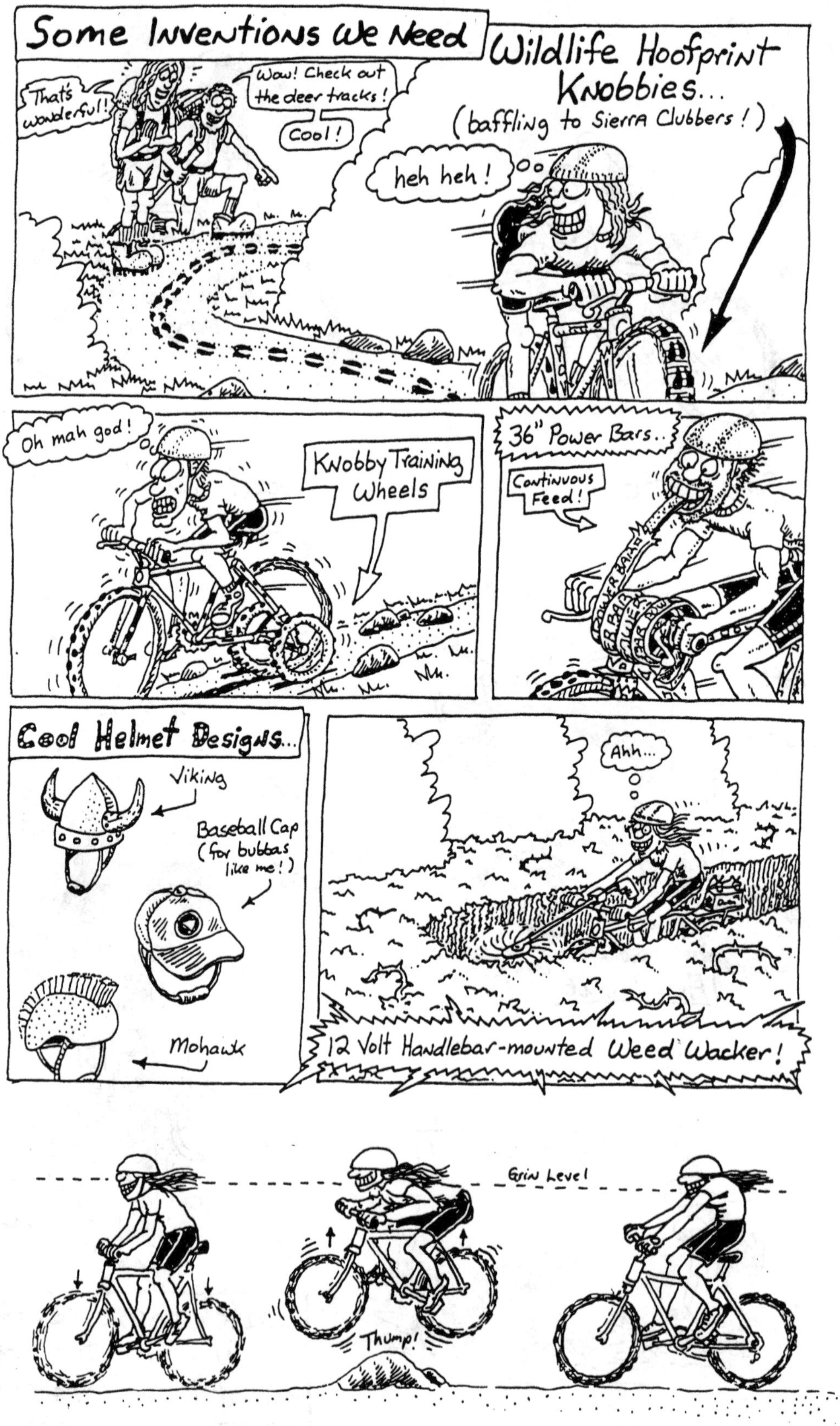
Some Inventions We Need
Wildlife Hoofprint Knobbies...
(baffling to Sierra Clubbers!)
That's wonderful!
Wow! Check out the deer tracks!
Cool!
heh heh!
Oh mah god!
Knobby Training Wheels
36" Power Bars..
Continuous Feed!
Cool Helmet Designs...
Viking
Baseball Cap (for bubbas like me!)
Mohawk
Ahh...
12 Volt Handlebar-mounted Weed Wacker!
Grin Level
Thump!

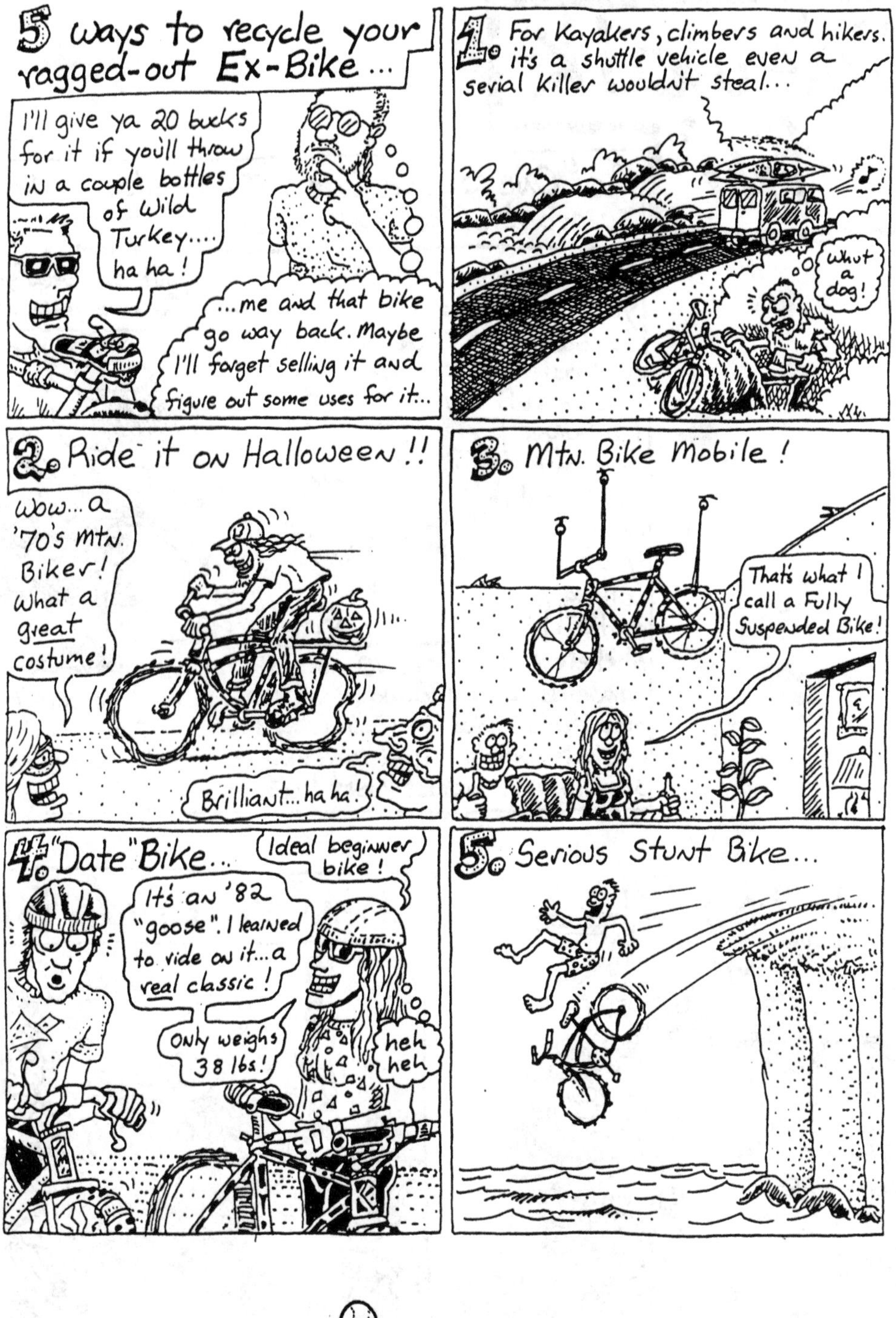
5 ways to recycle your ragged-out Ex-Bike...
I'll give ya 20 bucks for it if you'll throw in a couple bottles of Wild Turkey.... ha ha!
...me and that bike go way back. Maybe I'll forget selling it and figure out some uses for it...
1. For Kayakers, climbers and hikers. it's a shuttle vehicle even a serial killer wouldn't steal...
Whut a dog!
2. Ride it on Halloween!!
Wow... a '70's mtn. Biker! What a great costume!
Brilliant... ha ha!
3. Mtn. Bike Mobile!
That's what I call a Fully Suspended Bike!
4. "Date" Bike...
Ideal beginner bike!
It's an '82 "goose". I learned to ride on it... a real classic!
Only weighs 38 lbs.!
heh heh
5. Serious Stunt Bike...

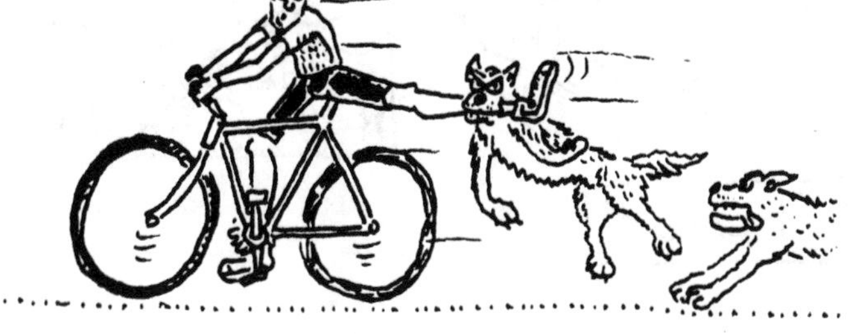

Sidewalk Surfin'

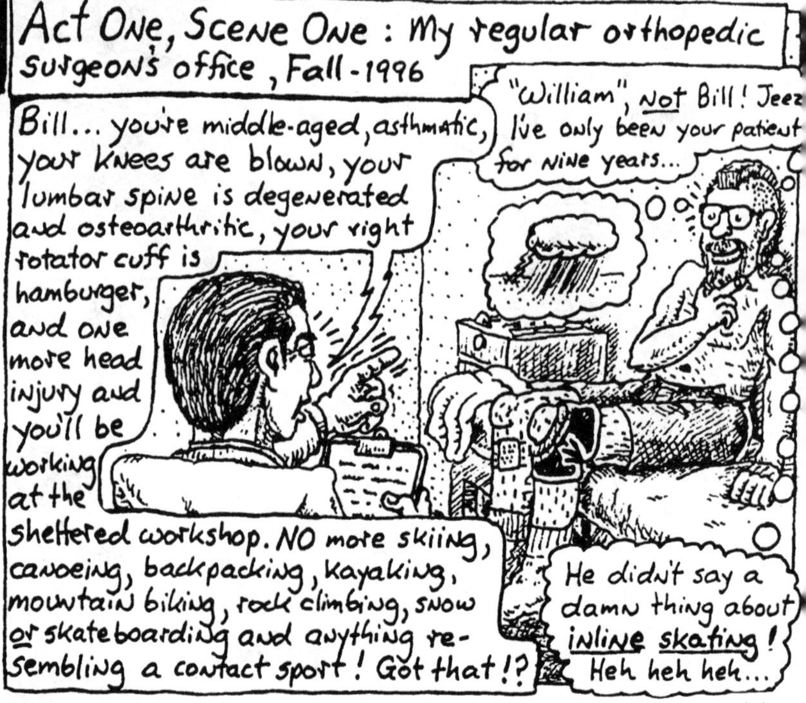
Act One, Scene One : My regular orthopedic surgeon's office, Fall-1996
Bill... you're middle-aged, asthmatic, your knees are blown, your lumbar spine is degenerated and osteoarthritic, your right rotator cuff is hamburger, and one more head injury and you'll be working at the sheltered workshop. NO more skiing, canoeing, backpacking, kayaking, mountain biking, rock climbing, snow or skateboarding and anything resembling a contact sport! Got that!?
"William", not Bill! Jeez I've only been your patient for nine years...
He didn't say a damn thing about inline skating! Heh heh heh...

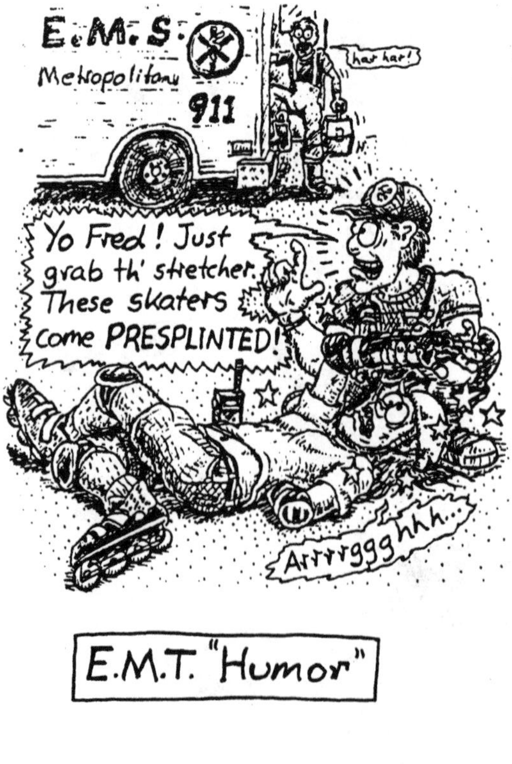
E.M.S.
Metropolitan
911
har har!
Yo Fred! Just grab th' stretcher. These skaters come PRESPLINTED!
Arrrrggghhh...

E.M.T. "Humor"

Doin' th' "Linda Blair"[1]

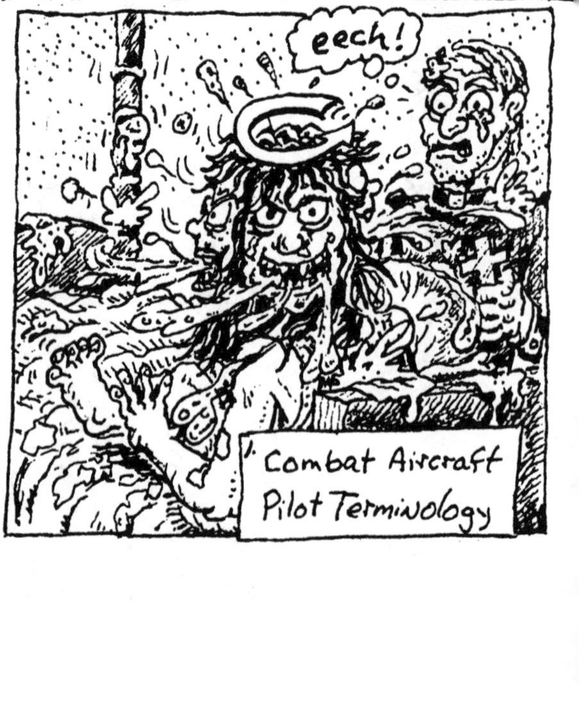
eech!
[1] Combat Aircraft Pilot Terminology

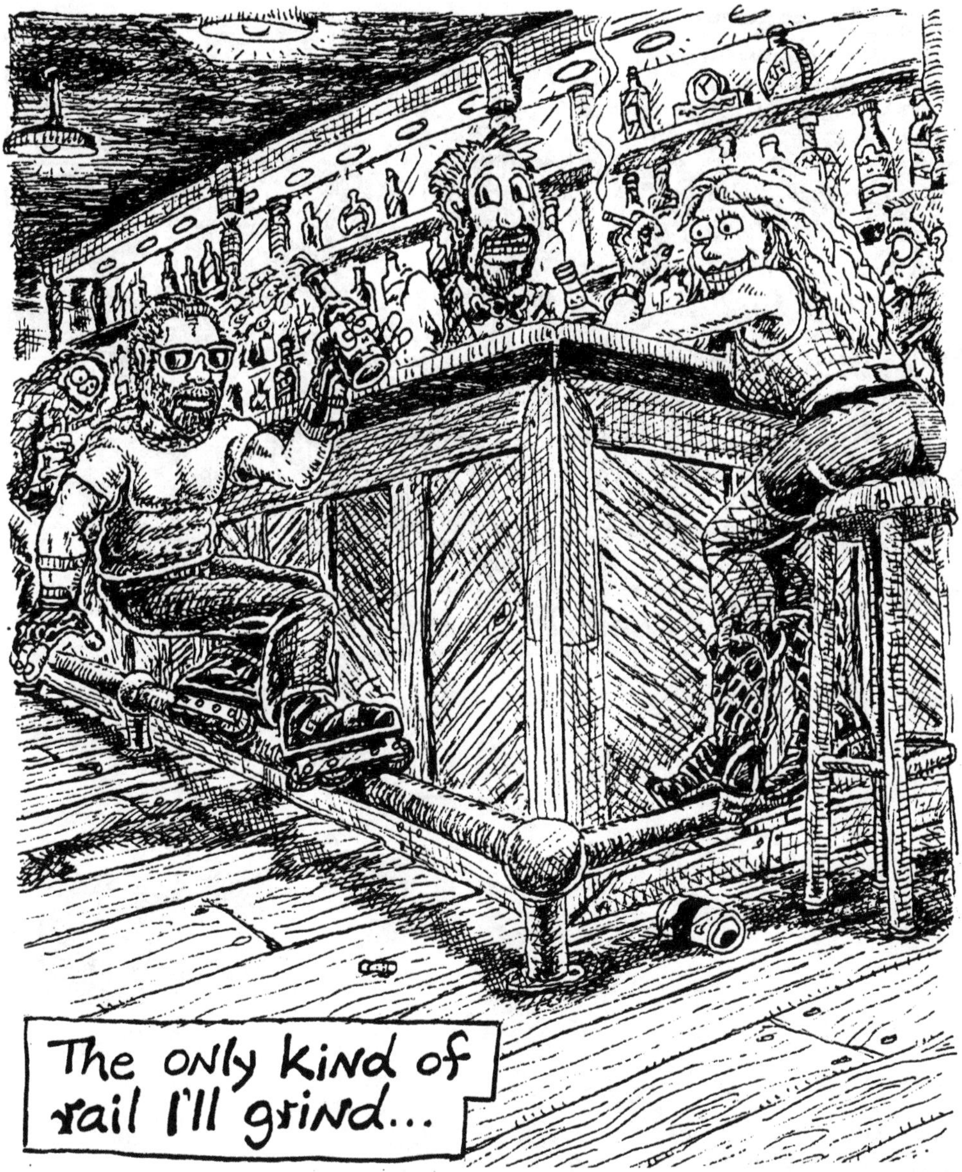
The only kind of rail I'll grind...

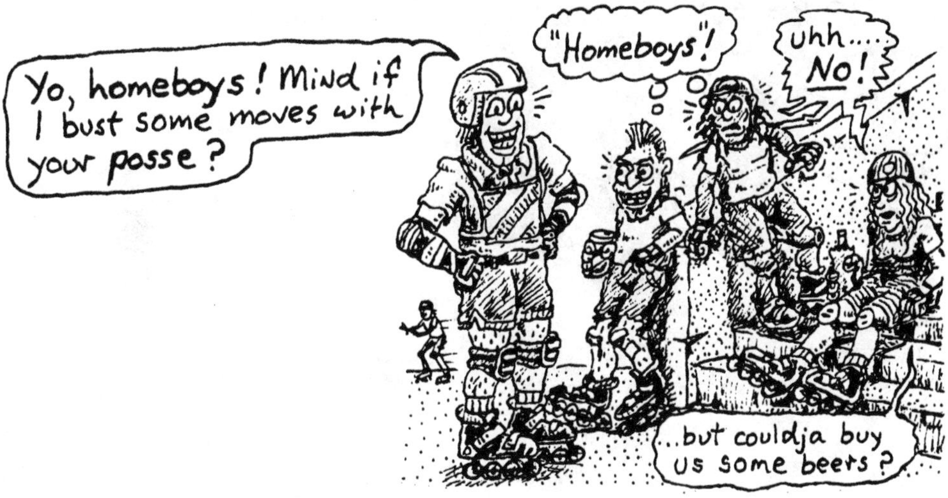
Yo, homeboys! Mind if I bust some moves with your posse?
"Homeboys"!
uhh.... No!
..but couldja buy us some beers?

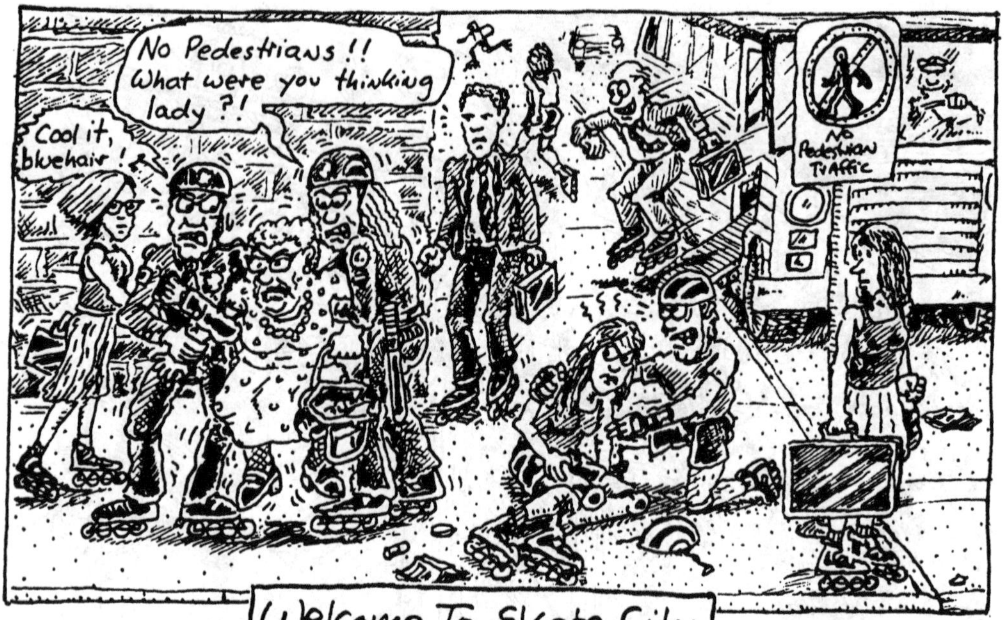
Cool it, bluehair!
No Pedestrians!! What were you thinking lady?!
No Pedestrian Traffic

Welcome To Skate City

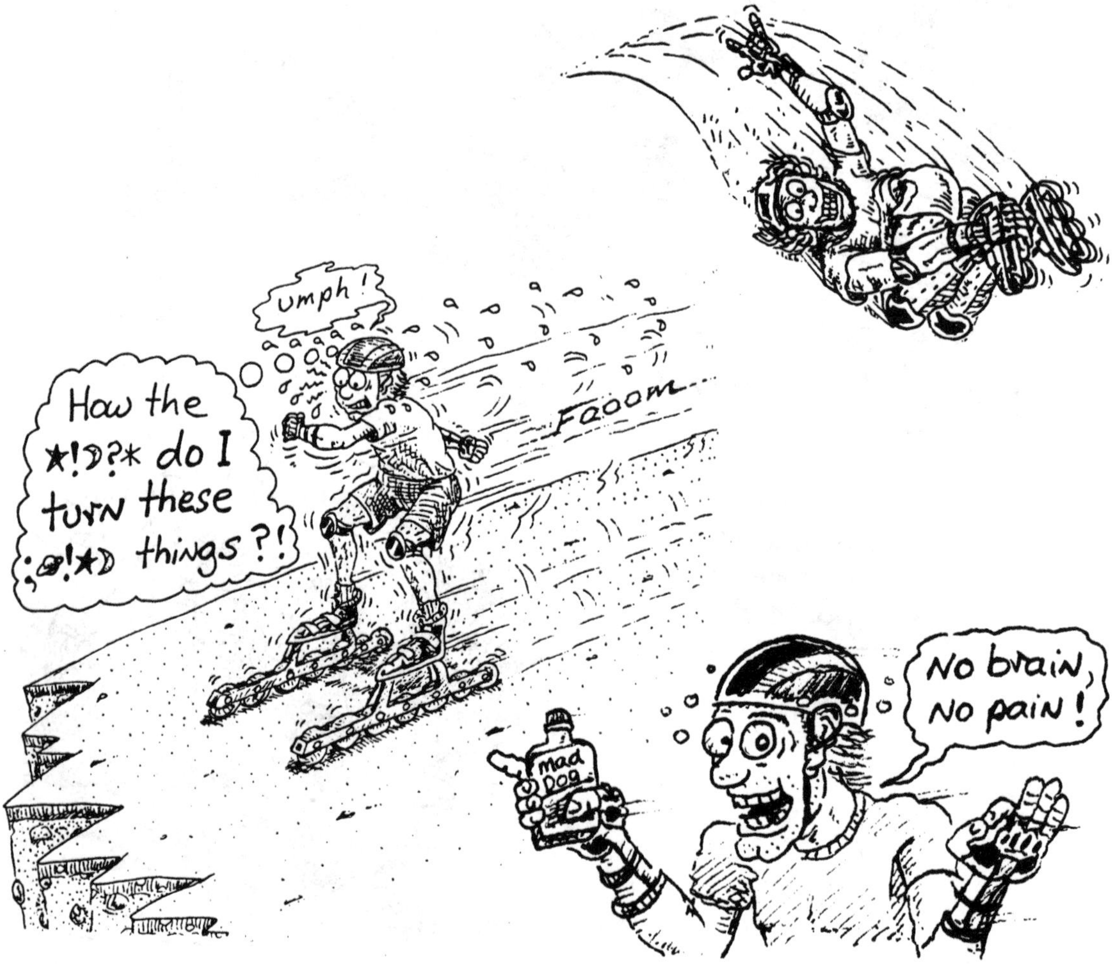
umph!
How the ★!Ɗ?* do I turn these ;@!★Ɗ things?!
Fooom
mad Dog
No brain, No pain!

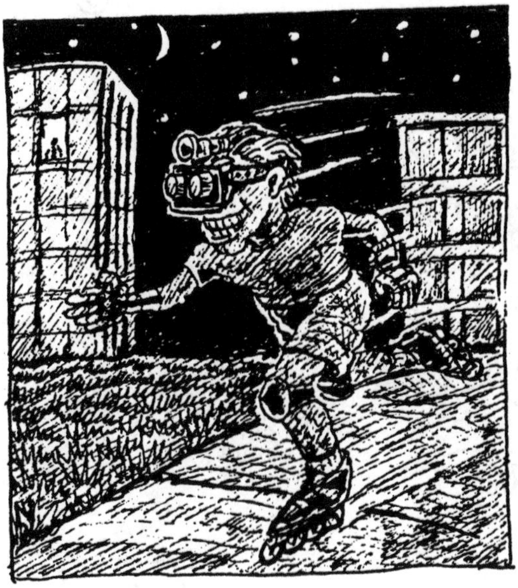

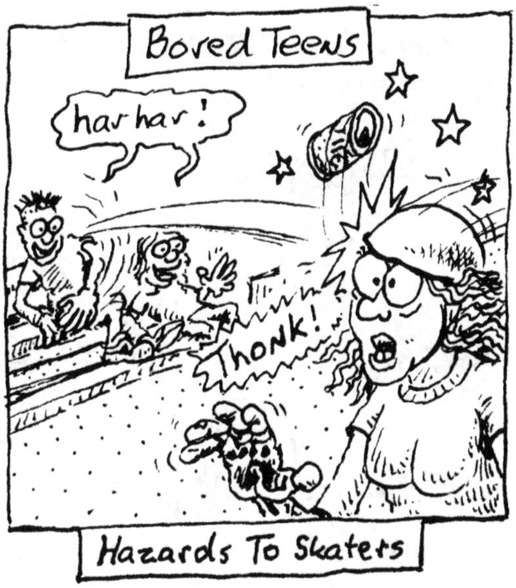
Bored Teens
har har!
THONK!
Hazards To Skaters

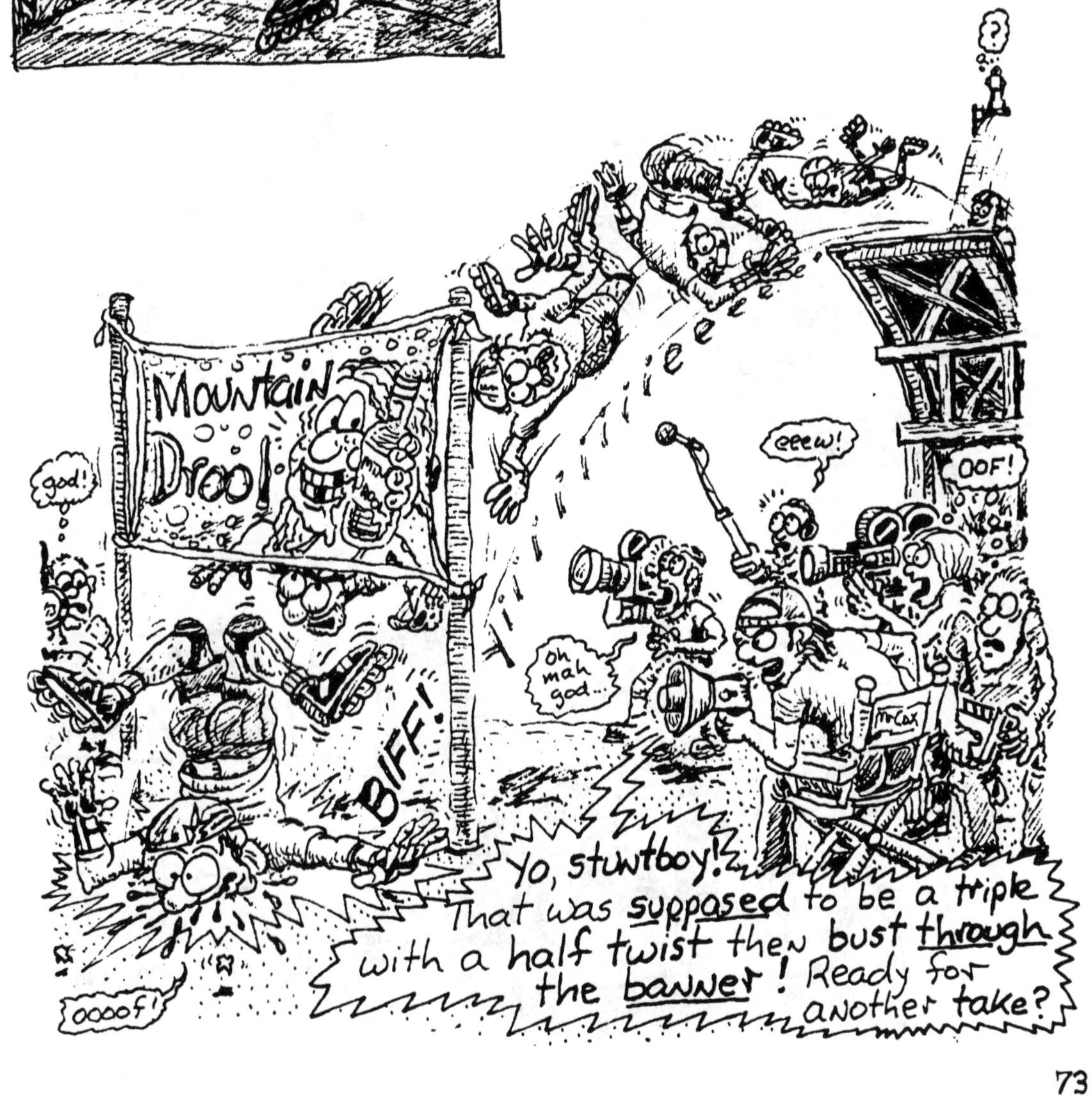
god!
Mountain Drool
eeew!
OOF!
oh mah god...
BIFF!
Yo, stuntboy! That was supposed to be a triple with a half twist then bust through the banner! Ready for another take?
ooof!

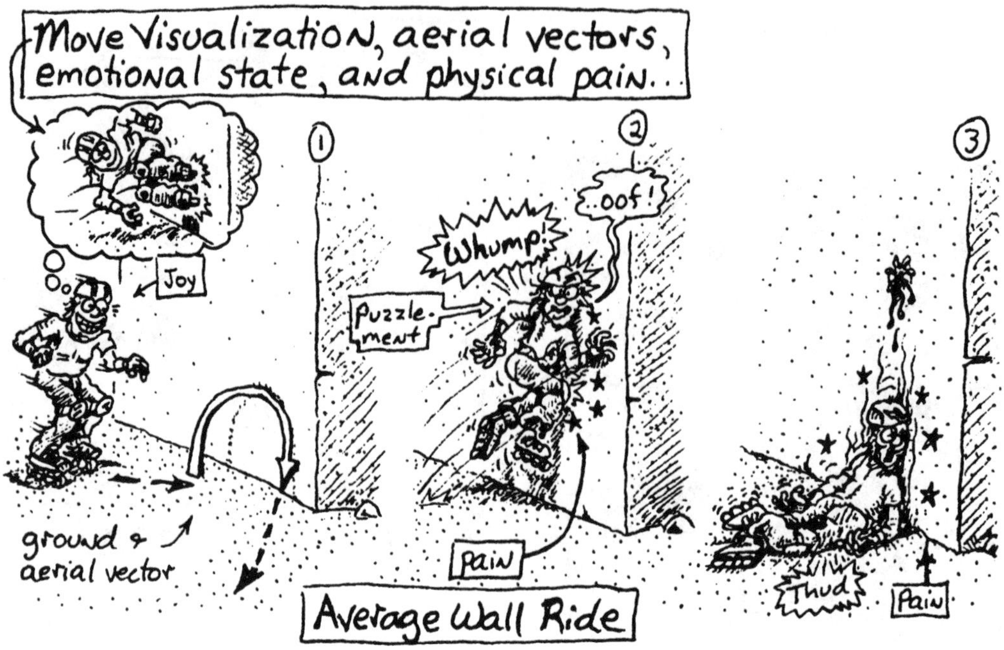
Move Visualization, aerial vectors, emotional state, and physical pain...
Joy
ground & aerial vector
1
2
Whump!
.oof!
puzzle-ment
pain
3
Thud
Pain
Average Wall Ride

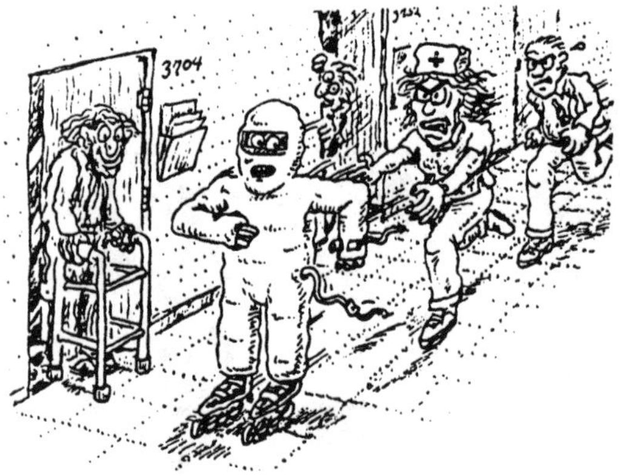
3704

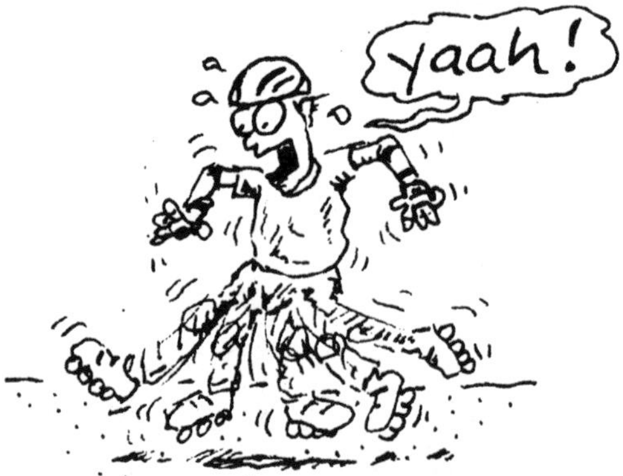
yaah!

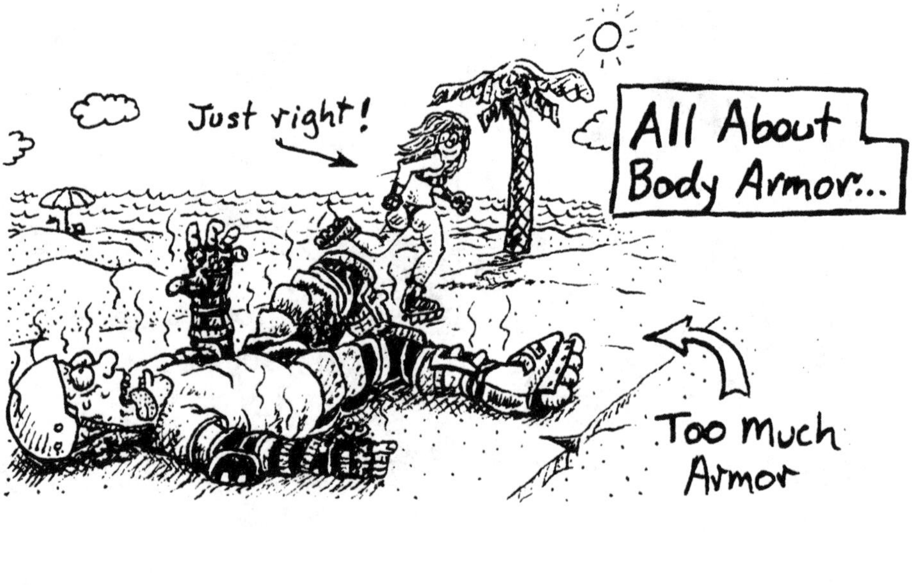
Just right!
All About Body Armor...
Too Much Armor

Racerheads

If you're only going from point A to point B fast, you can afford to see in two dimensions (like the, uh... racerheads.)

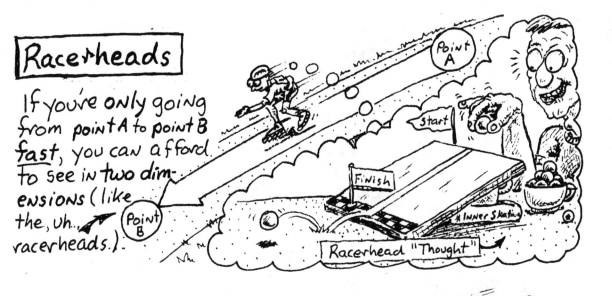

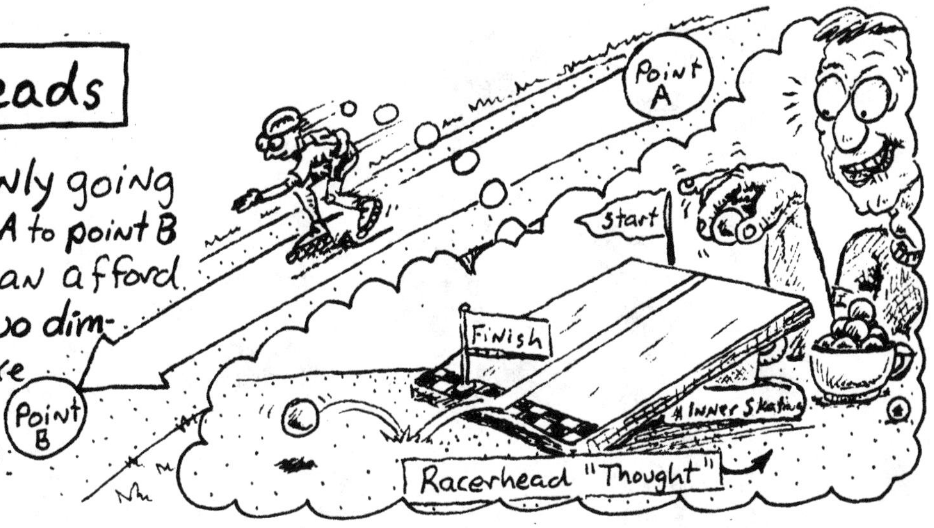
Point A
Start
Finish
Inner Skating
Point B
Racerhead "Thought"

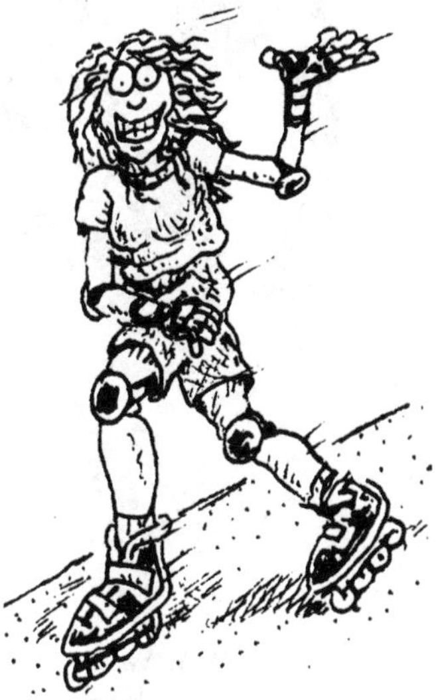

The Age Of Tubism*

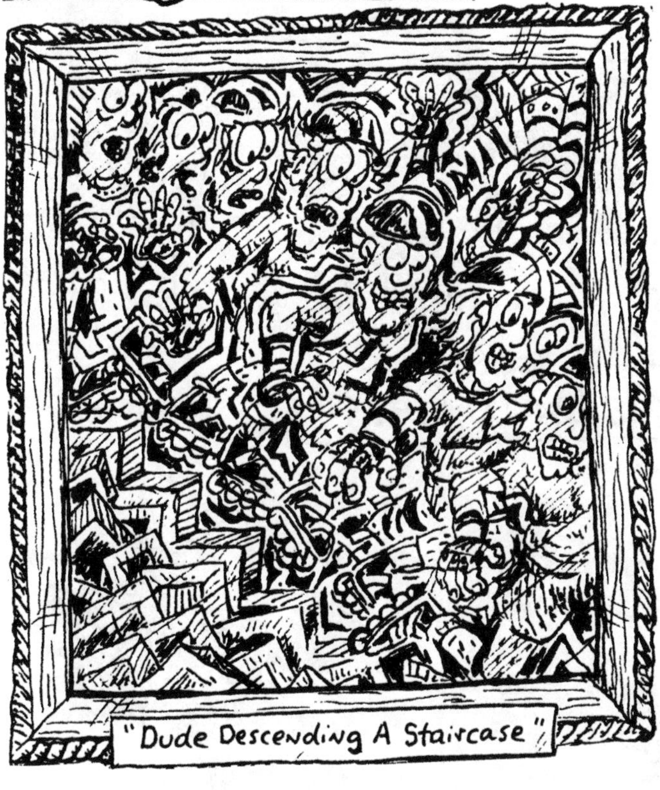

"Dude Descending A Staircase"

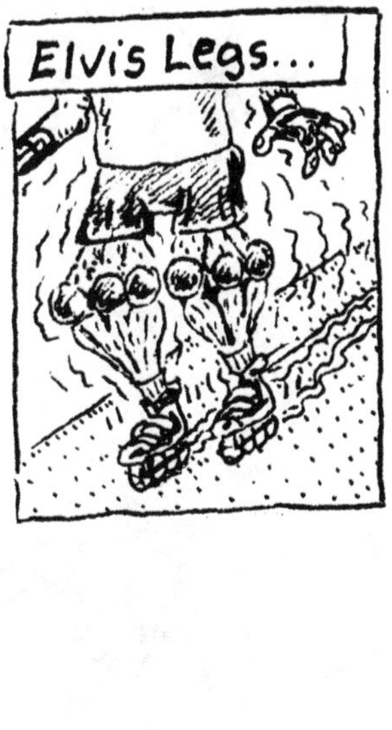
Elvis Legs...

*Apologies to marcel Duchamp

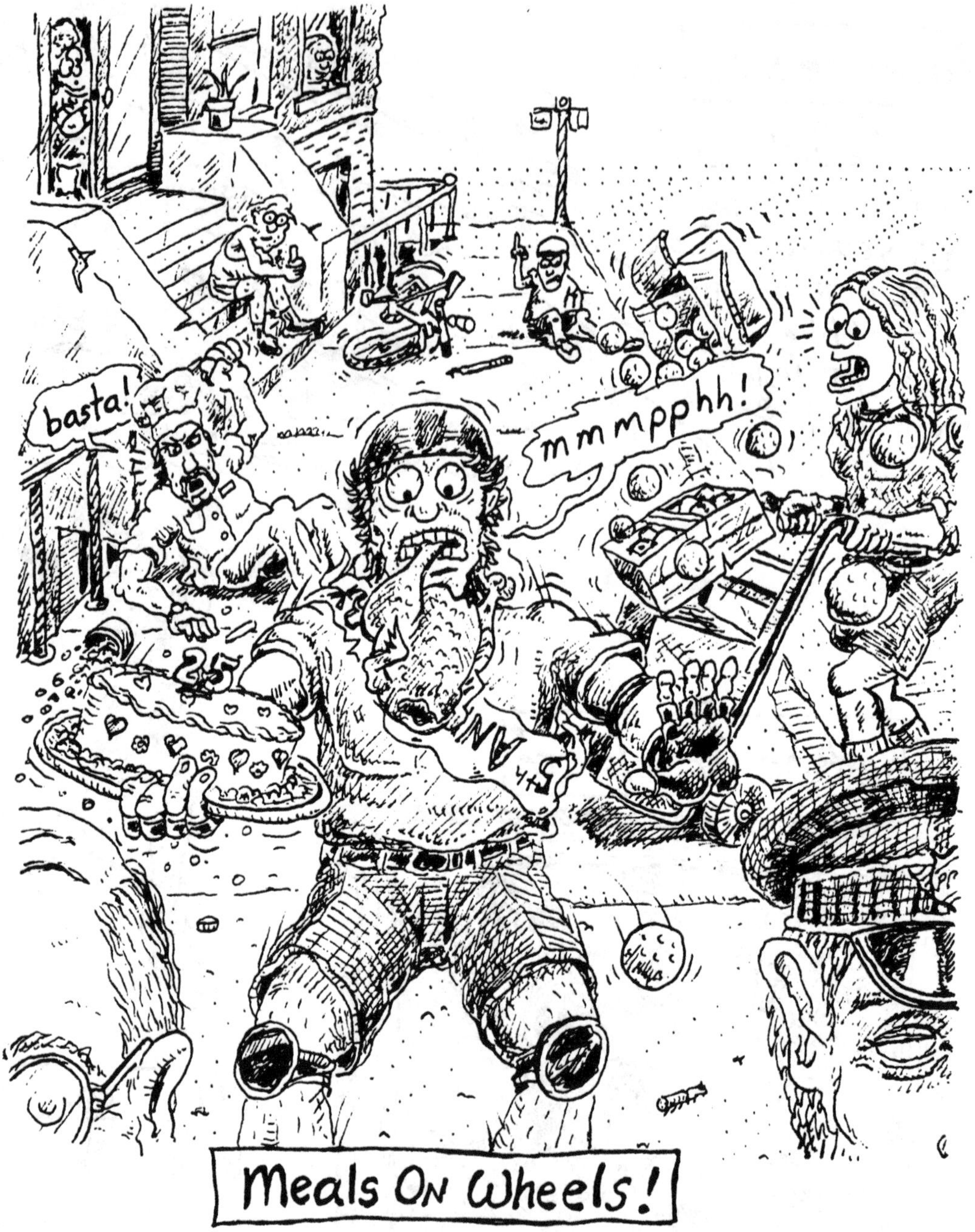
basta!
mmmpphh!
Meals On Wheels!

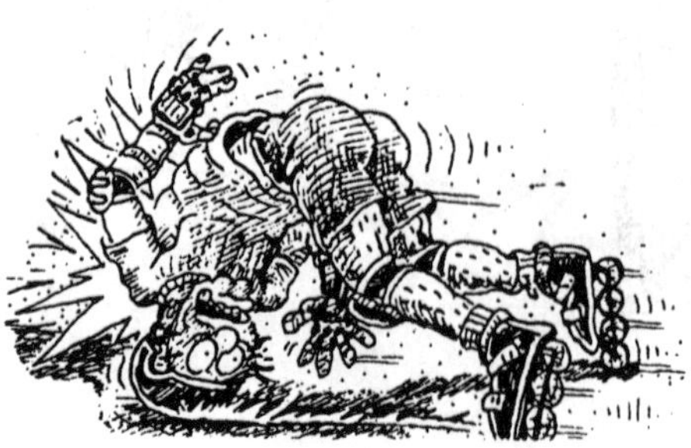

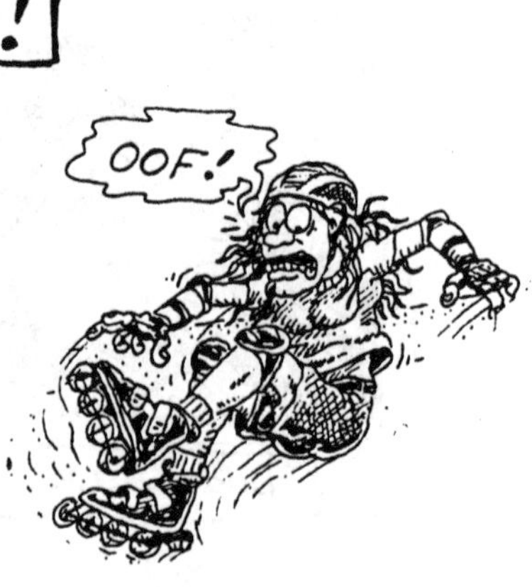
OOF!

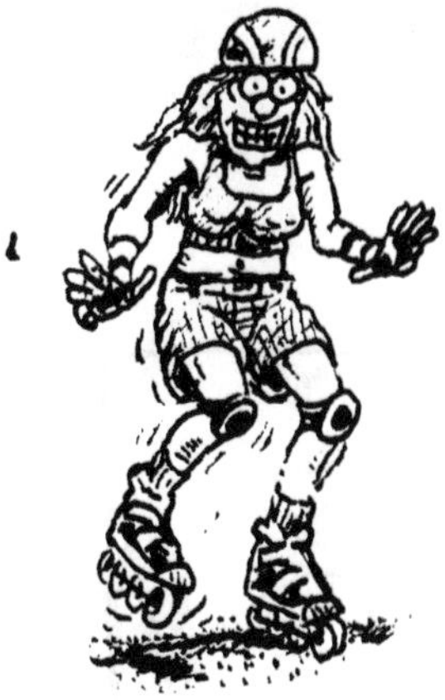

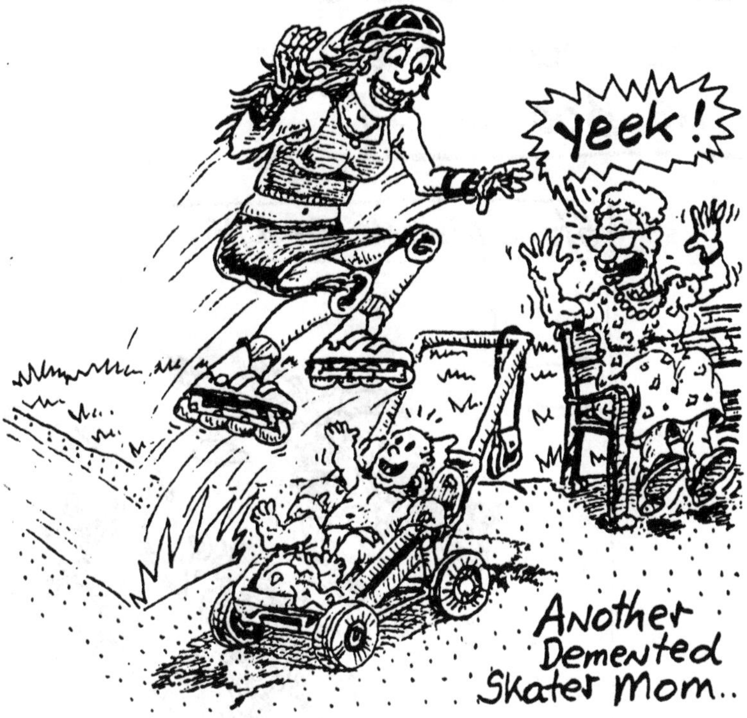
yeek!
Another Demented Skater Mom..

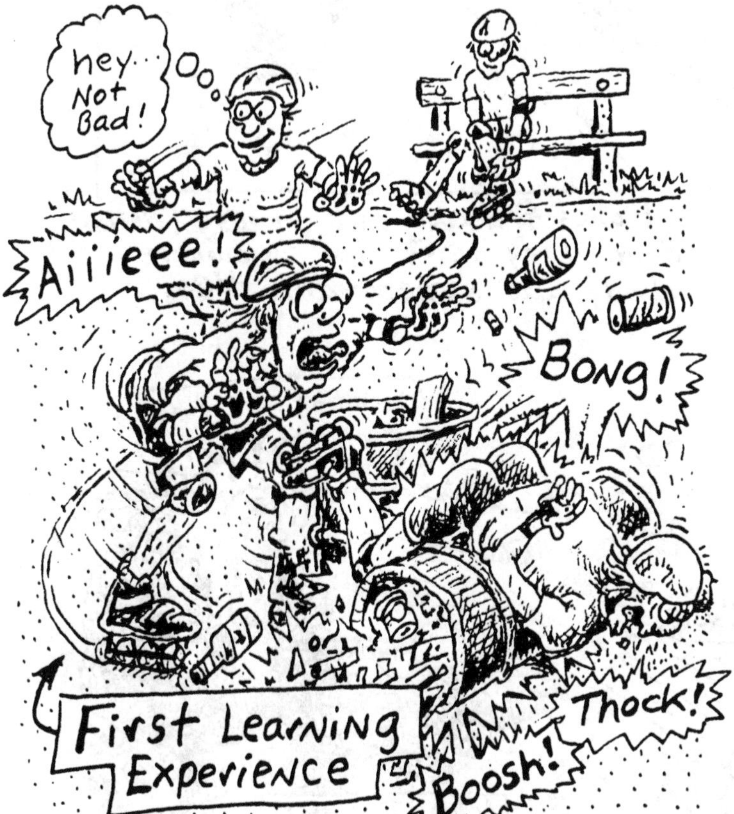
hey.. Not Bad!
Aiiieee!
Bong!
First Learning Experience
Thock!
Boosh!

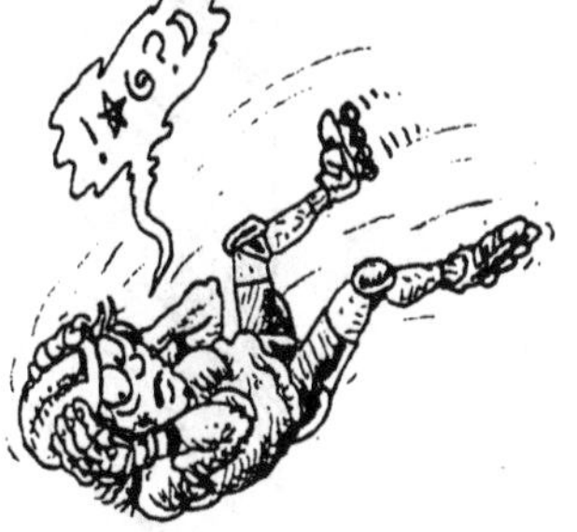

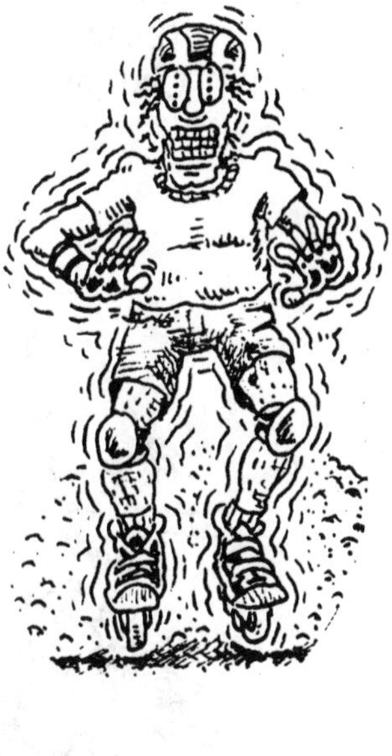

The Young And The Board...

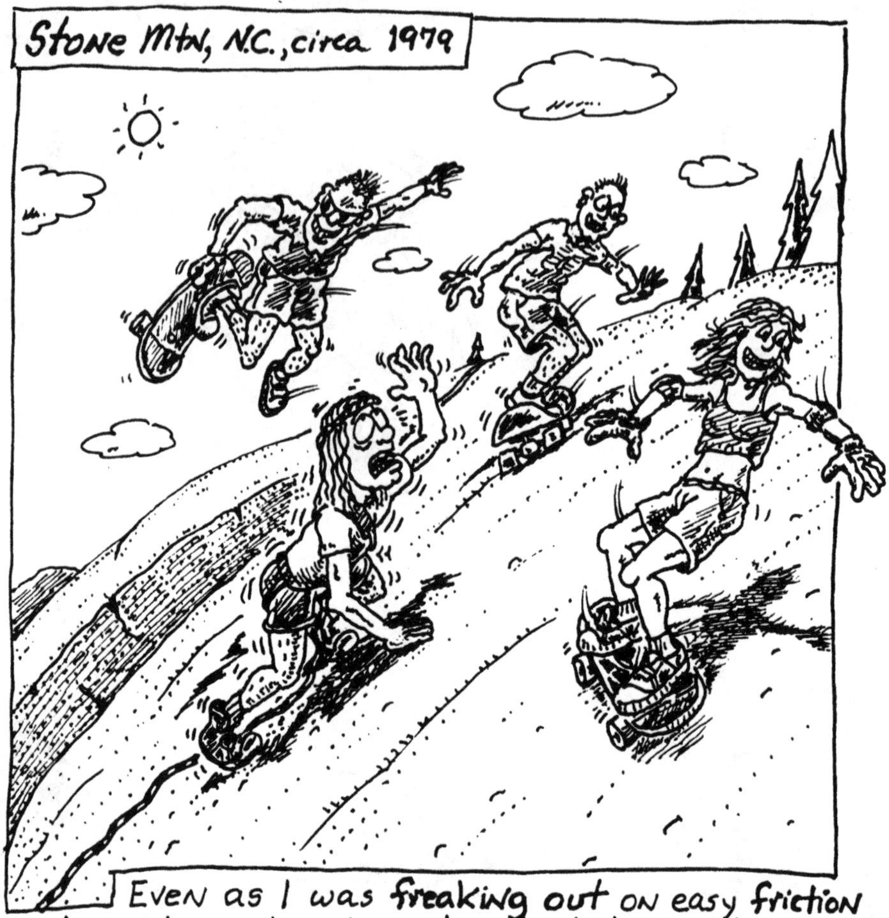
Stone Mtn, N.C., circa 1979

Even as I was **freaking out** on easy **friction** routes, I knew deep in my heart that somewhere in California, somebody was **skateboarding** this...

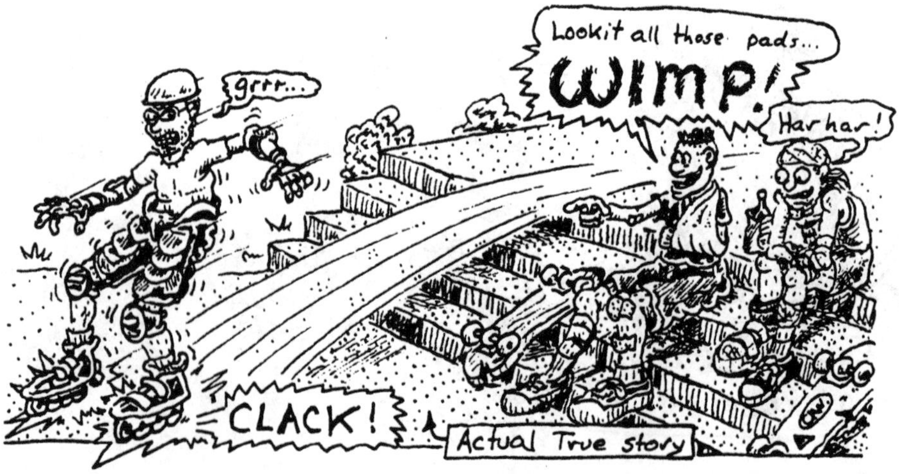
grrr...
Lookit all those pads...
WIMP!
Har har!
CLACK!
Actual True story

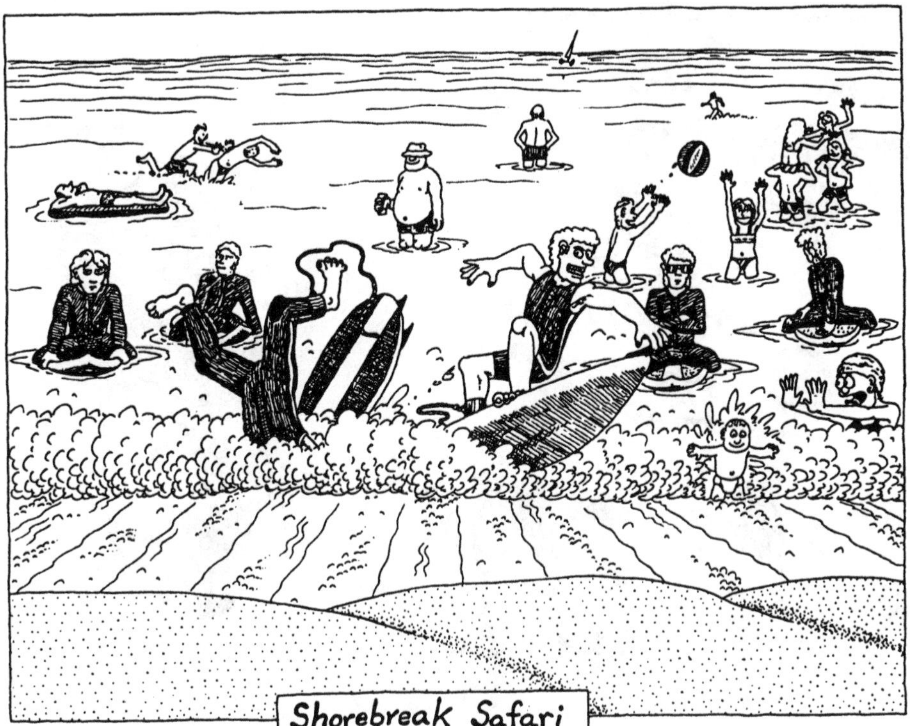

Shorebreak Safari

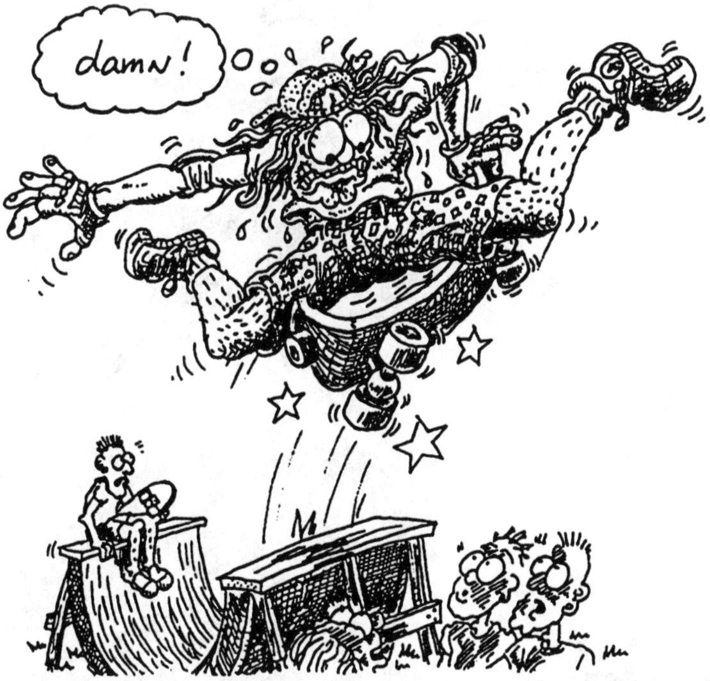

damn!

Suddenly Billy found himself yearning for some **crotch** armor...

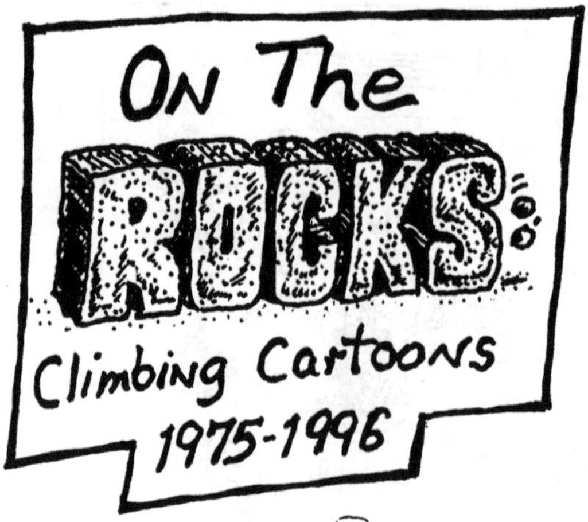
On The
ROCKS
Climbing Cartoons
1975-1996

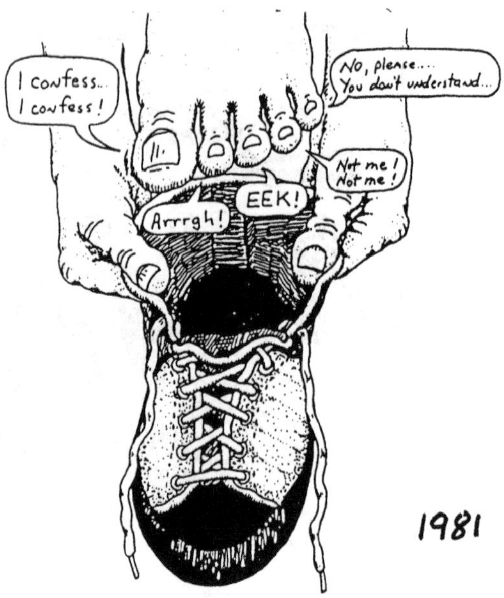
I confess...
I confess!
No, please...
You don't understand...
Not me!
Not me!
EEK!
Arrrgh!

1981

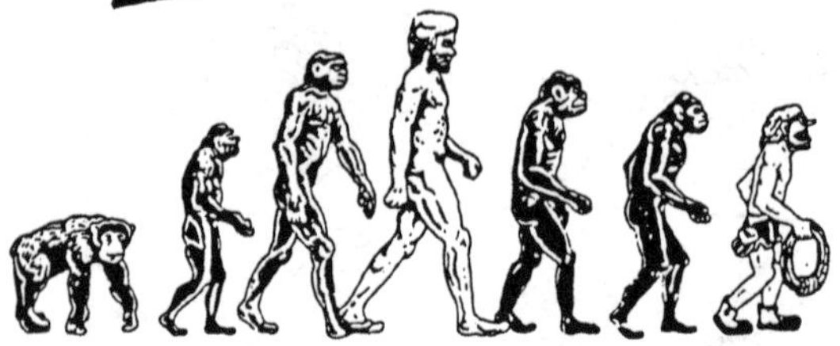

1983

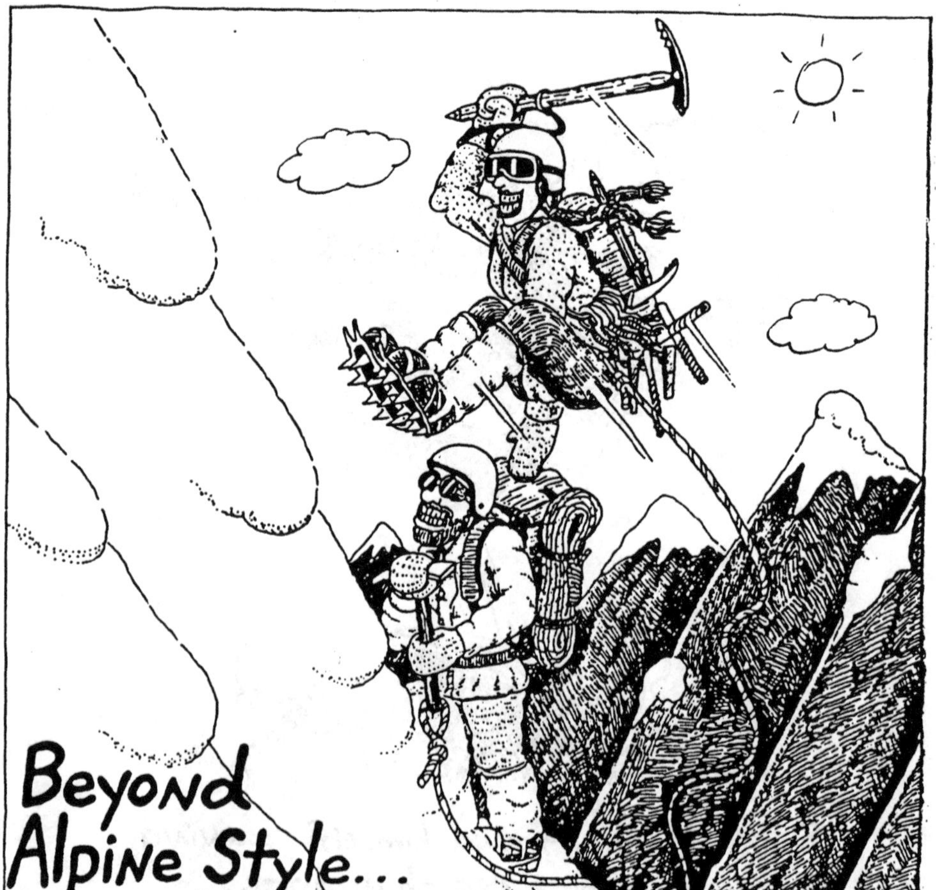
Beyond
Alpine Style...

1979

Rock Climbing
First AID

1975

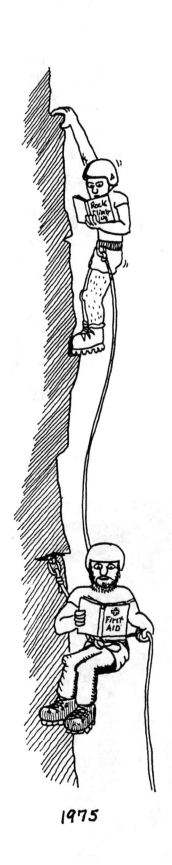

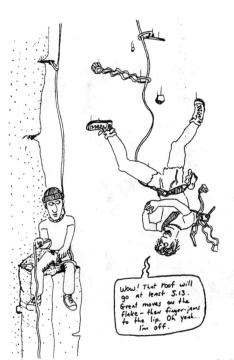

Wow! That roof will go at least 5.13. Great moves on the flake – then finger-jams to the lip. Oh yeah... I'm off.

1975

"Bicuspid Direct," A-4

1978

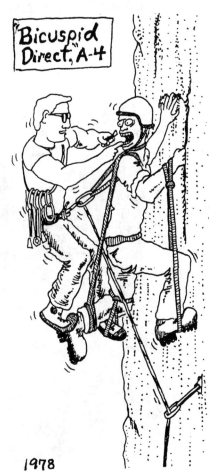

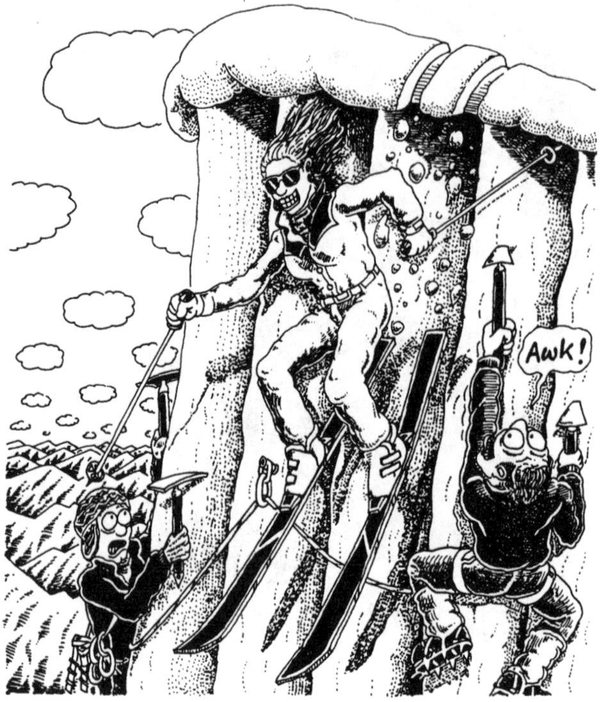

Awk!

Why Ice Climbers Hate Extreme Skiers

1990

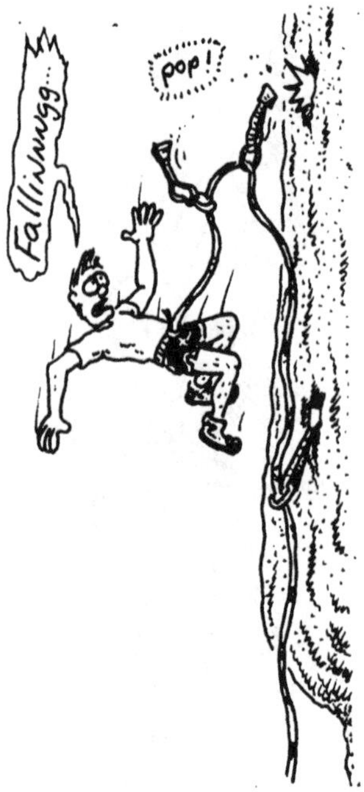

pop!
Fallinnnngg...

1995

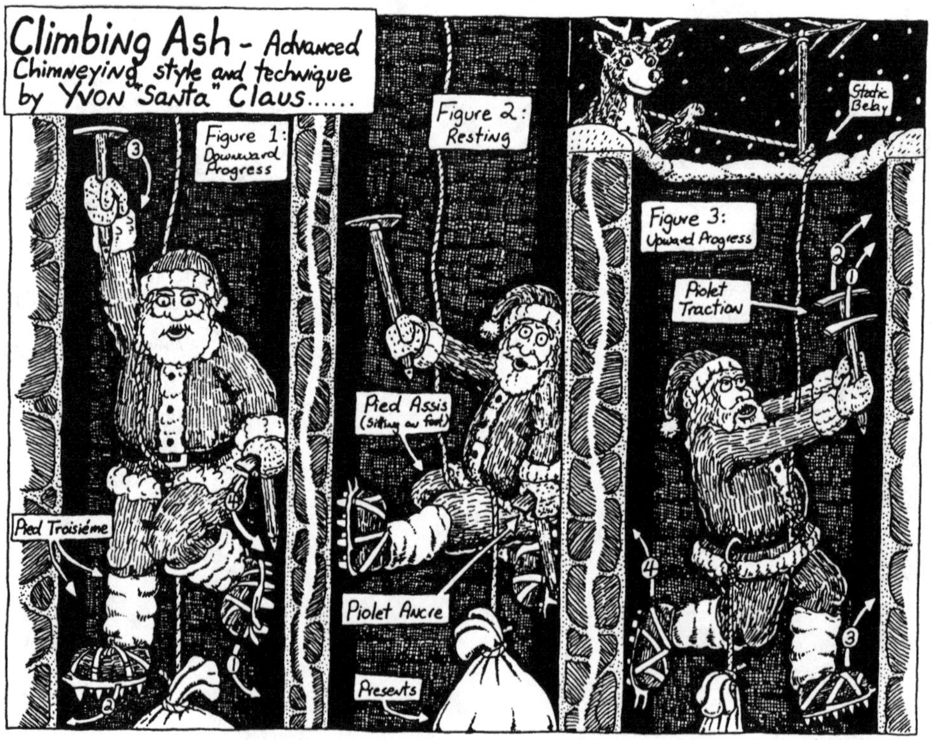

Climbing Ash - Advanced Chimneying style and technique by Yvon "Santa" Claus......
Figure 1: Downward Progress
Pied Troisiéme
Figure 2: Resting
Pied Assis (sitting on foot)
Piolet Ancre
Presents
Static Belay
Figure 3: Upward Progress
Piolet Traction

1984

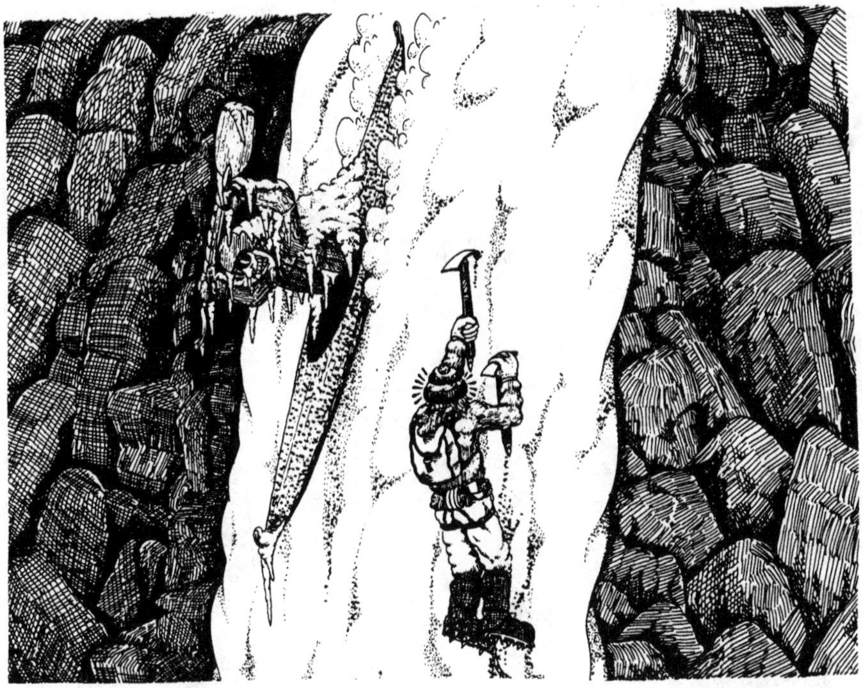

1983

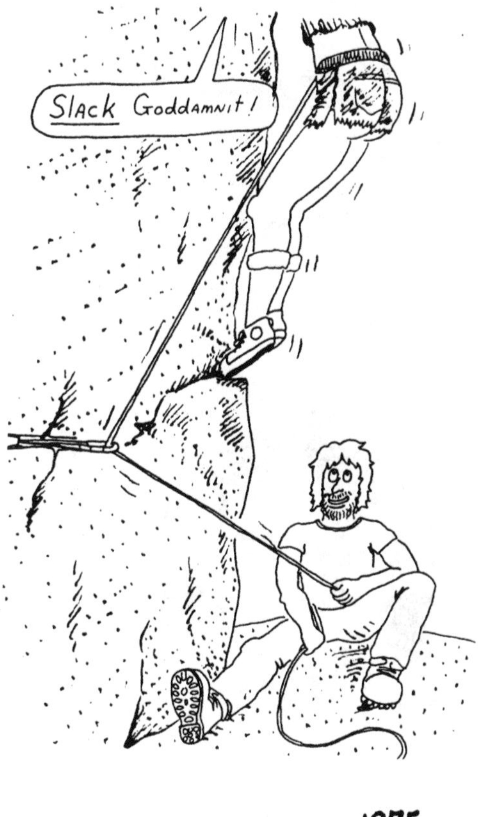
Slack Goddamnit!

1975

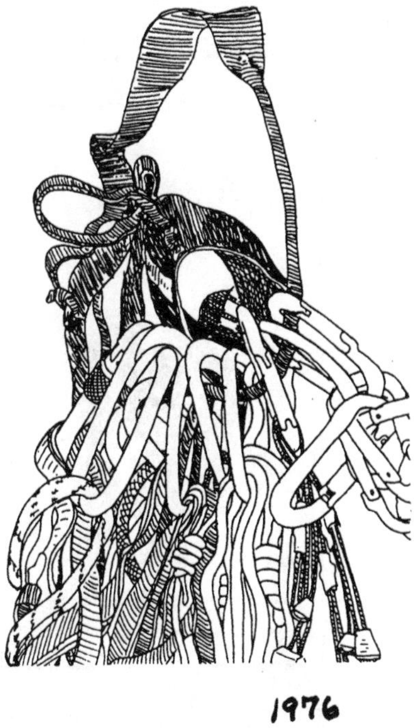

1976

Snow Abuse

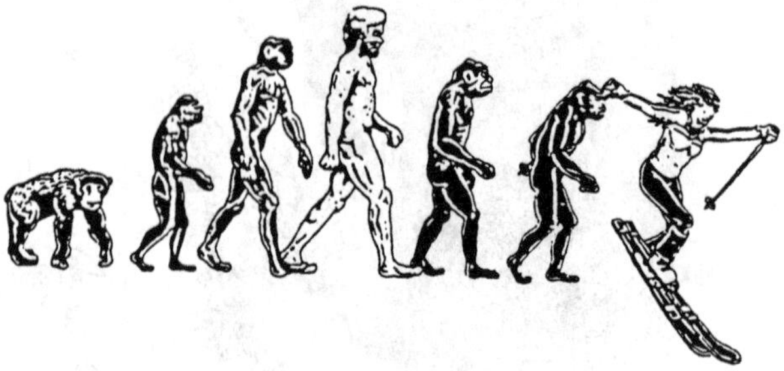

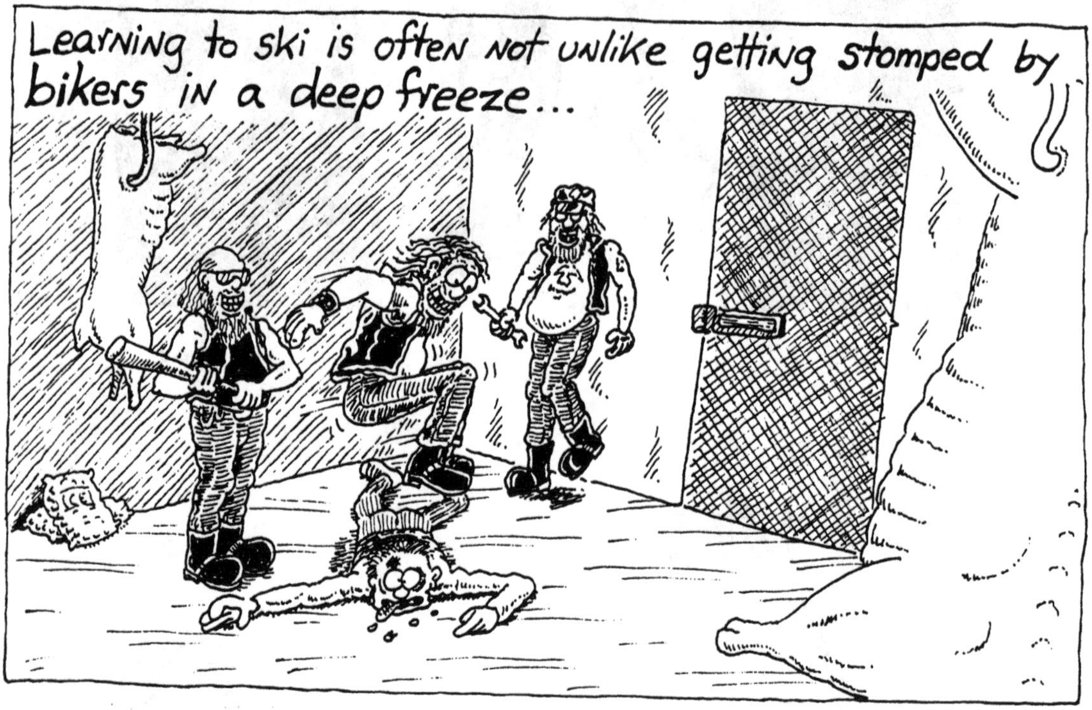
Learning to ski is often not unlike getting stomped by bikers in a deep freeze...

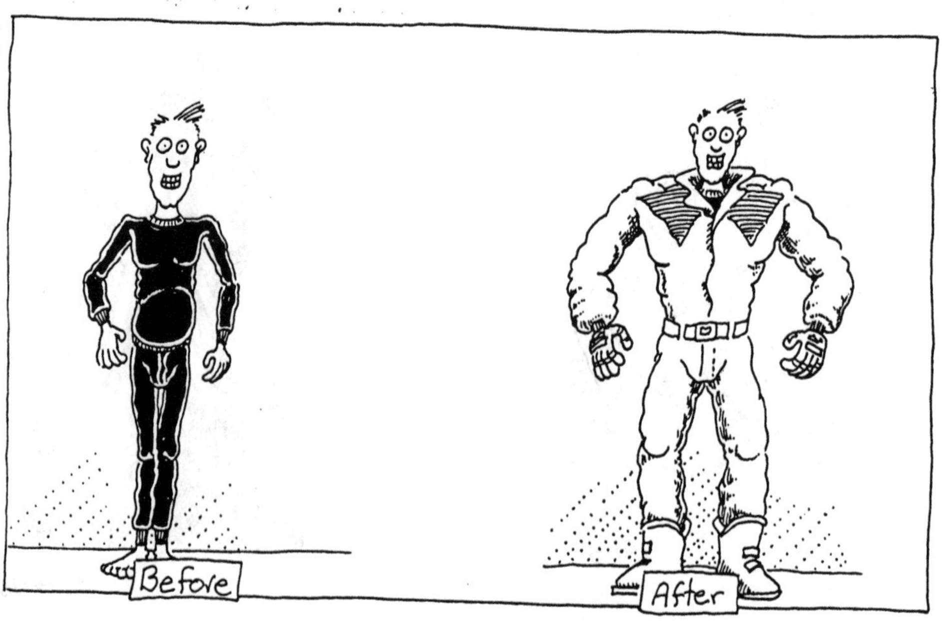
Before
After

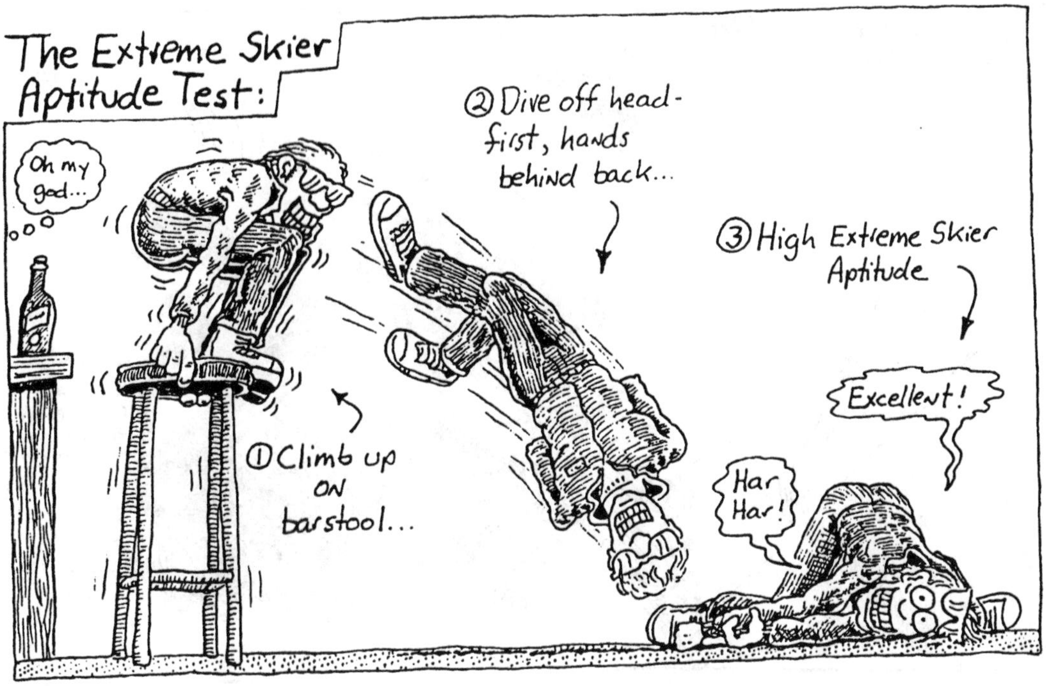
The Extreme Skier Aptitude Test:
Oh my god...
① Climb up on barstool...
② Dive off head-first, hands behind back...
③ High Extreme Skier Aptitude
Excellent!
Har Har!

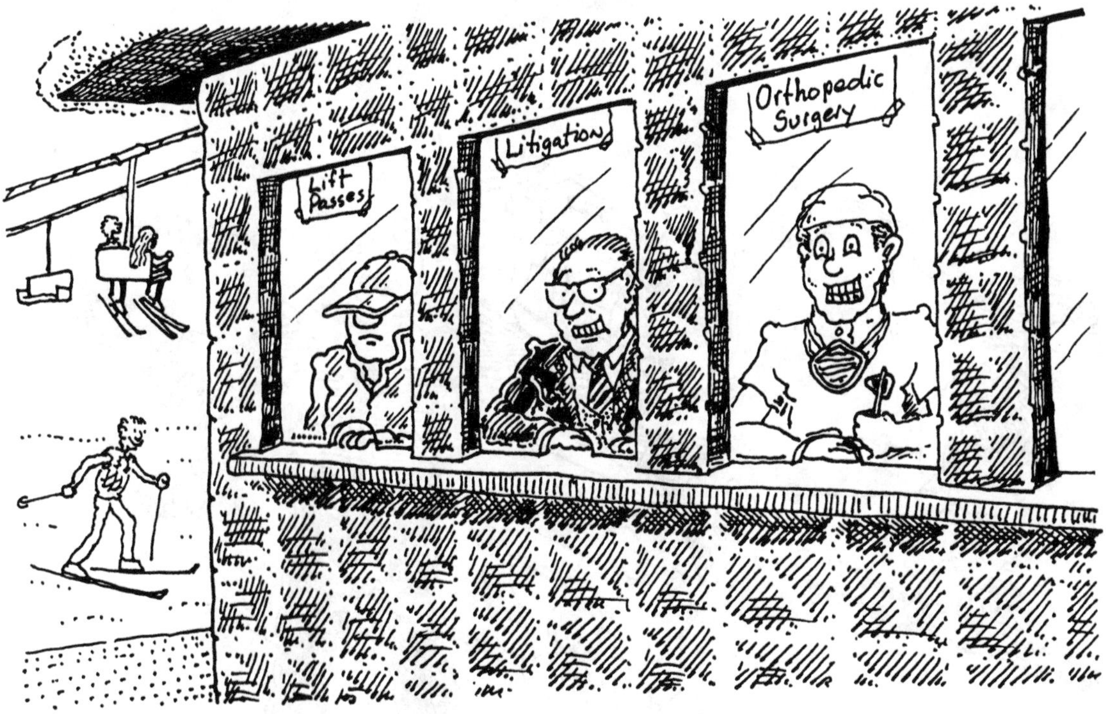
Lift Passes
Litigation
Orthopedic Surgery

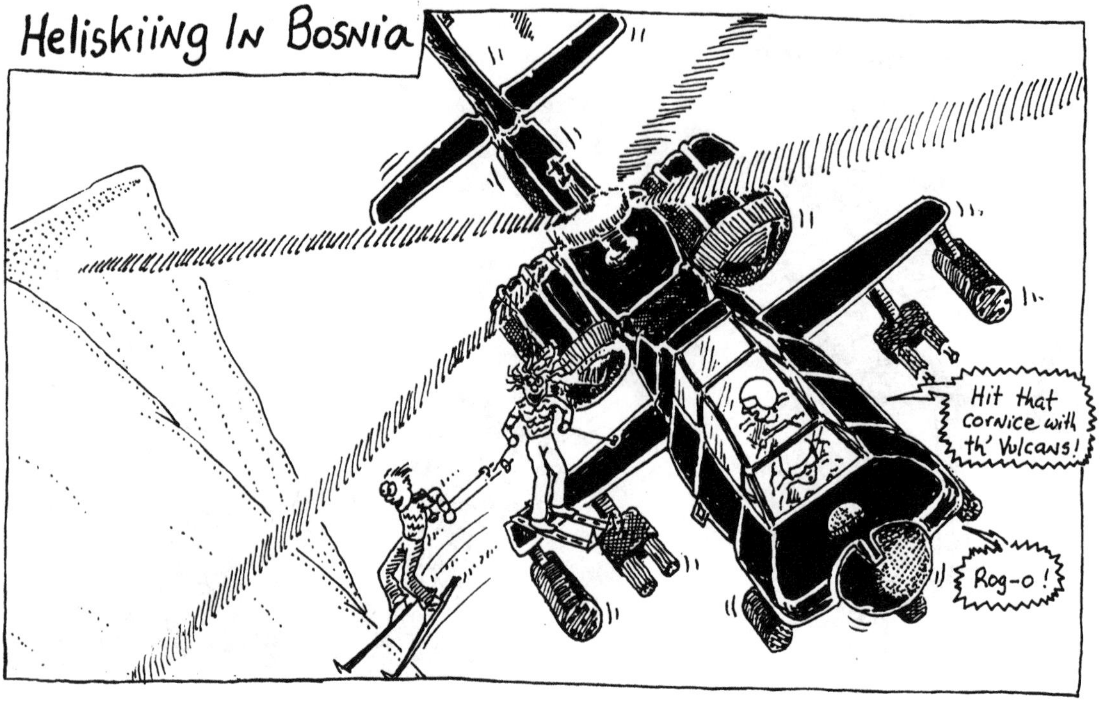
Heliskiing In Bosnia
Hit that cornice with th' Vulcans!
Rog-o!

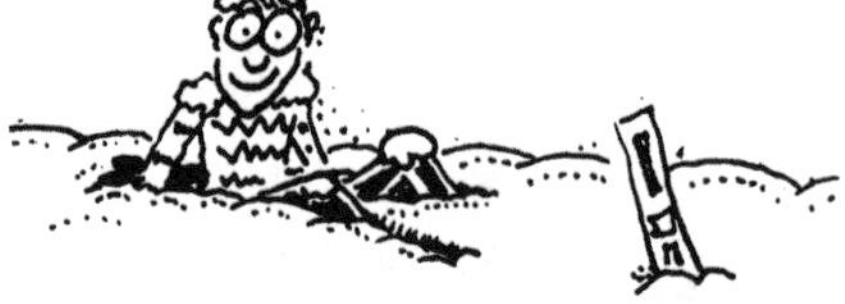

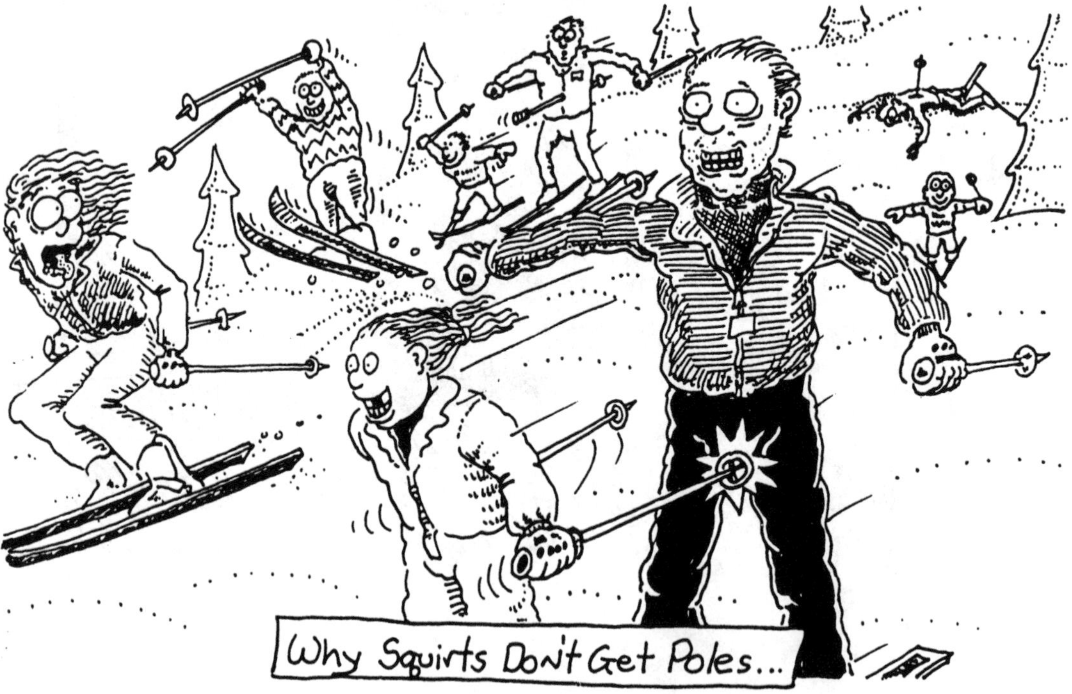
Why Squirts Don't Get Poles...

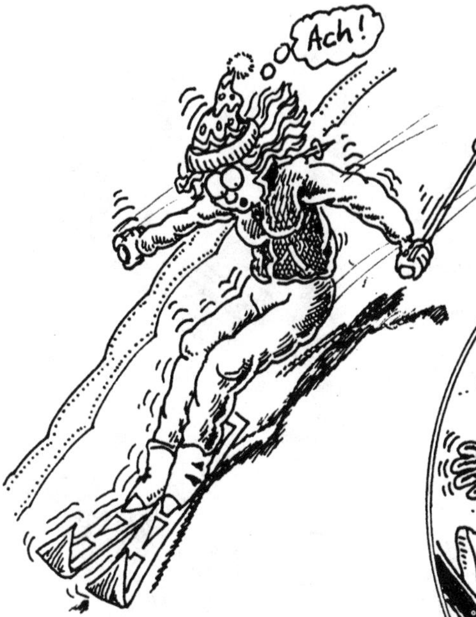

Ach!

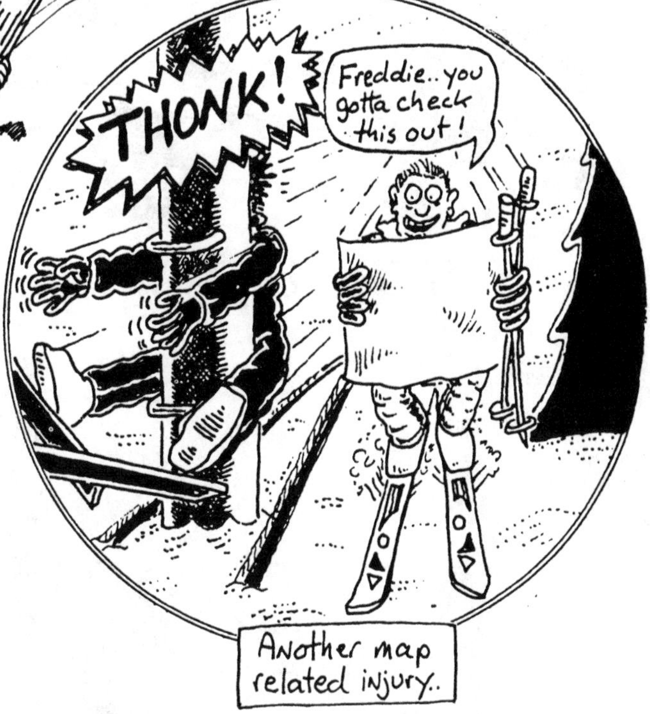

THONK!
Freddie.. you gotta check this out!
Another map related injury..

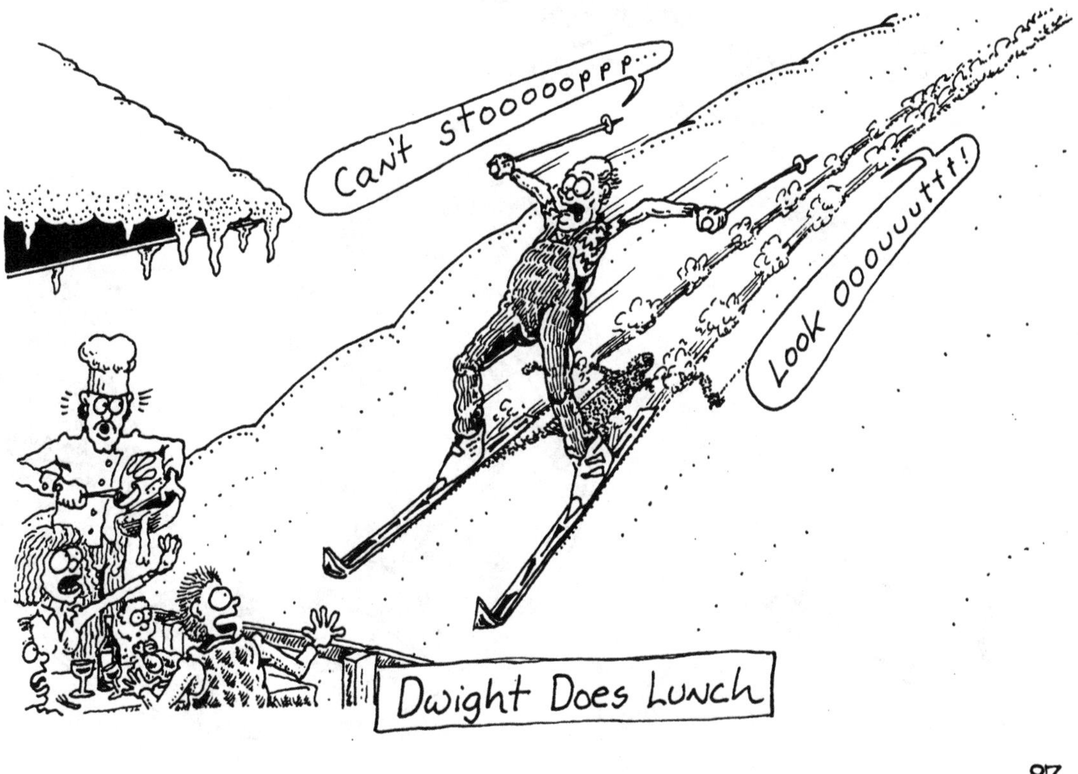

Can't stoooooppp...
Look ooouuuttt!
Dwight Does Lunch

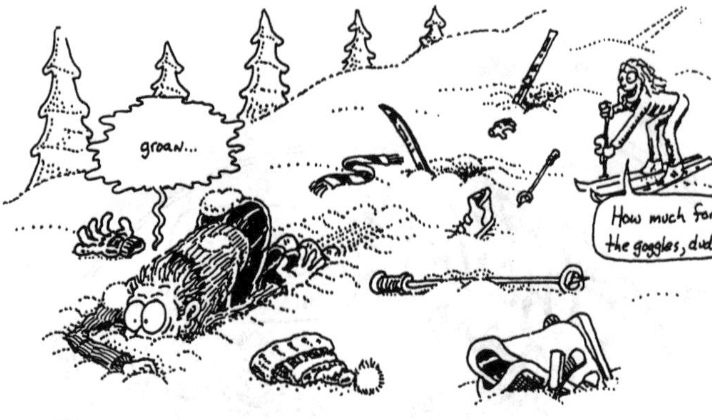
groan...
How much for the goggles, dude?

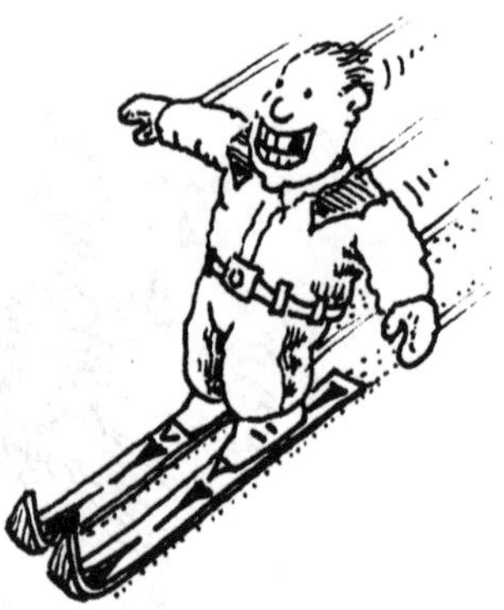

"Yard Sale" Crash

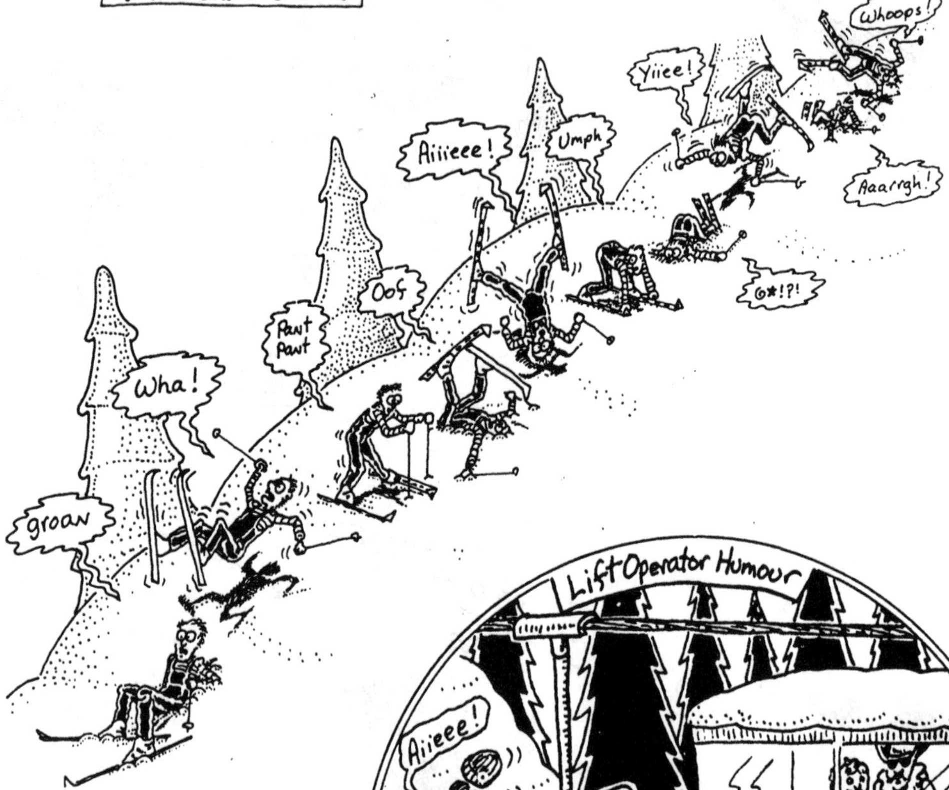
Whoops!
Yiiee!
Aiiieee!
Umph
Aaarrgh!
Oof
Pant Pant
G*!?!
Wha!
groan

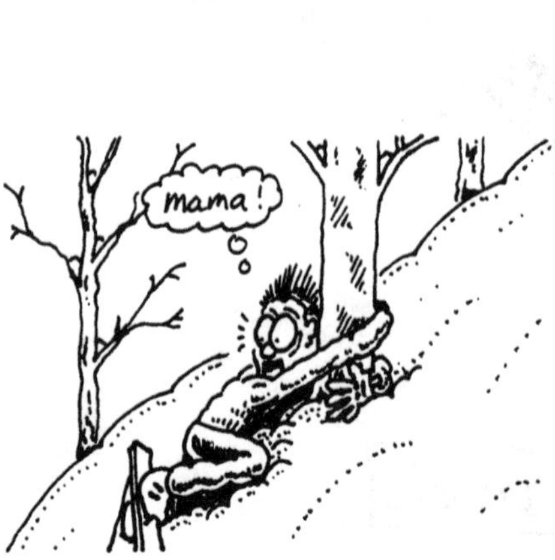
mama!

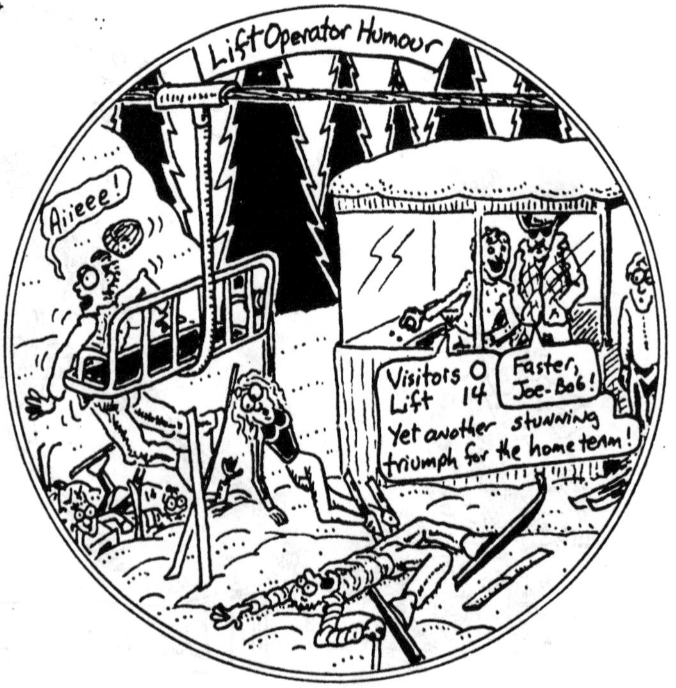
Lift Operator Humour
Aiieee!
Visitors 0
Lift 14
Faster, Joe-Bob!
Yet another stunning triumph for the home team!

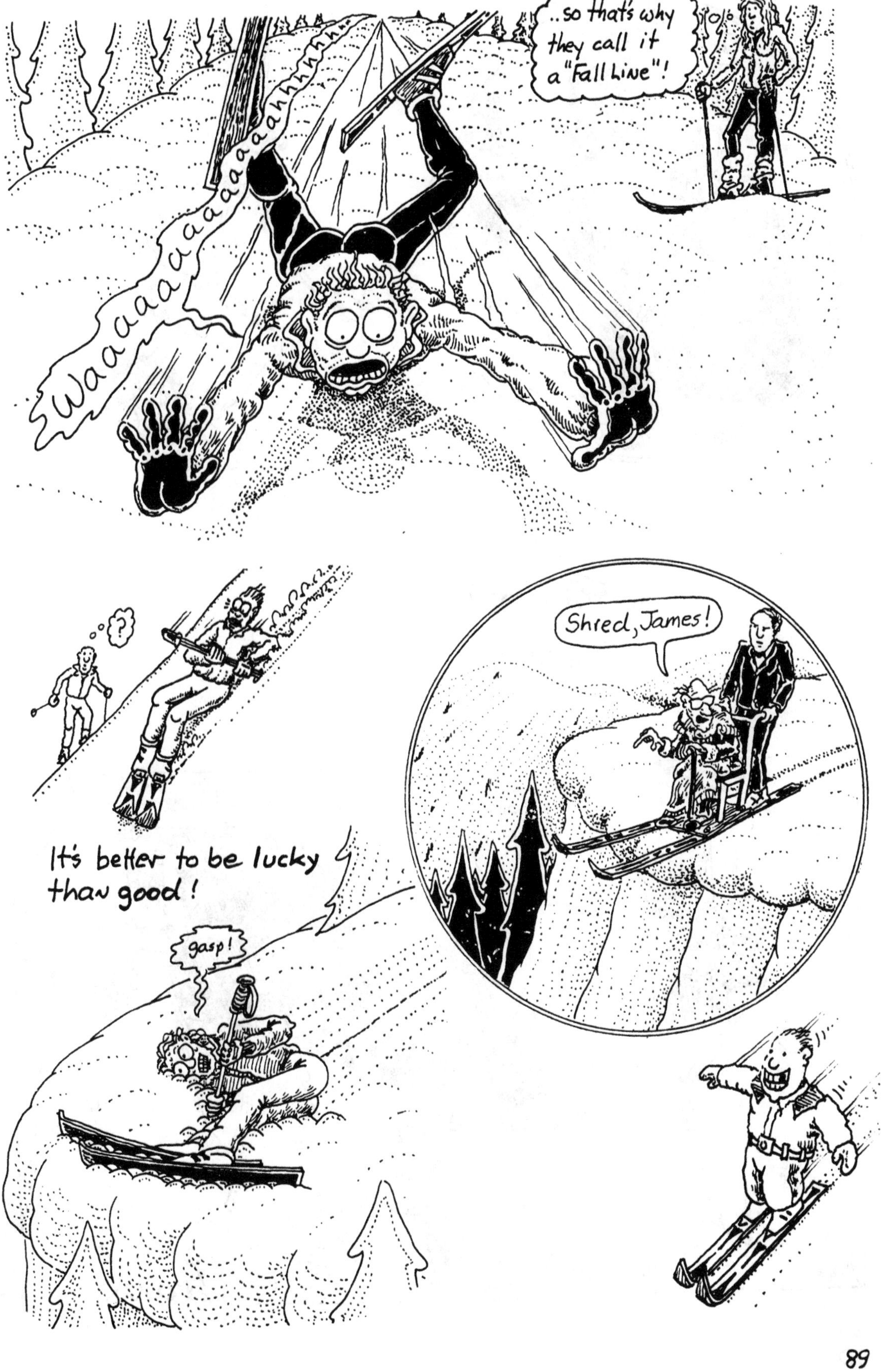
Waaaaaaaaaaaaaaaaahhhhhhhh...
..so that's why they call it a "Fall Line"!
?
Shred, James!
It's better to be lucky than good!
gasp!

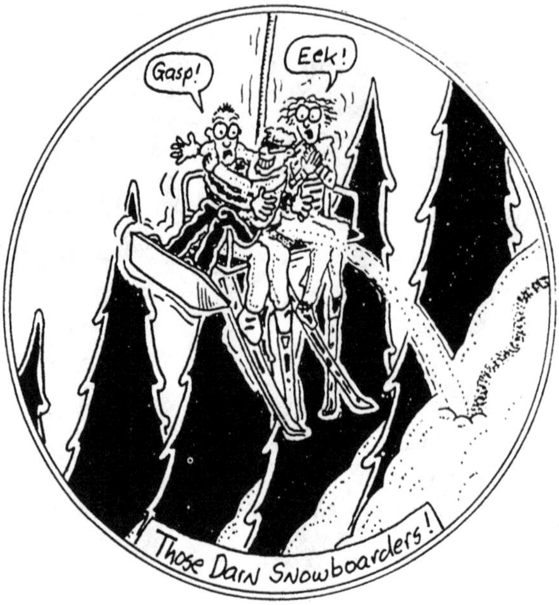
Gasp!
Eek!
Those Darn Snowboarders!

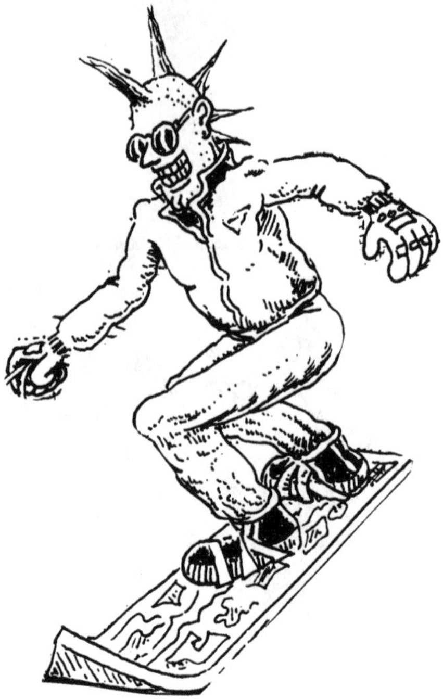

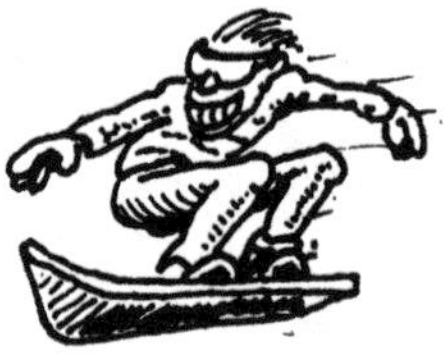

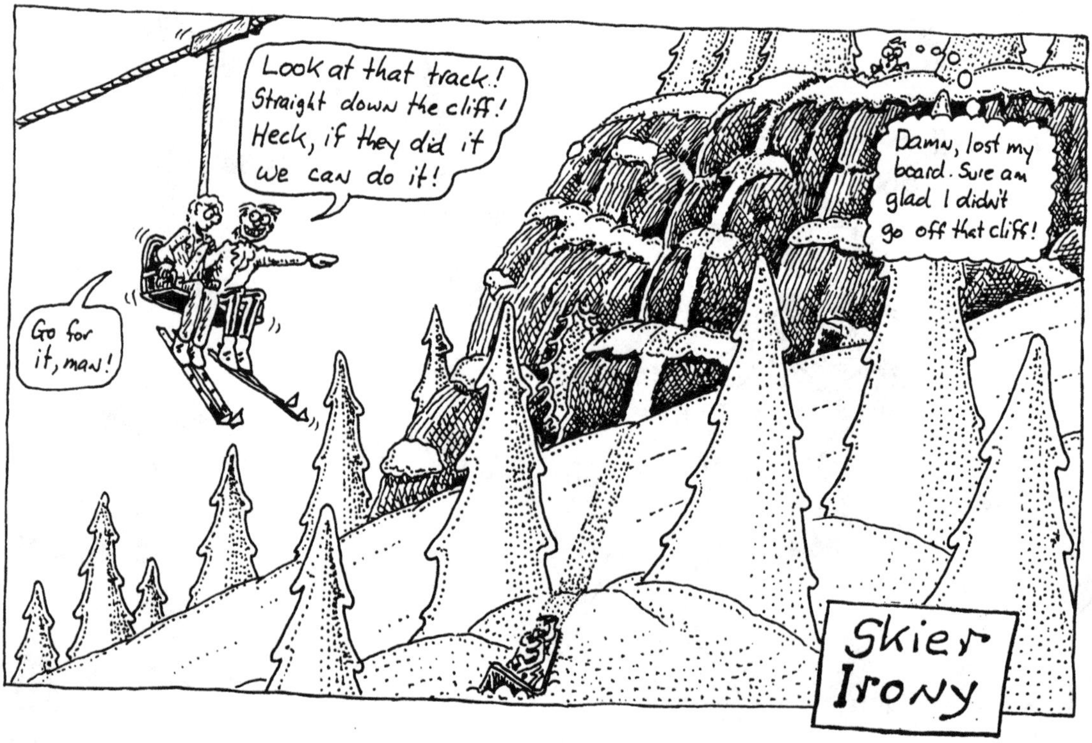
Look at that track! Straight down the cliff! Heck, if they did it we can do it!
Go for it, man!
Damn, lost my board. Sure am glad I didn't go off that cliff!
Skier Irony

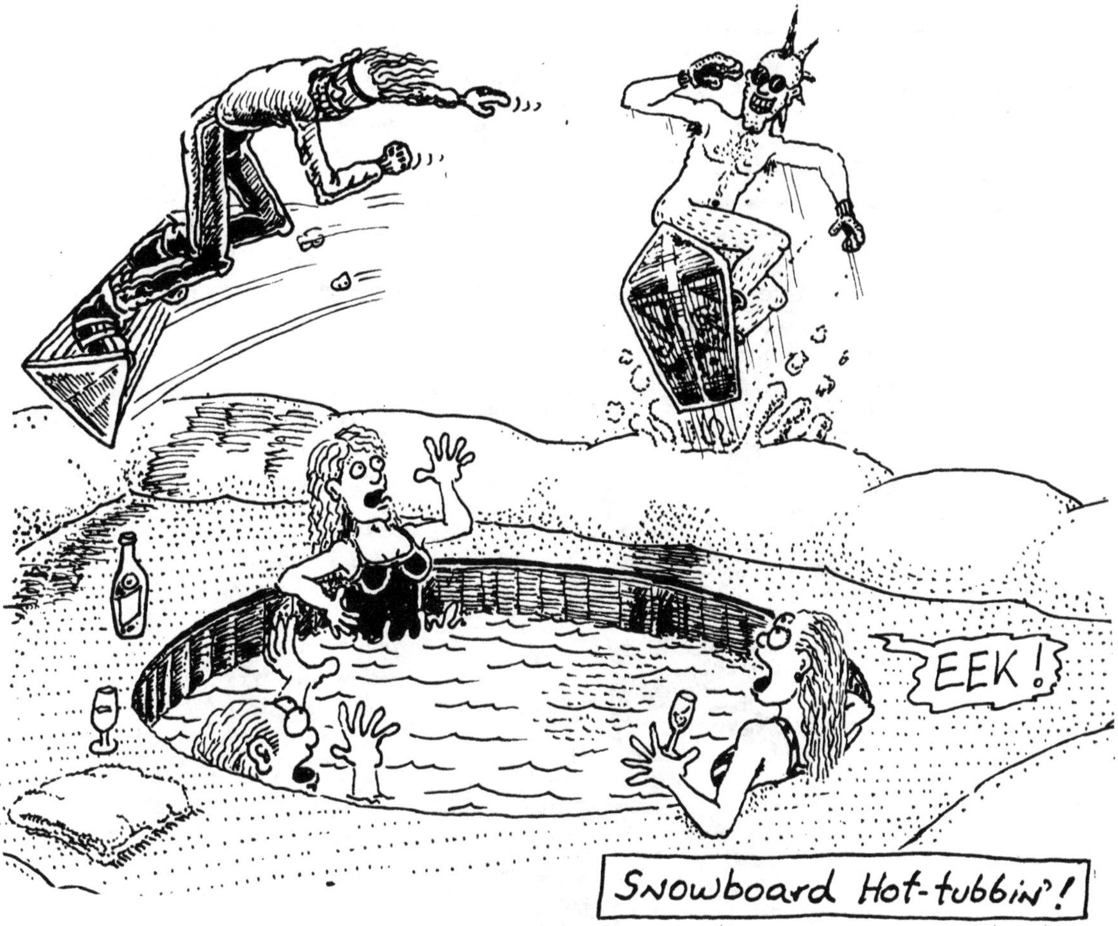
EEK!
Snowboard Hot-tubbin'!

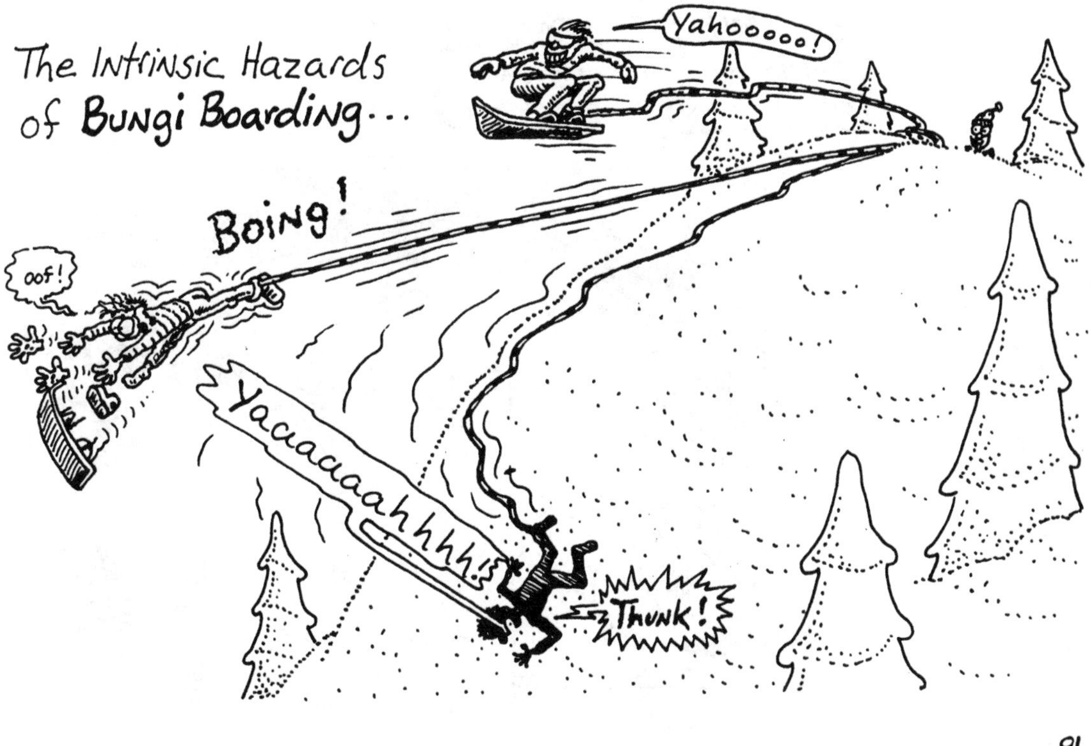
The Intrinsic Hazards of Bungi Boarding...
Yahoooooo!
Boing!
oof!
Yaaaaaahhhhh!
Thunk!

Jumping Out Of Perfectly Good Airplanes...

Things they don't teach you in tandem parachute groundschool...

splat!

grrr...

Hurl Handsignal *

I'm gonna cut yer sorry ass loose!

Wrong!

oof.

(one hand, hurl side)

Oh shit

Translation: "I'm gonna hurl on my left side very soon!"

Instructor has time to bank right, avoiding spew altogether →

Right!

ARF!

* Also a handy signal for nervous leadclimbers, relative-work, aerobatic student pilots, etc..

* Instructors hate being puked on & they carry cut-away knives!

① Parayakking

②

③ Quick release for super "Endo"

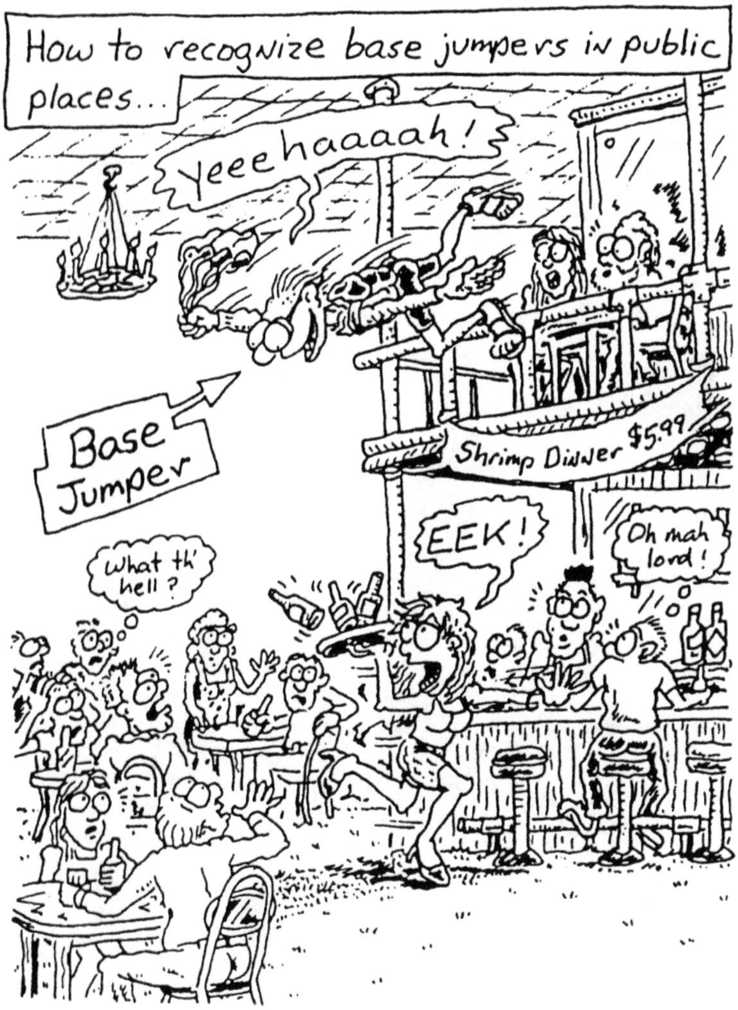
How to recognize base jumpers in public places...
Yeeehaaaah!
Base Jumper
Shrimp Dinner $5.99
What th' hell?
EEK!
Oh mah lord!

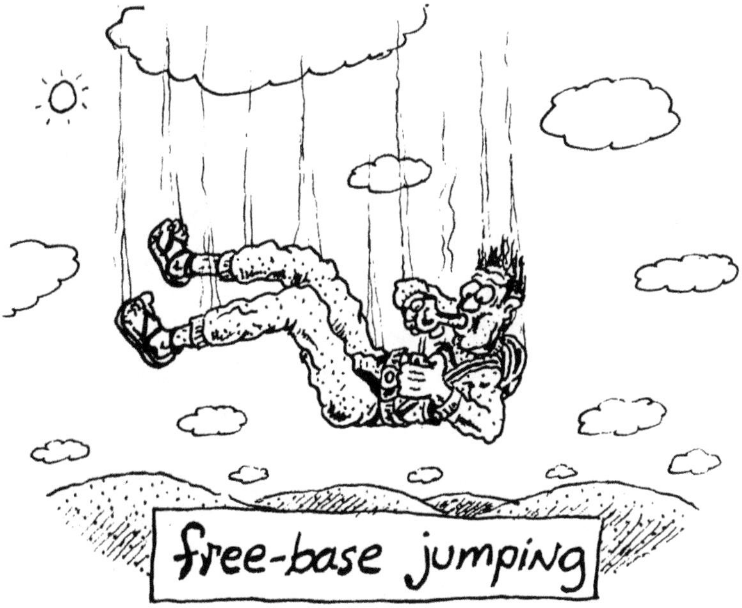
free-base jumping

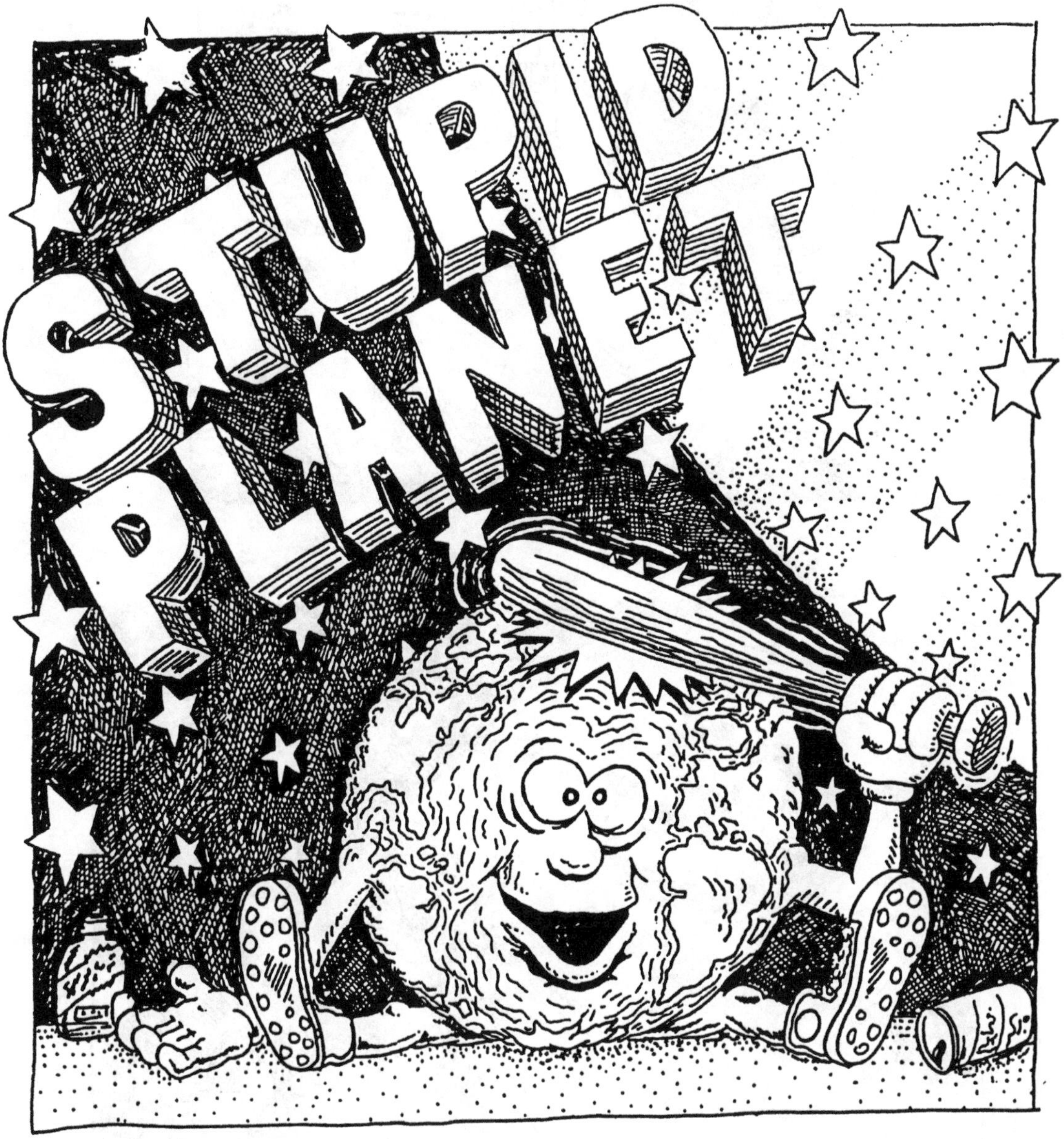
STUPID PLANET

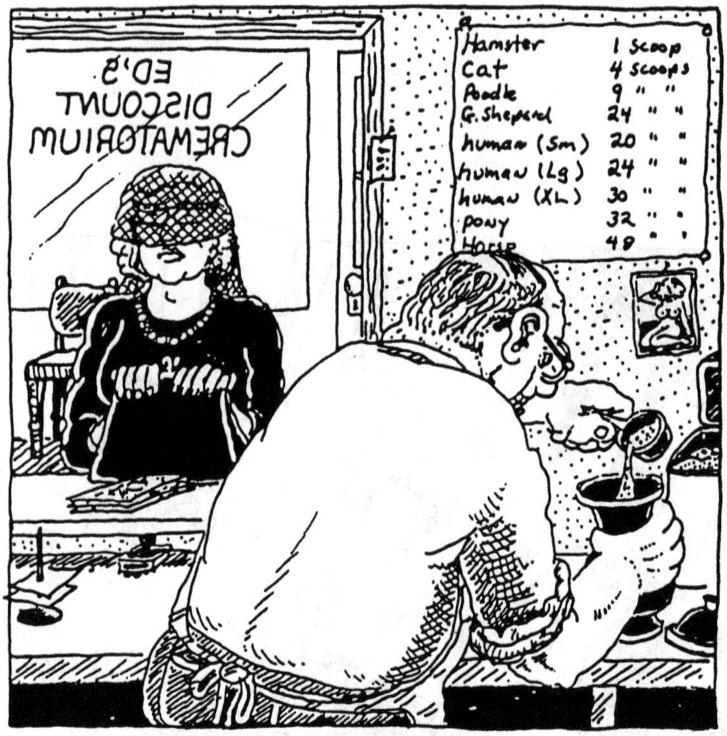
ED'S
DISCOUNT
CREMATORIUM
Hamster 1 Scoop
Cat 4 scoops
Poodle 9 " "
G. Shepard 24 " "
human (Sm) 20 " "
human (Lg) 24 " "
human (XL) 30 " "
pony 32 " "
Horse 48 " "

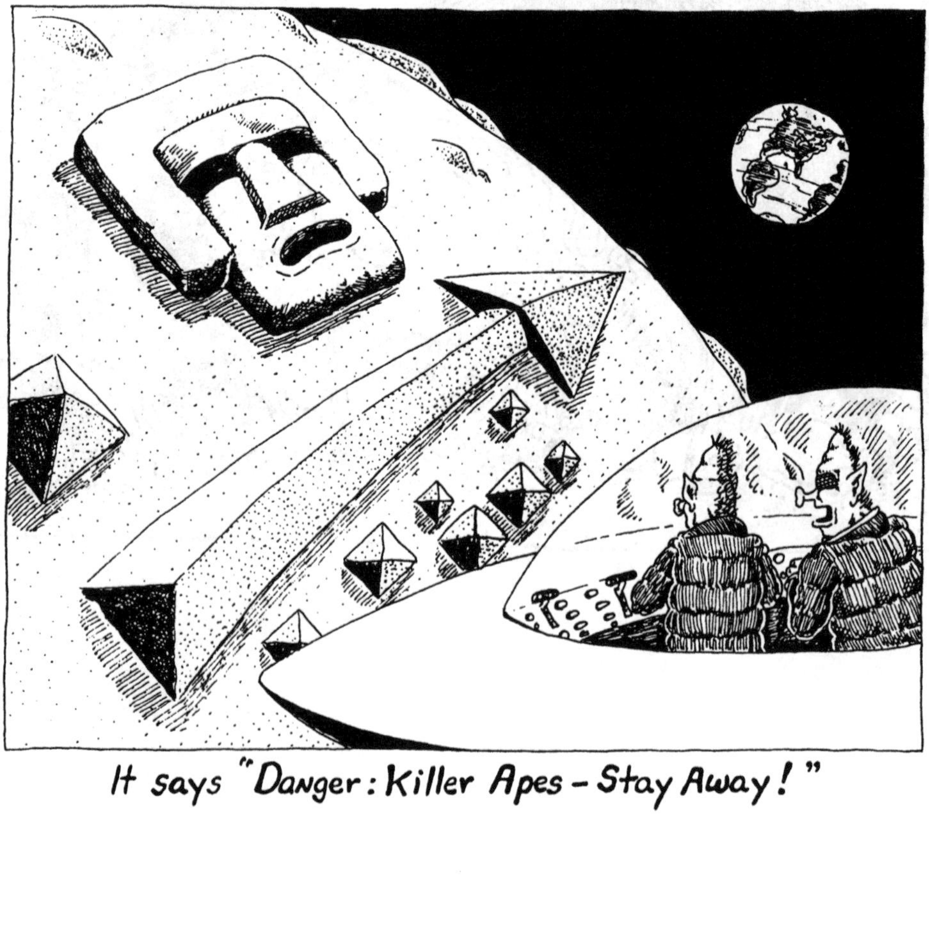

It says "Danger: Killer Apes - Stay Away!"

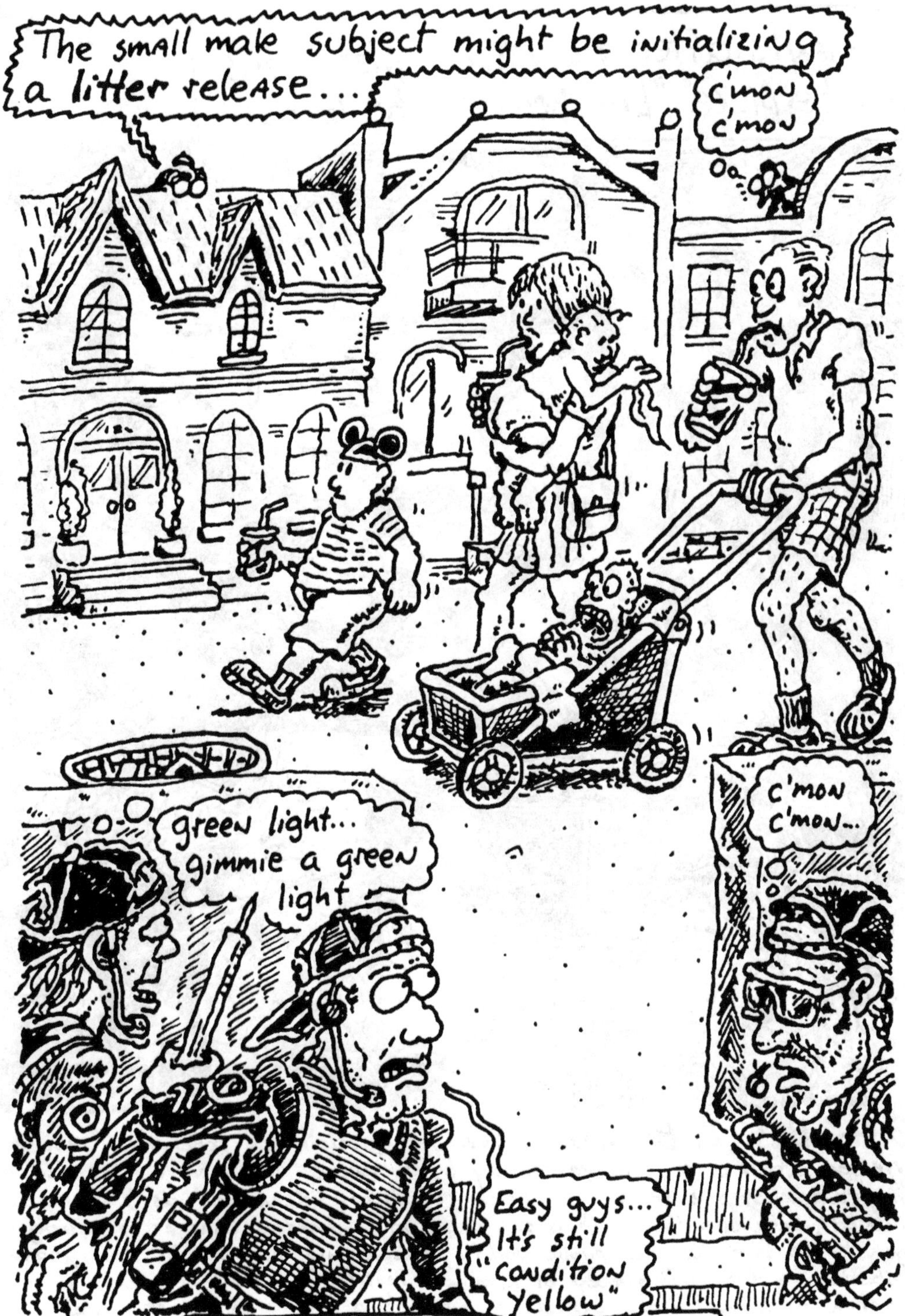
The small male subject might be initializing a litter release...
C'mon c'mon
green light... gimmie a green light
C'mon c'mon...
Easy guys... It's still "condition yellow"

Litter S.W.A.T.

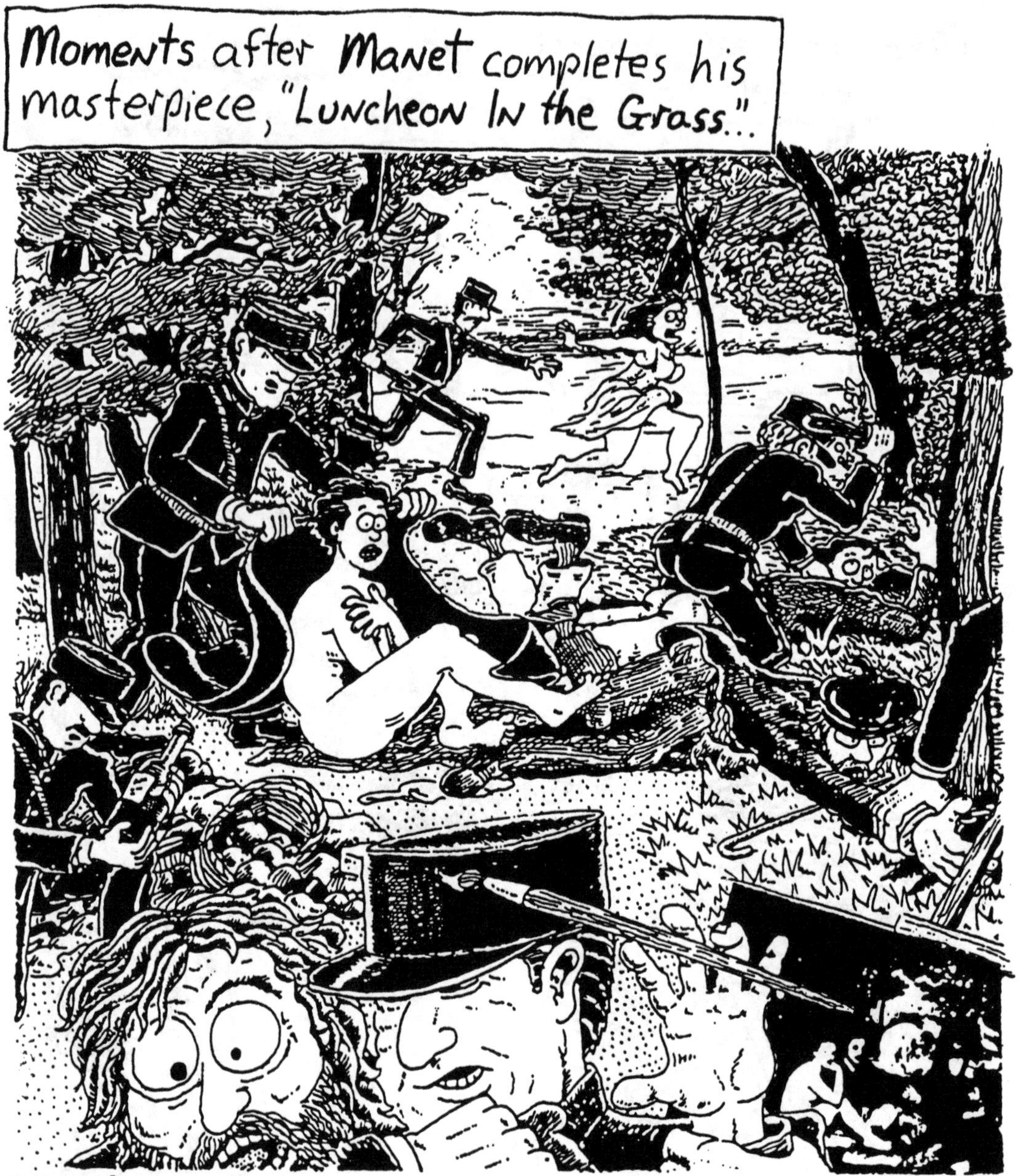
Moments after Manet completes his masterpiece, "Luncheon In the Grass."..

'Boho' Bust In Brionne - Five self-proclaimed "bohemians" were arrested after a scuffle yesterday by authorities in Brionne. The alleged ringleader of the band has been tenatively identified as Edouard Manet, an unemployed Parisian painting contractor. Charges pending against the five include public nudity, trespassing, public intoxication, contributing to the delinquency of a minor, resisting arrest, vagrancy and violation of a local health ordinance prohibiting luncheons on the grass.

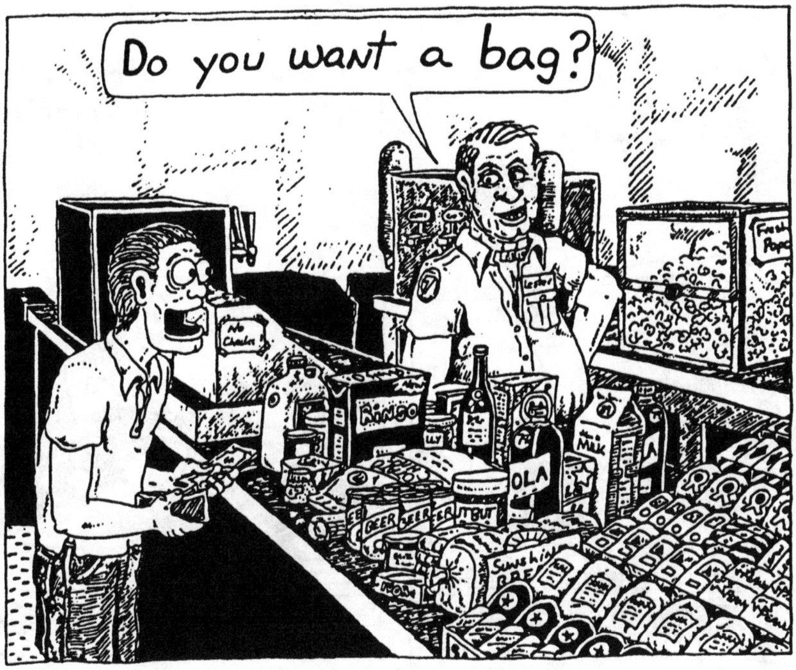
Do you want a bag?

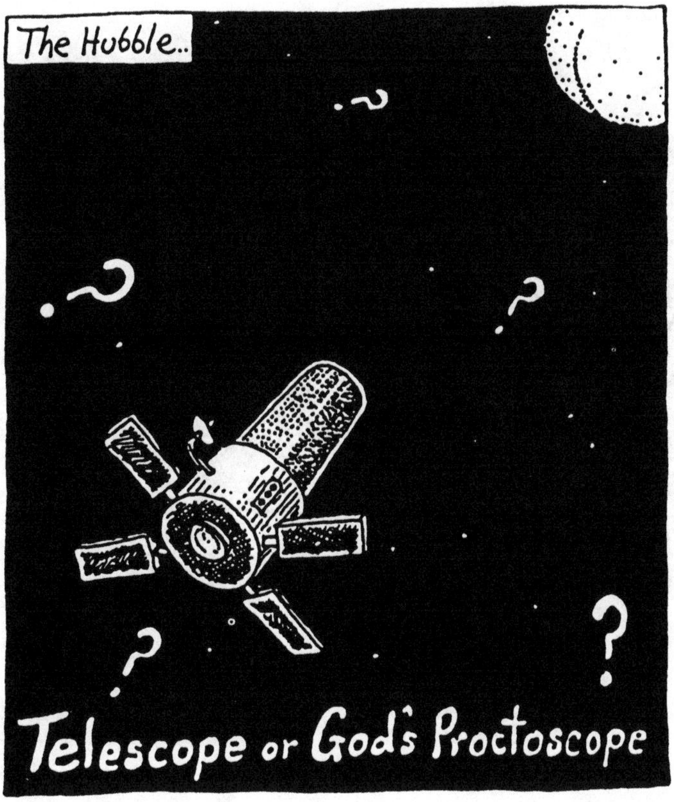
The Hubble..
Telescope or God's Proctoscope

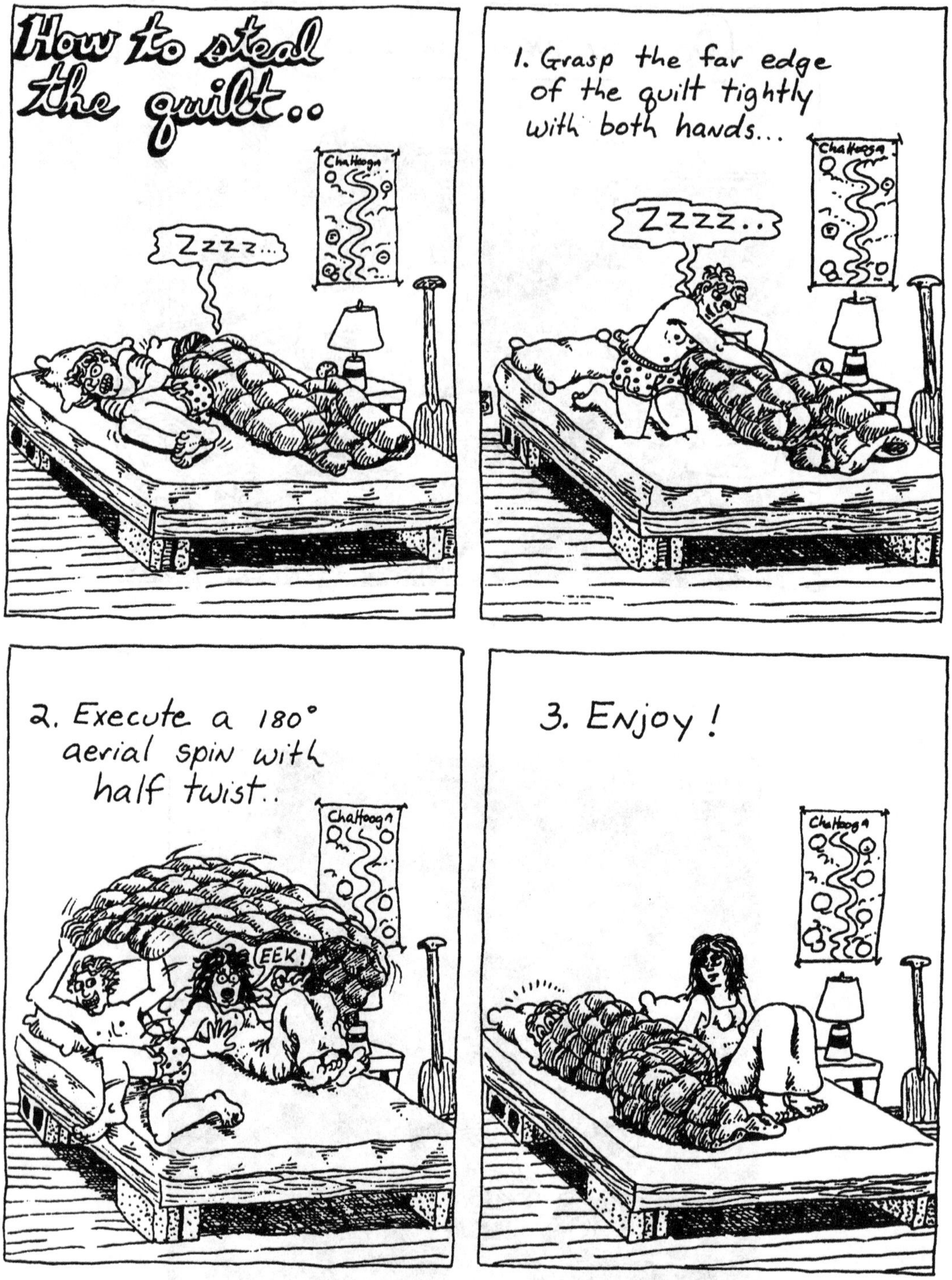
How to steal the quilt..
Zzzz...
1. Grasp the far edge of the quilt tightly with both hands...
Zzzz..
2. Execute a 180° aerial spin with half twist..
EEK!
3. Enjoy!

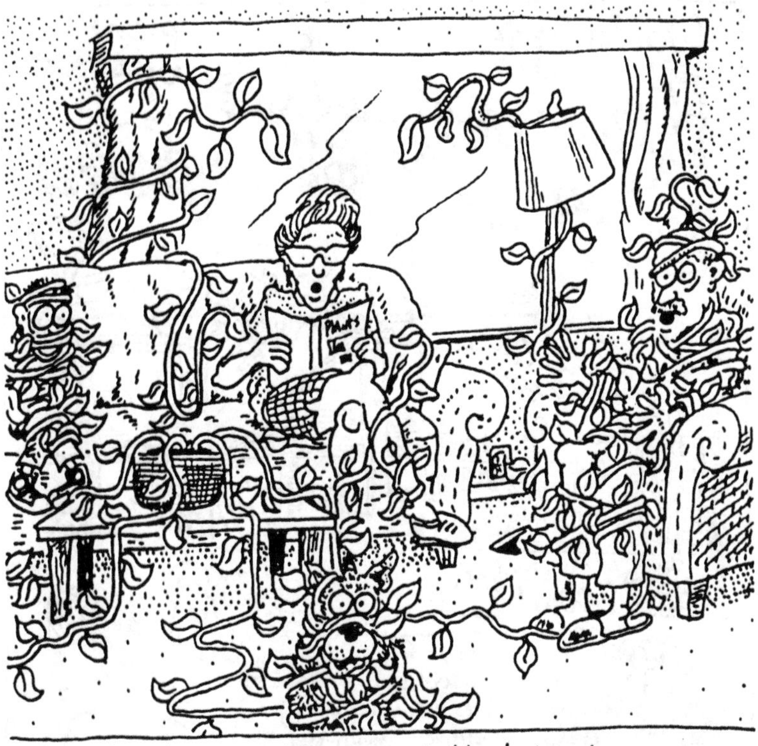

By the time Edna read that Kudzu was "at best an obnoxious and aggressive house-plant," it was too late for the Einbinder family...

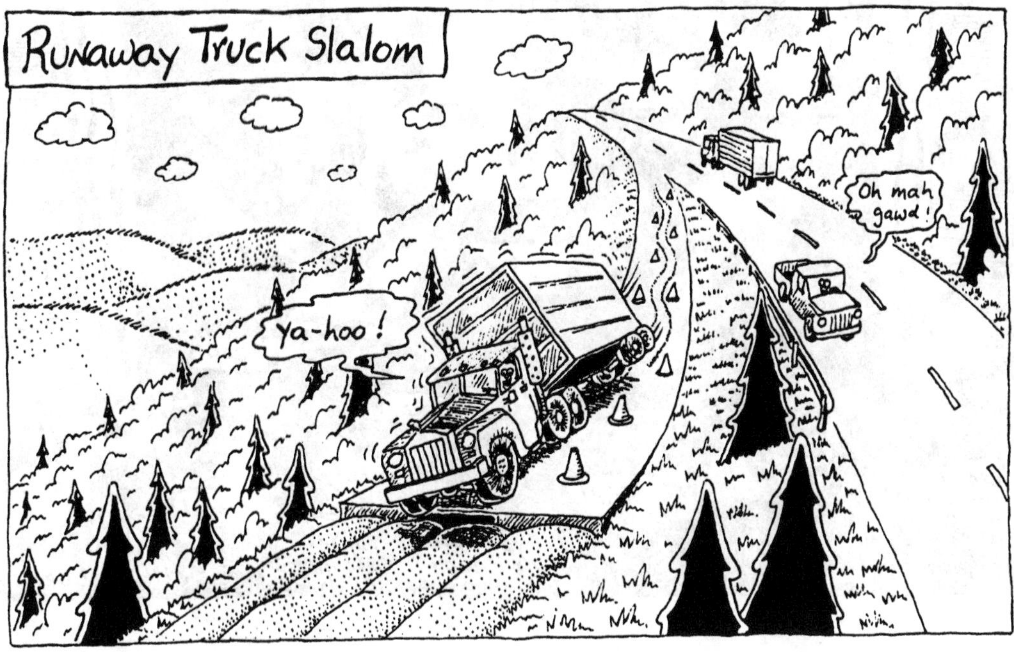
Runaway Truck Slalom
Ya-hoo!
Oh mah gawd!

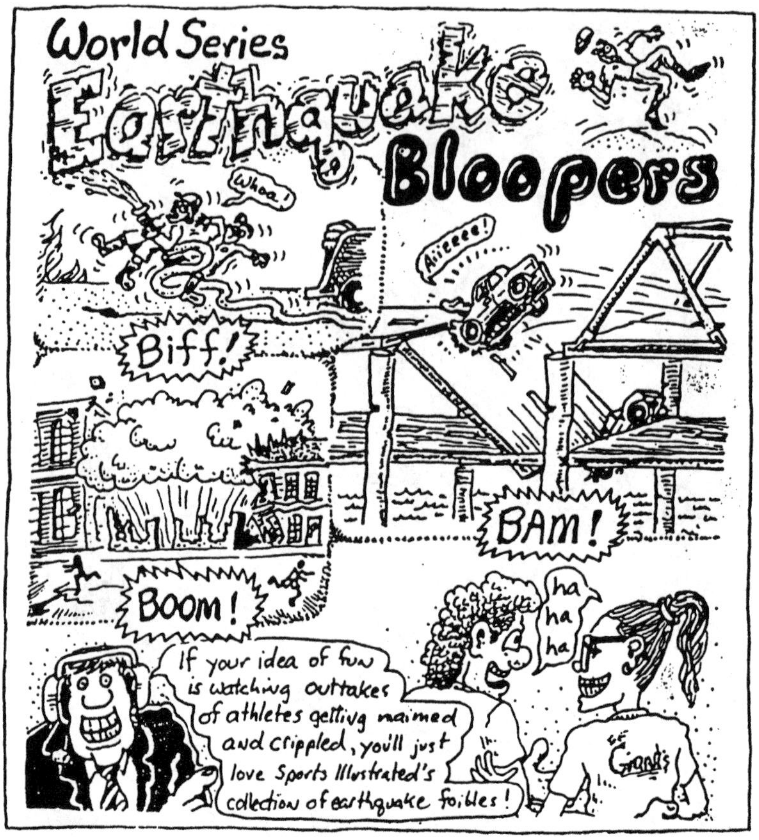
World Series
Earthquake
Bloopers
Whoa!
Aieeee!
Biff!
BAM!
BOOM!
ha
ha
ha
If your idea of fun is watching outtakes of athletes getting maimed and crippled, you'll just love Sports Illustrated's collection of earthquake foibles!

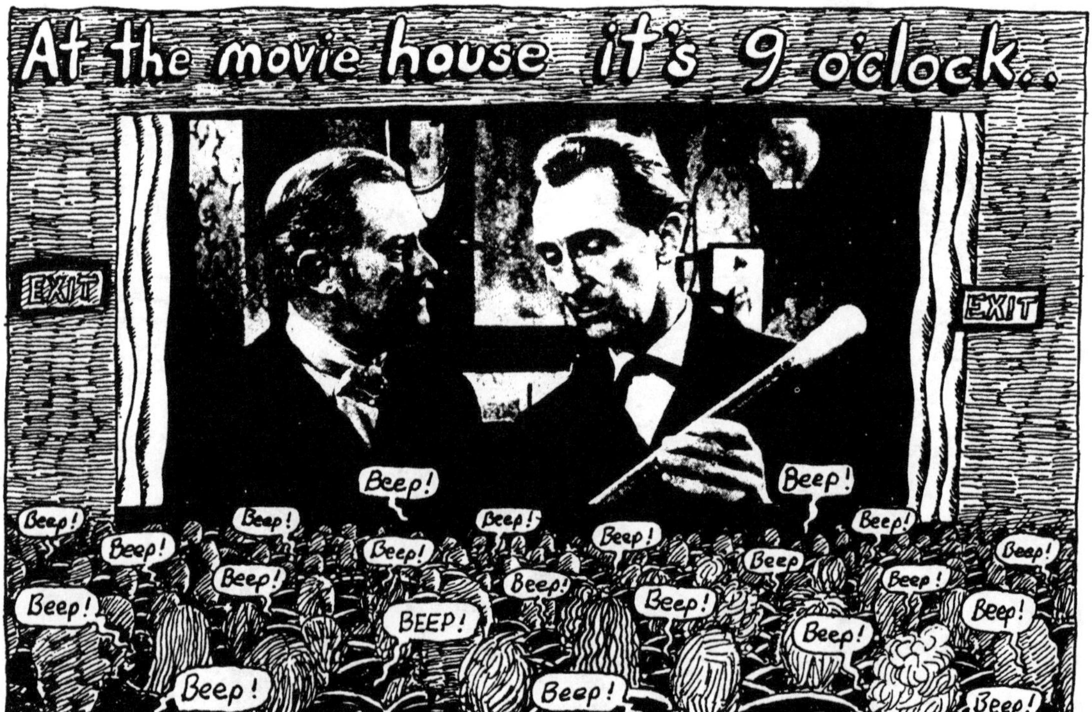
At the movie house it's 9 o'clock..
EXIT
EXIT
Beep!
Beep!
Beep!
Beep!
Beep!
Beep!
Beep!
Beep!
Beep!
Beep!
Beep!
Beep!
Beep!
Beep!
Beep!
Beep!
BEEP!
Beep!
Beep!
Beep!
Beep!
Beep!

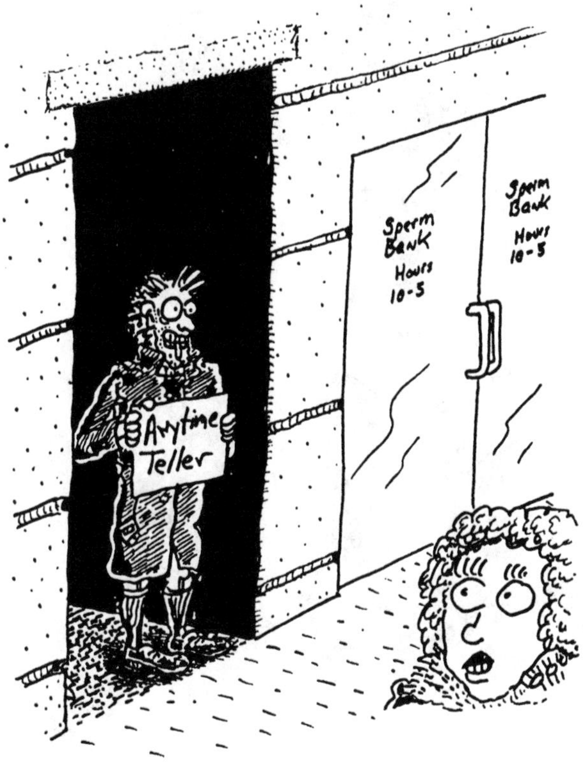
Sperm Bank Hours 10-5
Sperm Bank Hours 10-5
Anytime Teller

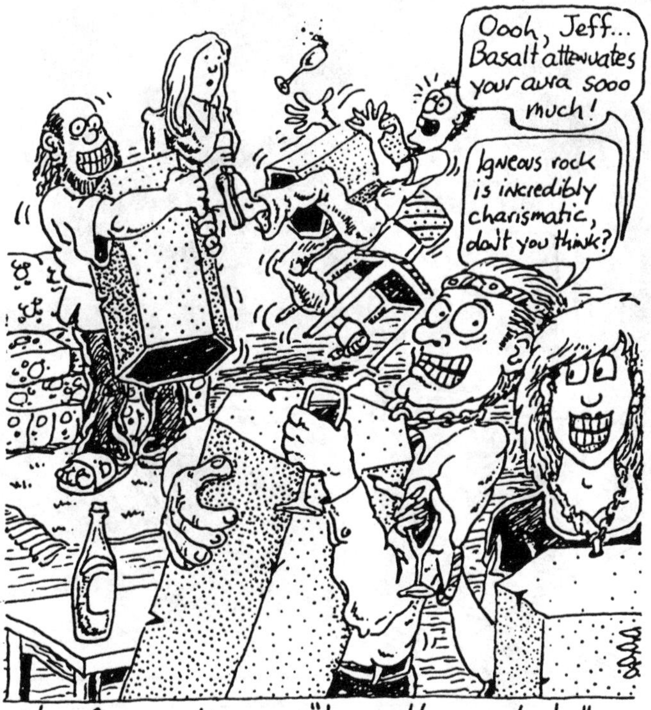
Oooh, Jeff... Basalt attenuates your aura sooo much!
Igneous rock is incredibly charismatic, don't you think?

New Agers discover "basalt crystals."..

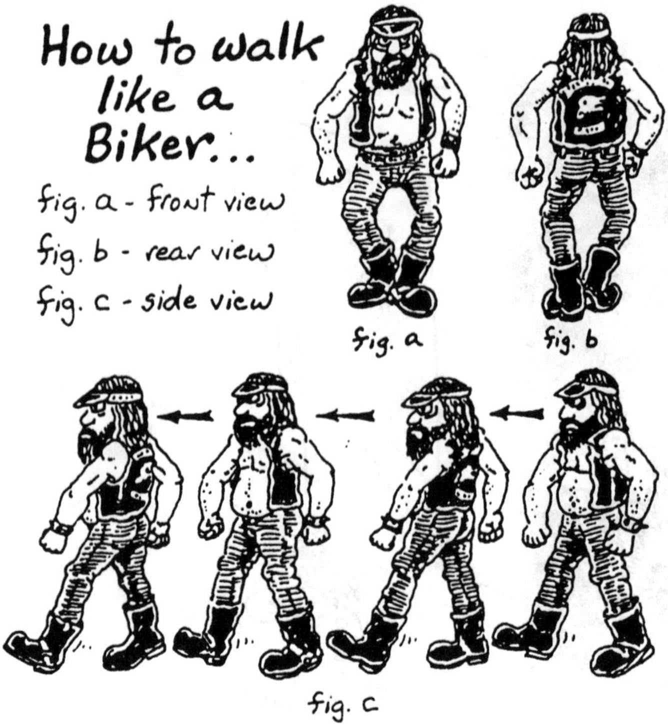
How to walk like a Biker...
fig. a - front view
fig. b - rear view
fig. c - side view
fig. a
fig. b
fig. c

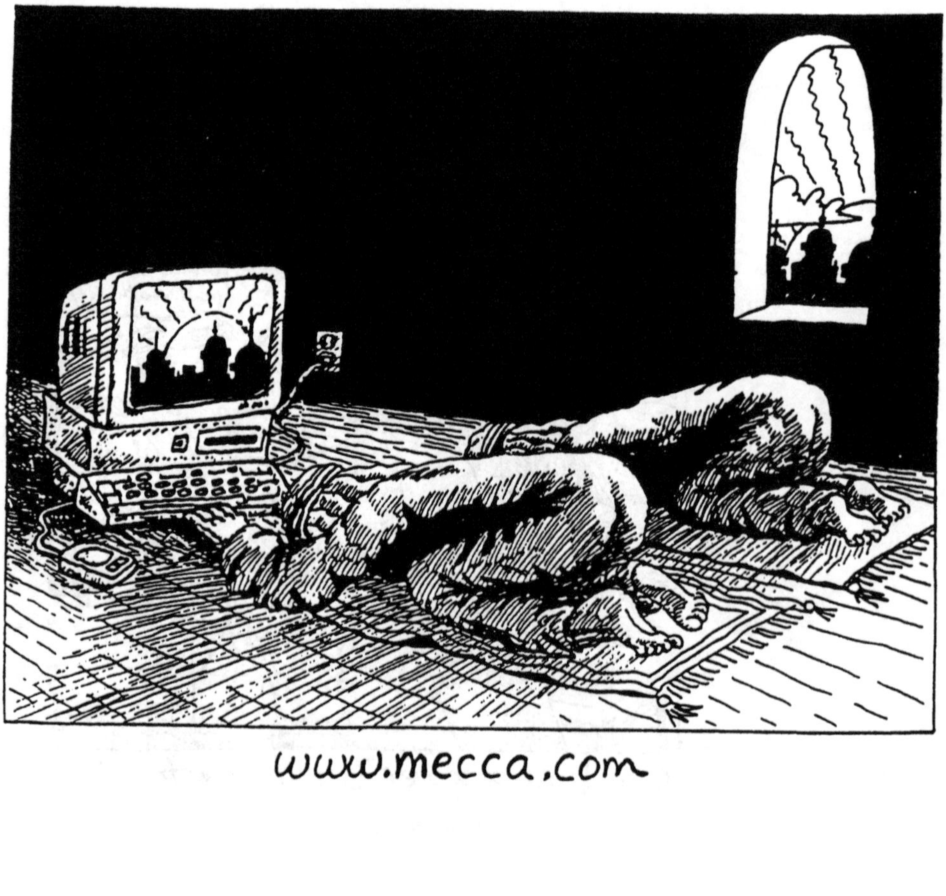

www.mecca.com

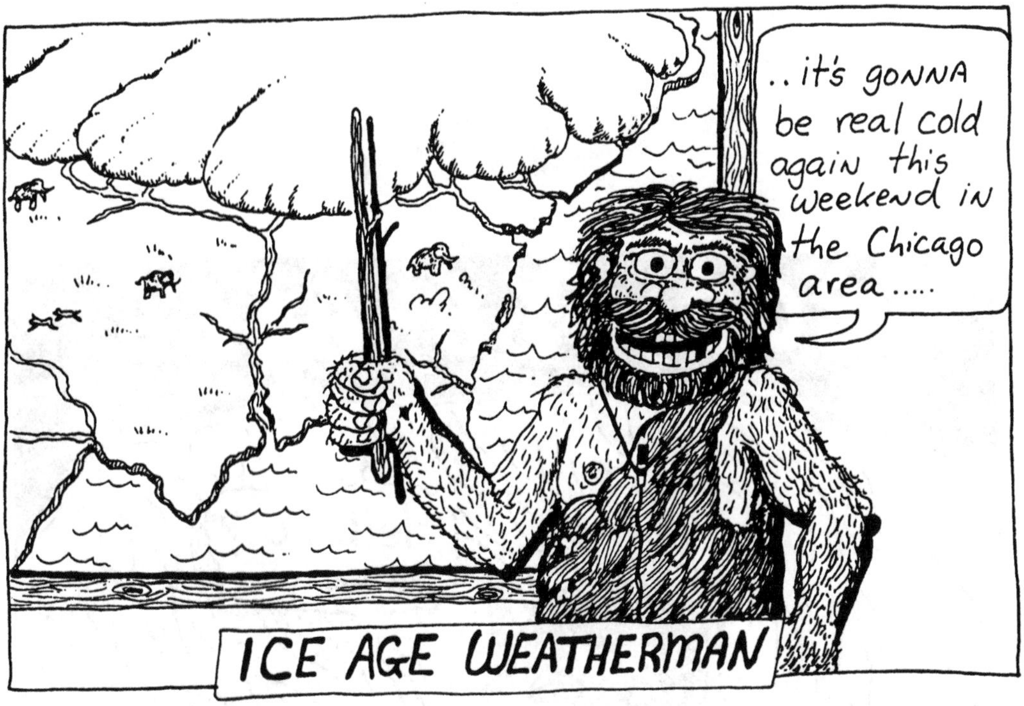
..it's GONNA be real cold again this weekend in the Chicago area.....
ICE AGE WEATHERMAN

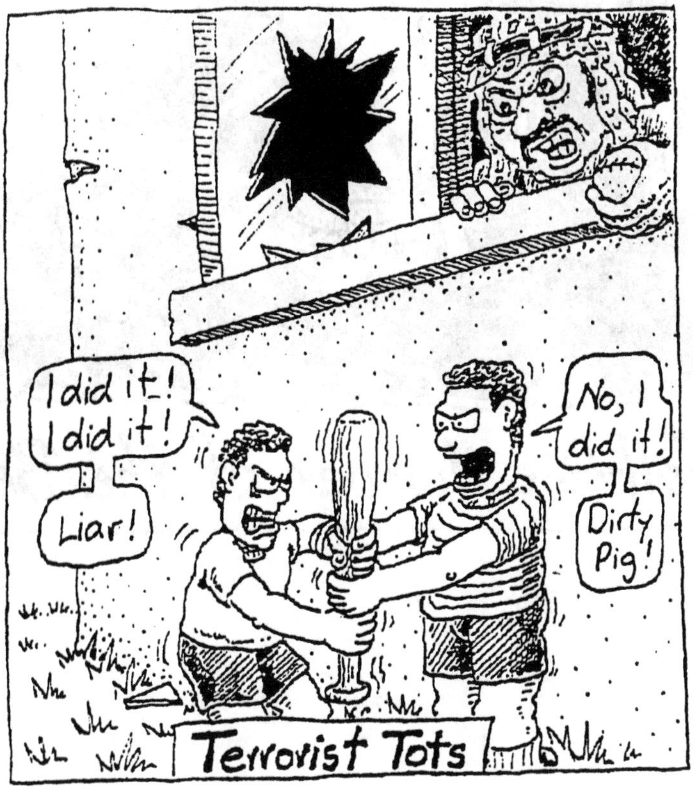
I did it! I did it!
Liar!
No, I did it!
Dirty Pig!
Terrorist Tots

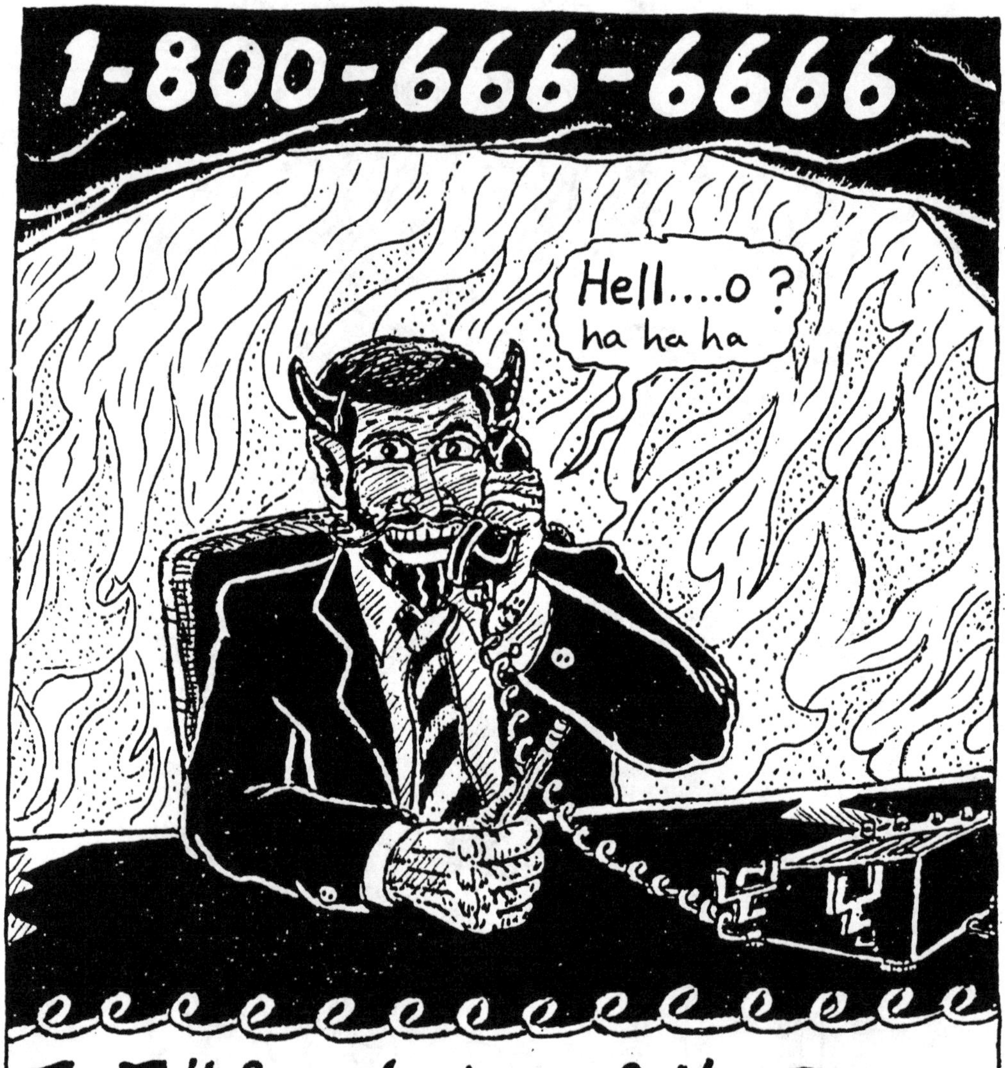
1-800-666-6666
Hell....o ?
ha ha ha
The Toll-free Number of the Beast

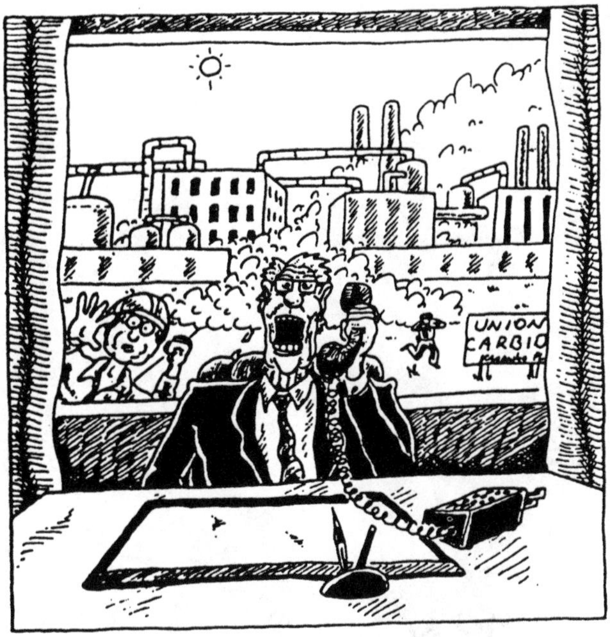
UNION

Gas leak! Quick... call Legal!

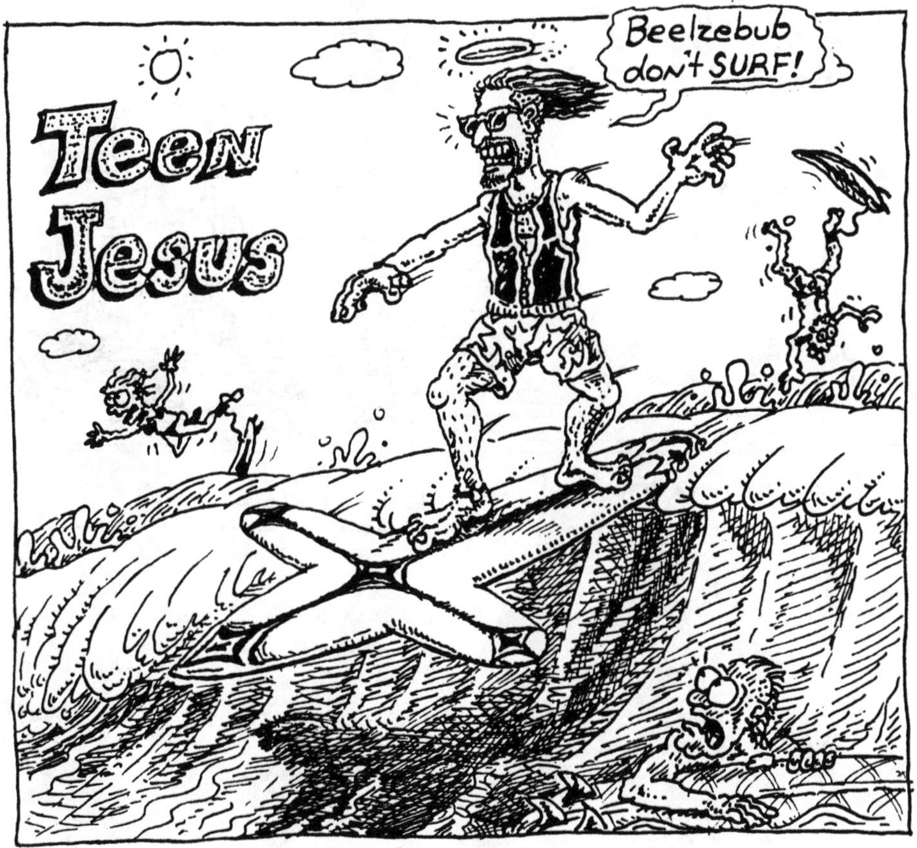
Beelzebub don't SURF!
Teen Jesus

...He doesn't just walk on water anymore!

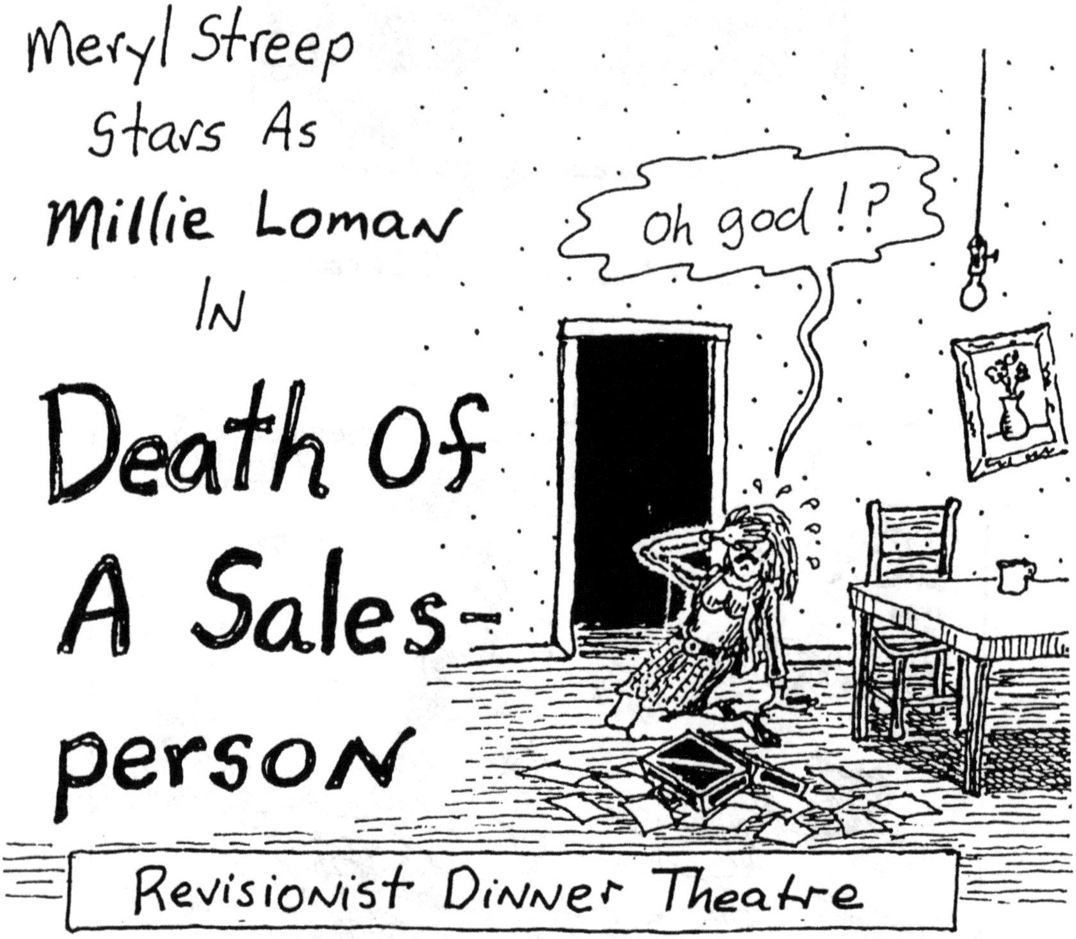
Meryl Streep
Stars As
Millie Loman
IN
Death Of
A Sales-
person
Oh god!?
Revisionist Dinner Theatre

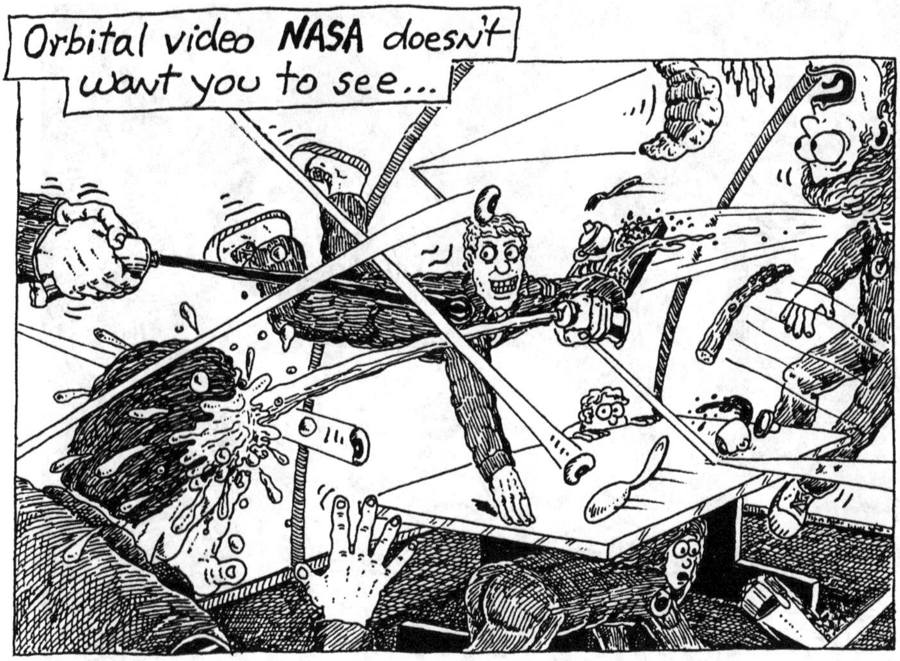
Orbital video NASA doesn't want you to see...

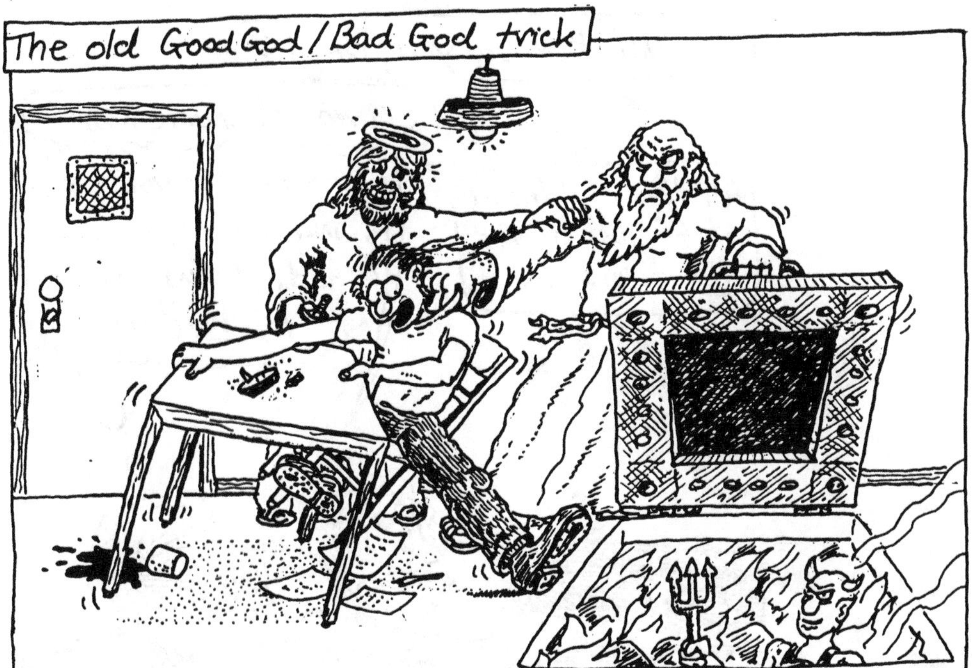
The old Good God / Bad God trick

Easy Jehovah! Be cool... why don't you get Mr. Kimbro some fresh coffee... take your time, OK?... Bob? Can I call you Bob? Have a smoke. The Big Guy's a little P.O.'d today... some trouble in Paradise.. ha ha. Let's have a little pow-wow while Mr. Grouchy goes to the canteen. Y'know, I was mortal once myself and I know it's tempting...

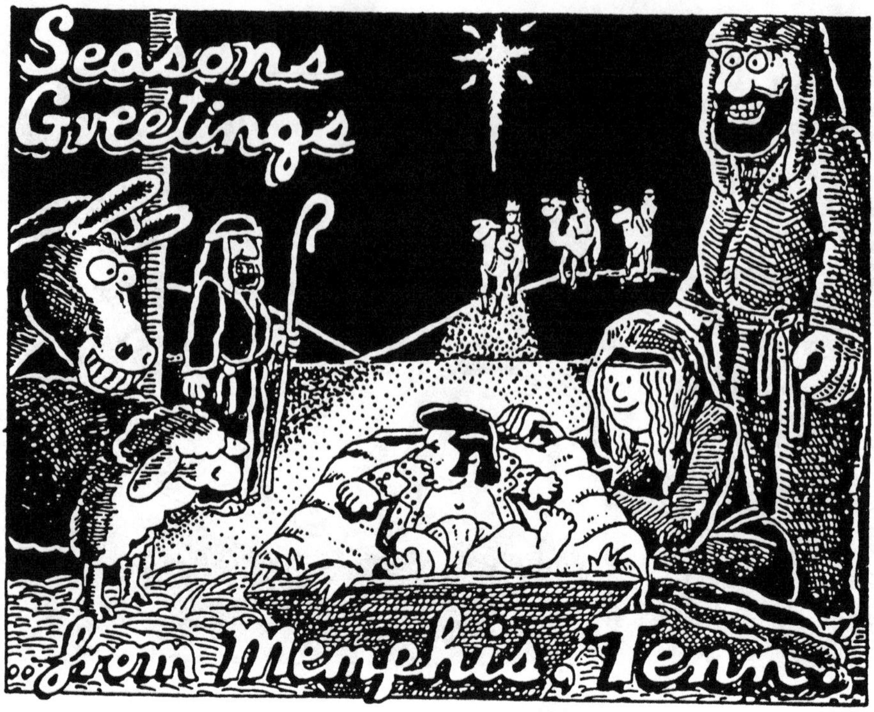
Seasons Greetings
from Memphis, Tenn.

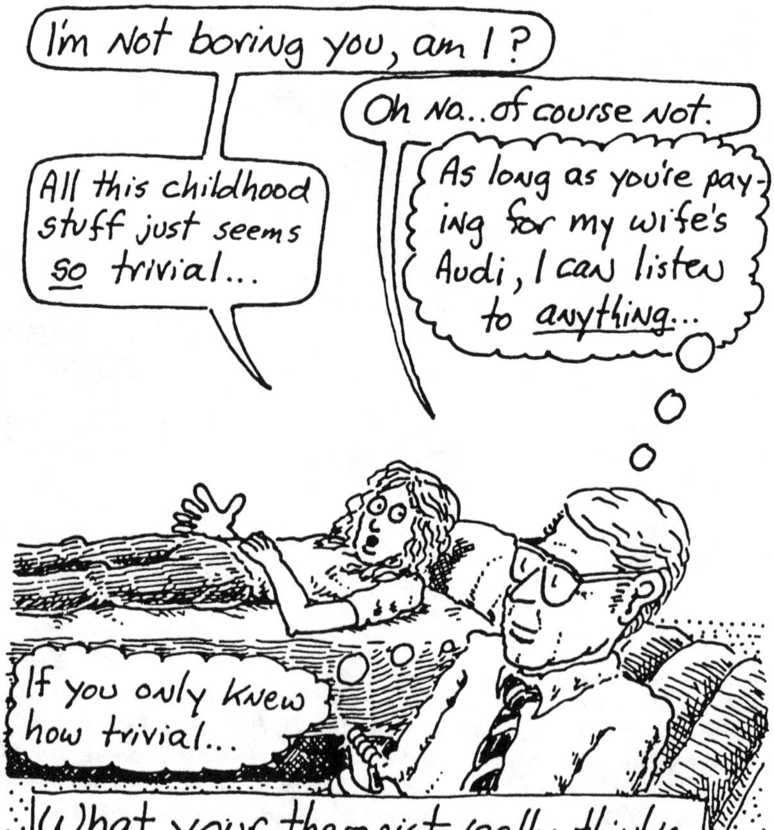
I'm Not boring you, am I?
All this childhood stuff just seems so trivial...
Oh No...of course not.
As long as you're paying for my wife's Audi, I can listen to anything...
If you only knew how trivial...
What your therapist really thinks

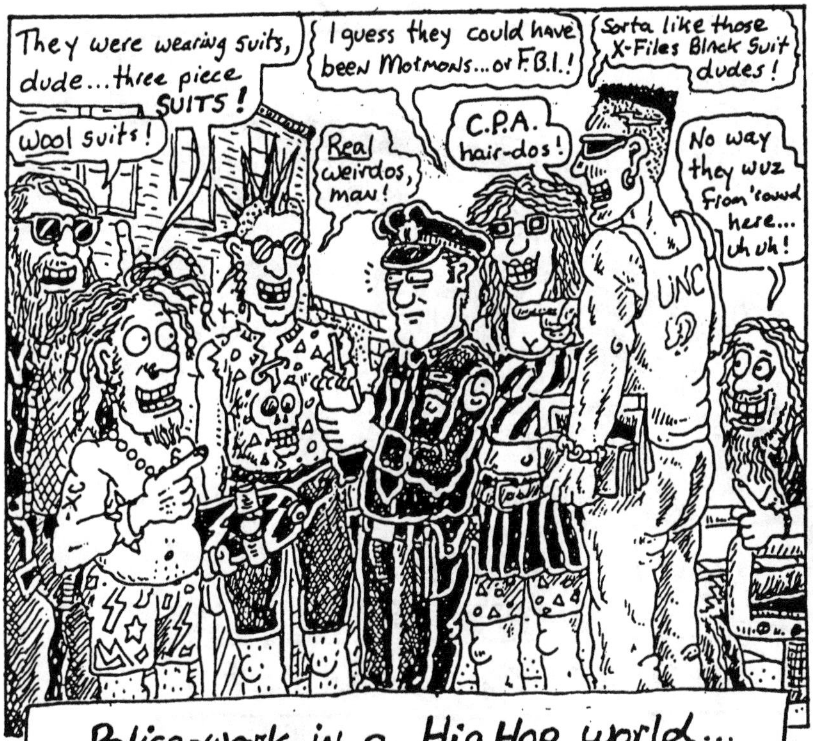
They were wearing suits, dude... three piece SUITS!
Wool suits!
I guess they could have been Mormons... or F.B.I.!
Real weirdos, man!
C.P.A. hair-dos!
Sorta like those X-Files Black Suit dudes!
No way they wuz from 'round here... uh uh!
UNC

Police-work in a Hip Hop world...

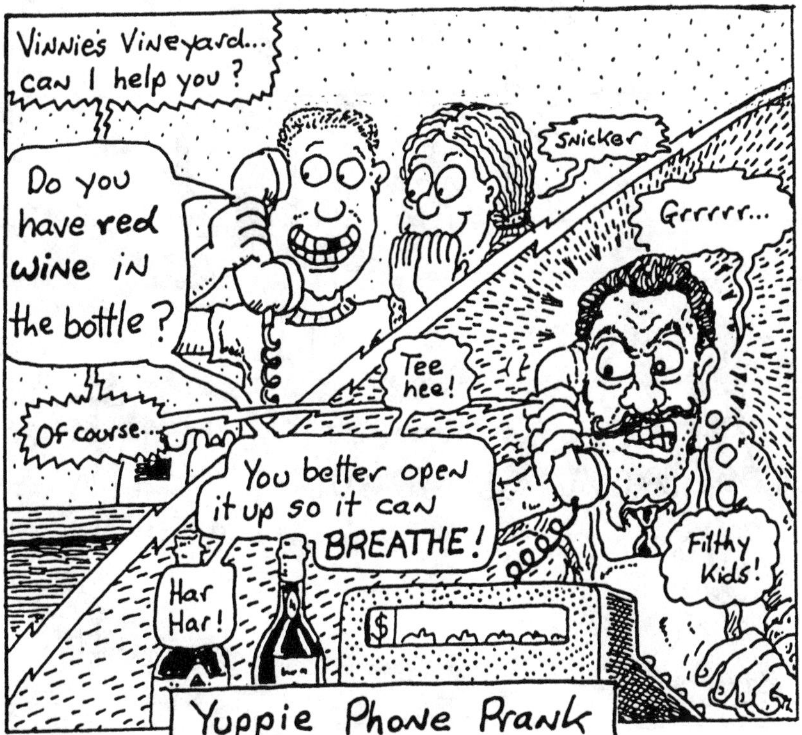
Vinnie's Vineyard... can I help you?
Do you have red wine in the bottle?
Snicker
Grrrrr...
Tee hee!
Of course...
You better open it up so it can BREATHE!
Har Har!
Filthy Kids!
$

Yuppie Phone Prank

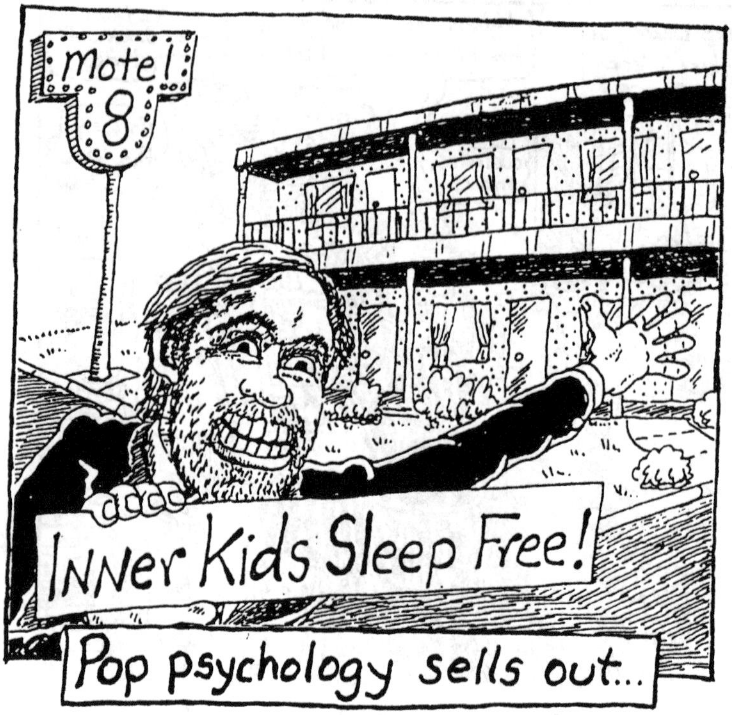
motel 8
Inner Kids Sleep Free!
Pop psychology sells out...

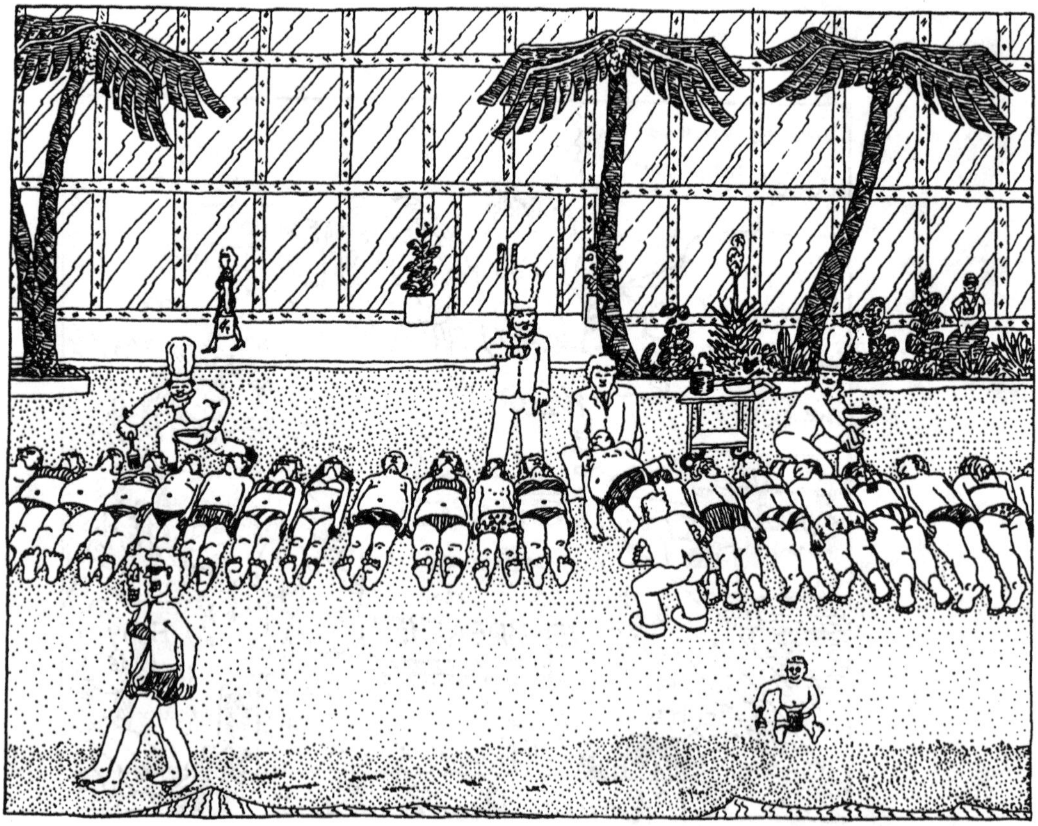

Home Bungi Jumping

..and then what did God tell you to do?

He... He told me to defraud a whole lot of people and live like Johnny Carson...

Anything else?

He told me to set up a string of safe houses, to buy two Rolls Royces for Him and his associate, Mr. Jesus...

And?

...He told me to evade taxes or They would take Tammy Faye to Heaven!

Jim Bakker turns state's evidence...

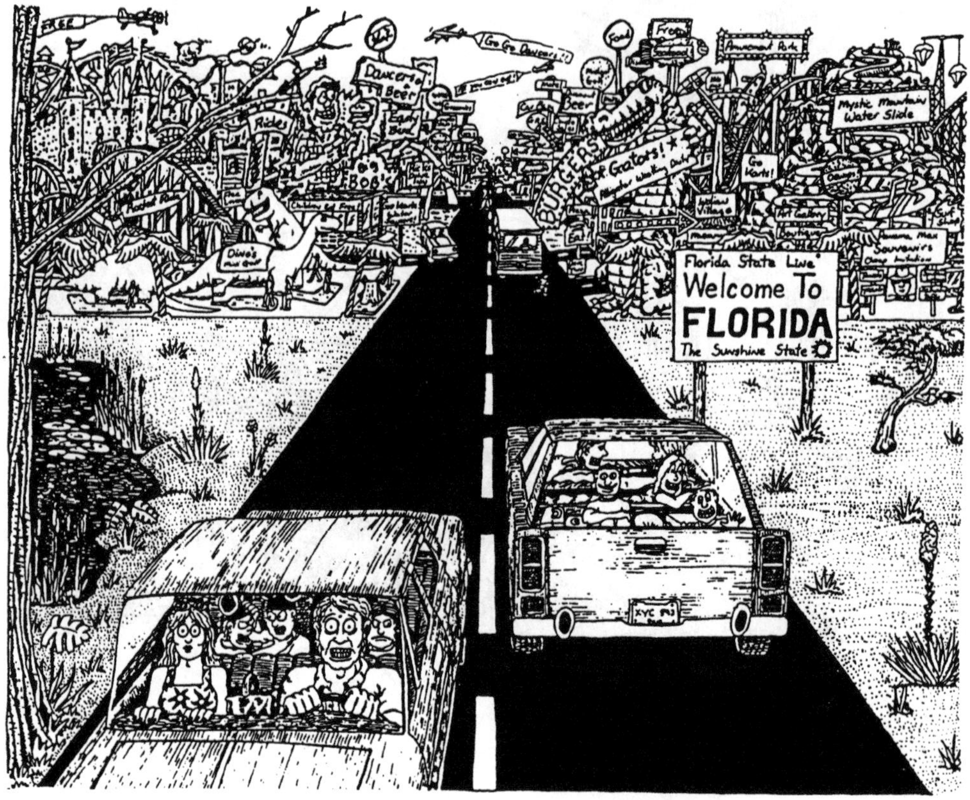

Florida State Line
Welcome To
FLORIDA
The Sunshine State
Dancers Beer
BURGERS
Gators!
Mystic Mountain Water Slide
Go Karts!
Rides
Art Gallery
Souvenirs

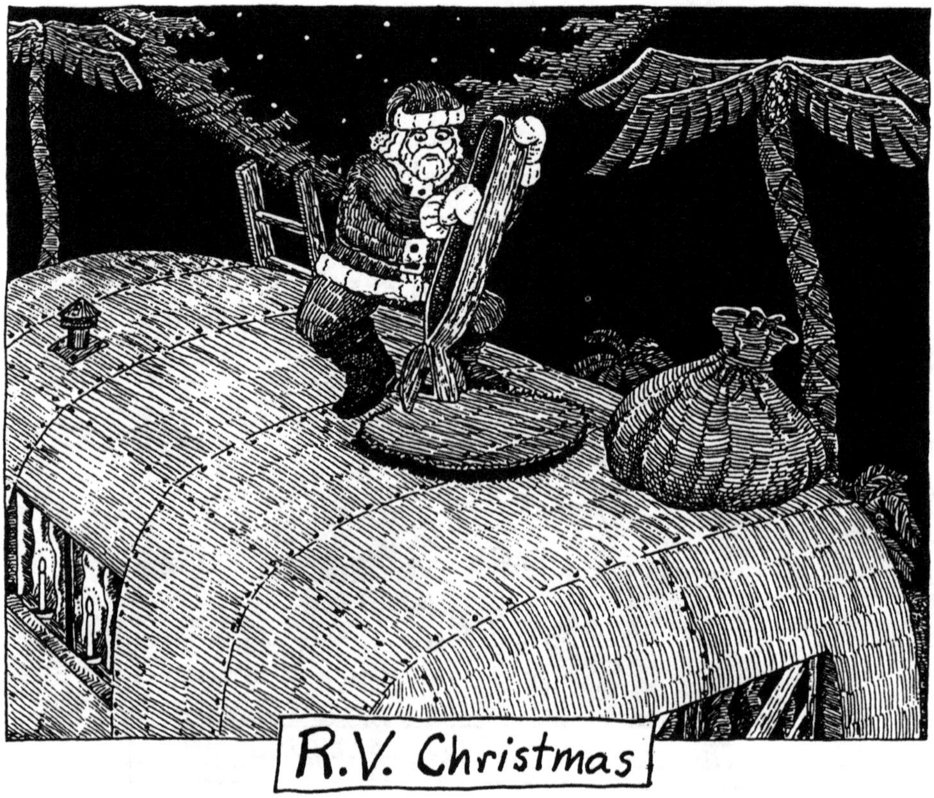

R.V. Christmas

Man vs. Mollusk! It's Conch Wrestling, Florida Style . . .

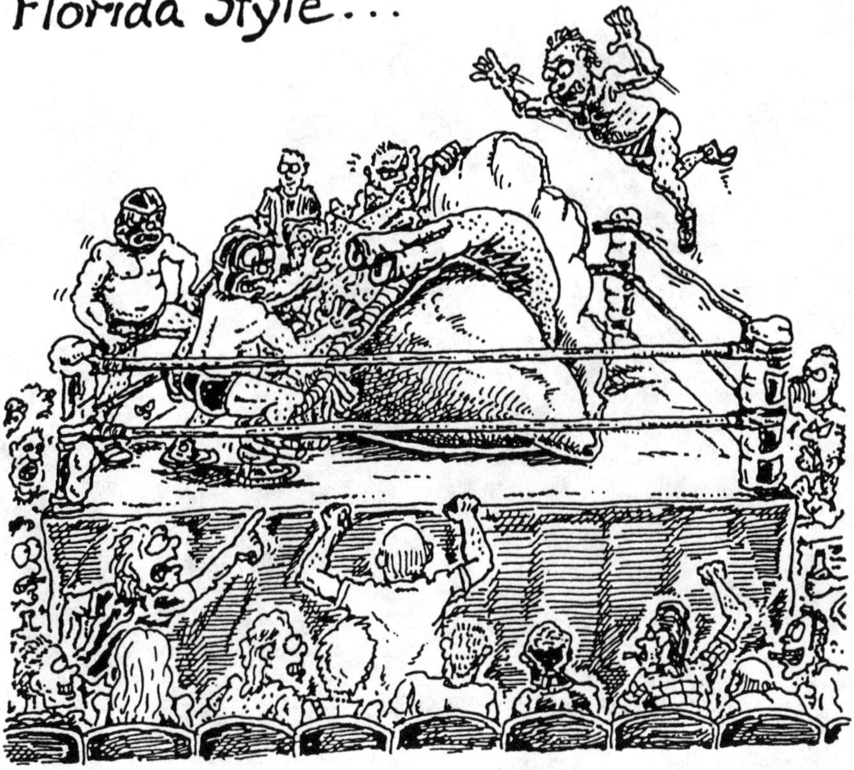

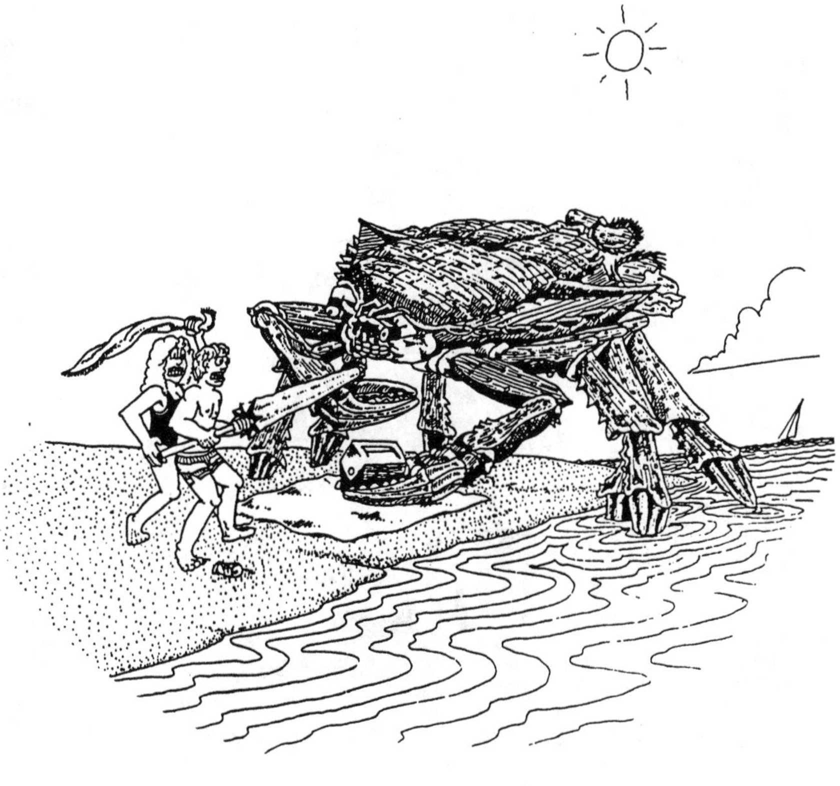

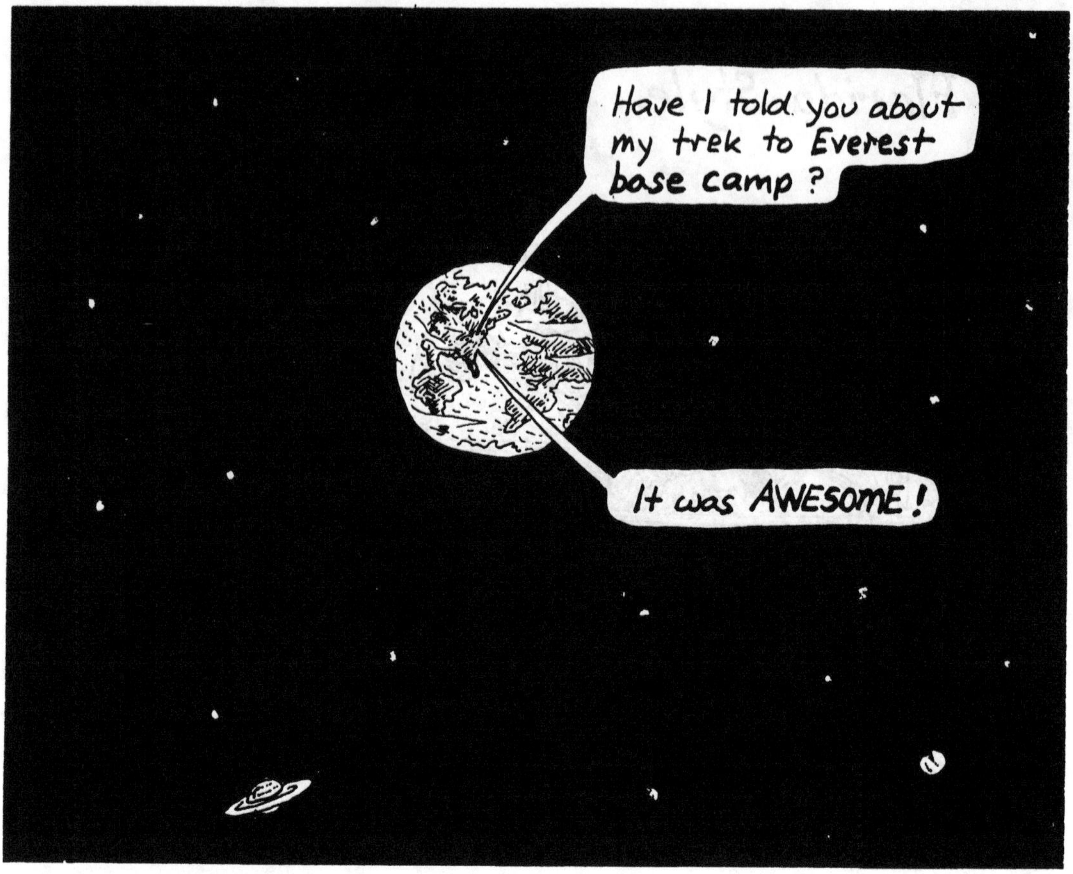
Have I told you about my trek to Everest base camp?
It was AWESOME!

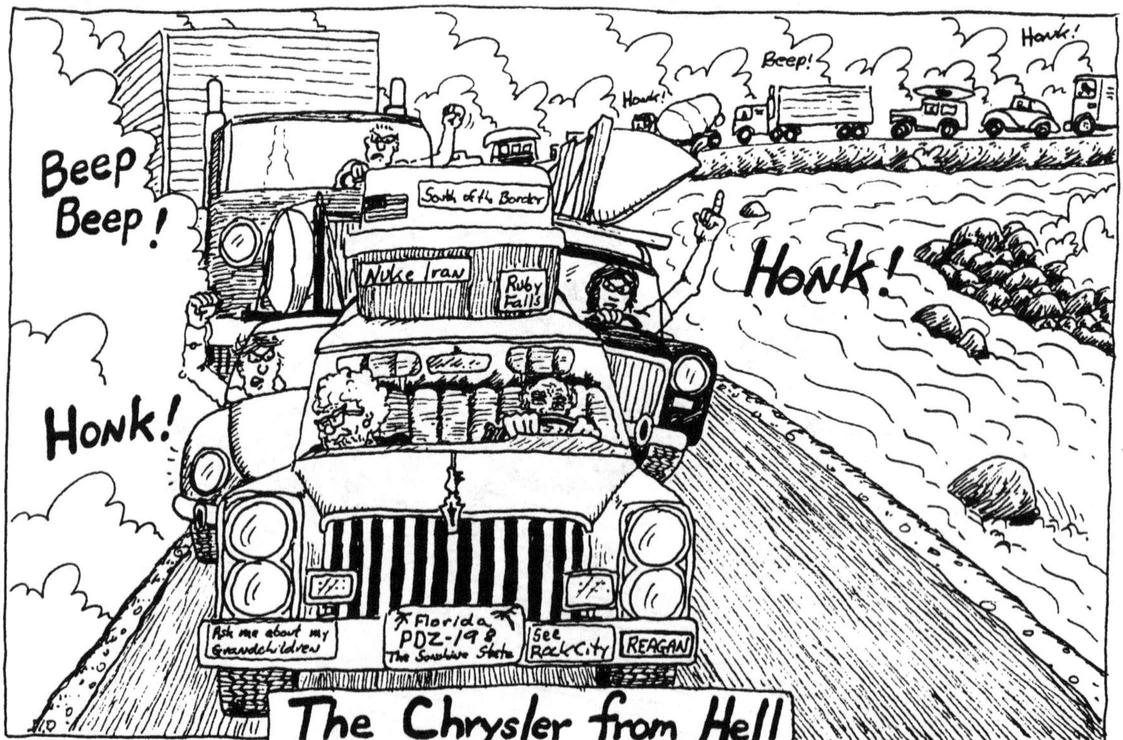
Honk!
Beep!
Honk!
Honk!
Beep Beep!
South of the Border
Nuke Iran
Ruby Falls
HONK!
Honk!
Ask me about my Grandchildren
Florida PDZ-198 The Sunshine State
See Rock City
REAGAN
The Chrysler from Hell

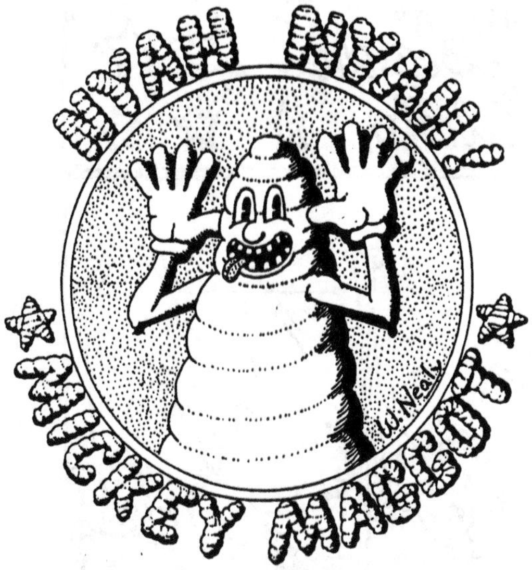
NYAH NYAH!
MICKEY MAGGOT
W. Nealy

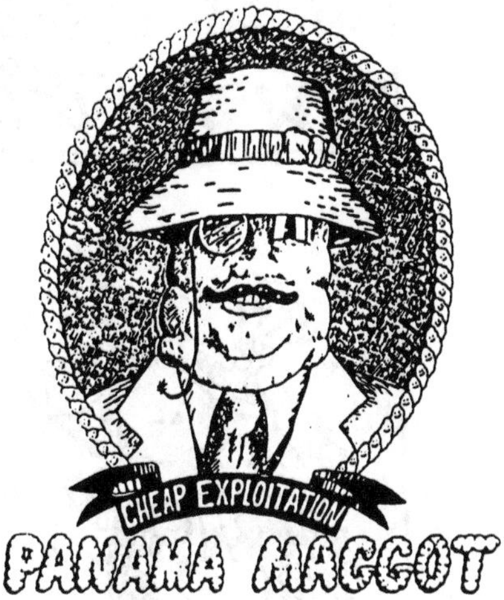
CHEAP EXPLOITATION
PANAMA MAGGOT

Welcome To LarvaLand

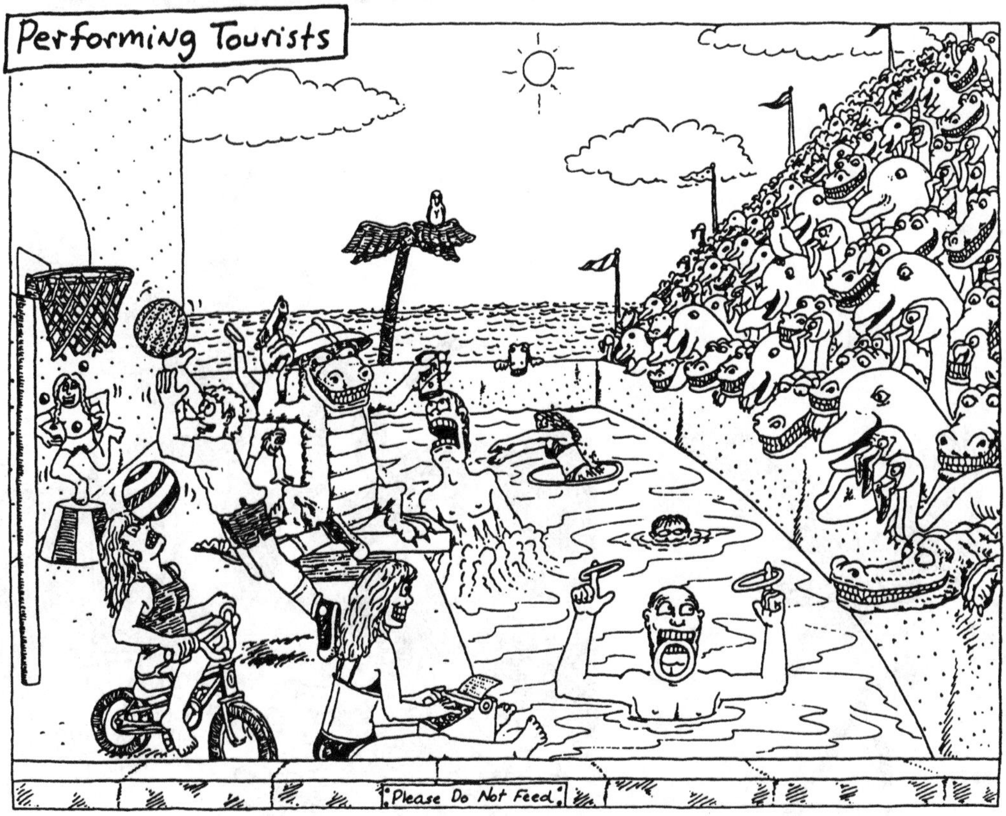
Performing Tourists
Please Do Not Feed

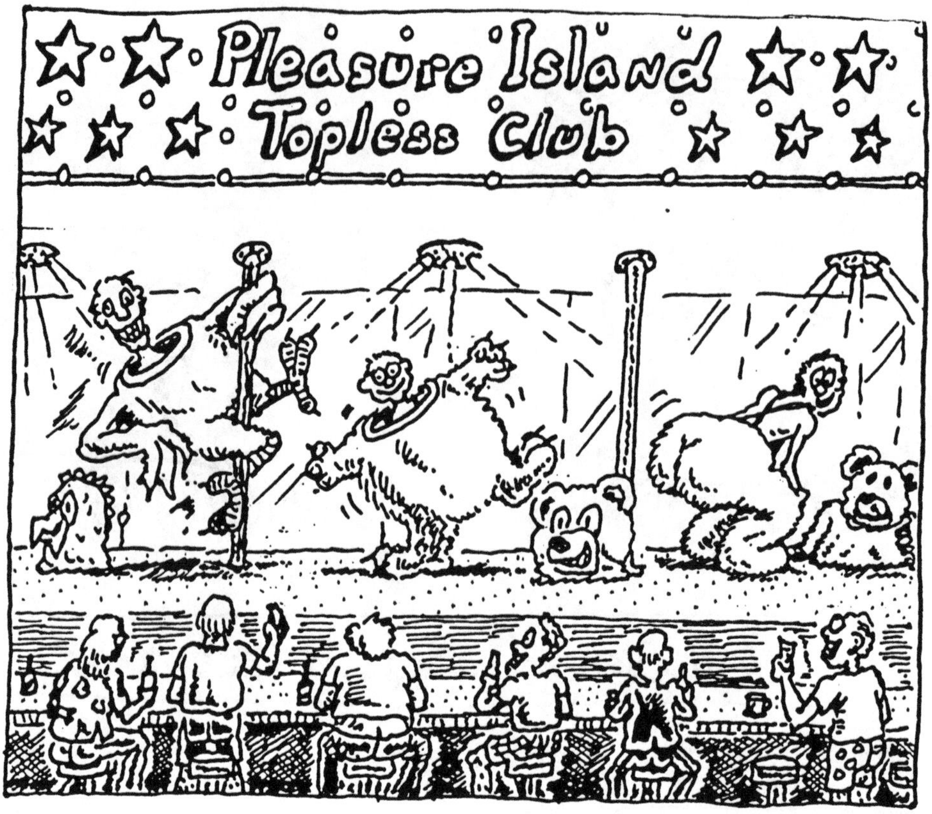
Pleasure Island
Topless Club

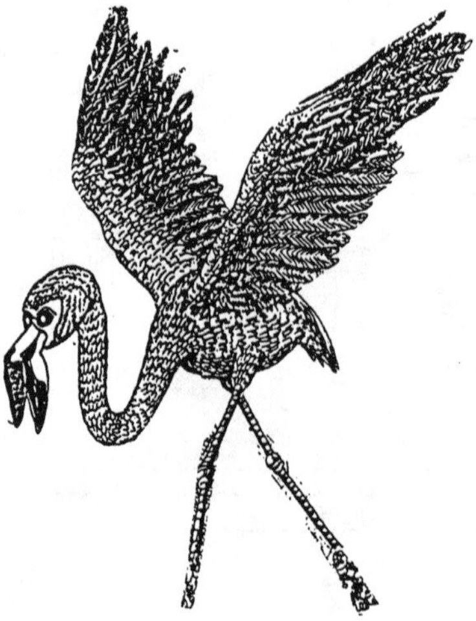

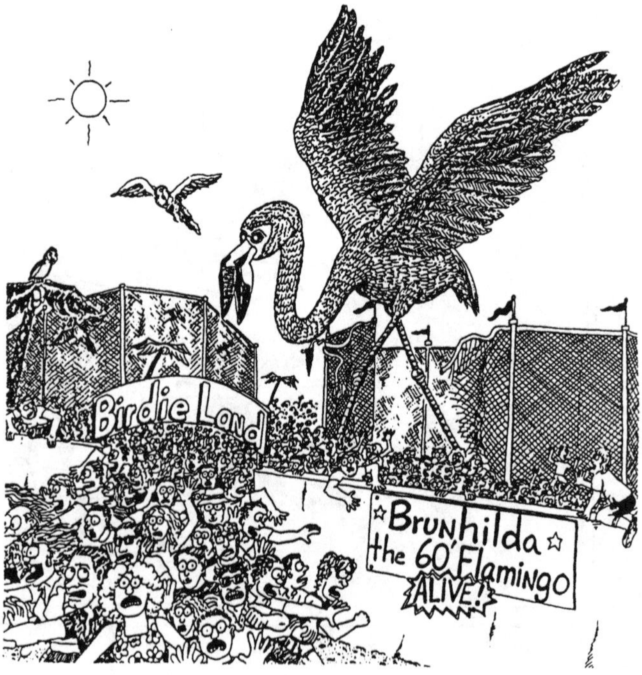
Birdie Land
Brunhilda
the 60' Flamingo
ALIVE!

Whips and Chains

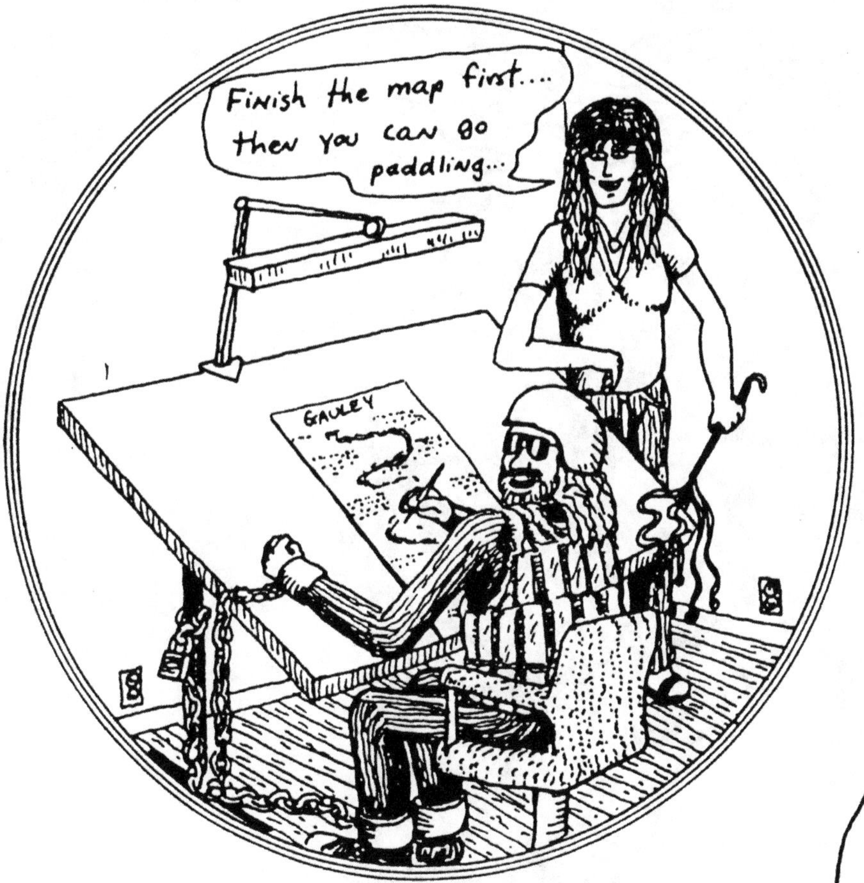
Finish the map first....
then you can go
paddling...
GAULEY

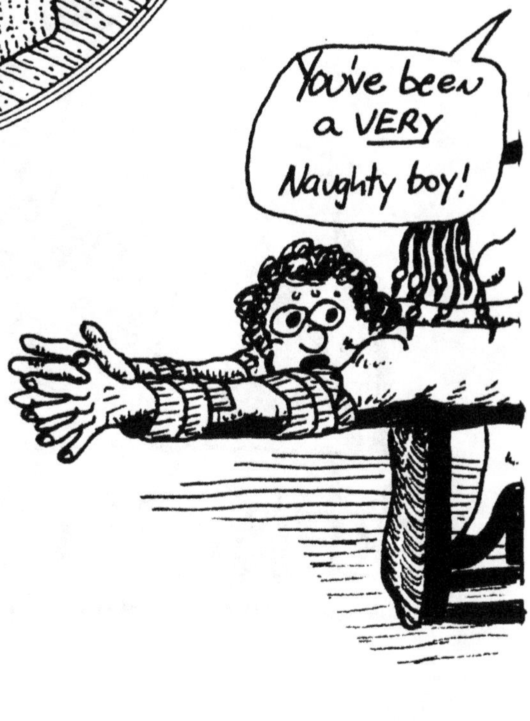
You've been
a VERY
Naughty boy!

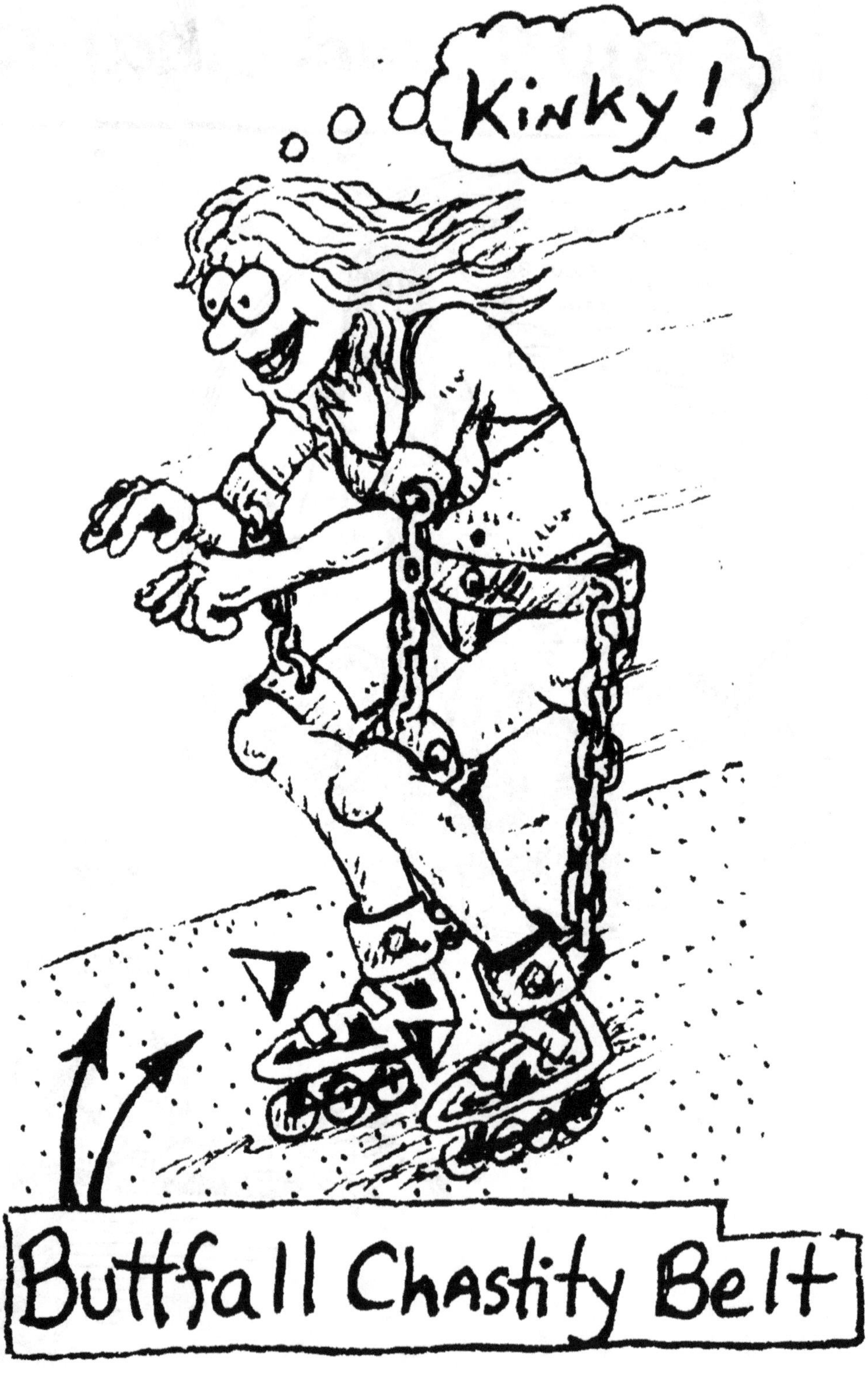
Kinky!
Buttfall Chastity Belt

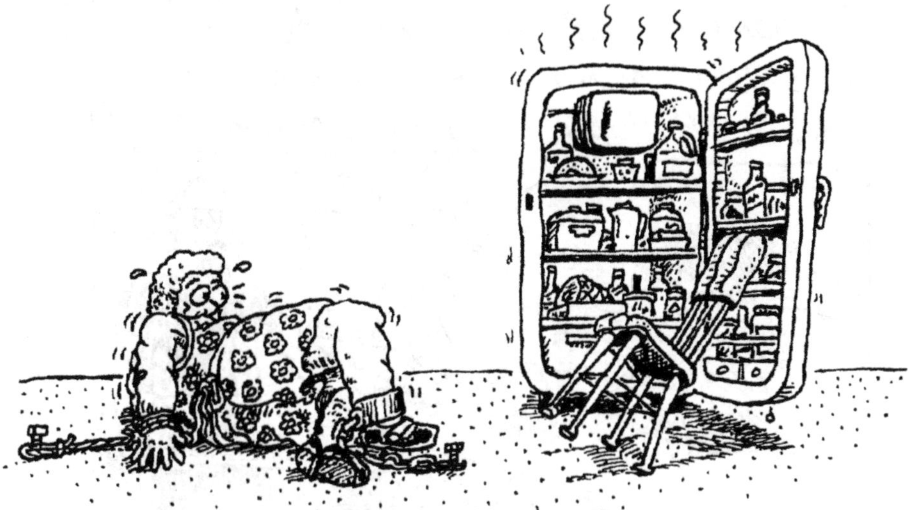

Mom Torture

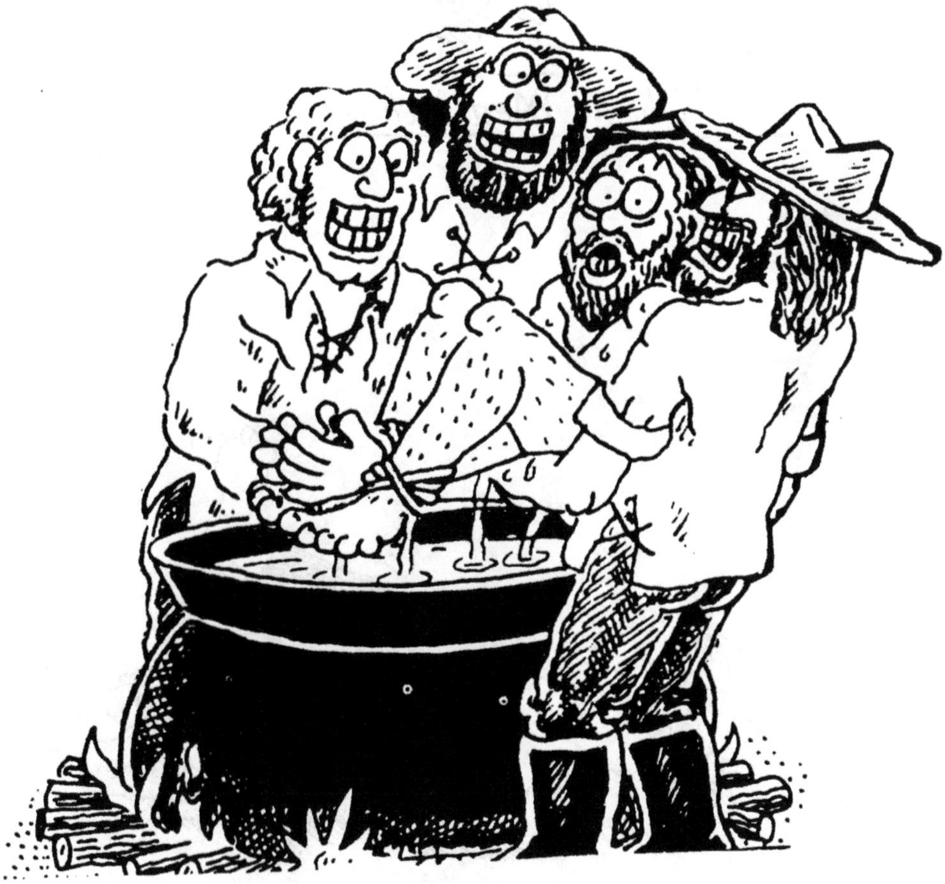

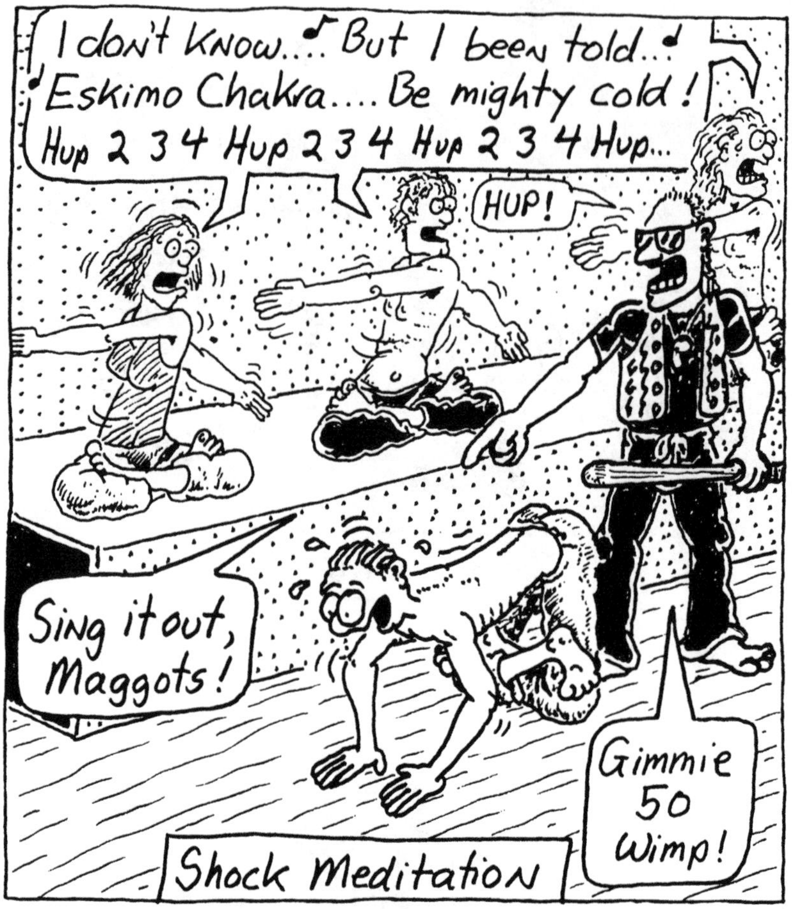
I don't know... But I been told...
Eskimo Chakra.... Be mighty cold!
Hup 2 3 4 Hup 2 3 4 Hup 2 3 4 Hup...
HUP!
Sing it out, Maggots!
Gimmie 50 Wimp!
Shock Meditation

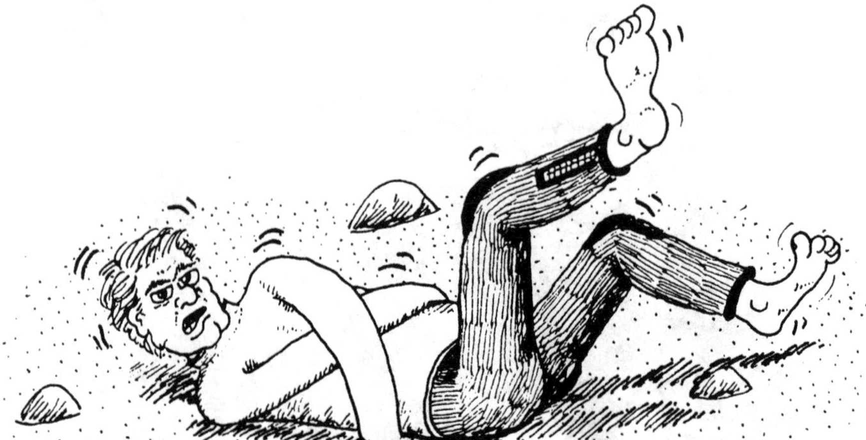

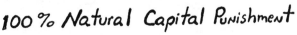

Shock Collars For Kids

100% Natural Capital Punishment

Politics As Usual

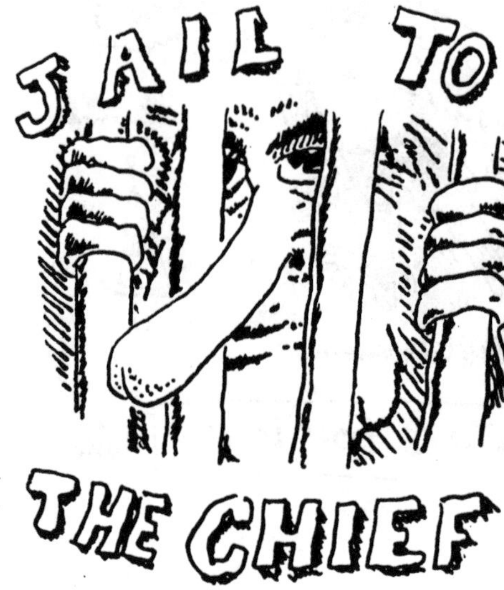
JAIL TO
THE CHIEF

Watergate T-Shirt Design 1972

Three Mile Island 1979

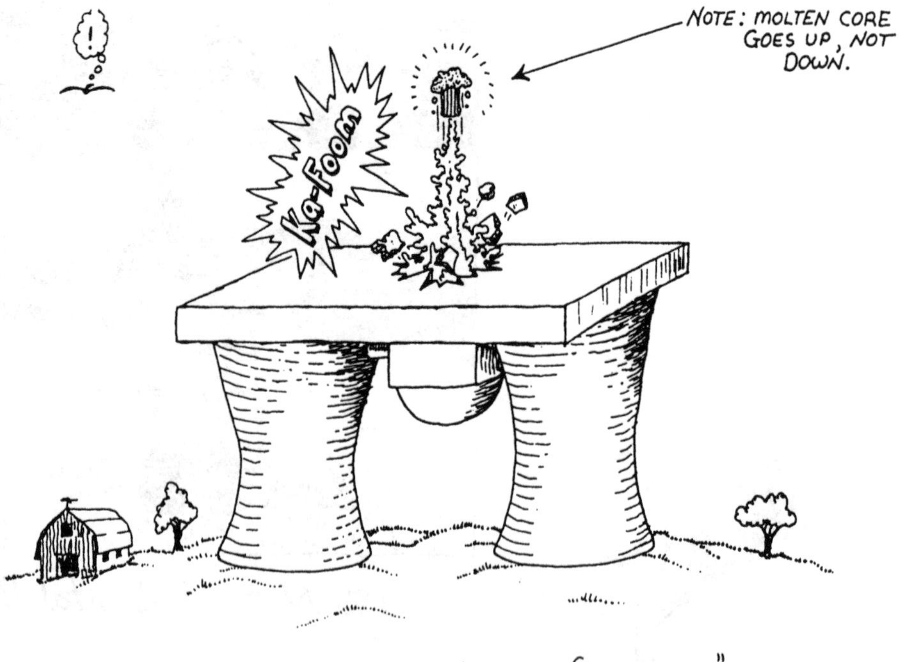
!
Ka-Foom
NOTE: MOLTEN CORE GOES UP, NOT DOWN.

Solution to dreaded "China Syndrome"... build reactors upside-down.

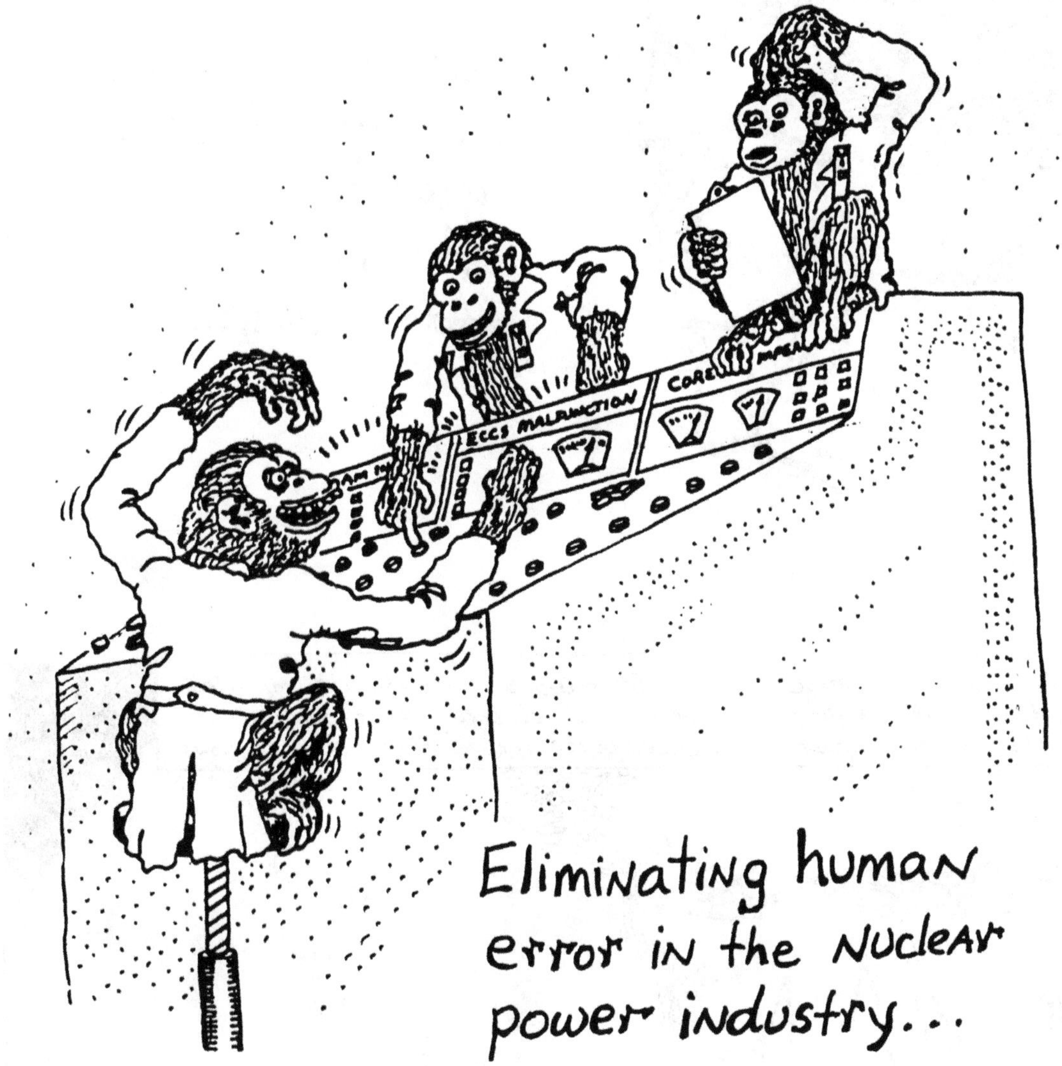
ECCS MALFUNCTION
CORE

Eliminating human error in the nuclear power industry...

Cartoonists owe a huge debt of gratitude to the Reagan Administration!

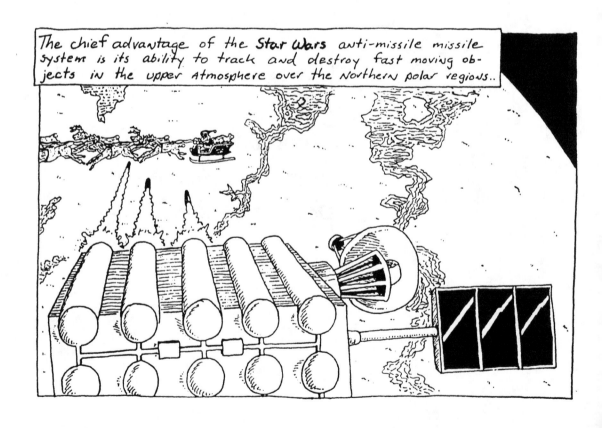

The chief advantage of the **Star Wars** anti-missile missile system is its ability to track and destroy fast moving objects in the upper Atmosphere over the Northern polar regions..

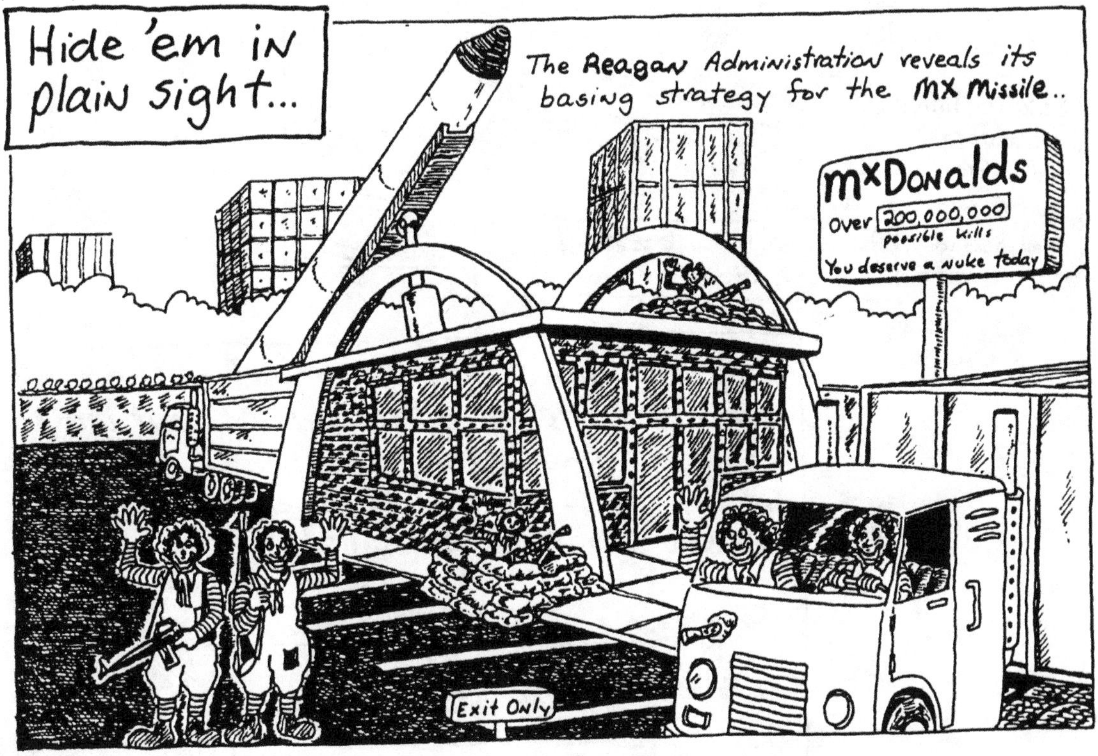
Hide 'em in plain sight...
The Reagan Administration reveals its basing strategy for the MX Missile..
mxDonalds
Over 200,000,000 possible kills
You deserve a nuke today
Exit Only

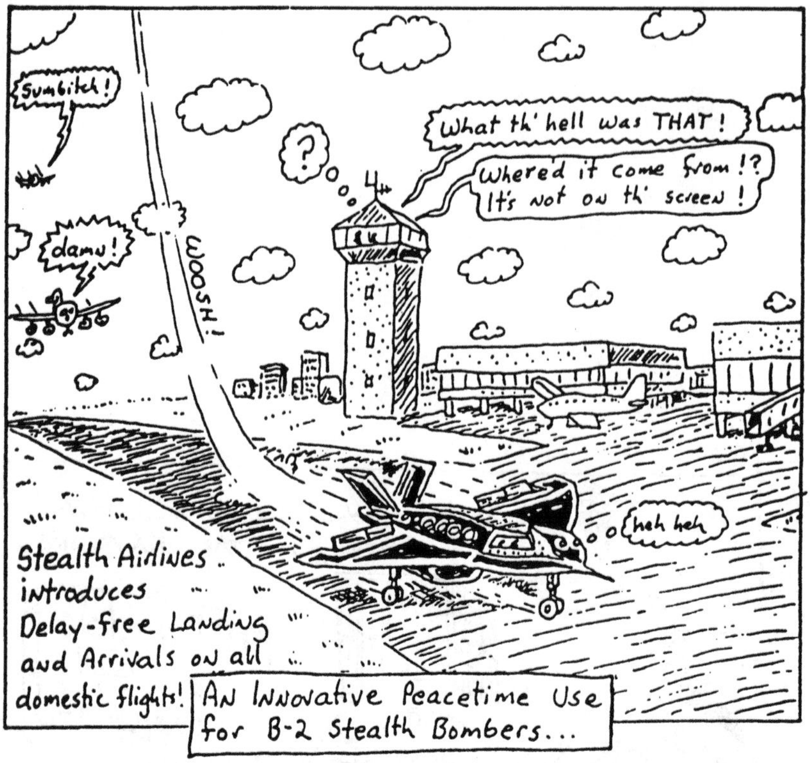
Sumbitch!
damn!
WOOSH!
?
What th' hell was THAT!
Where'd it come from!? It's not on th' screen!
heh heh
Stealth Airlines introduces Delay-free Landing and Arrivals on all domestic flights!
An Innovative Peacetime Use for B-2 Stealth Bombers...

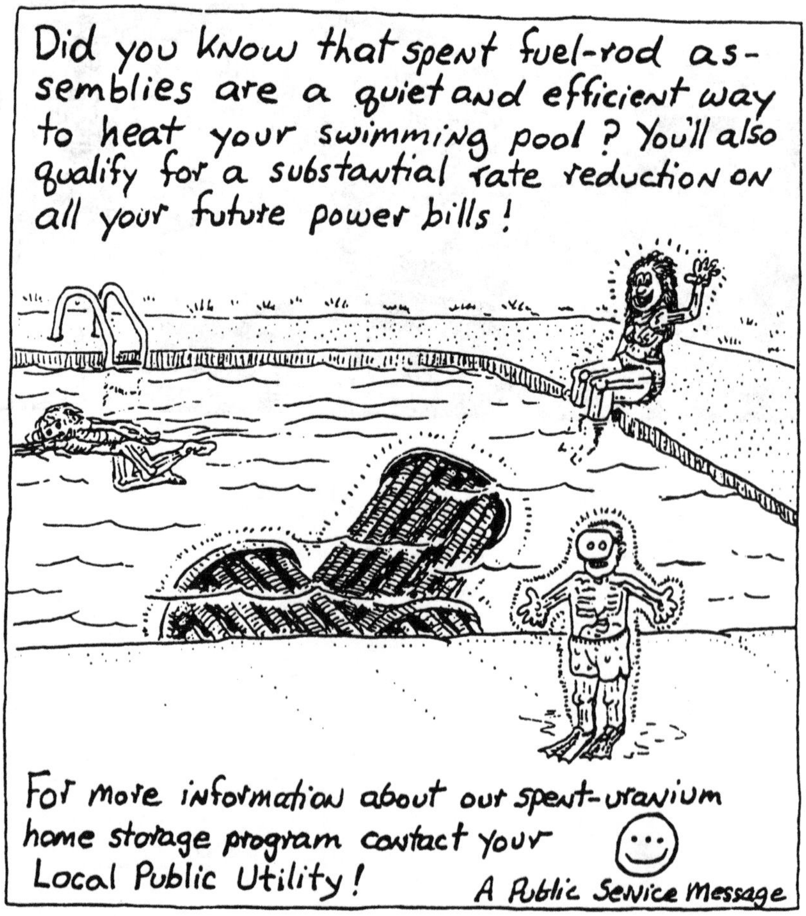
Did you know that spent fuel-rod assemblies are a quiet and efficient way to heat your swimming pool? You'll also qualify for a substantial rate reduction on all your future power bills!
For more information about our spent-uranium home storage program contact your Local Public Utility!
A Public Service Message

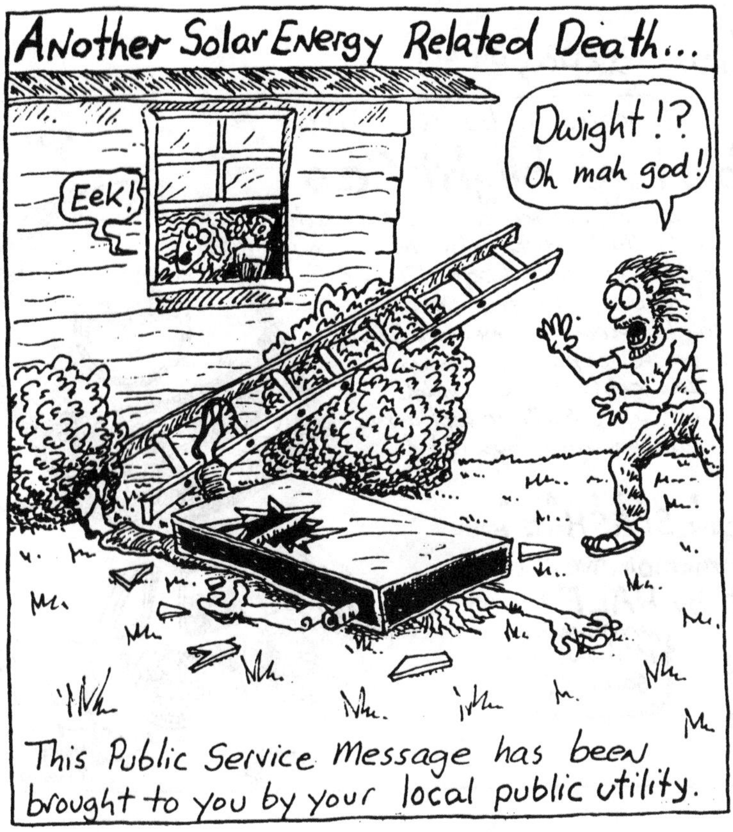
Another Solar Energy Related Death...
Eek!
Dwight!? Oh mah god!
This Public Service Message has been brought to you by your local public utility.

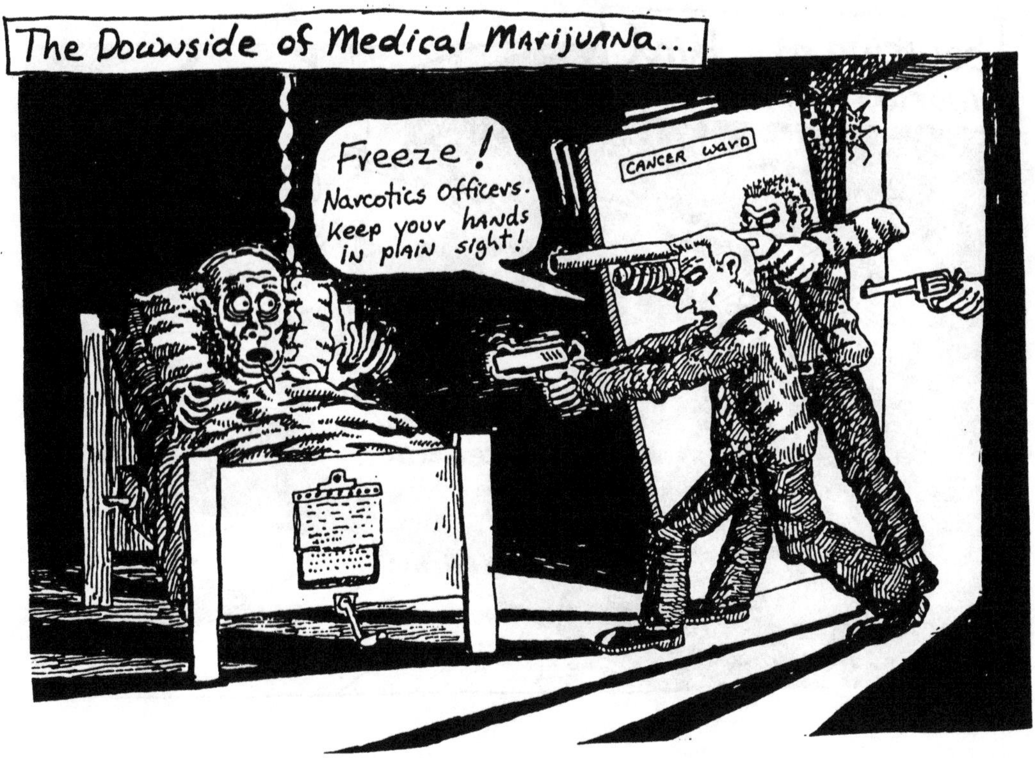
The Downside of Medical Marijuana...
Freeze! Narcotics officers. Keep your hands in plain sight!
CANCER WARD

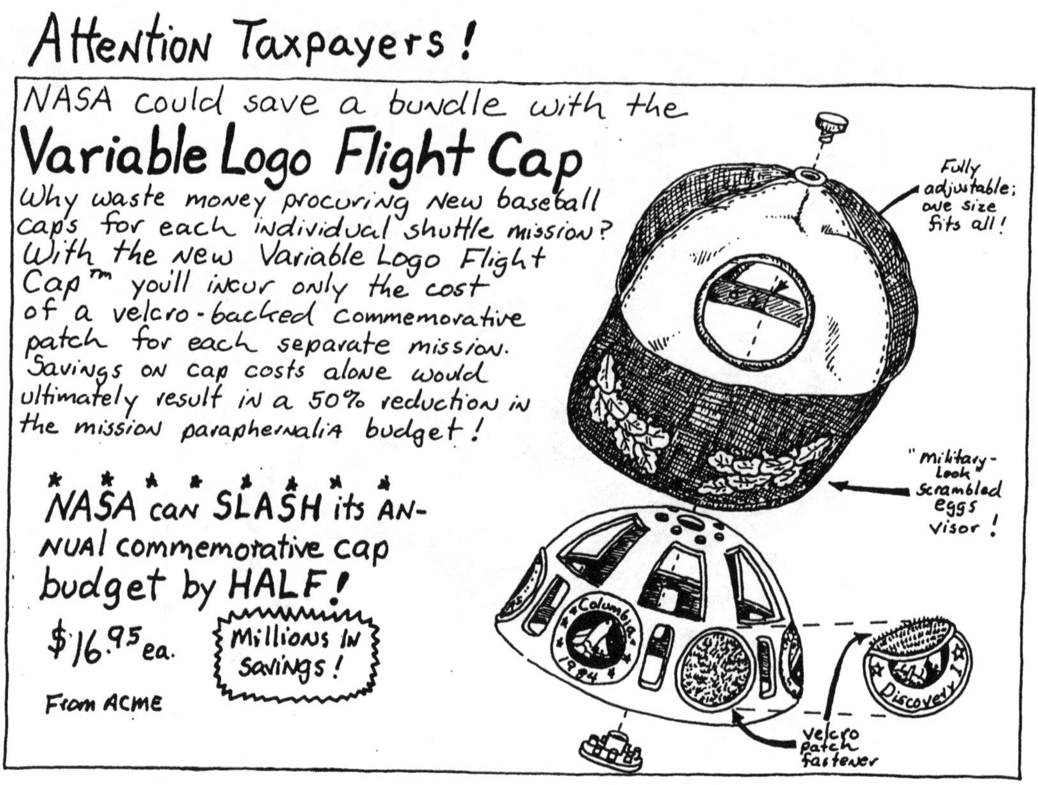
Attention Taxpayers!
NASA could save a bundle with the
Variable Logo Flight Cap
Why waste money procuring new baseball caps for each individual shuttle mission? With the new Variable Logo Flight Cap™ you'll incur only the cost of a velcro-backed commemorative patch for each separate mission. Savings on cap costs alone would ultimately result in a 50% reduction in the mission paraphernalia budget!
NASA can SLASH its ANNUAL commemorative cap budget by HALF!
$16.95 ea.
Millions in savings!
From ACME
Fully adjustable; one size fits all!
"Military-Look" scrambled eggs visor!
Columbia 1984
Discovery
Velcro patch fastener

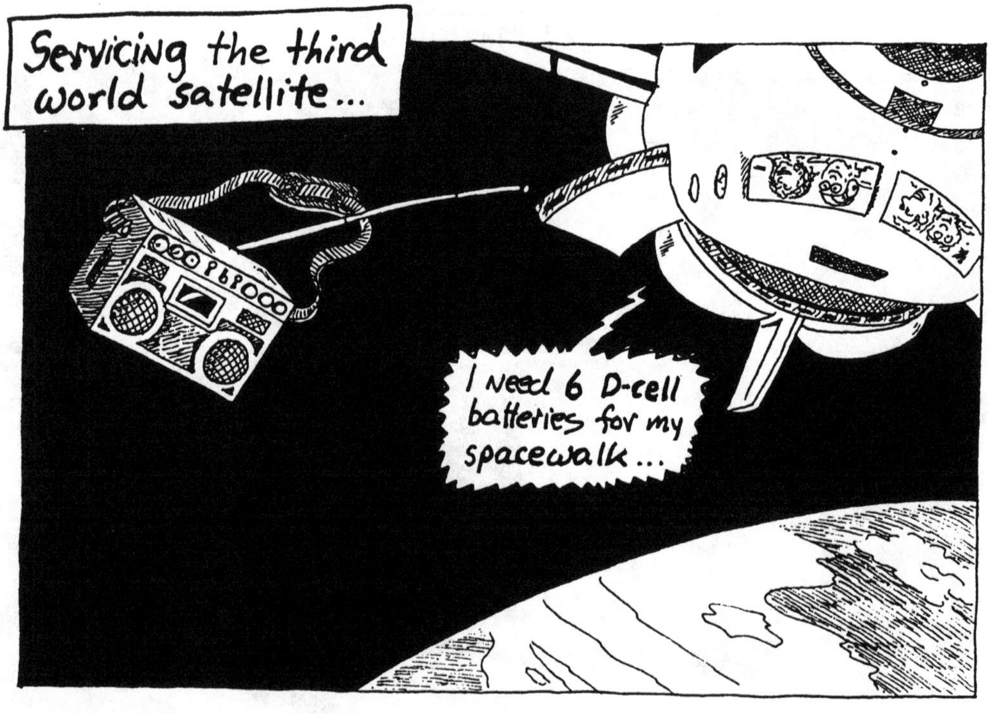
Servicing the third world satellite...
I need 6 D-cell batteries for my spacewalk...

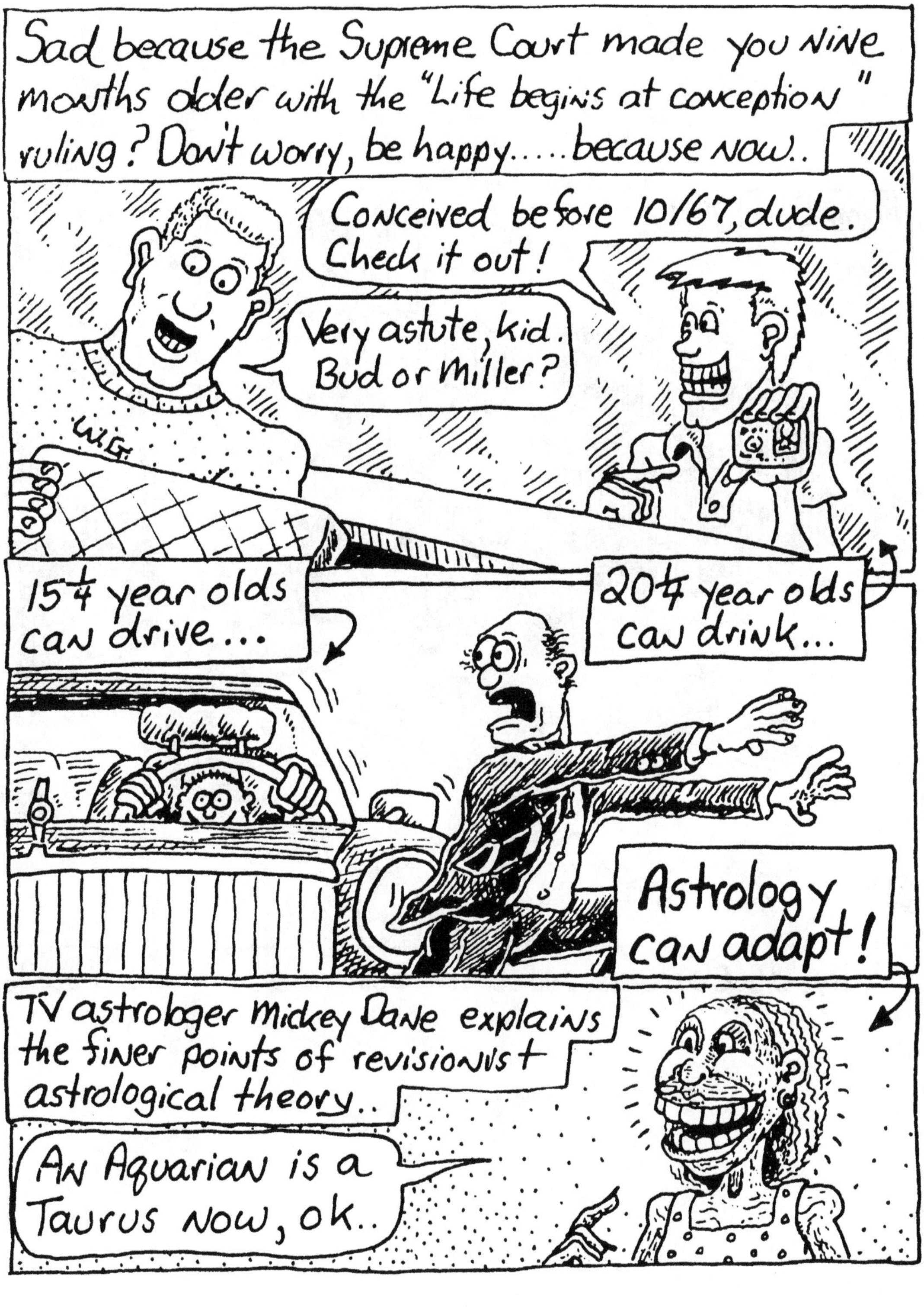
Sad because the Supreme Court made you NINE months older with the "Life begins at conception" ruling? Don't worry, be happy.....because now..
Conceived before 10/67, dude. Check it out!
Very astute, kid. Bud or Miller?
W.G.
15¼ year olds can drive...
20¼ year olds can drink...
Astrology can adapt!
TV astrologer Mickey Dane explains the finer points of revisionist astrological theory..
An Aquarian is a Taurus now, ok..

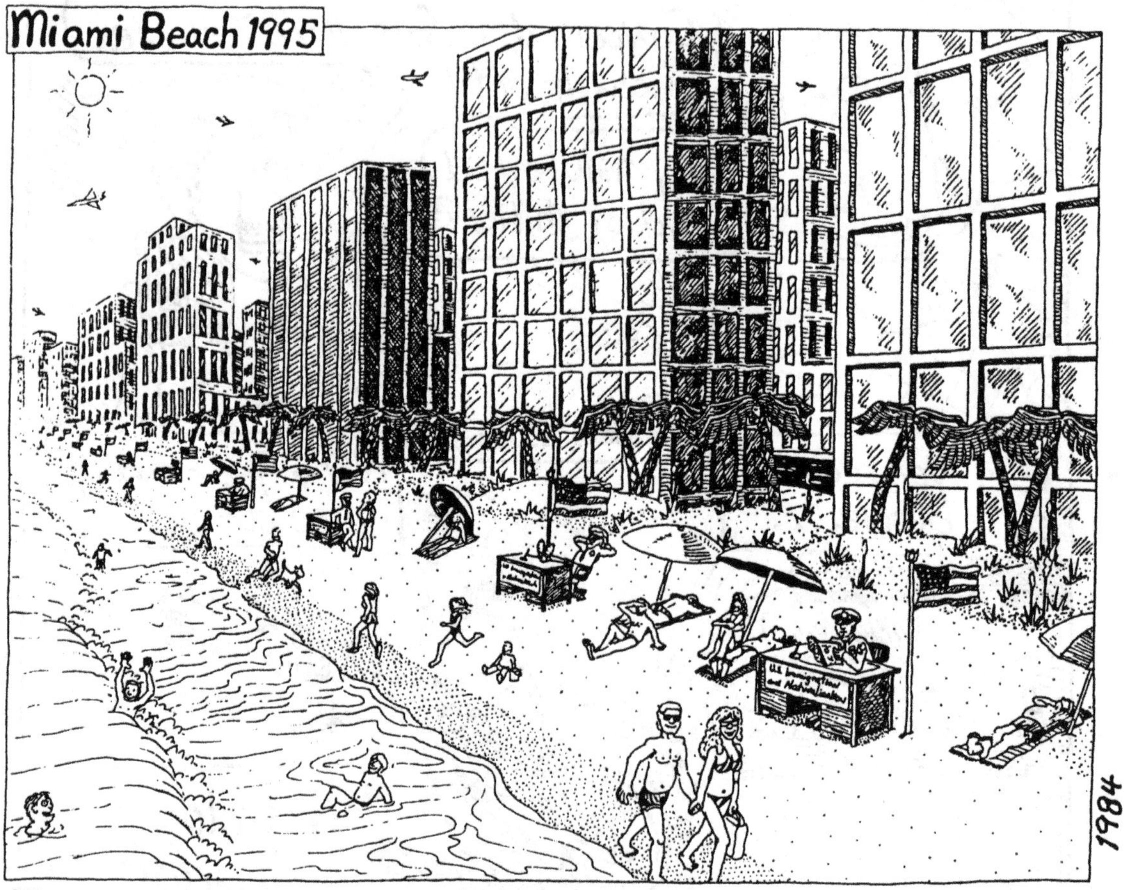
Miami Beach 1995
1984

Finally, U.S. Customs opens for business on the beach.

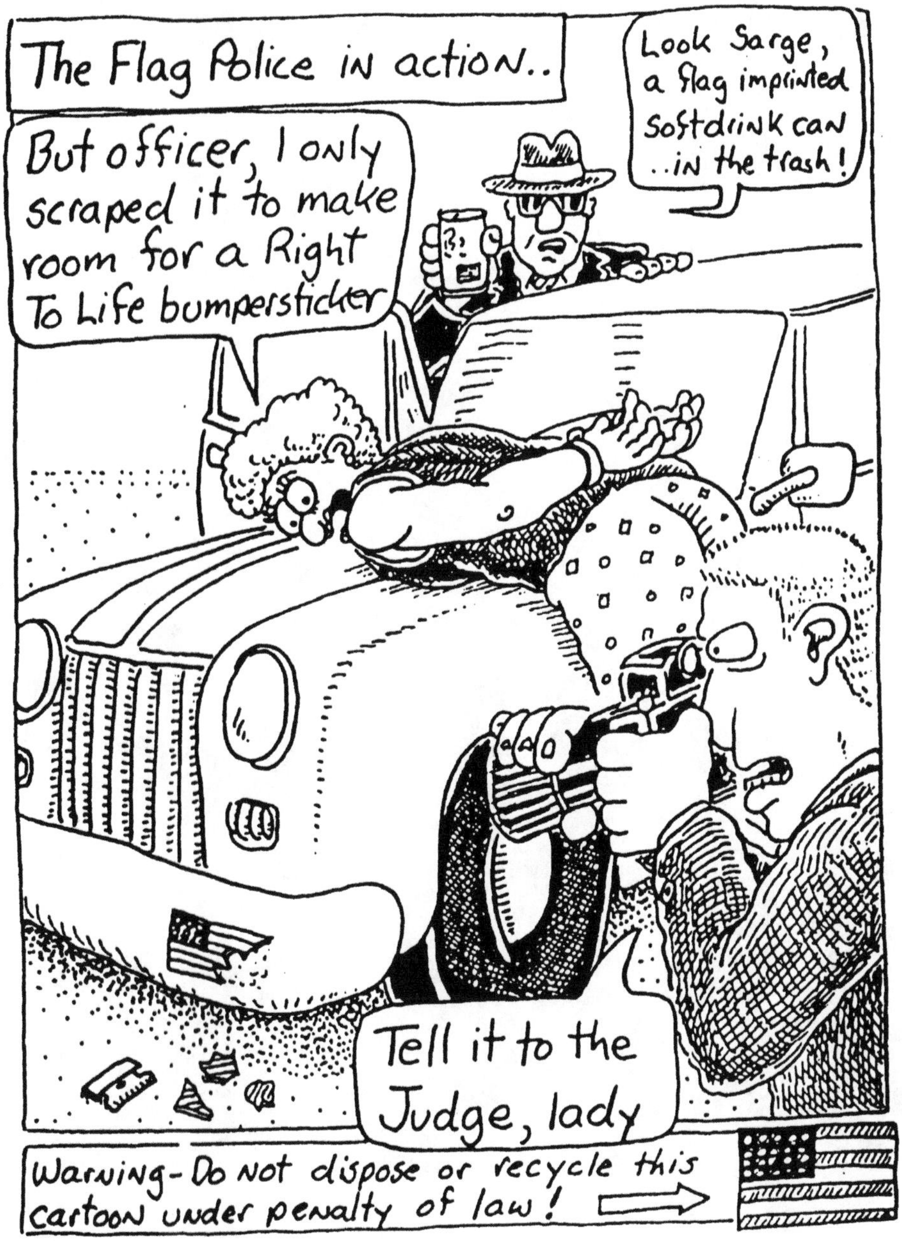
The Flag Police in action..
Look Sarge, a flag imprinted softdrink can ..in the trash!
But officer, I only scraped it to make room for a Right To Life bumpersticker
Tell it to the Judge, lady
Warning- Do not dispose or recycle this cartoon under penalty of law!

Baby, we were born to pun...

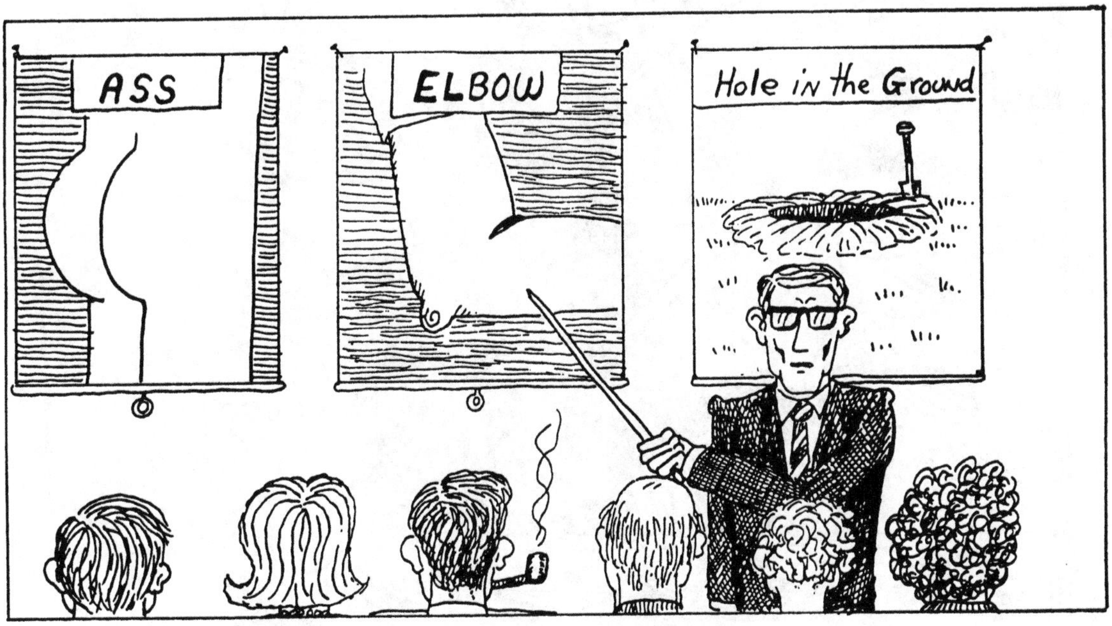

ASS
ELBOW
Hole in the Ground

Word Play

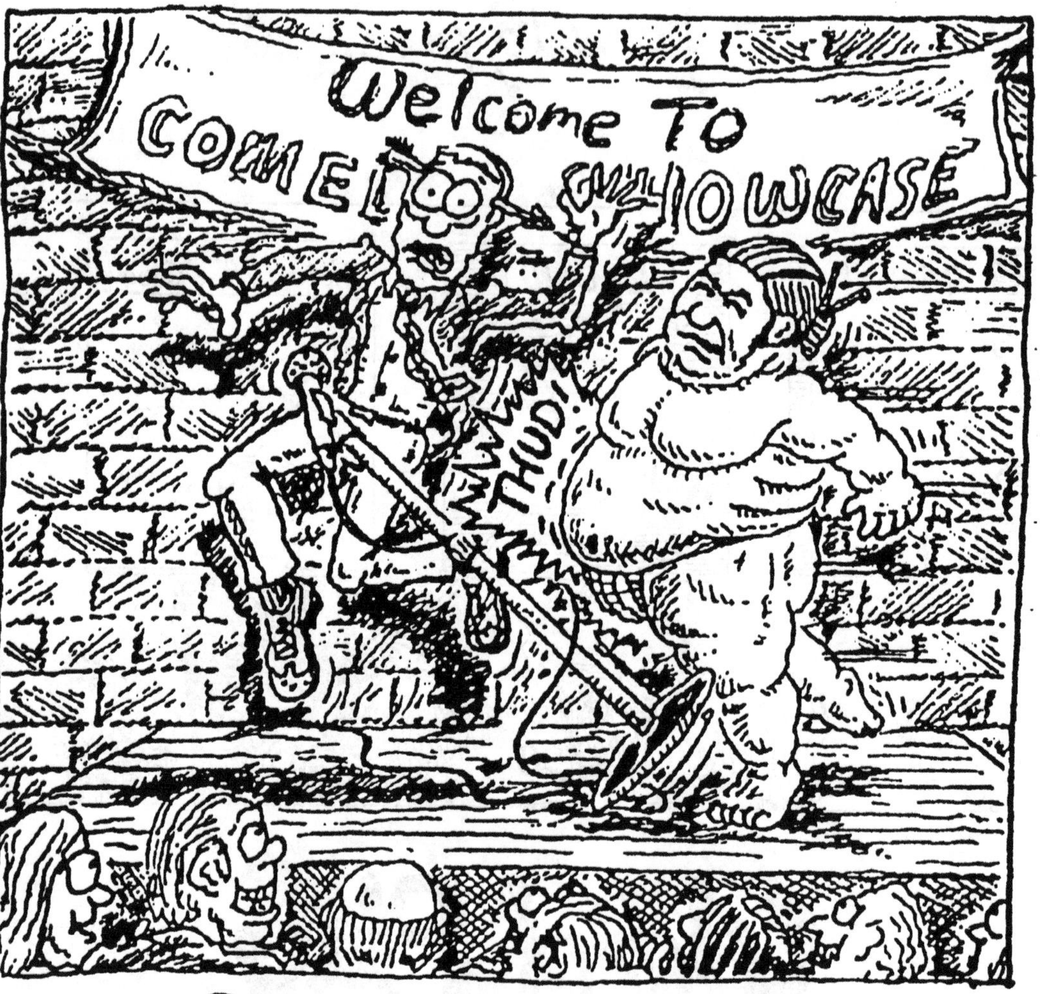
Welcome To
COMEDY SHOWCASE
THUD!

Sumo Heckler

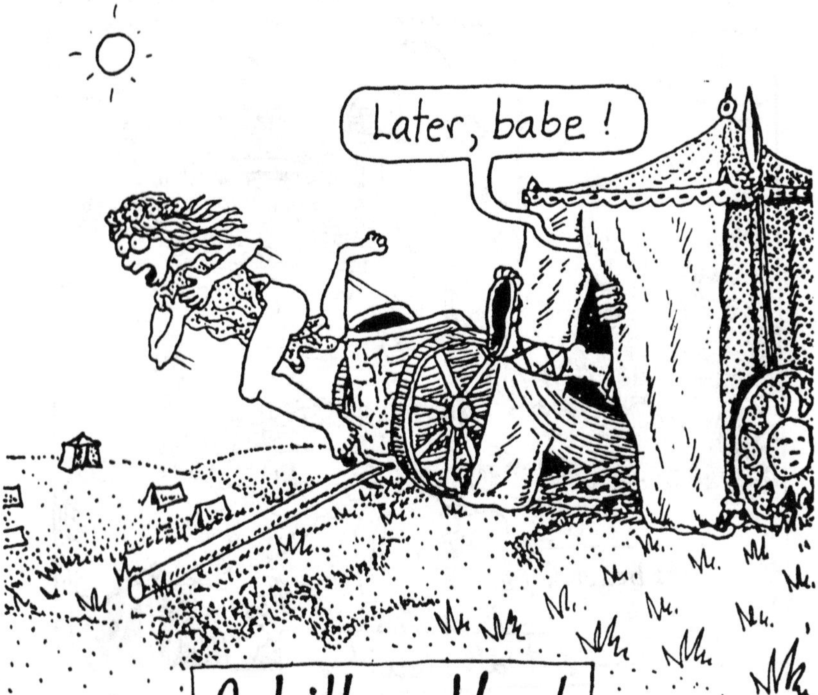
Later, babe!

Achilles, Heel

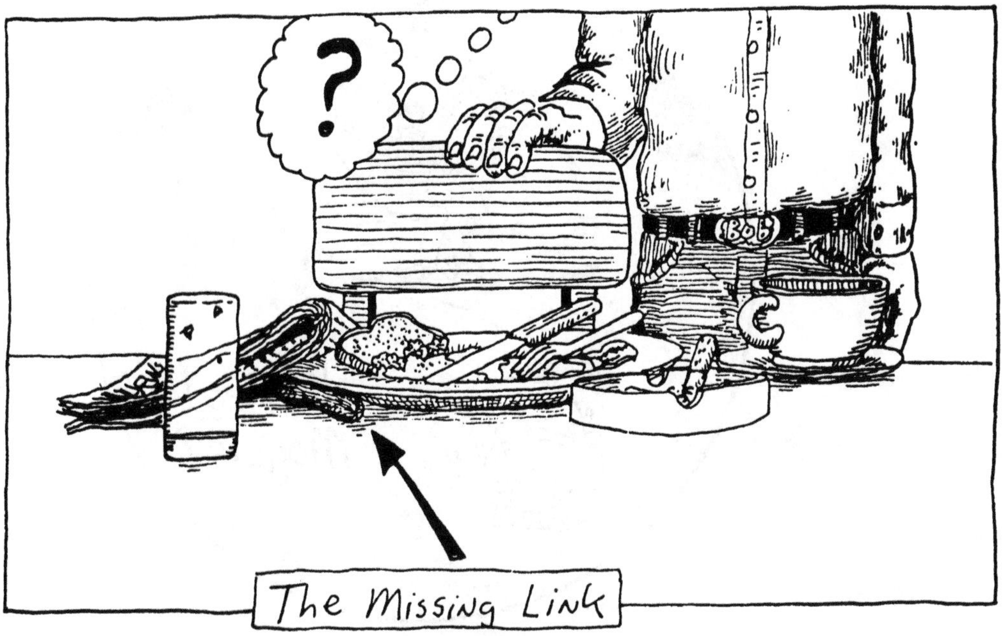
?

The Missing Link

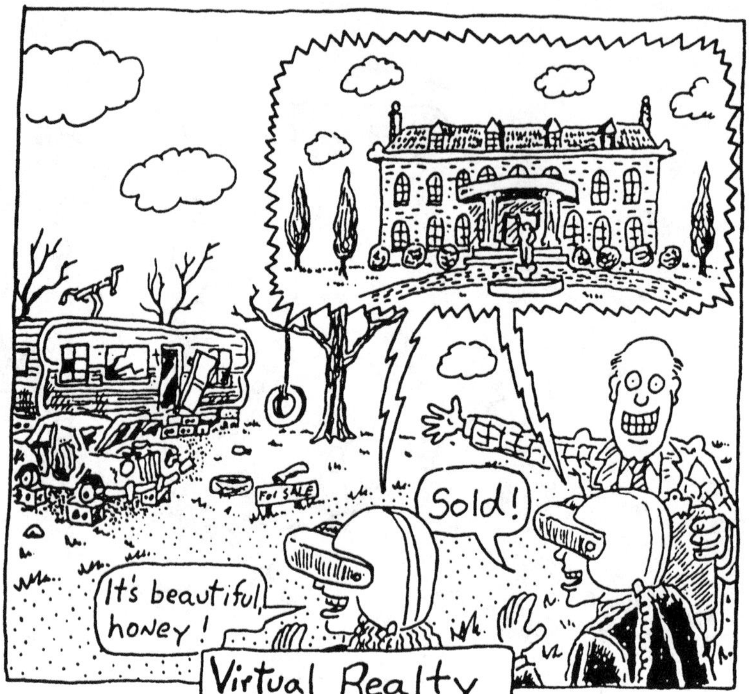
For SALE
Sold!
It's beautiful, honey!

Virtual Realty

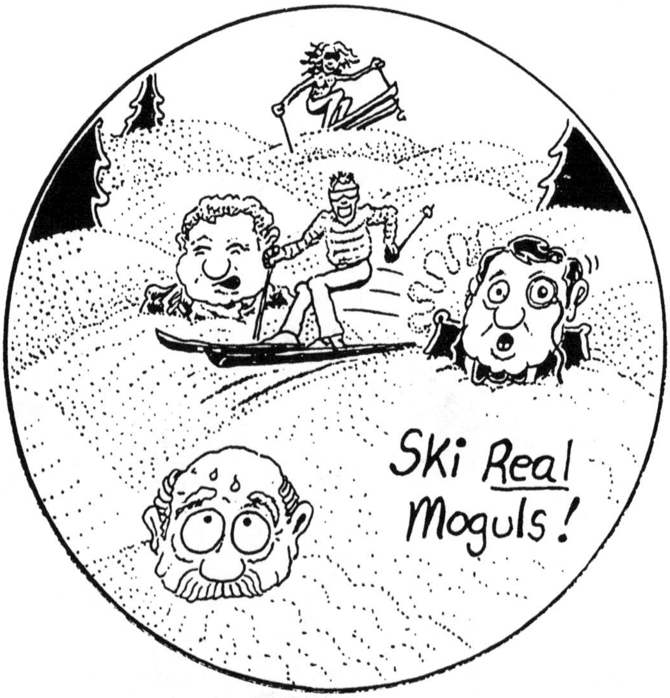
Ski Real Moguls!

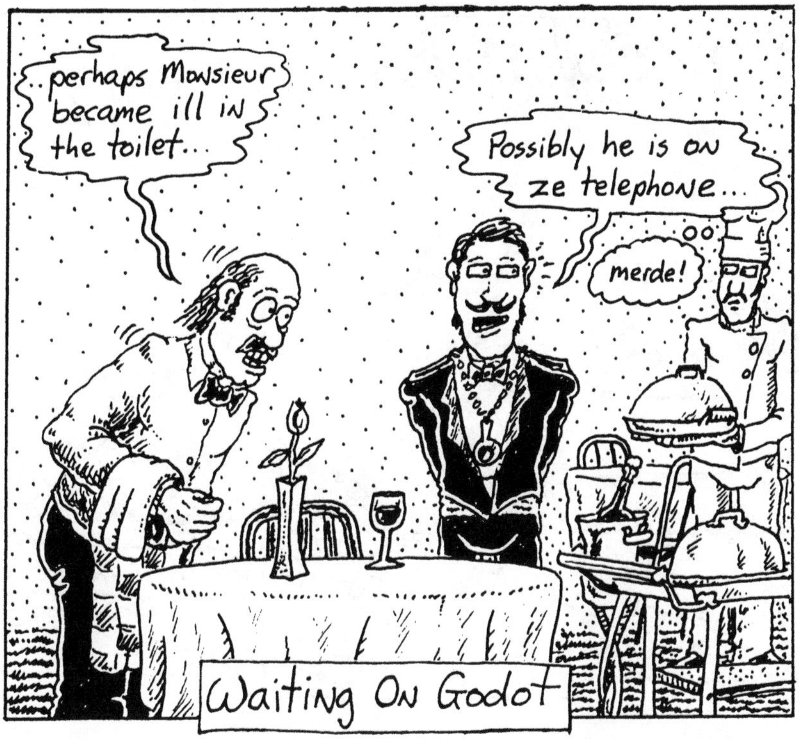
...perhaps Monsieur became ill in the toilet...
Possibly he is on ze telephone...
merde!
Waiting On Godot

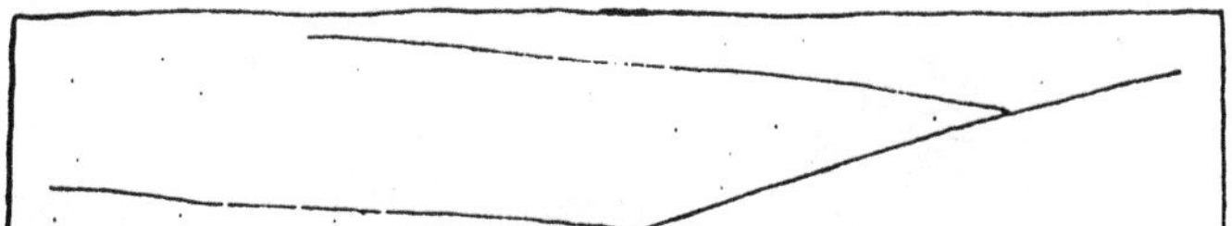
Grain Elevator

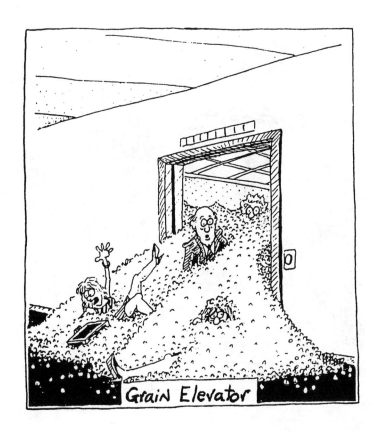

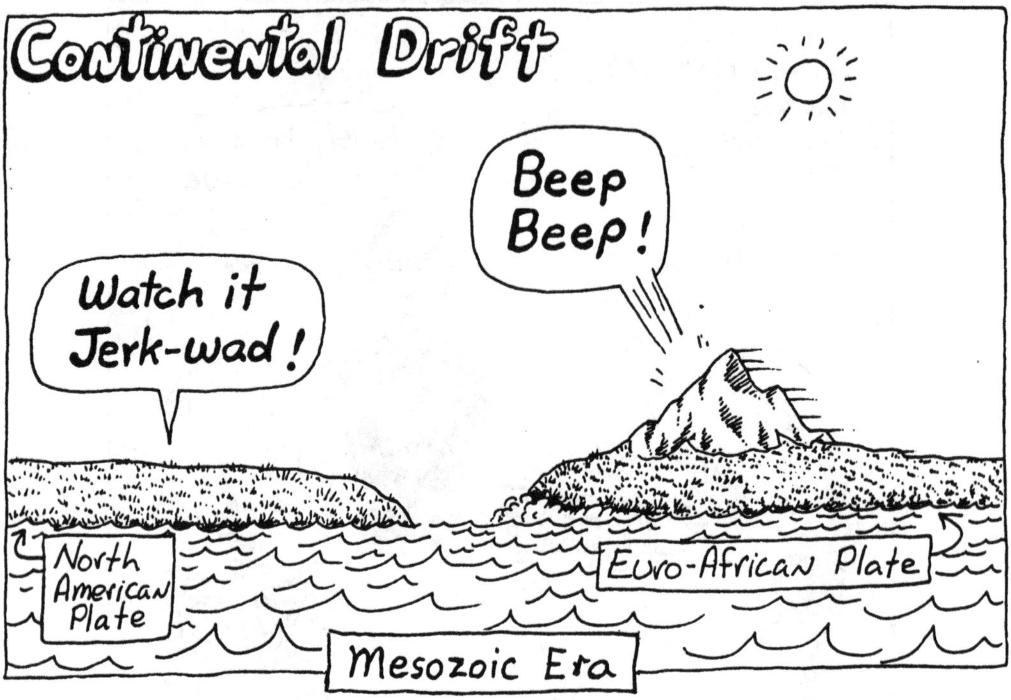

Continental Drift
Beep Beep!
Watch it Jerk-wad!
North American Plate
Euro-African Plate
Mesozoic Era

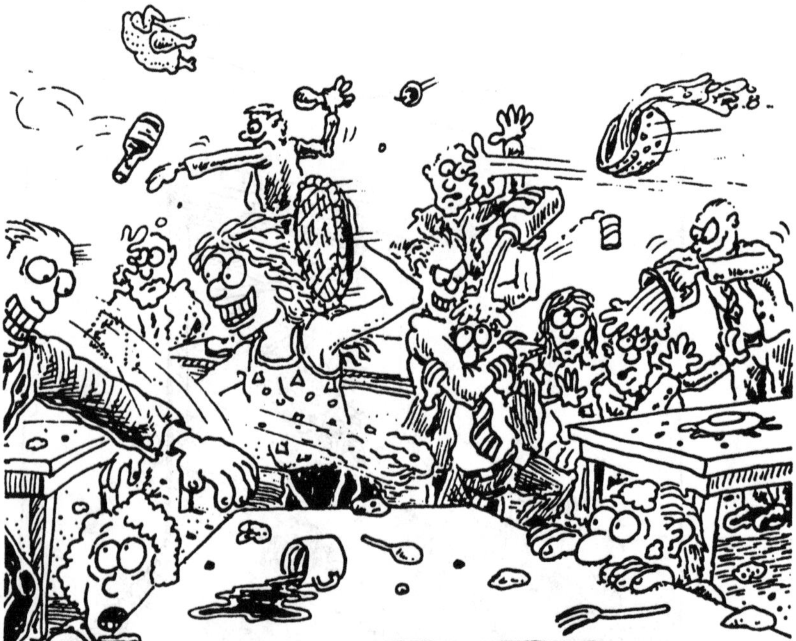

Mass Eating Disorder

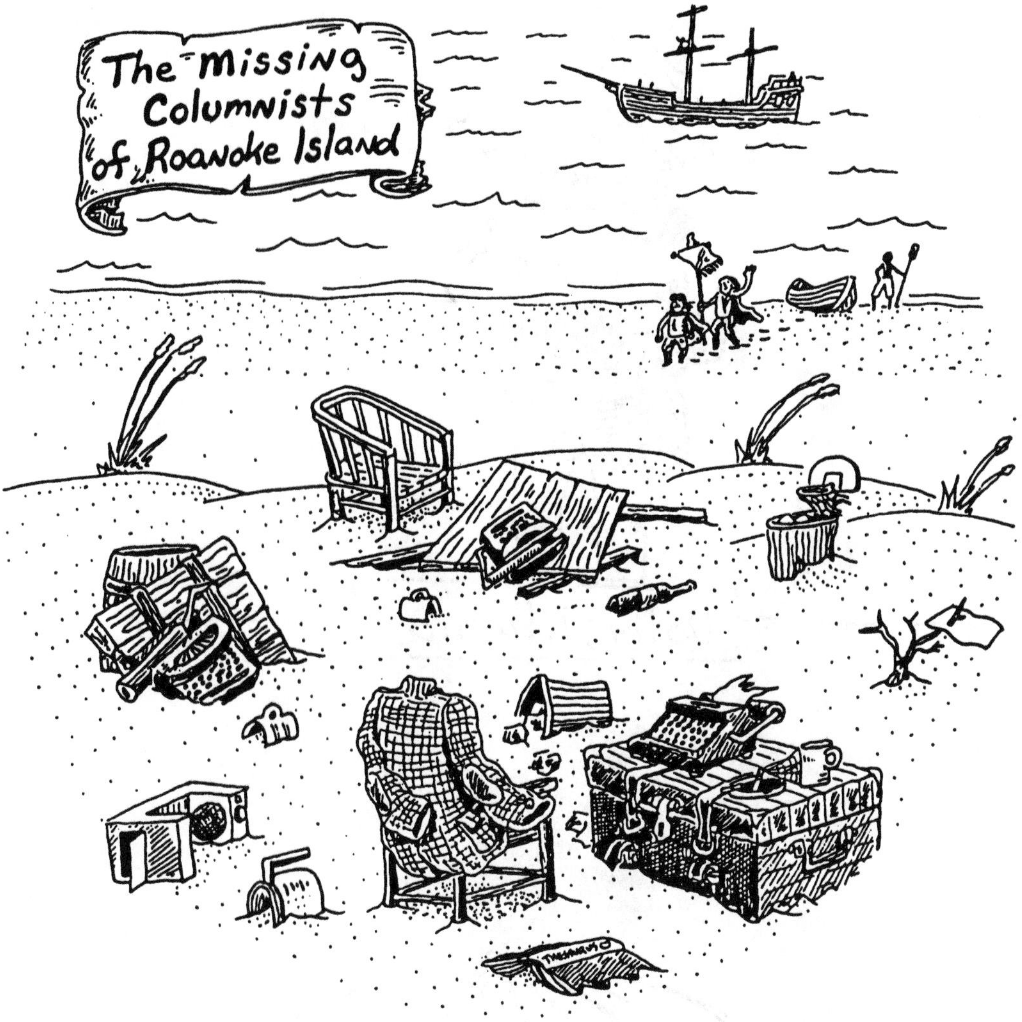
The missing Columnists of Roanoke Island

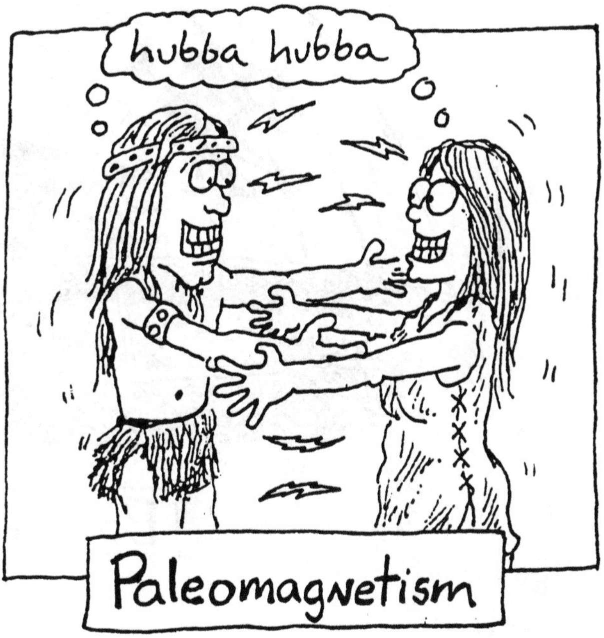
hubba hubba
Paleomagnetism

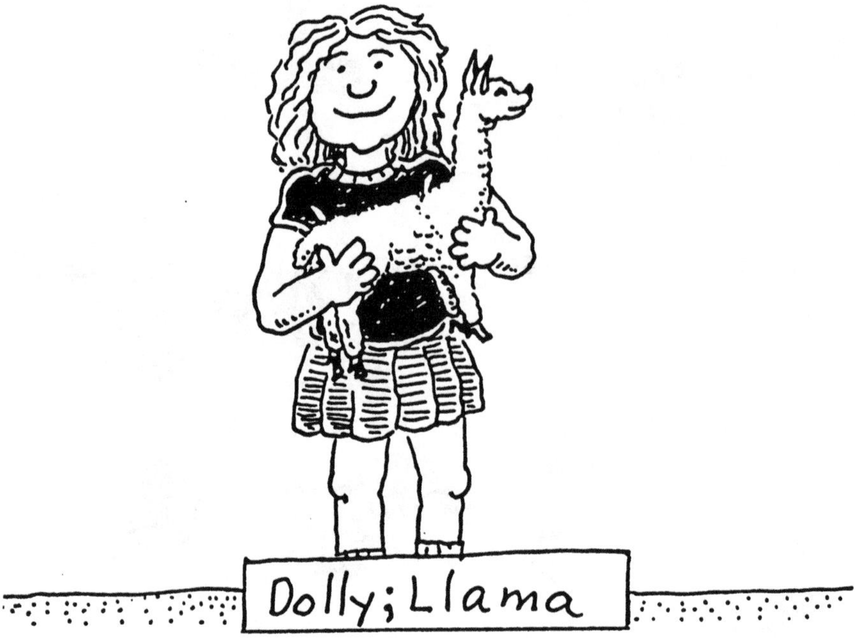
Dolly; Llama

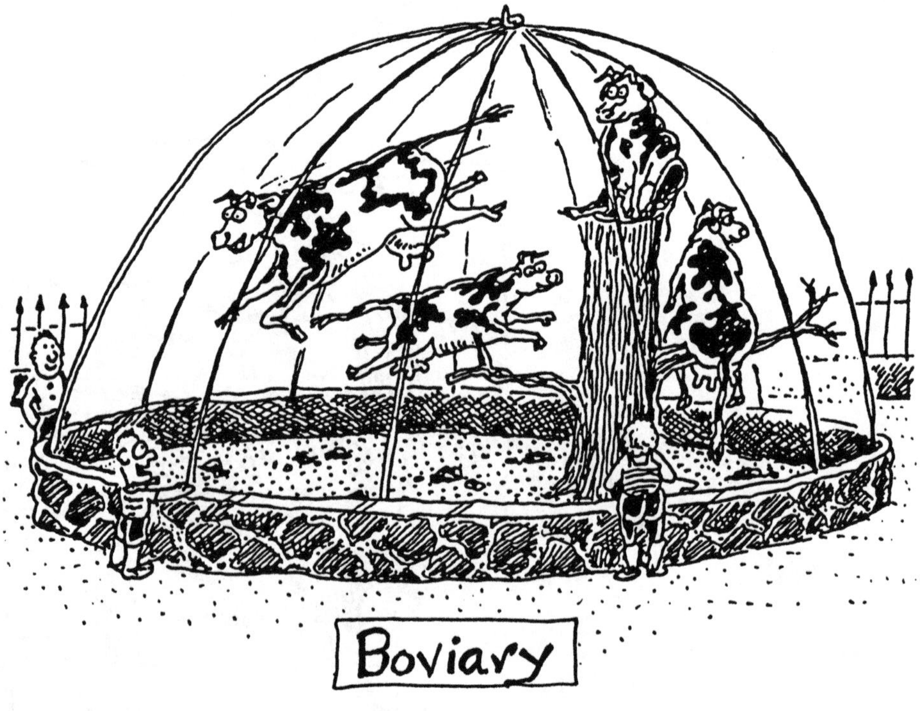
Boviary

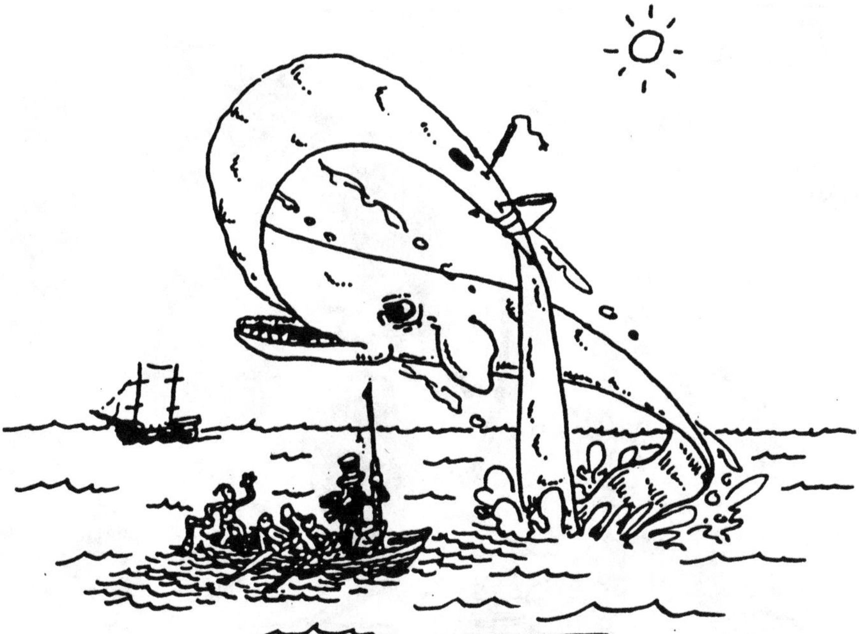

Möbius Dick

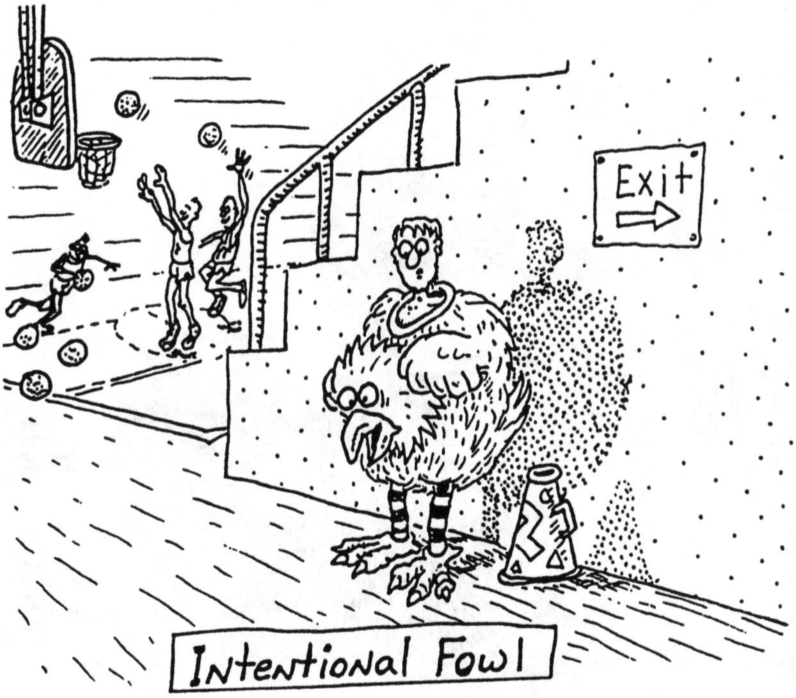
Exit

Intentional Fowl

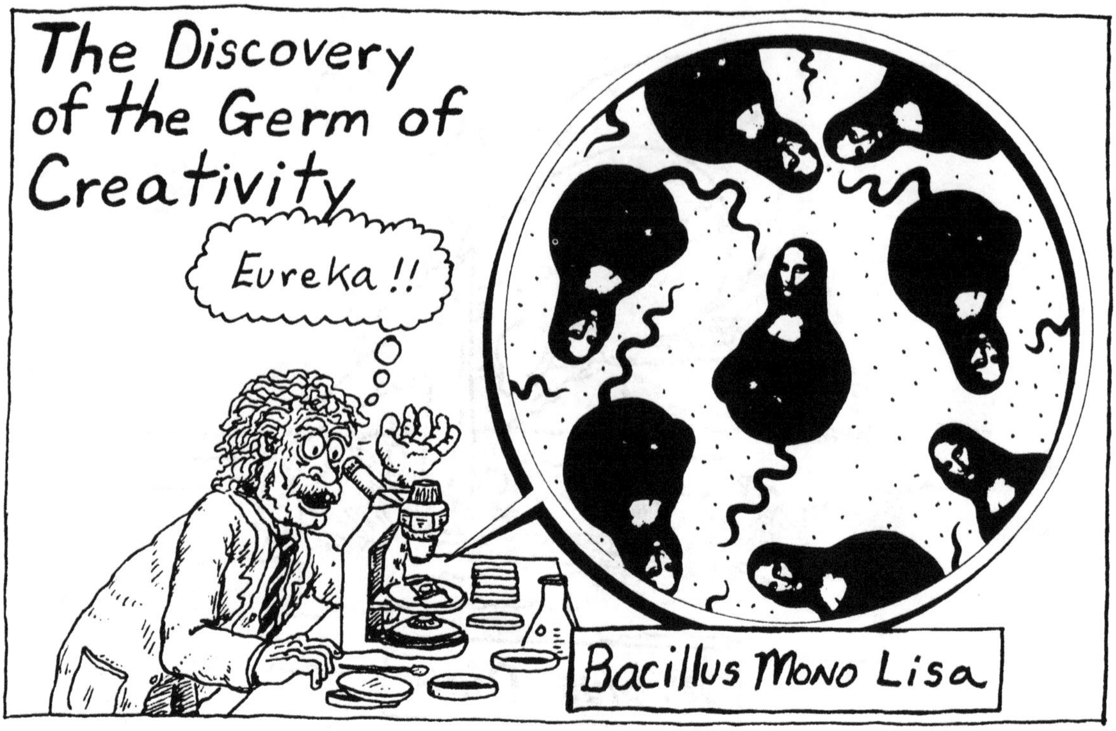
The Discovery of the Germ of Creativity
Eureka!!
Bacillus Mono Lisa

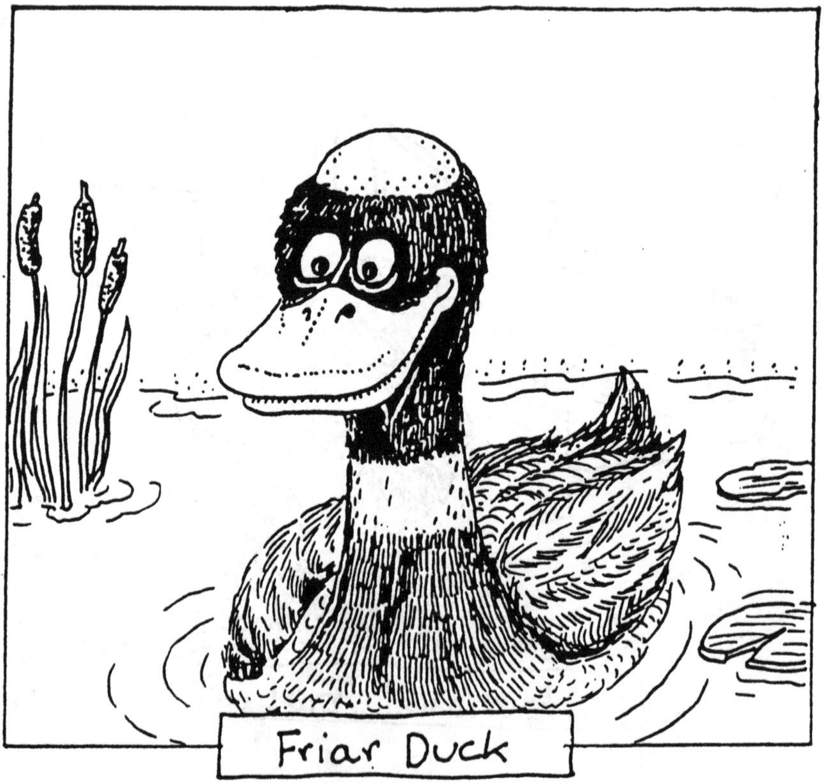
Friar Duck

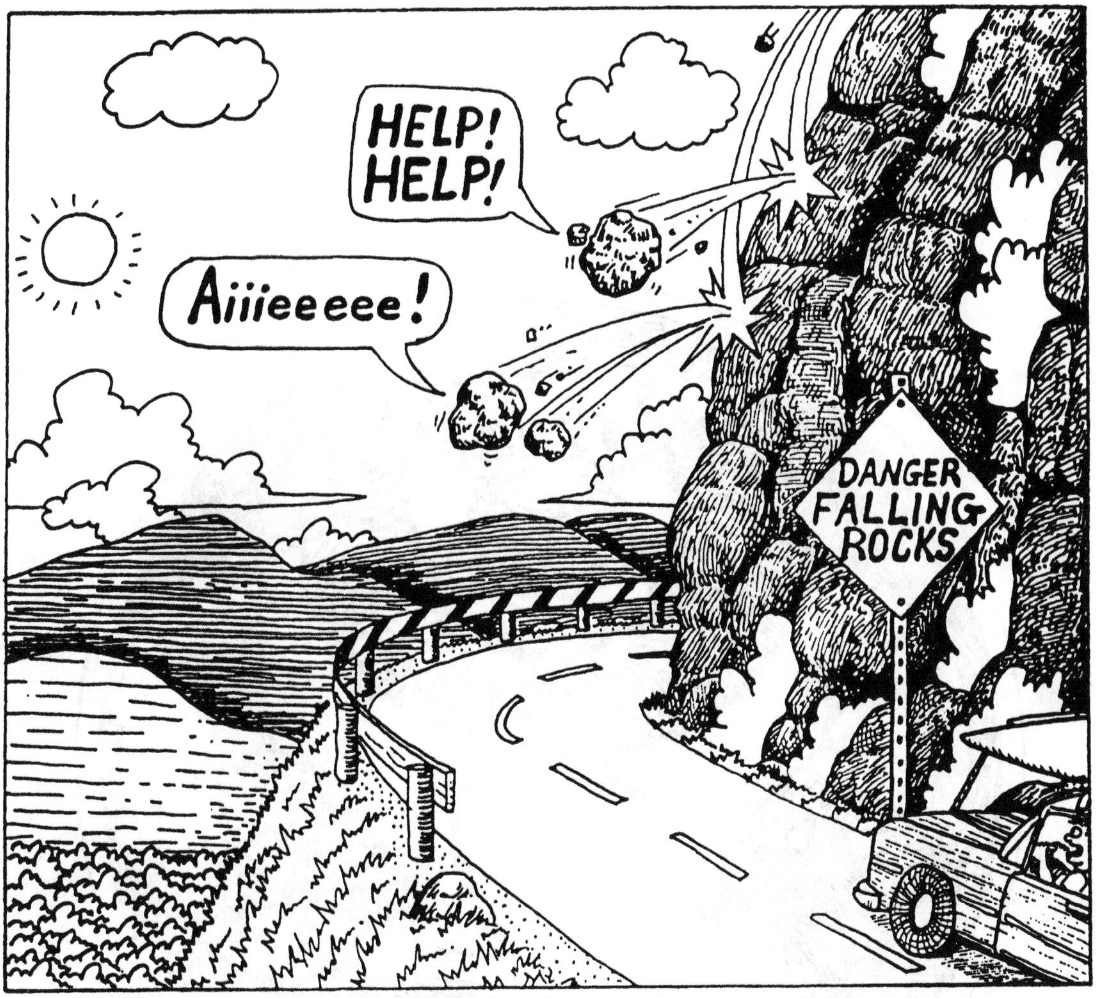
HELP! HELP!
Aiiieeeee!
DANGER FALLING ROCKS

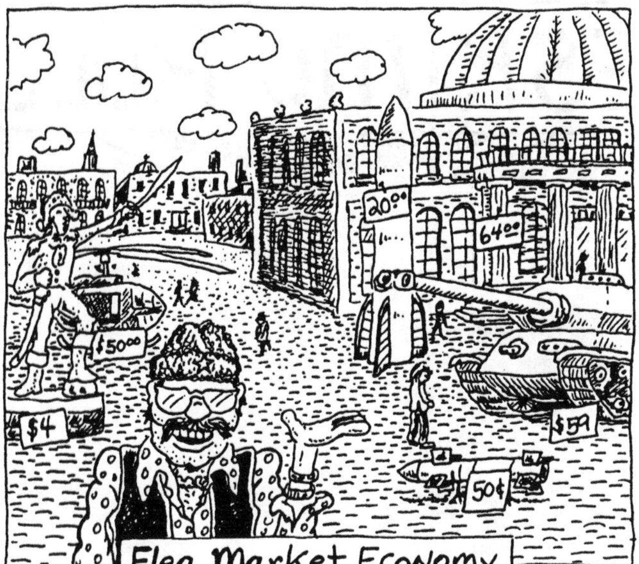
$4
$59
50¢

Flea Market Economy

ESKIMO ROLL

I went to the Animal Fair...

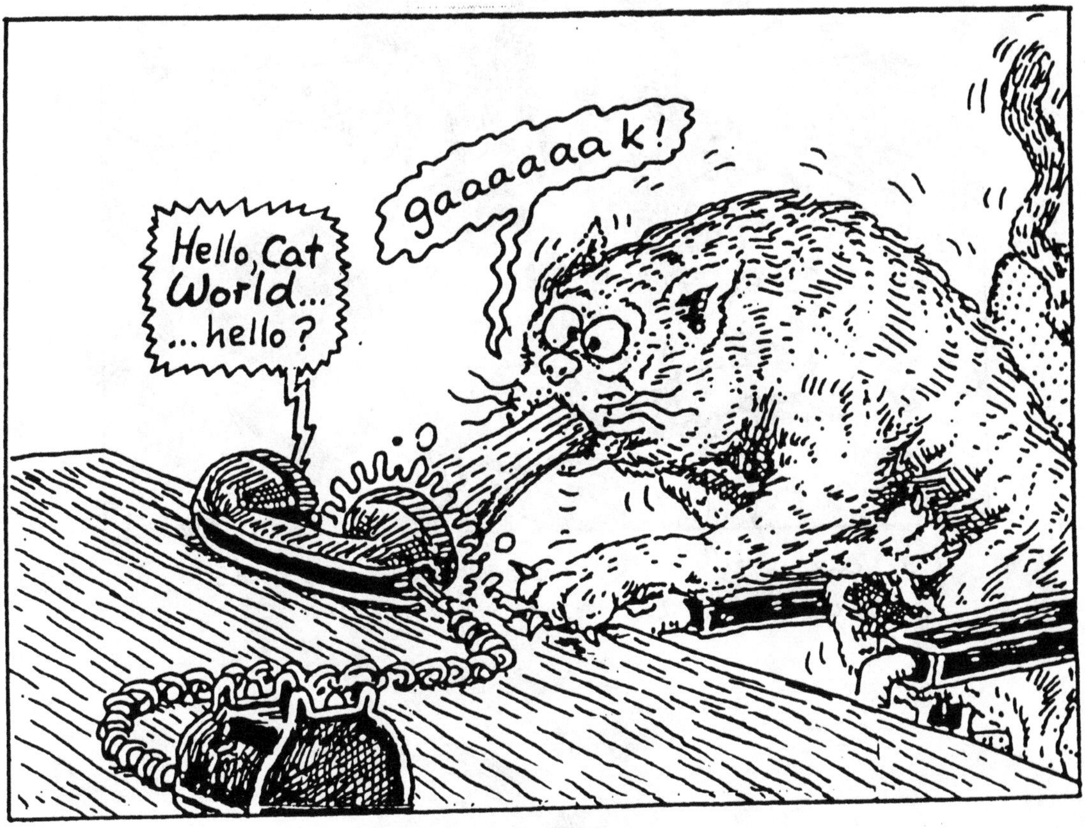
Hello, Cat World... ...hello?
gaaaaaaak!

the birds and the bees were there...

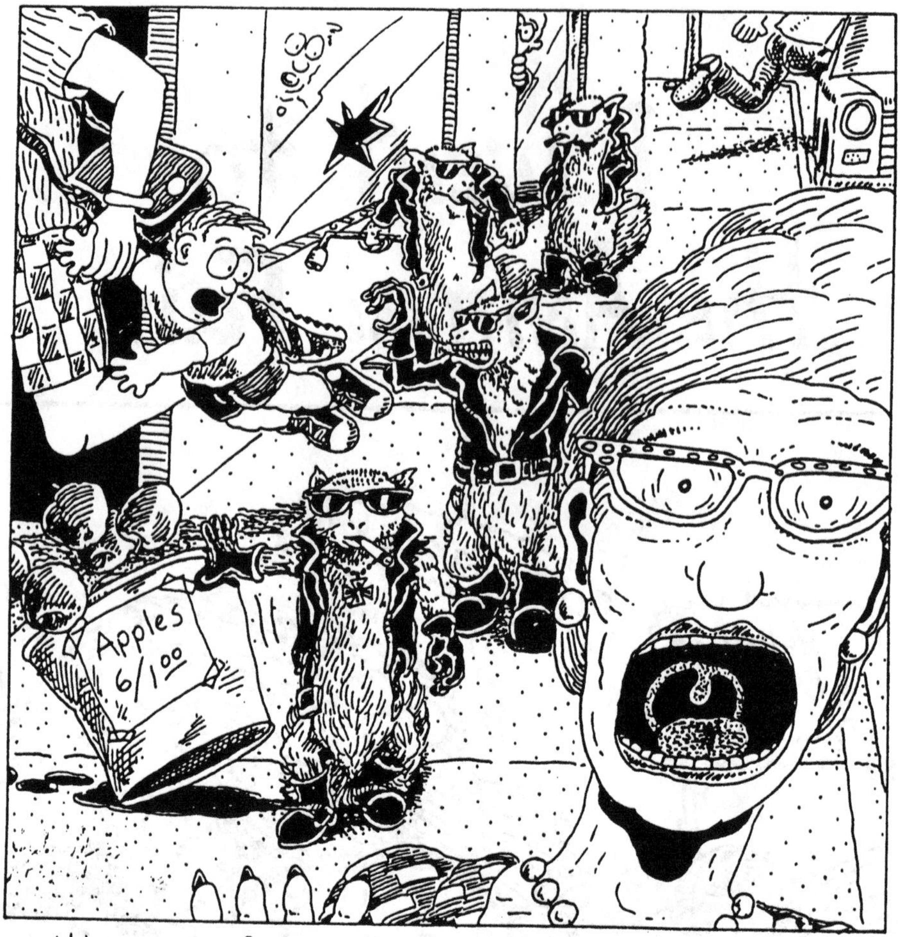
Apples
6/1^{00}

It's nearly fall and once again squirrels downtown are running amuck.

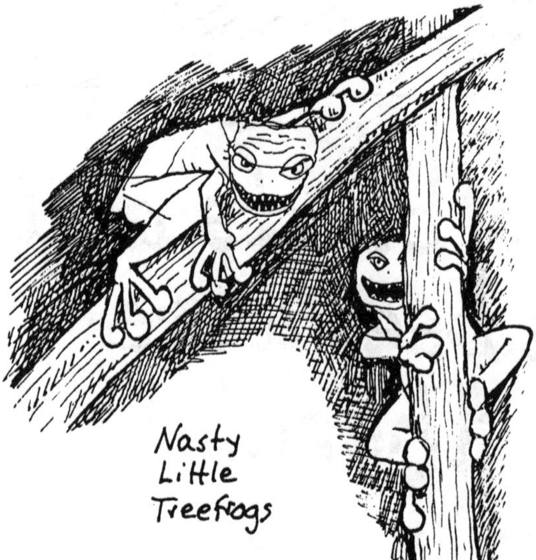
Nasty
Little
Treefrogs

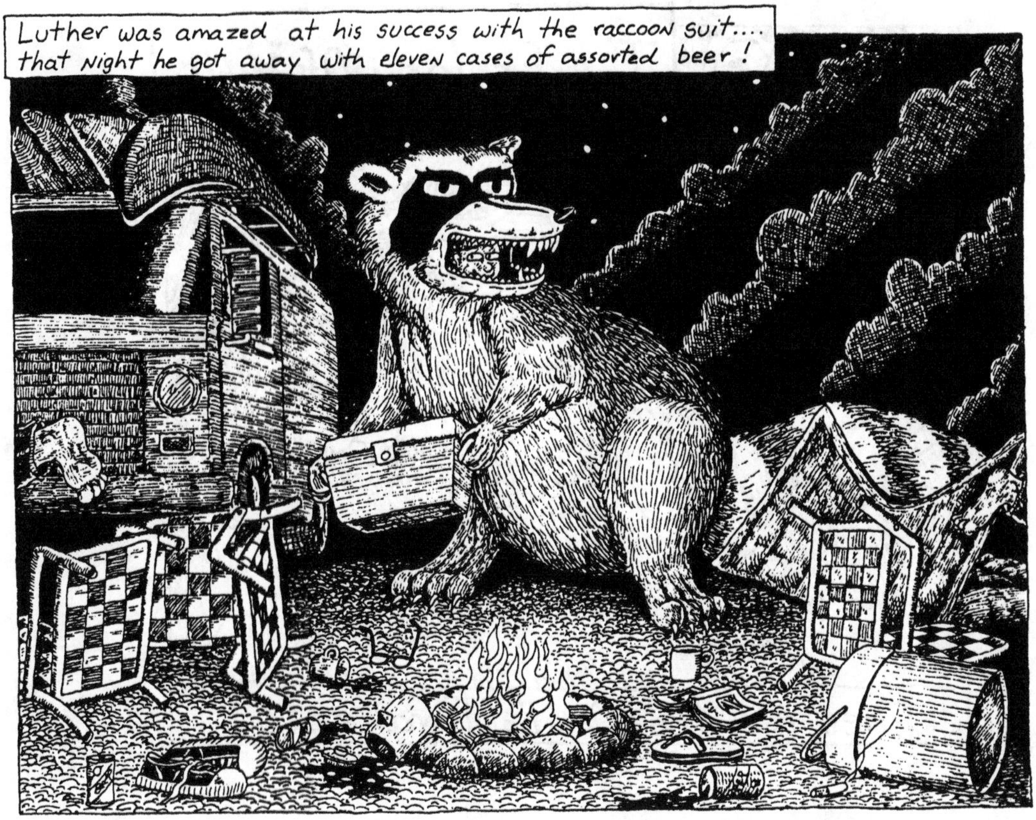
Luther was amazed at his success with the raccoon suit... that night he got away with eleven cases of assorted beer!

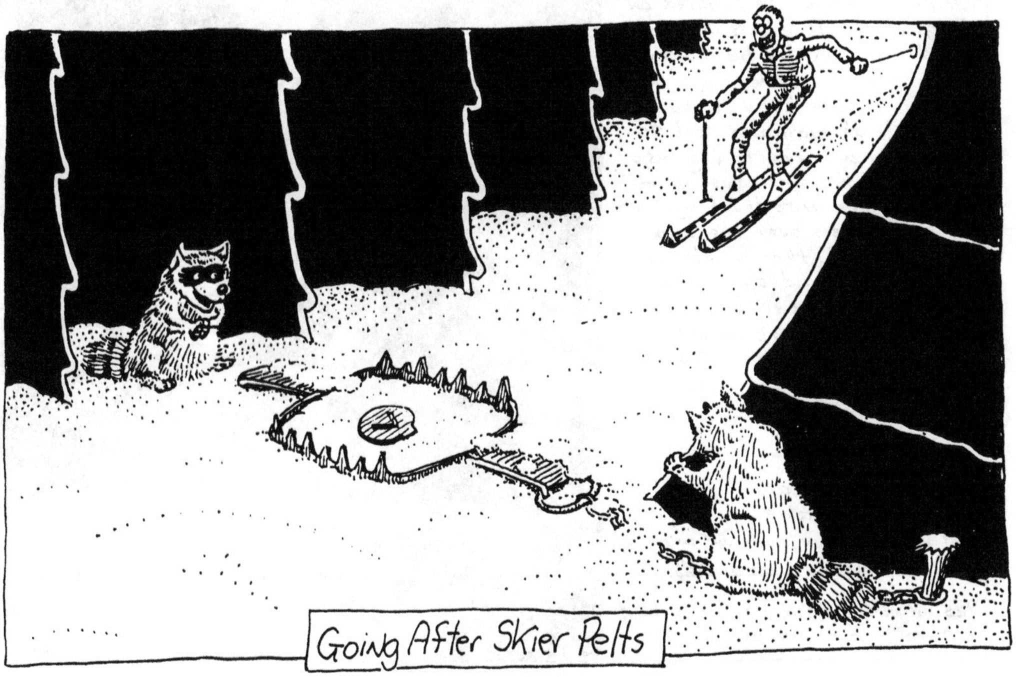
Going After Skier Pelts

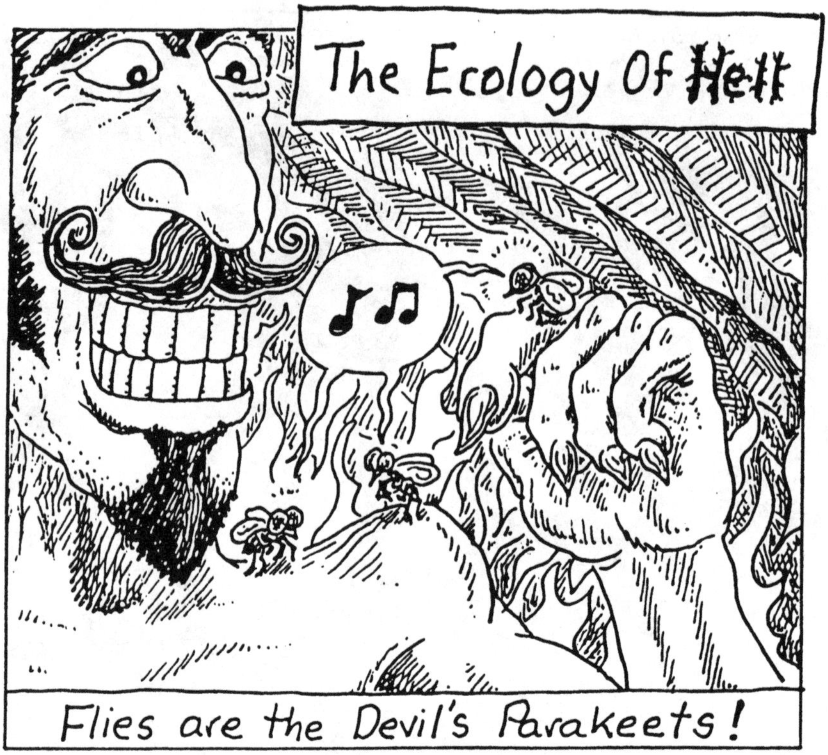
The Ecology Of Hell
Flies are the Devil's Parakeets!

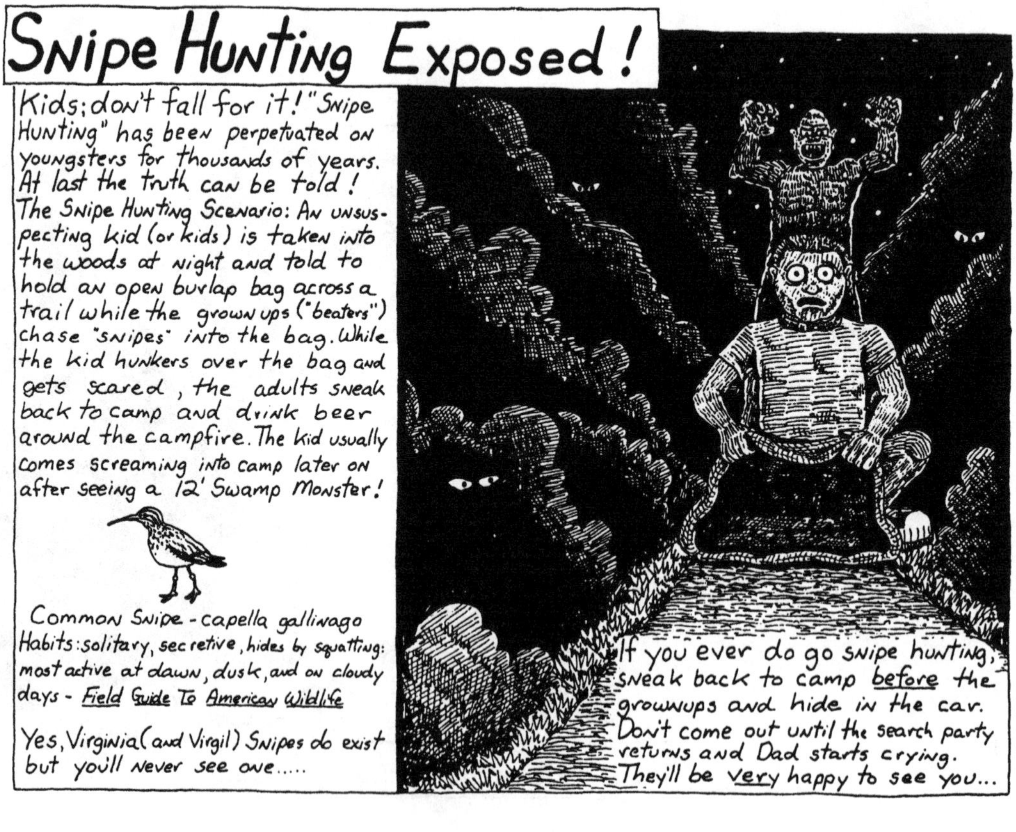
Snipe Hunting Exposed!
Kids: don't fall for it! "Snipe Hunting" has been perpetuated on youngsters for thousands of years. At last the truth can be told!
The Snipe Hunting Scenario: An unsuspecting kid (or kids) is taken into the woods at night and told to hold an open burlap bag across a trail while the grown ups ("beaters") chase "snipes" into the bag. While the kid hunkers over the bag and gets scared, the adults sneak back to camp and drink beer around the campfire. The kid usually comes screaming into camp later on after seeing a 12' Swamp Monster!
Common Snipe - capella gallinago
Habits: solitary, secretive, hides by squatting: most active at dawn, dusk, and on cloudy days - Field Guide To American Wildlife
Yes, Virginia (and Virgil) Snipes do exist but you'll never see one.....
If you ever do go snipe hunting, sneak back to camp before the grownups and hide in the car. Don't come out until the search party returns and Dad starts crying. They'll be very happy to see you...

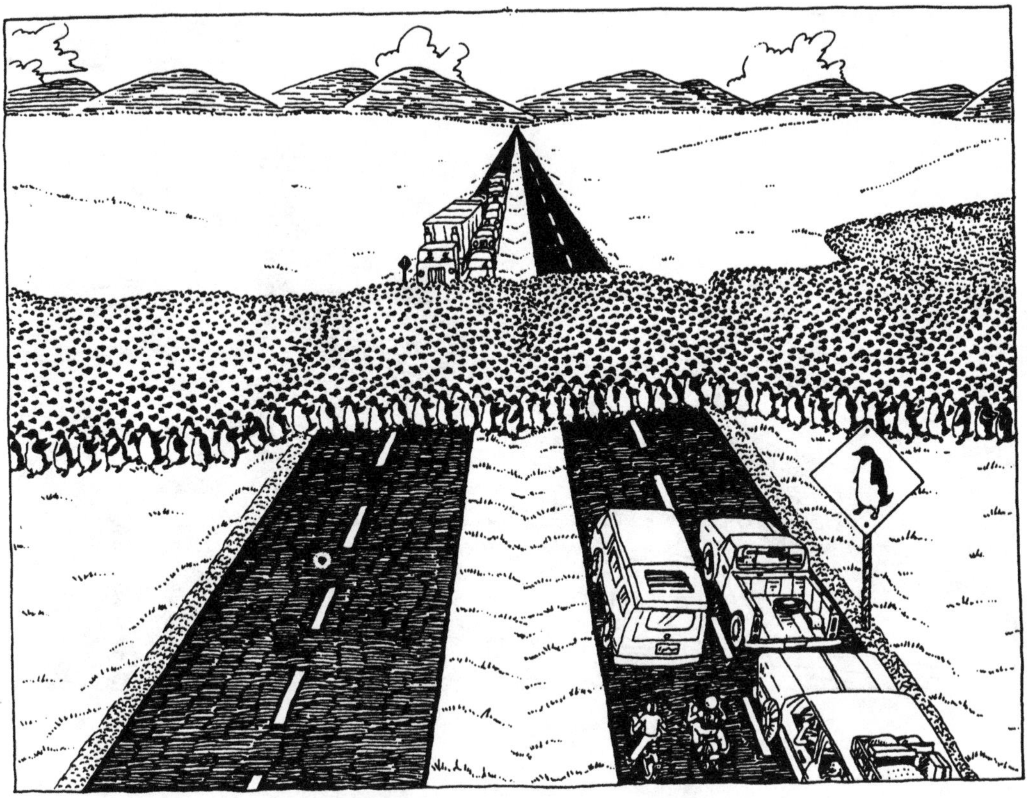

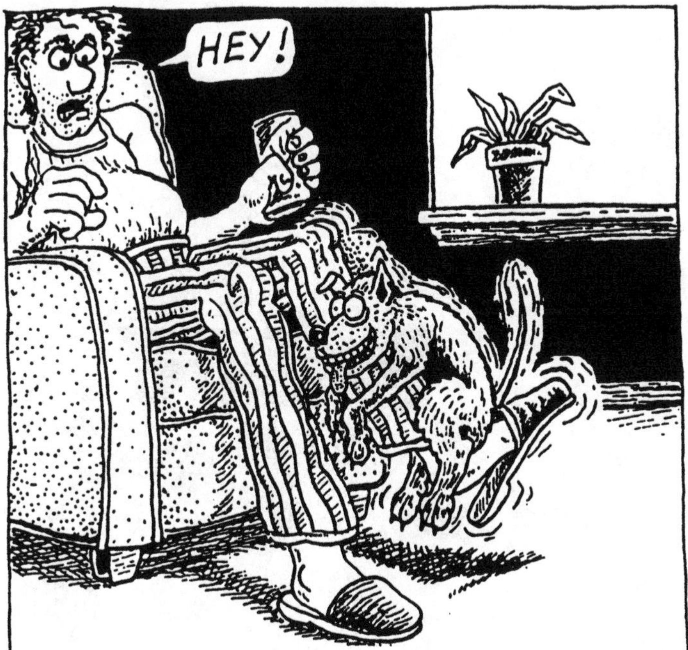
HEY!

Buster does the Lambada...

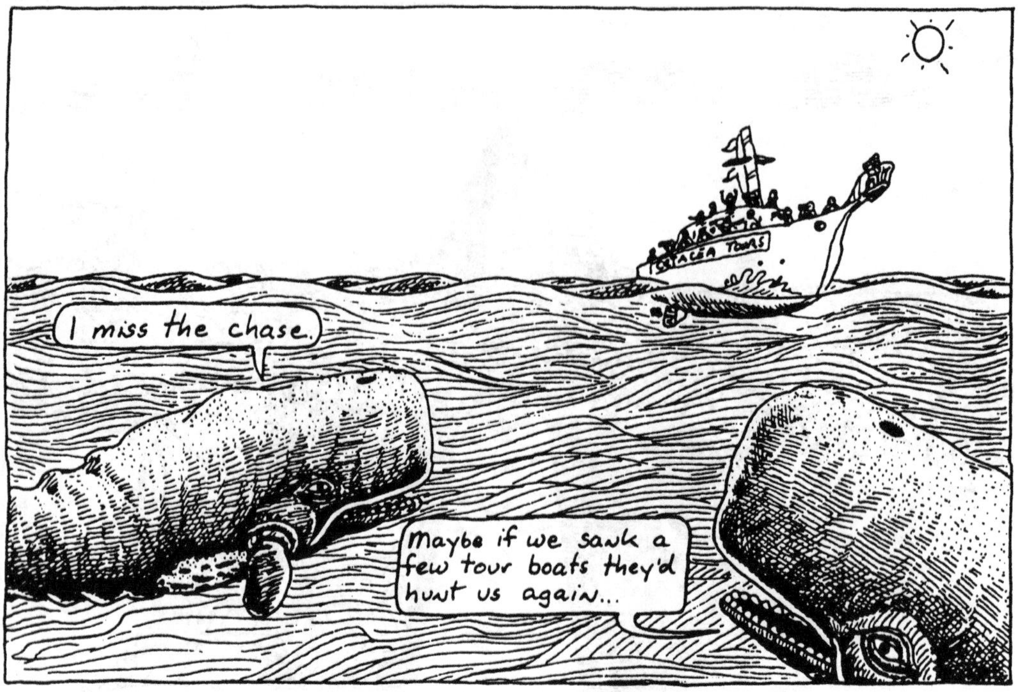
I miss the chase.
Maybe if we sank a few tour boats they'd hunt us again...

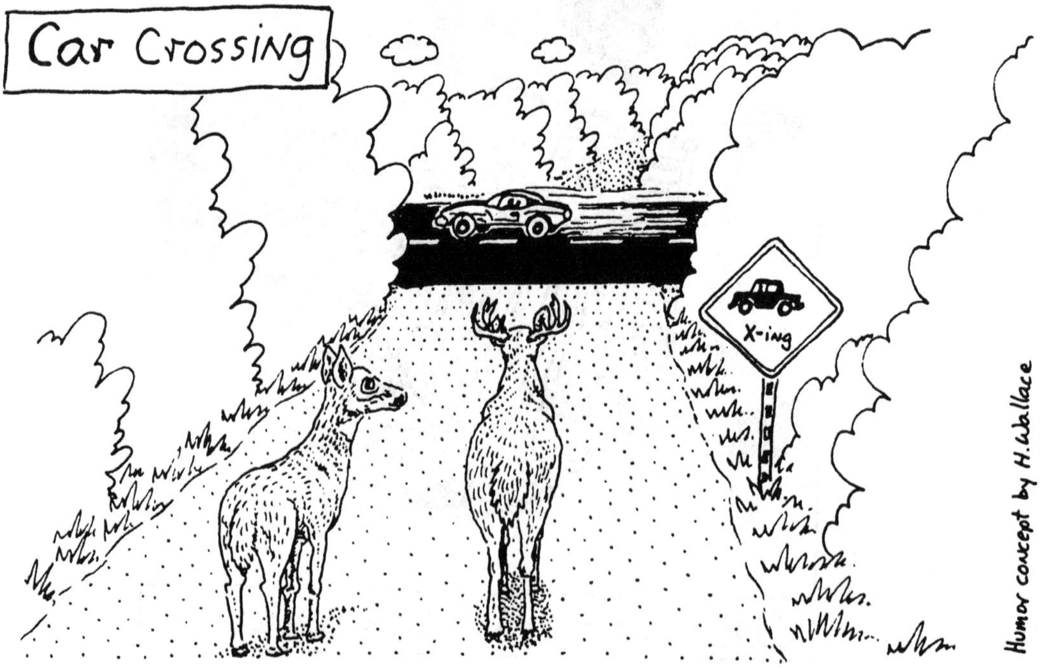
Car Crossing
X-ing
Humor concept by H. Wallace

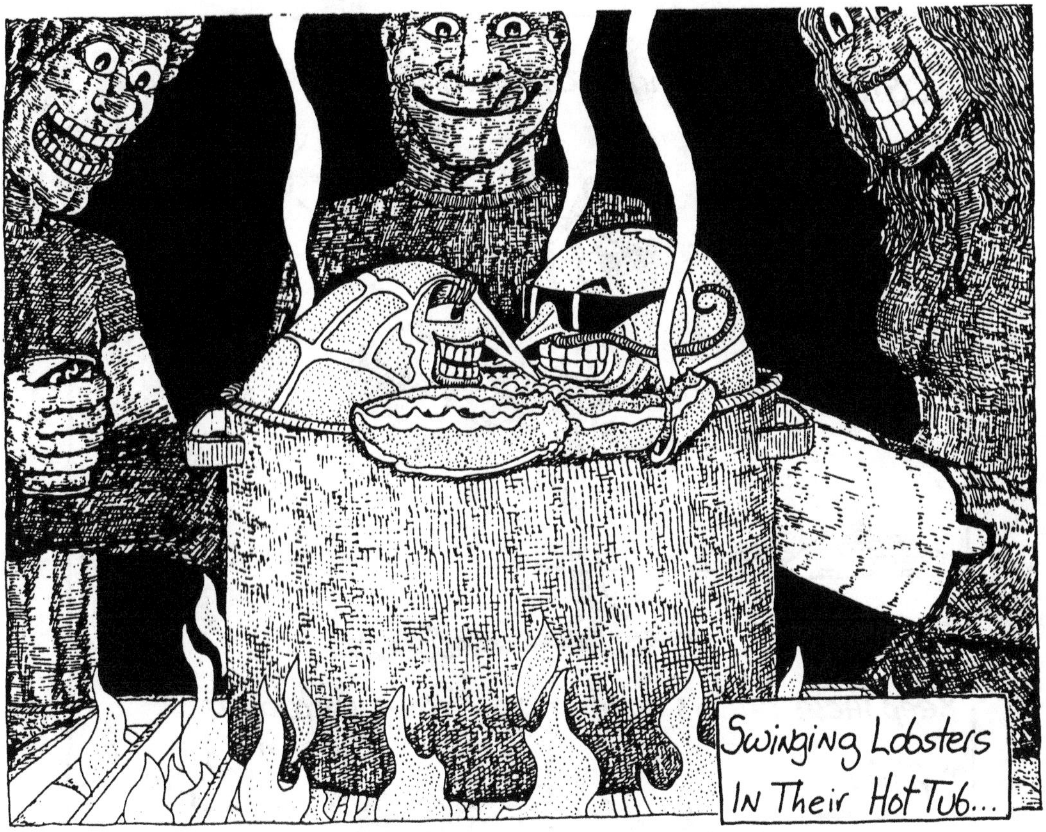
Swinging Lobsters
In Their Hot Tub...

Raccoon Empire

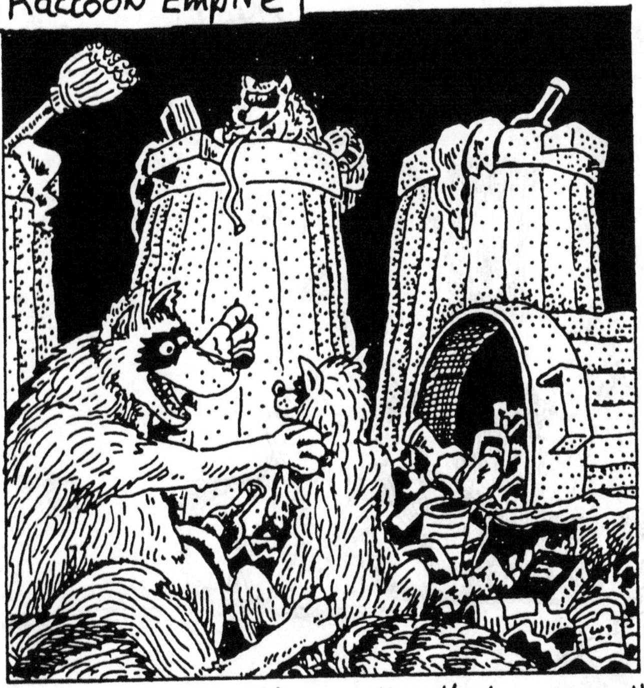

"Someday son, this will all be yours..."

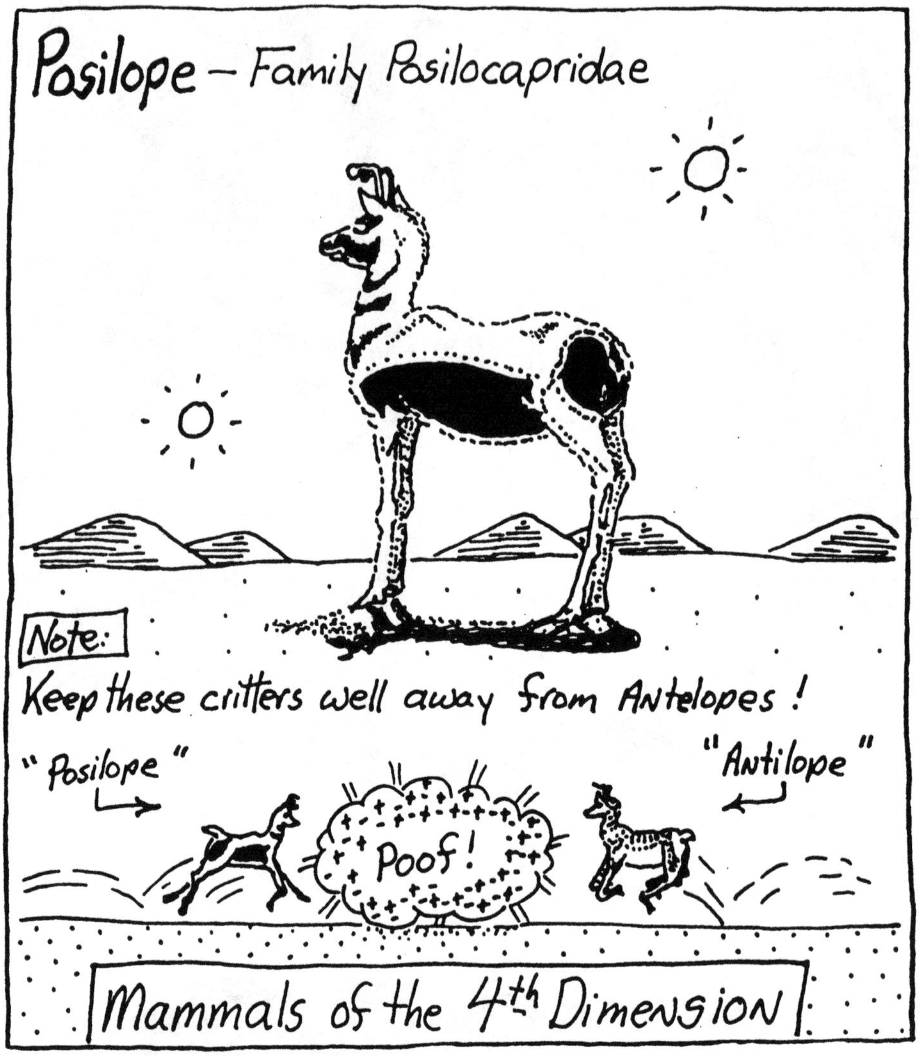
Posilope – Family Posilocapridae
Note:
Keep these critters well away from Antelopes!
"Posilope"
Poof!
"Antilope"
Mammals of the 4th Dimension

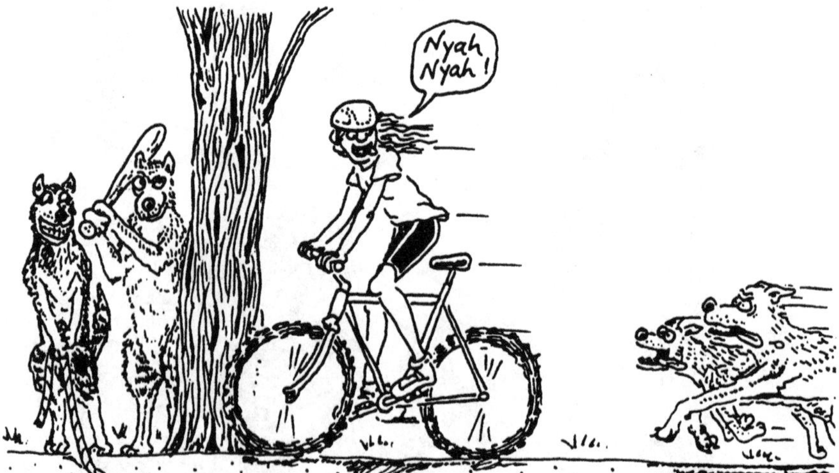
Nyah Nyah!

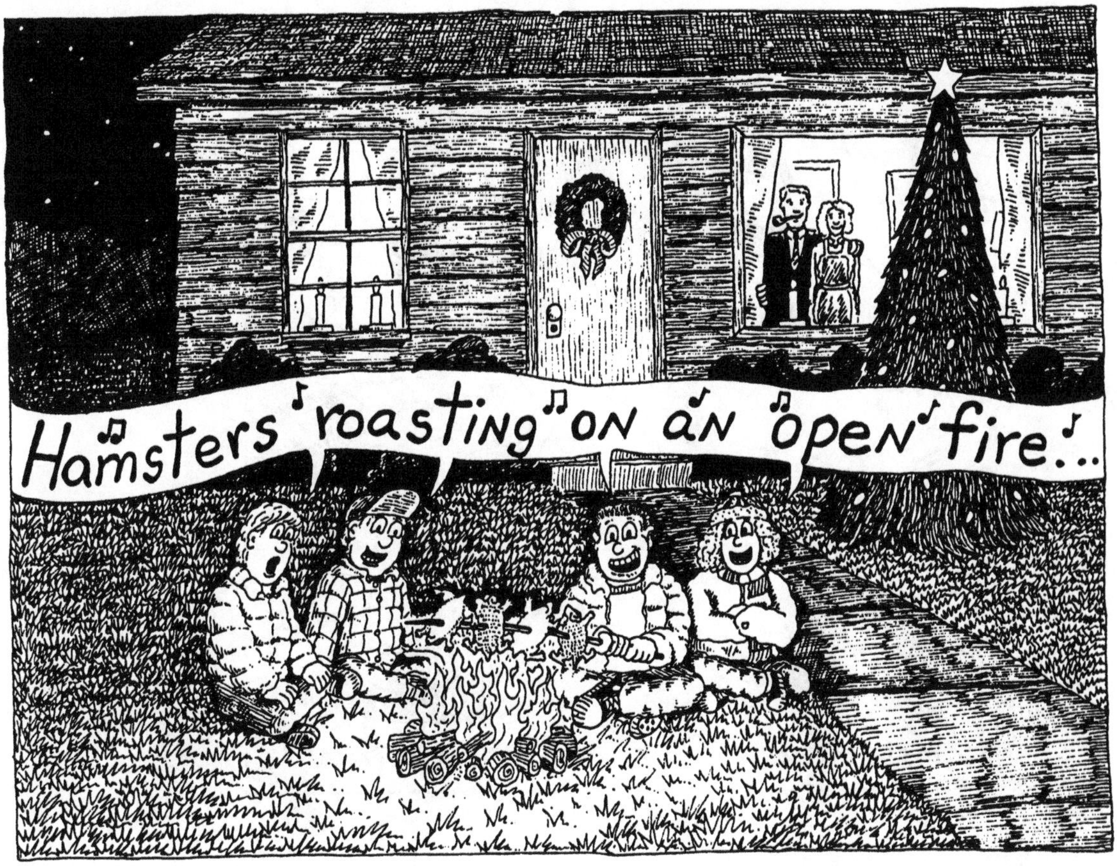
Hamsters roasting on an open fire...

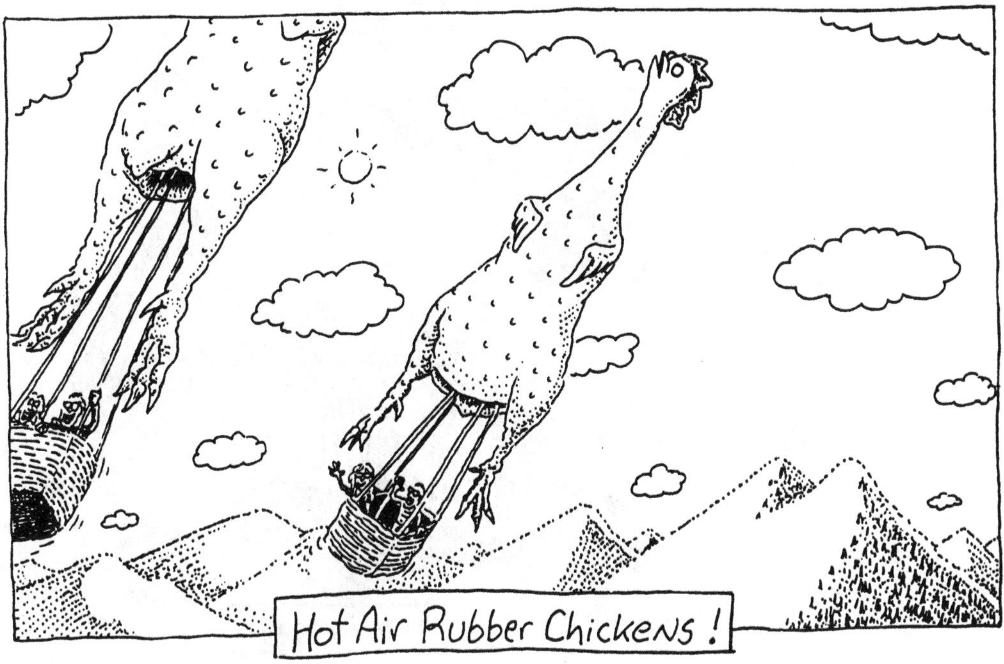
Hot Air Rubber Chickens!

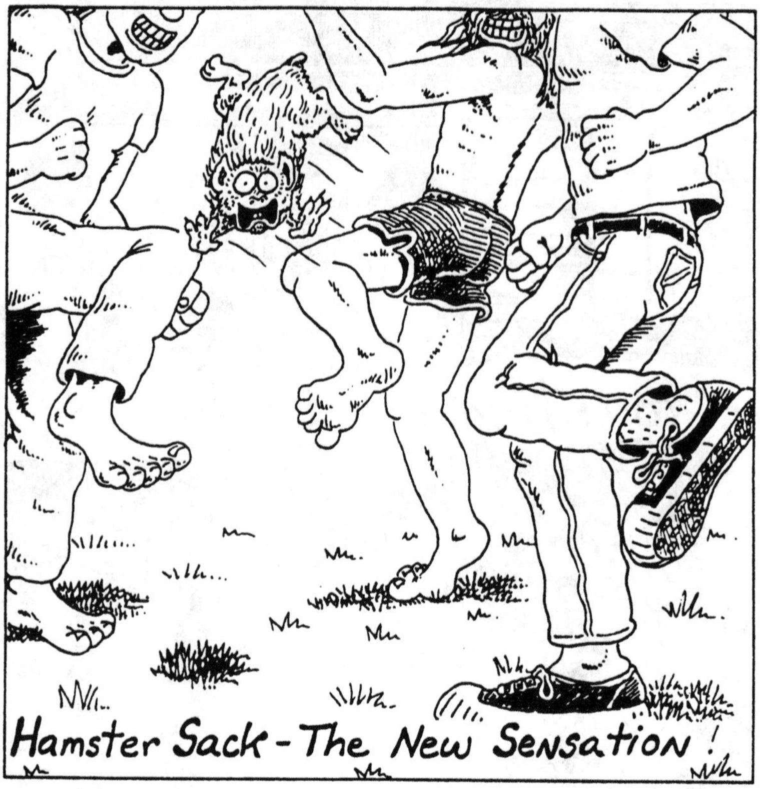
Hamster Sack - The New Sensation!

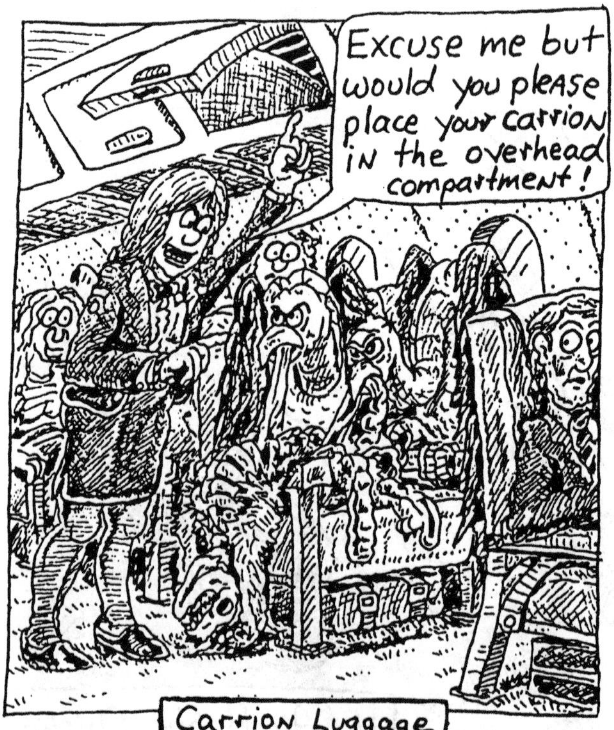
Excuse me but would you please place your carrion in the overhead compartment!

Carrion Luggage

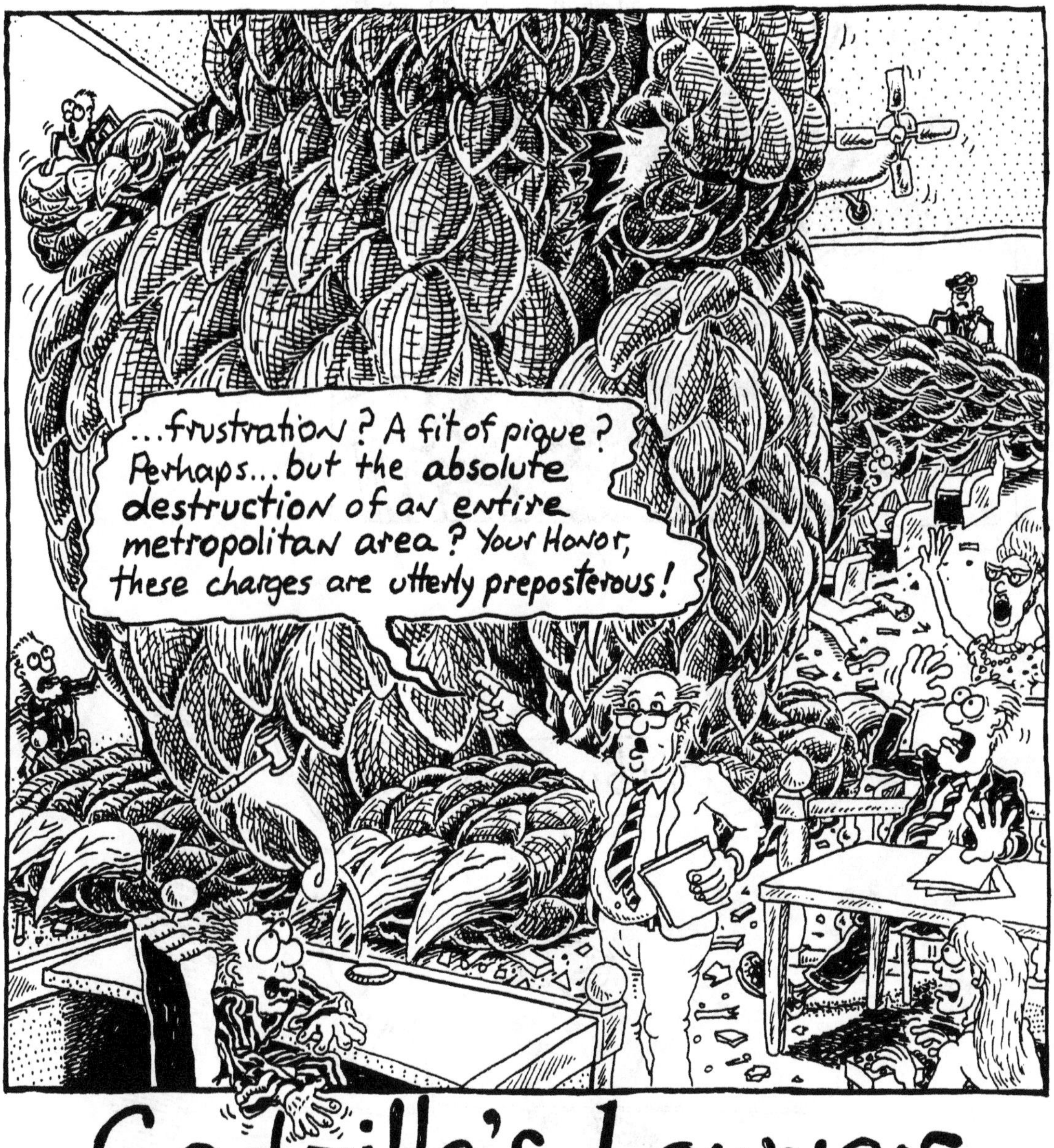
...frustration? A fit of pique? Perhaps...but the absolute destruction of an entire metropolitan area? Your Honor, these charges are utterly preposterous!

Godzilla's Lawyer

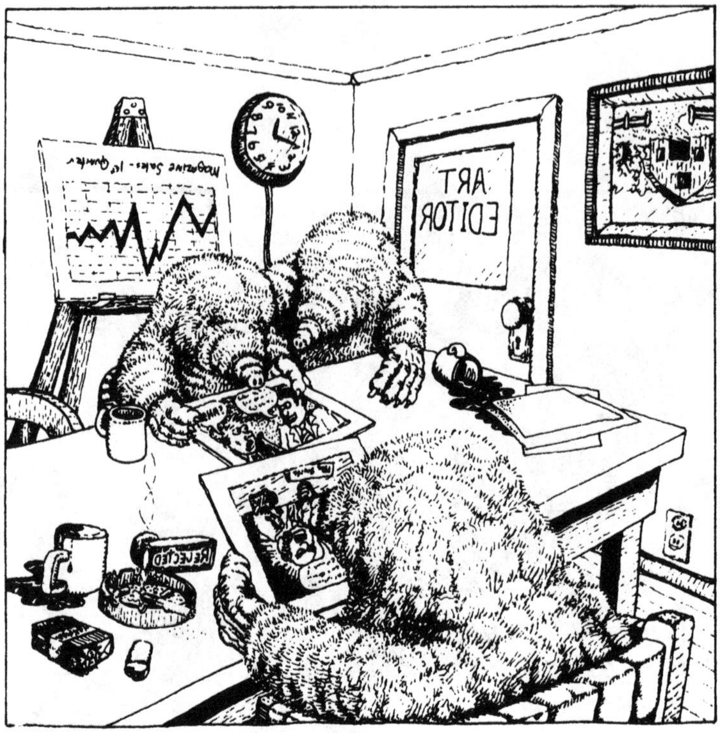
ART
EDITOR
REJECTED

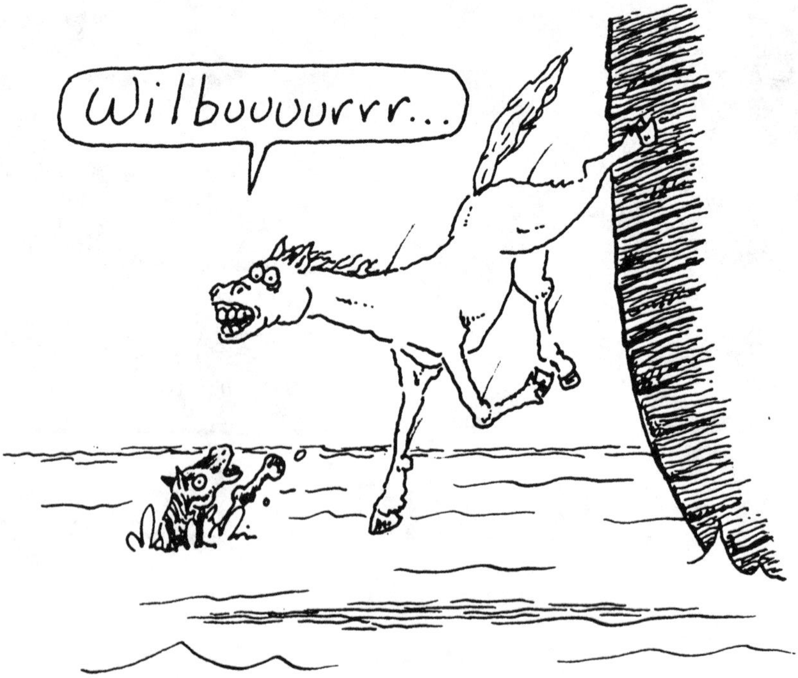
Wilbuuuurrr...

Mr. Ed visits the Horse Lattitudes

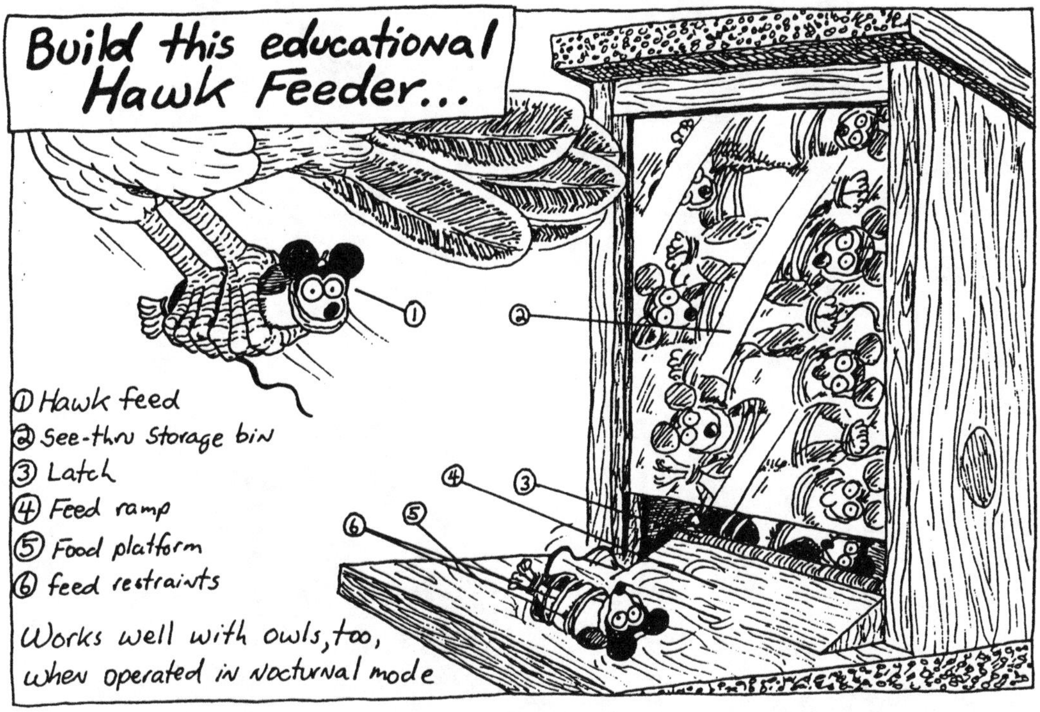
Build this educational Hawk Feeder...
① Hawk feed
② See-thru Storage bin
③ Latch
④ Feed ramp
⑤ Food platform
⑥ feed restraints
Works well with owls, too, when operated in nocturnal mode

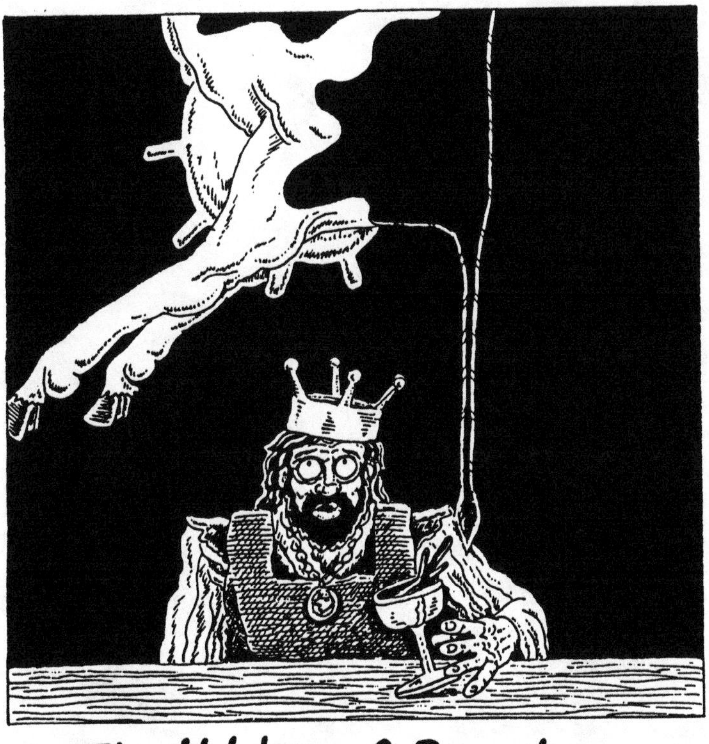

The Holstein of Damocles

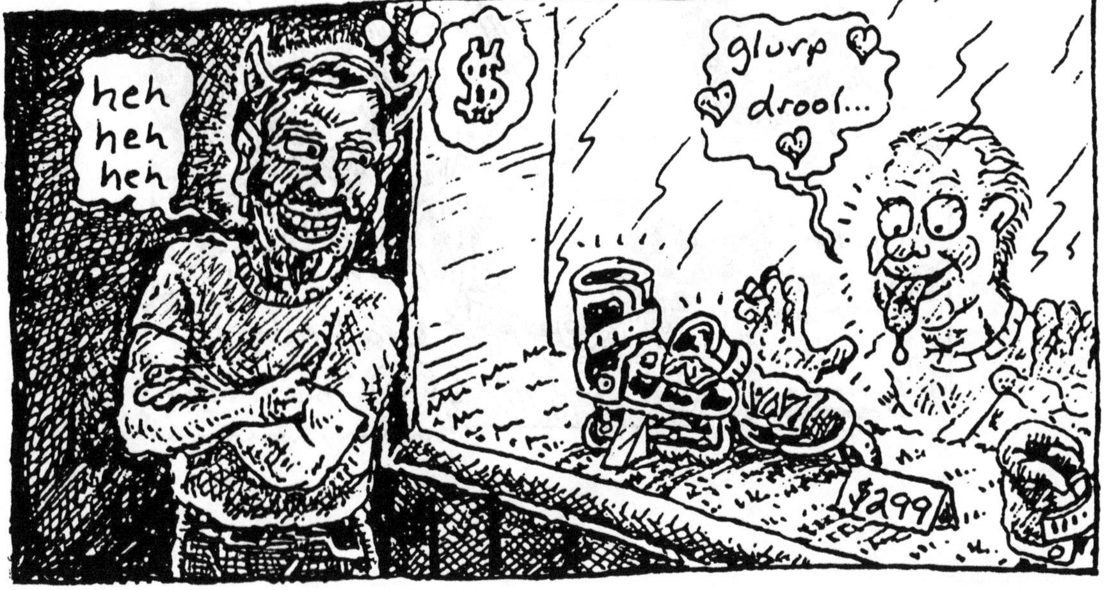
heh
heh
heh
$
glurp
drool...
$299

Operators Are Standing By...

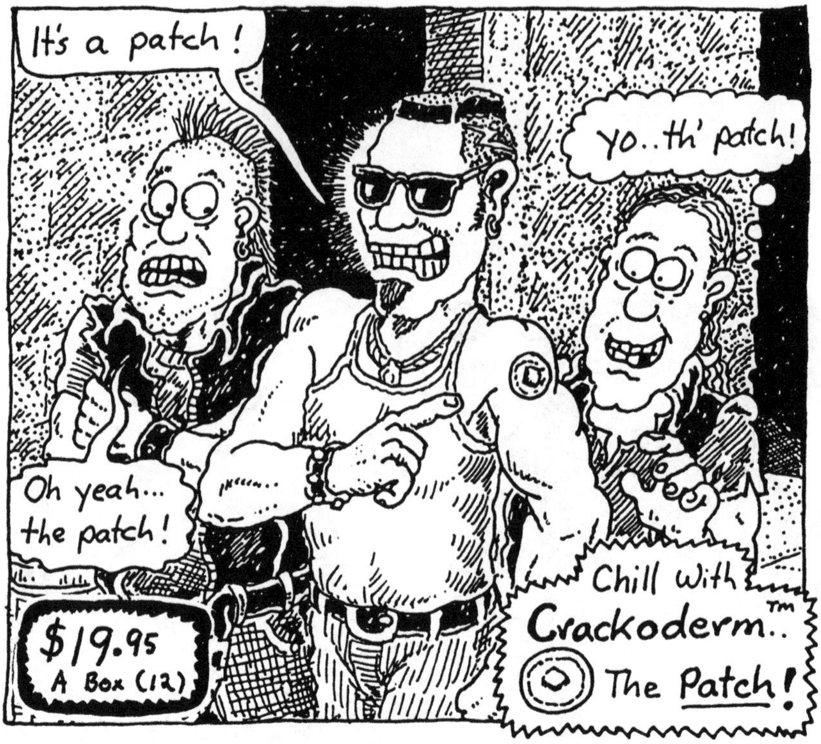
It's a patch!
yo.. th' patch!
Oh yeah... the patch!
$19.95 A Box (12)
Chill with Crackoderm™.. The Patch!

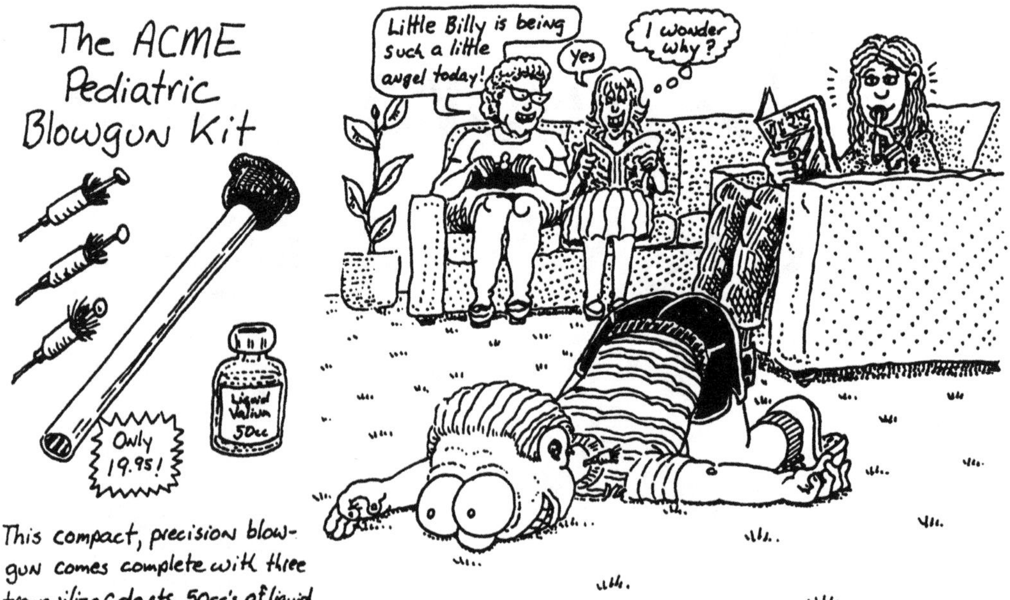
The ACME Pediatric Blowgun Kit
Only 19.95!
Liquid Valium 50cc
Little Billy is being such a little angel today!
Yes
I wonder why?

This compact, precision blowgun comes complete with three tranquilizer darts, 50cc's of liquid valium and instruction booklet.

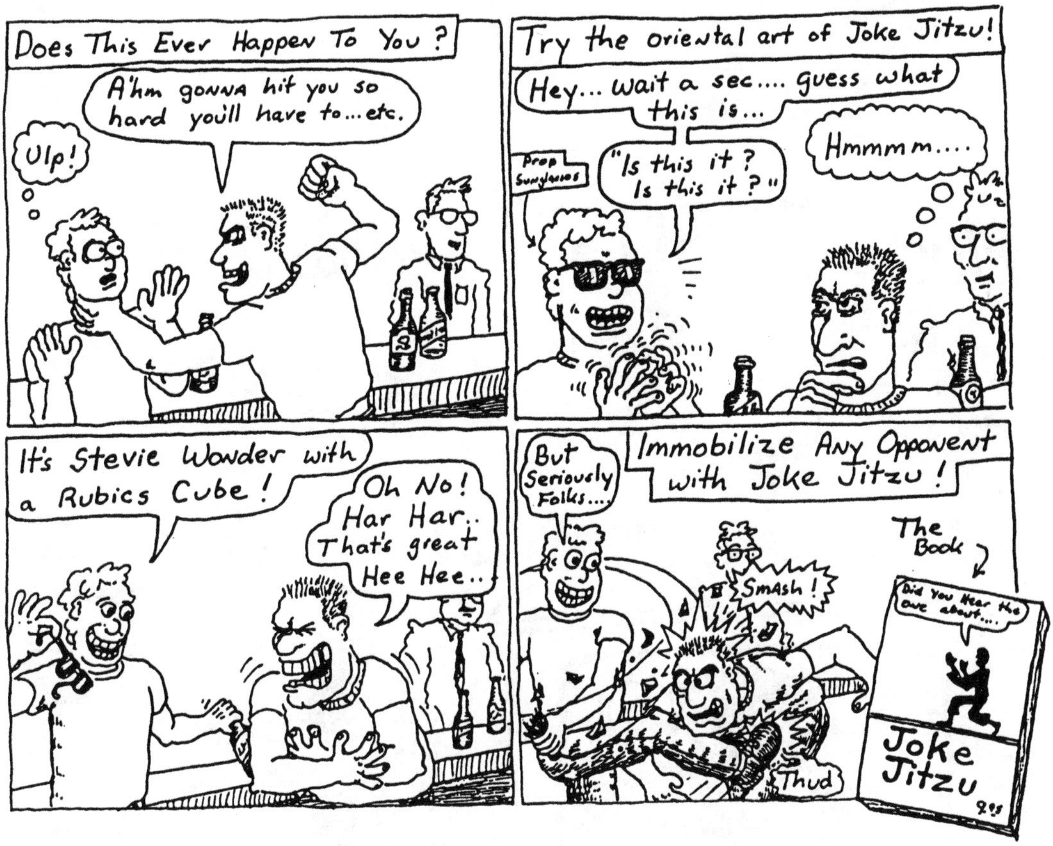

Does This Ever Happen To You?
Ulp!
A'hm gonna hit you so hard you'll have to... etc.
Try the oriental art of Joke Jitzu!
Hey... wait a sec.... guess what this is...
Prop Sunglasses
"Is this it? Is this it?"
Hmmmm....
It's Stevie Wonder with a Rubics Cube!
Oh No! Har Har.. That's great Hee Hee..
But Seriously Folks....
Immobilize Any Opponent with Joke Jitzu!
The Book
Did You Hear the one about....
Joke Jitzu
Smash!
Thud

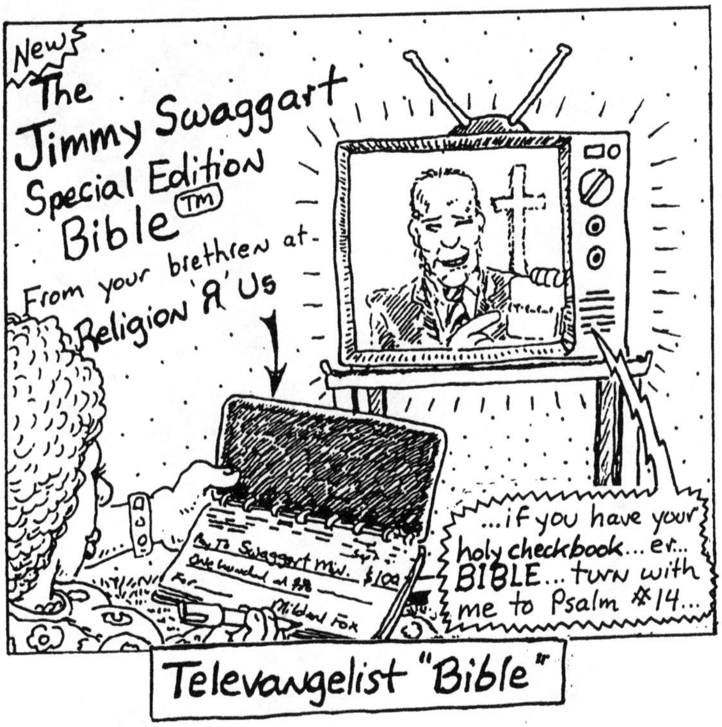

New
The Jimmy Swaggart Special Edition Bible TM
From your brethren at Religion 'R' Us
...if you have your holy checkbook... er... BIBLE... turn with me to Psalm #14...

Televangelist "Bible"

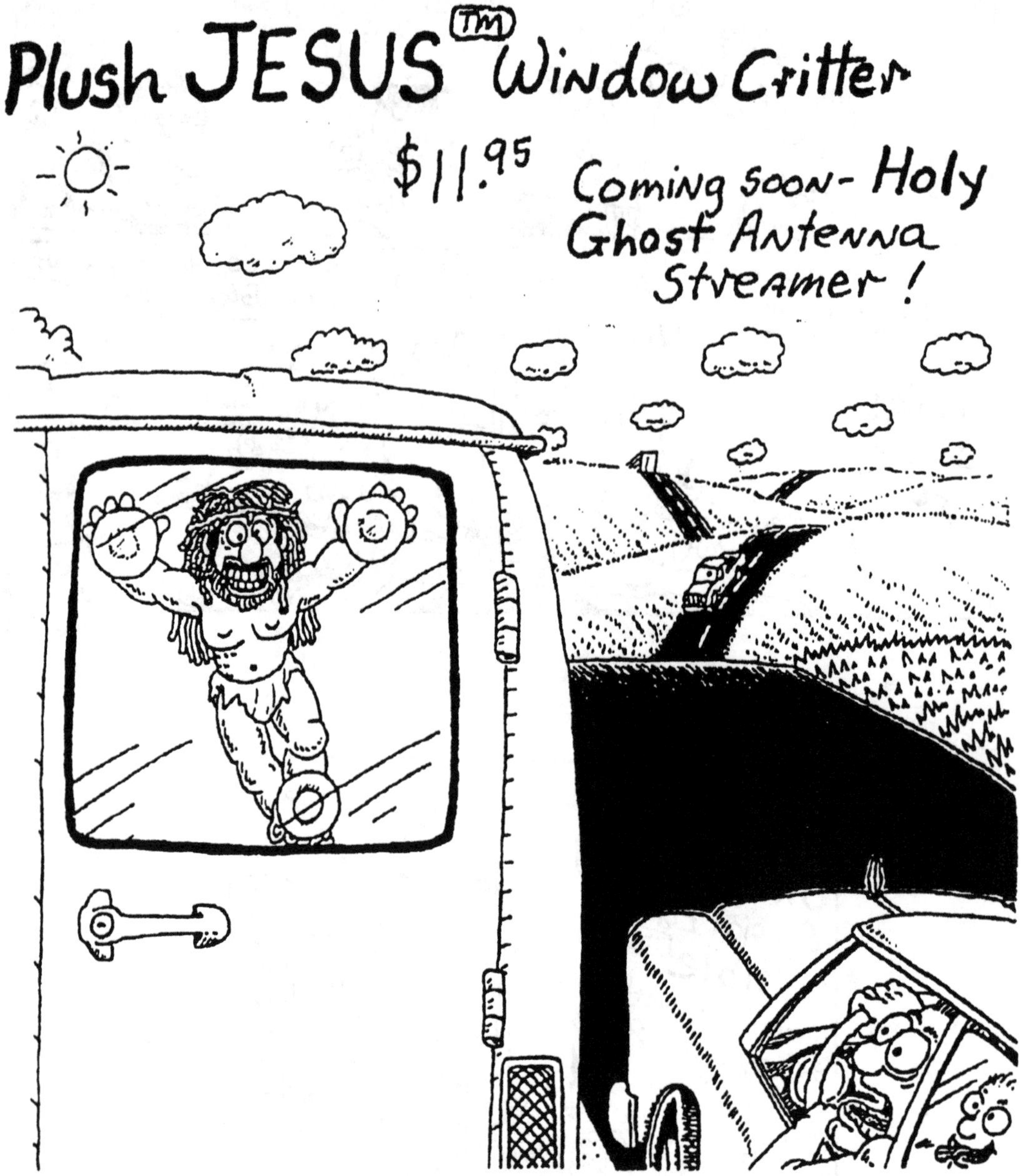
Plush JESUS(TM) Window Critter
$11.95
Coming soon- Holy Ghost Antenna Streamer!

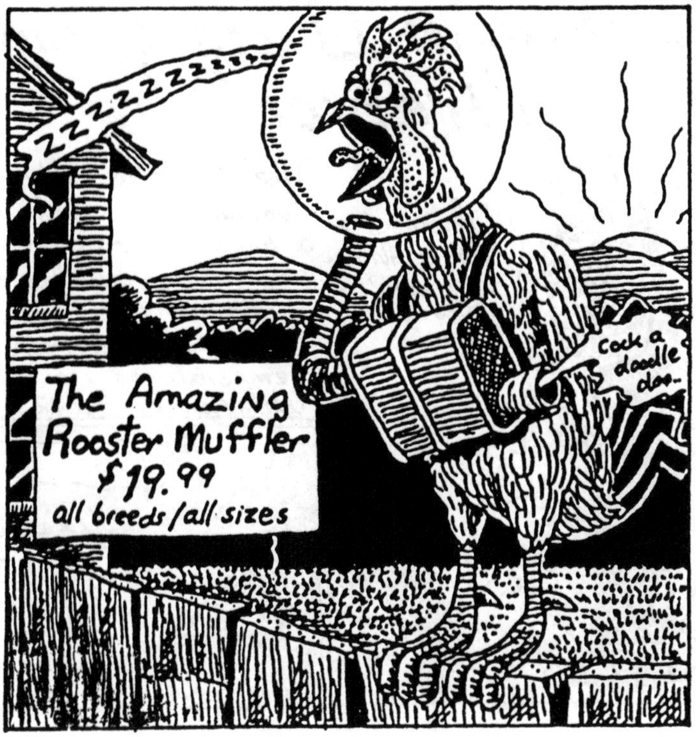
ZZZZZZZZZZZ
The Amazing
Rooster Muffler
$19.99
all breeds/all sizes
Cock a doodle doo..

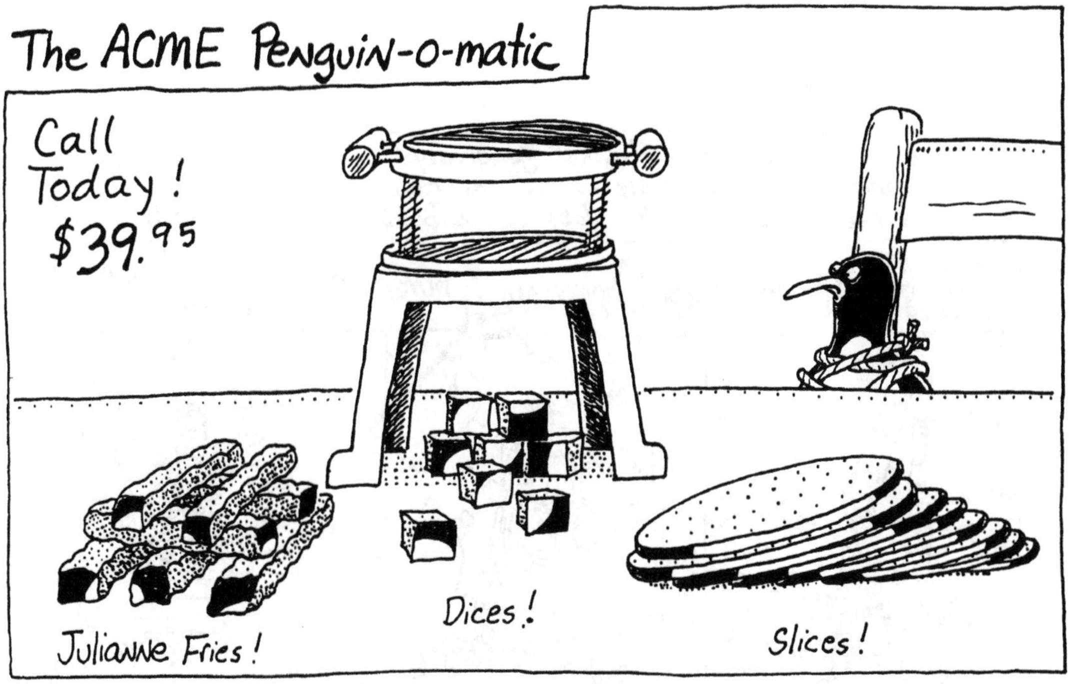
The ACME Penguin-o-matic
Call
Today!
$39.95
Julianne Fries!
Dices!
Slices!

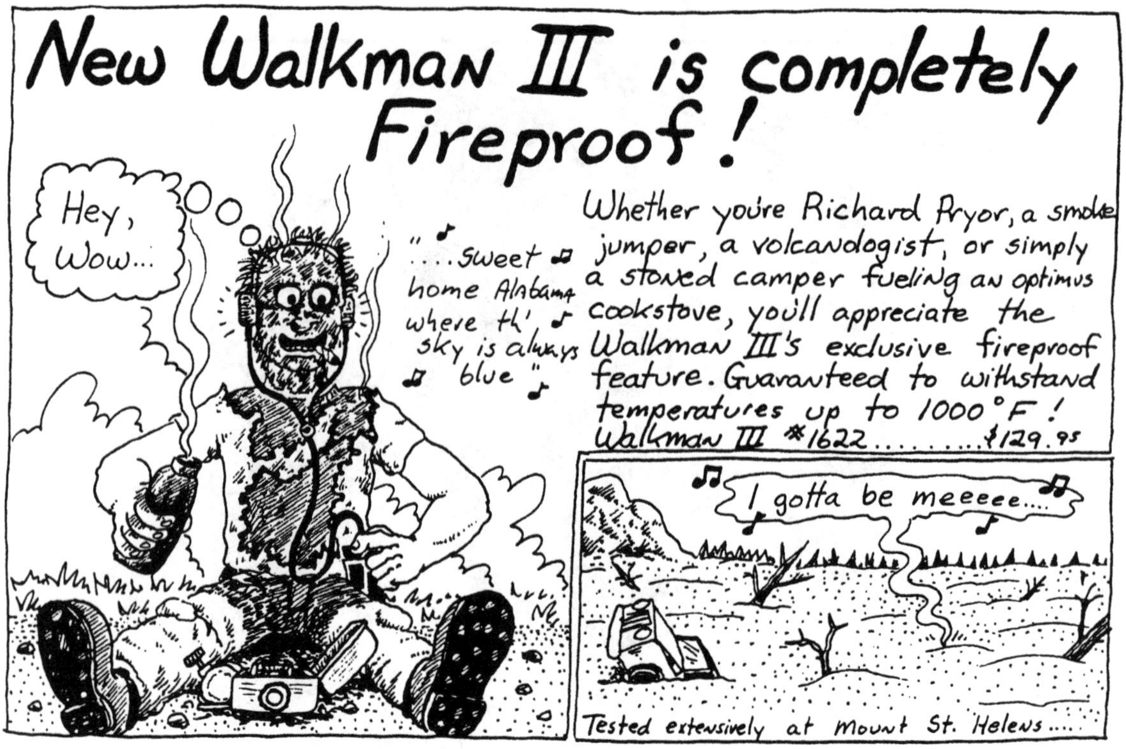
New Walkman III is completely Fireproof!
Hey, Wow...
"...sweet home Alabama where th' sky is always blue"
Whether you're Richard Pryor, a smoke jumper, a volcanologist, or simply a stoned camper fueling an optimus cookstove, you'll appreciate the Walkman III's exclusive fireproof feature. Guaranteed to withstand temperatures up to 1000°F!
Walkman III #1622 .... $129.95
I gotta be meeeee....
Tested extensively at Mount St. Helens....

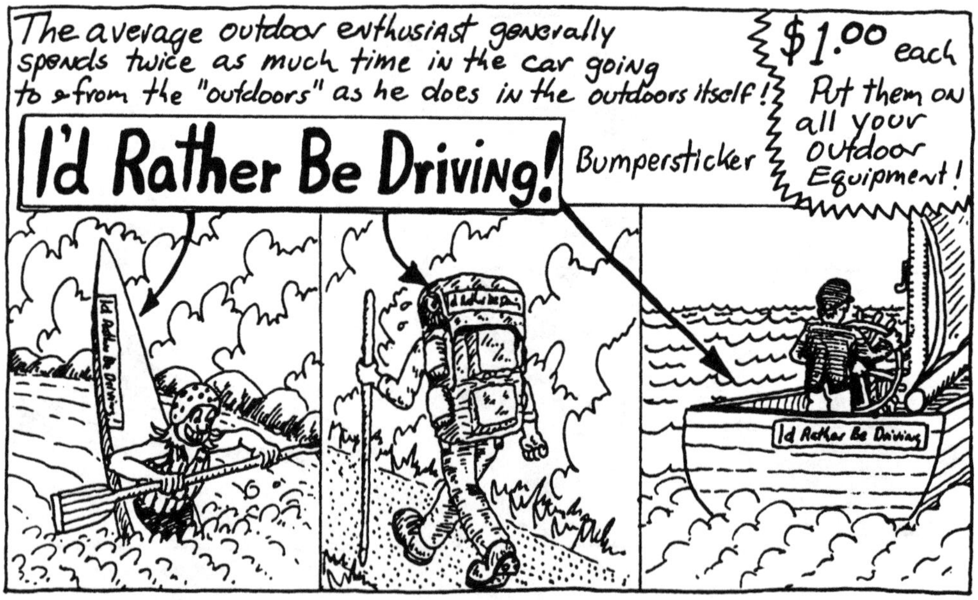
The average outdoor enthusiast generally spends twice as much time in the car going to & from the "outdoors" as he does in the outdoors itself!
I'd Rather Be Driving!
Bumpersticker
$1.00 each
Put them on all your outdoor Equipment!
I'd Rather Be Driving
I'd Rather Be Driving

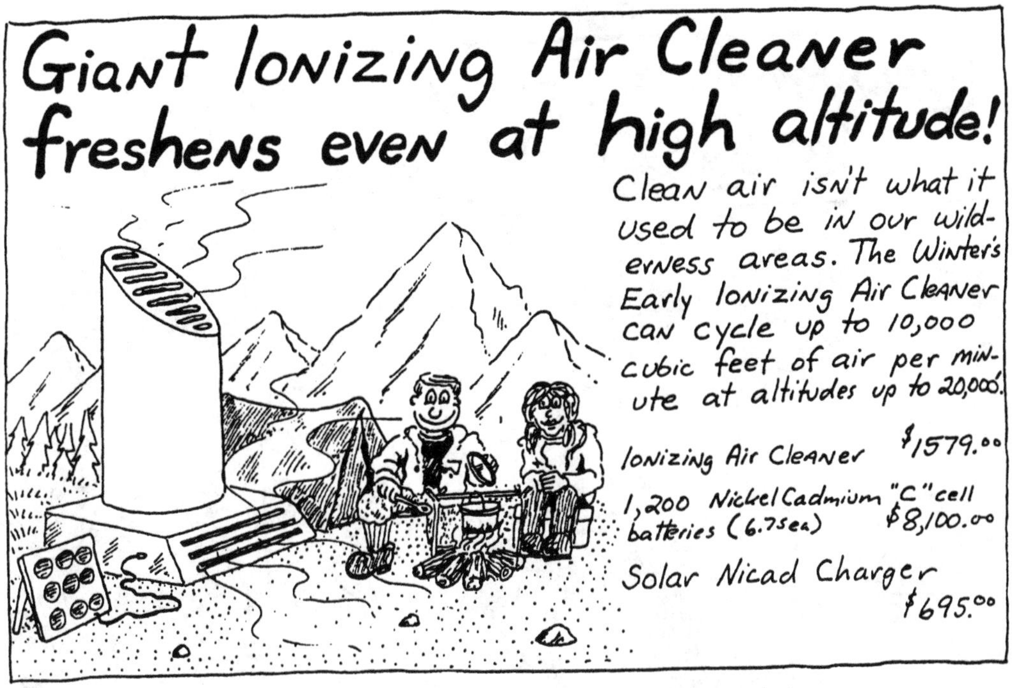
Giant Ionizing Air Cleaner freshens even at high altitude!
Clean air isn't what it used to be in our wild-erness areas. The Winter's Early Ionizing Air Cleaner can cycle up to 10,000 cubic feet of air per min-ute at altitudes up to 20,000'.
Ionizing Air Cleaner $1579.00
1,200 Nickel Cadmium "C" cell batteries (6.75ea) $8,100.00
Solar Nicad Charger $695.00

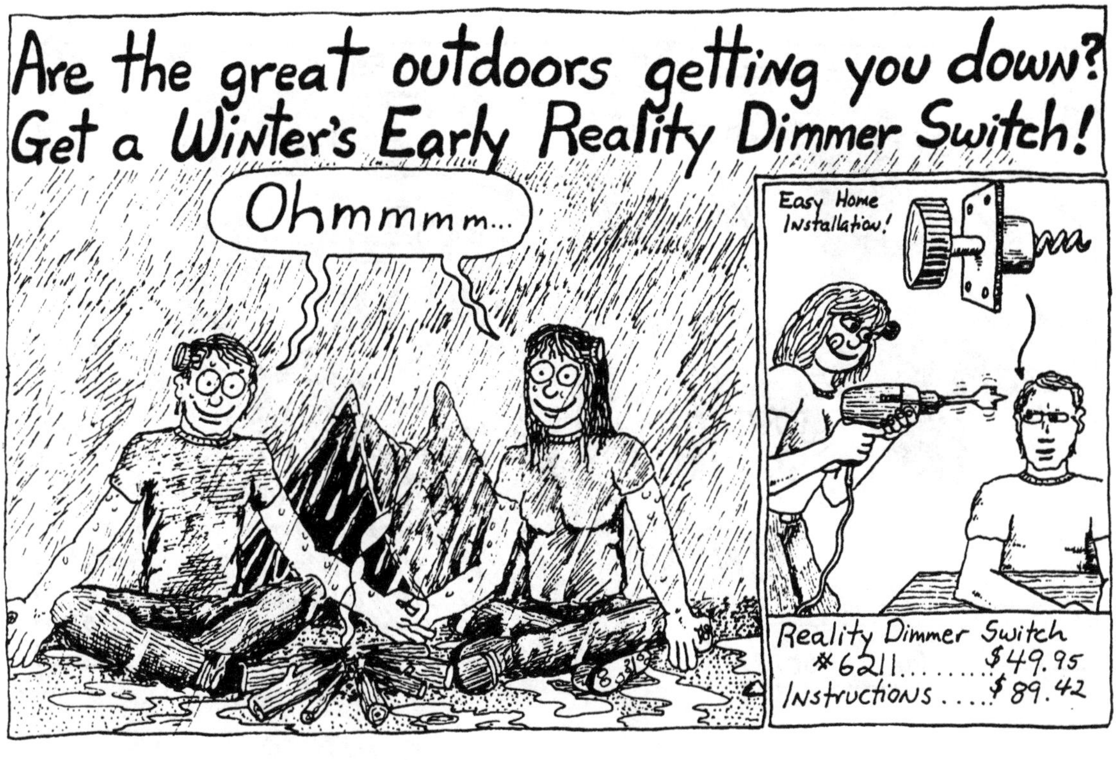
Are the great outdoors getting you down? Get a Winter's Early Reality Dimmer Switch!
Ohmmmm...
Easy Home Installation!
Reality Dimmer Switch
#6211.........$49.95
Instructions....$89.42

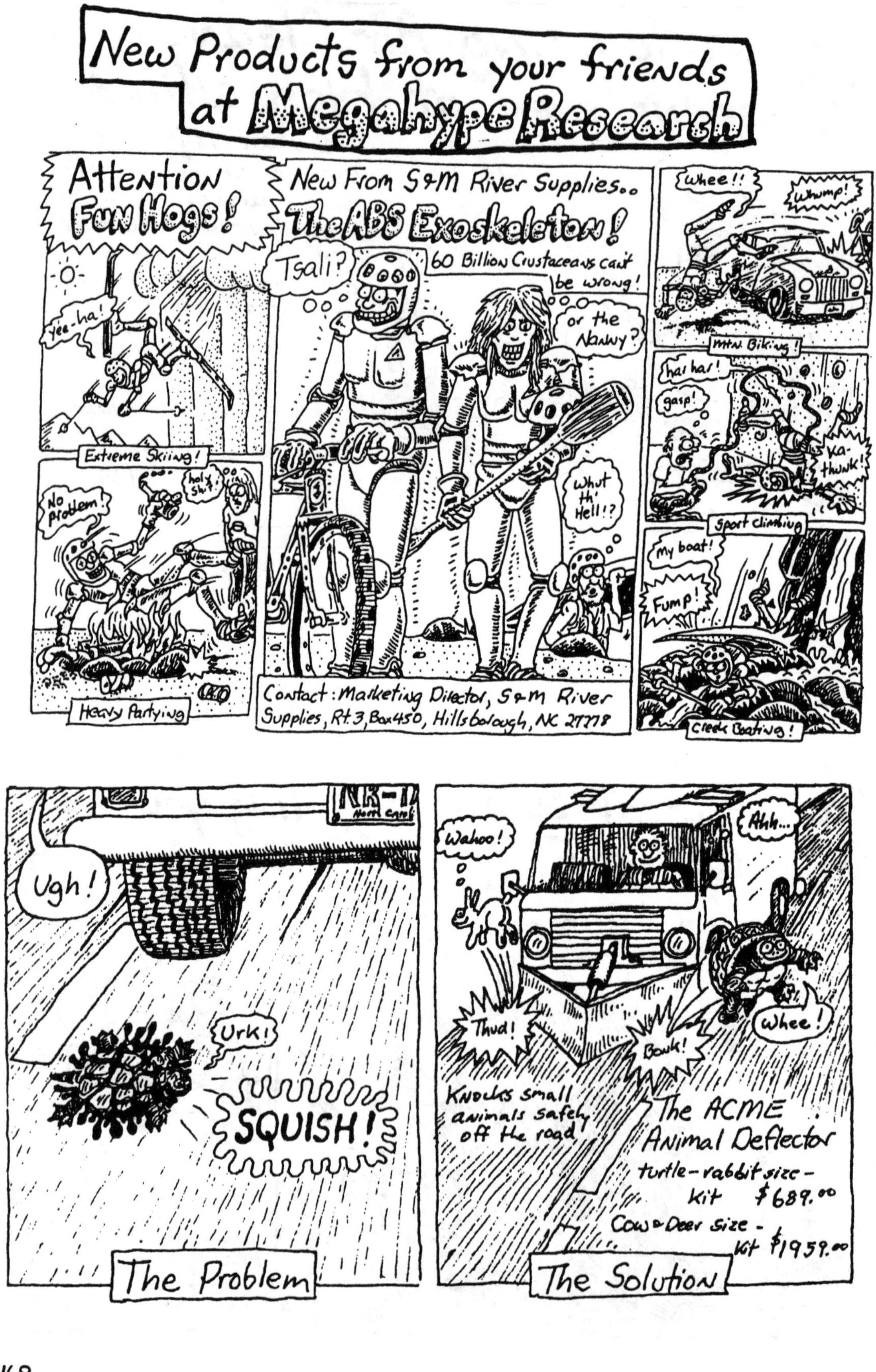
New Products from your friends at Megahype Research
Attention Fun Hogs!
Yee-ha!
Extreme Skiing!
No problem!
holy Shit!
Heavy Partying
New From S&M River Supplies..
The ABS Exoskeleton!
Tsali?
60 Billion Crustaceans can't be wrong!
or the Nanny?
Whut th' Hell!?
Contact: Marketing Director, S&M River Supplies, Rt.3, Box450, Hillsborough, NC 27278
Whee!!
Whump!
Mtn Biking!
ha! ha!
gasp!
Ka-thunk!
Sport climbing
My boat!
Fump!
Creek Boating!
Ugh!
Urk!
SQUISH!
The Problem
Wahoo!
Ahh...
Thud!
Bonk!
Whee!
Knocks small animals safely off the road
The ACME Animal Deflector
turtle-rabbit size - kit $689.00
Cow & Deer size - kit $1959.00
The Solution

The Megahype Offroad Exercycle Has It All!!

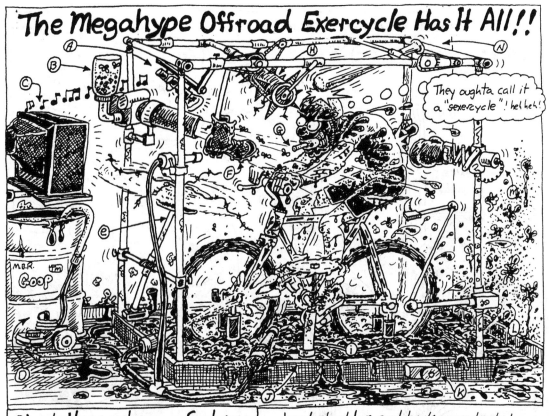

They oughta call it a "sexercycle"! heh heh!

Check these outrageous features:

(A) Heat lamps elicit instant **nausea**!

(B) Bug Gun™ shoots venomous **insects** into eyes, nostrils, ears and shirt! Eeek!

(C) Kamikaze Uphill Video synchronizes with exercycle features for **ultra-masochistic** riding simulation. Music by Wagner, of course!

(D) Goop™ Blower utilizes six jet nozzles to fire an omni-directional stream of **filth** and gunge under tremendous pressure into every nook and cranny of bike and rider!

(E) Barbed Wire Weedeater **scourges** rider's hands, arms and face! Yow!!

(F) Pneumatic **Steel-toed Boot** mimics trees, branches and P.O.ed Sierra Clubbers!

(G) 4 micron breathing tube transports you instantly to 18,000" above sea level (gasp)!

(H) Spike-studded Traversing Roller **flagellates** head, shoulders and back mercilessly!

(I) Seismo Resonators™ vibrate the bike frame at the exact frequency that causes total paralysis of the peripheral nervous system!

(J) Shin Scourge ~~dyno~~-buffs shins & ankles!

(K) Spiked Variable Resistance Roller guarantees a rear **flat** every 90 seconds!

(L) Flesh Hook works on crucial outer thigh area!

(M) 30 Oz. Boxing Glove Attachment **pounds** kidneys and lower back into something resembling pate'!

(N) Louisville Slugger Attachment **hammers** away superfluous **brain cells** without drugs!

Before — Have a Nice day!

After — Yo! beer!

For More Information Write; Marketing, Megahype Bicycle Research, Rt. 3 Box 450 Hillsboro, NC 27278

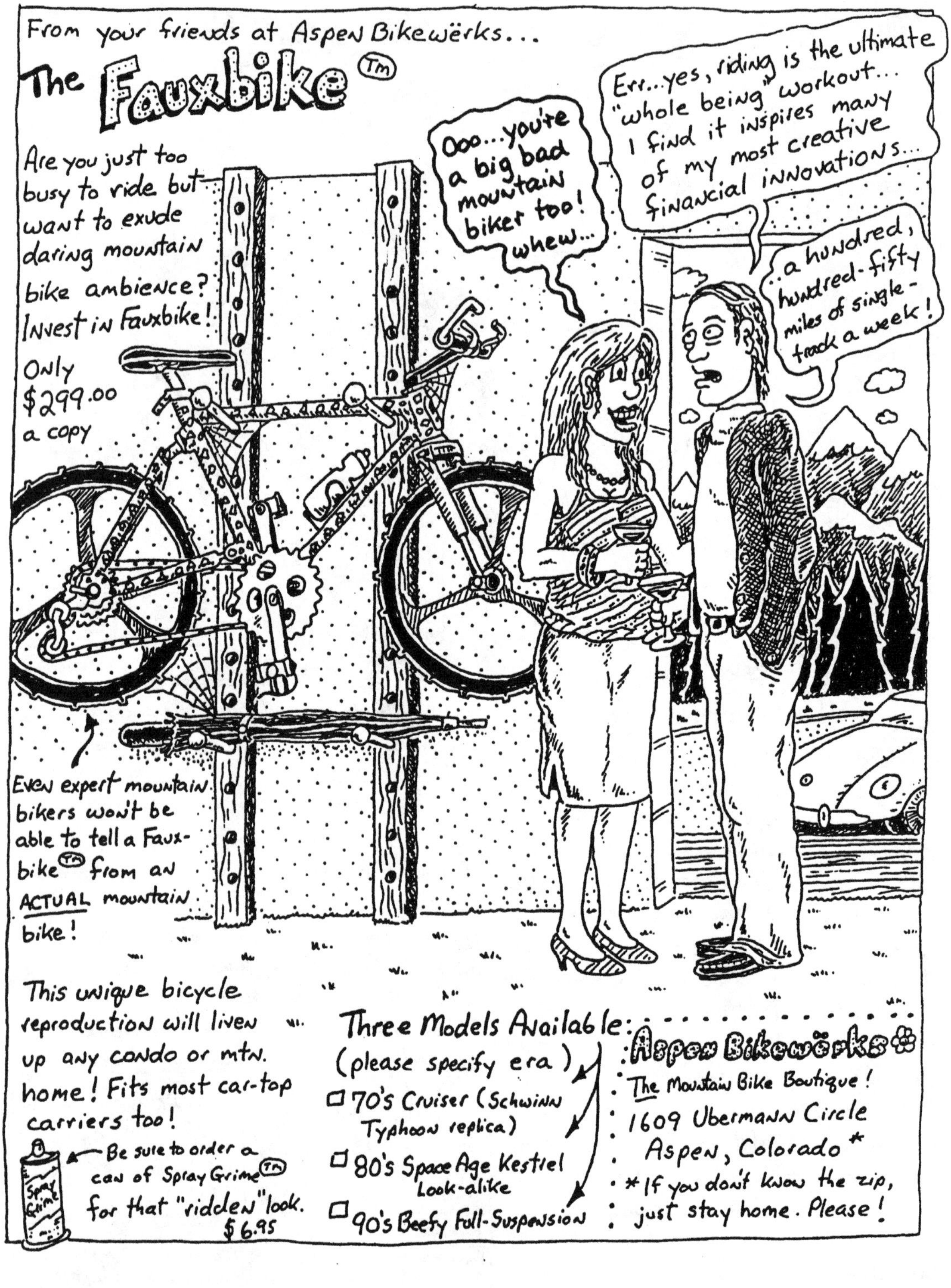

From your friends at Aspen Bikewërks...
The Fauxbike (Tm)
Are you just too busy to ride but want to exude daring mountain bike ambience? Invest in Fauxbike!
Only $299.00 a copy
Ooo...you're a big bad mountain biker too! whew...
Err...yes, riding is the ultimate "whole being" workout... I find it inspires many of my most creative financial innovations...
...a hundred, hundred-fifty miles of single-track a week!
Even expert mountain bikers won't be able to tell a Fauxbike(Tm) from an ACTUAL mountain bike!
This unique bicycle reproduction will liven up any condo or mtn. home! Fits most car-top carriers too!
Spray Grime
Be sure to order a can of Spray Grime(Tm) for that "ridden" look. $6.95
Three Models Available:
(please specify era)
☐ 70's Cruiser (Schwinn Typhoon replica)
☐ 80's Space Age Kestrel Look-alike
☐ 90's Beefy Full-Suspension
Aspen Bikewörks
The Mountain Bike Boutique!
1609 Ubermann Circle
Aspen, Colorado*
*If you don't know the zip, just stay home. Please!

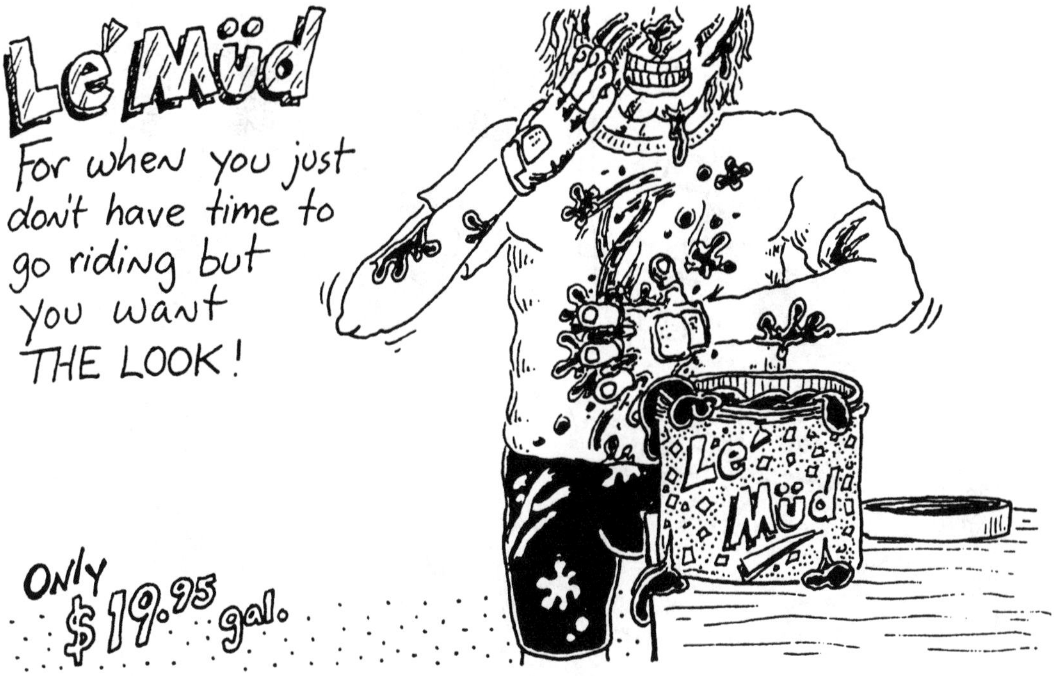
Le Müd
For when you just don't have time to go riding but you want THE LOOK!
Le Müd
ONLY $19.95 gal.

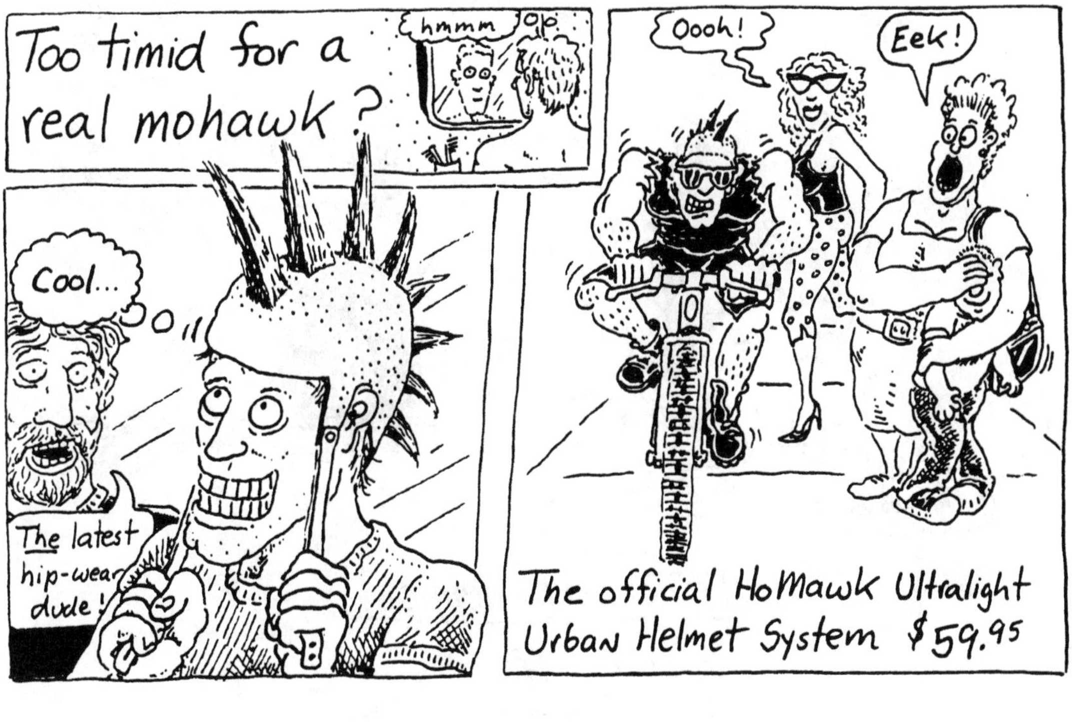
Too timid for a real mohawk?
hmmm
Cool...
The latest hip-wear dude!
Oooh!
Eek!
The official HoMawk Ultralight Urban Helmet System $59.95

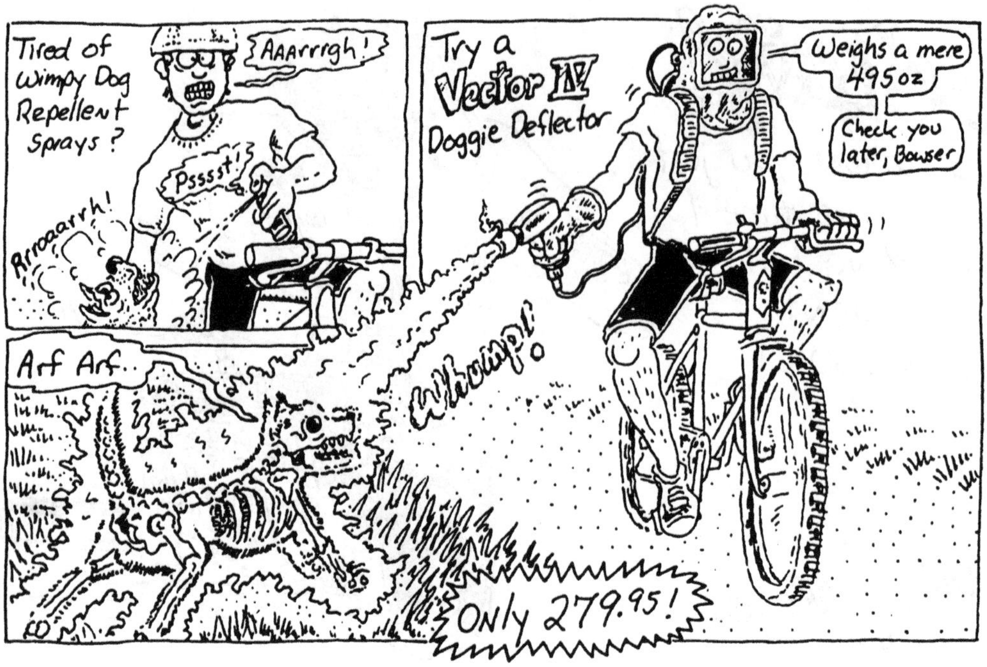
Tired of Wimpy Dog Repellent Sprays?
AAArrrgh!
Psssst!
Arrooaarrh!
Try a Vector IV Doggie Deflector
Weighs a mere 495 oz
Check you later, Bowser
Arf Arf
Whoomp!
Only 279.95!

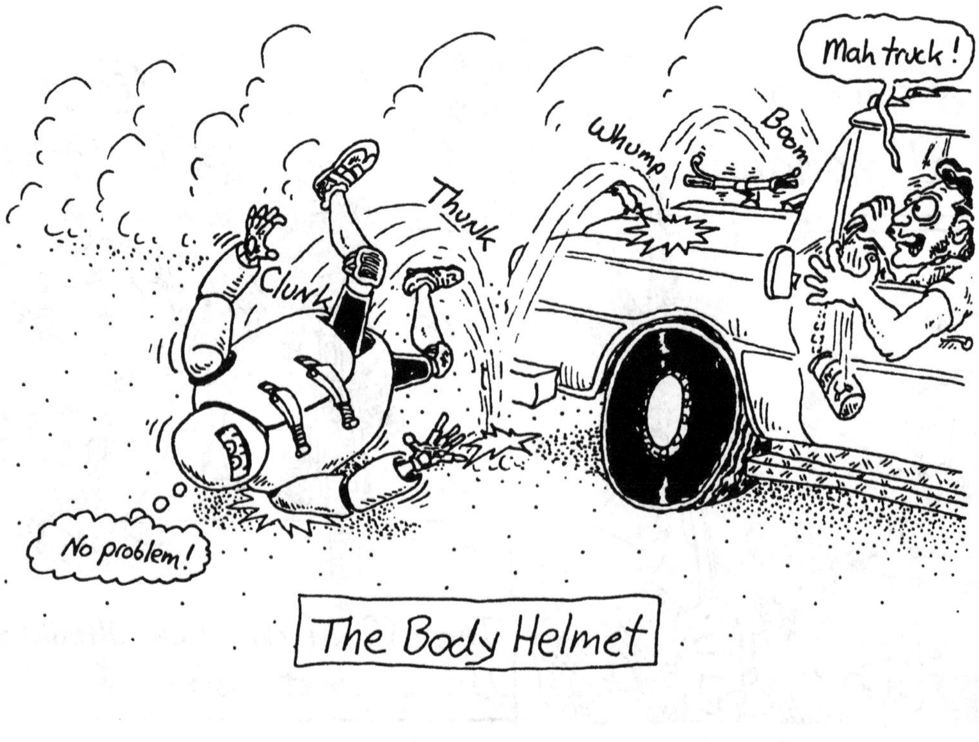
Mah truck!
Whump
Boom
Thunk
Clunk
No problem!

The Body Helmet

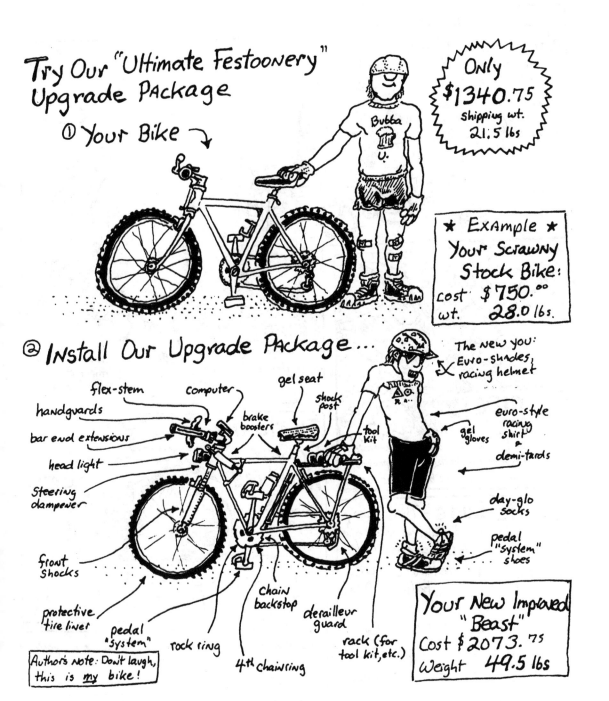

Try Our "Ultimate Festoonery" Upgrade Package

① Your Bike →

Bubba U.

ONLY $1340.75
shipping wt. 21.5 lbs

* EXAMPLE *
Your Scrawny Stock Bike:
Cost $750.⁰⁰
wt. 28.0 lbs.

② Install Our Upgrade Package...

The New you: Euro-shades, racing helmet

flex-stem
computer
gel seat
shock post
handguards
brake boosters
bar end extensions
tool kit
head light
euro-style racing shirt
gel gloves
demi-tards
steering dampener
day-glo socks
front shocks
pedal "system" shoes
protective tire liner
pedal "system"
rock ring
chain backstop
derailleur guard
4th chainring
rack (for tool kit, etc.)

Your New Improved "Beast"
Cost $2073.⁷⁵
Weight 49.5 lbs

Author's note: Don't laugh, this is my bike!

173

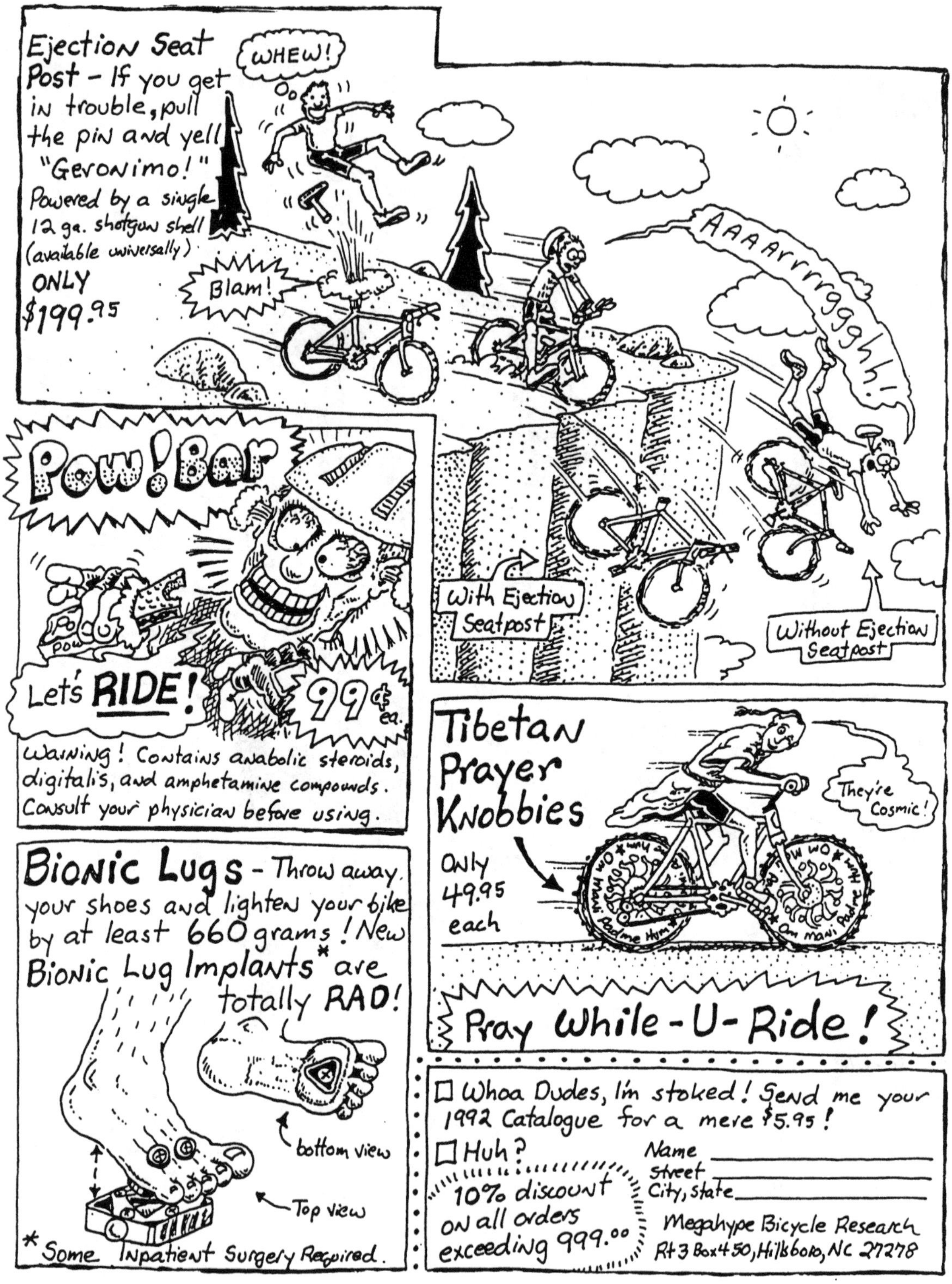

Ejection Seat Post - If you get in trouble, pull the pin and yell "Geronimo!" Powered by a single 12 ga. shotgun shell (available universally)
ONLY $199.95
WHEW!
Blam!
AAAArrrrggghh!
With Ejection Seatpost
Without Ejection Seatpost
Pow! Bar
Pow
Let's RIDE!
99¢ ea.
Warning! Contains anabolic steroids, digitalis, and amphetamine compounds. Consult your physician before using.
Tibetan Prayer Knobbies
Only 49.95 each
They're Cosmic!
Pray While-U-Ride!
Bionic Lugs - Throw away your shoes and lighten your bike by at least 660 grams! New Bionic Lug Implants* are totally RAD!
bottom view
Top view
* Some Inpatient Surgery Required.
☐ Whoa Dudes, I'm stoked! Send me your 1992 Catalogue for a mere $5.95!
☐ Huh?
10% discount on all orders exceeding 999.00
Name
street
City, state
Megahype Bicycle Research
Rt 3 Box 450, Hillsboro, NC 27278

S&M River Supplies

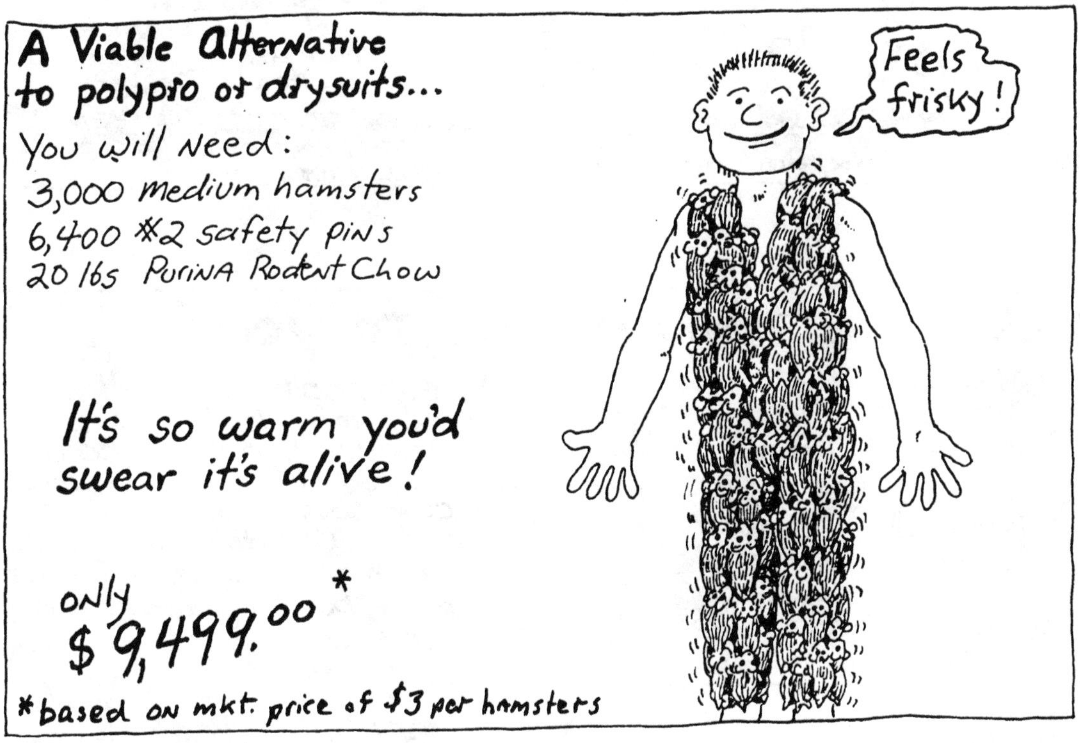

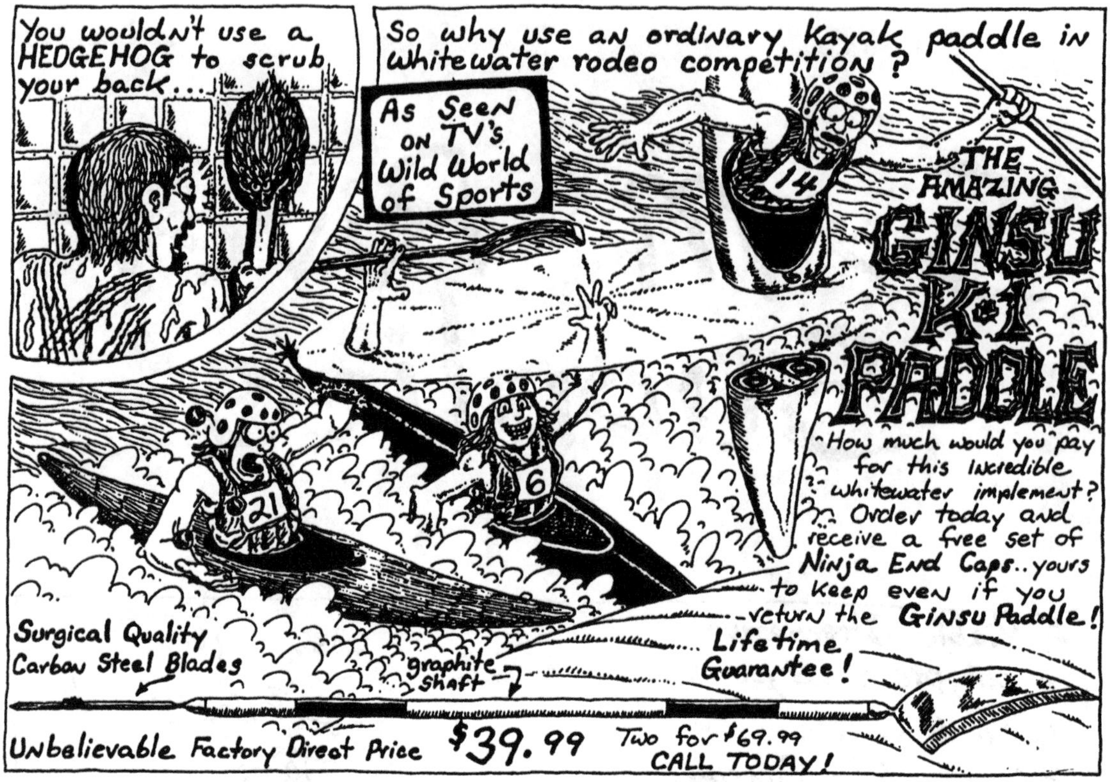
You wouldn't use a HEDGEHOG to scrub your back...
So why use an ordinary kayak paddle in whitewater rodeo competition?
As Seen on TV's Wild World of Sports
THE AMAZING GINSU K-1 PADDLE
14
21
6
How much would you pay for this incredible whitewater implement? Order today and receive a free set of Ninja End Caps.. yours to keep even if you return the GINSU Paddle!
Lifetime Guarantee!
Surgical Quality Carbon Steel Blades
graphite shaft
Unbelievable Factory Direct Price $39.99 Two for $69.99
CALL TODAY!

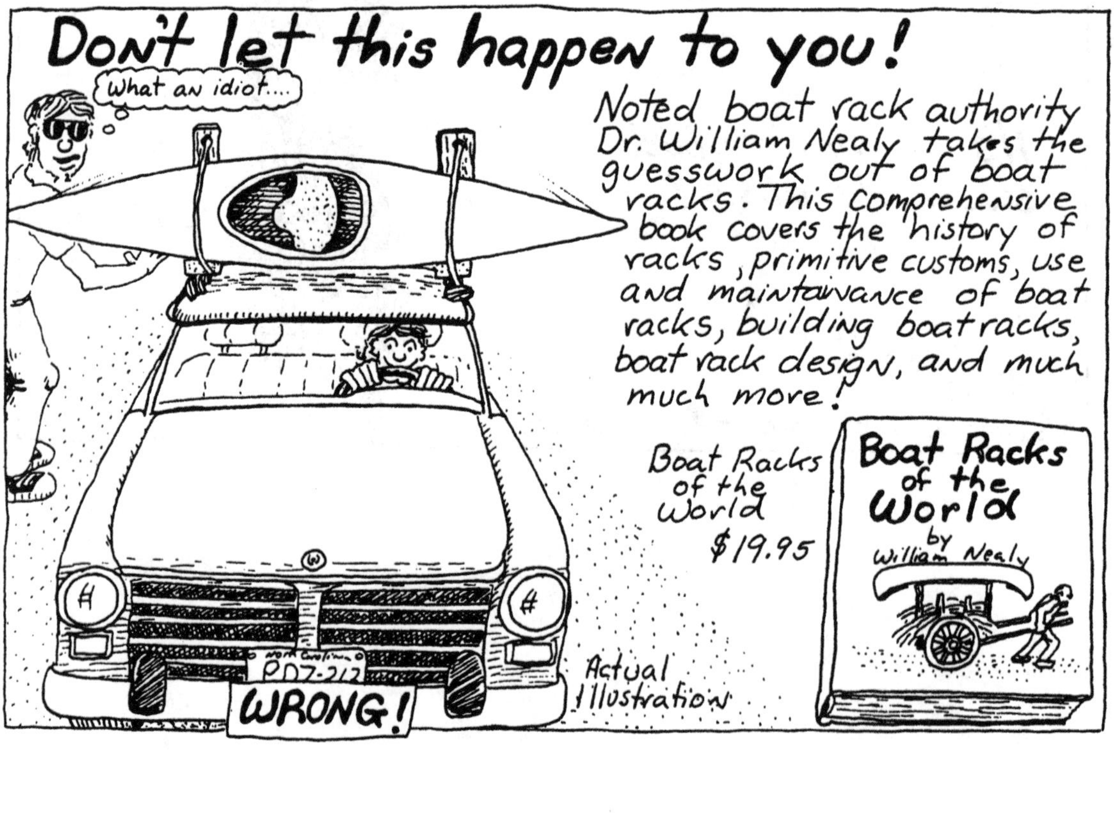
Don't let this happen to you!
What an idiot....
Noted boat rack authority Dr. William Nealy takes the guesswork out of boat racks. This comprehensive book covers the history of racks, primitive customs, use and maintainance of boat racks, building boatracks, boat rack design, and much much more!
Boat Racks of the World $19.95
Boat Racks of the World by William Nealy
Actual Illustration
WRONG!

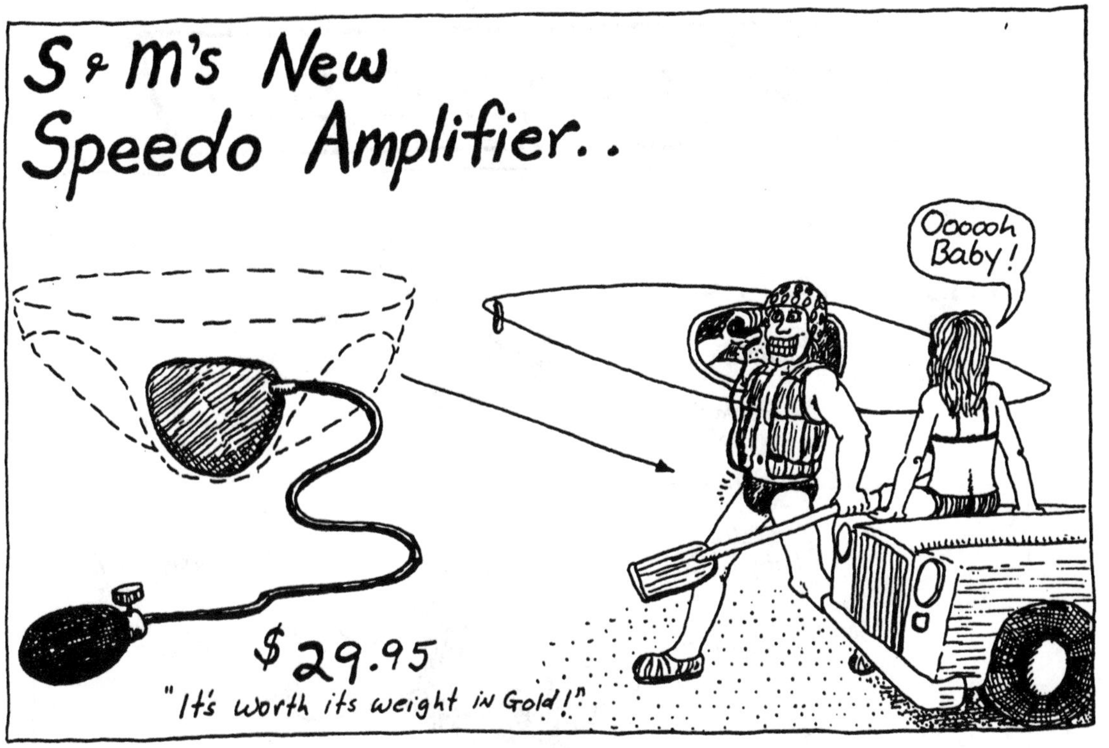
S & M's New Speedo Amplifier..
Oooooh Baby!
$29.95
"It's worth its weight in Gold!"

★ Porsche 928-S ★

Old shuttle time records for the New and Gauley Rivers fell like center-shot mallards last month when we road-tested the 928-S on an actual paddling trip. Despite its 4.7" ground-clearance, our test car took all West Virginia's treacherous mountain roads could dish out and more! But for a freak mechanical problem caused by a chicken somehow getting sucked into an engine air intake, the state troopers would never have come close to catching our test vehicle.

Since our sentencing for various driving-related felonies we've had lots of time to reflect on both the design and performance of the amazing 928-S... Positive Assets - speed, power, great cornering ability, ease in shifting, ease with which possession of said vehicle causes attractive members of the opposite sex to desire a short-term physical relationship in a seedy rural motel, phenomenal braking ability.. Negative Assets - lack of space for camping & boating gear, lack of rain gutters, lack of space for backseat passengers, cost.

The aforementioned design flaw (lack of rain gutters for attaching boat racks to) is easily overcome by gluing or spot welding rack brackets directly to the roof of the vehicle. Caution: high wind velocity and g-forces may cause shearing of rack brackets between the weld & the crossbar mount. However, as we discovered in testing, loss of boats is only a minor inconvience since a paddler looses all interest in boats and boating once seated behind the wheel of the 928-S!

Vital Statistics	
Builder - Porsche	
Type - medium volume cruiser	
cost - $50,000.00	
Materials	
body - welded steel & aluminum	
engine - V-8 aluminum block & heads	
Performance	
0-60 mph	5.7 seconds
Stndg ¼ mile	14.6 sec. @ 94 mph
horsepower	288 bhp
Top Speed	154 mph

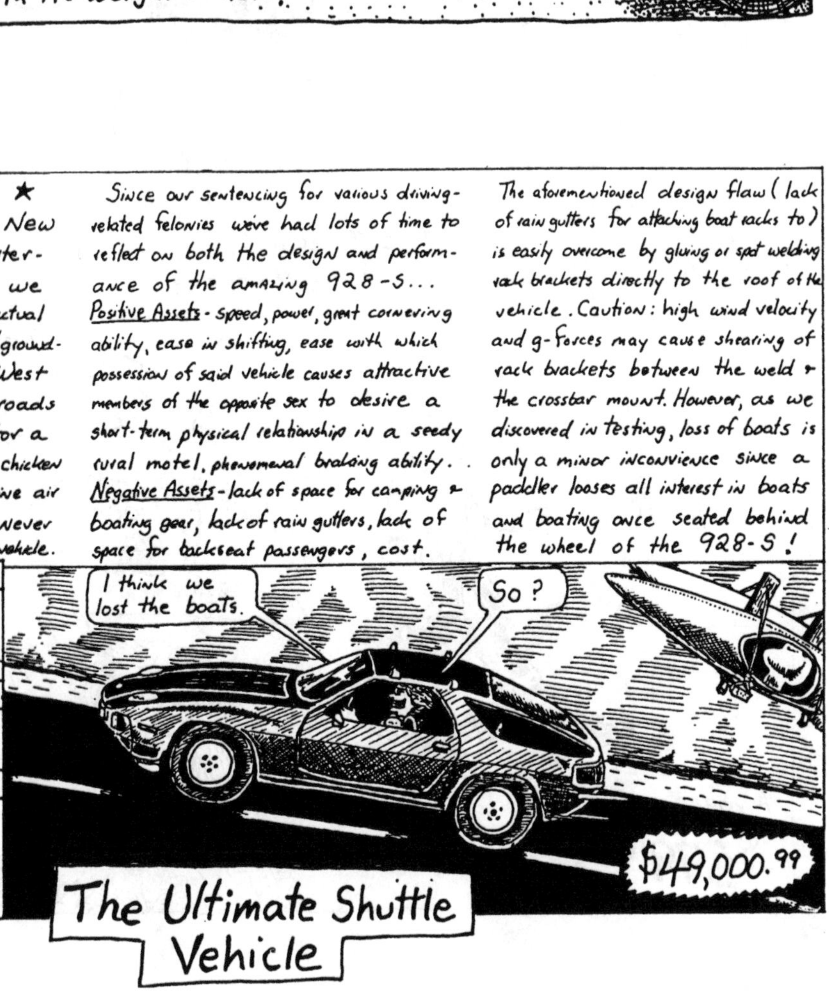
I think we lost the boats.
So?
$49,000.99
The Ultimate Shuttle Vehicle

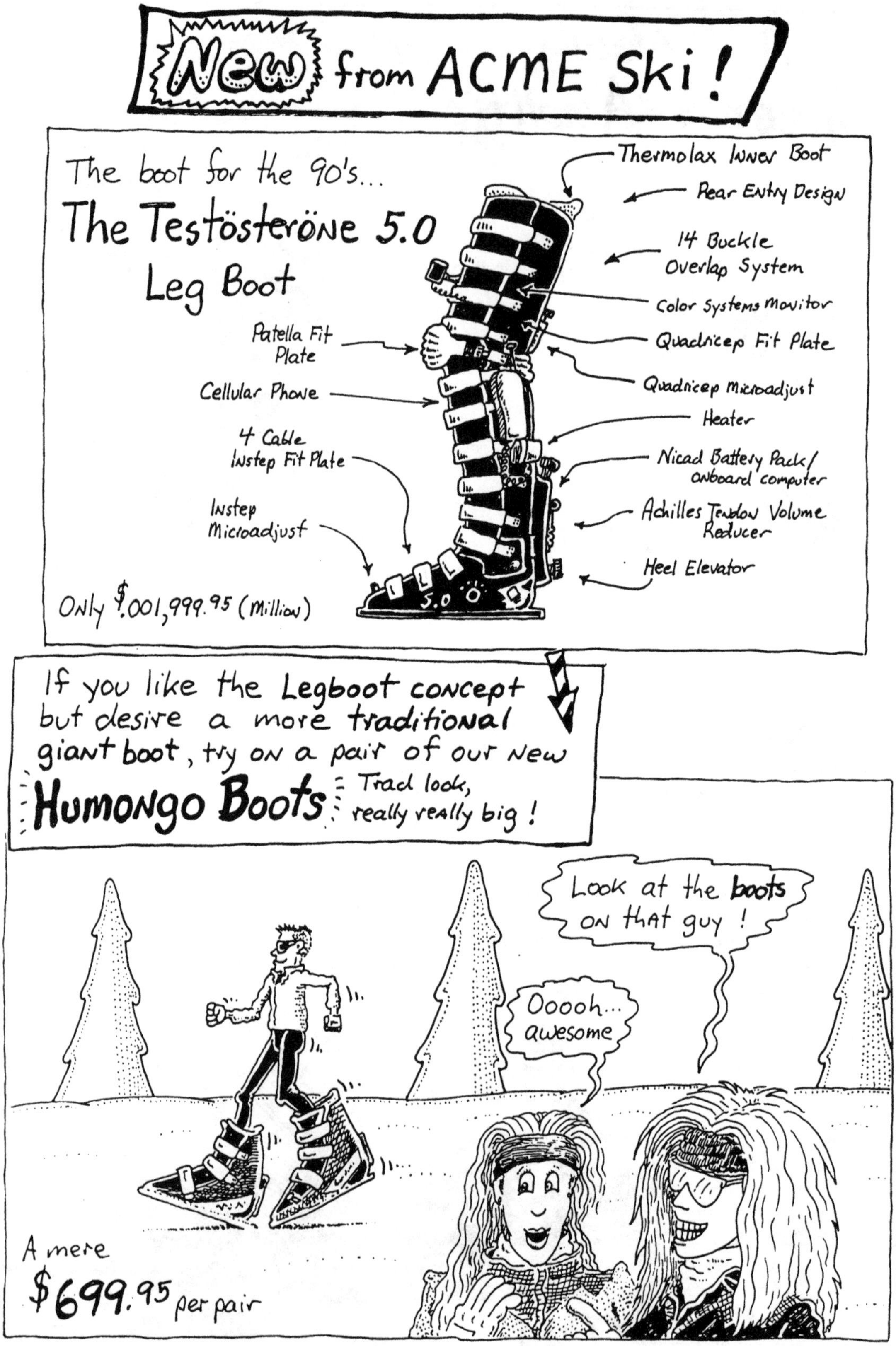
New from ACME Ski!
The boot for the 90's...
The Testösteröne 5.0 Leg Boot
Thermolax Inner Boot
Rear Entry Design
14 Buckle Overlap System
Color Systems Monitor
Quadricep Fit Plate
Quadricep Microadjust
Heater
Nicad Battery Pack/ onboard computer
Achilles Tendon Volume Reducer
Heel Elevator
Patella Fit Plate
Cellular Phone
4 Cable Instep Fit Plate
Instep Microadjust
5.0
Only $.001,999.95 (Million)
If you like the Legboot concept but desire a more traditional giant boot, try on a pair of our new Humongo Boots
Trad look, really really big!
Look at the boots on that guy!
Ooooh... awesome
A mere $699.95 per pair

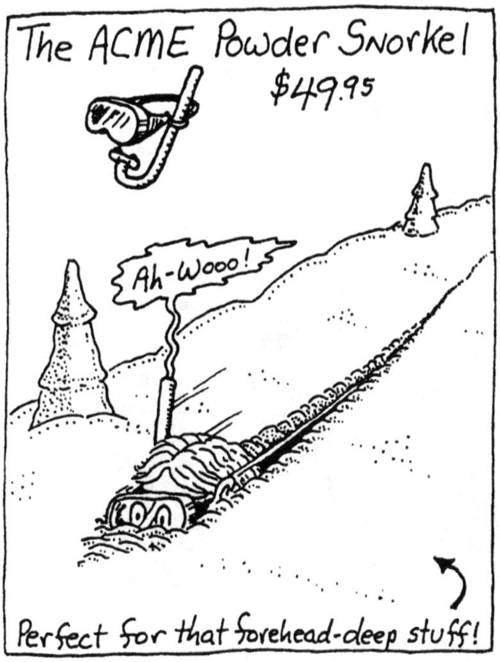
The ACME Powder Snorkel
$49.95
Ah-Wooo!
Perfect for that forehead-deep stuff!

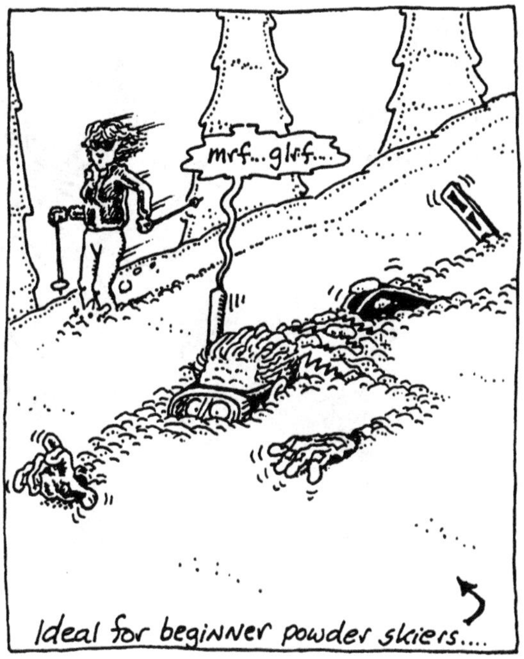
mrf...glrf...
Ideal for beginner powder skiers....

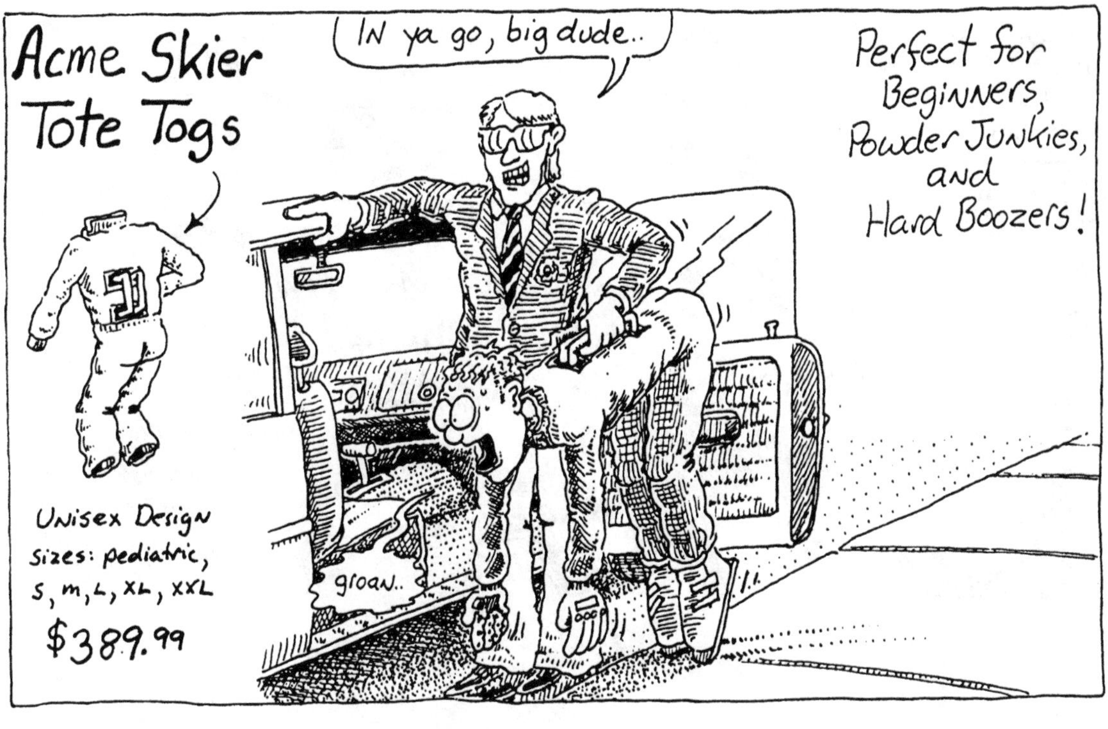
Acme Skier Tote Togs
IN ya go, big dude..
Perfect for Beginners, Powder Junkies, and Hard Boozers!
groan..
Unisex Design
sizes: pediatric, S, M, L, XL, XXL
$389.99

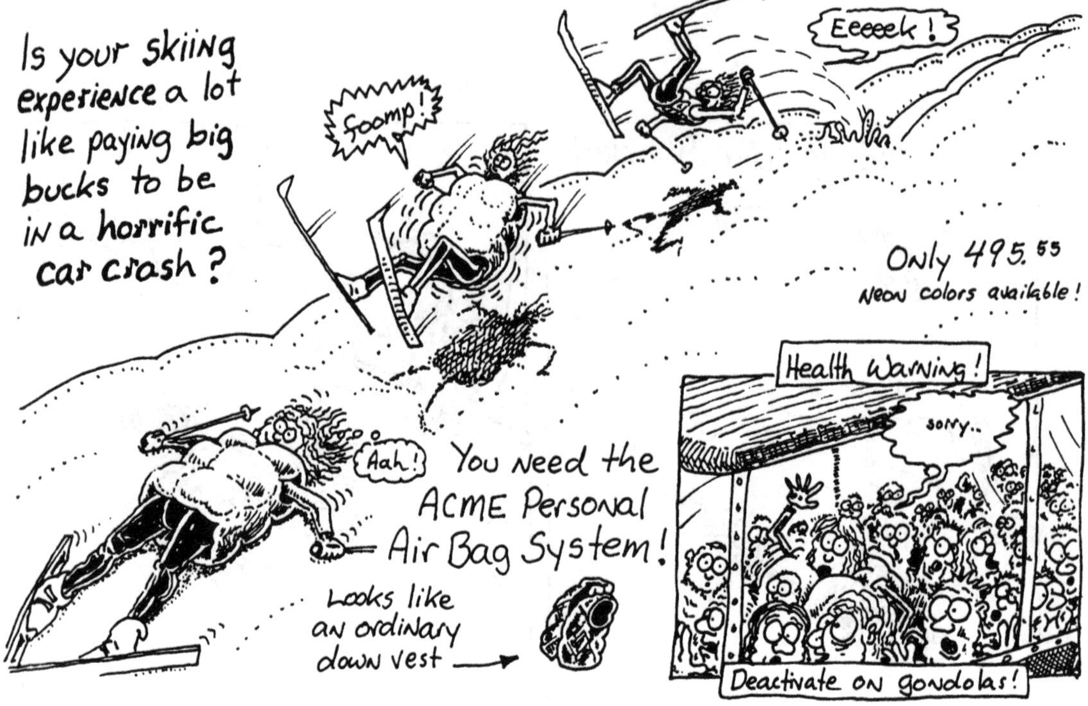
Is your skiing experience a lot like paying big bucks to be in a horrific car crash?
foomp!
Eeeeek!
Only 495.55
Neon colors available!
Aah!
You need the ACME Personal Air Bag System!
Looks like an ordinary down vest
Health Warning!
sorry..
Deactivate on gondolas!

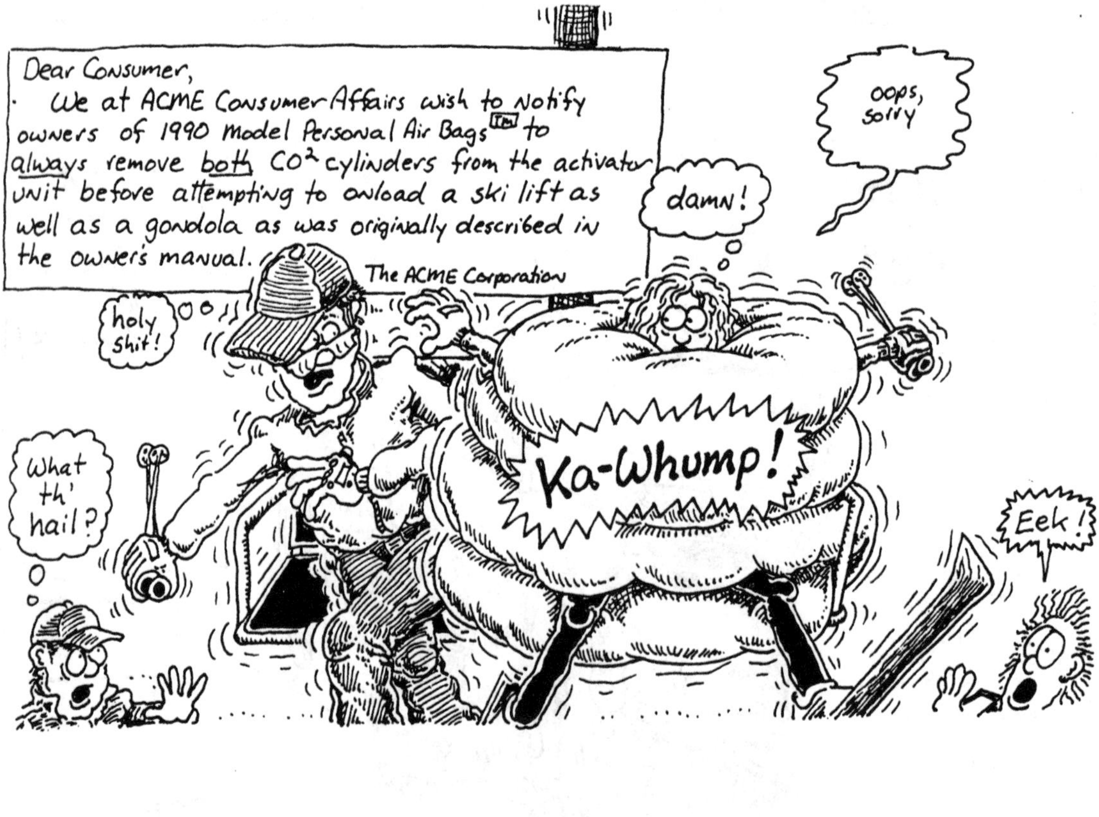
Dear Consumer,
We at ACME Consumer Affairs wish to notify owners of 1990 Model Personal Air Bags TM to always remove both CO2 cylinders from the activator unit before attempting to onload a ski lift as well as a gondola as was originally described in the owner's manual.
The ACME Corporation
oops, sorry
damn!
holy shit!
What th' hail?
Ka-Whump!
Eek!

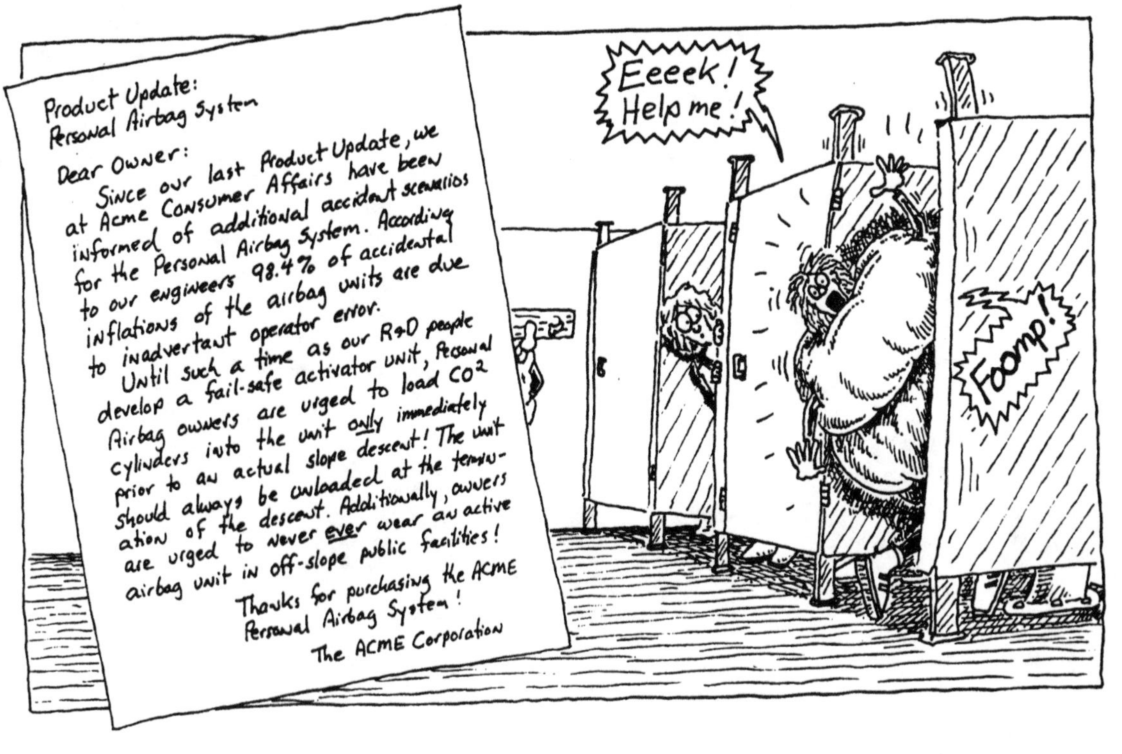
Product Update:
Personal Airbag System
Dear Owner:
Since our last Product Update, we at Acme Consumer Affairs have been informed of additional accident scenarios for the Personal Airbag System. According to our engineers 98.4% of accidental inflations of the airbag units are due to inadvertant operator error.
Until such a time as our R&D people develop a fail-safe activator unit, Personal Airbag owners are urged to load CO2 cylinders into the unit only immediately prior to an actual slope descent! The unit should always be unloaded at the termination of the descent. Additionally, owners are urged to never ever wear an active airbag unit in off-slope public facilities!
Thanks for purchasing the ACME Personal Airbag System!
The ACME Corporation
Eeeek! Help me!
Foomp!

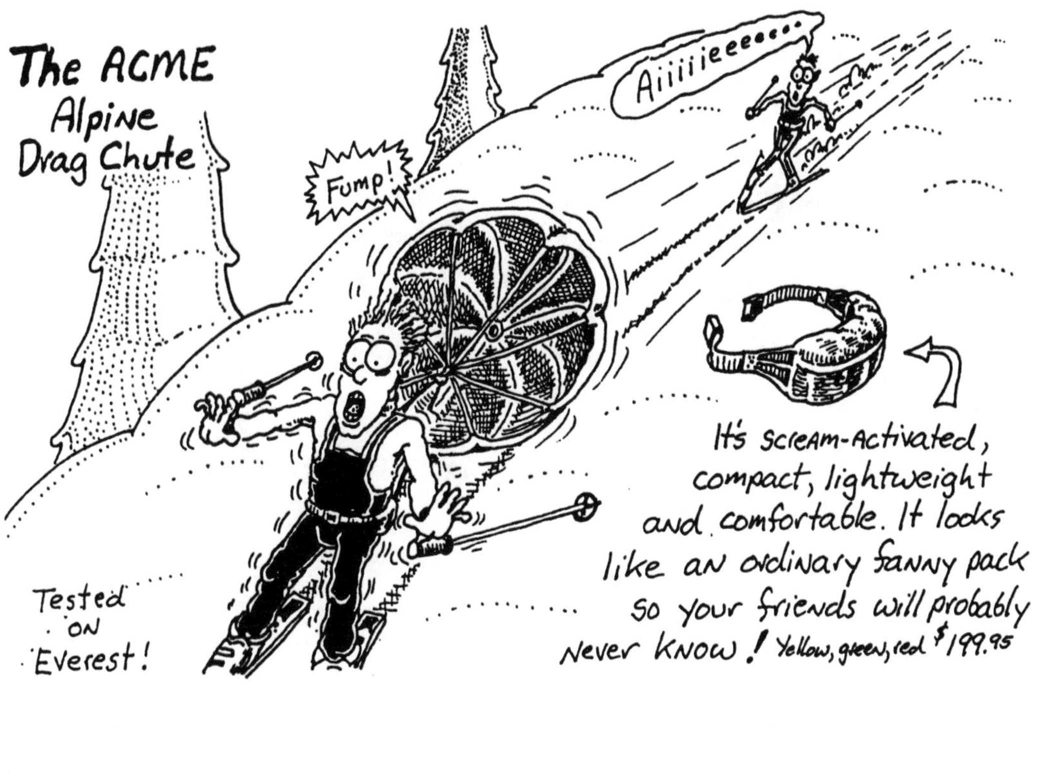
The ACME Alpine Drag Chute
Aiiiiieeee....
Fump!
It's scream-activated, compact, lightweight and comfortable. It looks like an ordinary fanny pack so your friends will probably never know! Yellow, green, red $199.95
Tested on Everest!

Learning Channel

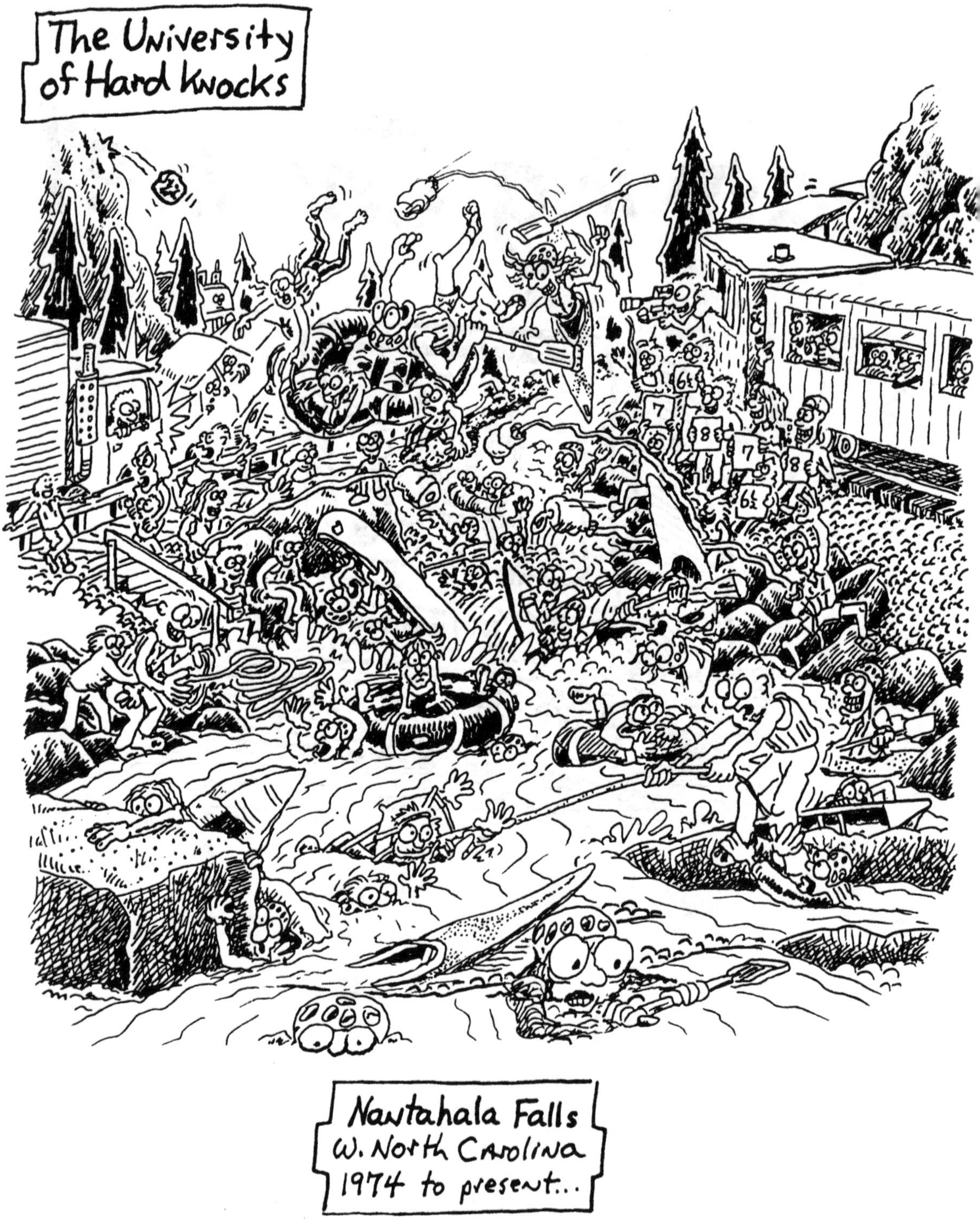
The University of Hard Knocks
7
6½
8
7
8
6½

Nantahala Falls
W. North Carolina
1974 to present...

Learning Channel

Getting to observe beginners crashing and burning (as well as the experts stylin' to humiliate the beginners) has always been a key aspect of my outdoor experiences. Not quite as important as the **adrenaline/dopamine rush**, but close.

While what we physically do in these pursuits is often dangerous and bodily miserable, the <u>really</u> interesting part is the individual's psychological response and growth. Thinking you're going to **die** will put you through a serious emotional wringer. You evolve mentally as well as physically as you progress from beginner to expert; a blob of quivering ectoplasm to demigod in just under 1,000 easy lessons!

It's not the flipless ultra-clean run down the Upper Gauley that sticks in your mind over the years. It's the **horrendous** thrashing you received in Nantahala Falls (or equivalent) in front of 200 spectators when you were a drooling beginner that you remember, **always**. A possum floating on a piece of driftwood can run a 30' drop with ease but it takes real **courage** and mental

Zen Learning Experience...

Tha-wap!

Thank you master...

discipline for a novice to strategize and then run a 7' drop. We all get hammered initially, the important thing is what you **learn** from the beating. You evolve or go extinct (figuratively, I hope). And all this while wet, cold, and dirty... whew! Misery loves comedy. And vice versa...

185

Learning To Learn

Most mtn. bike learning is of the self-instructed experiential variety. To wit, you ride progressively harder & harder stuff, wipe out a lot and learn from your mistakes (see below).

Eureka!

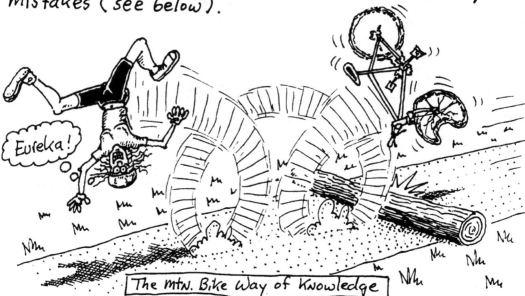

The mtn. Bike Way of Knowledge

Eventually you will train your body to react quickly and instinctively to a wide variety of obstacles and trail conditions while having loads of fun. Mountain biking is a never-ending learning process and as long as you're having fun you are on the learning curve (see below).

Skill
Fun Plane
Mega Fun
Success
Fun
No Fun
Failure
"No Fun" Training Slump
Time

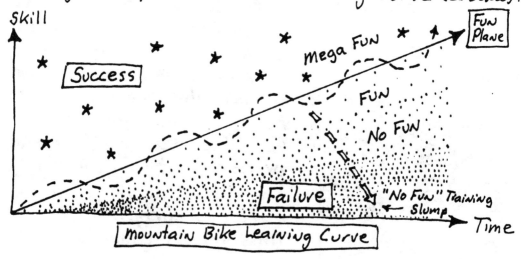

Mountain Bike Learning Curve

Brain Knowledge
Hmm.. 6" log, loose surface, speed: 10 mph, two seconds to impact..
Analysis
Cranks horizontal, coil body, load wheels... pull up on bars... shove bars forward...
Skill Protocol
Yiii?!
Thonk

fig. 1

Body Knowledge
Yo!
response
internalized Hop Protocol
Stimulus
Boink!

fig. 2

Pedal, you *!G? Weenie! Move! You're gonna hop that log or die trying!
gasp!

fig. 3, Training To Fail

How your mind perceives an obstacle after more than three consecutive failures...
Aiiieee!
gasp!

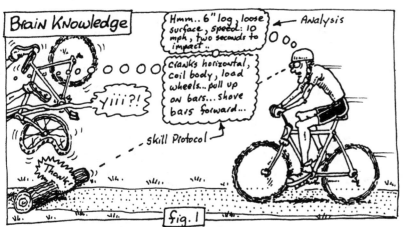

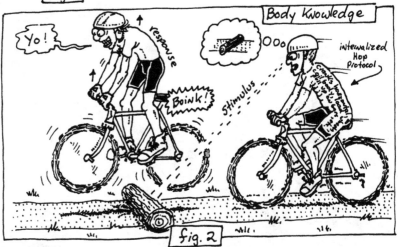

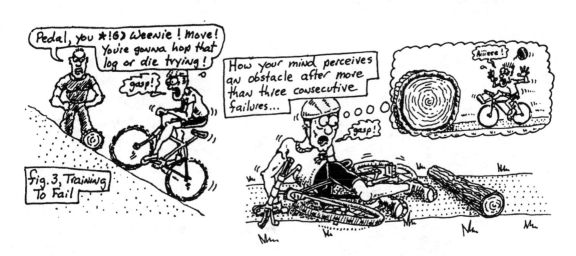

Inevitably, as you learn and progress...

Falls Happen...

As we get older, not only do we get brittler, fatter, clumsier, and even stupider, we develop an uncanny knack for analyzing and reflecting on our mistakes milliseconds before hitting the ground...

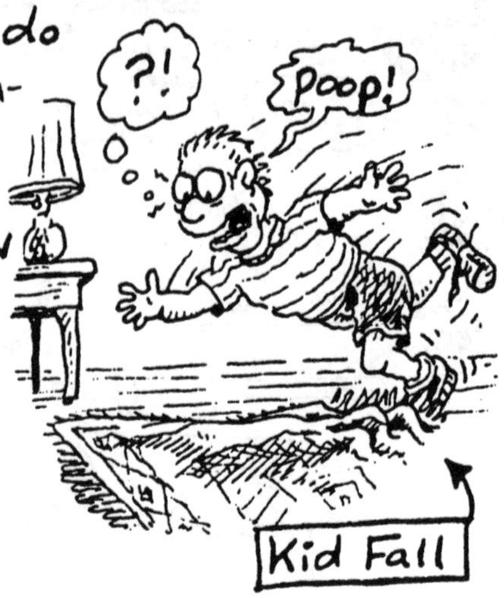
?!
Poop!
Kid Fall

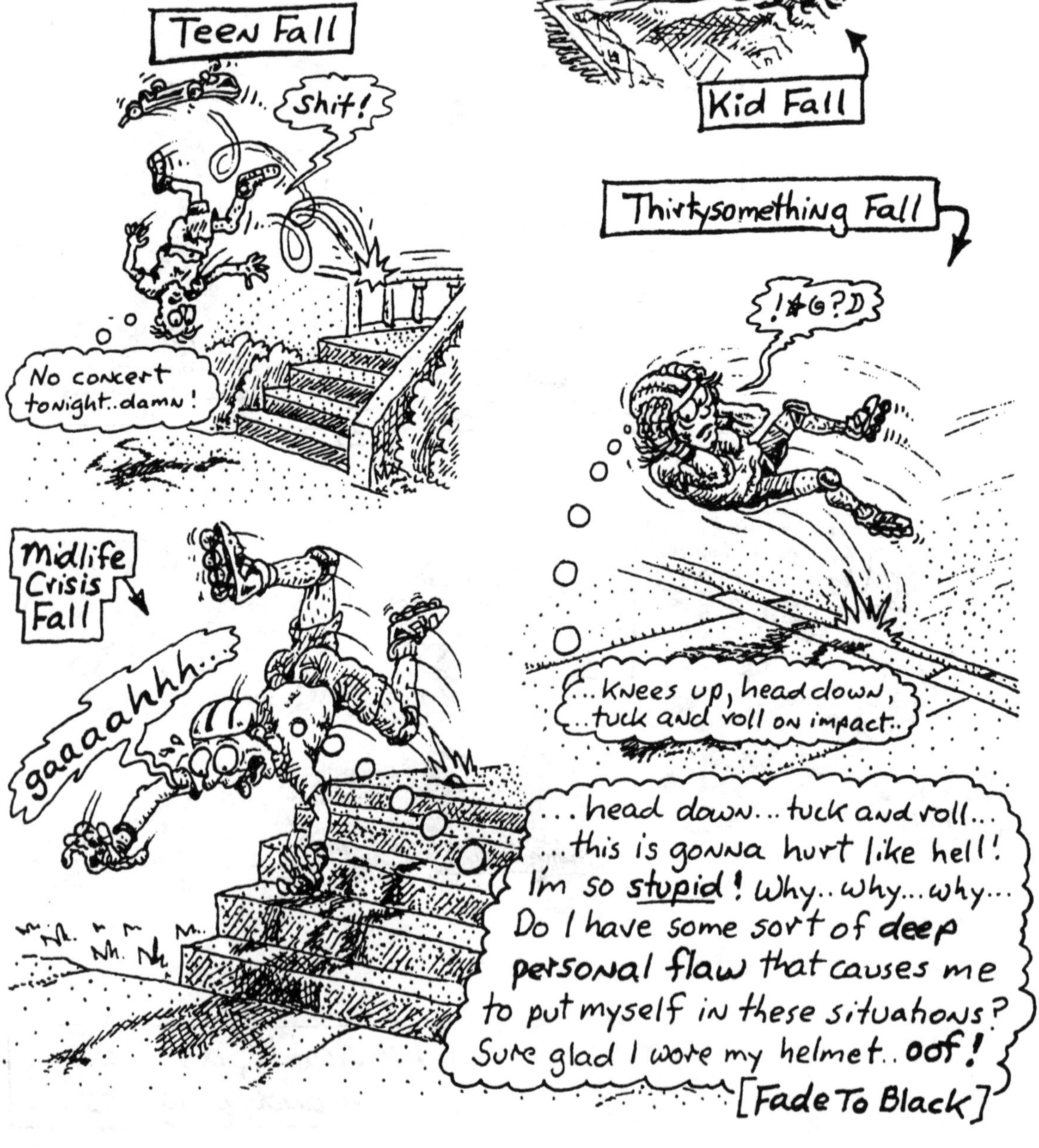
Teen Fall
Shit!
No concert tonight..damn!
Thirtysomething Fall
!#G?D
..knees up, head down, ..tuck and roll on impact..
Midlife Crisis Fall
gaaaahhh...
...head down...tuck and roll...
...this is gonna hurt like hell!
I'm so stupid! Why..why...why...
Do I have some sort of deep personal flaw that causes me to put myself in these situations?
Sure glad I wore my helmet..oof!
[Fade To Black]

Post-crash Psychic Trauma Recovery...

After a truly bad mountain bike trashing there's likely to be a period of depression while the former rider lies around waiting for the bones to knit back together. The recovering rider may even develop something akin to a phobia related to mountain biking (fig. 1) and may (god forbid!) consider selling his/her bike and taking up some nebbish retro-sport like roadcycling or frisbee football.

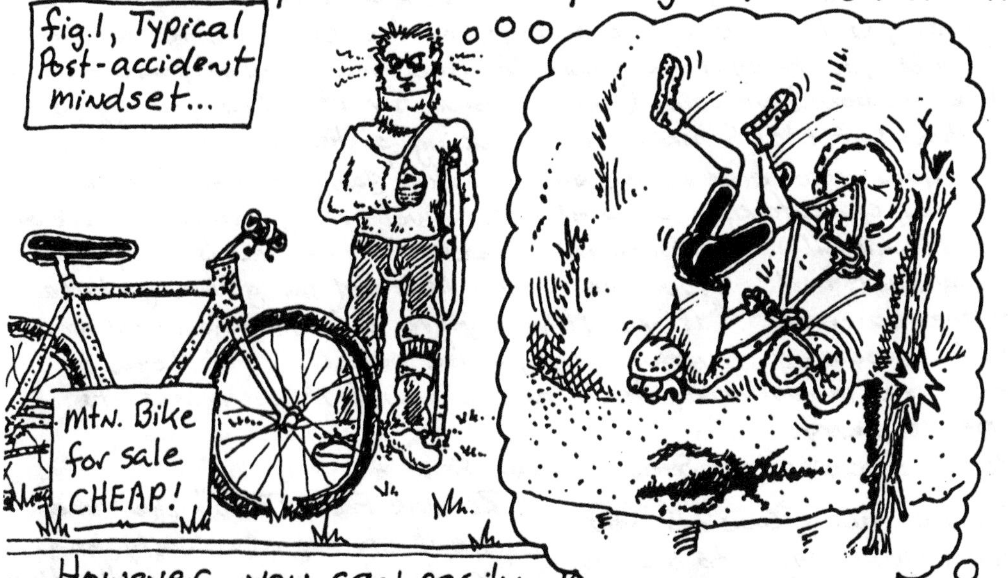

Mtn. Bike for sale CHEAP!

fig.1, Typical Post-accident mindset...

However, you can easily make a bad crash a positive experience by analyzing and learning from it.* A crash can bring on a conceptual leap in technique like a whack upside the head from an old zen master. The following pages document my most serious wipe-out so far and what I learned from it. The crash made me a much better rider albeit a slower and more conservative one... [* fig. 2]

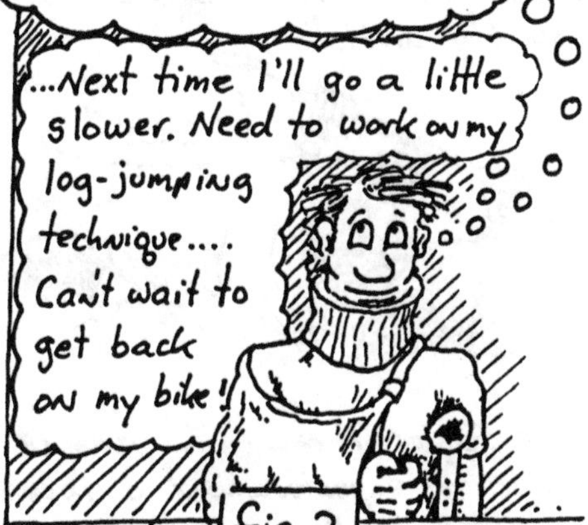

...Next time I'll go a little slower. Need to work on my log-jumping technique.... Can't wait to get back on my bike!

fig. 2

The Crash & Burn theory of education leads to...

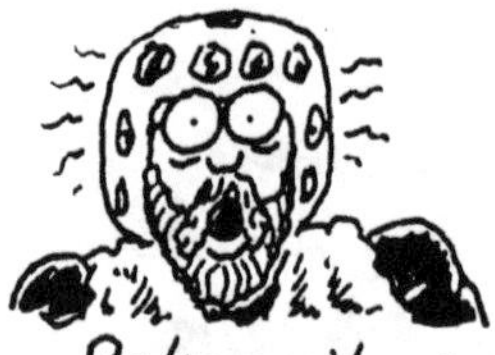

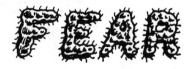

FEAR

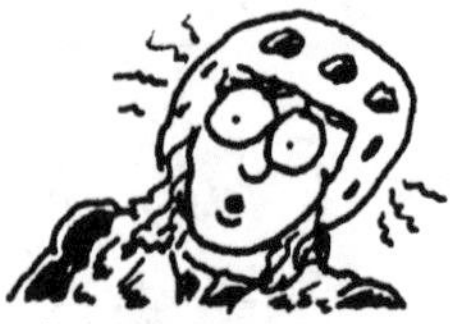

Believe it or not, sometime or another all kayakers experience fear... unless they're very very stupid. Fear is a perfectly natural and normal response to what is perceived to be a physical threat to life and/or limb. Recognizing the whitewater environment to be ultimately hostile to human life, it's obvious we have to learn to control fear a good bit of the time. "Good" fear makes you think.. it gives you the courage to portage or the concentration to run a rapid you thought you couldn't. "Bad" fear causes panic, elevated pulse, irrational behavior (such as "going for it" when you know you shouldn't, etc). A person experiencing a heavy dose of bad fear goes into preemptive shock (aka. "going to sleep", "zombied out" etc.), characterized by numbness, tunnel vision, inability to talk or paddle skillfully, etc. Preemptive shock is your brain's way of telling your body "Run this if you like but I'm gonna go hide in the basement!" If you think you're out of control and you maybe shouldn't try this drop, you're probably right. Learn to recognize immobilizing fear and channel it... it means it's time to carry.

Basic Precepts of Serious "River Fear" -

Zombie Factor One - "If you think you're going to die, you probably will."

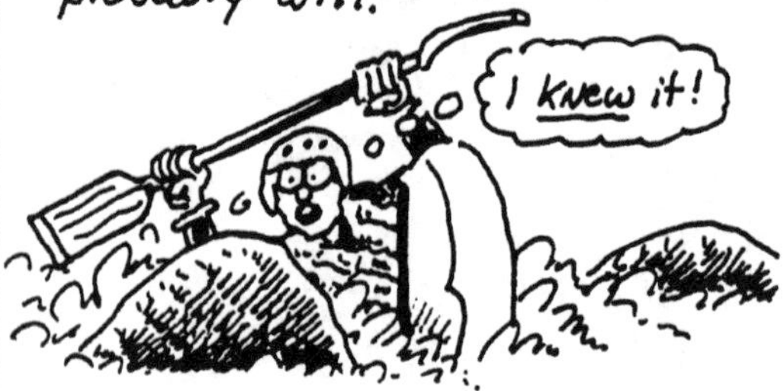
I knew it!

Zombie Factor Two - "The time spent staring at a nasty hole is directly proportional to the time you'll spend getting trashed in it."

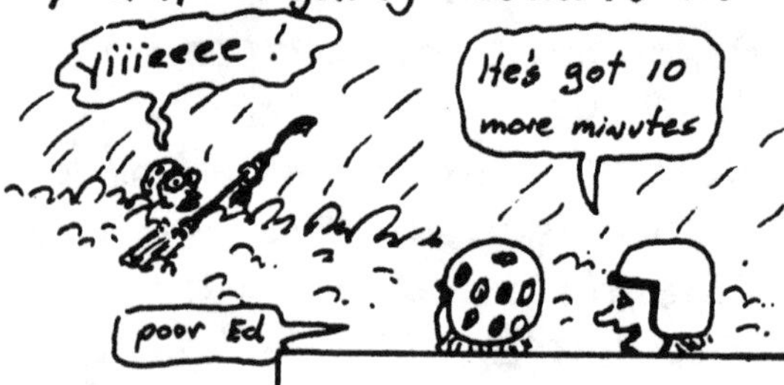
Yiiiieeee!
He's got 10 more minutes
poor Ed

Zombie Factor Three - "The amount of saliva available for expectoration is inversely proportional to the paddler's tendency to loose control." (ie- If you can't spit you should consider carrying that nasty rapid).

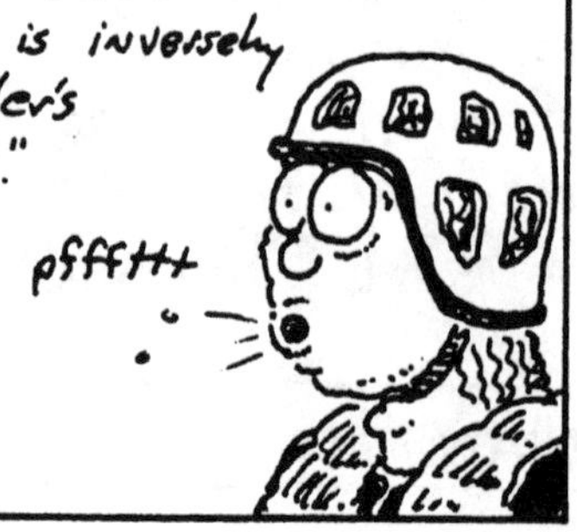
pfffttt

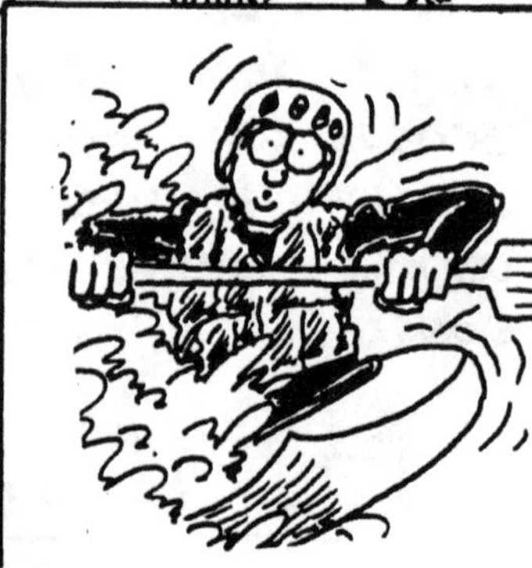

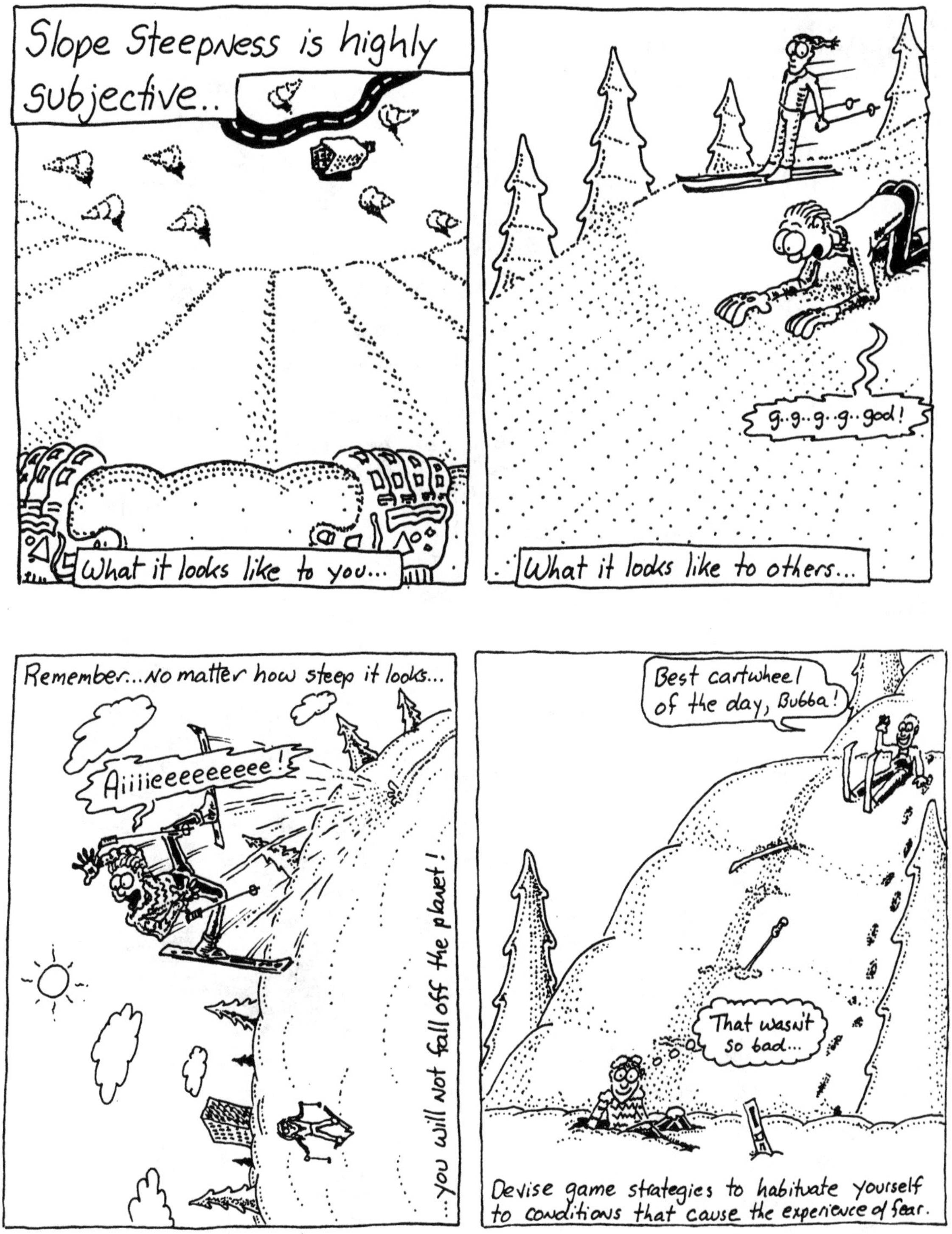
Slope Steepness is highly subjective..
What it looks like to you...
g..g..g..g..god!
What it looks like to others...
Remember...No matter how steep it looks...
Aiiiieeeeeeeee!
...you will not fall off the planet!
Best cartwheel of the day, Bubba!
That wasn't so bad...
Devise game strategies to habituate yourself to conditions that cause the experience of fear.

And...

Aggression...

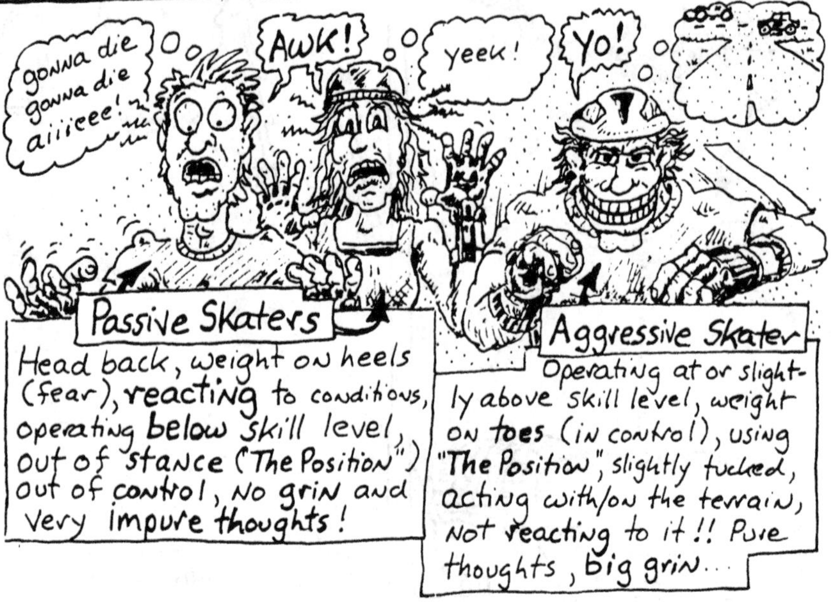

gonna die
gonna die
aiiieee!
AWK!
yeek!
Yo!
Passive Skaters
Head back, weight on heels (fear), reacting to conditions, operating below skill level, out of stance ("The Position") out of control, no grin and very impure thoughts!
Aggressive Skater
Operating at or slightly above skill level, weight on toes (in control), using "The Position", slightly tucked, acting with/on the terrain, not reacting to it!! Pure thoughts, big grin...

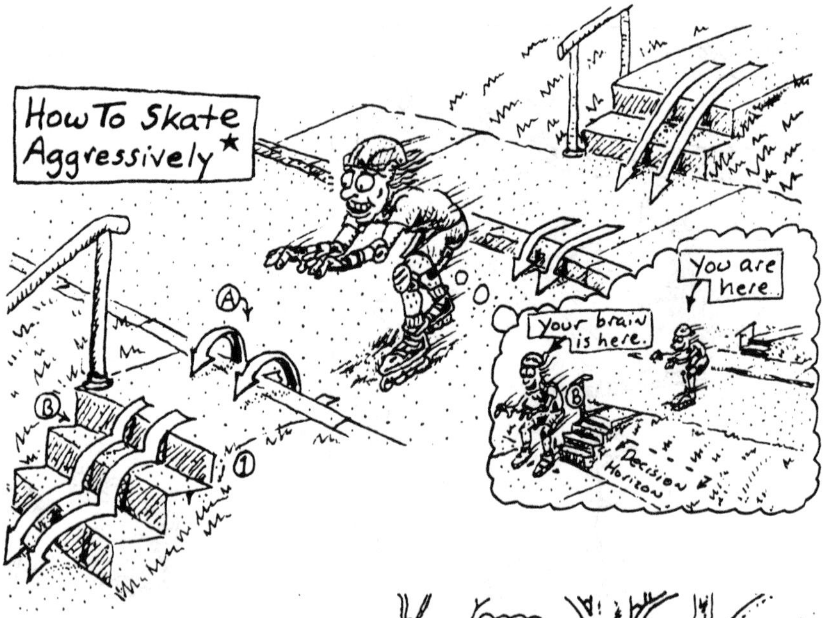

How To Skate Aggressively*
A
B
1
You are here
Your brain is here.
B
Decision Horizon

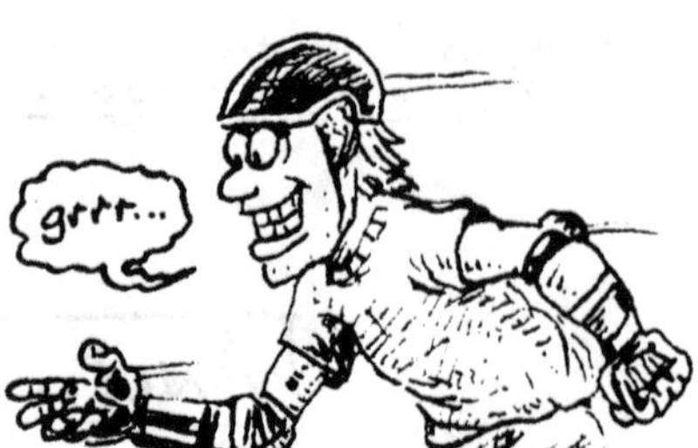

grrr...

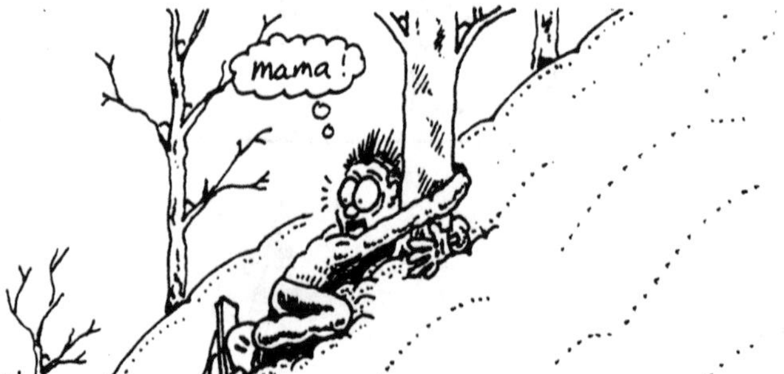

mama!

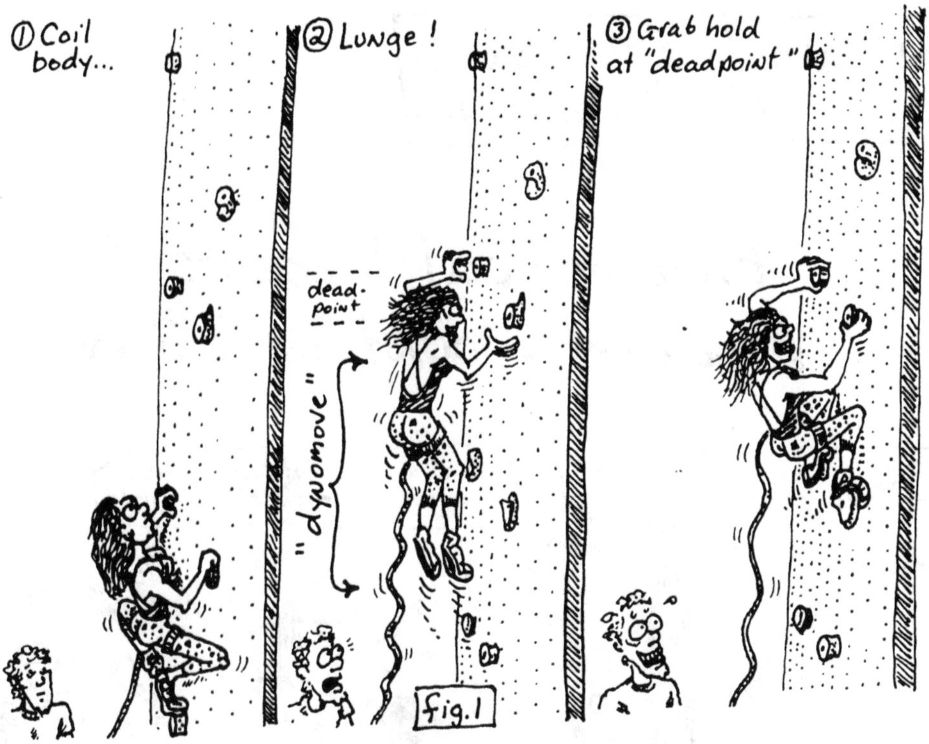
① Coil body...
② Lunge!
③ Grab hold at "deadpoint"
dead-point
"dynomove"
fig. 1

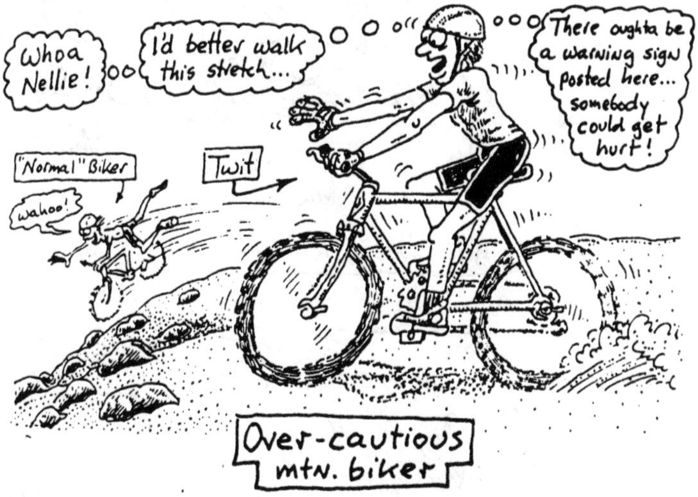
Whoa Nellie!
I'd better walk this stretch...
There oughta be a warning sign posted here... somebody could get hurt!
"Normal" Biker
wahoo!
Twit
Over-cautious mtn. biker

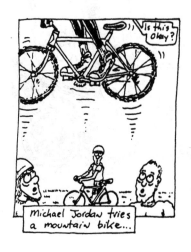

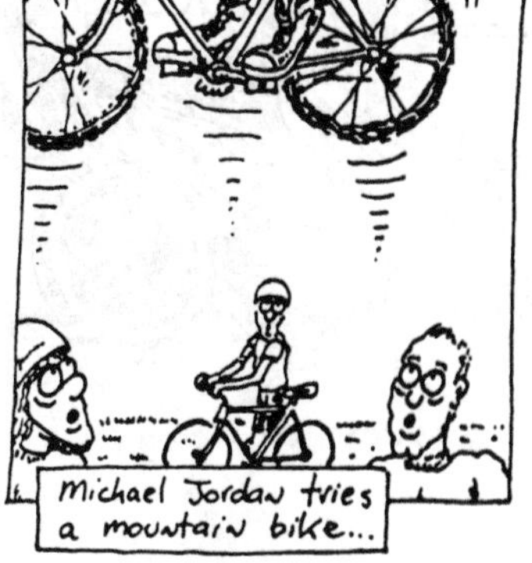
Is this Okay?
Michael Jordan tries a mountain bike...

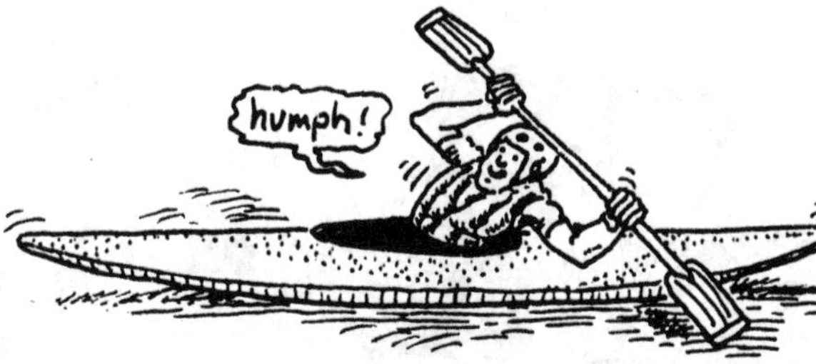
humph!

Eventually you develop an entirely new world view...

The Path To Expertdom Begins With Philosophy...

The Philosophical Precepts Of Modern Mountain Biking...

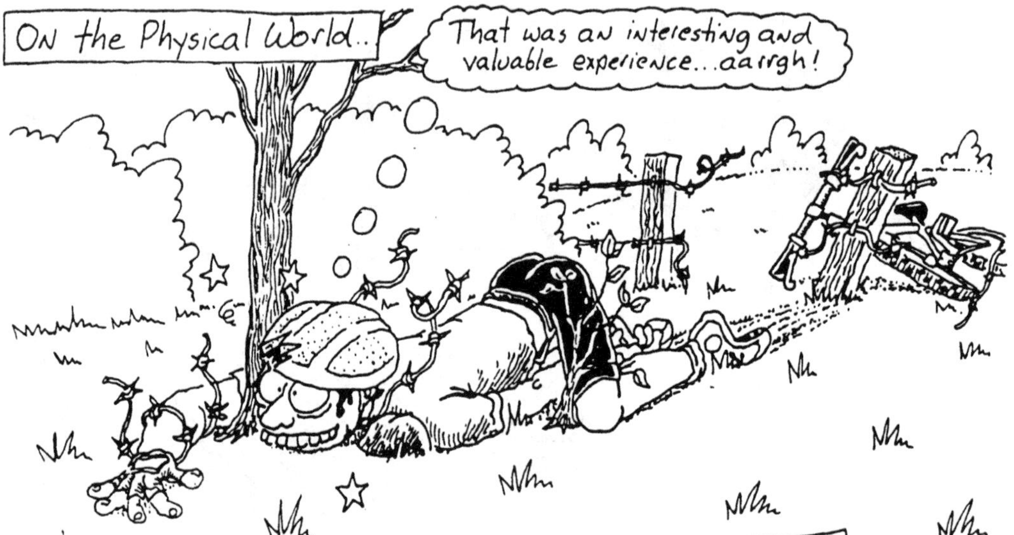
On the Physical World..
That was an interesting and valuable experience...aargh!

What doesn't kill you makes you stronger. Apologies To Fied Nietzsche

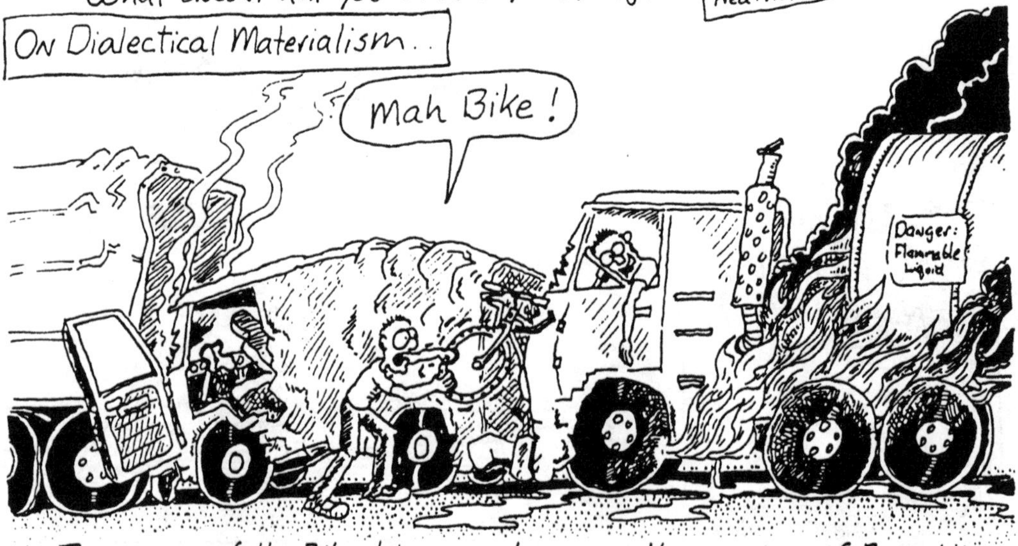
On Dialectical Materialism..
Mah Bike!
Danger: Flammable Liquid

The oneness of the Bike takes precedence over the oneness of Being!

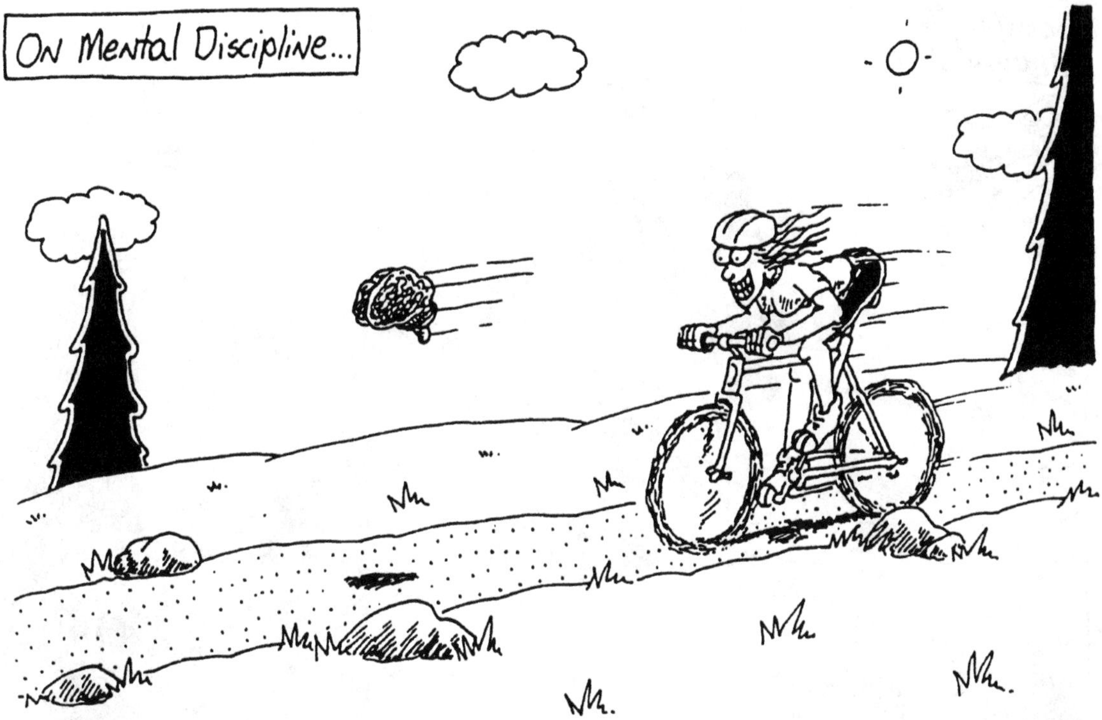
On Mental Discipline...

When riding, the mind should preceed the rider by one bike length (figuratively speaking)

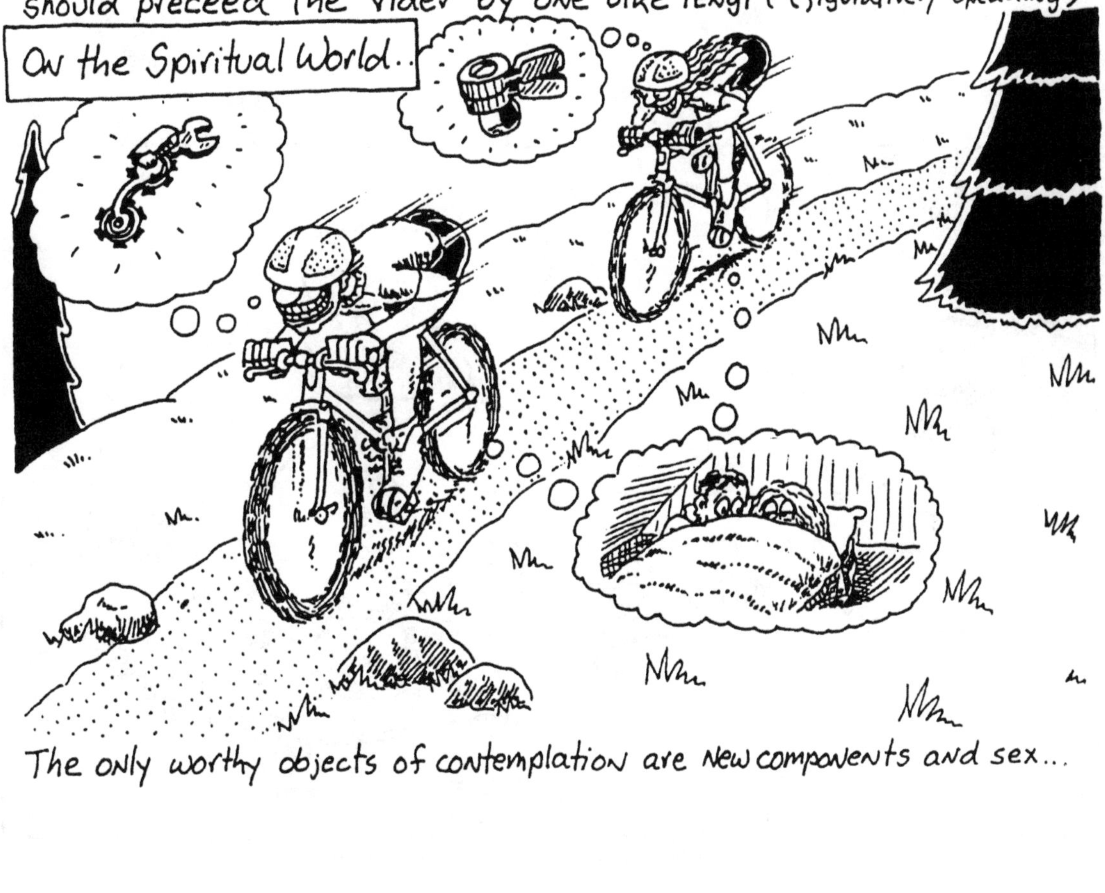
On the Spiritual World...

The only worthy objects of contemplation are new components and sex...

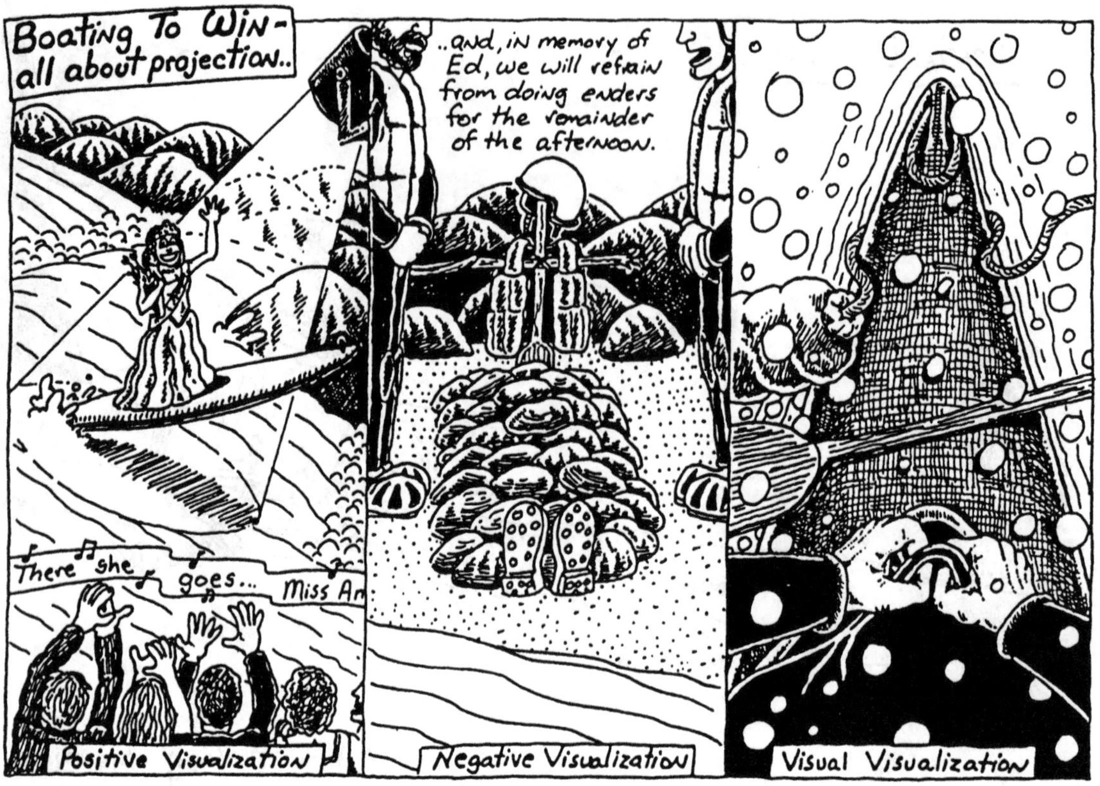
Boating To Win-
all about projection..
There she goes... Miss Am
Positive Visualization
..and, in memory of Ed, we will refrain from doing enders for the remainder of the afternoon.
Negative Visualization
Visual Visualization

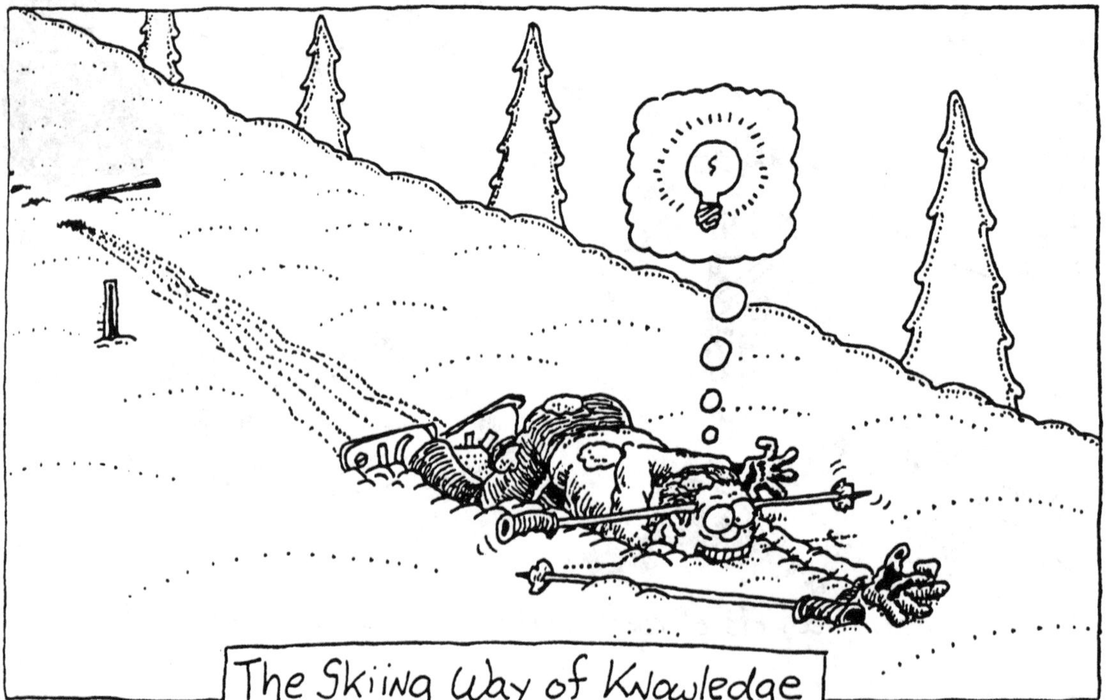
The Skiing Way of Knowledge

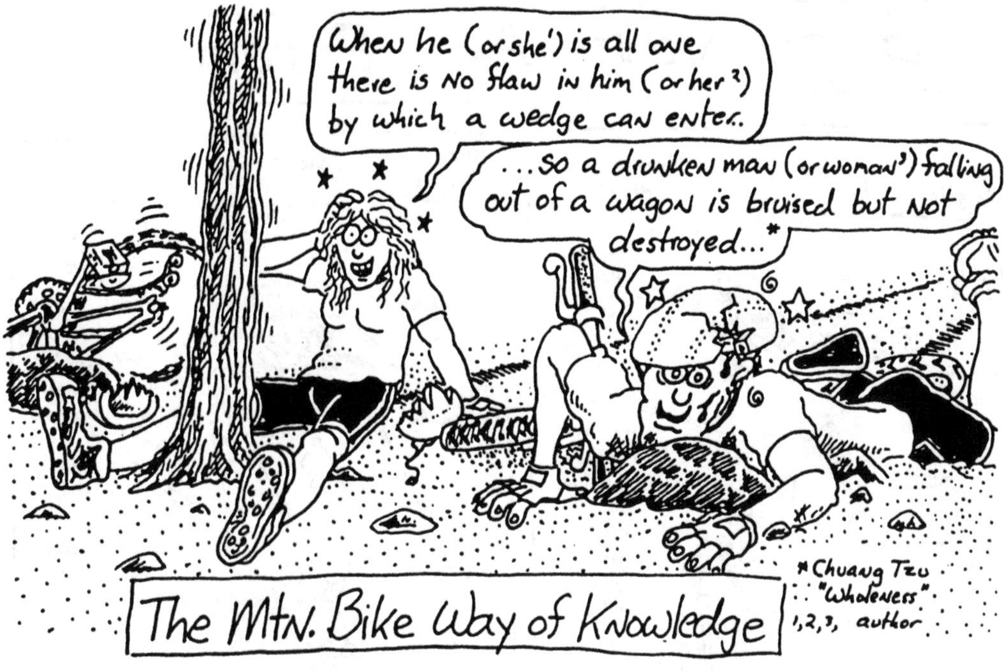
When he (or she¹) is all one there is no flaw in him (or her²) by which a wedge can enter.
...so a drunken man (or woman³) falling out of a wagon is bruised but not destroyed...*

The Mtn. Bike Way of Knowledge

*Chuang Tzu "Wholeness" 1,2,3, author

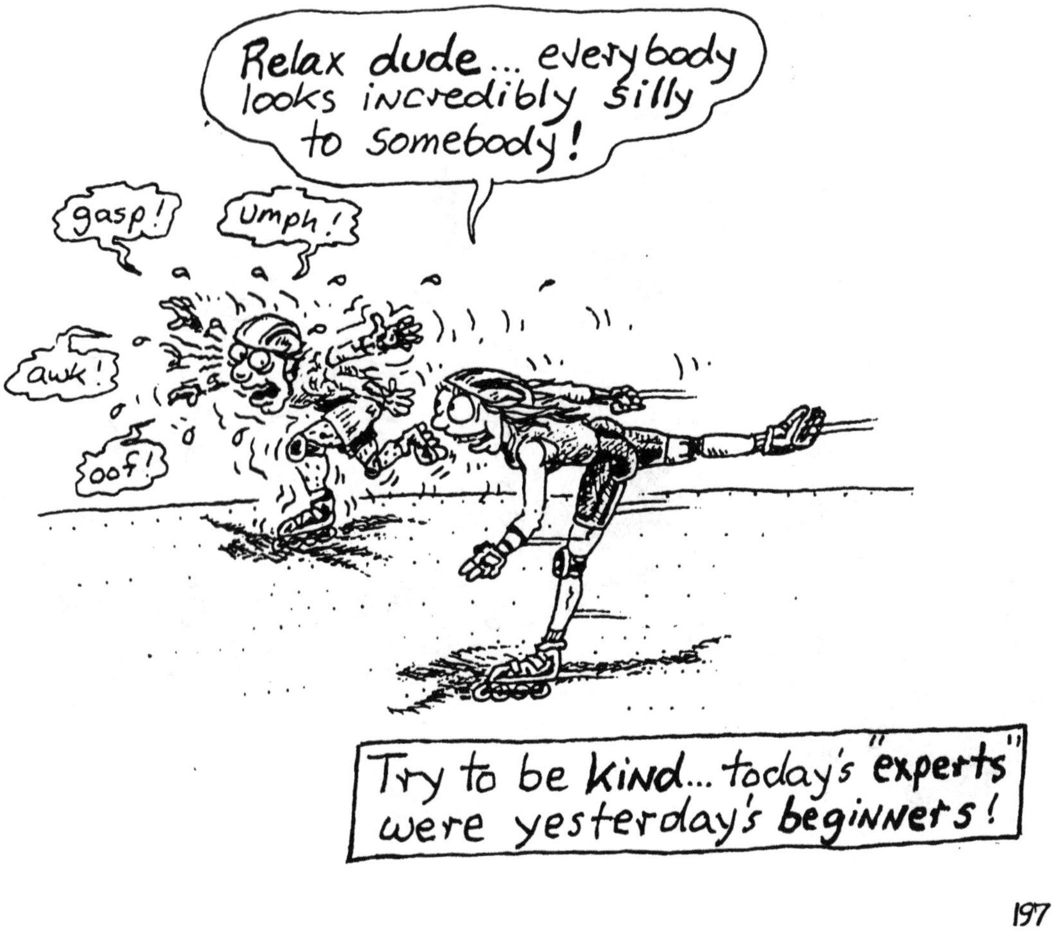
Relax dude... everybody looks incredibly silly to somebody!
gasp!
Umph!
awk!
oof!

Try to be **kind**... today's "**experts**" were yesterday's **beginners**!

Beginners And Experts

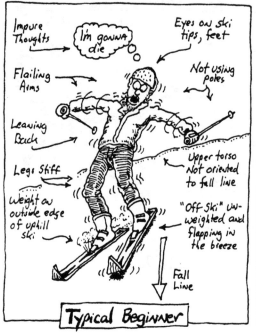

Impure Thoughts →

"I'm gonna die"

Eyes on ski tips, feet →

Not using poles

Flailing Arms →

Leaning Back →

Legs Stiff →

Weight on outside edge of uphill ski

Upper torso Not oriented to fall line

"Off Ski" unweighted and flapping in the breeze

Fall Line

Typical Beginner

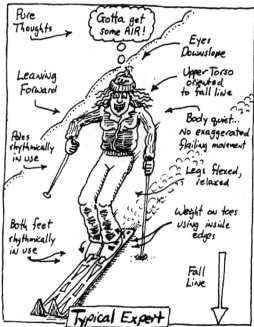

Pure Thoughts →

"Gotta get some AIR!"

Eyes Downslope

Upper Torso oriented to fall line

Leaning Forward →

Poles rhythmically in use

Body quiet... No exaggerated flailing movement

Legs flexed, relaxed

Both feet rhythmically in use →

Weight on toes using inside edges

Fall Line

Typical Expert

Basic Crash and Burn...

oof!

erk!

ow!

unh!

Awk!

Arf!

oh my god!

pathumpa thumpa thumpa thumpa thumpa. woooooooooooooooosssshhh.. fumph!

OUCH!

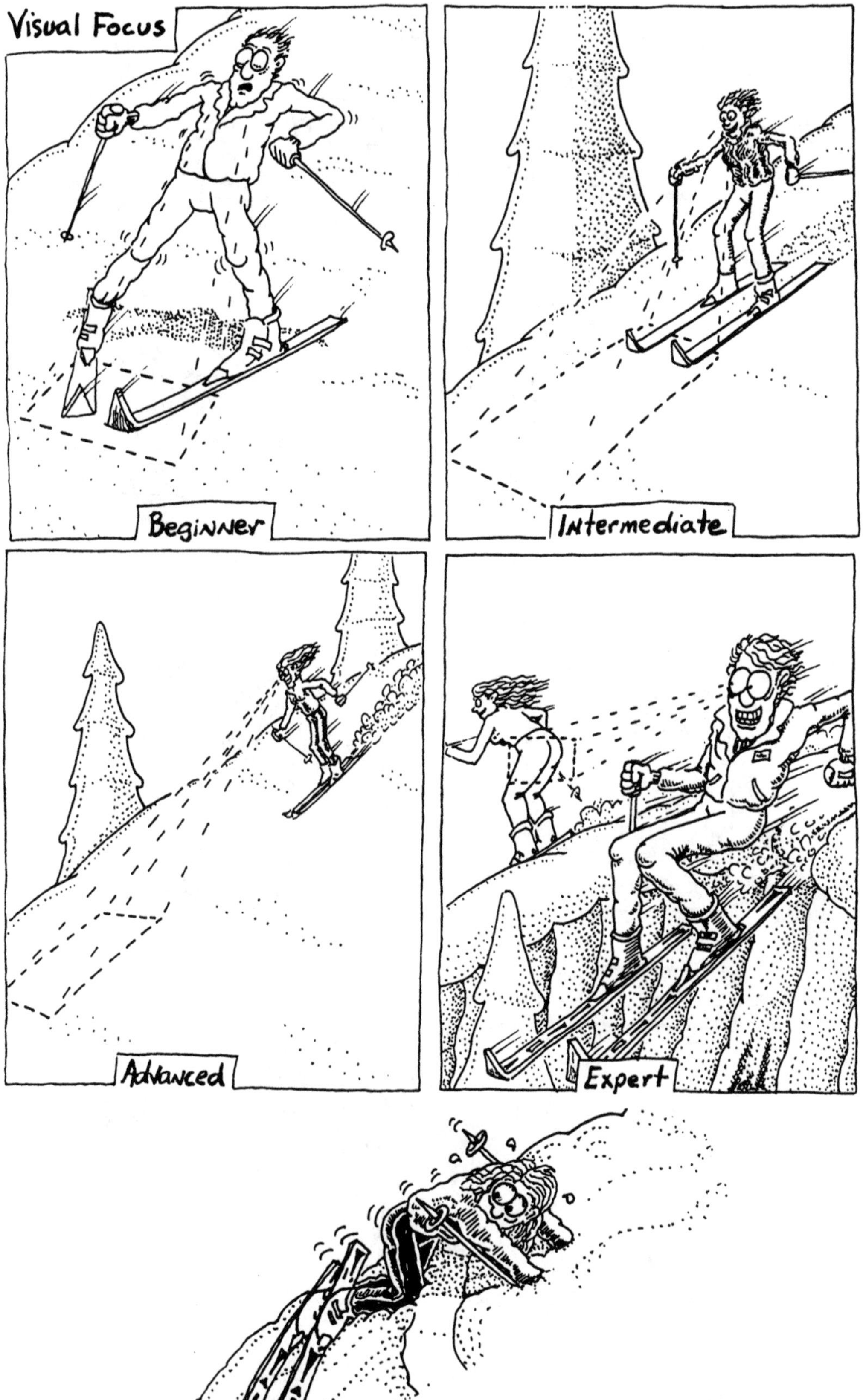
Visual Focus
Beginner
Intermediate
Advanced
Expert

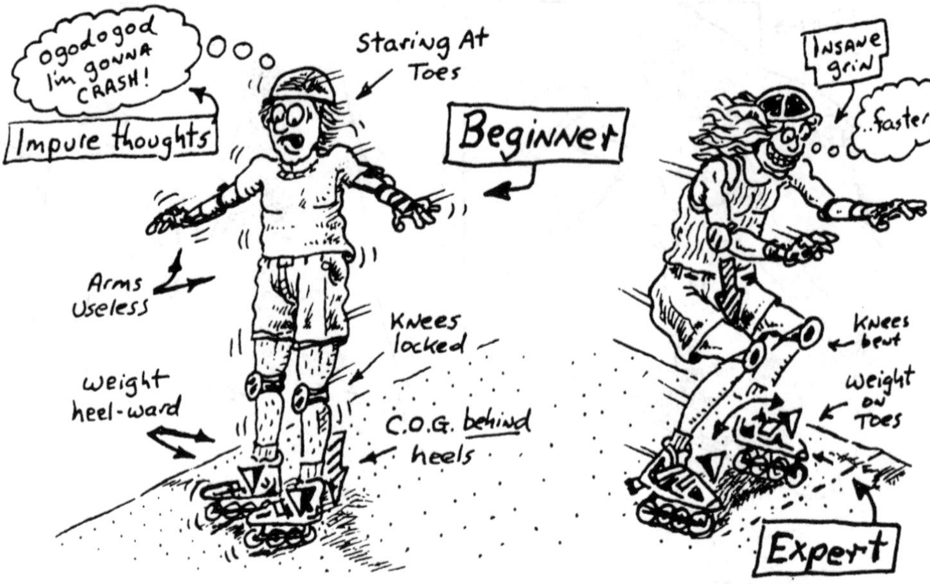
ogodogod I'm gonna CRASH!
Impure thoughts
Staring At Toes
Beginner
Arms Useless
Knees locked
weight heel-ward
C.O.G. behind heels
Insane grin
..faster!
Knees bent
weight on Toes
Expert

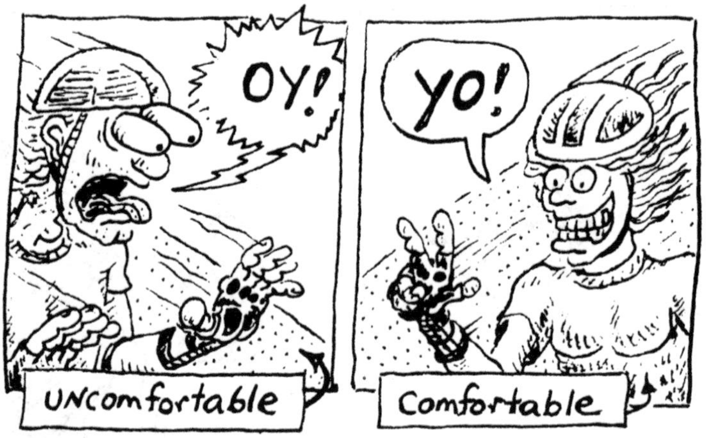
OY!
UNcomfortable
YO!
Comfortable

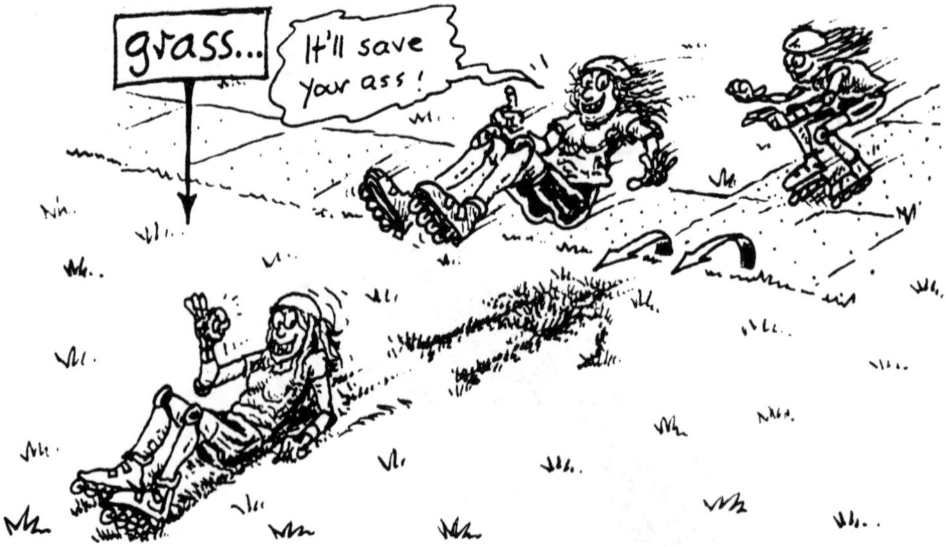
grass...
It'll save your ass!

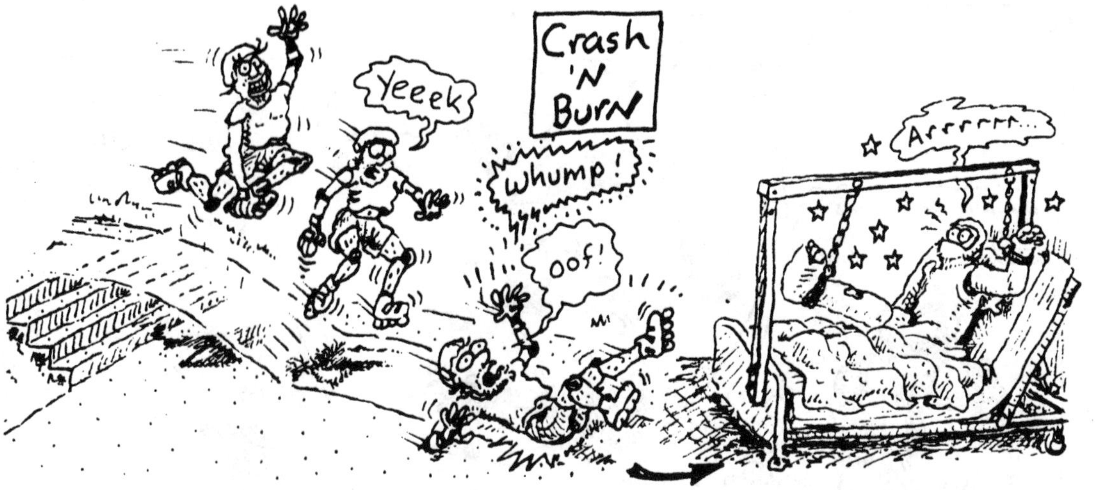
Crash 'N Burn
Yeeek
whump!
oof!
Arrrrrr...

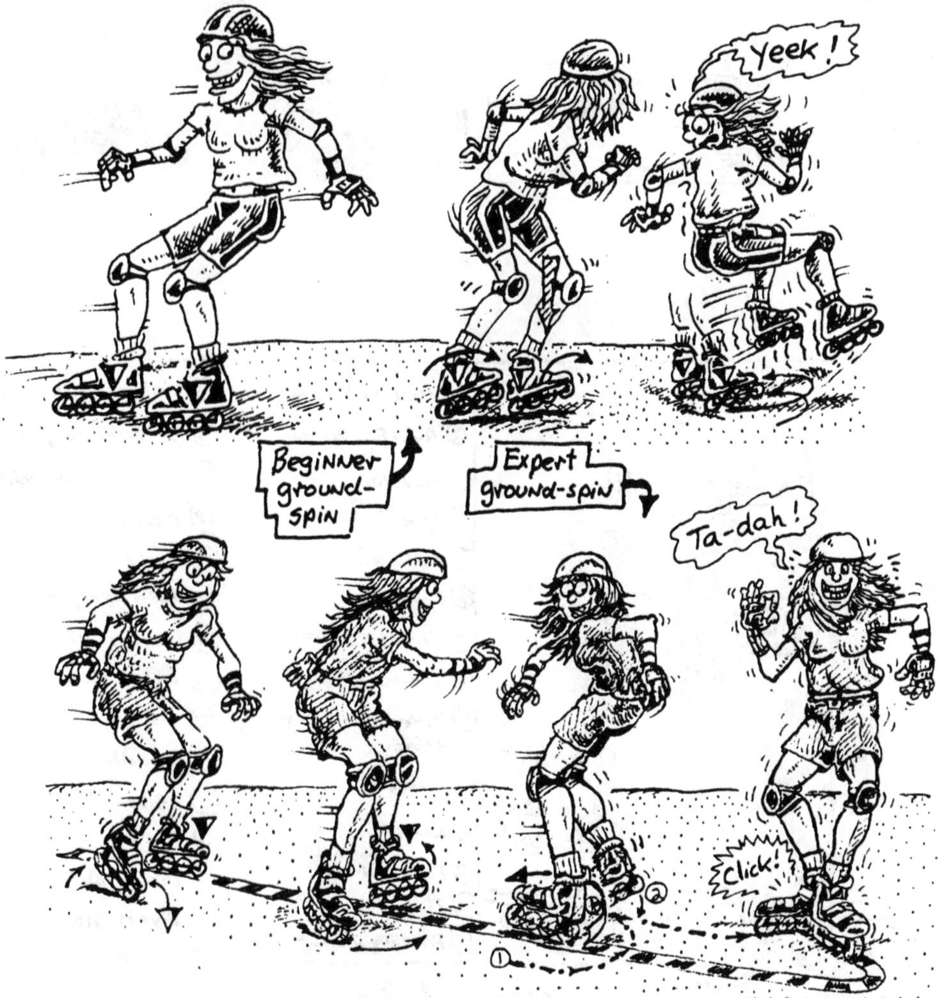
Yeek!
Beginner ground-spin
Expert ground-spin
Ta-dah!
Click!

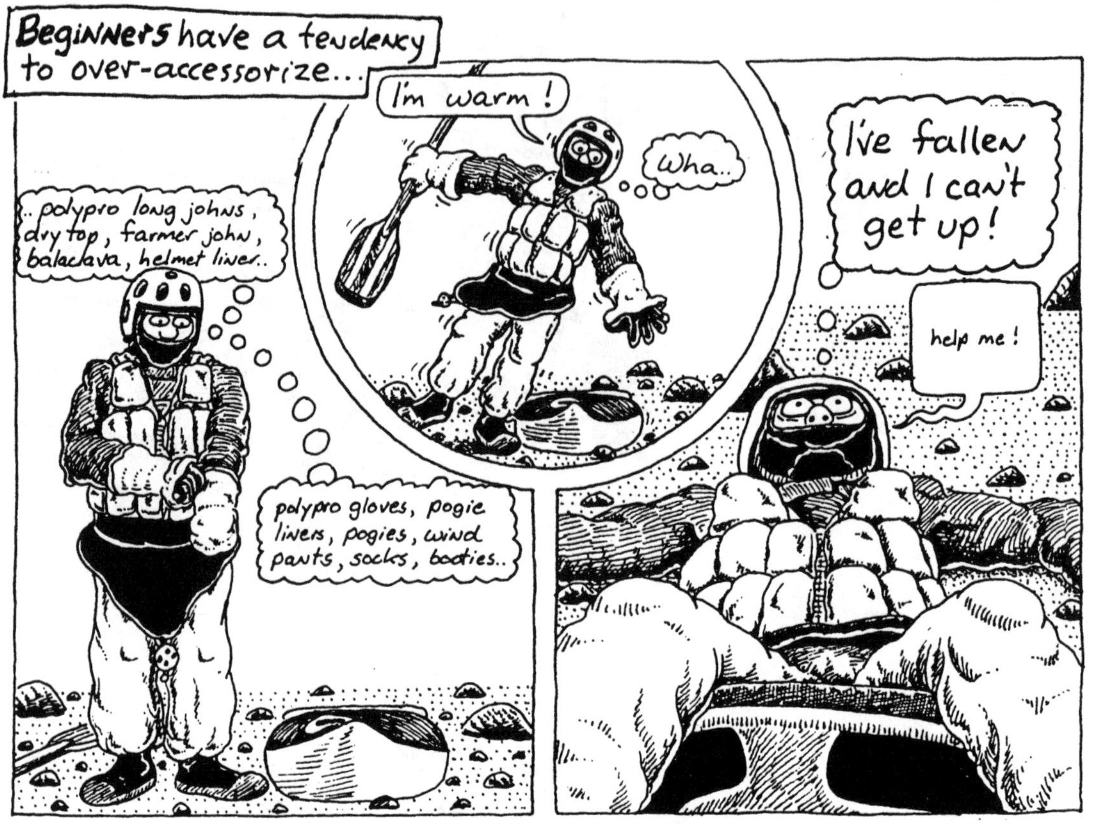
Beginners have a tendency to over-accessorize...
..polypro long johns, dry top, farmer john, balaclava, helmet liner..
polypro gloves, pogie liners, pogies, wind pants, socks, booties..
I'm warm!
Wha..
I've fallen and I can't get up!
help me!

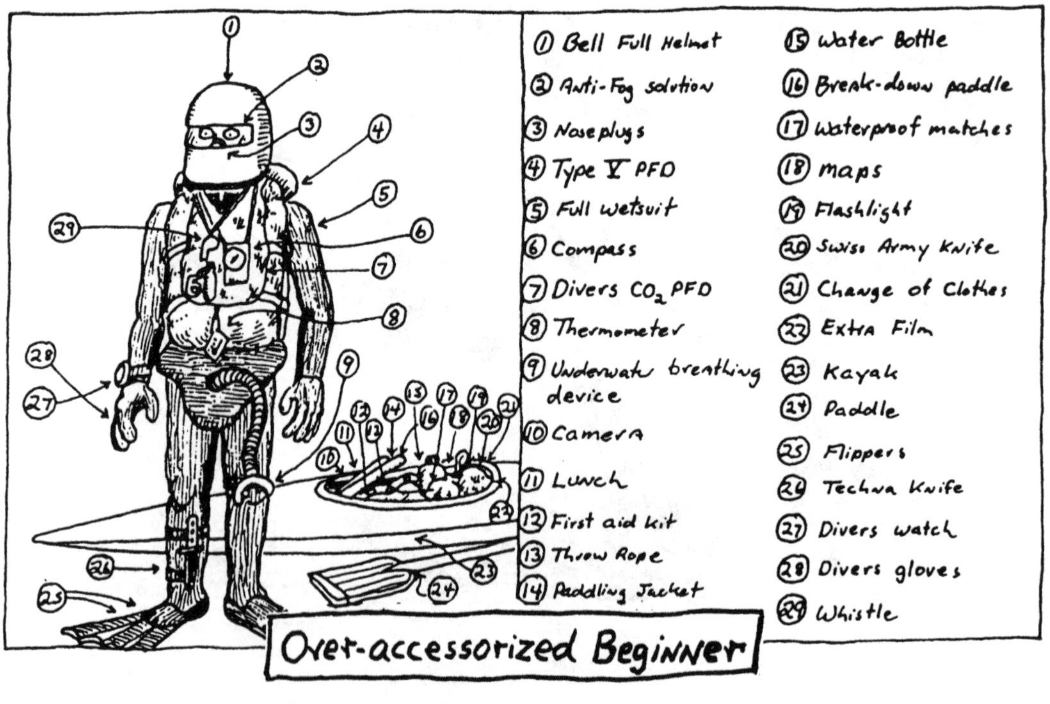
① Bell Full Helmet
② Anti-Fog solution
③ Noseplugs
④ Type V PFD
⑤ Full wetsuit
⑥ Compass
⑦ Divers CO_2 PFD
⑧ Thermometer
⑨ Underwater breathing device
⑩ Camera
⑪ Lunch
⑫ First aid kit
⑬ Throw Rope
⑭ Paddling Jacket
⑮ Water Bottle
⑯ Break-down paddle
⑰ Waterproof matches
⑱ maps
⑲ Flashlight
⑳ Swiss Army Knife
㉑ Change of Clothes
㉒ Extra Film
㉓ Kayak
㉔ Paddle
㉕ Flippers
㉖ Techna Knife
㉗ Divers watch
㉘ Divers gloves
㉙ Whistle

Over-accessorized Beginner

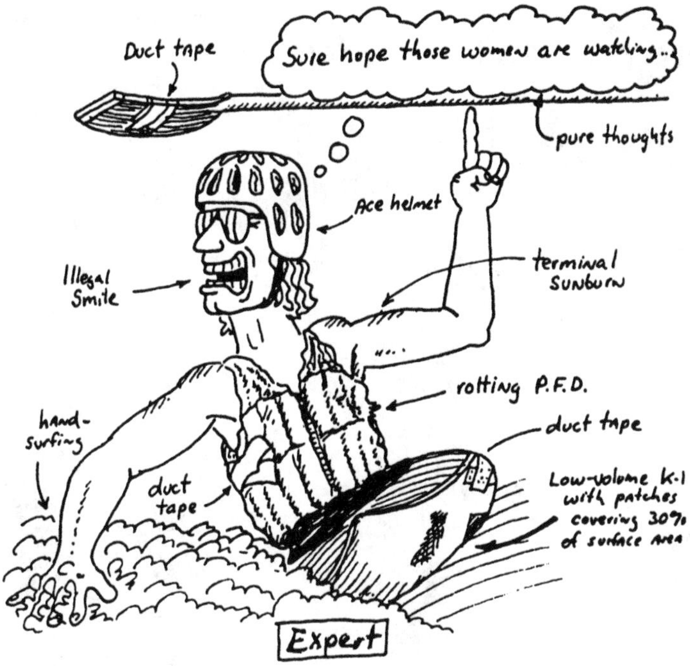
Duct tape
Sure hope those women are watching..
pure thoughts
Ace helmet
Illegal Smile
terminal sunburn
rotting P.F.D.
hand-surfing
duct tape
duct tape
Low-volume K-1 with patches covering 30% of surface area
Expert

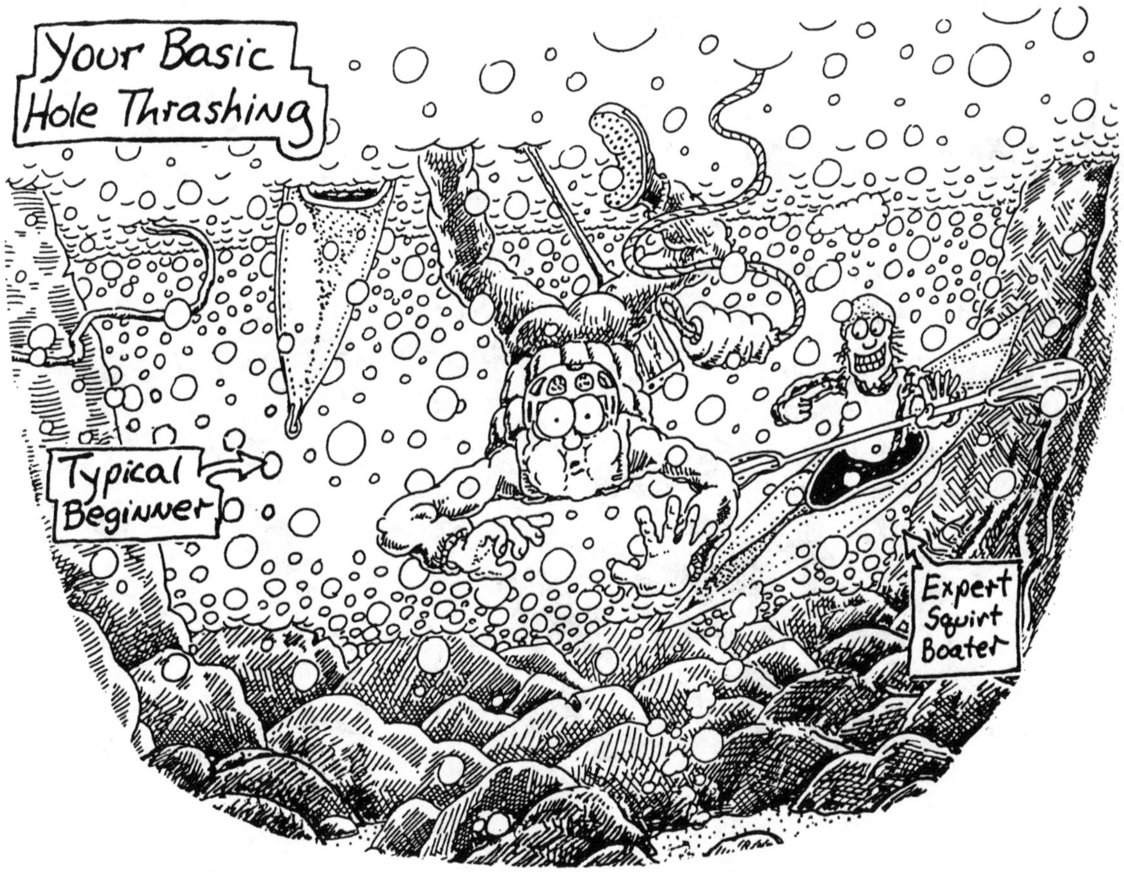
Your Basic Hole Thrashing
Typical Beginner
Expert Squirt Boater

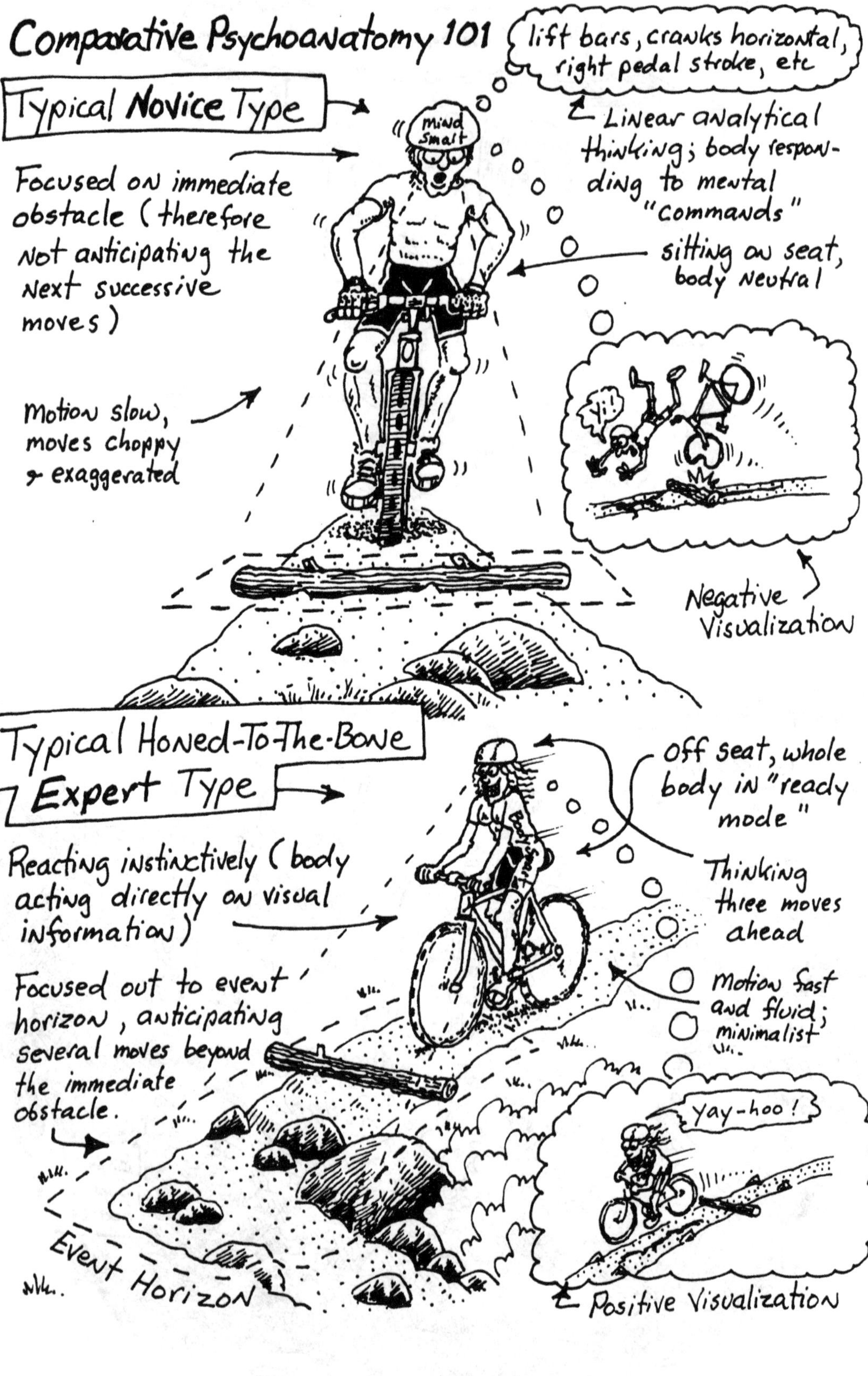
Comparative Psychoanatomy 101
lift bars, cranks horizontal, right pedal stroke, etc
Typical Novice Type
mind smalt
Linear analytical thinking; body responding to mental "commands"
Focused on immediate obstacle (therefore not anticipating the next successive moves)
sitting on seat, body neutral
Motion slow, moves choppy & exaggerated
Yi!
Negative Visualization
Typical Honed-To-The-Bone Expert Type
Off seat, whole body in "ready mode"
Reacting instinctively (body acting directly on visual information)
Thinking three moves ahead
Focused out to event horizon, anticipating several moves beyond the immediate obstacle.
Motion fast and fluid; minimalist
Yay-hoo!
Event Horizon
Positive Visualization

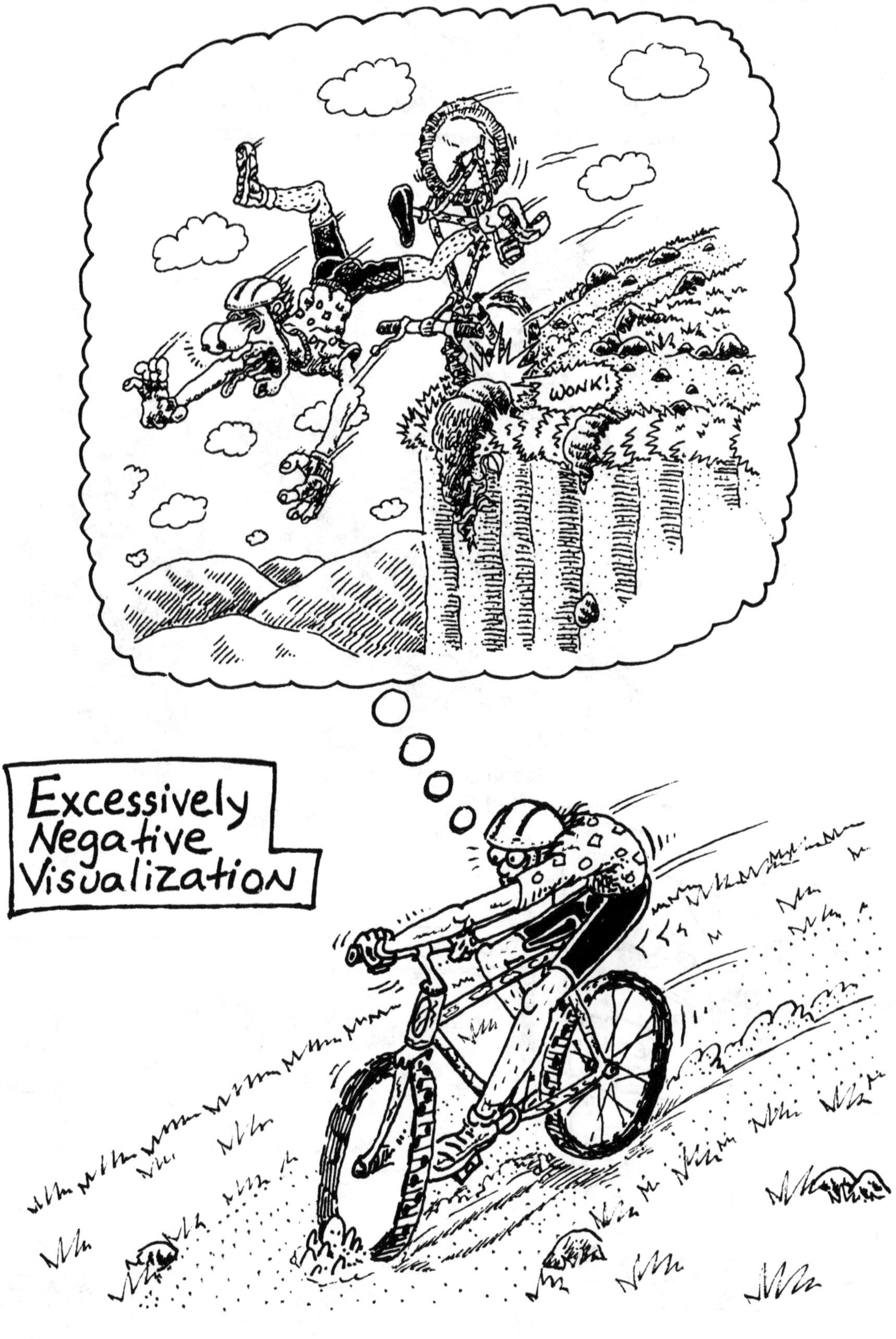
WONK!
Excessively Negative Visualization

Once You've Mastered A Sport, It's Time For Tricks And Stunts...

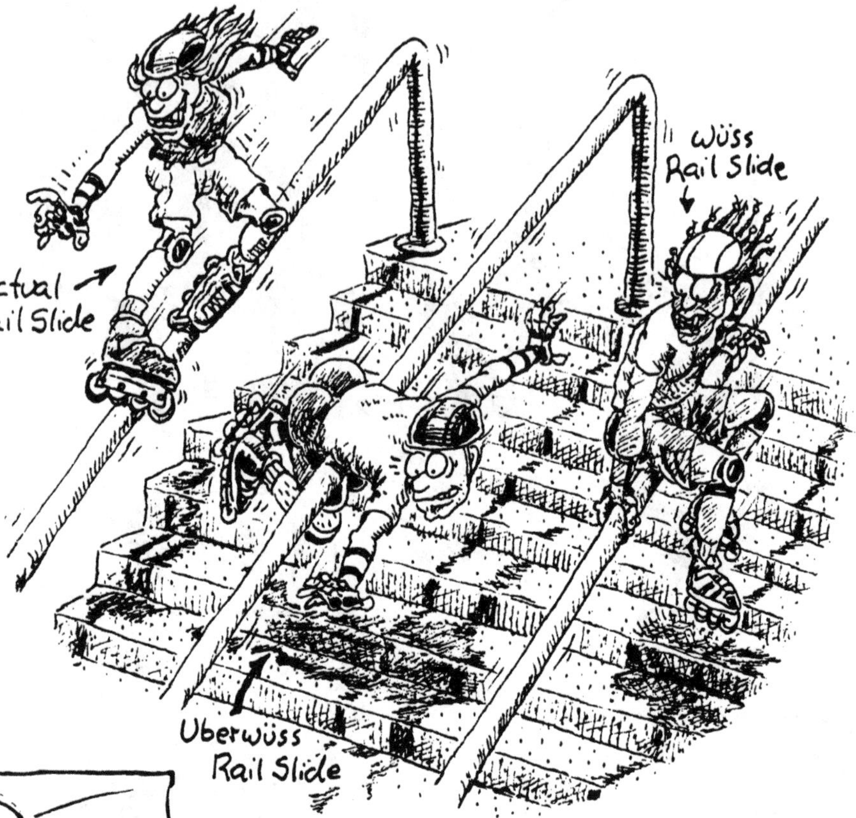

Actual Rail Slide
Wüss Rail Slide
Uberwüss Rail Slide

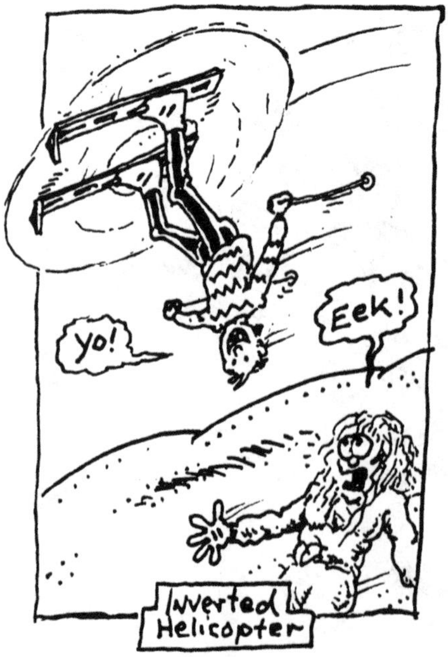

yo!
Eek!
Inverted Helicopter

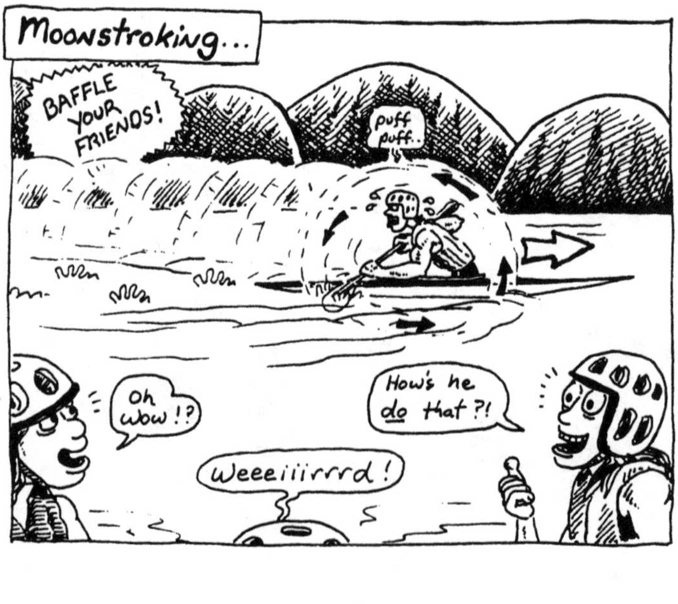

Moonstroking...
BAFFLE YOUR FRIENDS!
puff puff..
Oh wow!?
How's he do that?!
Weeeiiirrrd!

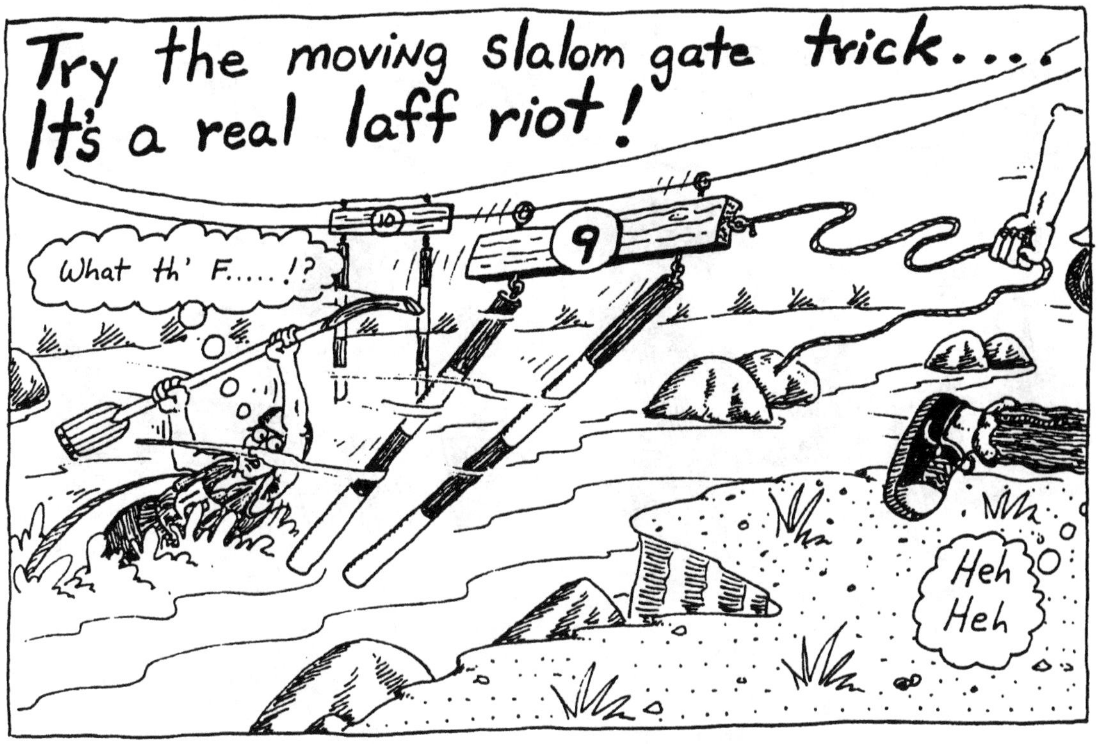
Try the moving slalom gate trick.... It's a real laff riot!
10
9
What th' F.....!?
Heh Heh

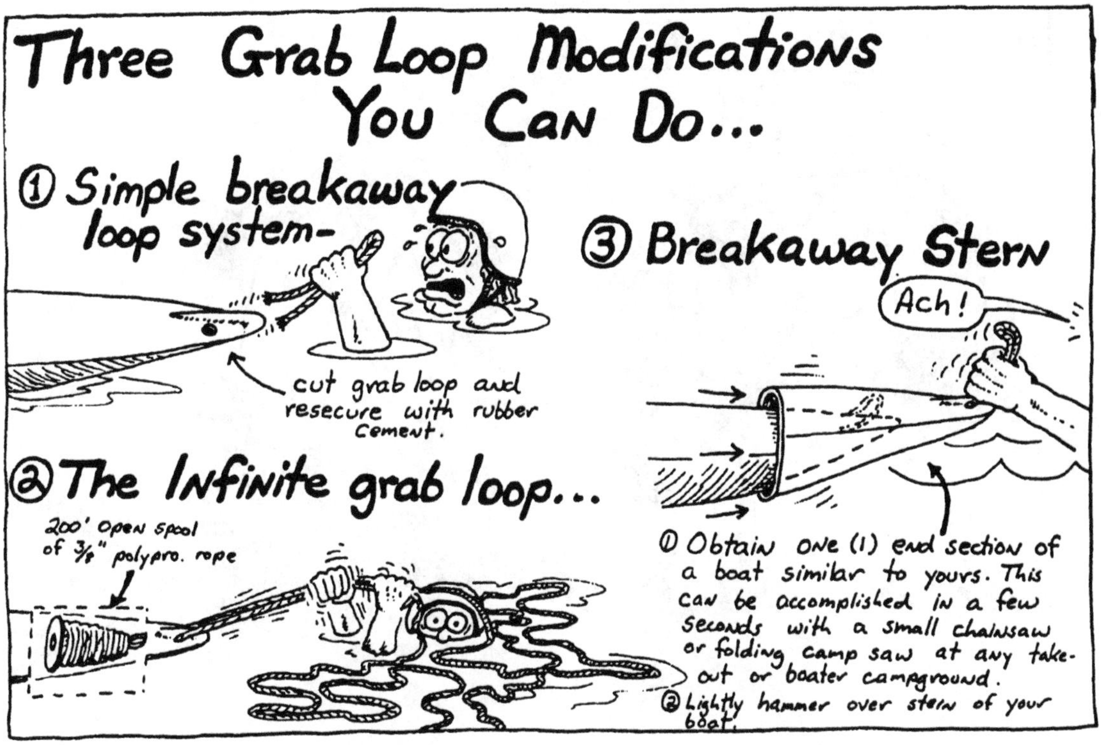
Three Grab Loop Modifications You Can Do...
① Simple breakaway loop system-
cut grab loop and resecure with rubber cement.
② The Infinite grab loop...
200' open spool of 3/8" polypro. rope
③ Breakaway Stern
Ach!
① Obtain one (1) end section of a boat similar to yours. This can be accomplished in a few seconds with a small chainsaw or folding camp saw at any take-out or boater campground.
② Lightly hammer over stern of your boat.

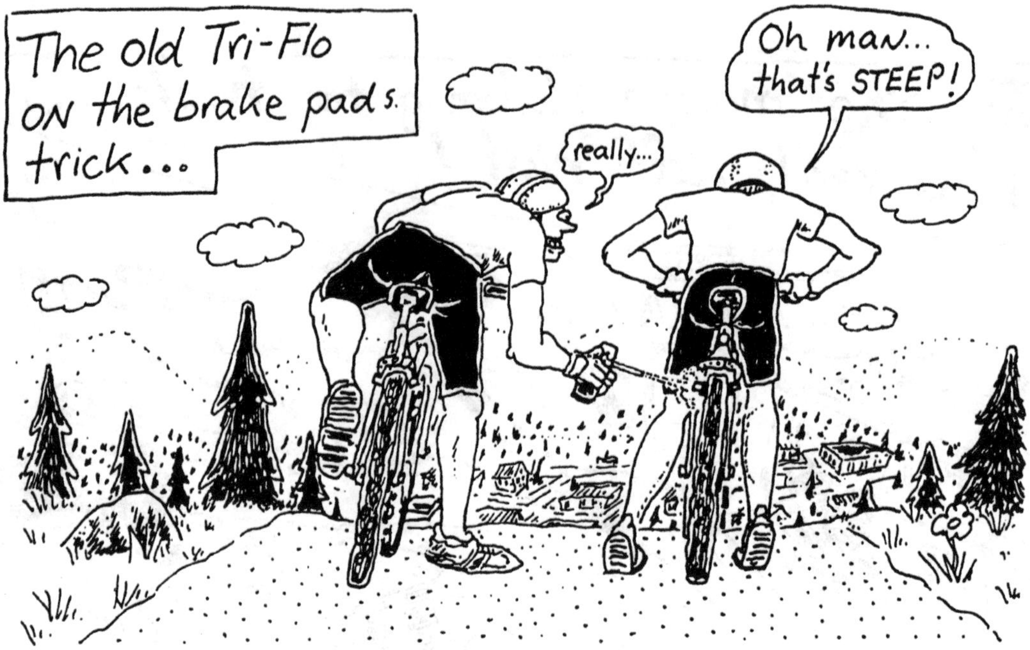
The old Tri-Flo on the brake pads trick...
really...
Oh man... that's STEEP!

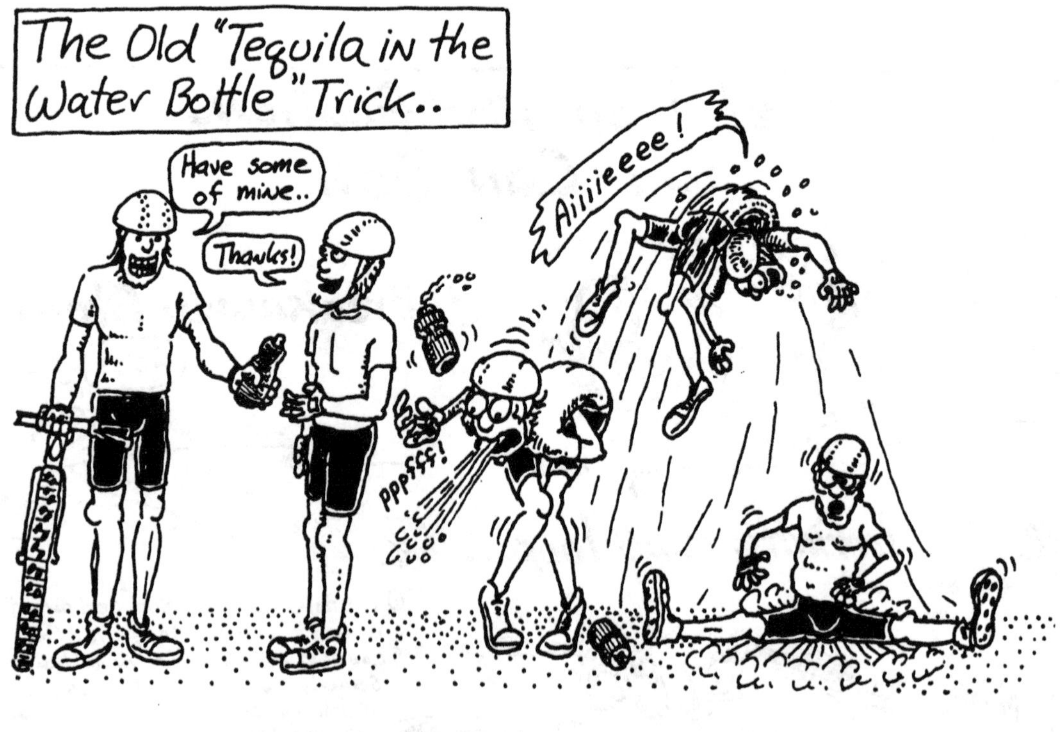
The Old "Tequila in the Water Bottle" Trick..
Have some of mine..
Thanks!
Aiiiieeee!
ppppfff!

More Stupid Bike Tricks... The Diabolical Creek-ford Trick:

Wherein the prankster endeavours to get ahead of the pack, set up a minor illusion and trick the others into riding into way-deep water!

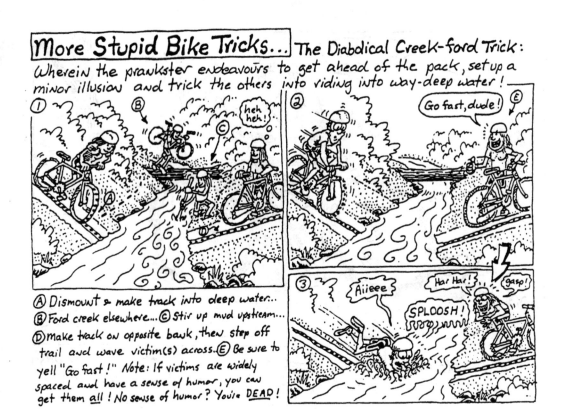

heh heh!

Go fast, dude!
Aiieee
Har Har!
gasp!
SPLOOSH!

Ⓐ Dismount & make track into deep water... Ⓑ Ford creek elsewhere... Ⓒ Stir up mud upstream... Ⓓ Make track on opposite bank, then step off trail and wave victim(s) across.. Ⓔ Be sure to yell "Go fast!" Note: If victims are widely spaced and have a sense of humor, you can get them all! No sense of humor? You're DEAD!

The Texas Chainsaw Dismount

whew.. I'm fried!

YEEK!!
Did I startle you?
Note: Look contrite!
I'm Sorry!
gurgle gurgle...

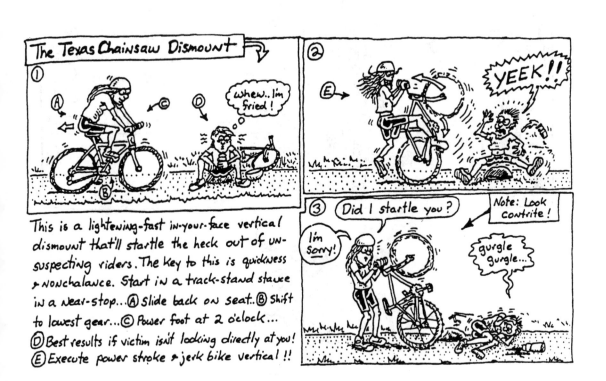

This is a lightening-fast in-your-face vertical dismount that'll startle the heck out of unsuspecting riders. The key to this is quickness & nonchalance. Start in a track-stand stance in a near-stop... Ⓐ Slide back on seat.. Ⓑ Shift to lowest gear... Ⓒ Power foot at 2 o'clock... Ⓓ Best results if victim isn't looking directly at you! Ⓔ Execute power stroke & jerk bike vertical!!

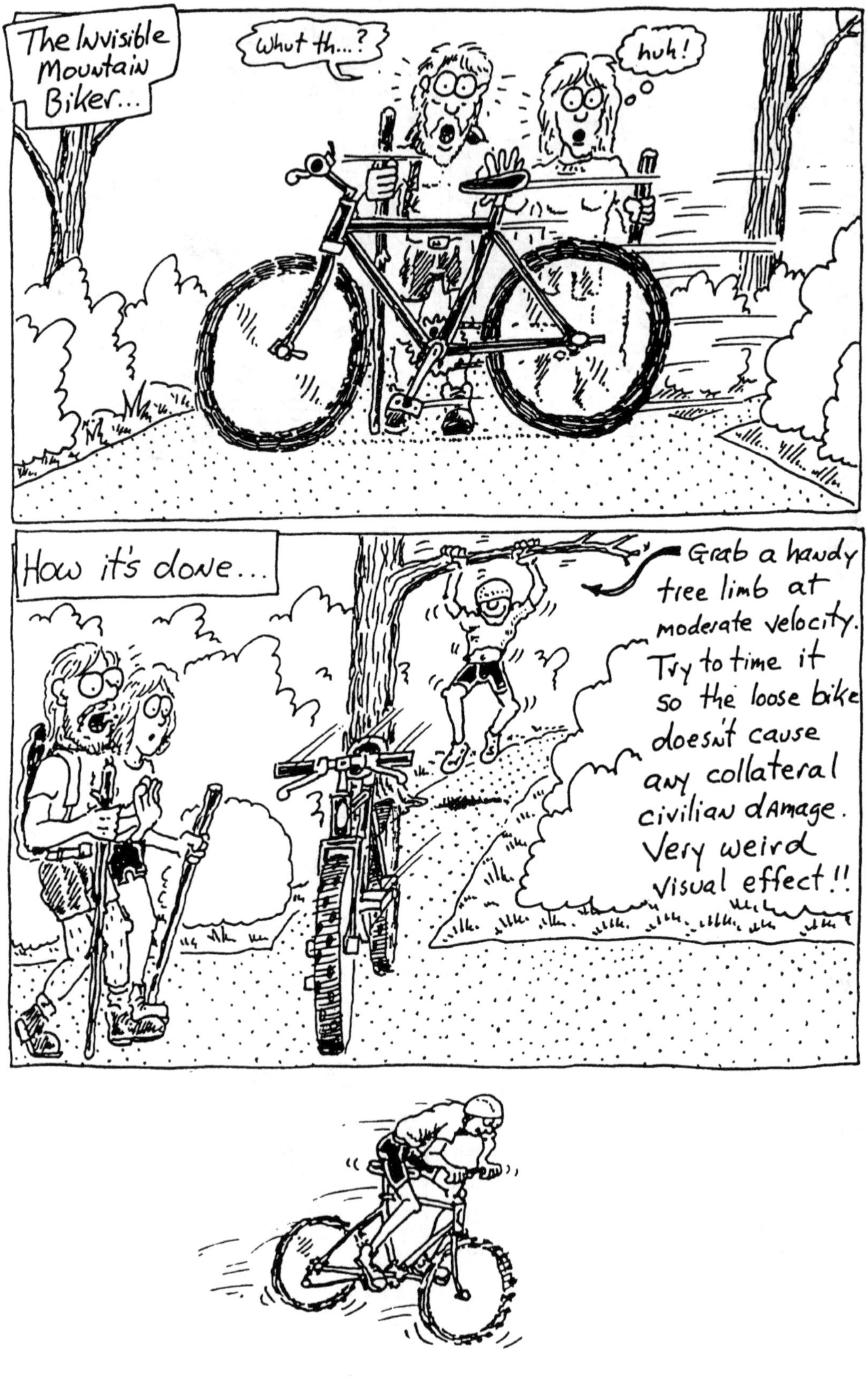
The Invisible Mountain Biker...
Whut th...?
huh!
How it's done...
Grab a handy tree limb at moderate velocity. Try to time it so the loose bike doesn't cause any collateral civilian damage. Very weird visual effect!!

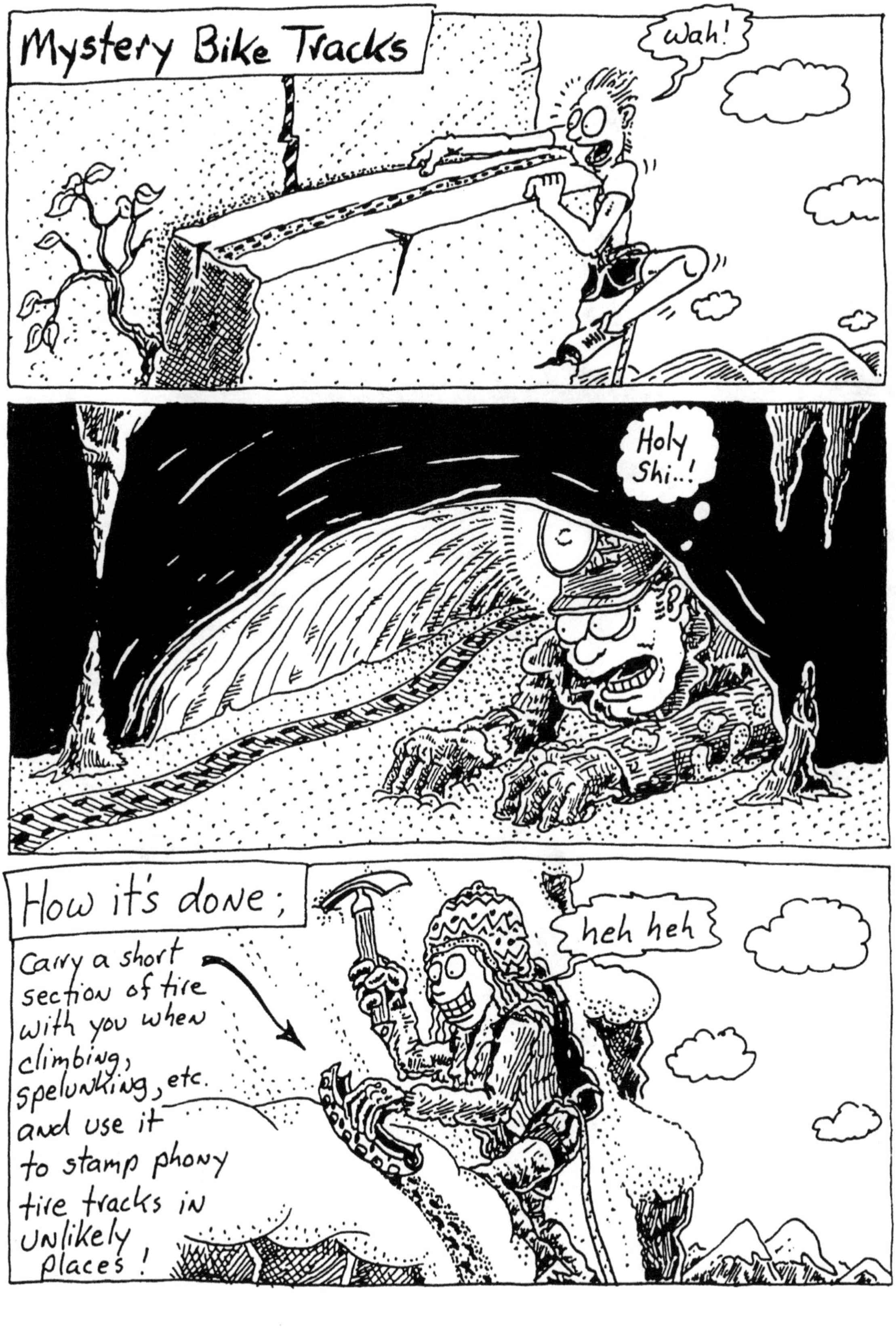
Mystery Bike Tracks
Wah!
Holy Shi..!
How it's done;
Carry a short section of tire with you when climbing, spelunking, etc. and use it to stamp phony tire tracks in unlikely places!
heh heh

My Cartoon Life...

Self Portraits

1978-2000

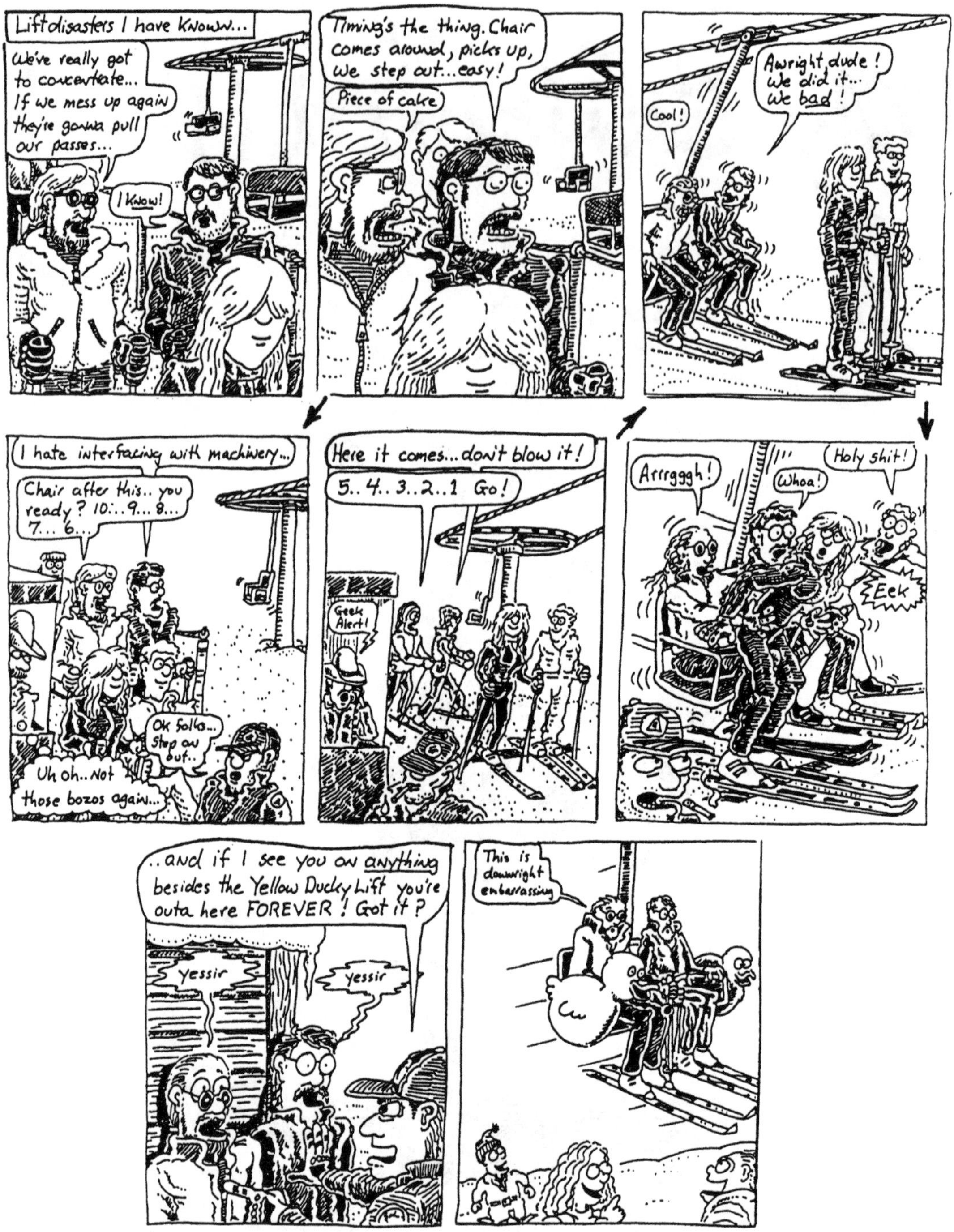
Liftdisasters I have Known...
We've really got to concentrate... If we mess up again they're gonna pull our passes...
I know!
Timing's the thing. Chair comes around, picks up, we step out...easy!
Piece of cake
Cool!
Awright dude! We did it... We bad!
I hate interfacing with machinery...
Chair after this.. you ready? 10:..9...8... 7...6...
Ok folks... Step on out..
Uh oh.. Not those bozos again...
Here it comes... don't blow it!
5..4..3..2..1 Go!
Geek Alert!
Arrrgggh!
Whoa!
Holy shit!
Eek
..and if I see you on anything besides the Yellow Ducky Lift you're outa here FOREVER! Got it?
yessir
yessir
This is downright embarrassing

Skiing with my publisher
Bob "Crash" Sehlinger

1986

Self Portraits

Since I'm the **head guinea pig** in my recreation "**research**", I put myself in the cartoon picture pretty often. I'm not egotistical, I'm just particularly talented at getting into **jams** and getting myself **trashed** bigtime. I also make frequent use of Holly, friends, paddling partners and other animals I know. They deserve the recognition* 'cause they provide the bulk of my cartoon material. I'm pretty good at taking surreptious notes and scribbling quick diagrams. Some have called me **SNEAKY.**

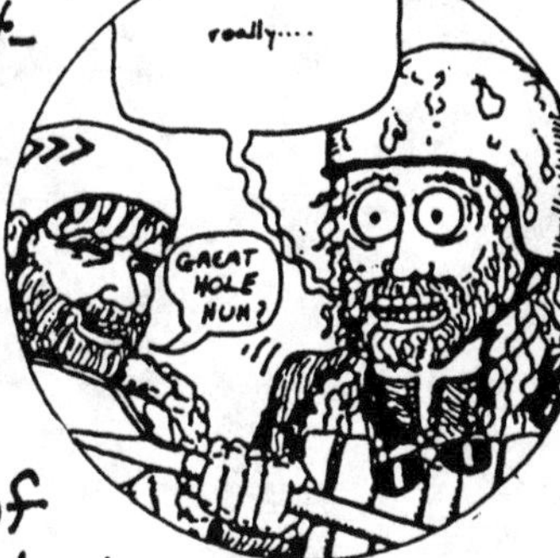
really....
GREAT HOLE HUH?

I used to think I was the only **cretin** tumbling down black diamond slopes, <u>and</u> getting terrified rockclimbing, and getting hammered paddling. I felt alone and sort of "special" for my record of swimming every major rapid in the southeast (twice!), busting collarbones, and occasionally setting my van (or tent) **on fire** while camping. That is, until I started using Nantahala Falls as a demented "**research station.**" In a single afternoon I could observe hundreds of boaters and rafters who were at least **as bad as me**. Over the years I met lots of climbers, boaters, skaters, mtn. bikers, skiers, and funhogs of every persuasion who would say "Hey, that's **me** in that cartoon... were you on my trip?". It turns out, I'm not alone after all, just a klutzy outdoor Everyman with a felt-tip pen.

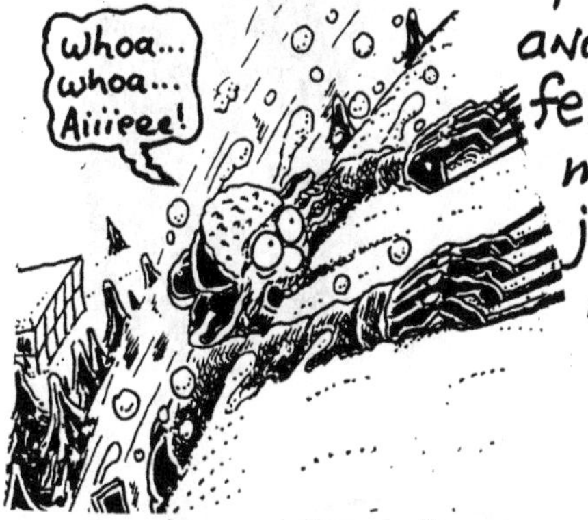
whoa...
whoa...
Aiiieee!

---

*Though sometimes, they make me change their names...

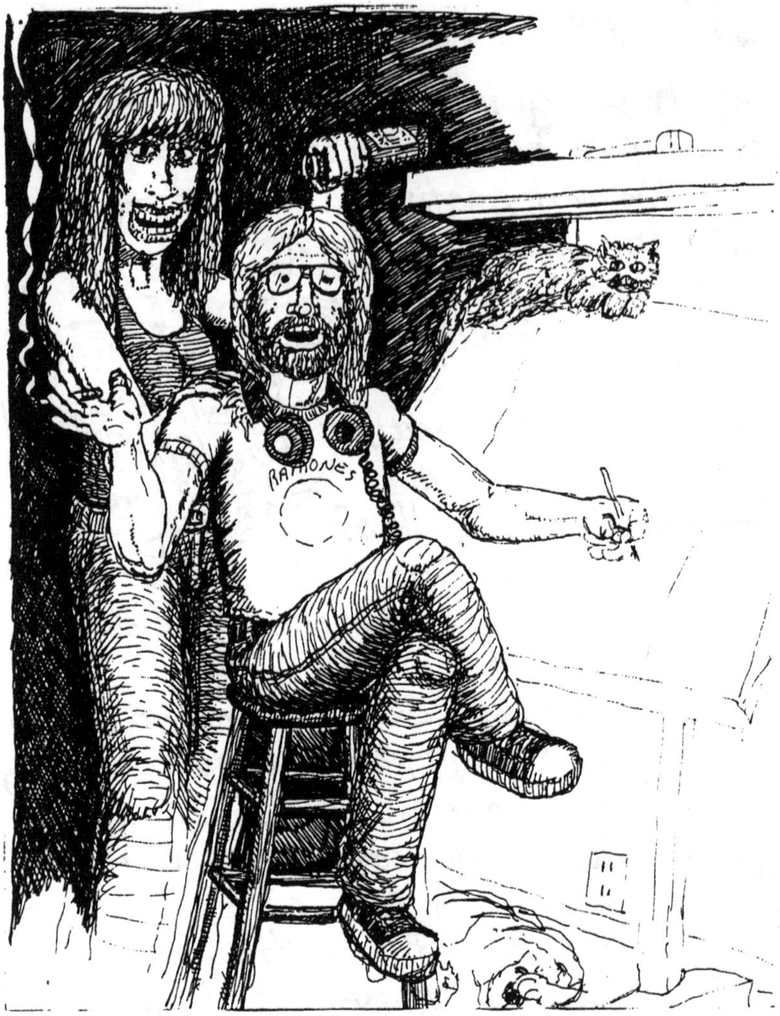
RAMONES

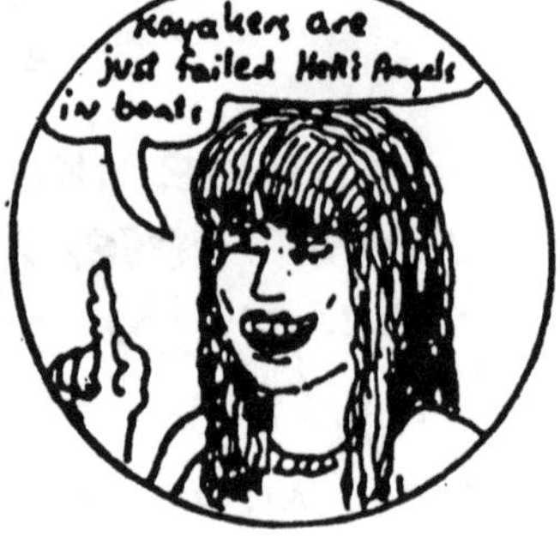
Kayakers are just failed Hell's Angels in boats

My Chapel Hill studio, 1978

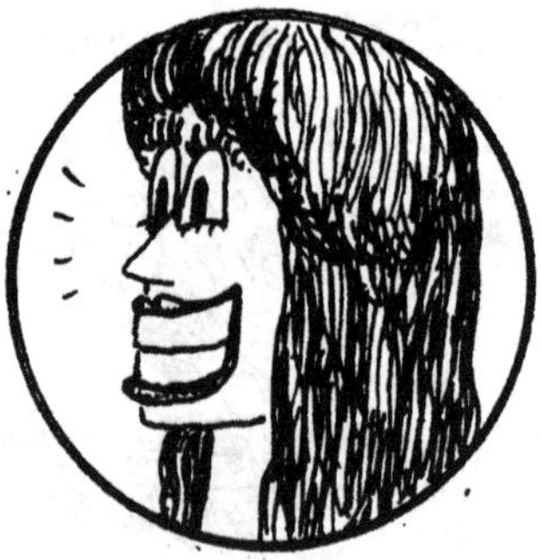

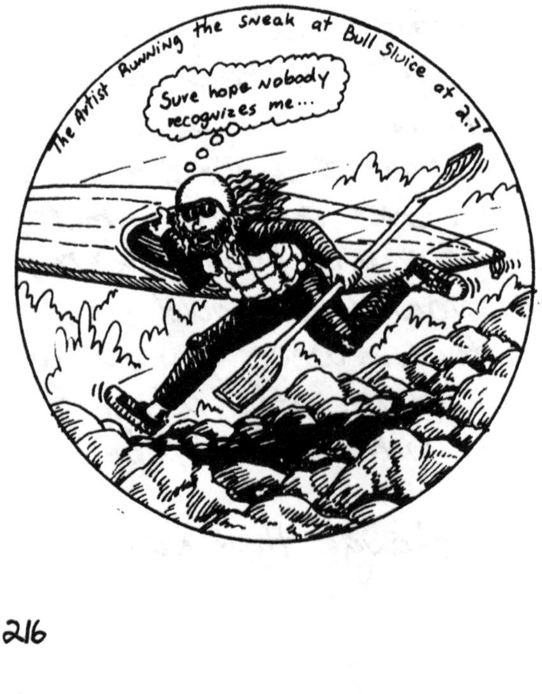
The Artist Running the Sneak at Bull Sluice at 2.7
Sure hope nobody recognizes me...

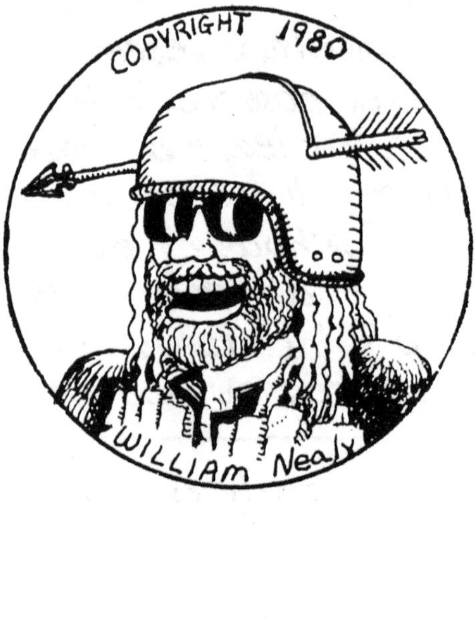
COPYRIGHT 1980
WILLIAM Nealy

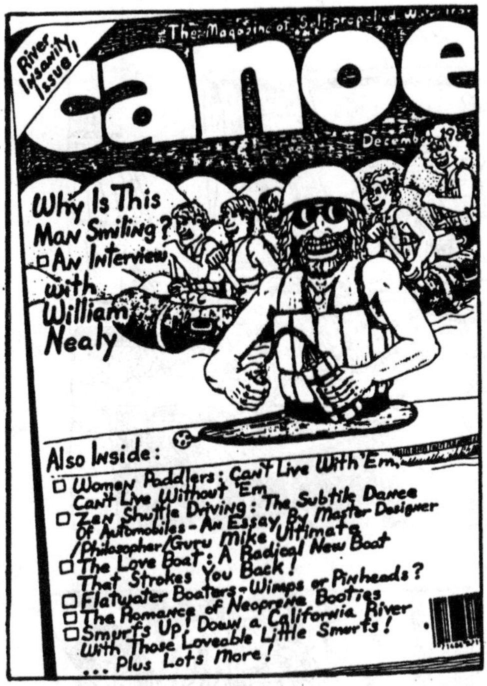
The Magazine of Self-propelled Water...
canoe
River Insanity Issue!
December 198?
Why Is This Man Smiling?
An Interview with William Nealy
Also Inside:
Women Paddlers: Can't Live With 'Em, Can't Live Without 'Em
Zen Shuttle Driving: The Subtle Dance Of Automobiles - An Essay By Master Designer /Philosopher/Guru Mike Ultimate
The Love Boat: A Radical New Boat That Strokes You Back!
Flatwater Boaters - Wimps or Pinheads?
The Romance of Neoprene Booties
Smurfs Up! Down a California River With Those Loveable Little Smurfs!
... Plus Lots More!

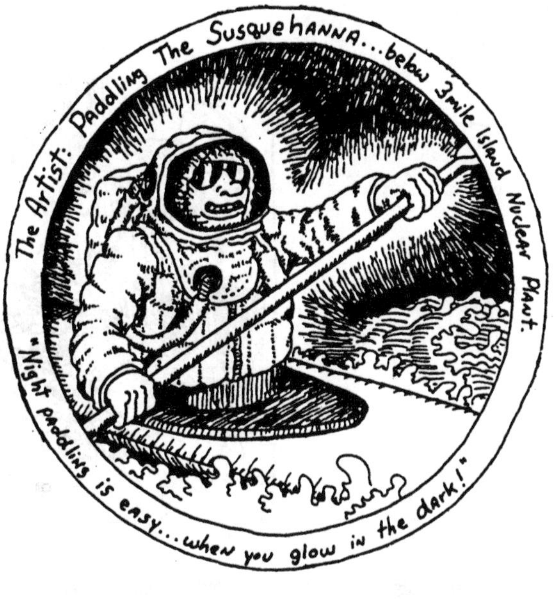
The Artist: Paddling The Susquehanna... below 3mile Island Nuclear Plant.
"Night paddling is easy... when you glow in the dark!"

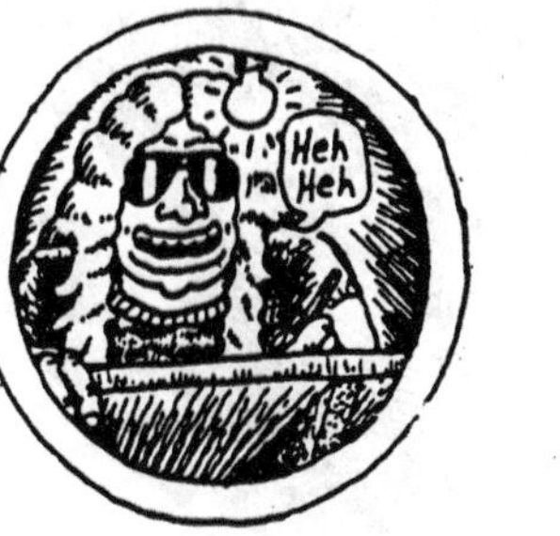
Heh Heh

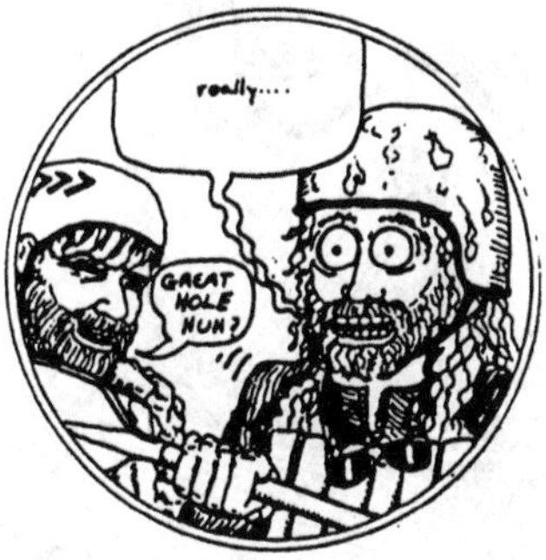
really....
GREAT HOLE HUH?

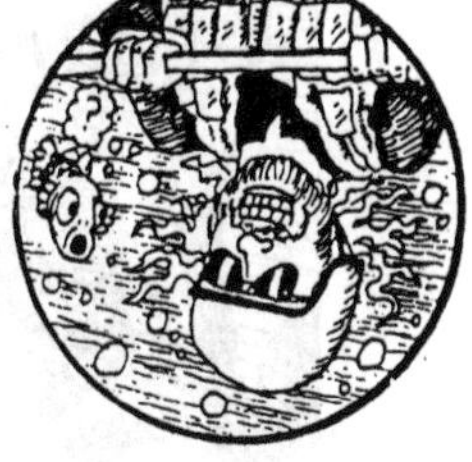

1980-81

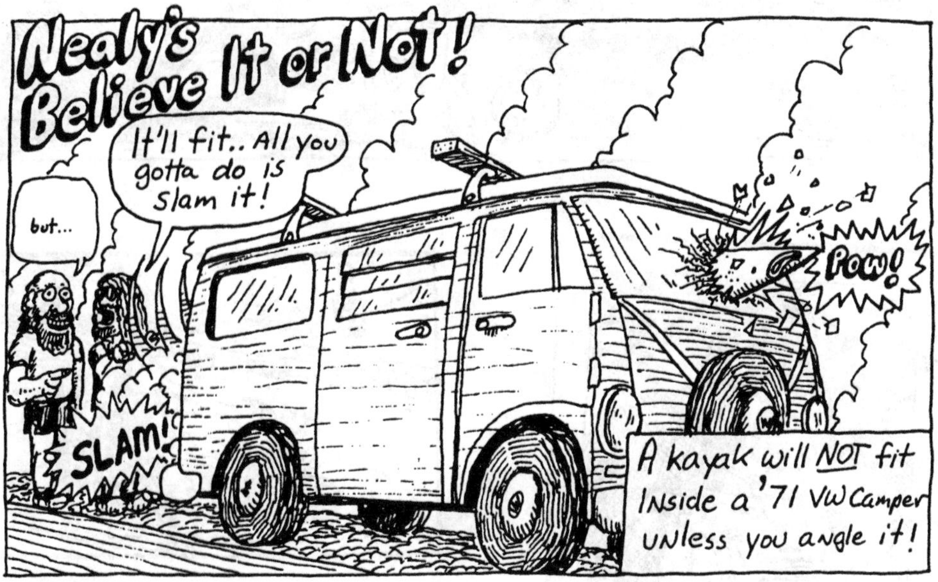
Nealy's Believe It or Not!
but...
It'll fit.. All you gotta do is slam it!
SLAM!
POW!
A kayak will NOT fit Inside a '71 VW Camper unless you angle it!

The 80's

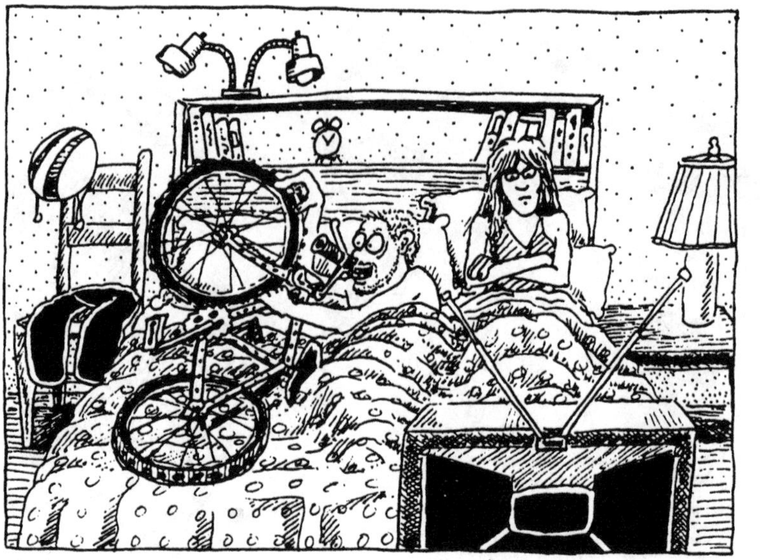

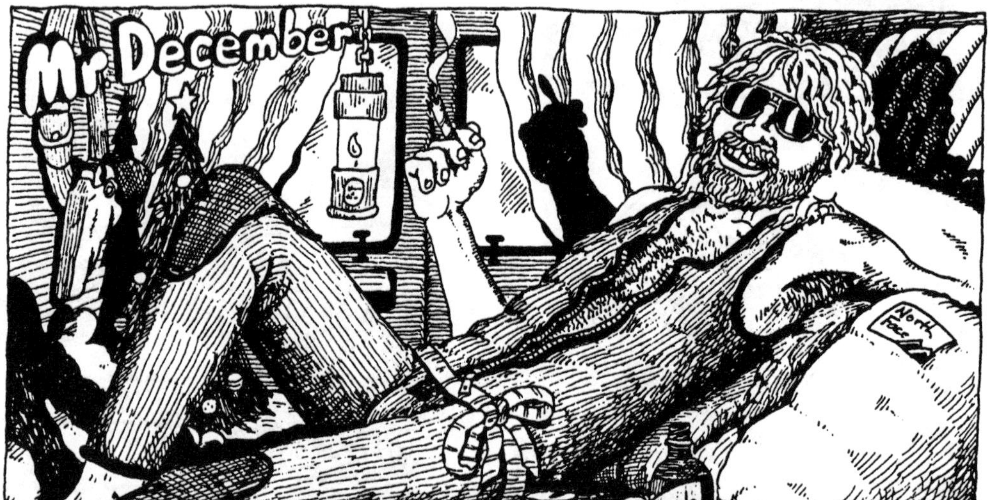
Mr. December
North Face
Coors
Ripple

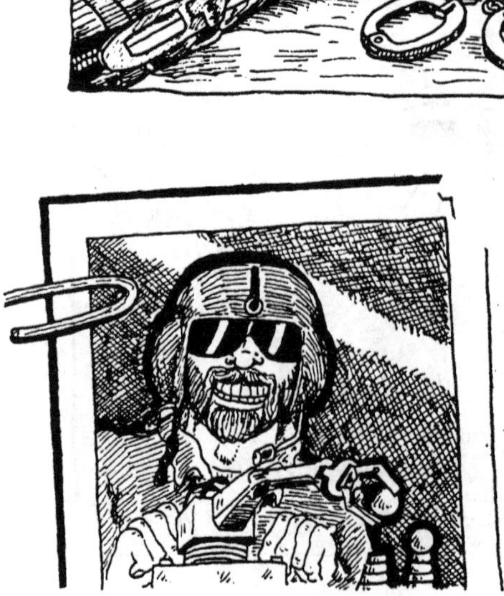

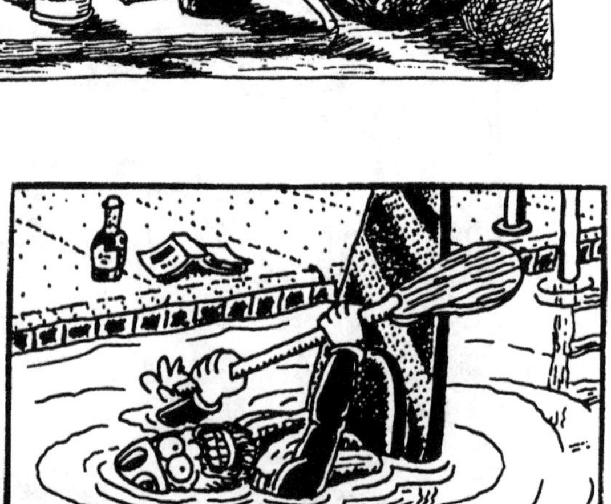

Troubleshooting Body Pain

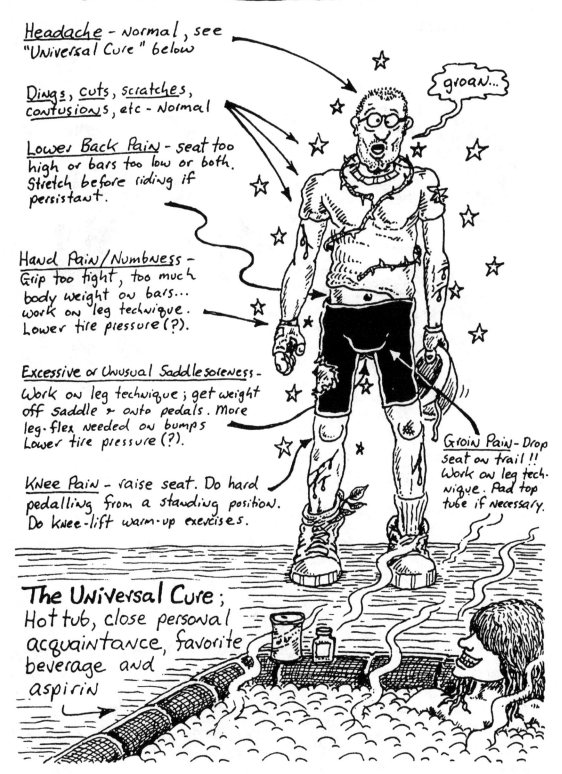

Headache - Normal, see "Universal Cure" below

Dings, cuts, scratches, contusions, etc - Normal

Lower Back Pain - seat too high or bars too low or both. Stretch before riding if persistant.

Hand Pain/Numbness - Grip too tight, too much body weight on bars... work on leg technique. Lower tire pressure (?).

Excessive or Unusual Saddle soreness - Work on leg technique; get weight off saddle & onto pedals. More leg-flex needed on bumps Lower tire pressure (?).

Knee Pain - raise seat. Do hard pedalling from a standing position. Do knee-lift warm-up exercises.

groan...

Groin Pain - Drop seat on trail!! Work on leg technique. Pad top tube if necessary.

The Universal Cure; Hot tub, close personal acquaintance, favorite beverage and aspirin

The 90's

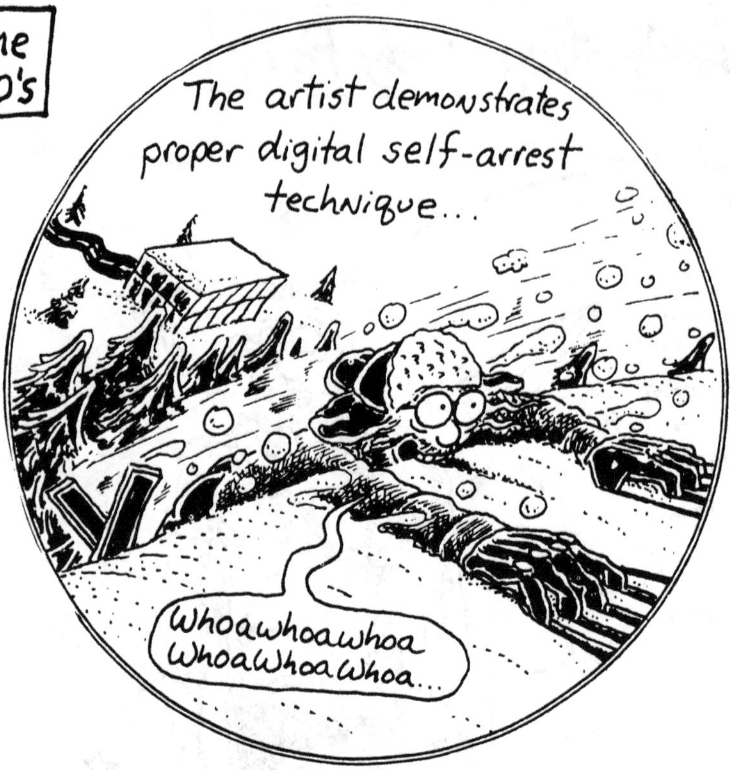
The artist demonstrates proper digital self-arrest technique...
Whoawhoawhoa WhoaWhoaWhoa...

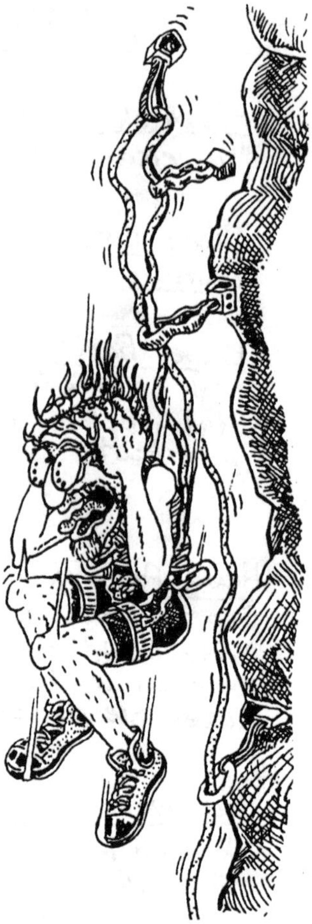

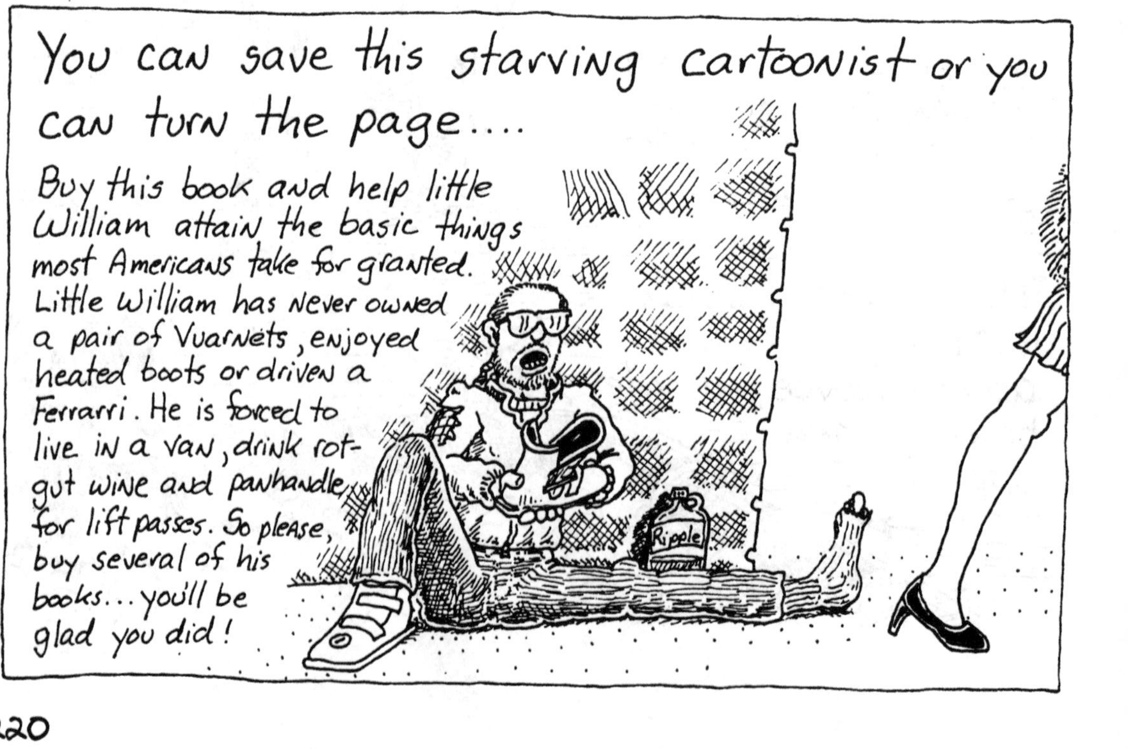
You can save this starving cartoonist or you can turn the page....
Buy this book and help little William attain the basic things most Americans take for granted. Little William has never owned a pair of Vuarnets, enjoyed heated boots or driven a Ferrarri. He is forced to live in a van, drink rot-gut wine and panhandle for lift passes. So please, buy several of his books... you'll be glad you did!
Ripple

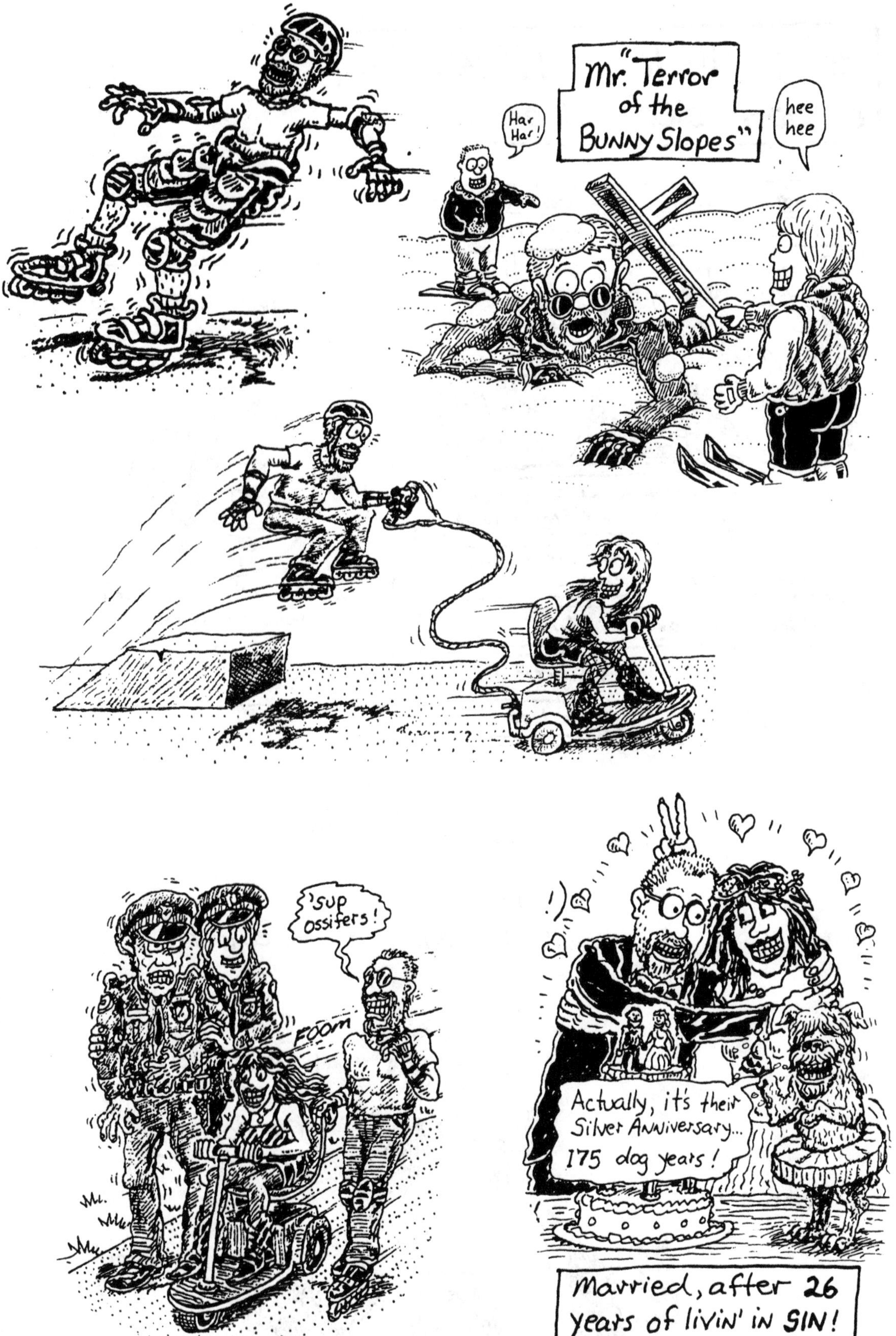
Har Har!
Mr. "Terror of the BUNNY Slopes"
hee hee
'sup ossifers!
FOOM
Actually, it's their Silver Anniversary... 175 dog years!
Married, after 26 years of livin' in SIN!

Holly will lobby HARD for a book dedication...

Dedicate the book to river guides? Name 10...

Never mind!

John, Mark, Kathy.....

Why not dedicate it to your dog?!

I'm sure someday you'll dedicate one to me.... posthumously

I'm sure your mom would like another book dedication....

OK – I'll do it

If you put this conversation in a cartoon I'll die! You're not serious? Please don't.

Those guys at EPRO will harass me for 100 years at least! Dooooonnn'''''t!?

You are kidding.....

Right?

Am I right?

This book is dedicated to my "special friend", Holland Wallace

Without whom life itself would be impossible....

This book is dedicated to
Holly
My permanent girlfriend and main editor

Sherman

Dedication! me? Oh goody!

Harold

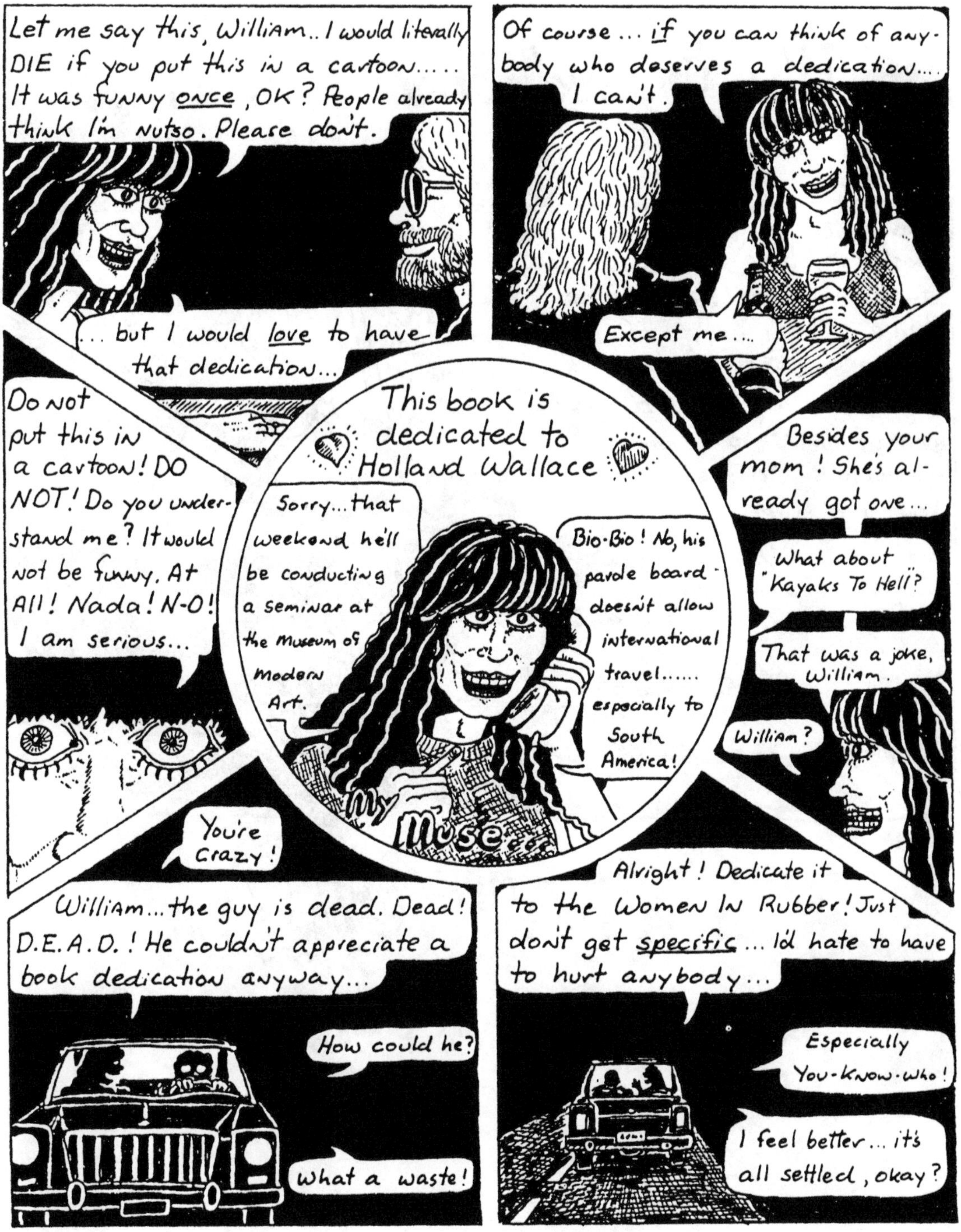

Let me say this, William.. I would literally DIE if you put this in a cartoon..... It was funny ONCE, OK? People already think I'm nutso. Please don't.
... but I would love to have that dedication...
Of course... if you can think of anybody who deserves a dedication.... I can't.
Except me....
Do not put this in a cartoon! DO NOT! Do you understand me? It would not be funny. At All! Nada! N-O! I am serious...
You're Crazy!
This book is dedicated to Holland Wallace
Sorry... that weekend he'll be conducting a seminar at the Museum of Modern Art.
Bio-Bio! No, his parole board doesn't allow international travel...... especially to South America!
My Muse
Besides your mom! She's already got one...
What about "Kayaks To Hell"?
That was a joke, William.
William?
William... the guy is dead. Dead! D.E.A.D.! He couldn't appreciate a book dedication anyway...
How could he?
What a waste!
Alright! Dedicate it to the Women In Rubber! Just don't get specific... I'd hate to have to hurt anybody...
Especially You-Know-Who!
I feel better... it's all settled, okay?

Illustrated Short Stories...

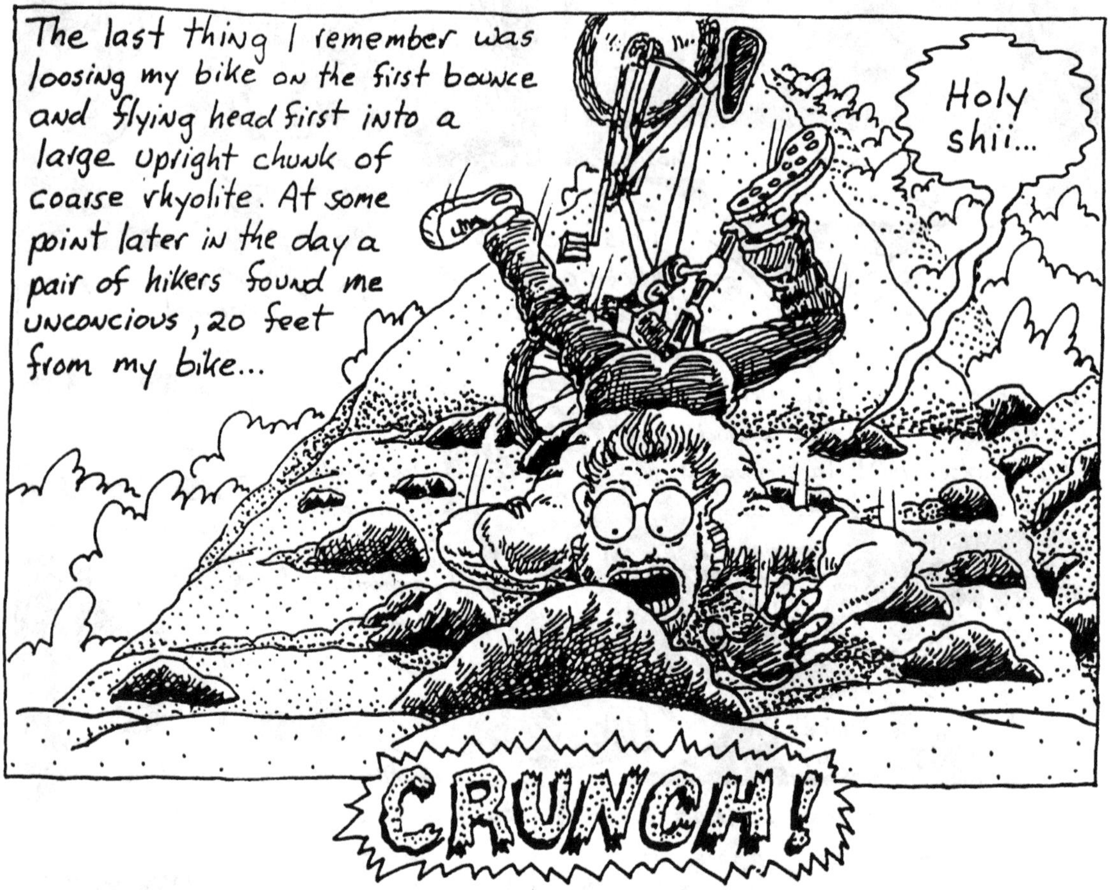
The last thing I remember was loosing my bike on the first bounce and flying head first into a large upright chunk of coarse rhyolite. At some point later in the day a pair of hikers found me unconcious, 20 feet from my bike...
Holy shii...
CRUNCH!

...In Chronological Order

Circa 1965...

POLIO CREEK

Us kids called it Polio Creek, as in: "You better stay out of that ditch or you'll get polio." It drained the eastern slopes of Red Mountain, the southernmost extent of the Appalachian foothills in Alabama's central piedmont. It ran through my backyard in Homewood, one of Birmingham's many bedroom communities. Before World War I Polio Creek had been a meandering brook with gentle curves and gentler gradient. By 1950 it had been engineered, channelized, and civilized, walled on both banks eight feet high, first with sandstone, later with concrete.

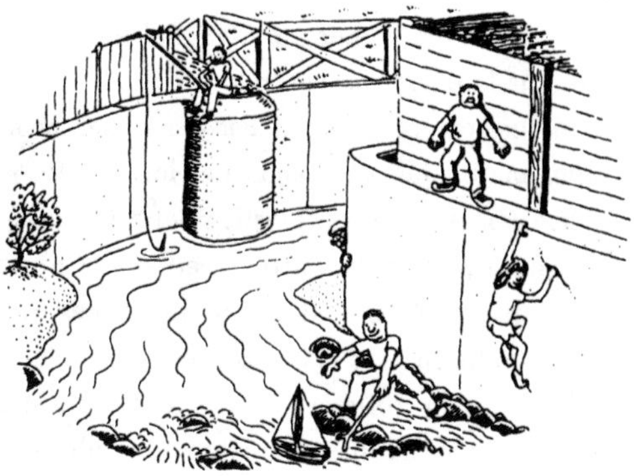

Polio Creek was a crack in suburbia, a kid Ho Chi Minh Trail, the forbidden zone. Within its sheer cool walls a youngster could walk for miles without once falling under an adult's reptilian gaze. Here and there were tunnels connecting other neighborhoods to the creek, tunnels big enough to walk upright in and, on occasion, big enough to run like hell in when being pursued by adults or worse, teenagers. Naturally we were forbidden to play in the creek by the mom and dad units. "Typhoid!" "Rats!" "Snakes!" and, obviously, "Polio!" Practically the worst thing that could happen to one of us would be to slip and fall into Polio Creek. It was a long sad walk home, dripping with the incontrovertible evidence of a sure whipping offense. Despite the hazards, I lived in Polio Creek.

Once or twice a year a flash flood would pump Polio Creek up eight or ten feet, turning it into a watery freight train whipping through Homewood faster than you could pedal a bike, light speed to a kid. We would be herded into the houses and our parents would stand looking out kitchen windows at the astonishing sight, smoking cigarettes and silently praying the furnace didn't get flooded. To the grown-ups the creek had become a limbless Godzilla, a hell snake unleashed on Homewood, slithering between the houses, hissing and throbbing. Sometimes a section of the retaining wall would get peeled off by the force of the current and entire backyards would be lost, scoured down to the old streambed. Dolls, basketballs, tires, jugs, paint cans, lumber, lawn furniture, shrubs and other suburban flotsam would begin the long journey south to the Gulf of Mexico on the crest of the flood. For years I had been contemplating just such a journey for myself.

I had a boat: a one-kid plastic rowboat-looking affair from K-Mart that also served as a wading pool, turtle pond or sled, as circumstances dictated. Conditions had to be just right to run Polio Creek: daylight, mild weather, sufficient water and absence of adult supervision. One blustery spring day in 1965 everything came together. It had rained all day and from my sixth-grade classroom I could see parents arriving early to pick

up their children, headlights on in the afternoon darkness—a good omen.

My friend Tommy and I rode our bikes home in the rain. Rainwater was gushing out of storm drains, and when we got to the bridge we saw that Polio Creek was high and going higher. We made a plan; I would float the creek and Tommy would stay ahead of me on his Schwinn Typhoon, checking my progress at each successive bridge. Since this was merely a run-through and not the actual Gulf of Mexico expedition, equipment and supplies were kept at a minimum. A boat, a paddle, and a paddler. I was only going a few blocks.

With Tommy stationed at the first bridge on my home street, I carried my boat upstream through backyards to where a smaller creek fed into Polio Creek through a break in the wall. Moving in a brisk but stealthy manner (a kid carrying a boat anywhere near a flooded creek was fair game for any nosey grown-up), I got into position on the feeder creek and slid down, out of sight. I got in the boat and paddled up to the break in the wall. Polio Creek shot past the breach with a low sucking moan, and as I cleared the wall I was snatched downstream. This was like some

demented new ride at the state fair—a Mad Mouse with no brakes and no end, an insane machine. I was falling down a shaft with walls of concrete, water and air.

The first rapid was a 90-degree bend to the right with a huge sewage tank protruding from the left wall at the middle of the bend. The entire flow was slamming straight into the tank and folding over itself in its rush to turn right. Despite a frantic stroke or two I was heading straight into a wall of very angry-looking water. Something grabbed the boat, stood it practically on end and shoved me right at the instant before I hit the tank. Then I was bailing with my hands; water had surged over the transom into the boat as I

was tossed to the right. A huge shadow flew over me and someone yelled my name. I looked up toward the sound and saw I had just streaked under the first bridge. I could see Tommy pony-express mounting his Typhoon, heading for bridge number two.

Next bend, 90 degrees left, trying to stay to the inside of the turn. Into the wall instead, nearly vertical, then whipped left just before impact. Bailing frantically now, like those cartoons where Sylvester the cat suddenly has 50 arms. . . . My predicament is dawning on me. First it is a trickle, then a torrent of realization: I am going to drown today. Probably in the next few minutes. The walls are smooth, unbroken. Unless I can somehow stand up in the boat. I can't reach the top of the wall. The water's too deep to stand in and too fast to tread. Ninety-degree bend to the right, stayed inside the turn and only shipped a little water this time. Long curve to the left. The creek is still rising . . . I can see windows, back porches now. Great. If I don't drown I'm going to get caught. Bridge number two is coming up to meet me . . . it's like sitting in a bathtub of cold water and having the world roll over me. Tommy rides onto the bridge, drops his bike and runs to the upstream rail. He's crying now. The bridge has a center piling with a tree and some boards stuck to it. The right side would be better because there's a curve to the right just below and that would put me inside the curve. I take the left side, which looks safer, and I'm into the curve before Tommy can run to the other side of the bridge. Boat spinning, I hit the wall this time and I'm full of water. Got to bail.

Third bridge, no sign of Tommy. Water still rising and it will be a squeeze to make it under this bridge . . . less than two feet. For one second I consider grabbing the bridge and climbing up on it. Then I'm scrunched into the bottom of the

boat, flying into the penumbra of the bridge. I'm clear, on a long straightaway; ahead is bridge number four. Just below this bridge is a steel waterpipe about a foot in diameter that crosses the creek about six feet above the creek bed. I've fished from it. Now it is right at the surface, splitting the flow horizontally like a planer. A huge boil just below where the flows reunite throws steam and froth into the air. It is the end of the world. I remember a concrete storm drainpipe on the right wall just above the bridge. That is how we climb in and out of the creek here when the creek is running a trickle. It's about halfway up the wall. Right now only the top of the pipe is visible, a six-inch ledge curving into brown water. I've got to grab the pipe, roll out of the boat and climb out. There is silence and I'm looking down a dark tunnel at the top edge of a pipe and the black underside of the bridge. Nothing else exists but that little piece of concrete. I'm there . . . drop paddle . . . grab pipe . . . roll out of the boat. I swing below the pipe, planing on the surface, water tearing at my jeans. Lost a shoe, then the other. I hear a crunch as the boat is bisected by the pipe. I can't bring myself to look downstream.

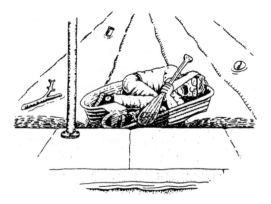

I get a leg in the pipe, then a foot on top and a hand on top of the wall. I bring my head up slowly . . . no fire trucks . . . no Tommy. The coast is clear. I cross to the far side of the bridge. Boat gone. Just brown boiling water. I hope Tommy shows up soon . . . we've got to prepare a good story in case we're interrogated later on tonight. Went wading, slipped and lost shoes. Some other kids swiped boat and sent it down creek, etc.

I see my mom's VW headed toward me, coming fast. There's my mom . . . there's Tommy. Holy crap.

circa 1977...

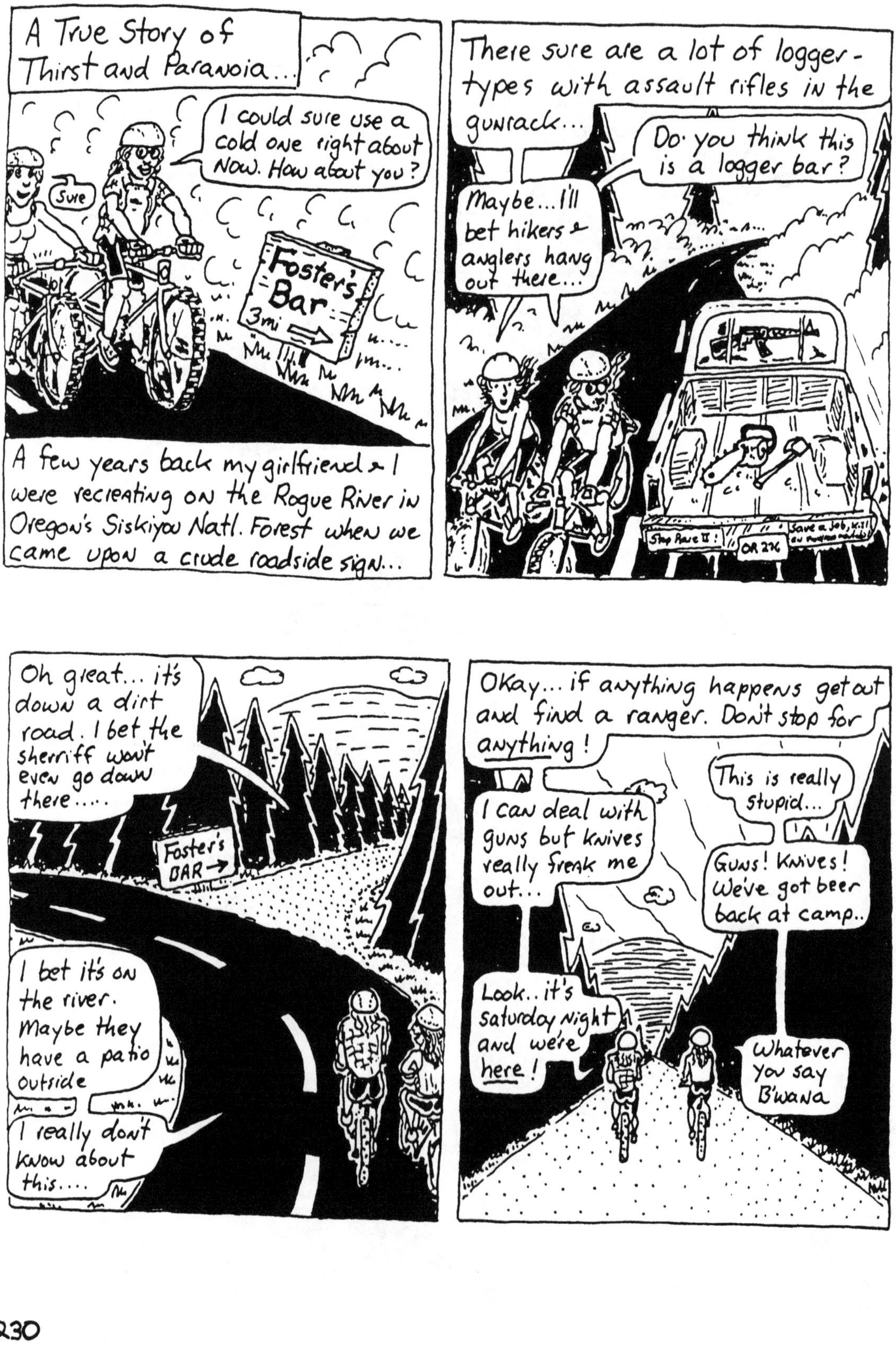

A True Story of Thirst and Paranoia...
I could sure use a cold one right about now. How about you?
Sure
Foster's Bar 3mi
A few years back my girlfriend & I were recreating on the Rogue River in Oregon's Siskiyou Natl. Forest when we came upon a crude roadside sign...
There sure are a lot of logger-types with assault rifles in the gunrack...
Do you think this is a logger bar?
Maybe... I'll bet hikers & anglers hang out there...
Oh great... it's down a dirt road. I bet the sherriff won't even go down there....
Foster's BAR
I bet it's on the river. Maybe they have a patio outside
I really don't know about this....
Okay... if anything happens get out and find a ranger. Don't stop for anything!
I can deal with guns but knives really freak me out...
This is really stupid...
Guns! Knives! We've got beer back at camp..
Look.. it's saturday night and we're here!
Whatever you say B'wana

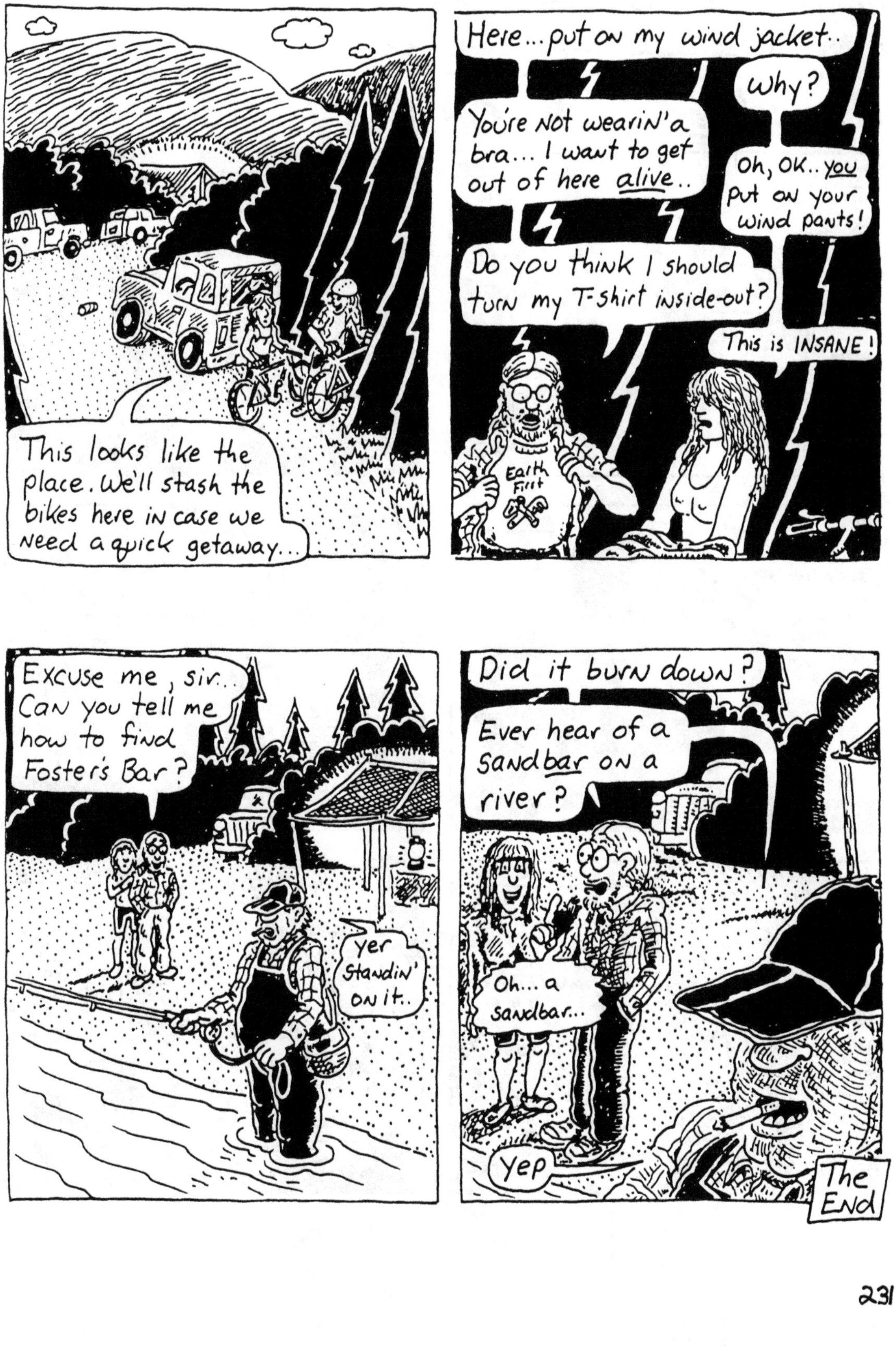
This looks like the place. We'll stash the bikes here in case we need a quick getaway...
Here... put on my wind jacket..
Why?
You're not wearin' a bra... I want to get out of here alive..
Oh, OK.. you put on your wind pants!
Do you think I should turn my T-shirt inside-out?
This is INSANE!
Earth First
Excuse me, sir.. Can you tell me how to find Foster's Bar?
yer standin' on it.
Did it burn down?
Ever hear of a sandbar on a river?
Oh... a sandbar...
Yep
The End

Circa 1979 To me, 3 boats on a river trip is a **crowd**; cluster-paddling with 10 or more boats is a **bloody nightmare**! This is the story of one season paddling with the _____ Canoe Club...

Standard Club Trip

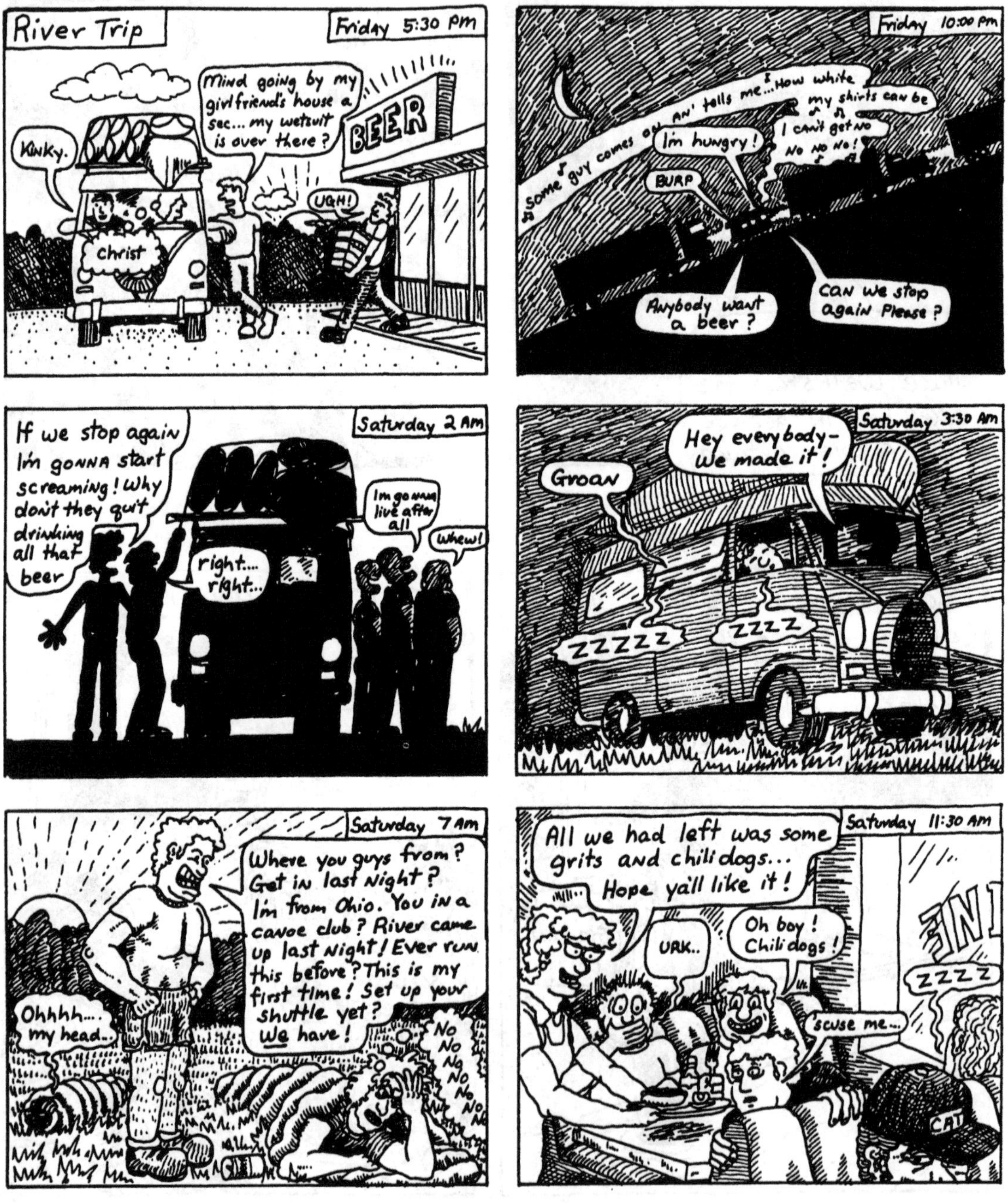
River Trip
Friday 5:30 PM
Kinky.
Mind going by my girlfriend's house a sec... my wetsuit is over there?
BEER
UGH!
Christ
Friday 10:00 PM
Some guy comes on an' tells me... How white my shirts can be
I'm hungry!
I can't get no No no no!
BURP
Anybody want a beer?
Can we stop again please?
Saturday 2 AM
If we stop again I'm gonna start screaming! Why don't they quit drinking all that beer
right... right...
I'm gonna live after all
Whew!
Saturday 3:30 AM
Groan
Hey everybody- We made it!
ZZZZZ
ZZZ
Saturday 7 AM
Where you guys from? Get in last night? I'm from Ohio. You in a canoe club? River came up last night! Ever run this before? This is my first time! Set up your shuttle yet? We have!
Ohhhh... my head..
No No No No No No
Saturday 11:30 AM
All we had left was some grits and chili dogs... Hope ya'll like it!
URK..
Oh boy! Chili dogs!
ZZZZ
'scuse me...
CAT

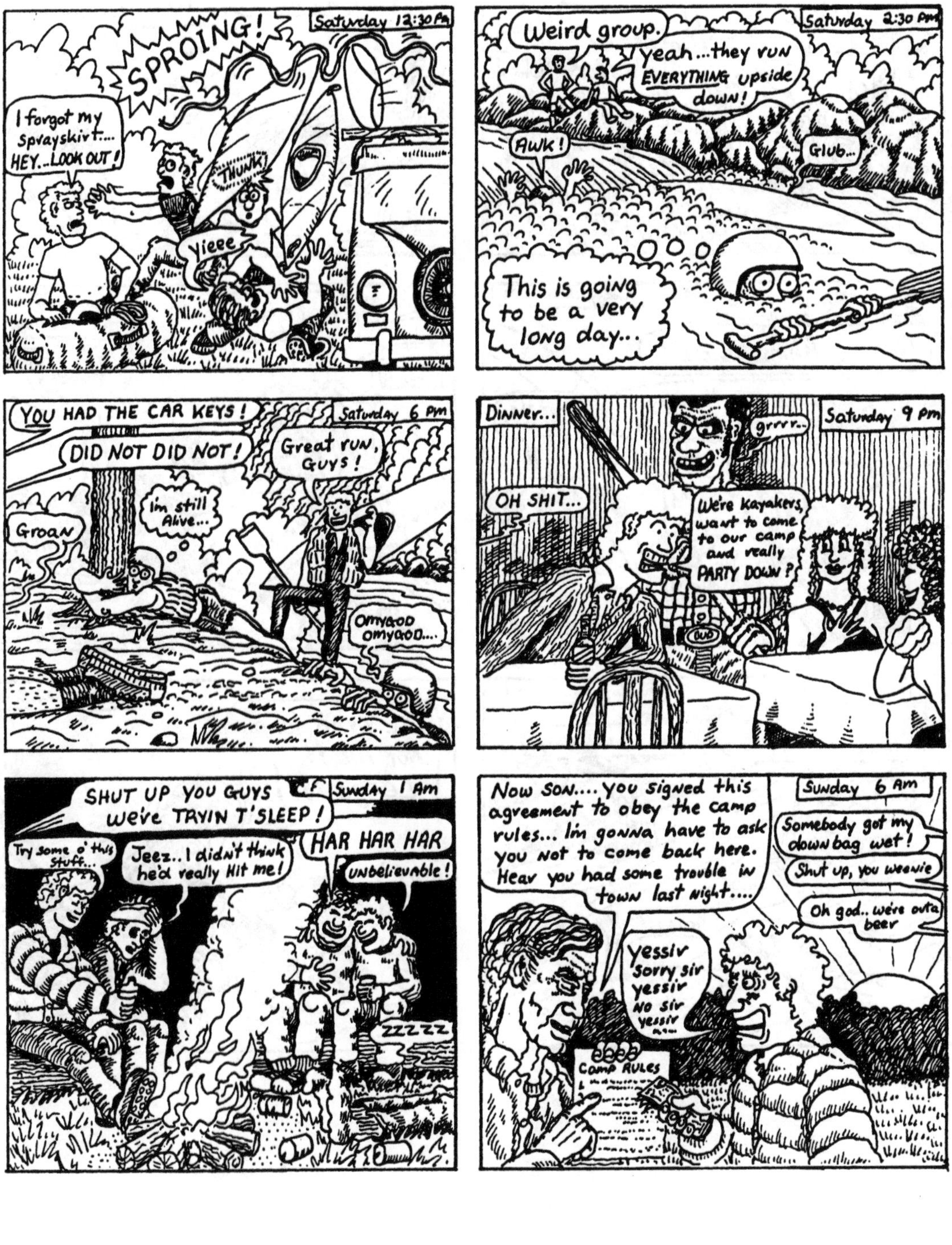
Saturday 12:30 PM
SPROING!
I forgot my sprayskirt.... HEY...LOOK OUT!
THUNK
Yieee
Saturday 2:30 PM
Weird group.
yeah...they run EVERYTHING upside down!
Awk!
Glub...
This is going to be a very long day...
YOU HAD THE CAR KEYS!
Saturday 6 PM
DID NOT DID NOT!
Great run, GUYS!
Groan
I'm still Alive...
OMYGOD OMYGOD...
Dinner...
Saturday 9 PM
grrrr..
OH SHIT...
We're kayakers, want to come to our camp and really PARTY DOWN?
SHUT UP YOU GUYS we're TRYIN T'SLEEP!
Sunday 1 AM
Try some o' this stuff...
Jeez..I didn't think he'd really hit me!
HAR HAR HAR
unbelievable!
ZZZZZ
Now son.... you signed this agreement to obey the camp rules... I'm gonna have to ask you not to come back here. Hear you had some trouble in town last night....
Sunday 6 AM
Somebody got my down bag wet!
Shut up, you weenie
Oh god.. we're outa beer
yessir sorry sir yessir no sir yessir
CAMP RULES

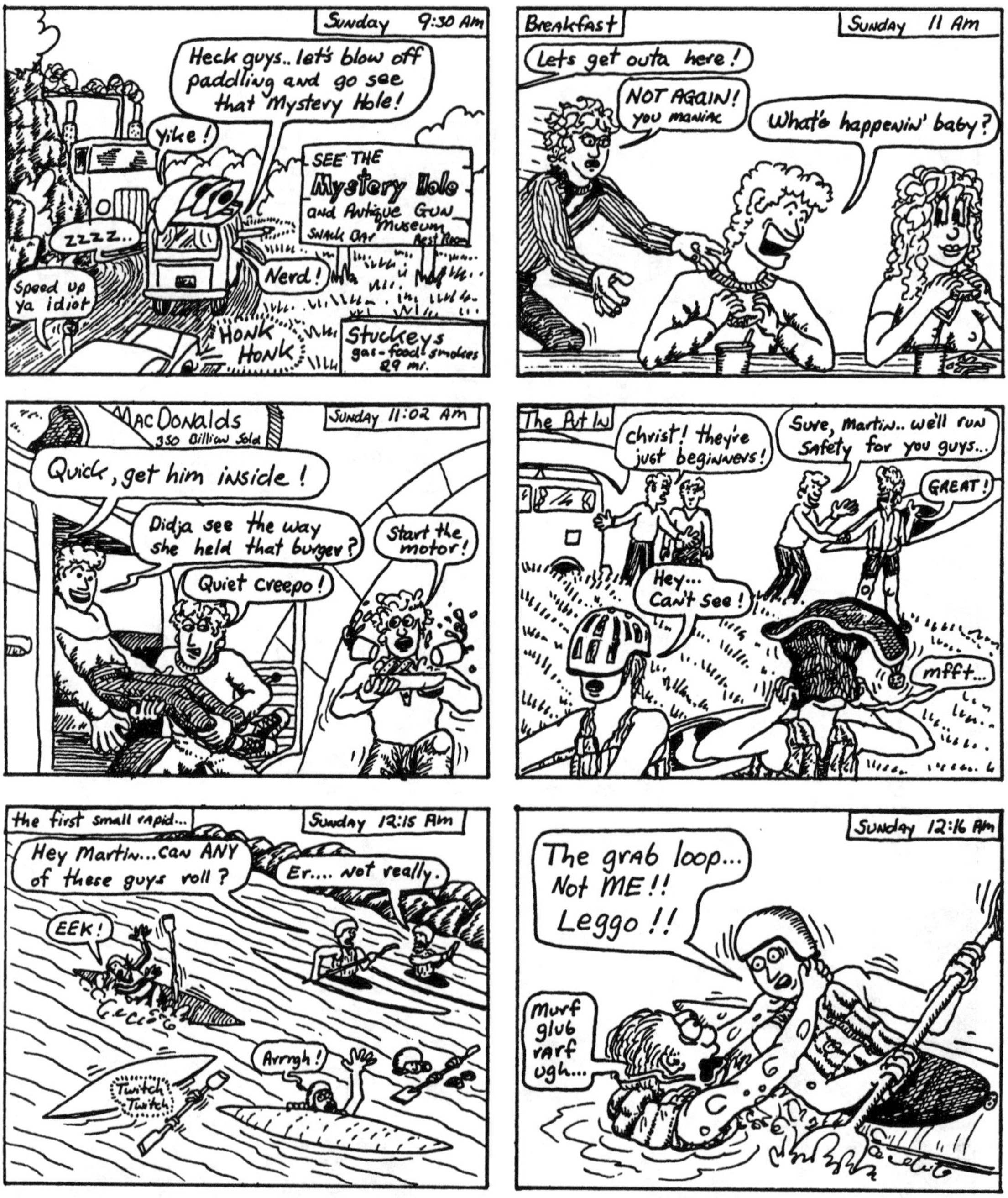
Sunday 9:30 Am
Heck guys.. let's blow off paddling and go see that Mystery Hole!
Yike!
SEE THE Mystery Hole and Antique GUN Museum
Snack Bar Rest Room
ZZZZ..
Nerd!
Speed up ya idiot
HONK HONK
Stuckeys gas-food-smokes 29 mi.
Breakfast
Sunday 11 Am
Lets get outa here!
NOT AGAIN! you maniac
What's happenin' baby?
MacDONALDS 350 Billion Sold
Sunday 11:02 Am
Quick, get him inside!
Didja see the way she held that burger?
Quiet creepo!
Start the motor!
The Put In
christ! they're just beginners!
Sure, Martin.. we'll run safety for you guys...
GREAT!
Hey... Can't see!
mfft...
the first small rapid...
Sunday 12:15 Am
Hey Martin...can ANY of these guys roll?
Er.... not really.
EEK!
Arrgh!
Twitch Twitch
Sunday 12:16 Am
The grab loop... Not ME!! Leggo!!
Murf glub varf ugh....

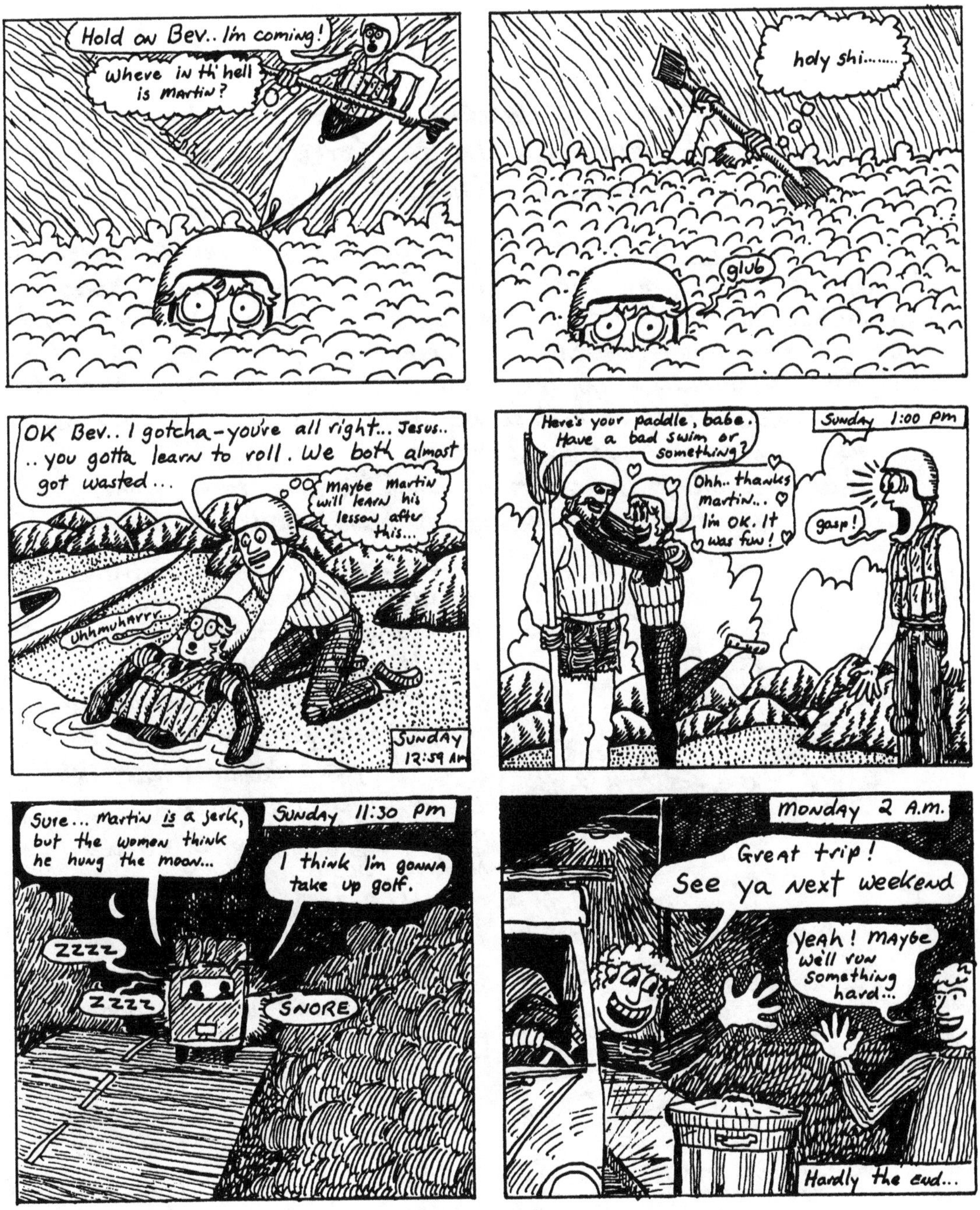

Hold on Bev.. I'm coming!
Where in th' hell is martin?
holy shi.......
glub
OK Bev.. I gotcha - you're all right... Jesus.. ..you gotta learn to roll. We both almost got wasted...
maybe martin will learn his lesson after this...
Uhhmuhurrr..
SUNDAY 12:59 AM
Sunday 1:00 pm
Here's your paddle, babe. Have a bad swim or something?
Ohh.. thanks martin... I'm OK. It was fun!
gasp!
Sunday 11:30 pm
Sure... martin is a jerk, but the women think he hung the moon...
I think I'm gonna take up golf.
ZZZZ
ZZZZ
SNORE
Monday 2 A.M.
Great trip! See ya next weekend
Yeah! maybe we'll run something hard...
Hardly the end...

Circa 1979...

The First Winter Descent of the Third or Fourth Highest Peak in the Great Smoky Mountains National Park

After the Outside article on mountain biking appeared in the Spring of '79, my friend Bruce* and I acquired a couple old Schwinns and proceeded to demolish both the bikes and ourselves. Our favorite activities were high-speed pedestrian slalom and staircase-riding on the campus of the University of North Carolina in Chapel Hill. And drinking beer. In short, we were bad boys in need of serious punishment.

That December Bruce, Holly and I drove to Alabama for Christmas via the Great Smokies National Park. Bruce and I had been planning a little side excursion. On the eastern end of the park there's a foottrail running off Mt. Sterling (5,842') to Big Creek Campground with an average gradient of 1,000 feet per mile for six odd miles. A couple years earlier I had hiked it. Baxter Creek Trail was a grunt, pure and simple, going up. Bruce and I planned to bomb down it.

At 3:30 pm we unloaded the bikes on a saddle a forest service road crossed within a couple miles of the Mt. Sterling Firetower, visible 1,000' above the saddle. We told Holly we'd see

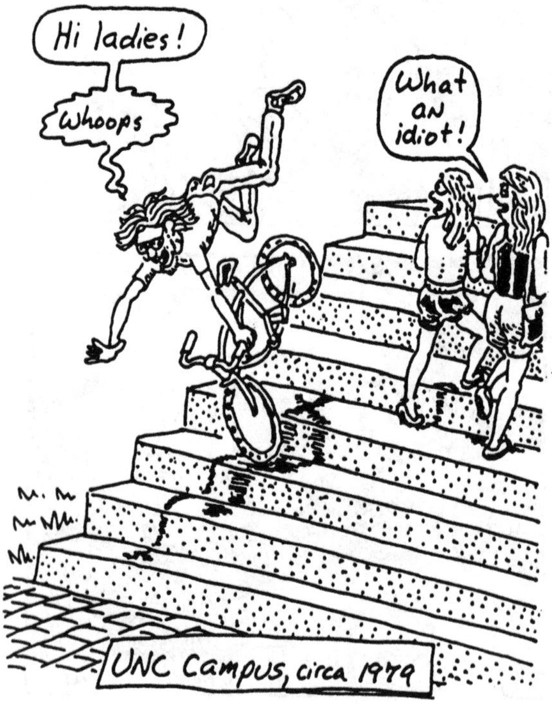
Hi ladies!
Whoops
What an idiot!

UNC Campus, circa 1979

* Bruce has an actual "job" now with NASA so I can't use his last name 'cause he'd get fired if they found out what a crazy bastard he really is!

her in an hour or so at the campground in the valley below. Bruce and I figured we'd surely beat the car down. After about 200 yds. the jeep trail to the firetower got too steep to pedal a 1-speed cruiser... we began a push/carry bike ascent epic. At about sundown we staggered into the clearing below the firetower. There was snow on the ground and, because Bruce and I had wisely elected to wear only T-shirts and blue jeans (now sweat-soaked) we were getting very cold. Now all we had to do was to select the correct trailhead to the campground from a number of trailheads leading out of the

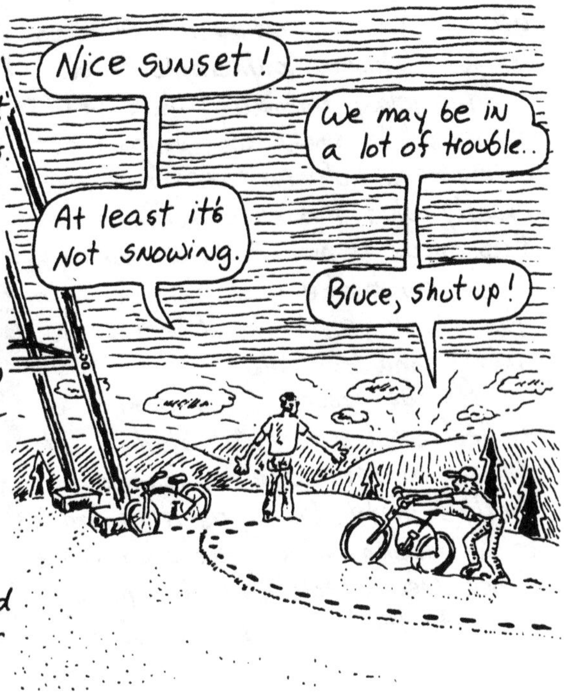
Nice sunset!
At least it's not snowing.
We may be in a lot of trouble..
Bruce, shut up!

clearing, all unmarked. Being hippie radicals, we chose the trailhead farthest left. In fading daylight we said a prayer to the bike gods and took off down the mountain. Bruce led because I couldn't see too well in the gloom in my ultra-dark prescription sunglasses. About ten minutes later I slid around a corner and ran over Bruce's arm, which was lying across the trail where Bruce lay sprawled after having been clotheslined by a fallen spruce tree hanging across the trail. After we finally located Bruce's glasses, which had been knocked off his head in the crash, we resumed the descent.

The trail was so steep we had

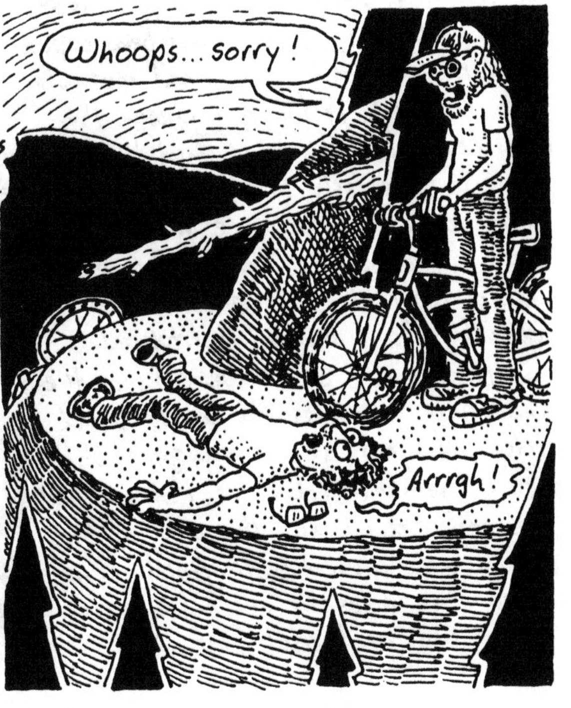
Whoops... sorry!
Arrrgh!

to ride standing on our coaster brakes, coming down Mt. Sterling in a continuous dynamic skid.

"Mayday! Mayday! I'm ON FIRE!" Dense white smoke was pouring out of my rear hub. Neither of us knew exactly what this phenomenon meant. I assumed it meant I was fixing to loose my brake and plummet into Big Creek, a thousand feet below in the shadows. Ulp.

As we resumed our semi-controlled skid down Mt. Sterling we began to speculate on ours and Holly's fate. Being as it was dark, below freezing and we were way overdue, Bruce speculated; "Holly has probably begun to think seriously about finding

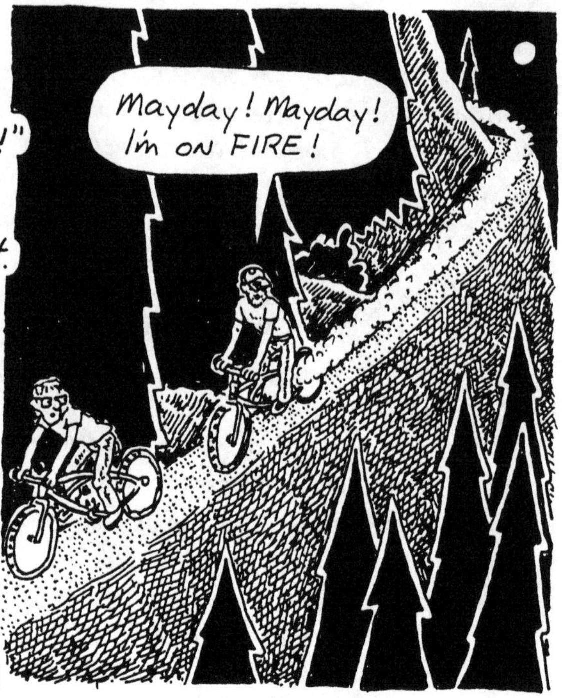
Mayday! Mayday! I'm ON FIRE!

a ranger and organizing a rescue party." "If she hasn't been raped and murdered by the local mutants," I countered. If we had chosen the correct trail at the top (and therefore weren't hopelessly lost and hypothermic) then, technically, we were merely late and hypothermic. Surely the rangers would only fine us and not cart us directly to a mental institution...

At around 6:30 PM we crossed the swinging bridge at the campground. No Holly, no car, no rangers. Shit! Bruce remembered that, it being late December and all, this end of the park was closed until April. It was two more miles to the entrance gate and we went real fast.

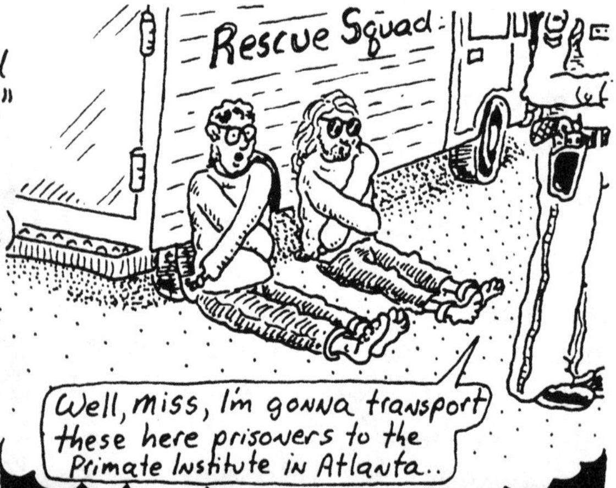
Rescue Squad
Well, miss, I'm gonna transport these here prisoners to the Primate Institute in Atlanta..

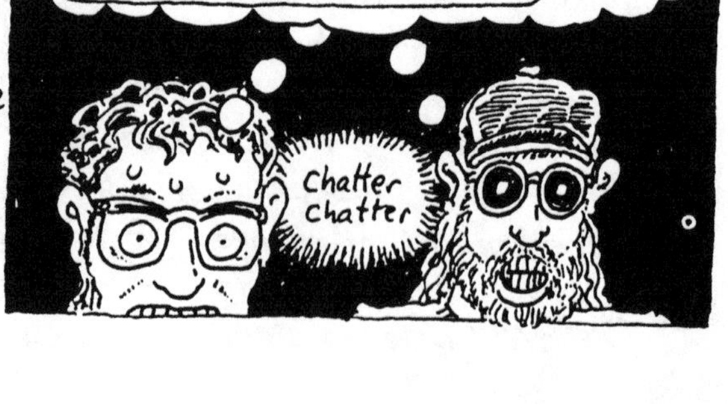
Chatter chatter

A vision of Beauty awaited us at the gate: Holly, warm car, cold beer and no rangers in sight. "You are late late late!" Holly said after opening her window about two inches. She took a sip of a steaming cup of coffee and scotch. "I thought you guys were hurt or lost or dead." "Please unlock the doors... pleeeaaassse!" I whimpered "Bruce and I are both very sorry and awfully cold to boot. And we will never even <u>think</u> about doing anything like this ever again!" "Amen" said Bruce.

She started the car. "See you two in Birmingham". She put the car in drive. "It is 350 @★$! miles to Birmingham" I choked, hanging onto the car with chattering teeth. "Hmm... 350 miles..." she said "Well guys, enjoy!"

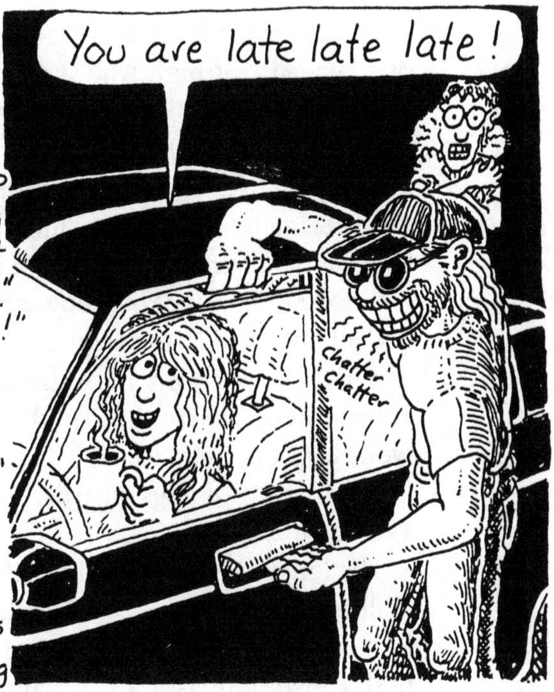
You are late late late!
Chatter chatter

Epilogue - She eventually allowed two penitant, frozen mountain bikers into the car after a little more well-deserved humiliation. Bruce has a real job now but rides when he can. I've become a helmeted, lycra-clad safety weenie and, between crashes and injuries, ride in a responsible and dignified manner. For me...

The End

P.S. Holly, to this day, refuses to run shuttle!

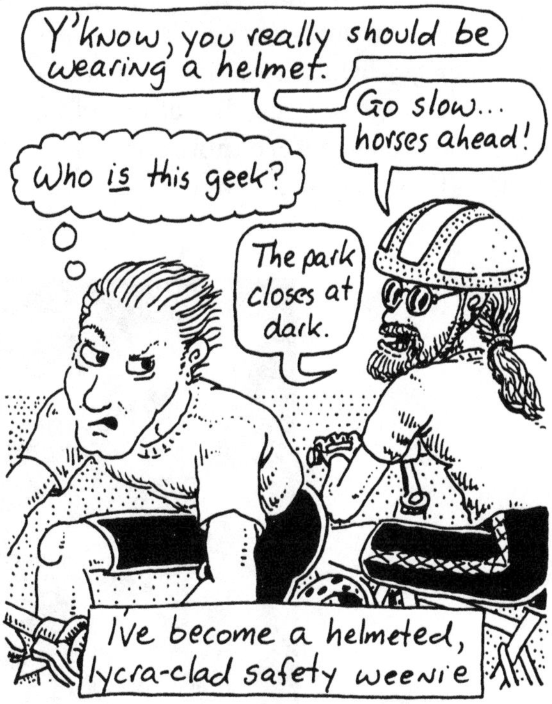
Y'know, you really should be wearing a helmet.
Go slow... horses ahead!
Who <u>is</u> this geek?
The park closes at dark.
I've become a helmeted, lycra-clad safety weenie

ABOUT THE AUTHOR

William "Not Bill" Nealy was a wild, gentle, brilliant artist and creator turned cult hero who wrote 10 books for Menasha Ridge Press from 1982 to 2000. William shared his hard-won "crash-and-learn" experiences through humorous hand-drawn cartoons and illustrated river maps that enabled generations to follow in his footsteps. His subjects included paddling, mountain biking, skiing, and inline skating. His hand-drawn, poster-size river maps of the Nantahala, Ocoee, Chattooga, Gauley, Youghiogheny, and several other rivers are still sought after and in use today.

William was born in Birmingham, Alabama. He and his wife, Holly Wallace, spent their adult years in a home William built in the woods on the outskirts of Chapel Hill, North Carolina, along with an assortment of dogs, lizards, pigs, snakes, turtles, and amphibians. William died in 2001.

His longtime friend and publisher, Bob Sehlinger, wrote: "When William Nealy died in 2001, paddling lost its poet laureate, one of its best teachers, and its greatest icon. William was arguably the best-known ambassador of whitewater sport, entertaining and instructing hundreds of thousands of paddlers through his illustrated books, including the classics: *Whitewater Home Companion Volumes I and II, Whitewater Tales of Terror, Kayaks to Hell,* and his best-known work, *Kayak,* which combined expert paddling instruction with artful caricatures and parodies of the whitewater community itself."

You can learn more about William, his art, and his many books at thewilliamnealy.com.

photo: MAGPIE

CPSIA information can be obtained
at www.ICGtesting.com
Printed in the USA
JSHW050054210423
40663JS00001B/1